# RAVEN MEN

# OF THE YELLOWSTONE

# RAVEN MEN OF THE YELLOWSTONE

*THE TRUE STORY OF CHIEF SORE-BELLY,*

*WAR-LORD OF THE CROWS.*

*[HIS LIFE AND TIMES]*

**By**

**BRIAN L. KEEFE.**

**By the same Author.**

The Battle of Rainy Butte. "The English Westerner`s Society." 2008.

Red Was the Blood of Our Forefathers. "The Caxton Press," Idaho. 2010.

Making Pacts with Old Enemies. "The English Westerner`s Society." 2012.

A Double Defeat for the Atsina. "The English Westerner`s Society;" 2014.

"Apsarokee" "The Choir Press," Gloucester, England. 2014.

My Good Friend Joe Medicine Crow. "English Westerner`s Society;" 2016.

Ma`heo`s Children. "The Choir Press," Gloucester, England. 2018.

Raven Men of the Yellowstone. "The Choir Press," Gloucester, England. 2020.

First Published by The Choir Press in 2019

ISBN 978-1-78963-071-8

Cover design;
Artist`s impression of Sore-Belly from Tribal oral descriptions.

# CONTENTS

## PART 1.

### Defenders of the Yellowstone Country.

## PART 11.

### Denizens of the Upper Missouri.

# CONTENTS

## PART 111.

### Decline of the Crow Ascendency.

## MAPS

## LIST OF ILLUSTRATIONS

## INTRODUCTION AND ACKNOWLEDGEMENTS

It was the *"Moon Weasels Turn White,"* * 1925.

A dozen canvas tepees stood adjacent to a cottonwood grove at Lodge Grass on the Crow Reservation, Montana. It was the festive period at the beginning of the winter season. The Apsaalooka people of that district had come together to hold an annual celebration, at which time they would feast, dance and tell stories as had been the custom of their forebears. So it was whilst lounging on elk-skin robes draped over adjacent pallets, Joe Medicine-Crow twelve years old, and Winona Plenty-Hoops four years younger, listened again to old ones of the buffalo days as they reminisced on days long past. [1]

How well in their octogenarian years could Joe and Winona still remember those times when, in the warmth of a central fire, they had listened to such men as White-Man-Runs-Him, Sacred-Raven and Plenty-Coups. The same who had ridden with Son-of-Morning-Star Custer in 1876, and bedecked in feathers and paint had cried `Koo-Koo-Hey` when fighting horseback against Lakota, Striped-Arrows and Pikuni enemies.

Oh, what stories those old fighters told. Of days when their people had been horse-riding hunters and warriors roaming free across the Northern Plains. Collectively, they called themselves *Apsaalooka* [Children of the Large-Beaked Bird], but to the Lakota they were known as *Kangi Wicasa* [Raven Men]; to the French, *Gens du Corbeaux* [People of the Raven]; to the Blackfoot, *Isahpo* [Rock People], and to the Cheyennes, *On-on-it-to* [White-Earth Robes]. But more commonly they were known, and are still known today as Raven Men or Crows.

In addition to the story-teller chiefs mentioned above, were Joe and Winona`s Great Grandmother Kills-in-the-Morning [b.1815 – d.1932], along with the old-time fighters, Cold-Wind [b.1841 - d.1961], Plain-Feather [b.1870 – d.1965], Yellow-Brow [b.1865 – d.1945], Charles Ten-Bear [b. c,1880 – d. c,1965] among others, all who likewise, have long since crossed to `The Other-Side Camp,` where those who have gone before reside.

The nomadic days of which they spoke are also gone. But when those old-time warriors narrated their stirring tales, young Joe and Winona had been carried into a world they could only imagine. A world which filled them with adulation as they experienced in their minds the thrill of a buffalo chase, while the high-pitched Indian war-whoop reverberating above the clash of tomahawk and lance, seemed to be ringing in their ears.

It is the stories pertaining to the origins, migrations and intertribal warfare of their Crow ancestors that Joe and Winona remembered, as they heard them repeated again and again by old-timers of their acquaintance.

Graciously, Joe of the Greasy-Mouth Crow clan and Winona of the Sore-Lips, along with fellow tribal members, Alex Bird-In-Ground, Barney Old-Coyote

*December

and Pius Real-Bird, have imparted to the present Author over the course of twenty-two years many of the details recorded in this volume.

Among such details one name often mentioned was that of *"Alapooish"* or *"Elapooish,"* i.e. Sore-Belly, arguably the greatest war-chief the Crow Nation produced. As a young boy Sore-Belly, too, had listened attentively to the stirring tales of his mentors and had been an inquisitive pupil, eager to learn all he could about his ancestors, before he himself was at an age to contribute his own deeds to Crow history.

Much erroneous information has appeared in print and, especially so, on modern-day electronic media concerning Crow history and their old-time chiefs. Some such data obscures the true details, while certain historical events have, not a few times, been shamefully misconstrued. This work attempts to correct those misnomers, so that what follows is a true history of the Crow people during the time of their becoming fierce equestrian warriors as shown through the life and times of the aforesaid Sore-Belly, when the Apsaalooka or Raven Men ruled supreme across the Montana and Wyoming High Plains.

The information contained herein, is an admixture of the more responsible published and unpublished documented data, along with much oral and traditional history, imparted to the present Author by Native informants among the Crow and other tribes in contact with them. Of the published sources, particular attention is given to James P. Beckwourth`s *"Life and Adventures,"* the James H. Bradley manuscripts on the Crow, and Robert H. Lowie`s *"Crow Texts"* [See bibliography]. I have, however, been selective with the Beckwourth material, and only those events pertaining directly or indirectly to Chief Sore-Belly and to the current theme have been included. The wording throughout apart from where verbatim quotes are given, is necessarily, my own. I have further endeavoured to render the contents in a more readable style than would usually be employed by academics writing for a limited circle of colleagues, and as such, it is hoped that the proper Indian idiom is here expressed, without the distraction of academic jargon. Having said this, the gist of actual words accredited to certain persons, have been preserved in either original primary documents or in the tribal oral accounts themselves, and are in no way imaginative.

Research for the present volume has been long and varied, and without the encouragement, faith and invaluable information offered freely by my revered mentors Joseph Medicine Crow and Winona Plenty-Hoops, the finished work could not have seen the light of day. Grateful thanks are additionally extended to my special friends and informants among the Crows which include the Alex and Susan Bird-in-Ground family, Vernon and Gail Whiteman, Elias Goes Ahead, Truman Jefferson, and Lawrence Flat-Lip, and to James King, Wayne Medicine-Elk, Bill Tall-Bull and Clarence `Bisco` Spotted-Wolf of the Northern Cheyennes. Also, to a host of persons and informants from various tribes met and befriended along the way, albeit too numerous to mention here, I offer my unbounded thanks and certainly, they are not forgotten.

Among the libraries and archives that have made their unpublished collections available for my personal use, hearty thanks are duly given to the Smithsonian Institution, Washington D.C., The British Library, London; The Dull Knife College Library and Archives, Lame Deer, Montana; Magdalen Mountain Horse, Jon Ille, Tim McCleary and Tim Barnardis of the Little Bighorn College Library and Archives, Crow Agency, Montana; the Denver Historical Society and the Denver Public Library Archival Collections, Denver, Colorado, the Hudson`s Bay Company Archives, Winnipeg, Canada, and the Braun Research Library, Southwest Museum, Los Angeles, California. To the staff of all these Institutions the Author is forever indebted.

Brian [Spotted-Tail-Eagle] Keefe,
Lodge Grass, Montana. 2013.

– 0 – 0 –= 0 – 0 – 0 – 0 – 0 – 0 – 0 – 0 – 0 – 0 – 0 – 0 – 0 -

Chief Long-Hair defending the rear at Otter Creek, 1820. [Detail from a water-colour by the Author.]

# PART 1.

# DEFENDERS OF THE YELLOWSTONE COUNTRY

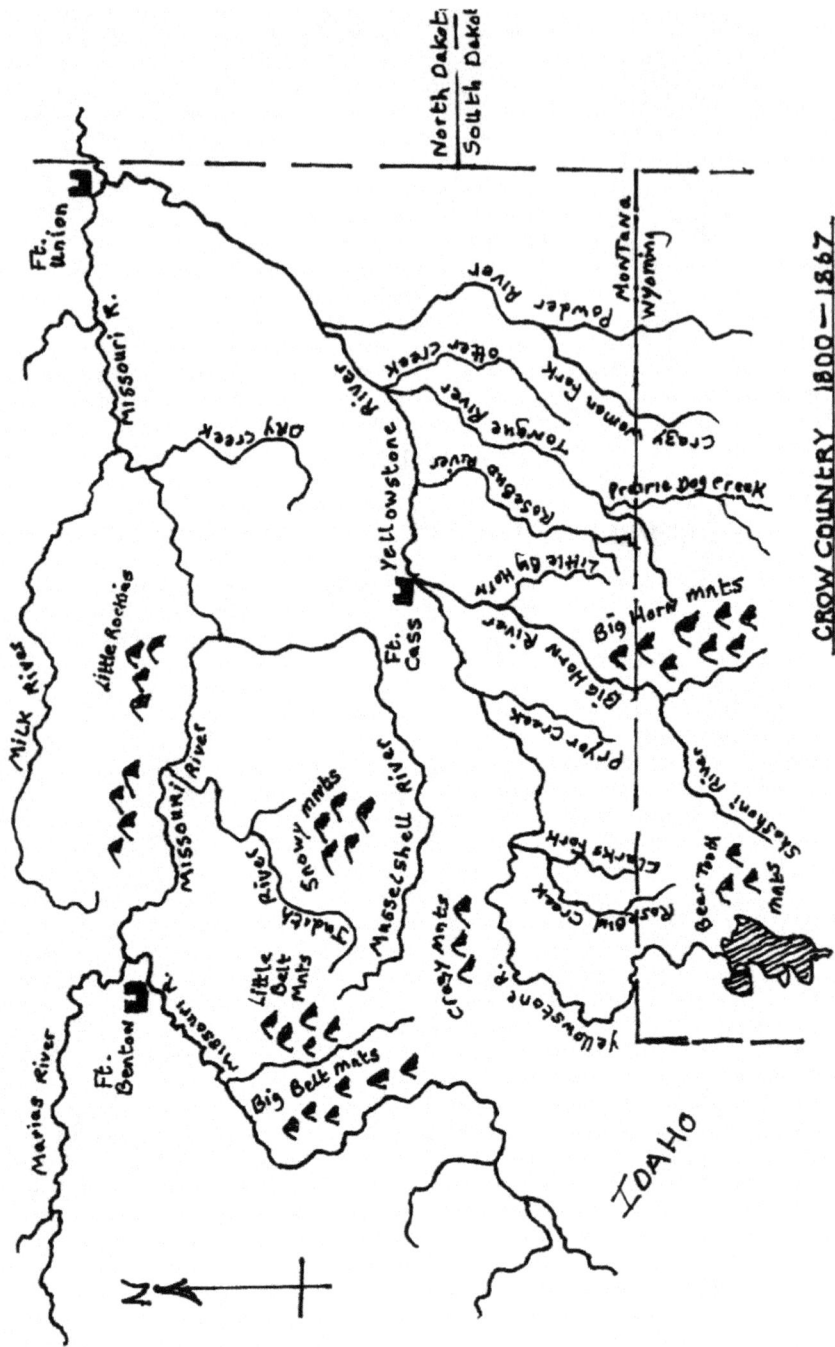

CROW COUNTRY 1800 — 1867

# CHAPTER 1.

## RISE OF THE APSAALOOKA.

Indian country was the best country, and the
best of Indian country belonged to the Crows.

Since before the beginning, *Akbaa-tadia* * was there. And with *Akbaa-tadia* was his secondary persona, *Isaah-ka-wauta* - Old-Man Coyote;- the winged inhabitants of the sky, and Mother Earth covered with water.

Old-Man Coyote, through whom *Akbaa-tadia* bestows its benevolence, bade the duck bring up mud from the watery depths. And with mud Old-Man-Coyote created the land upon which all things live. Old-Man-Coyote wandered over the land which was without form. So he fashioned the rivers and streams; the lakes, the rocks and mountains; the hills and valleys, canyons and defiles; the prairies, the forests and deserts, and in addition, he created everything that grows in those places, including the trees and grasses, the plants, fruits and tubers, all as he saw fit to do so.

Old-Man-Coyote then looked around for people to populate what he had done. But no people could he find. Thus he molded human figures from the red earth and clay around him and each of the creature species in turn. And hence, there came into being everyone and everything that breaths, walks and crawls in and over the places Old-Man created. Old-Man Coyote next chose a group of people he favored from the rest, and these became the Apsaalooka; "The Children of the Large-Beaked-Bird" who are also known as Raven Men and Crows. Old-Man-Coyote transported these people through the air and set them down in a bountiful place, abundant with buffalo and other game both large and small, along with fish-filled streams running like silver threads across the land.

All around chokecherries and other fruits blossomed, in addition to tubers of many kinds, and timber; sufficient for every need. During the sweltering heat of summer, cool breezes from the mountains blew across the grasslands, and when the geese fly south and "The-Great-North-Giant" spreads its white robe upon the land, the shadow of those mountains sheltered the people and gave respite from the biting winds of winter. In that bountiful place there thrived everything conducive to the people's needs and the people were thankful for what they had been given. When a Big-Horned sheep saved one later named Big-Metal from what had seemed like certain death, the people promised that the new land in which they dwelt, would evermore be known as Big Horn in that animal's honour. And Old-Man-Coyote was pleased with his chosen people. The Apsaalooka, he said, shall be the special guardians of *Echeta Casha*,** and they alone, `*Awaxawi ak iassee;*` - "Keepers of the Land."

Since that time forward the Apsaalooka have held the land which Old-Man-Coyote gave them, although once obliged to battle constantly against many

* **Great Spirit.**
** **The Yellowstone Country.**

foes. The bones of their Grandfathers and Great Grandfathers before them lie scattered around. For the Apsaalooka who walk that land today, do so by the blood of their ancestors shed upon it. Truly, it is Apsaalooka blood mingled with that of their enemies which impregnates the very ground upon which one treads. For Old-Man-Coyote had said,

> "I shall surround you with enemies who will try to take this fine land from you. To hold it your descendants must be brave and prove themselves deserving. Then, whenever you are in dire need you may call upon me, and I shall assist to preserve your country, your people and your name." [1]

These words of Old-Man-Coyote are burned deep into Apsaalooka minds, so even today they know them well, and will remember them always.

So it was that old-time Crow historians told only as much when first briefly explaining the origin of their people and their coming into *Echeta Casha*, the Yellowstone and Big Horn country. An explanation which includes an element of myth, but nonetheless, does infer that the Apsaalooka have long occupied the land in which they live, and true it is, the Crows have always fought hard and consistently in order to keep the land which still they call their own.

There is, however, another more historically correct and much more detailed account of Crow origins and migration to be gleaned from tribal oral history and tradition. A story corroborated in part by archaeological findings along with fragments of complementary evidence which, when taken together, offers a more plausible if not more graphic version. This oral tradition has been handed down over the course of at least sixteen generations [as of 1990], so that all adult persons of Apsaalooka blood should know the true history of their people. For in a time past, when buffalo and deer supplied both their material and physical needs while inhabiting the game-filled Montana region, Crow historians would narrate the earlier wanderings and life-style of their ancestors, and in such a way, the people were made aware that their forefathers had not always been the equestrian, buffalo-hunting nomads they eventually became.

Thus it is also told that as long ago as circa, AD. Ten-hundred, by the white man's calendar, the ancestors of the Apsaalooka had resided beyond two wide rivers far southeast of the Yellowstone and Big Horn country, in a land where it was always summer and trees grew standing in the water. In those same waters, Crow tradition relates, there then lived huge beasts - fearless and ferocious -which hunted the people and ate them. Such creatures, it is said, were very hard to kill, owing to their tough scaly skin and snapping jaws lined with razor-sharp teeth. It is not known today where exactly this place of habitat was. One suspects it refers to the southern parts of what are now the states of South Carolina and Georgia, and including, perhaps, the swamp lands of northern Florida, if not indeed, much further south across the Gulf of Mexico. Anciently, each of these regions were occupied predominately by Siouan-speaking peoples among whom the

Apsaalooka must be included. But in Apsaalooka tradition, this early place of habitat is merely referred to as, *"The land of Long-Ago Time."* [2]

In the words of the Author's adopted Grandfather, Joe Medicine-Crow,

> "In the long ago time, when our ancestors lived far to the southeast of this Big Horn country, our people had been hunter-gatherers and sometimes agriculturists. Often they were at the mercy of powerful enemies and fierce man-eating beasts, and were forced from one place of habitat to another in order to prevent their being exterminated." [3]

In that period the people were not known as Apsaalooka, but were members of three separate, albeit closely related and confederated bands much later known collectively as Hidatsa. These latter bands in the Long-ago time, constituted one of a number of cognate groups belonging to a much larger conglomerate of similar-speaking peoples, whose indigenous generic name has long since been forgotten. They were then a part of those known historically as Winnebago which also included the ancestral Mandan, Iowa and Oto, and only after an eon of circuitous migration, did the Proto-Crow in individual bands separate from their respective parent Hidatsa-speaking groups, and arrive in the country they now occupy to become the Apsaalooka Nation in their own right.

Notwithstanding an Athapaskan-stock element among them, what we do know from dialectical comparisons, in conjunction with traditions from other tribes and some archaeological evidence, is that the majority of Crows belong to the great Siouan linguistic family, members of which include the Dakota and Lakota [Sioux], Hidatsa, Mandan, Assiniboine, Winnebago, Omaha, Oto, Iowa and others, and with each of whom other than the Hidatsa and Mandan, the Crows at a much later date, were engaged in a state of chronic warfare.

A long-kept tradition among the Hunkpapa Lakota only recently imparted to outsiders, states that they, along with certain other Siouan-speaking groups which included the Winnebago, Mandan and Hidatsa, had, in their ancient time, resided far south in lands beyond the Gulf of Mexico. They were, the tradition continues, then in close contact with, if not a component part of ancient Mayan peoples from what are now the regions of Guatemala and Yucatan. Certainly the Winnebago and Mandan each have near identical traditions relating to an ancient residence far south across the Gulf of Mexico, and along with the Lakota, they show a number of unique comparisons in their mythologies and religious observances with those of the Maya. It cannot, though, be determined from these traditions alone, if the ancestors of the aforementioned Siouan tribes first traveled north through Mexico then east across southern Texas and Louisiana, or actually crossed the waters of the Gulf itself in sea-going craft. [4]

Whatever the scenario, the Mandan claim to have next settled adjacent to the mouth of the Mississippi River in the present-day state of Louisiana, and if this was so, then their nearest linguistic relatives later known as Hidatsa must have been close by. From the mouth of the Mississippi the Mandan moved upriver on their own volition in staggered phases, whilst other Siouan groups including the Hidatsa element which by then had separated from the Mandan, seem to have spread northeast into Alabama, Georgia and South Carolina.

As the above applies to the aforementioned Siouan groups which include Hidatsa-speaking peoples, then it must by definition also apply to the early progenitors of our Crow subjects who evolved from them, and thereafter, wandered northwest across the vastness of the land, until after the course of many generations and their separating from the Hidatsa, they finally claimed the southern Montana country as their own.

Prior to becoming the Crow Nation of more recent time, their Hidatsa ancestors had broken away from the parent Winnebago-Mandan group and divided into three separate entities, each of which spoke similar dialects to one another. These three affiliated but autonomous Hidatsa-speaking groups, had then claimed adjacent hunting areas whilst roaming on foot as nomadic hunter / gatherers, and over the course of generations, other factions split from these groups to become themselves additional independent bands, each of which wandered off on its own volition at different periods and in different directions to experience their respective ills and fortunes. It was only after these later-date independent bands eventually united, that they became known as Apsaalooka, i.e. Raven Men or Crows, and their separate migration stories then inter-woven to create a single, semi-constant narrative. [5] Hence forward, it would suffice for the newly established Crow Nation which, during the late historic time of circa, 1830 comprised four major divisions known as,

> Mountain Crow [Aka "Many Lodges"]
> River Crow [Aka "Raven-Men,*" Gens de Panse"* or Paunch Indians,
>     and "Dung-on-the-River-Banks"]
> Kicked-in-the-Bellies [Aka "Whistling-Waters"]
> Beaver Dries its Fur Band, or "Dried-Hairs" [now extinct].

As did their Hidatsa kin-folk, the Crows as a Nation adhered to a rigid clan system [i.e. all members of a particular group claiming a common ancestor] which among the Crows, was matrilineal in structure. Originally, there had been only four separate clans representing the original four autonomous bands, but by the 1800s, the clans had expanded to eight and at an even later date, had further increased to twelve. These clans were grouped together in pairs as follows,

| | |
|---|---|
| [1] Greasy-Mouths. | [3] Whistling-Waters. |
| [2] Sore [Burned] Lips. | [4] Poor-War-Deeds. |
| | |
| [5] Streaked-Lodges. | [7] Newly-Made Lodges. |
| [6] Dried-Out-Furs. | [8] Big-Lodges. |
| | |
| [9] Piegans. | [11] Ties-the-Bundle. |
| [10] Treacherous Lodges. | [12] Brings-Home-the-Game. |

It was, say the Crows, late in the 17$^{th}$ century after their split from the Hidatsa and their taking up residence between the mouth of the Yellowstone and Little Missouri, that they first met the Kiowa, a Tanoan-speaking people, and with whom ever since, the Crows have been firm friends and associates.

Friendship with the Kiowa, also opened the way for Crow friendship with another group of foreigners of Plains Apache Athapaskan-speakers, then known as Gattacka, but at a later date, referred to as Prairie or Kiowa-Apache.

The Kiowa for their part had long known the Gattacka, since their two peoples at a much earlier time had inhabited the same Rocky Mountain district of eastern Alberta, Canada, and had continued in some degree of harmonious contact even after the Gattacka left that region and migrated southeast into the Nebraska Plains. Crow friendship with the Kiowa thus automatically brought friendship with the Gattacka, a relationship through which the Crows – even though at loggerheads with most other Plains Apache groups, - were later to benefit from in no small way.

At that time the Gattacka were comparatively rich in horses, obtained from Lipan-Apache relatives and Pueblo traders from the south who brought Spanish horses north of the Rio Grande and into the Southern and Central Plains. It was the Gattacka initially, who not only became the main suppliers of horses to the Northern Tribes, but also brought them iron weapons, tools and domestic metal items, likewise obtained from Spanish and Pueblo contacts.

Before this, however, the most important thing the Crows, Kiowa and Gattacka had in common, was that all three were then in conflict with other horse-riding peoples, who came up from the south and also east from the Great Basin region and into the Western and Central Plains searching for isolated camps to raid. These ferocious enemy war-bands likewise had trading contacts with Pueblo Indians and Spanish-speaking peoples further south, and as early as 1680, they owned a few horses and had iron-bladed weapons with which to terrorize the pedestrian stone-using Northern Tribes, who as a consequence, reeled under such attacks and were invariably defeated.

In the early French and English documents these nomadic equestrian marauders are designated *Gens de Serpent* and *Snakes* respectively. The same who came careering out of the prairie haze wielding long-handled stone-headed war-clubs called `Pomegons,` iron axes and twelve-foot lances tipped with Spanish sword blades. Their bodies and horses were encased in a kind of overlapping leather armor reinforced with a mixture of sand and glue that rendered them virtually impervious to the stone-headed arrows of their victims. Mercilessly, they killed all the men folk they could find; destroyed their victim's lodges and crops, and carried off the latter`s women and children to be sold in the Spanish slave markets in exchange for more horses and iron weapons needed to pursue their aggression. Collectively, the term Snakes most often, referred to those mounted war-bands of allied Shoshoni, Flathead and Kutenai, but was sometimes extended to include the latter`s own mounted enemies comprising the Ute and numerous Athapascan-speaking Apache bands of the Central and Southern Plains. This is apparent from the LaVerendrye brothers` report of 1743, wherein it is stated that the greater part of the Snakes live in forts, while others wander about occupying a

5

large extent of territory, and adds that they were often at war with the Spaniards. We know that the Shoshoni, Flathead and Kutenai did not live in `forts,` they being nomadic buffalo hunters. But several Ute and Plains Apache bands did then reside in permanent villages surrounded by some kind of hide and timber stockade, and it was the Ute and Apaches who were regularly at war with the Spanish provinces, rather than the Shoshoni and Flatheads, who went south moreover, with the intention to trade.

From the middle of the seventeenth century, successive Governors of what was then known as New Spain, had encouraged the holding of annual intertribal trading fairs at several of the Pueblo towns, particularly those of Picuris, Santa Fe and Taos along the Rio Grande in what are now the states of Arizona and New Mexico. To these `fairs` came nomadic pedestrian tribes from the North, carrying tanned hides of buffalo, deer and elk; buckskin garments and dried buffalo meat to exchange with the Pueblos for woollen blankets, vegetables and corn. In addition, the nomadic tribes, or `Nortenos` [Northerners], as the Spaniards called them, obtained metal knives and hatchets, iron cooking pots, arrow heads and sword blades of Spanish manufacture, but no firearms or horses. Since many years earlier, the Spaniards had in place a `bandio` or embargo against supplying the *Nortenos* with such weapons and animals, and anyone caught trying to do so was severely fined or punished. This was in order to diminish the effectiveness of the same nomadic tribes when the latter chose to conduct hostilities against the Pueblos and Spaniards, with whom at other times, they had been trading in apparent harmony and friendship. Not until after the revolt of 1680, when Pueblo peoples rose up against their Spanish overseers and acquired a vast number of horses from the then abandoned Spanish stock, did such animals become diffused in some quantity among tribes such as the Snake, Apache, Ute and Gattacka, and who thereafter, could afford to trade off their surplus stock to other tribes of their choice.

The Spaniards themselves had little use for most of what the *Nortenos* offered for barter, apart that is, for slaves. These were needed by the Spanish land owners to work in their fields and as servants in their haciendas and on their sprawling cattle Rancheras. It was much cheaper to acquire such beings from the *Nortenoes* than from the regulated slave auctions held in Spanish, French and even Anglo-American territories elsewhere, and the *Nortenos* were only too pleased to exchange their captives for much sought after wares of European manufacture. In such a way the slave trade, certainly in the Southwest, became a regular commercial activity which involved certain Northern Tribes as middlemen, so to speak. In the pursuit of this commercial interaction, all those involved [apart from the slaves we might assume] were highly satisfied with their role and subsequent profits. Thus tribal raiding of more remote nomadic peoples in order to take captives to feed the Spanish slave trade soon become endemic, and was a major factor in further advancing the intertribal war culture of the inhabitants of the Southern, Central and Northern Plains, which persisted late into the historic era.

The result of constant hostility and incursions by horse-riding Snakes, particularly from Shoshoni-speaking groups and their Flathead and Kutenai allies in their search for slaves, became so overbearing that both the Crows and Kiowa found themselves being pushed further east and southeast, as they endeavoured to extricate themselves from Snake aggression.

It is indicative to note that according to their own traditions, the Crows only first heard of horses whilst inhabiting an area near a *"Great Medicine Lake,"* and it is further said, that such animals originally came out of that same body of water. Perhaps this statement is meant to apply to a time when Crows resided far to the northeast in the vicinity of the fresh water expanse known as Devil's Lake in northeastern North Dakota, as stated to the present Author by more than one contemporary tribal informant. An alternative Crow tradition, however, infers that the first horses their people actually saw, came from the direction of Great Salt Lake in present-day Utah, either from the west or south, and indeed, these were the two directions from whence - more often than not - appeared their mounted Ute and Shoshoni foes. Other modern-day Crow informants admit that their ancestors had once been acquainted with horses during some early period in their history, but are adamant that they did not until much later, keep any such animals for their own use.

The Author's Crow relative Alex Bird-In-Ground on the other hand, narrated yet another old Crow tradition, which states that while residing somewhere adjacent to the eastern foothills of the Rocky Mountains in what is now the west-central part of Colorado [thus indicating a date between 1715 and 1720], a party of Crows once spied what they thought was a long reptile-like monster with many legs and glistening body, winding its way across the prairie expanse, intent, so the Crows thought, on doing harm to their people. The strange sight proved to be a column of horseback riders, which included a small band of Apache-speaking people on their way north into the western Nebraska Plains, and in which country, some broke off from the main body and continued northwest to their kindred the Sarsi around what is now the city of Calgary in Alberta, Canada. Others among this band of horsemen wore metal helmets and breastplates and carried shields burnished bright to reflect the sun. The horses themselves were encased in body armor fashioned from large pieces of leather, each shaped like the letter 'D' which overlapped one another in rows. The strangers had asked permission from the Crows to travel through their country; to which the latter agreed, and hereafter their two peoples became good friends.

The above story seems to relate to the first time Crow Indians came face to face with Spanish-speaking peoples, who are indicated in the tradition as having accompanied the aforesaid small Apache-speaking band into the Central Plains. It is known that the ill-fated Lieutenant Colonel Pedro de Villasur's Spanish expedition, that went north from Santa Fe to the Loup Fork of the Platte in mid-summer of 1720, did include a large contingent of Pueblo Indians and some sixty Apache warriors with which the expedition had supplemented its smaller number of Spanish soldiers. The expedition, subsequently, met with disaster at the hands of hostile Pawnee and the latter's allies, supposedly at the Forks of the Platte. This was country frequented by the Gattacka, whose permanent villages stood along Dismal River not far to the east. The Crow tradition then, as recounted above, is important here, as it confirms an early Crow connection with the Gattacka, i.e.

7

Kiowa-Apache, who, it is said, in these early days were friends of the Crows and often visited their Sarsi Apache-speaking kin-folk then resident in the Calgary, Alberta region. As noted earlier, it was the Gattacka at a later date who supplied horses and mules to the Northern Tribes, although neither does this particular account suggest the Crows obtained any horses for their own use at the time in question.

Some few horses – it is also said in Crow tradition – were obtained throughout the early 1730s and after years when; periodically, one or another band of Crows participated in intertribal trading fairs in the north, held annually by the Gattacka and certain more Northern Tribes on or near Horse Creek, a southern tributary of the North Fork of the Platte just west of the present Wyoming – Nebraska state line. At such times, peoples who generally met each other only on the field of combat, then came together briefly to trade. And so Taos and Picuris Pueblos and both Lipan and Gattacka Apaches brought horses and mules, metal items and blue glass beads from the south, to exchange with the Crows, Kiowa and Arapaho for dried buffalo meat, furs, pelts and quill-worked leather garments. Since their first visits to these `fairs,` both the Crows and Kiowa had realized the obvious benefits to their everyday existence which a regular supply of horses and European trade goods could bring, and certainly from that time on, both the Crows and their Kiowa friends were fully aware that unless they themselves acquired such animals in sufficient quantity, they could not hope to defend their people adequately against their more numerous and ferocious mounted Snake foes. Thus, sometime during the early 1730s, one or more of the several Kiowa bands started south on foot, in order that they themselves might obtain their own horses by more direct means. With them filled with an equal desire and determination, went a large party of Crows.

An historical anecdote narrated to the present Author by the Crow elder Barney Old Coyote, tells how long ago, when the Crows and Kiowa were *Awala-diile* * and lived together in the northeastern Wyoming country, a part of the Kiowa decided to leave their hearths, lured by horses that were available for the taking from Pueblo and Spanish-speaking peoples in the south. At first these Kiowa involved moved through the Big Horn Mountains, until they came to the well-known pass near present-day Dayton, Wyoming not far from the eminence known as Cloud`s Peak. Traveling over the pass they continued south on foot, and embarked on a journey that would keep them away from home nearly two years before returning to the North country and reuniting with kinfolk they had earlier left behind. According to the present-day Crow version, when this Kiowa group had been about to leave the Big Horns, a number of Crow youths who had fallen in love with Kiowa maidens, followed up the Kiowa in a body in order to be with their sweethearts. When arrived among the traveling Kiowa, this party of amorous Crows was told in no uncertain terms to go back to their own people empty-handed. This the Crows refused to do, and not being able to persuade them further, the Kiowa finally allowed the Crows to join their lovers. By so doing, a number of Crows stayed with these Kiowa and endured a prolonged time of wandering through the southern country.

**\*Literally, `Earth walking,` i.e., on foot.**

Of course, what the above anecdote commemorates, is that a body of Crows; evidently a raiding party, was included among the particular Kiowa group in question, and rather, it was the lure of horses and mules which had encouraged this first Crow war-party to undertake such a long and hazardous journey south.

The story falls silent at this point, although whether or not this Crow war-party was successful in its venture, several albeit small adventurous groups of Crows thereafter, also trekked on foot far south to the Spanish Possessions in order to procure such animals for themselves. Early Spanish Colonial documents mention in 1732 and again in 1735, that among the Northern peoples or *Nortenos* suddenly appearing at the Pueblo towns, were included Kiowa with pole-drags pulled by dogs, and who were then hostile to Spanish-speaking peoples.

Once the Crows had their own access to the Spanish Rancheras and settlements in what then embraced the present-day states of Arizona, Nevada, Texas and New Mexico, horses, mules and Spanish European artifacts soon became common in Crow camps.

An old Indian road commonly known as "The Great North Trail," ran north to south along the tree line close to the eastern foothills of the Backbone of the World [Rocky Mountains]. This trail stretched some two-thousand miles from a starting point in the region of the Mackenzie Delta of the far north [Canada], and extended south to the Rio Grande and even further south through what is known as the Raton Pass and into Sonora, Mexico. Likely, the road had been utilized at least as early as the 9th century AD., during the southern migration of Navaho Indians from the north, and at a much later date, by both Plains Apache and Comanche bands when driven south from the Northern and Central Plains. Such was the road's near constant use that as late as 1896, ruts made by countless Indian pole-drags over hundreds of years, were still plainly visible at certain points along the trail.

During the early decades of the eighteenth century, the aforementioned road had already become a well-worn trade and war route for Indians both north and south, and moreover, for Mexican and Pueblo traders seeking out customers among the Northern Tribes, In later years, the Kiowa used the same route when visiting their Crow friends in the north; as did the Crows when reciprocating these visits to the Kiowa, while more adventurous warriors continued south along the trail, in order to raid outlying Spanish haciendas in the Mexican provinces of Sonora and Durango.

Traveling the trail was, though, a dangerous business for the Crows. Numerous war-bands of Apache, Ute and Navaho habitually scouted the route where it passed through their own territories, hoping to rob or massacre one or another of the traveling parties. Mexican traders, customarily, were immune to such danger, as it was not in the Indian's interest to deter the latter from bringing much desired wares to their camps. But the Crows of all tribes apt to travel the road were particularly vulnerable, as they seem to have had many more enemies to contend with, and because such trips back and forth might occupy a period of between one and two years duration, only the bravest of Crow parties traveled so far.

Crow oral tradition relates, that when first these early war-parties went on foot far south specifically to raid, they came face to face with mounted Spaniards clad in iron The Crows had then stood motionless; rooted to the spot with fear, or – as the Crow idiom has it,

*"...the warriors suddenly had frog legs which could not run."* [6]

This had made the Crows easy prey to the Spaniards who merely ran their horses into them and struck them down with swords and lances. During this period, say the Crows, their warriors would actually kill the horses to get at the riders, and this statement concurs with the report of the Sieur de LaVerendrye, who when among the Mandan towns on the Missouri late in 1738, heard stories of mounted men to the south who wore beards and Spanish cuirasses made of iron net [chain mail]. These people sometimes crossed the Plains, he was told, but actually lived a whole summer's journey away. Arrows were useless against them and one had first to shoot their horses after which the iron-clad riders could easily be run down and killed, being too encumbered on foot to affect a speedy escape. They [the people of the south] had metal bucklers [shields], very light in color and fought with lances and sabers in the use of which they were very skillful. Sometime later, La Verendrye was further told by an Assiniboine warrior,

"Last summer I killed one of the people who was covered with iron.
If I had not first killed the horse; I could not have got the man." [7]

After a while the Crows learned how to avoid the flying hooves, and soon became adept in roping the iron-clad riders from their saddles or pulling them to the ground with their bare hands. Surprisingly, the Crows did not then often kill the riders, being content merely to take some of their victim's metal accouterments and, of course, the horse which they then rode home in triumph. It was when one such Whistling Waters Crow war-party returned to the Yellowstone country with several Mexican horses in tow, a curious tribal member pulled vigorously on the long tail of one of the beasts as he compared it with his own long hair. For his pains, he received a severe kick from the animal's hind legs which crippled him for life. It was because of this singular event, that the family group to which the unfortunate belonged was thereafter, dubbed the Kicked-in-the-Belly band, and by which name they are still known today.

Such raids upon the Spaniards and expeditions against southern tribes of horse-using Indians, along with their occasional attendance at the aforesaid intertribal trading fairs on Horse Creek, did allow the Crows to build up their own herds, which in turn, enabled them to confront their Snake and other enemies on more equal terms. Prior to their acquisition of horses, the Crows and their pedestrian neighbors had been obliged to site their villages in the foothill regions of the mountains, or along the rivers and streams crisscrossing the Plains. Thus their Snake enemies had merely to follow a particular river's course, or scout out the foothill country in order to find their quarry.

Now, however, with horses in significant number, the Crows had the means of unprecedented mobility and from then on, it seems, the Crows could never get enough such animals to satisfy their want.

10

Moving from one camping site to another; on the hunt or at war, with the horse the Indian could now survive as a nomad on the open Plains. A man's wealth became assessed by the number of horses he owned, and with horses he bought himself a wife and hauled his heavy buffalo-hide tepee covers and domestic belongings on pony-drags, transporting himself and his family as they traversed the grasslands in pursuit of the herds. To increase one's wealth, the raiding of another tribe's stock became the regular past-time for almost every adult male. But if caught by the indignant owners the thieves were invariably killed, which in turn, would necessitate a retaliation raid in order to avenge the loss of fellow tribesmen. At such times the prize was then the scalps of their quarry and the capture of women and children to be adopted as tribal members, in order to compensate their own losses suffered in previous engagements.

Such activity became the means by which any lowly warrior could achieve prestige as the heroic defender of his tribe and, not least, as the fearless nemesis of his people's enemies.

Overnight, so to speak, war became the main focal point in the social structure and ideology to which the Indian subscribed, and to the wild unconstrained Plains nomad, performing upon the field of conflict became the very breath of his nostrils. Warfare became his reason for living; his livelihood; and the continuous unbroken reality of his being. By harbouring such a concept it allowed his tribe to survive in a naturally aggressive environment, while social standing and renown were more easily obtained through one's heroic deeds achieved in battle, or on the horse-stealing trail.

Thus the pursuit of intertribal warfare became an inseparable dimension to that of the Plains Indian's day to day existence. One hostile act merely being reciprocated by another, inevitably creating a never-ending cycle of aggression between the tribes and to such degree, that even the original episode which had initiated a feud in the first place was, in most cases, entirely lost from memory. Tribe continued to fight against tribe for successive generations, simply because they supposed they had always done so in the past.

So it was that during the period between circa, 1740 and 1750, the Crows and Kiowa were not the only peoples in direct confrontation with the Snakes. Other Plains Tribes were also suffering Snake attacks and sometimes, several of these discomfited tribes actually united their forces, in order to combat the common enemy in a joint undertaking.

During late summer, 1742, two sons of the aforementioned Sieur de LaVerendrye, whilst travelling southwest from the Mandan villages at the mouth of Heart River on the Missouri, met a mixed band of Crows and Arapaho which people they termed *"Beaux Hommes"* or `Handsome Men.` [8] Ostensibly, this meeting took place in the vicinity of Bear Butte in the north-western part of what is now South Dakota, and after more than a month with their hosts, one or more of the *Beaux Hommes* conducted the brothers southward, meeting and joining several foreign tribal groups along the way, until eventually, they arrived at a grand gathering of allied camps, among whom were included Kiowa, Kiowa Apache [Gattacka] and Cheyennes. The allied bands had come together in order to launch a combined crusade against the Snakes, who – the brothers were told – were the enemies of all. The grand crusade actually came to naught, as the allied host broke up before meeting the enemy and dispersed in their separate bands back to their respective territories. However, the event does indicate that the Crows were not then facing the Snakes alone, but rather, along with the aforementioned tribes, were presenting a united front against a mutual foe. The event also indicates that the Snakes were still then regarded as formidable opponents to have incited such a large allied gathering in the first place, and as late as 1772 /`73, the Hudson`s Bay Company employee Mathew Cocking when on the south Saskatchewan Plains with a mixed band of pedestrian Cree and Assiniboine, mentioned that when horses were seen in the distance, his hosts were much afraid, supposing them to indicate the presence of Snake Indians, *"...with whom"* Cocking said,*" they* [his hosts] *were then at variance."* [9]

The same traveller had earlier been shown a coat without sleeves of six-fold quilted leather which, he was told, was used by the Snakes as protection against the arrows of their adversaries. Sometime later he met with a small band of Gros Ventres [Atsina], some of whom he noticed were themselves wearing, *"... jackets of moose leather six-fold quilted and without sleeves."* [10] [Presumably a fashion either captured or adopted from Snakes who they had met in battle].

No wonder by the date 1780, at which time the Crows themselves and other Plains Tribes had acquired a significant number of horses to accommodate their every need, in addition to iron-bladed weapons and a small number of flintlock guns through contacts both along and northeast of the Missouri, that they retaliated in kind against their erstwhile nemesis. Even later when guns came among them in quantity, all those once on the receiving end of Snake attacks beset the latter repeatedly without the least show of mercy. The Crows and others then began destroying Snake camps at random, and reciprocated by killing and enslaving that people. This being said, the eventual demise of Snake and Plains Apache peoples as prominent forces in the Northern and Central Plains, was not entirely due to the Crows and others alone. Such had been exacerbated by an even more destructive element, unseen and silent moving, which finished the work the Crows and their allies had begun, finally destroying forever Snake and Plains Apache power in the buffalo country east of the Rocky Mountains.

This silent killer was `xaxibaleshee,` the white man's "Spotted death,"as the Crows called it, more commonly known as Smallpox.

Similar devastating outbreaks had occurred in earlier years, but appeared in more virulent form between 1781 / `82. This time, it swept the entire North American Continent and carried off the Indians in their droves. The occupants of the Missouri River towns lost more than half their numbers and villages, whilst the more nomadic Lakota and Cheyenne, being able to outrun the disease and isolate themselves in scattered camps far from the source of contagion, did not succumb to the same degree, although their numbers were also reduced. The Crows, however, suffered diabolically. Of their estimated two-thousand lodges comprising some ten-thousand persons which the combined Crow bands could boast prior to 1781, after the outbreak had run its course; coupled with several albeit less severe maladies throughout the rest of that decade and the early 1790s, the entire Nation just prior to 1800, could muster little more than four-thousand persons, residing in some eight-hundred lodges distributed among the four semi-autonomous Crow bands.

Both the Blackfoot and Assiniboine - old adversaries of the Crows – also lost heavily in the same contagion and as a result, for a few years thereafter, they remained north of the Missouri whilst recuperating from their decimating ordeal.

In addition, the contagion devastated age-old tribal political structures, resulting in a general breakdown in social and tribal cohesion which in itself, created a great upheaval among all peoples roaming the buffalo country west of the Mississippi. Tribe now pushed upon tribe, as each took advantage of a weakened neighbor whose disparity in number and military prowess, made them vulnerable to a stronger, more determined foe, endeavouring to extend its hunting grounds, or simply to gain the ascendency over long-time antagonists.

As above mentioned, the Shoshoni-speaking Snakes, along with their Kutenai and Flathead allies and the Plains Apache, also suffered. In fact, they, too, succumbed in their thousands, due to their even closer contact with Spanish and Pueblo settlements where the disease was particularly prevalent. In total they lost more than three-fifths of their entire populations and withal, Snake and Apache power on the Plains came to an abrupt and decisive end. Never again would they prove themselves military powers to be reckoned with. Hereafter, they reaped the whirlwind from those they had once terrorized and slaughtered without compunction.

By 1790 the Shoshoni had lost the advantage completely. Unlike their enemies they could not obtain guns in any appreciable quantity, owing to the continuation of the age-old Spanish embargo which still prohibited supplying Indians such weapons, while in addition, their eastern and northern trade routes were blocked by avenging Crows and Blackfoot, who now stood between the Snakes and those few English and French-speaking traders both along and north of the Missouri. As a consequence, the Snakes began suffering constant, vigorous assaults upon their villages, which they themselves could not match in any comparable manner. Soon they were pushed out of the Plains and west across the mountains, where for many years they were debarred altogether from re-entering the buffalo country by their better armed foes and for a time, were prevented from attending the intertribal trading fairs still being held annually on Horse Creek and also sometimes from attending comparable `fairs` on Green River in the west-central part of Wyoming. The Comanche Shoshoni-speaking bands for their part, who appear to have fared slightly better than their Eastern Snake cousins, fled south to and below the Arkansas River, while the Shoshoni, Flathead and Kutenai remained in situ west of the Rocky Mountains, in an effort to escape complete annihilation.

Some years later in 1805, when met on the Columbia River in present day Washington State by the Lewis and Clark expedition, Shoshoni remnants of their once powerful Nation complained bitterly to the explorers that in recent time they had roamed with impunity over the Northern Plains, but the guns of their enemies, they said, had driven them west beyond the Big Horn and Wind River Mountains and prevented them hunting buffalo as had been the habit of their fathers.

In 1831, the white trapper Warren A. Ferris, was told by a Flathead Indian how his tribe likewise, had been terrorized by gun-toting enemies when residing in the buffalo country east of the Rockies,

> "...They had firearms and we had none. We knew nothing about guns except their effects. Often they attacked us when we went on the Plains to hunt buffalo. With their thunder and lightning they killed many of our bravest warriors, but they never came in reach of our arrows. Sometimes their young warriors closed in with us and were defeated, but their friends never failed to repay us fourfold, from a safe distance......one time when we were in the buffalo country, we saw our best warriors falling around us almost daily for several moons. But we were never able to avenge their deaths. Goaded by thirst for revenge, we often rushed forth upon our enemies. They retreated as we advanced, and so remained at the same distance, where our arrows could not reach them...At last Big-Foot, the head chief of our tribe, gathered his warriors in a council and made a speech to them. He reminded them of their helplessness before their enemies, and he persuaded them to leave the country and to find a safe retreat in the mountains. For one whole moon we traveled southwestward...We went through a gap in the mountains and down to a river that flows toward the setting sun." [11]

Here, though, in the above extract, Ferris's Flathead narrator was referring also to Blackfoot enemies, rather than to disagreements with the Crows and Kiowa alone.

It is indicative, however, that a Brule Lakota winter-count once kept by Baptist Good, records for the year 1781 / '82 that this was the last time lance-wielding enemies on horseback from the Western Plains came to attack them. The enemies referred to, no doubt, represent Shoshoni, Plains Apache and even Arickara when all three, although not as allies, had for many years previously been raiding Lakota villages at random adjacent to and east of the Missouri.

The Crows, conversely, have a tradition that it was their people alone who finally drove the hated Snakes from the Big Horn and Yellowstone regions, forcing the Snakes to seek refuge west across the mountains. This was after a great battle had been fought between their tribes lasting three days, and during which event, the Crow chief had caused the sun to stand still, enabling his people to win a great and decisive victory. Having said this, it does appear that once the Shoshoni, Flathead and Kutenai were no longer regarded as a serious threat, the Crows temporarily patched up their quarrel with them, and sometimes, even joined together against common foes such as the Assiniboine and the several Blackfoot-speaking tribes, and the Cree, who the Crows knew as *"Sahiia."*

Thus we are informed by the Reverend Robert Rundle from what Pikuni Blackfoot told him in 1847, that fifty or sixty years prior to the latter date, a large-scale battle had been fought on the banks of what has since become known as Sly-Shooting River not far from the present-day city of Edmonton in central Alberta,

14

Canada. On the one side, Rundle was told, were five-hundred Flathead, Kutenai, Nez-Perce, Snakes [Shoshoni] and Crows, then acting as allies against a similar force of combined Pikuni, Blood, Siksika, Sarsi and Cree along with two or three Stony Assiniboine. As it was the Blackfoot and their allies were well-supplied with guns, while those opposing them had only two guns in their entire arsenal. The victory then, not surprisingly, was with the Blackfoot and their allies, who lost only one man killed. This being a Pikuni chief who had actually been slain early in the morning during a sly attack before the main battle had begun. The opposing force of allied combatants which included Crows, lost upwards of one-hundred killed in the engagement proper, and were driven forty or fifty miles south from the battleground. [12]

Be this as it may, once entrenched in the rich hunting grounds vacated by the Snakes between the Missouri on the north and the Forks of the Platte in the south, and from the mouth of the Yellowstone in the east, to the Big Horn and beyond in the west, the Crows set up their tepees and claimed title to all that land which they referred to in its entirety as *"Eechee-likakasha-Aasha,"* i.e., "Elk River Country," but known to others as `*Absaroka,*` " Home of the Crows."

From that time on as new inhabitants of the Big Horn and Yellowstone country, the Crows soon became middlemen *par excellence* in the ongoing intertribal trading network involving both northern and southern tribes. Regularly, Crows attended the above mentioned trading fairs held annually on Horse Creek and at various points along Green River, where again, both friend and foe among whom were included Pueblo and Spanish-speaking Mexicans and erstwhile enemies such as Flathead, Nez-Perce and Ute, and at times, even one and another band of Shoshoni and Comanche, continued to come together for brief periods each year to reap the benefits of mutual commerce. To the fairs on Green River, the Flathead and Nez-Perce brought great numbers of horses which they now raised themselves on the lush grasslands west of the Rockies, while the Pueblos continued to supply woolen blankets and garden produce, and the Comanche brought animals they had stolen during their southern raids. The Mexicans for their part, offered their usual assortment of Spanish-made domestic items and iron-bladed weapons, while the Crows in turn, instead of bringing dried buffalo meat and leather quill-embroidered garments as they had of old, now brought much sought after guns, powder and ball obtained from Hidatsa relatives and Mandan friends on the Missouri, who themselves, acquired such items in their own trade with the more northern Assiniboine and Cree, and even from French Canadian traders actually domiciled in Mandan and Hidatsa towns. Thus a small quantity of the guns and ammunition which the Hidatsa and Mandan passed on to the Crows in exchange for horses and mules, the Crows then bartered to the Comanche, Shoshoni and Ute in exchange for more horses and Spanish commodities at the Green River fairs.

In such a way, a continuous cycle of intertribal trade which revolved around horses and European goods was extant not only in the Pueblo towns of the south, but was now established in the north through the innovation of the Northern Tribes, and the Crows as one of the leading entrepreneurs in such commerce, became rich and formidable through their transactions, relative to what Indians then considered as constituting wealth in their native state.

Notwithstanding, however, their new-found affluence and being entrenched firmly in lands which, they believed, had earlier been promised to their ancestors by Old-Man-Coyote, the Crows were not immune from repeated attacks upon their villages, or relieved in any discernible degree from hostile pressure directed against them. Rather, they were beset by numerous tribes from both far and near, some of whom such as the Shoshoni, Flathead and Kutenai, oft-times continued to resist Crow occupation of the country, while others including the several Blackfoot-speaking tribes of Blood, Pikuni and Siksika, in common with the Assiniboine and Cree after recuperating from the recent contagion, not only constantly endeavoured to increase their pony herds from Crow stock, but were intent separately upon coveting for their exclusive use great tracts of rich hunting ground, teeming with buffalo, antelope and other game, which comprised a significant part of the newly acquired Crow domain.

So it was, the Crows became fully occupied in stemming ever increasing inroads into their country by a host of enemies, and among whom were soon included antagonists from the east such as the *Aashua-pashko* or Cut-Heads – i.e., the Lakota, and the *Isaashupshe* or Stripped-Arrows – the Cheyenne, although these latter did not then act as allies.

The Crows state that at least three decades prior to the opening of the nineteenth century, the Lakota were already attacking Crows for no better reason than when receiving a fresh supply of iron points, hatchets and guns at the annual Lakota trading fairs held on James River east of the Missouri, they would say among themselves, *"Let us try them out on the Crows."* [13]

Thus was the beginning of the endemic warfare between Crows on one side and Lakota on the other, while the Crows were also forced to defend themselves against the Cheyennes and Suhtaio, after these tribes likewise, commenced raiding Crow camps during their own steady encroachment west.

This statement is at variance to the Cheyenne view, who declare it was Crows who first opened hostilities against the Cheyenne, by assaulting the latter's camps and hunting parties in order to obtain women captives, personal war-honours and prestige, if not merely for the excitement of doing so before any official declaration of war had been entered into. The Cheyennes do admit, though, that before the coming of the great smallpox of 1781-`82, such raids by the Crows were not during those early days of a significant nature, and the Lakota for their part, state that neither did they themselves then regard the Crows as an enemy of importance. Notwithstanding that a Lakota winter-count mentions that a large Lakota war-party went west as far as the Big Horn Mountains as early as 1726, and the Yankton Sioux count of John K. Bear records that in 1771, an important battle then took place during which the Yankton Killed many Crow Indians. Yet another big Sioux–Crow fight is noted in the Oglala Lakota count of John Colhof for 1774, during which event when the Lakota were in retreat, an Oglala of the Heyoka or Clown Society stayed behind and shot arrows at his own fleeing comrades before eventually being killed by the Crows. Three years later, as recorded in the Oglala count of Left-Heron for 1777, Owns-the-Club and three

16

others who had been sent out as scouts, were killed by Crows, and the Oglala 'count' of American-Horse records for 1779 / '80, Crows killed a Lakota chief named Long-Pine. [14]

These last named events, nonetheless, were sporadic occurrences and it is true that prior to the mid-seventeen-seventies, only seldom had the Lakota and Crows been in contact with one another owing to the intervening distance between them. But in the aftermath of the epidemic of 1781 / '82, the Lakota were everywhere; raiding Crow horse herds and clashing with Crow hunters on a regular basis. Thus American-Horse also recorded for 1785 /'86 that Crows killed a Brule Lakota chief named Bear's-Ears when attempting to steal horses from a Crow camp, and in 1786 /'87, an Oglala named Broken-Leg-Duck was killed while attempting to do the same. The following year a grand Lakota war-party went searching for Crows to exact revenge for the death of Broken-Leg-Duck, but failing to find their quarry, the Lakota attacked a party of Mandan instead and killed many, and in another count kept by the Hunkpapa Lakota No-Two-Horns, it is recorded for the same year of 1787-'88, *"They killed some Crows in the winter time."* [15]

In those days the Lakota referred to the Crows by the mixed term Psa-Toka [Dakota or Eastern Sioux dialect] or Psa-Loka [Lakota or Western Sioux dialect], perhaps having derived from one or another Hidatsa name for the Crows of *Adah-pakoa* and *Apsa-roka*. At a later date, both Sioux terms were used indiscriminately by the latter to designate other enemy groups as well, but according to Lakota tradition, it was sometime between the years 1790 and 1800, that the Lakota drove the Psa-Toka west from the Little Missouri region, and certainly, by 1790, Crow conflicts with the Lakota and Dakota had become constant and large-scale. One of the earliest such fights recalled in any detail in the oral history of the Crows, and which involved a great number of opposing Lakota and Crow warriors, is said to have taken place near the mouth of Powder River sometime between the last mentioned dates.

It had happened that a band of Kiowa which had recently migrated from the Black Hills country to the Southern Plains, was on a return visit to a remnant of their people known as "Cold Men" in the Black Hills of western South Dakota and to their Crow friends in the lower Powder district. During that time the combined Crow and Kiowa village was suddenly confronted by a host of Lakota massed a short distance away on the open prairie. The Crow and Kiowa warriors at once mounted their war-ponies and like the Lakota opposing them, formed a long line facing the enemy in a defensive mode. For a while neither side did anything more than shake their weapons and hurl abuse at their opposite numbers. But at length, a Kiowa war-chief rode out from his line and into the no-man's land between the opposing forces. There he reined in his mount, and shouted a challenge to any among the enemy who would dare face him in single combat. After a significant pause, one among the Lakota finally accepted the challenge and likewise, on horseback, met his Kiowa adversary in a savage one to one mounted encounter to the death. [16]

This, say the Crows, was the first time the Lakota experienced such an event during the course of a battle, when champions from each side would fight

17

one to one from the backs of their horses whilst their respective tribesmen looked on. Previously, opposing champions had always dismounted and fought on foot, but this new innovation made a deep impression on the Lakota. Thereafter, the advent of single combats whilst remaining horseback during the course of large-scale confrontations became the order of the day. It allowed the contestants to show off their acrobatic riding skills, and was a sure way to gain prestige and honour which, to the Indian mind, only enhanced the well-beloved game of war.

In later years, even the old-ones could not remember life as being any other way. An entire system had since evolved by which a tribal member's war-deeds could be numbered and recognized. Thereby, causing one to rise to great heights within the tribe with its attendant authority and respect from one's mentors and peers. Thus if a Crow accomplished four specific war deeds [*dakshey*], he or she could rise to the position of a chief among the people. One was then eligible to join the seventeen-member council which, as a body, discussed and decided all important issues concerning the united tribe. These four specific war deeds were as follows,

[1]    Striking a first coup, i.e. being the first to touch an enemy with either the hand or a slender willow-wand commonly known as a `coup-stick.
[2]    Taking a gun or other weapon from the hands of an enemy.
[3]    Stealing a tethered horse from the camp of the enemy [usually requiring cutting the halter rope fixed to a picket pin at one end and to the wrist of its sleeping owner at the other].
[4]    Leading a successful foray against the enemy without losing any party members.

In their military organization the Crows, like most other tribes, had a sophisticated system of warrior societies or clubs, each of which had its own fraternity regalia; dances; ceremonies and taboos. Throughout the first half of the nineteenth century there existed among the Crows nine such societies, which could be listed as follows,

Stone-Hammers.
Ravens.
Foxes [Kit-Foxes].
Lump-Woods [Knob-Sticks].
Half-Shaved-Heads.
Little Dogs.
Big Dogs.
Muddy-Hands.
Bulls.

These clubs were not age-graded in their make-up as were their counterparts among the Hidatsa and Mandan, although the Stone-Hammers were composed mainly of youths between fifteen and twenty years of age, while the Bulls, for the most part, consisted of veteran warriors of forty-five years and over.

18

Membership was usually by invitation, although few were turned away from their society of choice. Each spring, one society would be selected by the chief's council to act as camp police throughout that season and ensuing summer. Their duties included the control of communal buffalo hunts; arbitrating in both personal and band or clan disputes and generally keeping order within the tribe. The main purpose of these clubs, moreover, was to protect the women, children and old-folk and to defend the camp against its enemies. Many [although not all males of fighting age] belonged to one society or another and members of a particular fraternity considered themselves brothers, no matter what band or clan they were affiliated to.

There was withal, intense rivalry between the different societies as they competed against each other to achieve renown and prestige. So for a period in time, one society might be predominant whilst another fell into decline and at a later date, when a decline in members or renown had become profound, certain clubs disbanded altogether and ceased to exist, their few redundant members joining another society en masse. Such was the case of the Half-Shaved-Heads, which about the year 1835 became obsolete among the Crows, as also did the Muddy-Hands and the Bulls some thirty-five years later. The surviving members of these defunct societies joined the Lump-woods in their stead, whilst the number of effective warrior societies overall was then reduced to three, namely, the Foxes, Lump-woods and Dogs.

Whether a society member or not, the individual Crow warrior always endeavoured to present himself somewhat as a dandy among his peers. His appearance when wishing to create effect during ceremonial occasions or on the battlefield, was often far superior in the quantity of beads, feathers, paint, ermine tails and artificial hair which he attached about his person to that of neighbouring tribes. Prominent overall, however, was the raised clay-adorned hair roach above the forehead and dantalium hair-pipe side pieces, in conjunction with a long matted hair-queue extending from the crown of the head and down one's back, sometimes reaching the ground by the addition of horse hair and pine-gum decorated with beads or the breast feathers of an eagle. Often the forehead itself was plastered with bright vermilion or red ochre; and this along with the singular hairstyle aforementioned, distinguished the Crow warrior from all others on the Plains.

It was into this new era of Plains Indian evolution during the late eighteenth century, of what might be termed the 'Horse culture period,' that there was born among the Crows one to become the war-lord and saviour of his people. His name has come down to us as *"Alapooish"* or *"Elapooish,* often mistranslated as Rotten-Belly, but more properly meaning, Sore-Belly. A name suggesting that he went to war so many times, the saddle girth of his war-pony was constantly in use, and in such a way, caused the animal's belly to become chaffed and sore.

Old Crow veterans of the buffalo days considered Sore-Belly the greatest war-chief their Nation produced. Even today his name is held high in esteem and reverence. Stories are still told of his great *medicine* power and of his heroic exploits on the field of battle. My good friend Joseph Medicine-Crow, last of the

19

true Apsaalooka chiefs and elected tribal historian, along with the grand Crow matriarch Winona Plenty-Hoops – herself a direct descendent of the aforesaid Sore-Belly, - in many interviews with the Author during numerous visits to Crow country, provided much information regarding their illustrious ancestor.

- 0 - 0 - 0 - 0 - 0 - 0 - 0 - 0 - 0 - 0 - 0 - 0 -- 0 - 0 - 0 -

## CHAPTER 2.

### SORE-BELLY`S CHILDHOOD YEARS.

By what name Sore-Belly was known in his childhood days, Winona and Joe could not recall. Only that his father was a Flathead taken captive by Crows when young and married to a Crow woman named Four-Times-Four, who herself, was a member of the Sore-Lip clan among the *"Peelatchi Bilaxpake,"* i.e. Raven People, known to the French as *"Gens de Panse"* [Paunch Indians], and at a later date, as `River Crow.` [1]

Said Winona Plenty-Hoops,

> "Now let me see. It was the `winter three came home` when Sore-Belly was born. I think that was forty years or so before the time we Crows call, `Stars fell from the sky." [2]

This event refers to a well-known occurrence recalled among many Plains Tribes. It pertains to November of the white man's year 1833, when a "Leonid" Meteoric shower had been observed in the night sky over the entire Northern and Central Plains. A complete winter-count history in material form does not now exist among the Crows and today, only a few years are remembered by name. Both Winona and Joe, therefore, could not be sure of the exact date of Sore-Belly`s birth, although the event when "Three came home" had once been memorable in Crow history. Winona narrated to the effect,

> "...Thirty-five Crows went north on a raid. The warriors were `Awala-diile` [land walking]. Somewhere along the way they were surprised by a superior force of enemies and put to a hard fight. The Crows retreated to the top of a rocky outcrop where they were besieged for some time. Most of the party was killed. Only three warriors of the original thirty-five escaped and returned safely to their home camp. Hence our Crow name for that year, `Three came home." [3]

This alas, was all Winona could say on the matter, although it does appear there is yet extant a contemporary reference which may date the same episode more specifically.

20

# SORE-BELLY'S CHILDHOOD YEARS

The English Fur-trader, Peter Fiddler, when in the employ of the Hudson's Bay Company during the latter part of the eighteenth century, was in a Piegan [Pikuni] Blackfoot village when a victorious war-party came in. He reported in his journal that seventeen Blood Blackfoot Indians whilst on a friendly visit to the Shoshoni, with whom the Piegan Blackfoot had made a temporary peace the previous summer, had joined a Shoshoni war-party and gone south. They crossed the Missouri River and a short time later, met and attacked a party of thirty-five Mountain Crows.

The seventeen Bloods – their faces painted black as a sign of victory, - finally returned to the Piegan camp where the Hudson's Bay trader was then visiting at the end of January 1793. The Shoshoni war-party, Fiddler said, of which these returning Bloods had been participating members, had taken thirty-two Crow scalps along with several guns of Spanish manufacture; twenty Spanish swords; a number of painted bull-hide shields, bows and arrows and an assortment of clothing, all obtained from the vanquished foe as booty. [4]

If the above account does refer to the same event as mentioned by Winona, and as one "winter" in the Indian idiom actually covered part of a two-year period of the white man's conventional way of reckoning, we might construe that the Crow chief, Sore-Belly, was likely born sometime late in 1792 or early 1793.

What both Winona and Joe Medicine Crow did know was that as a child, the young Sore-Belly proved to be somewhat precocious and endowed with a strong-willed personality. He deliberately pushed himself in order to excel among his peers, both in the children's games he played and in survival training such as hunting and learning the ways of the warrior. By the time he entered his early teens he was, even then, showing signs of leadership, and as one who could cajole and influence those around him.

There was at that time a proven warrior named Hanging-Raven, who was also a favourite storyteller within the camp in which Sore-Belly resided. This man took the boy under his wing and for hours at a time, would recite to his attentive listener the legends and heroic history of the Apsaalooka. So was instilled in the youthful Sore-Belly a strong sense of national pride, along with a desire to emulate great and heroic Crow warriors and chiefs who had gone before to the Spirit World beyond.

So it was that the infant Sore-Belly practiced with bow and arrow; learned to crawl stealthily among the horses so not to give alarm, and to ride as if man and horse were one. Eager he was to reach an age when he himself could go to war and destroy the antagonists of his people. All his childhood learning and training was designed to prepare him for that day.

During the formative years of Sore-Belly's upbringing, he watched Crow war-parties constantly going out and coming in. Sometimes in order to protect their hunting grounds from foreign interlopers, or to avenge some earlier mishap in battle when a chief or kinsman had been rubbed out. Moreover, though, such belligerent escapades were undertaken merely for the thrill of adventure, and to increase one's pony herd from some other tribe's stock. Not least was the quest to

21

count *dakshey* [war honours], which would earn prestige and elevate one's standing and influence within Crow society.

When Sore-Belly was seven or eight years old, there occurred an event which had an important and lasting effect upon his character; an experience which caused him to decide there and then, his avowed ambition in life.

Regarding Crow relations with other tribes during Sore-Belly's early years, both Blackfoot and Assiniboine above the Missouri, constantly forayed south into Crow country in an endeavour to steal horses and obtain Crow scalps. At the same time, tribes from the east including Lakota, Cheyenne and Arickara, were conducting numerous raids into the western country and were fast becoming a serious threat to contend with. Certainly at this period, the Crows could only regard the Mandan, Hidatsa and Kiowa - and sometime the Arapaho - as their friends. Rarely, though, did they act in concert, while the neighbouring Arapaho's Atsina brethren, being confederated with the Blackfoot, were also regarded as potential enemies. Likewise were the fickle-minded Shoshoni, who were ever alternatively at war or peace with the Crows, and to make matters worse, about the year 1800, the Cheyenne and Teton Lakota made peace with one another and, thereafter, joined as allies against mutual foes, which included a stepping up of their erstwhile separate wars against the Crows.

As a consequence of this increased hostility on the Crow front, in late summer 1800, the Crows gained what they considered was a great victory over their enemies. A thirty man war-party of Oglala Lakota out after horses and scalps, was discovered by a Crow force somewhere near the mouth of the Powder and, *"...rubbed out to a man."* [5]

Joe Medicine Crow described to the present Author how in his youth, old tribal members would still recall the grand spectacle presented when the aforesaid Crow party returned.[6] Thus it had happened a few hours before the victorious warriors re-entered their home camp in which young Sore-Belly resided, a lone horseman arrived, bringing word tthat the people's brave men were coming in and had taken many scalps. The village occupants were excited and there was joyous uproar among the lodges. Many of the women, children and old ones along with young men who had not yet earned war honours of their own, suddenly stopped what they were doing and all at once ran from the encampment ready to welcome their home-coming heroes. Others donned ceremonial clothing; mounted their best ponies and rode out to join the victorious party, with the intent of accompanying its triumphant entry through the camp.

The returning warriors meanwhile, had earlier ensconced themselves behind a nearby hill overlooking the village below. Here, out of sight from the camp occupants they repainted their faces and donned their finest attire as befitted their triumphant status. After several hours of preparation they re-mounted their ponies, and numbering close to one-hundred warriors, arranged themselves along the crest of the hill. Silently they sat their ponies, poised in a long undulating line in full view of the waiting villagers. The latter in turn, hurriedly positioned themselves in two parallel rows extending from the camp entrance and across the prairie floor, and along the centre of this human avenue the victorious party would be expected to ride.

At length, the warriors on the ridge top bunched themselves together in a tightly packed mass, then began coasting their ponies slowly down the grassy slope towards the encampment. On other occasions, the victorious group would have careered their ponies down the slope, yelling war-cries and shooting guns in the air as they charged. But this time they moved at a leisurely trot, albeit many warriors singing war-songs, while others blew on eagle-bone whistles and in response, the watching womenfolk sang praise songs and trilled the tremolo in their honour. This was why, Joe Medicine Crow said, the event was still recalled many years later, because of the uncustomary procedure at that time.

At the base of the hill, the returning warriors changed formation, and arranging themselves four abreast in a long column, they continued forward over the shimmering prairie and rode along the avenue formed by the two rows of watching villagers. Some among the on-looking women rushed forward; running up to loved ones among the returning party in order to touch them. Others snatched willow wands from the hands of the warriors, from the ends of which dangled either a scalp, a severed hand, foot, arm or leg, not to mention a number of enemy heads impaled on the end of lance-points, all taken as trophies in the recent engagement. These the women carried aloft into camp and paraded on high among the jubilant spectators.

We are not told how many if any Crow warriors had been slain in the fight. But whatever the number it must have been small, for any mournful wailing from bereaved kinfolk was quickly drowned out by the triumphant revelry in camp. Scalp dances were held for many weeks thereafter, as the participating warriors told and retold - and acted out in grim pantomime - the deeds they had performed that day.

It is said that young Sore Belly was filled with pride as he watched with adulation the warriors parading within the inner circle of lodges. Later, he actually joined with them in their victory dances, as they stomped around in time to heavy beating on hide-covered drums and the sound of praise-songs emanating from the people. Sore-Belly was enthralled by the martial spectacle going on around him. Already he yearned to lead a war-party himself, so that his own name would be heralded through the camp and his people honour him as their protector and destroyer of foes. He had yet to learn, however, that for every victory gained; there was often a price to pay. [7]

Indeed, while such joyous celebrations were going on in Crow country, far to the east in lands abutting the west bank of the Missouri, there was no such revelry. Only cries of anguish and mournful keening for lost relatives resounded among the Oglala lodges, many of which would be dark with sorrow that coming winter. A greater calamity had not befallen their people for many a year. The whole Lakota Nation was aroused and shared the grief harboured by the relatives of those slain. Throughout the coming moons the Oglala chiefs deliberated upon the matter, and at length, it was decided to eliminate the Crows as a military power on the Northern Plains.

23

Now among the Lakota, it was the custom when planning a revenge expedition to wait one winter after the provocative event, and the following year, to start forth in a grand body against the foe. So it was that during the time of the snows, Oglala couriers carried a war-pipe to other Lakota bands, including the Miniconjou, Sans-Arc and Brule and even to their recently acquired Cheyenne allies, inviting all to join together and avenge the loss of the thirty Oglala. The chiefs and headmen of each band accepted the pipe and inhaled its symbolic smoke, thereby pledging themselves and their warriors to accompany the proposed crusade.

Thus come mid-summer 1801, the grasslands around the Oglala camp on Cherry Creek flowing into the Big Cheyenne east of the Black Hills, became a moving mass of colour, as the various allied bands congregated in preparation for a grand offensive against the Crows.

From the east, south and north the war bands came, all eager to shed the blood of a common foe. Gorgeous feathered bonnets nodded in the breeze, whilst gaudy patterns of dyed porcupine quills and beads decorating hair-fringed war shirts and leggings, splashed bright hues amid the hundreds of conical smoke-tanned tepees pitched in their respective band circles, and which together covered many acres on a verdant sea of grass. Close to each camp vast herds of ponies milled around, looking from a distance like a huge patchwork of brown, black and white.

The coming together of the different bands was treated as a festive occasion. But at the same time, new arrows were made; lance points and battle-axes re-ground, and among those who had not received a protective Spirit Helper, war *medicines* were earnestly sought to watch over them during the coming conflict, and give them power to bring honour to both themselves and their people.

It was to be a large force to invade the very heart of Crow country, and the camps buzzed with anticipation of how many heads [scalps] their warriors would take, along with the vast number of ponies and women and children captives they would drive home before them. And so it was, after several weeks of singing, dancing and feasting, the grand war-party at last started out on its *"Red road to war."*

This must have been one of the largest host of warriors seen on horseback west of the Missouri since many a year. Certainly, the largest the Crows themselves were yet to see sent against them by their now combined Lakota and Cheyenne enemies. Here were gathered over one thousand allied warriors; many armed with bows and arrows, lances and stone-headed war clubs, whilst in addition, some carried short barrelled, smoothbore trade muskets, iron headed axes and even French and English sword blades, and all were of a mind for vengeance; all set against the Crows.

As the huge cavalcade moved forward it followed a course northwest and when reaching what the Crows called *Bilapchashe* – Ash River, [i.e. Powder River], scouts were sent out to locate the nearest Crow village.

It was not long before the scouts returned, reporting they had discovered a Crow camp of thirty lodges nestling peaceably along a river bank, and that the

24

occupants appeared to be ignorant of impending danger. A council of war was convened, during which the allied chiefs agreed their forces should march out that very night; surround the Crow camp and launch their attack at dawn. In response, the entire conglomerate of allied warriors immediately prepared themselves for battle, and when all were ready, the grand host started forth, heading directly towards the foe. Come dawn, the Allies were positioned in a long colourful line, almost encircling the still sleeping Crow village.

As the first rays of sunlight appeared above the eastern hills and lit up the prairie floor, a single high-pitched war-cry rang out, instantly followed by a tumultuous roar arising from a thousand throats. Then was heard the thunder of four thousand hooves pounding the earth, as the entire allied host urged their ponies forward and charged headlong toward the camp. The sound of war-whoops coupled with the clatter of weapons beating on hide-covered shields, along with the shrill of eagle bone whistles amid the random discharge of guns, brought the villagers from their lodges and panic seized them all. Some of the older Crow warriors called to their comrades to stand and fight, at least in an attempt to save the women and children, who began running in every direction in frantic efforts to escape. A number of Crow menfolk did indeed, sacrifice their lives by making a stand and facing the overwhelming number of enemies, merely that their non-combatants might have a better chance of survival.

Such, however, was the complete surprise attending the attack, that the Cheyennes and Lakota carried their charge right in amongst the tepees. Smashing into them and other camp paraphernalia, trampling all and sundry under hoof. The Crow warriors, who along with teenage boys and old men constituted little more than one-hundred persons bearing arms, were, of course, grossly outnumbered. Very soon the Crows were falling back under the sheer weight of enemy pressure. In fact, many of the fleeing Crows were obliged to leave their kinfolk where they had fallen, although others continued to fight desperately in bitter hand to hand struggles before one by one they sank to the ground - either dead or dying - until all resistance was subdued. Some Crows escaped, but they were few, and these went running to another Crow village further west along the Yellowstone with word of the attack. But their brother Crows were a long way off from being able to give immediate or any practical military assistance.

In the meantime, the Allies dispatched the enemy wounded and cut the bodies into pieces, and in this there was reason. More as an act of expediency rather than malice, the victors believed it ensured one's own self-preservation in the Spirit World beyond. For in that 'Other World' where those who had gone before resided, life continued as it had on Earth. If one's body was not whole, one could no longer be an enemy to fear. Without arms, hands or fingers, no bow could be drawn; no gun fired and no lance or tomahawk wielded. Without legs or feet, no chase could be given and without eyes to see and ears to hear, all was invisible and unintelligible to them. Without a tongue, no cries could be raised to bring assistance to an enemy's plight, and who therefore, was immobilized and impotent; never again to pose a threat, even in the 'After Life' beyond.

Thus, after indulging in their gory acts of mutilation, the Allies looted the tepees then set them ablaze, along with all domestic belongings they themselves deemed worthless. Following this, they packed their plunder on the backs of little less than one-hundred Crow women and children captives and vacated the scene, driving their prisoners before them like a herd of wild ponies.

Whilst returning east and in order to humiliate the enemy further, the victorious Allies heaped abuse upon their captives, especially on the adult women to show how inadequate the latter's defeated menfolk had been in protecting them, and in this also there was reason. Indian philosophy held that one's tribal entity was made manifest through the women, they being the lynch-pin of tribal society and of the people's very existence and identity. For the victors to undermine this concept among their enemies was a profound disgrace to inflict upon them, and moreover, it broke the sacred connection of the enemy's continuity with nature and the cosmos which women were also thought to personify. Thus, the enemy's women-folk were initially subjected to degrading and cruel treatment before reaching the victor's home camp. However, at that point, the red road of war being temporarily concluded, and the victors having undertaken purifying rituals in sweat-lodges to cleanse themselves from what they considered, was the evil of their excessive blood-letting on fellow beings, the captives were relieved of their torments and allowed a high degree of equality as adopted members of the captor's tribe.

Among the aforesaid female captives taken during the event, were two young women having been stolen by Crows from the Shoshoni some short time previously, and who were later traded by the Allies to the Hidatsa. The Crows had known one of these women as Frog-Woman, who was a sister to another Shoshoni captive already among the Hidatsa and known by the name of Sacagawea. The same who later accompanied Lewis and Clark on their epic journey west across the Continent. [8]

Meanwhile, after returning to the base camp from which they came, the Allies dismantled the lodges; packed the covers on pole drags and hastily returned to their own country east of the Black Hills. Before, that is, the whole Crow Nation could organize a formidable war-party and exact revenge.

It was long after the victors had left the field of carnage, that a number of Crow survivors who had taken refuge among nearby hills, came sauntering back to the smouldering remains of their village and inspected the ruined scene. They gathered up their dead, and after salvaging any personal belongings overlooked or discarded by the enemy, they set out in a mournful body, heading for the main camp of their people some distance west.

The arrival of this sad and dejected group of survivors at the main Crow village, caused great concern among the people. Upon hearing the gory details of the affair, news of the disaster was carried to all other Crow bands, and the whole Nation lapsed into a prolonged period of mourning. There was not one family among the entire population, it is said, that had not now lost a loved one, either killed or carried into bondage by the foe. Such a catastrophe had not attended the Crows for many a year, and the people's expressions of sorrow knew no bounds. Many of the warriors cut their long braids short or tore great hanks of hair from their heads with their own hands. They covered their faces and bodies with a mixture of dirt and ashes and donned worn-out skins and robes, in order to show their extent of grief by self-humiliation.

The womenfolk did likewise, but also stabbed themselves in the forehead and limbs until the blood flowed freely. Some lopped off a finger joint or two indicating the personal loss of close family members, whilst others thrust bone skewers through their tormented bodies piercing the breasts or shoulders, and to these they attached long rawhide thongs from the loose ends of which hung a dead kinsman's shield or a buffalo skull, to be dragged laboriously over the rocks whilst the mourners continued to bleed from numerous self-inflicted wounds. Alone both night and day they screeched their pitiful, heart-rending laments until they became hoarse or simply collapsed from sheer exhaustion. Finally they dispersed themselves among the hills, each to suffer in solitude their personal torment and anguish, shunning the comforts of camp life and the sympathy of their kin-folk and in such a state, they wandered aimlessly for many weeks; sometimes months, still bewailing their monotonous dirges.

Perhaps this was the first time Sore-Belly – then eight or nine years old – witnessed his people's extreme expressions of grief. The sight of which, initially, could only have made him sick to the stomach and filled him with a sense of profound sadness and pity for the plight of those in mourning. This was, of course, deliberate on the part of the women, not less, in order also to move the warriors into seeking revenge and - more often - it had the desired effect. Certainly the whole affair had a lasting effect upon young Sore-Belly, who hereafter, became even more determined to become a great warrior and *"Ipache-akee"* [i.e. war-chief], with the ability both to avenge and protect his people from any comparable woe in the future.

As far as the Crow chiefs were concerned, their people had suffered a dire calamity on this occasion. In the immediate aftermath, they temporarily gave up their claim to that part of their hunting grounds between the Little Missouri and Powder River. Instead, they retreated west to the Big Horn Mountains, there to lick their wounds and better defend themselves if attacked again by the same or another allied war-band.

Cheyenne oral tradition states it were they, the Cheyennes alone, who drove the Crows west around this date of 1801.[9] But true it is, as a direct result of the above mentioned disaster in which Lakota were also involved, the Crows did temporarily take up residence west of Powder River as far as the Pryor country, in order to escape further raids from both Lakota and Cheyenne enemies.

This particular event attending the Crows, is the earliest surviving memory in tribal oral history relating to the complete destruction of an entire Crow village by an enemy force. Alas, it was to prove but one of several similar episodes destined to befall that Nation over the next fifty years. To the Lakota and Cheyennes on the other hand, it was considered an important victory, and the Oglala American-Horse`s "winter-count" for that year records,

"Winter 1800/1801 The Oglala, Sans-Arc, Miniconjou, Brule and Cheyenne, destroyed thirty Crow lodges." [10]

For the Crows and young Sore-Belly, however, there was yet more sorrow to come. If the above event had not been disastrous enough, later that same year and continuing into 1802, smallpox again spread its deadly tentacles across the Northern and Central Plains. This outbreak like its predecessor twenty years earlier was also severe, and carried off in its wake many among the Crows. Thus the latter's already diminished population over the previous two decades, was further reduced from an estimated 800 lodges in 1800, to around six-hundred lodges in total by the end of 1801, constituting an effective fighting force of little over one-thousand warriors to defend the people and their still extensive country.

It was at this time that the ten year old Sore-Belly lost both his parents to the smallpox, thereby rendering him *"baakedeeta"* [orphan]. Fortunately, he still had surviving relatives who were wealthy and influential members within the tribe and as a consequence, did not suffer the pangs of extreme poverty or of social ostracism commonly associated with parentless children. Even so, as was usual regarding orphans among the Crows, he would often go from lodge to lodge, staying for a while first with one family then another, whilst at the same time, his personal appearance was customarily dirty and his clothes ragged, and whatever his previous potential, he was then generally believed to be *"Itchila,"* i.e., worthless, and in adult life, it was said, *"...He will not amount to much."* [11]

- 0 - 0 - 0 - 0 - 0 - 0 - 0 - 0 - 0 - 0 - 0 -- 0 - 0 - 0 –

## CHAPTER 3.

## HOSTILE INTERLUDES and THE YELLOW-EYES COMETH.

Among the survivors of the thirty-lodge Crow camp recently destroyed, was a man named Strikes-enemy-with-his-brother. He had lost a number of close clan relatives both killed and captured on that occasion and, it is said, *"...his heart lay heavy on the ground."* [1] Filled with sadness and despondency, he decided to take the vow of a Crazy-Dog warrior. This was a drastic action, as Crazy-Dogs were also known as "Those-wishing-to-die," and thus, this man was promising to sacrifice his life in the next fight with the enemy and, "give his body to the wolves."

One's commitment, however, after taking such an oath did not extend more than a season, which usually embraced the summer moons when warfare was more intense and warriors enthusiastic in its pursuit. Among the Crows, an avowed Crazy-Dog during his term of office, was obliged to do things backward and speak in such a way that it was opposite to what was really meant. At the same time, he was allowed to be intimate with any woman of his choice, even if it be another man's wife - and could take victuals from anyone's kettle without being invited to do so. Because of his promised undertaking, such a person was accorded utmost attention and respect from the whole tribe, who believed that by sacrificing his life in battle, it would cause his people to be victorious.

So it was that Strikes-enemy-with-his-brother dressed himself as befitted such a warrior. On his head he wore an eagle-feathered bonnet and tied skunk tails

28

to the heels of his moccasins. Two long strips of red flannel were tied each side of his waist belt, and his face, torso and legs were daubed with a sacred red paint. In one hand he held a buffalo paunch rattle filled with small stones, and in the other, a long lance wrapped in the hide of a coyote. Thus attired and mounted on a fine spotted pony decorated with red and green flannel and its tail bobbed up, Strikes-enemy-with-his-brother rode among the lodges several times a day, singing a Crazy-Dog song with the words,

> "There is nothing to keep me from dying, I am looking for death.
> Only the sky and rocks last forever." [2]

The people came out of their lodges to watch him, the men shouting Aho, Aho" in recognition of his presence, while the women raised the tremolo in his honour. It was not, though, until mid-summer the following year [1802], before Strikes-enemy-with-his-brother actually had the opportunity to carry out his vow. By that time the smallpox scourge which had ravished Crow camps had released its hold, and at last, the Crows proposed that a war-party should go against the Lakota to avenge the thirty lodges destroyed the previous year. This was the chance Strikes-enemy-with-his-brother had been waiting for, and he eagerly joined as a member of the expedition.

The war-party was formidable comprising just over one-hundred warriors, and on the first stage of its journey, there was included the warrior`s women and children and their lodges, all travelling in a southeast direction across the open Plains. Somewhere west of the Little Missouri the cavalcade stopped and went into camp along a stream known today as Sand Creek, not far from the present North / South Dakota state line. Leaving their non-combatants and lodges at this point, the warriors started out on foot, and included among their number was the Crazy-Dog, Strikes-enemy-with-his-brother. They headed south towards the Belle Fourche branch of Cheyenne River in the northwest corner of South Dakota where they hoped to find one or another Lakota band, then in the habit of visiting the sacred site of Bear Butte of that region for religious purposes.

`Alee, kaashi-kaashi alee,` * it is said, and as they travelled day after day, they found no water along the route. At length, the party including two of Sore-Belly`s surviving uncles, came to where two buttes stand close together isolated in the prairie expanse. One of these buttes is shaped like a sugar-loaf, and next to it is an elongated butte easy to scale. A number of Crows climbed to the top of the elongated butte to get a better view of the surrounding country, and to see if a stream or pool of water was nearby where from they could slake their thirst. The rest of the warriors, meanwhile, rested in the long grass below, half asleep in the noon-day sun. Those on top of the butte must also have been dozing, for a horde of Lakota; horseback and painted for war, suddenly appeared from nowhere, it seemed, and at once charged on those resting in the grass. The Crows quickly jumped to their feet and immediately began scrambling up the butte where were their comrades, being their only chance of a defensive position. It was at this point,

***

\* **Very hot [Literally, "Hot, much, much hot."]**

29

while his companions were scrambling up the butte, that Strikes-enemy-with-his-brother, being obliged to do things backward to what others would do, actually ran towards the enemy before making his suicide stand. After staking the ends of the two red sashes attached to his waist belt to the ground with his lance, he stood with shield and stone-headed tomahawk facing the oncoming foe alone.

The Lakota galloped forward to count coup on such a brave man, and very soon the lone Crow; as the Indian idiom has it,

*"... was covered up by the enemy and killed."* [3]

With the death of the Crazy Dog warrior, the fight around the bluff top began in earnest. For a while, the Crows and Lakota shot many arrows at each other, the Lakota by arching their bows and firing skywards so their shafts fell like rain onto the unprotected Crows entrenched along the summit. The Lakota had completely surrounded the butte, but not wishing to incur unnecessary casualties by storming the position head on in the face of missiles fired at point blank range, they set up brush and hide bivouacs around the base of the butte and prepared to wait patiently until the entrapped Crows succumbed through lack of water and fatigue owing to the gruelling heat. This indeed is what happened, and it is told that after four or five days when the Lakota finally scaled the height, they met no opposition and found one-hundred and more Crows already dead. Some present-day tribal informants state that some of those entrapped committed suicide, rather than being taken alive by the Lakota. [4] It is further said, however, that germs of smallpox from the recent contagion afflicting the Crows, must still have lingered on some of the garments the dead Crows were wearing. For the Lakota, having taken items of clothing from their victim's corpses as spoils of war, themselves contracted the malady and many among their number soon began dying, one after the other, as the contagion ran like wildfire through their ranks.

A significant number of human bones and skulls since discovered in a small canyon immediately northwest of the buttes, are said to be from the dead Lakota who died of the contagion, and as late as the 1950s, local ranch-hands could point out rock rings around the base of the butte where some of the besieging Lakota lodges had likely been pitched. At that time many flint and iron arrowheads were also found on top and around the base of the butte, evidence of a great fight having once taken place at the site.

Whatever the number of Lakota having died as an indirect result of the fight, the number of Crow warriors killed was a loss their people could ill-afford after their own recent depopulation due to smallpox. Thus it was an event which brought more grief and despondency upon the people; and to Sore-Belly especially, who thereby, had lost two more of his immediate kinfolk.


Notwithstanding these concurrent setbacks befalling the Crows, their situation was such that being constantly beset by numerous foes - albeit that the latter's own populations had likewise been reduced by the aforesaid contagion - the Crows could not afford to languish in their sorrow. The longer their warriors remained inactive, the more vulnerable they were to a comparable assault upon one or another of their villages as had occurred in the summer of 1801.

It was not long therefore, before Crow warriors again took to the war trail. On the one hand to avenge recent losses; on the other, in an attempt to curtail the ardour and confidence of their foes and throughout the ensuing years, the Crows did achieve a number of military successes of which young Sore-Belly would have been fully acquainted with. Indeed, a resume of Lakota winter-counts coupled with certain reports from white traders of the period, substantiate the degree of hostile activity involving Crows during the first decade of the nineteenth century.

According to several Lakota winter-counts it was also in 1802, that the Crows and Lakota had another big fight, albeit this time southeast of the Black Hills in southwestern South Dakota, and during which event, the latter escaped with a number of curly-haired ponies from the Crows. Commemorating the same year, a Miniconjou Lakota named Big-Missouri recorded in his 'count' yet a third serious confrontation between his people and Crows. In this case two hunting parties; one Lakota, the other Crow, met accidentally whilst attempting to run the same herd of buffalo and a fight broke out between them. During the actual conflict a blinding snow storm came up which caused the opposing parties to break off the engagement prematurely. Each group then moved away in opposite directions and supposing their two parties were then separated by a respectful distance; they set up their camps for the night. Come morning the storm had passed and it was discovered they had erected their camps very close to each other, whereupon another fight ensued. We are not told the outcome of this second contest, although its peculiar circumstances commemorated the event in the Miniconjou 'count. '

In late summer or early fall 1802, according to the Charles LeRaye memoir of his wanderings through the Big Horn and Yellowstone country, a war-party from the *Nootso-pah-zsah* Crow band conducted a raid across the Rocky Mountains against the *Pal-lo-lo-Path* Indians, who LeRaye referred to as Flatheads. The Crows were victorious and returned with several scalps and sixteen prisoners in tow comprising men, women and children. However, the description given by LeRaye pertaining to the captives, such as the men bearing tattoos on their chests and wearing bones through the septum of their noses, along with their half-shaved heads and other peculiar hairstyles, suggest they were not Salish-speaking Flatheads in the proper sense of the term, but actually of the latter's allies the Shahapitian-speaking [Nez Perce] Palouse tribe, whose territory then straddled the borders of what are now the states of Washington and Idaho. It was also while still encamped with the Crows and their captives, that LeRaye witnessed a visit from a large party of "Snake" Indians, of whom LeRaye said,

"...This Nation resides principally on the head waters of the Big Horn River, and the most inaccessible parts of the Rocky Mountains, where they have frequently to hide in caverns from their enemies. Owing to their defenceless situation, they become an easy conquest to any Nation disposed to attack them, and they are frequently attacked for no other reason than the pleasure of killing them...... [We] came to a camp of the Paunch Indians...These Indians reside mostly towards the head waters of the river Jaun [i.e., the Yellowstone] and the branches of the Big Horn....They call

31

themselves "All-ah-kaa-wiah."...Their arms consist of bows and spears, with buffalo skin targets [shields], much larger than those made use of by the Snake Indians, and so thick and firm, that an arrow will not pierce them. They use a short dagger and the war-club. A few of them had guns, but no ammunition. Many Crows and Gross-Ventres [Hidatsa] are armed in the same manner." [5]

So here we learn that Crows were then at peace with the Snakes, and apparently, from documentary evidence in the Hudson`s Bay journals, were also still on friendly terms with the Atsina, as it was late that same year [1802], when the Atsina sent a delegation with a war-pipe south to their Arapaho cousins and also to the Crows, requesting they join the Atsina in a grand crusade against the *"Yellow-Legs"* [Assiniboine], and the latter`s confederated *"Sahiia"* [Plains Cree] allies. There is no way of knowing if Crows did join the proposed crusade or what the outcome was, although it does confirm that Crows were still at peace with both the Atsina and Arapaho at that time.

On the other hand, Crow conflicts with the Lakota and Cheyennes continued unabated. During the following year [1803], the Arapaho along with the Kiowa and Gattacka - old friends of the Crows, - whilst indulging in some kind of intertribal trading fair in the Black Hills of south-western South Dakota, were suddenly attacked by Lakota accompanied by Cheyenne allies, and were driven southwest into the mountain foothills between the heads of the South Platte and Arkansas River. [6] It is likely that at least a part of the Crows also suffered on this occasion, as they invariably attended the same trading fairs as did the Kiowa and Arapaho. If this had been the case then the Crows evidently gained some compensation soon after the event, as according to the journal of the French Canadian trader, Pierre Antoine Tabeau, Crow warriors later that same year succeeded in rubbing out between twenty-five and thirty Cheyennes who had entered the Crow domain in search of horses and scalps. [7]

At the same time, other Crow war-parties were vigorously raiding Blackfoot villages north of the Missouri, and even Comanche pony herds far south on the Arkansas. It was probably from the last-named people that the Crows obtained a number of shod horses originally stolen by the Comanche from Spaniards further south, as several Lakota winter-counts record that when themselves raided Crows that year of 1803, they managed to run off a number of ponies wearing iron footwear. A circumstance which caused the Lakota to believe the Crows were then `confederate` with white men in one way or another. Additionally, Crow parties were foraying against the Arickara and Omaha far down the Missouri, and again according to the aforementioned trader Tabeau, the Crows would attack any foreign people they encountered on the trail.

Indeed, Tabeau reported that in early June the following year [1804], a Crow war-party scouting adjacent to the middle Missouri looking for enemies to raid, came across two Arickara tepees pitched some distance from the latter`s earth-lodge villages overlooking the mouth of the Grand. In the event, the Crows destroyed the two tepees; slaughtered the male occupants and took six women and children captive. A number of Arickara warriors had fought desperately, thereby facilitating the escape of two Arickara women who with their children, jumped into a nearby stream and hiding among the reeds keeping only their noses above water to breathe, managed to evade capture and finally returned safely to their people. At the time of this Crow attack, a number of white men had been busy cutting wood only two leagues [six miles] distant, and Tabeau, who wrote of the encounter some few years later, had been in no doubt that the Crows would have fallen upon the whites in identical manner if, that is, they had not first stumbled upon the Arickara tepees in their path. Needless to say, after committing their grisly deed the Crows hastily vacated the area, suspecting that when discovering their loss, the Arickara would dispatch a great force in pursuit eager to avenge themselves on the killers. It seems, though, that before Arickara vengeance could be had and before the year was out, the Arickara suffered yet another, more serious defeat at Crow hands. It is an episode still related in Crow oral tradition when referring to Chief Sore Belly's younger days.

The story tells how one year prior to the time the French-speaking white man Francois Larocque first visited Crow country in 1805, and remained among that tribe's lodges for a significant period, a twenty-strong war-party of Arickara dared enter Crow country *Awala-diile* * in an endeavour to steal horses and scalps. Forty Crow warriors, among whom was the eleven or twelve year old Sore-Belly acting as servant to the older men, happened to be out hunting buffalo when they discerned a number of people walking single file across the prairie.

The Crows knew by the manner of these people they were not Crows, while the fact they were afoot indicated a war-party most likely after horses; and Crow horses at that. A small herd of buffalo milled around nearby, and the Crows, each of whom was mounted on a fast buffalo-running pony, decided to trick their enemies and entice them in close so they would not be able to gain appropriate cover when attacked. To achieve this, the Crow warriors lay flat along the backs of their ponies, keeping lances and other weapons out of sight in the long grass, and waited patiently for their quarry to draw near.

Only when their enemies were but thirty or forty yards distant did the Crows pick up their lances, and rising suddenly from their prone positions; whooped the Crow war-cry "Koo-Koo-Hey." They then charged headlong into the Arickara; lance points flashing; tomahawks flaying, while at the same time, sending a shower of flint and iron-tipped arrows hissing through the air. The Arickara were taken by surprise. With no cover from which to defend themselves, they fought back as best they could, but only twenty strong, on foot and fully exposed, the Crows soon had them surrounded. They cut the Arickara down piecemeal in bunches of threes and fours, until all but one were killed. The victorious Crows then released the lone survivor, sparing his life so he could return to his own people with a message from the Crows that, "...Never again should the Arickar come with hostile intent into the country of the Apsaalooka." [8]

So it was, that an additional number of Arickara scalps came into Crow hands. An event the Arickara themselves would not forget in a hurry and, without

- **On foot.**

doubt, would endeavour to avenge. But in the meantime, although the Hunkpapa Lakota killed four Crows this year according to the winter-count of Left-Heron, Sore Belly`s people continued to mark up additional victories.

In late August 1804, the Lewis and Clark expedition then in the process of traversing the Continent from east to west, met a body of Yankton Sioux near the mouth of Beaver Creek on the Missouri below the Niobrara River. Captain Clark was then told of a particular warrior society which, he believed, existed only among the Yankton and Crow Indians, the latter of whom, Clark reported, *"…live further to the westward,"* [9] and from among whom the idea of the society had originally been conceived, and only afterwards copied by the Yankton.

From the brief description of the society as given by Clark, its peculiarities appear to correspond with that known as the "Big Dogs" once found among the Crows. Its members had taken a vow never to retreat in battle, or to deter in the slightest way from their original resolve no matter what the cost. Clark reported in his journal that the number of warriors belonging to the society`s Yankton equivalent, had recently been reduced to four. These being all that remained from twenty-two previous members who only a comparatively short time earlier, had composed the entire fraternity among the Yankton. But in a battle with the Crow de Curbo [sic; i.e. Corbeaux] Indians [Clark's original name for the Crows] from the Cout Noie [sic; i.e. Cote Noir] Black Mountains [an early name for the Laramie Mountains west of the Platte Forks], eighteen warriors of the Yankton fraternity had been killed, the surviving four members having been rescued, albeit dragged kicking from the field by others of their tribesmen.

This event, one assumes, would have been regarded among the Crows as a great victory. In all probability it refers to the same occasion mentioned in the Yankton winter count of John K. Bear, which states for the year 1803 / `04,

*"…There was a big battle with the Yankton at Heart River."* [10]

Although the opposing enemy`s tribal name is not given in the `count,` the fact that the occurrence warranted inclusion in the first place, indicates a large-scale conflict during which some unusual happening had taken place, such as the slaughter of eighteen members of one specific warrior society would have merited. We do, however, have another independent source which corroborates such a battle at`that time.

The Northwest Fur Company employee Alexander Henry the younger, when residing among the Mandan and Hidatsa during the summer of 1806, recorded in his journal that he then visited the site of a large-scale battle between the Mandan and Yankton Sioux which had taken place only two years earlier [1804] near the mouth of Heart River. In the event, a large body of Crows and Hidatsa along with a few Flathead allies then accompanying the Crows, had been very much involved.

It can be inferred from this, that as it was the Sore Lip clan led by Long-Hair which more often at this date, visited the Hidatsa and Mandan in the latter`s

34

earth-lodge villages along the Knife and Heart Rivers, then young Sore-Belly was most likely present when the actual battle took place.

According to Henry's information, a host of Yankton and Teton [Lakota] had banded together in order to launch a punitive attack upon the Mandan. Thus, not far from the mouth of the Heart, on a level Plain separating the Mandan villages on the north bank of that river from a line of low hills stretching to the west and north, a fierce contest took place on horseback between the opposing forces, with neither side at first gaining an advantage. Soon, however, from the west, a horde of warriors comprising Hidatsa, re-enforced by a small number of Flatheads and a very large number of Crows who just happened to be visiting their Hidatsa cousins at the time, raced their ponies to the scene of conflict from the neighbouring villages on the Knife.

This formidable body of Crow and Hidatsa reinforcements did not immediately engage the enemy. Instead, they decided to surround the latter by turning off to the left and riding unobserved behind the line of low hills to the north until they were positioned in the rear of the foe. Here, some distance behind the Yankton and Lakota men-folk were gathered the latter's women and other non-combatants, who had followed their husbands and sons with pack ponies and travois in expectation of carrying off much plunder from the Mandan villages they hoped to see destroyed. The Crows and their allies came upon these non-combatants by surprise, and careering into the rear of their huddled mass, they killed many and took a large number of captives. Having done this, the Crows and Hidatsa surmounted the crest of a nearby hill overlooking the Lakota and Yankton warriors, who were still battling with the Mandan to their front. The Crows and Hidatsa then charged horseback down the slope, and continued right in amongst the enemy spread out on the Plain below.

Already the Yankton and Lakota were fatigued from the morning's constant fighting with the Mandan, and now, being grossly outnumbered and assaulted both from front and rear, many of their warriors were killed and wounded while the rest succumbed to panic; gave up the fight and attempted to flee the field. Unfortunately, their route of retreat to the west and north was now blocked by the Crows and Hidatsa, so that the Yankton and Lakota were obliged to race directly toward the Missouri. Into the water they plunged their horses and themselves from that river's west bank, and attempted in any way possible to reach the far side and safety. In their scramble many more of their number were killed and wounded by the pursuing Crows and Hidatsa, and it had probably been at this point that the Yankton warrior society members - as mentioned by Lewis and Clark - had made their stand and were almost completely wiped out by the Crows. It was estimated by the victors owing to the amount of enemy corpses left on the Plain and along the route of retreat - so the trader Henry was told – that upwards of three-hundred Sioux had been slain in this one fight alone.

It was two years after the event when Henry actually visited the scene, and the bleaching bones of Sioux dead were then still to be seen, having been gathered up by the victorious villagers, Henry said, and deposited in one great pile on the prairie some short distance from the Mandan towns. But whatever the true number of enemy casualties, the Crows along with their Mandan and Hidatsa allies, had deemed the event a great victory on their part.

By such events, as Sore-Belly entered his early teens he acquired a more than usual interest in the military side of his people's activities, and for a number of years the Crows continued to achieve a degree of martial success. As mentioned earlier, Crow war-parties were then vigorously assaulting Blackfoot-speaking tribes above the Missouri and the Arickara much farther downstream. In addition, they were also raiding Comanche pony herds along the South Platte and Arkansas, and at times, even the Pueblos and Mexican haciendas both along and south of the Rio Grande. In most of these enterprises Crow warriors returned triumphant with scores of stolen ponies in tow, along with booty consisting of clothing and weapons in abundance; enemy scalps, and a number of captive women and children, to be adopted into the tribe as compensation for Crow relatives lost in previous engagements.

So it was that young Sore-Belly found enough excitement to keep him fully occupied. He matured quickly in understanding fully the ways of his people; much quicker, it is said, than other Crow boys of his age. He was in all ways a keen pupil, and by the time he was twelve years old, had already become an accomplished hunter of deer and elk. Unlike his childhood companions, he was oft-times a participating member on a buffalo hunt, each time assisting in the killing and butchering of several animals.

More important, though, was an occasion when as a teenager of thirteen years in the summer of 1805, he had the opportunity to observe at close quarters a party of White men that came into Crow country and stayed among his people's lodges for a significant period.

According to Crow legend, their people had seen their first white men when living in a far distant land to the northeast close to a large lake. So large, it is said, that its far shore could not be seen. The white men were then only two in number and were paddling a canoe close along the shoreline of the said lake. This event, traditionally, occurred as long ago as nine generations past, which by assessing an average of forty years per generation, perhaps refers to some three-hundred and sixty years prior to A.D.2010 when the statement was made. Such a date would be consistent with the presence of either the explorers Pierre Radisson and Jean Baptiste Grossiliers, both of whom, we know, traversed Lake Superior and Green Bay during the 1650s and 1660s, or to Nicolas Perrot, who visited the Upper Mississippi tribes and surrounding country during the 1680s and '90s. Whatever the case, from this circumstance, the Crows for a long time thereafter always referred to white men as *"Bille-baa-chii,"* meaning "People who live on the Water." Not until many years later did they adopt the Lakota name for white men of "Yellow Eyes," which term when rendered in Crow is *"Mahr-stah-she-dah."*

When first meeting face to face with white men, the Crows had held them in awe, supposing them to be magical or mysterious beings. However, in later years after becoming more familiar with the white man's ways, and by the time Sore-Belly was in his teens during the early years of the nineteenth century, the Crows, like most others of their nomadic, equestrian neighbours, harboured little respect for the white race in general. The Crows particularly, it was then believed, held all white men in a degree of contempt owing to what the Crows thought was the latter's apparent unwarlike disposition, and lack of knowledge when it came to enduring the more hostile extremes of everyday life in the Indian country. The Crows had openly shown this attitude in no uncertain way when in 1801, they had been visited in one of their camps by the French Canadian trader 'Old' François Menard. Menard was then resident on and off among all three of the sedentary Missouri River tribes of Hidatsa, Mandan and Arickara, as he had been for thirty or more years prior to that date.

At the time of which we speak, Old Menard had set out from the Hidatsa towns along the Knife to the Big Horn country, intending to trade with the Mountain Crows for horses and beaver skins. Arriving among the Crow lodges, he had been received in friendship and managed to procure nine horses; a number of beaver skins and two female slaves. However, on his return journey to the Hidatsa, a party of young Crows followed him and during his first night out, stole seven of his ponies. A few nights after this, his female slaves deserted taking the remaining two horses with them and the next day, another Crow party accosted him and robbed most everything he had left, including his gun and knife and even stripped him of his clothing, leaving him semi-nude and destitute to survive the hostile environment as best he could. Fortunately he retained his woollen blanket, from which he tore off strips to wrap around his feet as protection from the cold and the prickly pear over which he was obliged to travel. Only when more dead than alive did Menard eventually reach the Hidatsa town from whence he came, and so was saved from near certain death. The account goes on to relate how the Hidatsa were so incensed that the Crows should have treated their trader in such a treacherous manner that in their anger, the very next time a party of Crows appeared at their town the Hidatsa slew a number of the visitors in revenge. Thus the Hidatsa for one, we assume, did have some respect for certain white men at least, especially those who could supply them with much needed merchandise such as guns and ammunition, with which to hold an advantage over their enemies.

This act on the part of the Hidatsa, not surprisingly, had created a degree of hostility between the Hidatsa and Crows, which although not resulting in any immediate large-scale violent confrontation and, seemingly, smoothed over a short time later, it did, nevertheless, threaten to jeopardize the age-old amicable relationship between their peoples, and certainly, it fuelled dissention between certain persons among both tribes for several years to come.

Thus, both Paunch [*Gens de Panse*] and Mountain Crow bands continued to visit the Hidatsa villages in order to trade, and on such occasions, young Sore-Belly was often included.

Sore-Belly, no doubt, had seen non-Indians before 1805; Mexican traders surely, and perhaps, individual white men such as the above mentioned 'Old' Menard who for a long time had been domiciled among the Hidatsa lodges before being killed by Assiniboine in 1803. Other white traders then in the employ of both Spanish and French companies, had also been encountered among the Hidatsa and Mandan since as early as 1791 during the Crow's sporadic sojourns to the latter's towns. But such white persons who regularly cohabited with Indians - apart from few exceptions - were hardly representative of the more sophisticated white men from the settlements far east of Crow country.

The majority of white men customarily visiting the Missouri River villages, were usually of French Canadian stock; illiterate for the most part; dirty in dress and habits and more inclined to adopt the vices of the Natives, rather than what Sore-Belly himself might have deemed, were the more noble traits and attributes of his race. Indeed, those white men with whom Sore-Belly first became acquainted, appeared to be more interested in the company of promiscuous Indian women, rather than occupying themselves with hunting or the more manly pursuit of going to war in quest of horses, scalps and captives.

It was not then merely that white men were visiting the Missouri River towns, why Sore-Belly's people of the Sore-Lip clan among a large band of Mountain Crows, made a special trek to their Hidatsa cousins this summer of 1805. But moreover, by reason of the escalating Lakota and Cheyenne attacks upon them, not to mention irritating raids from both the Assiniboine and Cree [these last named affecting the Paunch Crow bands especially]. Coupled to this, the Mountain Crows had recently found it expedient to make peace with the Shoshoni, against whom they had previously been at war for one-hundred years and more, and now wished to include their Hidatsa cousins in the pact.

It has been noted previously how, in 1793 around the time of Sore-Belly's birth, a war-party of allied Blood, Pikuni and Shoshoni had raided deep into the Crow domain and escaped with thirty-two Mountain Crow scalps, along with their victim's weapons and other accoutrements including some of Spanish origin. Fortunately for the Crows, this Blood, Pikuni and Shoshoni alliance had been short lived and by 1795, a renewal of hostile pressure from the Blackfoot tribes combined, including the event of a Blood and Siksika war-party killing twenty-five Shoshoni warriors and two women in a pitched battle that year, contributed again in keeping the Shoshoni and the latter's Flathead allies west of the Rocky Mountains.

The Crows on the other hand, being themselves fully engaged against all Blackfoot-speaking peoples, found they now had common cause with the Shoshoni in repelling Blackfoot attacks upon their villages. So it was around the date 1803, when a band of Mountain Crows met the destitute survivors of a small Shoshoni village recently destroyed by one or another Blackfoot-speaking war-band, their two groups temporarily joined forces for mutual protection as they continued through the country. Soon after this, the Crows had been approached by an official delegation of Shoshoni chiefs holding out the red stone calumet as a proposal of peace between their tribes. The Crows had realized the benefits of accepting the offer in order to gain allies against the common enemy, and accordingly that coming summer, a more permanent pact between their peoples had been concluded. Thus for a period, there came into effect a cessation of Crow hostilities against all the Eastern and Northern Shoshoni-speaking bands. From here on, for a number of years at least, Shoshoni and Crows came together at intervals to socialize and sometimes to act as allies against mutual foes. The Shoshoni were even allowed to hunt freely east of the Rocky Mountains in Crow country once and sometimes twice a year. This concession, though, was only granted by the Crows after permission was sought by the Shoshoni each time they wished to enter Crow lands. In part this was considered an act of protocol, but also as a token of respect and acknowledgement that the said country still belonged to the Crows. Indeed, the latter wished it known among all tribes, that foreigners who entered their hunting grounds did so without the threat of serious chastisement, only if the Crows themselves had previously given their permission.

Such a truce was beneficial to all parties involved and was particularly beneficial in more ways than one to the Crows. Certainly it afforded a more formidable defence against the ever-encroaching Lakota, Cheyenne and Blackfoot into the rich game lands of the southern Montana country, but at the same time it allowed free trade with the Eastern Shoshoni and the latter's Flathead allies, who could supply the Crows with Spanish goods along with a regular supply of horses. Hereafter, the Crows no longer had to make their own journeys south to the Spanish Possessions, which had always proved a hazardous and time consuming undertaking.

It was for this last reason after making their pact with the Shoshoni, that other than the more adventurous among them, the Crows chose instead to attend grand intertribal trading fairs held annually at some point on the lower reaches of Green River in present-day Wyoming. As already noted in an earlier chapter, during the time of these "fairs," Shoshoni, Flathead, Nez Perce, Kutenai, Ute, Kiowa, Gattacka, Pueblos and Crows, and at times Arapaho when not at war with the Crows, congregated in perfect harmony in order to exchange their respective merchandise brought from different points of the compass.

The explorers Lewis and Clark were told of these intertribal fairs in 1805 / '06 and reported,

> "...They [the Crows] annually visit the Mandans, Minnetarees and Ahwahahaways [Awaxawi], to whom they barter horses, mules, leather lodges and many articles of Indian apparel, to which they receive in return guns, ammunition, axes, kettles, awls and other European manufactures. When they return to their country they are in turn visited by the Paunch and Snake Indians, to whom they barter most of the articles they have obtained from the Nations on the Missouri, for horses and mules of which these Nations have a greater abundance than themselves. They [Crows] also obtain of the Snake Indians, bridle-bits and blankets, and some other articles which these Indians purchase from the Spaniards....." [11]

The above observation confirms that Crows were then at peace with the Shoshoni. However, when Lewis and Clark referred to the "Paunch Indians," they were alluding to those at a later date known as River Crows specifically, as the Crow horses, so mentioned, came from the Flathead or, perhaps, from the Nez Perce with whom only the Crow-speaking Paunch Indians traded. In their turn, the metal items and mules referred to in the same account, undoubtedly came from the Spanish Possessions in the south via the Pueblos, Gattacka and Ute, as Indians did not themselves raise mules, and so the passage above alludes to the aforesaid intertribal gatherings then being held on Green River.

We cannot doubt that young Sore-Belly was present during these grand intertribal fairs, and one can well imagine how inquisitive he must have been, in order to learn all he could about the strange southern Indians and Spanish-speaking non-Indians alike, with whom at such times he came in contact.

As business entrepreneurs both Mexican traders and Pueblo Indians were represented at these gatherings, and at times - it is said in oral tradition among the Crows – they would afterwards accompany one tribe or another into the latter's own country in order to continue their trade. In the early 1880s an aged Indian from San Juan Pueblo recalled to the cavalry officer John G. Bourke, how in his youth he had often accompanied trading parties to the camps of Crows, Lakota and Cheyenne in the latter's own countries far north of the Rio Grande.

Indeed, the late amateur historian and archaeologist Glen L. Sweem of Sheridan, Wyoming, once showed the present Author several Spanish sword blades bearing the name `Toledo` with dates ranging from 1785 to 1799 etched upon them. These he had found in Indian burial caves and the like during his wanderings through the old Crow country of northern Wyoming and southern Montana. Quite likely the blades had been deposited with the corpses of their Indian owners, whose bones and other artefacts had long since been carried off by scavenging wolves and coyotes.

The presence of such blades does indicate that the Crows were recipients of Spanish trade goods, either directly or indirectly during the late eighteenth century, and corroborates the Fiddler report of 1793, wherein he mentioned Spanish items having been captured from the Crows by the Blood, Pikuni and Shoshoni war-party that year. Such infers also that young Sore-Belly - being himself of the Sore-Lip clan then often among the Mountain Crows - had likely become well-acquainted with both Pueblo Indians and Spanish traders at an early age.

It was then, more importantly for the reason of peace-making that come midsummer, 1805, a large band of Crows in the company of twenty lodges of Shoshoni arrived at the earth-lodge towns along the Knife, so that the Shoshoni themselves could make a comparable pact with the Hidatsa.

It was imperative that the Shoshoni resolve their differences with the Hidatsa. For the Crows, as the latter's close kinfolk, must be prevented from revenge-seeking if a Hidatsa relative be slain by a Shoshoni or visa-versa and which, undoubtedly, would have been the case if the feud be allowed to continue. It is also intimated in Crow oral tradition that the Crows wished to patch up their own recent spate of quarrels with the Hidatsa, instigated by the Crow's treatment of Old Menard and the subsequent act of revenge by the Hidatsa previously mentioned, before all-out warfare broke out between their peoples.

Fortunately for the historian, a literate Scots trader named Charles McKenzie and an educated French Canadian, Francois Larocque, were at that time, themselves on a trading expedition to the Knife River villages on behalf of the Northwest Fur Company. There they met this same party of Crows and Shoshoni which had travelled east from the Rocky Mountains in order to make

40

their pacts with the Hidatsa. It is from both these white men that we have our first written descriptions of the Crows.

The narrative of Charles McKenzie particularly, paints a vivid picture of the grand entry into the Hidatsa village made by the combined Crow and Shoshoni peace party. He noted as follows,

> "...About the middle of June the Rocky Mountain Indians [Crows] made their appearance. They consisted of more than three-hundred tents, and presented the handsomest sight that one could imagine - all on horseback. Children of small size were lashed to their saddles, and those above the age of six could manage a horse.....the women had wooden saddles - most of the men had none. There was a great many horses for the baggage, and the whole exceeding two thousand covered a large space of ground and had the appearance of an army; they halted on a rising ground behind the village; [Hidatsa] formed into a circle - when the chief addressed them, they then descended full speed - rode through the village, exhibiting their dexterity in horsemanship in a thousand shapes - I was astonished to see their agility and address - and I could believe they were the best riders in the world; They were dressed in leather; looked clean and neat - some wore beads and rings as ornaments. Their arms were bows and arrows, lances and round stones enclosed in leather and slung to a shank in the form of a whip. They make use of shields and they have a few guns....." [12]

In a later passage, McKenzie went on to state,

> "...in the meantime, Le Borgne [One-Eye, the Hidatsa head chief] sent for us in order to introduce Mr. La Roque [sic] to the Rocky Mountain chief whose name is *Nakesinia* or Red-Calf. When we offered to shake hands with this great man, he did not understand the intention, and stood motionless until he was informed that shaking hands was the sign of friendship among white men - then he stretched forth both hands to receive ours..." [13]

We are then told in the account how a *"big pipe"* was passed around between the white men and assembled Crow and Hidatsa chiefs, and after which, Francois Larocque presented Red-Calf with a flag and pipe, along with certain other articles as gifts. In response Red-Calf adopted Larocque as his father and vowed to honour and respect him evermore. The chief of the Hidatsa named One-Eye, then smoked the pipe with Red-Calf and each of the other Crow chiefs in attendance, and gave each of the latter one-hundred rounds of powder and ball, in addition to one-hundred bushels of corn; many iron kettles, axes and countless yards of red and blue strouding cloth among other things. In return, the Crows gave their hosts two-hundred and fifty horses and many large parcels of buffalo robes, along with tanned leather leggings and shirts in great number. [14]

Another account of these same events was also recorded in the day by day journal of Larocque himself, who stated there were included twenty lodges of Snake Indians comprising around 40 warriors accompanying the Crows, and further reported,

> "...Thursday 27th....I clothed the chief of the Ereokas [i.e. Crows] at the same time and gave him a flag and a wampaum belt and told them that our chief did not expect, that we would pass many different Nations and therefore had sent but one chief's clothing but that in the course of the summer we would fix upon a spot most convenient for them all where we would build and trade with them, if we saw that they wished to encourage the white people to go on their lands by being good hunters and that then all their chiefs who would behave well would get a coat..." [15]

The Larocque account also makes clear that the Crows were then divided into several bands, which is consistent with the organization of the four "paired clans" or bands which constituted the Crow Nation at that time.

As regards the number of warriors comprising the Crow party mentioned in Larocque's excerpt, his inclusion of the accompanying Shoshoni contingent of forty warriors, would be compatible with the generally accepted average of two adult males to one buffalo-hide tepee.

Larocque also mentioned that a grand adoption ceremony was then going on between the tribes, and this, we know, was a customary part of any peace-making between Indian peoples.

We are informed in the alternative McKenzie account, that the Crows were composed of two tribes, one under the aforementioned Red-Calf; the other led by a chief named Red-Fish, and McKenzie further stated that the band of Red-Fish was comparable in size to that of Red-Calf's band, and likewise, contained six-hundred warriors. Evidently, though, Red-Fish and his people were not actually present on this occasion. as only three hundred Crow tepees are mentioned.

Now the term "Red" as in the name Red-Calf, is said by Joe Medicine Crow to represent 'the first born' or 'original,' as is the Indian idiom of 'red' meaning 'real' or 'proper' and, therefore, this Crow chief's name should have been rendered, First-Born-Calf. This was another, albeit earlier name for the great Mountain Crow head chief originally known as Foolish-Boy, and at a later date, more commonly known as Long-Hair. At the time in question [1805], Long-Hair would have been close to forty years of age and already a leading figure within the tribe, although not as yet regarded as head chief of the entire Absaroka Nation. The fact that Long-Hair's first wife was known as Good-Calf-Woman, appears to add substance to Joe Medicine Crow's assertion, as this name has the added connotation of referring to the woman or wife of the Good-Calf, i.e. "Good" in this sense, meaning a brave and able warrior or chief, as in the Crow expression *"Itchi bachee,"* i. e. "A good man." [16]

The name Red-Fish on the other hand, must represent the Head chief of the Paunch band , as the name refers to the salmon specifically, and likely applies to Chief Paints-His-Face-Red who belonged to that Crow group, and was the overall Head chief of the Nation at that date. There were no salmon to be found in the rivers and streams east of the Rocky Mountains, but the country of the Flathead and Nez Perce was noted for such fish during the appropriate season, and it was the Paunch Indians who associated more regularly with the Flathead and Nez Perce in the salmon country, rather than their Mountain Crow kinfolk.

In addition to the above, McKenzie also reported that the chief of the Hidatsa had previously adopted Chief Red-Calf as his son, and that the Hidatsa chief recommended him highly to the white traders, saying,

*"...He is a great chief."* [17]

It was whilst still assembled among the chiefs in the Hidatsa lodge, that Larocque made his wishes known to the Crows that he intended to return with them to their own country, a proposal at first disagreeable to certain Crows present. The head chief of the Hidatsa One-Eye arose and addressed the Crows, telling them to treat the white man well, for only then would their people have the trade they so much desired. To this effect the Hidatsa chief told the Crows to rejoice that the white men wished to visit their country. He told them how the white men love beaver skins and give the Hidatsa many good things in return, including guns and ammunition, so that the Hidatsa now lived better and more secure than had their fathers. If their Snake enemies had such weapons, the chief continued, then they would not lose so many of their scalps to the Hidatsa. He then told the Crow Chief Red-Calf not to let the white men out of his sight, and asked why it was some among the Crows were telling the white men to go back because they, the Crows, were afraid.

In response, an elderly Crow chief rose to his feet and answered that they had at first been suspicious of the white men, believing they might cast evil among the Crows and on Crow lands. But, the old chief added, their fears were now subdued. The Crows, he said, are in two tribes and have two chiefs, Red-Calf, who has received favours from the white men, and Red-Fish who has received none, and it was Red-Fish who had told them to be suspicious. Red-Calf himself then turned to Larocque and addressed him thus,

"Father, if you are willing to go with us, we are willing to receive you - but should an enemy stand in our way, or attack us in our journey - you and your men must assist us in beating them off." [18]

Larocque agreed and early next morning; July 1, 1805, the French trader with two white comrades set off in the company of a host of Indians. They travelled in a southwest direction from Knife River and the Hidatsa town, prepared to live, hunt, and fight if necessary, alongside Chief Long-Hair`s [Red-Calf`s] band of Mountain Crows.

Larocque subsequently left an interesting journal pertaining to his period of wandering with the Crows; the first educated white man to have done so. He noted that there were three tribes of Crows, known in their own language respectively, according to Larocque's garbled rendition, as the *Apsarecha, Keetheresa* and *Ashcabcaber* [i.e. Mountain Crows, Paunch Indians, later known as River Crows, and the Dried-Out-Furs band]. These tribes, he added,

> "...are again divided into many other small ones [i.e., clans?] which at present consist of a few people in each, as they are the remainder of a numerous people who were reduced to their present number by the ravage of the Small Pox which raged among them for many years successively and as late as three years ago [1802]. They told me they counted 2,000 lodges or tents in their camp when altogether, before the Small Pox had infected them...Since the great decrease of their numbers, they generally dwell all together and flit at the same time and as long as it is possible for them to live, when together they seldom part." [19]

Here Larocque was referring only to the then still united Mountain Crow and Kicked-in-the-Belly bands with whom he was traveling, as he further noted that their number then comprised some 2,400 souls in 300 lodges, whereas in his earlier notation recorded at the Mandan and Hidatsa towns, he stated that the other branch of the tribe also contained 300 lodges in total.

It is not within the scope of this work to give a complete resume of Larocque's sojourn with his Crow hosts, only to note that he was disappointed somewhat at the Indian's lack of enthusiasm for hunting beaver, and only once, it seems, was he aware of any actual conflict between his hosts and their enemies during the time he remained among them. This latter event occurred on the morning of Saturday 24th, when three strangers were sighted atop *"...the first hill of the mountain."* [20] Buffalo were in motion indicating the presence of hunters nearby, and gunshots were heard coming from the direction of the Big Horn River. Thirty Crow warriors immediately mounted their war-ponies and rode off to ascertain the source of such activity, whilst those remaining in camp prepared themselves for battle; ready to follow up their comrades at a moment's notice if need arose. A few hours later, a number of riders belonging to the first party of warriors returned to camp, bringing news that they had espied thirty-five Assiniboine Indians walking along the far bank of the Big Horn River. Larocque went on to report,

> "...in less time than the courier could tell the news no one remained in camp but a few old men and women, all the rest scampered off in pursuit. I [Larocque] went along with them. We did not all set off together nor could we all keep together as some horses were slower than others, but the foremost stopped galloping on a hill, and continued on with a small trot as people came up. They did the same when a chief arrived, he and his band or a part of it galloped twice before the main body of the people who still continued their trot, intersecting the line of their course while some of his friends I suppose his aide de camp, harangued; they were all

44

dressed in their best clothes. Many were followed by their wives who carried their arms, and who were to deliver them at the time of battle. There were likewise many children, but only those who could keep their saddles. Ahead of us were some young men on different hills making signs with their robes which way we were to go. As soon as all the chiefs had come up and had made their harangues everyone set off the way he liked best and pursued according to his own judgment....All [of the enemy] escaped but two of the foremost who being scouts of the party, had advanced nearer to us than the others......They were surrounded after a long race, but killed and scalped in a twinkling. When I arrived at the dead bodies they had taken but his scalp and the fingers of his right hand with which the outer was cut off. They [the Crows] borrowed my hanger [knife] with which they cut off his left hand and returned it [the knife] to me bloody as a mark of honour....Men women and children were thronging to see the dead bodies and taste the blood....everyone was desirous of stabbing the bodies to show what he would have done had he met them alive, and insulted and scoffed at them in the worst language they could muster. In a short time the remains of a Human body was hardly distinguishable. Every young man had a piece of flesh tied to his gun or lance with which he rode off to camp singing, and exultantly showing it to every young woman in his way. Some women had whole limbs dangling from their saddles. The sight made me shudder with horror at such cruelties, and I returned home [to the camp] in quite a different frame from that in which I left it. The scalp dance was danced all night, and the scalps carried on procession throughout the day." [21]

In a later passage Larocque added that three days later, ten Crows were sent out to discover the intentions of the rest of the Assiniboine party which had eluded them, and from here on, the Crows were in constant expectation of their own camp being attacked by the enemy. However, four days later, another party of Crow scouts came upon an abandoned site of thirty lodges on the Big Horn. The occupants, apparently, had retreated in great haste, having left behind them, *"....chief's coats, Stroud wampaum, [sic] shells, and other items."* [22]

For three months more or less, Larocque traversed the Crow country, having travelled west across the Little Missouri, Powder and Tongue rivers. Thence over the *"Chee-tiish,"* i. e., Wolf-Teeth Mountains, before crossing the Big Horn River then continuing west to Pryor Creek. At this point the party turned north and followed the course of the Pryor down-stream until reaching the Yellowstone, and where on a small island in that river, Larocque held a final council with his hosts before bidding farewell and returning north to Fort Montagne a la Bosse on the Assiniboine River in present-day Saskatchewan, Canada.

In reality, other than recording the day by day routine of his hosts and being the first white man to have actually entered the far reaches of Crow country, the journal which Larocque left for posterity, from a purely historical perspective, does not seem to contain anything more exceptional than his mention of an old Crow war-chief whom he calls Spotted-Crow [but whose real name evidently, was Sits-Down-Spotted], along with the observation that on September 7th whilst encamped with his hosts somewhere in the vicinity of Pryor Creek, a band of Atsina then on the other side of the mountains at the mouth of the Big Horn, sent three emissaries to the Crow camp, requesting, so Larocque believed, that peace be made between them and the Crows. Crow oral tradition coupled with that of the Atsina also states, however, that other than coming to the Crow camp with the pipe of peace, the Atsina brought word that a formidable coalition of tribes; all enemies of the Crow, had smoked a war-pipe together and at that very moment, was travelling the "red road" in a great combined war-party, in order to exact vengeance upon the Crows for past grievances against them.

$$- 0 - 0 - 0 - 0 - 0 - 0 - 0 - 0 - 0 - 0 - 0 -$$

## CHAPTER 4.

## THE FIGHT AT PRYOR GAP.

So it was later that summer in mid-August 1805 after Larocque bade his farewells, that a significant battle occurred between Crow Indians on one side, and a formidable force of enemies composed of several allied tribes on the other. It was an event unreported by any white chronicler of the day, although the particular fight is still considered an important episode in Crow oral history, notwithstanding that it has long since become shrouded in myth and legend. It is, though, yet another episode in which, it is said, the young Sore-Belly was personally involved.
1

It had been five or more years prior to the fight in question, that a young Crow brave named Rolling-Thunder, being the son of the aforementioned council chief, Sits-Down-Spotted, had gone with a war-party as far east as the middle course of the Missouri River in what is now central South Dakota, intending to raid the Lakota of that region in search of the spoils of war.

During the course of its meandering, the war-party had detoured in order to pay a friendly visit to the Arickara at the latter's earth lodge villages at the mouth of the Grand, as at this particular time [1800] the Crows and Arickara – albeit temporarily – were enjoying a period of peace between their tribes.

The Crow party had tarried among the Arickara for two weeks or more, during which time the young man Rolling-Thunder fell in love with an Arickara maiden, and when finally his companions departed, Rolling-Thunder remained at the town. Soon after this he married the maiden whose name was Breeze-of-the-South-Wind, and thereafter, settled down as an adopted member of his wife's people. The woman it transpired, was the daughter of an Arickara chief named Red-Tomahawk, but as the Arickara tribe was then composed of many different factions between whom there was intense rivalry and often aggressive confrontation, this man Red-Tomahawk was not happy with his lot. Instead, he grew very close to his newly-acquired Crow son-in-law.

It was only a few years after this, that owing to some misunderstanding now forgotten, the Crows and Arickara renewed hostilities against each other. But still Rolling-Thunder remained among his wife's people, although refusing to involve himself in their feud with his own people the Crows. Then in Mid-August 1805, a great body of warriors including Lakota, Cheyennes and Arapaho arrived at the Arickara towns carrying a war-pipe. This they duly offered to their hosts, along with a request that the Arickara join them in a grand multi-tribal offensive against the Crows.

Thus the Arapaho were now also hostile against the Crows, who until recently had been friends and sometimes allies.

The reason for this allied visit to the Arickara seems to have been in part, a response to the aforementioned defeat of the combined Teton and Yankton force the previous summer at Heart River when Crows, by their personal involvement, had assured the former tribes' crushing and humiliating defeat. The Cheyennes, though, had their own good reason to want to avenge themselves on the Crows, owing to several recent defeats suffered at that people's hands which had brought much grief to their lodges, such as the twenty-five or thirty Cheyennes killed by Crows two years earlier. It does appear, in fact, that it was Cheyennes who had actually first proposed the idea of a hostile crusade, as during the previous winter, Cheyenne delegates had carried their own war-pipe to several tribes, among whom were included the Arickara and Lakota, and even to the Mandan, and this, we know, was the customary and singular procedure among Cheyennes when contemplating such a venture. As regards the Arapaho, during the month of August the previous year [1804] when in the company of Cheyennes, Padaux [Lipan Apache] and Gattacka [Kiowa-Apache] along with contingents from some other Plains Tribes, they had visited the Arickara towns for the first time, ostensibly, on a trading expedition, and whilst there, the Arapaho at the instigation of their Cheyenne allies had made peace not only with the Arickara, but also with a band of Lakota which happened to be visiting the Arickara at that time. Thus in order to show both the Arickara and Lakota their commitment to the recent pacts, the Arapaho had now included themselves in the proposed crusade against their erstwhile friends the Crows. The Arickara, we have seen, had likewise suffered recent reverses from the same enemy, and being at last at peace with the Cheyennes, Arapaho and Lakota, the Arickara chiefs willingly accepted the proffered pipe, and agreed to travel with their allies on the "red road" against the Crows.

Now it had happened that Rolling-Thunder had since become a member of an Arickara warrior society, and so was privy to the council then being held between the allied chiefs. Subsequently, he knew well that the intention of the proposed crusade was to destroy the Crow people as a power on the Northern

Plains, and further, to take the beautiful Yellowstone country from them along with the Crow women and children into captivity.

True it was that Rolling-Thunder did harbour a degree of affection towards his adopted people, but the innate loyalty towards the blood relatives of his birth was overriding. He could not stand idly by and let his own Crow people suffer the potential catastrophe being planned against them. He spoke of this to his wife, telling her that he would go to the Crows and warn them of the impending danger. To his surprise his wife agreed to accompany him on his mission. All she asked was that if things turned out bad for the Arickara during the coming contest, then the Crows should spare the life of her father Red-Tomahawk, as he would be obliged to accompany the allied war-party or lose face and prestige as a man. Rolling-Thunder agreed and that very night, he and his wife slipped out of the Arickara town and after mounting horses secreted some distance from the town earlier that day, they started on their long and hazardous journey to the Crow country.

When several days later the young man and his wife arrived at his father's Crow village which had recently played host to the Frenchman Larocque, and had since been joined by Paints-His-Face-Red and thirty lodges of the Paunch band, there was much rejoicing among the people celebrating the return of the long-absent son of Sits-Down-Spotted. Later, in his father's lodge, Rolling-Thunder told an assembled council among whom were Paints-His-Face-Red [i .e. Red-Fish] and Long-Hair [Red-Calf], that a great host was coming against them intending to take the sacred *Echeta-Casha* for themselves and the Crow women and children captive. He further told the council that even then, the enemy force which now included their erstwhile friends the Arapaho, was on the march, and only three or four days traveling distance from the Crow village. The council was alarmed and there was much earnest deliberation among the chiefs and headmen present.

Chief Paints-His-Face-Red, whose full name was, Paints-His-Face-Red-With-the-Blood-of-His-Enemies, had much to say on the matter. He harangued the council with words to the effect,

"...So they come again into Crow country. Now they come in great number and with them the Tattooed Breasts [Arapaho], who once we welcomed in our lodges and smoked and feasted as brothers. See now my chiefs how those dog-eaters repay our hospitality that they should prove themselves treacherous and see fit to unite with those who are traveling the red road against us. Let us pray to Old Man Coyote to assist us as once he promised, and in the meantime, summon our Crow bands to come together as one people. We shall place ourselves in a strong position and prepare to meet the foe. If it be our last sunrise, then we shall see it as a united people, and will shed enough enemy blood to stain the buffalo grass for many snows to come, long after we ourselves have fallen and our bodies devoured by the four-leggeds and their winged brethren of the sky."
2

Such stirring words put new heart into those who earlier, had voiced the opinion that the various Crow bands should disperse into many small groups to better elude the foe. Now, however, all were eager to resist and ready to sacrifice their lives, if need be, for the sake of their people and their country, and, not least, for their own tribal honour and prestige. It was thus agreed that all the scattered bands of Crows should be called in, and together, they should move without delay to a canyon-like gap in a range of sandstone bluffs a short distance from what the Crows knew as "Shoots-the-Arrow Rock," which overlooks what today is designated on modem-day maps as Pryor Creek.

This accordingly was done. And so it was that the whole Crow Nation congregated as a single body where; it was supposed, they could better defend their families and safeguard their vast herd of ponies.

The site chosen by the chiefs to make their stand had a particular defensive advantage. At the south end of the river valley, the aforesaid 'Gap' forms a low-walled narrow defile or canyon running east to west, and it was here in the deep recess of the canyon itself, that the Crows erected their tepees, while at the canyon mouth at its east end, they placed bushes and small trees to hide the opening from view. Having done this, all the able-bodied men folk with the exception of fifty hand-picked warriors, positioned themselves in battle array along each side of the canyon and awaited the arrival of the foe. The remaining fifty warriors were instructed to act as a decoy force, intending to lure the enemy into the narrow defile where they could be fought in smaller groups, and hopefully, slaughtered piecemeal by the main Crow body which would then take the allies by surprise.

In the meantime, the Crows had scouts out at all times, so that adequate warning could be given as soon as the enemy host appeared.

It was two days later before the enemy did finally come in sight. The fifty hand-picked Crow warriors - among whom was included the young man Rolling-Thunder – mounted their war-ponies and rode ahead from the mouth of the canyon and into the wide grassy valley where a small herd of buffalo was grazing. Just before the allied force drew near, these Crow warriors started to ride in amongst the herd in the pretence that they were starting on a hunt. The allies saw the fifty Crows scattered here and there across the valley, and thinking they could easily run down and kill them all, they at once urged their ponies forward, and yelling war-cries at the tops of their voices charged headlong towards them.

The fifty Crows waited until the allies were only forty or fifty yards distant, then bunched themselves together and rode pell-mell towards the canyon mouth, as yet still hidden from the foe.

The Crows appeared to be running, *"...like scared rabbits,"* [3] it is said - and the enemy in premature jubilation, sent a cloud of arrows after them, while those who carried fire arms of some description shot wildly, and thus expended their first shots before the battle proper began. Suddenly to the allies' bewilderment, the fifty Crows rode right through the trees and foliage concealing the canyon mouth, but convinced that they themselves would close up with their quarry in another moment, the allies rode blindly on, still shooting arrows and musket balls into the fleeing bunch ahead.

On they rode following the retreating Crows, straight into the mouth of the canyon and soon were between the canyon walls on either side. The fifty Crows who until this time had appeared frightened with no stomach to fight, now pulled up their mounts; wheeled them smartly around and not only faced the oncoming foe, but charged straight at them.

At this date the Crows owned very few guns, but as their fifty comrades bravely confronted the enemy, a number of gunshots rang out and hundreds of arrows whistled through the air from each side of the canyon. The Crow missiles smashed into allied riders and horses, toppling many a warrior from the saddle and creating general confusion among their ranks. The enemy could only turn and flee in an endeavour to escape the trap and this they managed to do, although leaving many of their comrades dead or dying in the wake of their retreat. The whole fighting force of Crows then joined in the fray; some shooting arrows and guns from the cover of rocks that dotted the landscape; others charging on their war-ponies in amongst the throng of enemies in order to count *dakshey,* or to perform reckless, and sometimes, suicidal deeds.

Among the Crows that day was the earlier mentioned leading sub-chief then known as Red-Calf, but who in later years took the name Red-Feather-on-the-Temple, albeit more widely known by the nomenclature, Long-Hair. At this date he was about forty years of age, and was recognized as a great and fearless fighter, who possessed strong *medicine* powers obtained from his sacred protectors Morning Star and Bear Spirit. It is said he was most prominent throughout the conflict, as time and again he rallied the Crow warriors to re-group and led them in several spirited charges against the massed ranks of the foe. Occasionally, Long-Hair himself dispatched an opponent and also knocked several enemies from their horses; one after the other, with his dexterous use of the lance.

A number of teenage Crow boys between fifteen and sixteen years of age, were not content to remain in the comparative safety of the Crow village protected by the women and old men. Instead, they ran onto the battlefield, capturing the loose horses of the enemy whose riders had been killed; seriously wounded or simply unseated from their saddles. These animals the Crow boys then drove deep into the far recess of the canyon as the spoils of war, and among those doing this brave thing, was the thirteen year-old Sore-Belly; the youngest of them all.

At one point during the melee, whilst the Crows and their enemies were all mixed up battling each other across the field, Rolling-Thunder spied the unhorsed Arickara Red-Tomahawk. In keeping with the promise earlier given to his wife, the young Crow raced over to his father-in-law; bade him climb up on his horse behind him and carried him safely to the Crow camp, where the Arickara chief remained throughout the rest of the fight.

Several times during the day-long contest the allies regrouped and charged anew. But having lost so many of their number both dead and wounded, along with many put on foot and unable to resist Crow cavalry in a significant manner, they could make no serious inroads on the field.

It was late afternoon when the entire Crow force made one last exerted effort, led by the indefatigable Chief Long-Hair, and this time they routed the allies completely. The latter turned their horses around and rode back the way they had come as fast as they were able, many riding double after picking up unhorsed companions as they fled.

Numerous Lakota winter-counts commemorate this fight, referring to it as, *"...a running battle with the Crows,"* [4] and in which event, a number of mounted allied warriors were forced to ride double, rendering them at a great disadvantage to those pursuing them. Conversely, a Hunkpapa Lakota winter-count entry for the same year, states that it had been a large Crow war-party consisting of warriors both mounted and on foot which had assaulted a Lakota village, and in the event,

> "The battle was long and well fought, but as the Crows were mounted two on a horse [so they could easily run down the Sioux, many of whom were on foot having had their horses killed from under them], the Crows were the victors and many [Sioux] were killed." [5]

Here it seems, the interpreter of this particular `count` misconstrued the true meaning of the entry, and it should rather be compatible with those other `counts` which state specifically, that it was the retreating Lakota who were forced to ride double in order to escape their pursuers on this occasion.

These same `counts` further mention that a white man trader among the attacking allied force was also killed, while during another stage of the fight, eight warriors had made a stand in some kind of enclosure or "dugout," but were surrounded by the enemy and eventually wiped out, although it is also said that *"...The Lakota killed many enemies too."* [6]

However, as is often the case regarding the earlier entries in the winter-counts themselves, there is here as elsewhere some discrepancy as to whether the mention of the eight surrounded and killed, actually refers to Lakota warriors or to Crows.

What is remembered by the Crows, is that most of the dead and seriously wounded from among the allied ranks were left where they had fallen, to be abused, humiliated and eventually butchered and mutilated by the victors. To leave one's comrades on the field whether they be alive or dead, was considered a dishonourable act among the Crows, as indeed, it was among the Lakota and their allies also. Thus having done so, it shows how completely demoralized and in such a state of disarray the retreating allies must have been at that time.

Nevertheless, the Crows did not let up. They rode after the fleeing foe; raced alongside them and fought hand to hand as they galloped across the prairie, and continued the running fight for several hours until, that is, it became too dark to distinguish friend from foe. Only then did the victorious Crows give up the chase, and return to the original scene of conflict at the canyon's mouth.

By the light of a full moon, the Crow women searched among the prostrate bodies lying scattered across the field. They killed all those of the enemy lying wounded and dispatched the many injured horses to put them out of their misery. Several Crow warriors also wandered among the dead, and to a number of enemy corpses lying face upwards looking at the sky, they turned the bodies over so their faces were buried in the ground. This was a sign that the particular warriors thus re-positioned had not fought well that day. Of their own dead and wounded, the Crows carried them back to their camp and gave the bodies over to the respective relatives to prepare for burial. Each Crow warrior then retired to his own family lodge, as there would be no victory celebrations until a day of mourning had been observed for loved ones slain. Still, though, a number of Crow scouts kept a sharp watch through that night and following day, lest the enemy should return in even greater force and again attempt to destroy the valiant Apsaalooka. But their fears were unfounded. The allied force by then was already far distant; long on its way out of the country - even before the Crows next day arose from their slumber.

The Crows gave thanks to *Akbaa-tadia* and to Old-Man-Coyote for ensuring their people's safe deliverance from potential annihilation and for the great victory achieved. Truly, it was said, Old-Man-Coyote had kept his ancient promise; to assist the Apsaalooka and protect the land of *Echeta Casha* in times of dire need. When, however, in the bright light of day, it was made known the names of those Crows who had fallen and of others, who having been seriously wounded in the conflict were likely to succumb to their injuries, there was much sadness among the people, which curtailed somewhat their initial feelings of jubilation.

Notwithstanding, however, a degree of despondency permeating the Crow camp because of loved ones lost, those who had shown themselves heroes in the fight were soon after honoured accordingly. The sub-chief Long-Hair was raised to even higher standing within the tribe owing to the brave deeds he had performed that day. He was, though, but one of those whose names were heralded around the camp, and among these others was young Sore-Belly who himself, had captured several horses from the foe. He, too, was duly recognized for his deeds that day and praise songs were sung in his honour around the lodges.

Regarding the Arickara Chief Red-Tomahawk, it is alleged that he remained among the Crows until his death from old age some few years later, whilst his son-in-law Rolling-Thunder, became a renowned warrior and eventually a chief among the Crows in his own right. It is further said that in the aftermath of the fight, the Crows collected together the bodies of their own slain kinsmen and even those of their enemies left on the field of battle. These they buried in several pits which they covered over with dirt and stones creating a number of small cairn-like structures, in order to protect the remains from scavenging beasts.

For many years after this time, any Crow - and indeed, members of those other tribes involved - when passing through the canyon, were apt to place a small stone on one or more of the cairns in commemoration of the event and to appease the spirits of the dead. Today these piles of stones can still be seen at the place called, Pryor Gap.

It was not long after this, while the Crows were still contemplating their deliverance from what might have been a disastrous defeat, that they agreed among themselves to accept the earlier mentioned Atsina offer of peace. The Atsina had a motive in parching up their quarrel with the Crows, in so much that other than wishing to hunt freely in lands abutting the north side of the Yellowstone, they had recently severed their trading links with Hudson's Bay Company posts, due to a series of hostile acts perpetrated by Atsina upon establishments of that company and its employees. Thus the Atsina wished to gain unobstructed access through Crow country in order to reach their Arapaho kinfolk on the South Platte, and from whom the Atsina hoped to obtain horses, Spanish weapons and other trade items which they were now debarred from obtaining in the north. In addition, the Atsina had recently fallen out with their erstwhile friends and allies the Siksika-Blackfoot, Cree and Assiniboine, so the Atsina at this particular time, were also in dire need of friends who could assist them against common foes.

The Crows, being ever willing to gain allies in their constant struggle against the Lakota and Cheyennes, agreed to the aforementioned peace and by so doing, lay the foundation for a renewal of friendship between themselves and the Arapaho, who it is said in Crow tradition, were included among those who congregated at Pompey's Pillar later that year to conclude the pact. Peace with the Atsina also inaugurated a temporary cessation of Crow hostilities with the most southern Blackfoot-speaking people, specifically the Small Robe Pikuni band, which tended to roam and hunt in and around the Three Forks of the Missouri on the very borders of Crow territory, and who unlike their Siksika cousins, still remained close allies and confederates of the Atsina.

So it was before the year was out, that the gathering at Pompey's Pillar went ahead and concurrent pacts were duly confirmed between the Crows, Atsina, Arapaho, Small-Robe Pikuni, and also some Flathead and a band of Shoshoni who had taken it upon themselves to attend. From then on, apart from sporadic minor horse-stealing raids upon each other's herds, the Crow peace effected at this time with both the Atsina and Arapaho and Small-Robe Pikuni held fast, that is for at least a year, which among such warring tribes was no mean achievement.

This being so, it was because of the Crow-Atsina-Arapaho pact that in spring the following year of 1806, the Crows endeavoured to extend the hand of friendship to the Cheyennes - who were then close allies and associates to both the Atsina and Arapaho - along with an invitation to the Cheyennes to join in yet another proposed intertribal peace-gathering that coming summer.

Accordingly, a delegation of twelve Crow braves was sent into Cheyenne country east of the Black Hills. They intended to offer their old-time enemies the calumet of peace, lest the recent escalation of hostility between their Nations should increase even further, at a time when the Crows were already fully engaged defending their hearths against the Assiniboine and more powerful Blood and Siksika [Blackfoot-Proper] tribes of the north.

Unfortunately at this period, the Cheyennes were not inclined to terminate their feud with the Crows, or to relax in their endeavour to wrest the eastern portion of Crow country for their own use. Indeed, the Cheyennes could well afford to be brash having the powerful Teton Lakota as allies, while at the same time, the Cheyennes themselves were conducting a vigorous war against the Shoshoni with whom, only a few years earlier, the Crows had made peace. As a consequence, the Cheyennes now regarded the Crows as allies to the Shoshoni and thus, enemies of the Cheyenne.

What the actual details were surrounding the fate of the twelve Crow emissaries, we are not told in either the documented or oral accounts. Crow tradition merely states that somewhere en route to the Cheyenne country, the Crow delegation was confronted by a large Cheyenne war-party and the entire embassy wiped out. [7]

Seemingly oblivious to such a treacherous act as then perpetrated by the Cheyennes, in early summer the same year, the Crows Hidatsa cousins and supposed allies, undertook a friendly trading trip to a Cheyenne village on the open prairie some distance south of the Hidatsa towns, and among the Cheyennes were then included contingents from both the Arapahoe and Lakota.

Such a move on the part of the Hidatsa was due in no small part to the persuasions of the explorers Lewis and Clark, who`s expedition just happened to then be on its return journey down the Missouri. Lewis and Clark whilst again visiting the Arickara towns at the mouth of Grand River, had held councils with that people and with several chiefs of the Lakota, Arapaho and Cheyennes who were then also in attendance. The explorers had urged the chiefs of those tribes present to keep the peace between themselves, and to extend the hand of friendship to the Mandan and Hidatsa further upstream. And so it was that the Hidatsa, in accordance with the explorer`s wishes, had at this time set out on a mission to make their pact with the Cheyennes and also, with the aforementioned contingents of Arapaho and Lakota.

The resulting pacts were not destined to last, although soon after the Hidatsa returned to their Knife River towns after meeting the Cheyennes, a body of thirty Crow warriors and their families along with a number of Flathead arrived on a friendly visit to their cousins. The Crows were on a trading trip and brought with them a great number of horses, skins, furs and slaves to barter for guns, ammunition, tobacco and axes etc. The trader Alexander Henry the younger who later met this same Crow-Flathead party, noted in his journal at the time that they [Crows], have no other means of procuring European articles and go toward the Spanish settlements with the Flatheads, but what they get in that way is too trifling to answer their purpose. Henry further recorded that the Crows offered to trade him a handsome slave girl about twelve years of age in exchange for a gun, 100 balls, and powder enough to fire them. But, remarked Henry,

> "The rascally Big Bellies [Hidatsa] would not allow us to purchase her, saying they wanted her for themselves." [7] ...The Crows have the character of a brave and warlike people, though obliged to put up with insults from the Hidatsa with whom they, the Crows, have been repeatedly at war and on many occasions, have displayed dauntless spirit. [8]

Whether Henry was referring to Atsina [also known as Big-Bellies] or to Hidatsa is unclear, although whatever the case, obviously the visiting Crows were informed of the Hidatsa peace-making enterprise. But there remains no record that the Crows themselves then wished to be included in the pacts, and especially so, after such a treacherous act on the part of the Cheyennes only recently committed against their earlier delegation.

Thus, Crow feuding with the Cheyennes continued and actually increased in its severity and consistency. Rarely did a week pass when there was not some kind of hostile confrontation between the two.

Crow hostilities against the Lakota also continued as fiercely as ever, and several Teton winter-counts refer to episodes relating to such conflicts for the year 1806, Some of these entries, however, may apply to the Pryor Gap fight previously recounted, and are recorded as follows,

*"In war with the Crows, a leader named Akile-Luta was slain."* [9]

In another Lakota winter-count the entry for 1806 / `07 records,

*"Black-Stone* [or Black-Rock`] *killed by Crows."* [10]

This man Black-Rock was an important chief among the Oglala Lakota, although there is some dispute between the several Lakota` counts` whether he was merely wounded at this time or killed.

In alternative `counts` it is also recorded for the year of 1806 / `07,

*"A Lakota leader* [spy or scout] *slain by Crows,"* [11]

and in yet another `count` it is noted,

*"Eight Lakota eagle trappers killed by Crows."* [12]

Here, likewise, there is some dispute between the several `counts` which mention this event, whether there had been eight, one, or two eagle trappers killed at that time, whilst in the so-called John Colhoff `count, ` it is said that an Oglala chief named Big-Crow and his son while engaged in trapping eagles, were surprised by Crows led by a chief named Sitting-Hawk, and were killed. The term Sitting-Hawk is a variant form of Sits-Down-Spotted an important Crow chief at the time, and was the same man Spotted-Crow with whom the trader Larocque had met whilst traveling through Crow country the previous year. Perhaps, also, this was the same man named Spotted-Water, alternatively known as War Eagle, later listed as being active in 1834 by the American trapper William M. Anderson in his journal notes for that year.

– 0 – 0 – 0 – 0 – 0 – 0 – 0 – 0 – 0 – 0 – 0 –

## CHAPTER. 5.
### HIDATSA SCALPS ON APSAALOOKA WAISTBELTS.

Concerning the aforementioned Crow-Atsina pact, it did not endure long. By spring 1807, both tribes were again raiding each other's camps. In early May that year the Atsina, while returning north to their Marias River homeland after time spent near the Spanish settlements with their Arapaho cousins, came across a small Crow camp in the Big Horn country. The Atsina were a fickle lot, often acting on impulse rather than taking account of the likely consequences of their actions. They thus found the temptation to steal a few Crow horses too strong to resist and in the event, one or more Crows were killed, after which the Atsina made a precipitous exit from the region. So much for the peace-making at Pompey`s Pillar little more than a year past.

In response, the Crows threatened to combine their forces and strike a punitive blow in the Atsina country itself. After receiving word of the impending invasion, the Atsina suddenly appeared at the gates of the Hudson's Bay post Fort Edmonton on the North Branch of the Saskatchewan. There they pleaded with the Factor to trade guns and ammunition with which the Atsina could defend themselves against the Crows. As it was the threatened invasion did not materialize, although it helped enhance the reputation given the Crows as a formidable fighting force on the Northern Plains, even though their more recent victories had not been of a particularly significant nature. It was, however, perhaps due to the mere threat of invasion that in late July, a large war-band of combined Siksika, Blood and Atsina pillaged and destroyed the Northwest Company post Fort Augustus, during which they obtained many guns and a large quantity of powder and ball with which to charge them. Considering themselves thus sufficiently armed, the same band of allies then went south to make war on the Crows. What the outcome was, we are not told, although one might assume that the Crows did not suffer to any great extent, or surely, there would be some mention in the many Company documents of that time.

Be this as it may, forth-coming days did bode well for the Crows as a whole. Such was especially so when in late autumn that same year, the first white man's trading post was erected in the very heart of Crow country. This enabled the latter for the first time to have regular access to an adequate supply of guns, powder and ball, metal axes and knives, along with sheet iron for the manufacture of arrow heads and lance points. Together, such commodities would allow the Crows to defend themselves on a more equal footing against their numerous foes.

Indeed, when in late 1806 the Lewis and Clark expedition which had traversed the North American Continent from east to west and west to east, had finally returned to the town of St. Louis on the Mississippi below the mouth of the Missouri, the explorers brought with them information regarding the great number of beaver and other fur-bearing animals to be found in the upper country. Such news had created an immediate incentive among certain traders to undertake their own expeditions, in order to take advantage of this untapped source of wealth.

First among these entrepreneurs was the Spanish born Manuel Lisa of the "Missouri Fur Company" that had been in operation far down the Missouri since 1793. Now, however, early in 1807, Lisa with a `brigade` of sixty-one men, sailed, hauled and poled two shallow-draught keel boats up the `Muddy Missouri` towards the rich trapping country of the Northwest.

Among Lisa`s employees at this time were two competent hunters named John Colter and George Drouillard, both of whom had been important members of the aforesaid Lewis and Clark expedition across the Continent.

Drouillard; of French Canadian and Shawnee Indian descent, had remained with the explorers until being formally discharged in St. Louis, where a short time later he had signed on with Lisa's brigade then preparing to ascend the river. Colter on the other hand, had taken leave of Lewis and Clark whilst on the expedition's return journey down the Missouri. At the Mandan towns, he had met two itinerant white men from the Illinois country preparing to go upriver on a trapping venture of their own. Joining with them, Colter and his new-found companions had then retraced the expedition's steps west in order to spend the winter of 1806 / '07; trapping the rich harvest of fur in the Upper Missouri district. Sometime during his sojourn and for reasons unclear, Colter soon after disassociated himself from his two companions and come the following spring, had paddled a canoe back down the Missouri intent upon returning to St. Louis and the comforts of civilization.

It had happened during his return trip that when reaching the mouth of the Platte, he met Lisa's brigade temporarily halted at that point. Perhaps from information supplied by Colter's old acquaintance Drouillard, Lisa realized that here was a man who could be of immense value to his enterprise, as Colter by then was well-acquainted with the upper country. At once Lisa set about persuading him to accompany the brigade in the capacity of hunter and guide and whatever the inducements offered, Colter agreed to join the flotilla. He and Droulliard were the only Company men present who had any real knowledge of the Yellowstone and Big Horn country, not to mention Colter's now singular knowledge of its Indian inhabitants.

Lisa's flotilla thereafter, continued upriver and reached the mouth of the Big Horn in late November that year of 1807. At once Lisa supervised the construction of a post which he named Fort Raymond [more properly the Spanish equivalent, 'Remon' after a son by that name recently born to his wife in St. Louis]. Thus, on the west bank of the Big Horn close to where it enters the Yellowstone, the Spaniard erected a two-roomed log cabin with an attic for extra storage, and from here he conducted his operations throughout the ensuing winter. So was built the first permanent white man's structure not only in Crow country, but in the whole of that vast expanse which is the present-day state of Montana.

Before the onset of snow, Lisa instructed three men, one of whom was Colter, to seek out the various Crow camps in their winter quarters and invite the Indians to bring their furs to the post. The other two emissaries included the above mentioned George Drouillard and a mulatto named Edward Rose, who himself, had spent some time among the Omaha Indians lower down the Missouri. All three men set out on foot in different directions just as the first flurries of snow heralded the arrival of the winter season. They carried their trade goods and personal accoutrements in bundles strapped to their backs, and one can imagine that their respective journeys were not an inviting prospect.

Both Drouillard and Rose accordingly, went up the Yellowstone and several of its tributaries searching out Crow camps thought to be in those areas. Colter, meanwhile, travelled a south-westerly course which took him over the Big Horn and Wind River Mountains. It was a gruelling journey, but he successfully made contact not only with the Mountain Crows, but with camps of Shoshoni and Flatheads also.

Among the Mountain Crows Colter was well received, they being only too pleased to have white men actually trading in their country. Now their people could be supplied with much needed guns and ammunition directly, rather than having to risk the long and hazardous journey to and from the Hidatsa towns, which had always invited attack from numerous enemy war-bands roaming the intervening country.

It seems that Colter remained among the Crows throughout the rest of that winter and coming spring. During that time he had encouraged his hosts to trap beaver and trade their pelts to his employer at the newly erected post near the mouth of the Big Horn. He also traversed the surrounding country on foot, and was the first white man to discover the Hot Springs and other natural phenomena in what are now the Yellowstone and Grand Teton National Parks.

It is evident, though, that a small number of Crows must earlier have visited the aforesaid Fort Raymond at the beginning of its construction. How else could either of those sent from the fort to the various scattered Crow camps know their exact locations? Of course, the Crows themselves would have been fully aware of the presence of strangers who had taken up permanent residence in the very heart of Crow territory, and having said this, we might reasonably assume that as was customary of white traders in those days, Lisa may have personally presented a so-called "chief's coat" to one of the leading Crow men who may have visited his fort, if not to an important chief among that tribe.

Certainly, various Lakota winter-counts record for the same winter of 1807 / '08, that a war-party composed of warriors from several Lakota bands had a big fight with Crows at that time. The fight was considered memorable by the fact that during the melee, a brave Crow having only one serviceable eye and wearing a conspicuous red coat was killed. The particular garment must have been fairly unique among Indians at that date to warrant mention in the first place. It likely refers to a red military-type frock coat, commonly known as a "chief's coat" as presented by white traders to prominent figures among the tribes and who in return, were then expected to influence others among their people to accommodate the trader's needs. It is reasonable, therefore, that if the garment had not been among booty taken from the abandoned Assiniboine war-camp mentioned in a previous chapter, then it had been obtained from Lisa himself. The Crow Indian wearing such a coat and killed by Lakota would have been an important member of his tribe. But, alas, other than the winter-count entries themselves, we have no further information pertaining to the slain man or indeed, regarding the occurrence. Several alternative Lakota winter-counts depict the same event, but say that this man was a Lakota and was killed by the Arickara, and another [the American-Horse count], has the event recorded for the winter of 1810 / '11.

Suffice to say, if Lisa did bestow his favour upon a Crow chief at the time in question, then it had not brought the wearer the good luck he might have expected. Although before the winter of 1807 / '08 had passed according to the Hunkpapa Lakota winter-count of Long-Soldier, two Lakota on the war-path were killed by Crows.

In the meantime, as far as Lisa was concerned, the resulting spring returns in beaver and other pelts had made a success of his first trading enterprise in Crow country. Later in the new year of 1808 following his return to St. Louis, he set his sights on the lands of the Blackfoot, in an endeavour to open trade with that people as he had with the Crows.

With such a prospect in mind, it was after returning to the Upper Missouri that Lisa dispatched his now most trustworthy and competent employee John Colter, to seek out the Blackfoot. It was hoped that Colter could persuade them to allow white traders to visit their camps, or better still, to agree to the establishment of a separate post in the Blackfoot country itself.

So it was that Colter with fellow employee John Potts, started out on horseback from Fort Raymond in late autumn that year, leading pack-horses loaded with gifts and an assortment of trade goods with which to entice the Blackfoot. It is thought that Colter and Potts followed the course of the Yellowstone upstream and continued over what today is known as Bozeman Pass which leads across the Bighorn Mountains into the valley of the Gallatin River. Certainly, they were heading towards the Three Forks district of the Upper Missouri on the first leg of their journey. Somewhere en route they fell in with two moving villages of allied Crows and Flatheads, leisurely meandering their way toward their intended autumn hunting grounds in the aforesaid Three Forks area. The Flathead contingent, Colter later reported, comprised around five-hundred warriors and was actually traveling ahead of their Crow friends, who were bringing up the rear about four or five miles behind. When only one day's travel from their desired destination [between twenty and thirty miles], a large war-band of Blackfoot enemies, *"...whooping and singing whilst prancing around on spirited ponies,"* [1] Colter said, suddenly appeared about one half-mile ahead of the Flatheads.

Albeit taken by surprise, the Flatheads were quick to react. At once they sent their non-combatants to the rear, where the latter instantly began arranging travois and camp baggage into a defensive circle. The Flathead warriors meanwhile, changed to war-ponies tethered at their sides, and arrayed their force in a long line facing the enemy, ready and eager for battle.

The opposing Blackfoot force in total boasted some fifteen-hundred braves - according to Colter's estimate, - and almost at once, at least half their number charged forward against the Flathead line, *"...in a great fury."* [2]

Outnumbered three to one, the Flatheads stayed their ground. They braced themselves to meet the attack and did not waver. Many of their warriors had firearms of some description, thanks to their newfound allies the Crows and Hidatsa who, only recently, had traded them numerous guns along with a liberal supply of powder and ball. Their arms were also supplemented, no doubt, with a quantity of iron-bladed weapons lately obtained from the Crows, who in turn had obtained them from Lisa's post near the Big Horn. As a consequence, the Flatheads acquitted themselves well. Their stolid resistance broke the Blackfoot charge and drove the enemy back, preventing the latter from overrunning the Flathead position in the first attack.

Several miles away the Crows caught the faint sound of battle carried on the wind. But not until a few Flathead non-combatants came galloping back to the Crow column and burst out the news that the main party of Flatheads was about to be overwhelmed, did between eight and nine-hundred Crow warriors whip up their ponies and race off to assist their beleaguered allies.

The arrival of the Crows evened up the unequal odds, and the fight soon settled down to that of two opposing forces of mounted warriors hurling abuse at their respective opponents. Every so often one side or the other would make a half-hearted charge which not once actually reached its objective, but even so, Colter said, *"...the contest was hard fought."* [3]

Colter was among the fighting men of the Crows - as he was expected to be by his hosts. At first he had endeavoured to remain neutral during the contest, so not to incur animosity from the Blackfoot with who his employer Lisa would wish to trade in more congenial circumstances. But the Blackfoot for their part had no such qualms. Seeing a white man among the ranks of their enemies, whether he was actually fighting or not, was enough for the Blackfoot to consider him their adversary also, and they had every intention of lifting his scalp. Inevitably, the lone white man was forced to defend himself when a number of Blackfoot warriors bore down upon him, shooting arrows and muskets as they rode. In the event Colter received a Blackfoot arrow in his thigh, upon which he raised his long-rifle to his shoulder; took aim and squeezed the trigger and managed to bring down the foremost of his attackers. From then on, Colter was fully engaged and fought as energetically as did his Crow and Flathead companions.

My Crow informant Winona Plenty-Hoops asserted, that she had heard that the teenage Sore-Belly then fifteen or sixteen years of age, was also prominent in this fight. Forever riding out in front of the Crow line in acts of sheer bravado with only a slender willow-wand in an upraised hand. As he did so, he hurled torrents of abuse into the massed ranks of Blackfoot warriors arrayed before him. Much to the distress, Winona added, to those who worried for his safety.

At length, after many hours of charging back and forth with little advantage to either side, the Blackfoot finally withdrew from the field. Albeit in good order and the Crows and Flatheads merely watched as their opponents slowly disappeared from view. The Crows and their allies were satisfied that their combined forces had won the day, although the enemy deemed themselves to have been the victors.

Soon after the battle, Colter and Potts took leave of the Crows and returned to the post from whence they came. At Fort Raymond Colter spent some time recuperating from his wound; the intended mission to the Blackfoot completely undermined and now indefinitely postponed.

This fight appears to be the same referred to by the trader Alexander Henry the younger, who noted in his journal that the first severe check the Piegan Blackfoot suffered from the Flatheads, was when the Piegans had met the Flatheads and the latter`s allies [Crows?] marching to the Plains in search of buffalo. The meeting, Henry said, had been so sudden and unexpected that the Piegans could not avoid giving battle. They had fought with great courage nearly all day until expending the last of their ammunition and had to resort to defending themselves with stones. A small rising ground between the opposing forces had enabled the respective contestants to come to close quarters with one another, but at length, the Piegans were forced to retreat leaving sixteen of their warriors dead on the field. Henry's account stated that the event had taken place in the summer of 1810, although here Henry was confusing a similar fight between Flatheads and Piegans which did occur in that year, but much further north than this earlier fight of 1808, which had been the first serious check by Flatheads against the Blackfoot and on which occasion, John Colter and the young Sore-Belly had been involved.

The aforesaid battle regarding Colter, must be considered as having been a large scale affair, which would have been a comparatively rare occurrence at that date. It was not customary for two such large forces to deliberately engage in battle on an open field, without one or the other supposing it had a clear advantage. It must be admitted, though, that when first the Blackfoot had espied the Flathead contingent, the Blackfoot; being numerically superior, would have thought they had the Flatheads at their mercy. Certainly, it was only the timely arrival of the Crows that turned the tide of conflict, preventing a situation which may well have transpired into a humiliating, not to say catastrophic defeat for the Crow's Flathead allies.

As regards the actual site of the battle, the area in question was then hotly contested between several Upper Missouri and Rocky Mountain tribes. Indeed, the Three Forks district was well-known for its abundant stocks of beaver and other fur-bearing animals and thus, was a favourite haunt for all three Blackfoot-speaking peoples, in order to obtain pelts to trade with Hudson's Bay posts in the Bow River and Upper Saskatchewan country, Canada. On the other hand, certain Crow and Flathead bands often used the Three Forks area as a summer camping ground and, of course, took full advantage of the trapping facilities so readily available. For this reason, when the Blackfoot entered that same area usually during the summer and autumn months, they came in formidable force in case of attack from Crow and Flathead enemies. The whole region, in fact, was a war-ground, wherein any tribal group wandered at their peril. If, however, a particular war-band remained undiscovered, it might well continue on in order to assault the nearest enemy camp, and hostile encounters between Crows and Blackfoot continued unabated and on a regular basis, as was also the case regarding Crow conflicts with their other foes.

Sometime during the same year 1808, a Crow war-party succeeded in taking captive a Pikuni Blackfoot woman. This probably refers to an event later recorded in the Bull-Plume Pikuni winter-count for that year, wherein it is stated that one or more Pikuni women while getting paint from Castle River near Turtle Mountain, were captured by Crows. In addition, a Lakota scout out looking for buffalo was killed by Crows, and late that year a formidable Crow party successfully drove off a great number of horses from a Pikuni village. During the following year of 1809, the Lakota suffered again at Crow hands when, according to the American-Horse winter-count [previously cited], an Oglala of some renown named Black-Rock who was either the same man mentioned in 1805, or having taken the name from a deceased relative killed that year by Crows - was slain during another big fight with that people.

It was in 1809 also, that another large-scale battle as reported by a Hudson's Bay trader, took place between a combined force of Blackfoot and Atsina on one side and Crows on the other. No additional details are given, although the event does corroborate that the Crow – Atsina pact so warmly effected in 1806, had by then, if not earlier, been irretrievably thrown to the wind.

Notwithstanding, however, the precarious situation in the Upper Missouri country, the trader Lisa continued to supply his post at the mouth of the Big Horn with both trappers and trade goods. Now, though, he was aware that there was more profit if he expanded the number of his own white employees to trap, rather than Indians, who not only showed little enthusiasm for such unmanly work as they saw it, but rarely presented pelts in a fit state for sale. As far as the Indians themselves were concerned, they had more pressing and rewarding business to conduct, such as undertaking hostile ventures against hereditary foes.

If then it was dangerous for Indians to be abroad in the upper country at this period, it must have been doubly precarious for white trappers searching for beaver. No matter that the Crow and Blackfoot welcomed the guns and ammunition white traders brought into their country, when it came to white men themselves taking beaver and other game at will, without permission or due compensation to the Indians, their presence was resented by all tribes that visited the region.

In early summer 1809, Lisa sent another brigade of trappers now led by Andrew Henry, overland from the Arickara villages near the mouth of Grand River to trap the Three Forks district of the Upper Missouri. It had been agreed that after the trapper's trade goods and powder and ball had become exhausted, the employees were to exist by their own means, until Lisa replenished them with necessary supplies the following spring.

Regarding Lisa's employees, it had been earlier during the winter of 1807 / '08, that Edward Rose, who had been one of those initially sent by Lisa to contact the Crows when first Fort Raymond had been constructed on the Big Horn, had not proved himself entirely conducive to the enterprise. On his own volition Rose had given away Company trade goods without any return, save the personal prestige generally accorded by Indians to such persons who showered generosity upon them.

The empty-handed return of Rose to Lisa's post the following spring, had occasioned a heated argument between the mulatto and his employer. The result being, that after Lisa made a precipitous departure to St. Louis, Rose, with all the trade goods he could cajole from the post stores, made his own departure, but for his part, he went straight back to the Crows he had recently left, intending to remain among that people and adopt the life of an Indian in all its aspects.

Once again, by a liberal distribution of goods among those he thought influential members of the tribe; Rose ingratiated himself among his hosts and became a welcome addition in their camps.

During his first years of permanent residence among the Crows, Rose was known as Cut-Nose, owing to a prominent scar which he carried on that part of his face. He indulged himself in Crow life and customs completely, soon picking up a tolerable understanding of the language, coupled with a smattering of words belonging to surrounding tribes both friend and foe alike. As such, he became well-known as a singular character and an important, albeit much detested go-between in the upper country; at least among those white men in the mountains with whom Rose and his adopted people came in contact. Such was his influence among the Crows that Rose could; and did, levy large quantities of merchandise from any party of white trappers and traders entering Crow country. In this way, he continued to keep on hand a regular supply of goods to distribute among his Indian associates when he thought fit to do so, and which in turn, kept him welcome among them.

Sore-Belly, it is said, being an impressionable youth at this time, became the constant companion of the flamboyant Rose. He appeared to follow him around as if mesmerized by the mulatto's assumed air of importance.

For the most part, however, Sore-Belly's fellow tribesmen were more inclined to give somewhat greater respect to one they deemed a brave and successful warrior. It was to this end that Rose felt obliged to show his hosts his propensity for belligerent action and merely waited a suitable opportunity to do so.

Perhaps Rose had already been an active participant on one or more horse-stealing raid upon an enemy's stock, and most likely, had shouldered arms when the occupants of the particular village in which he resided had been forced to defend themselves when attacked by a hostile force. By his own account, though, he did not gain any notoriety in the theatre of war until sometime during his third year of residence among his hosts. It was then, in the year 1810 that the opportunity finally presented itself, whereby, he could show his reckless fighting ability in some spectacular manner.

Now it happened that a Hidatsa horse-stealing party of twelve, including a young teenage novice on his first war-trip acting as servant to the older warriors, had, for no better reason than a desire to earn coups compatible with the Indian's desire to win prestige, was in the process of traversing Crow country on its way west to one or another Shoshoni camp on the far side of the Backbone of the World [Rocky Mountains]. Thus the Hidatsa-Shoshoni pact affected in 1805, had by now likewise, been thrown to the wind.

Whilst en route, these Hidatsa spied a man and woman casually passing through a shallow ravine cutting across the prairie floor before merging again with the level Plain. The man was on foot leading the way, whilst the woman who was mounted, followed behind leading a packhorse loaded with meat from a recent kill. These two persons were Crows who, evidently, had gone out early that morning to hunt. The village from whence they came was that of a small Crow band encamped some distance away in a small valley close to the Big Horn Mountains, although neither the camp occupants nor the Hidatsa party were aware of each other's presence. The Hidatsa were not then at war with their Crow cousins, although the dissension between their peoples over the Crow's treatment of 'Old' Menard and the Hidatsa response to that event prior to the peace-making in 1805, had still left some issues of resentment among their respective tribes which had not been fully resolved. Such was the attitude harboured by the Hidatsa war-party

63

now in question, and as the two Crows appeared easy prey with no other people nearby, the Hidatsa dismounted and concealed themselves at the head of the ravine, having decided to destroy the two Crows in order to "count their coups."

As the Crow couple moved up out of the ravine and onto the open Plain, several of the waiting Hidatsa shot arrows at the pair at almost point-blank range. By so doing, they toppled the man to the ground, but the woman was not hit. Immediately she let go of the lead rope attached to the pack-animal; whipped up her own mount with her quirt and raced off, bending low over her horse's neck as another flight of Hidatsa arrows whistled through the air in her wake.

The Hidatsa had been on foot when first making their attack, and now they ran to remount their horses and give chase. But the woman already had a good start and being astride a fine buffalo-runner, she easily outpaced her pursuers.

When at last the woman galloped breathless into the Crow camp and burst out the news of her husband's death; along with that of her own lucky escape, the village population was in uproar. Almost at once, at least fifty able-bodied warriors grabbed their weapons; jumped astride war-ponies and raced out of the village. They headed towards the place of the encounter as indicated by the woman, who having exchanged her mount for a fresh animal, was leading the way.

Among this band of warriors was the then seventeen or eighteen year old Sore-Belly. He followed dutifully behind his hero Edward Rose who himself, was now attired and painted so as to be indistinguishable from any other Crow warrior.

It was still early in the morning when the Crow party came to the shallow ravine where lay the now mutilated corpse of the woman's husband. At this point, Rose immediately took up the trail. He rode ahead of his companions and around noon, signalled back that he had sighted the offending Hidatsa, going at a slow trot on their ponies along the foot of a low ridge some distance ahead.

The Hidatsa, it seemed, supposed themselves safe from imminent pursuit, and were not observant enough to notice riders in their rear.

The Crows, meanwhile, crossed over to the far side of the ridge and continued unseen, intending to draw close to their quarry. When finally they deemed themselves opposite the latter, they all at once charged up and over the ridge-top and down upon the unsuspecting Hidatsa.

By this time the Crow horses having at first been ridden at speed in order to catch up with the enemy, had become somewhat jaded, whereas those of the Hidatsa had been ridden at a leisurely pace and were still comparatively fresh. Thus, as the Hidatsa whipped up their ponies when the Crows first appeared on the ridge top, they easily drew ahead and managed to avoid an immediate hand to hand contest. Instead, the Hidatsa raced across the prairie towards a rocky outcrop surrounded by trees, and from where they hoped to gain cover and make a stand. Rose and five companions were galloping ahead of the Crow party, and actually came up with the Hidatsa as the latter were jumping from their ponies and running through the trees to reach the rocky height.

By his own account, Rose came close to the last Hidatsa still mounted. He reached over his horse's neck; took hold of the tail of the animal the Hidatsa was riding and gave it a strong pull. At the same time he turned his own mount in the opposite direction and in such a way, brought both his and the Hidatsa`s horse crashing to the ground, throwing both riders in the process. Before Rose could regain his feet and deal his dismounted enemy a death blow with his tomahawk, a Crow companion raced up and killed the Hidatsa, whereupon the other four Crows dismounted and set about stabbing and beating the prostrate enemy as they counted *dakshey* on his corpse.

Such actions on the part of these five, gave respite for the remaining Hidatsa to gain appropriate cover, and by the time the main body of Crows reached the scene, the enemy were securely entrenched behind a low breastwork of stones with guns and bows at the ready. The teenage boy among them had managed to secrete himself behind a cluster of large rocks away from where his comrades were entrenched, and there he stayed, hidden throughout the ensuing conflict safe from harm.

The Hidatsa were protected on all sides in their rocky refuge and the Crows knew only too well, how difficult and costly to their own numbers it would be if they attempted to storm the place in force. They thus dismounted and sat around in a group, discussing among themselves whether to resume the fight or abandon it altogether.

Rose grew impatient. He began berating his comrades, calling them dogs and cowards and such was his tirade against them, that the Crows felt ashamed. In response, they plucked up courage and once again, began clamouring for Hidatsa blood.

To prevent their quarry escaping, the Crows from a distance picked off the Hidatsa horses left at the base of the rocks with well-aimed arrows and musket fire. Then, with Rose at their head, they rushed on foot towards the stronghold. When, however, only a short distance separated the opposing forces, the Hidatsa warriors suddenly rose up in a body and discharged a hail of musket balls and arrows into the Crow ranks. The foremost five Crows fell to the ground; some dead - some wounded, and only Rose among their number remained unscathed. Still undaunted, he was in the act of clambering over the first line of rocks ready to engage hand to hand with the foe, when he chanced to look behind him. To his utter disdain he saw that the rest of the Crows who he supposed were following in the rear, had actually turned on their heels and were running in the opposite direction in an effort to seek cover. Seeing this, Rose gave up his assault and walked slowly back to where his comrades were hovering some distance from the enemy position.

Indian nature being what it was, may have caused the Crows to blame Rose for the death and wounding of their comrades, as it had been Rose alone who had urged them to storm the position against their better judgment which would have involved more cautionary tactics. Instead, seeing that the mulatto now eyed them with contempt for their timidity, the Crows began accusing each other of cowardice and yet again, seemed eager to carry on the fight. They now looked to Rose to apprise them how best to achieve the destruction of the foe and once more, Rose rebuked them for their hesitation saying, *"Stay like deer where you are."* [4]

At the same time, he took hold of two bull-hide shields some nearby warriors were carrying. After placing one shield inside the declivity of the other so to render a double thickness of protection against arrows and musket balls, he took his iron tomahawk in hand, then proceeded at a run towards the rocks among which the Hidatsa were entrenched.

In a moment, Rose again had one foot on a rocky ledge of the breastworks, and was ready to hurl himself into the huddled bunch within. Just then a volley of leaden balls and iron-tipped arrows struck his double shield, knocking him backwards with the impact. Miraculously, Rose was not hurt. Immediately he regained his feet and before the enemy could reload their pieces or fix another arrow to the bowstring, he was over the breastwork and flaying about him with his tomahawk both right and left. Three Hidatsa fell to his deadly blows, and then a fourth as Rose was actually extricating himself from the enclosure before the enemy could surround him and bring him down.

Their refuge having been breached, those remaining among the Hidatsa fled every man for himself, and in so doing, lost yet another comrade to the blood-stained tomahawk of Rose. By this time the rest of the Crow force had come up, having followed the path of their mulatto champion, and now Rose merely stood back and watched as the remaining Hidatsa were run down and rubbed out by the overwhelming number of Crows.

In recognition of the mulatto's deeds that day, the Crows bestowed upon him another name. That of Cut-Nose was thrown away and he was thereafter, known among them as *"Chee-Xo-Binnee,"* i.e. "Five-Scalps." [5]

Only the teenage Hidatsa boy survived the slaughter, having remained hidden throughout the conflict and thus gone unnoticed by the Crows. Long after the victors had left the scene and darkness covered the land, this lone survivor crept away, and after many days during which he suffered greatly from fatigue, hunger and exposure, he finally reached his home village on the banks of the Knife where he told his kinfolk what had happened.

As far as the Crows believed, none of the enemy had escaped and they did not suppose the Hidatsa as a tribe, would be any the wiser as to the fate of their tribesmen. If known, then it would surely have deterred any Crows from visiting their cousins until the current troubles had been resolved. Rose, however, either did not care one way or the other, or alternatively, was of the opinion that the Hidatsa would be ignorant of the singular part he himself had played in the destruction of their warriors. Before the year was out, he voluntarily paid a visit to the Hidatsa villages.

At first he was welcomed in friendship as an old acquaintance. But it was not long before the young survivor of the Hidatsa party slaughtered earlier in the year, recognized Rose as having been prominent on that occasion and he informed his people as much. The Hidatsa chiefs discussed the matter among themselves and came to one accord, that the mulatto should forfeit his life for his perfidy.

Fortunately for Rose, before the chiefs could put their design into effect, he somehow got wind of their intention and made a precipitous exit from the village. Securing himself a bull-boat, he paddled his way down the Missouri to the mouth of the Grand and took up residence among the Arickara, who having heard through the moccasin grapevine of the mulatto's military prowess, were only too pleased to have such a great warrior living among them and in addition, one who was also at loggerheads with the Hidatsa with whom the Arickara themselves were then at war.

- 0 - 0 - 0 - 0 - 0 - 0 - 0 - 0 - 0 - 0 - 0 - 0 - 0 - 0 - 0 - 0 - 0 -

## CHAPTER. 6.

## SORE-BELLY BECOMES A PIPE-HOLDER.

The young warrior Sore-Belly had been fully involved in the slaughter of the Hidatsa party, although at that time he was without any personal *medicine* to protect him when in danger. Now, having grown out of his reckless behaviour when in his teens, he was discouraged somewhat from placing himself in too vulnerable a position which might bring about his untimely demise. Well he knew, he would have to acquire a strong Spirit-helper before realizing his ambition of becoming a great chief among his people; and only the lonely sufferings of a vision quest could give him what he yearned.

Indeed, notwithstanding his appearance, ability or talent, each Crow warrior believed that without obtaining `Maxpe` or "mystic power" [i.e., *medicine*], from some supernatural force, he could have no control over his personal destiny. As far as he was concerned, the lack of such power would contribute to much distress and bad luck through one's life and, ultimately, guarantee his untimely death due to some unfavourable circumstance. Such power was thought to emanate from the Great Spirit itself, though only made manifest through non-human forms and celestial bodies, including the sun, moon and stars, along with natural phenomena of nature such as thunder and lightning etc.; Each of these supposed mystic manifestations were thought to constitute a part of the Other World which, it was also believed, presented a parallel dimension to that where Mankind in his more lowly state, was obliged to exist.

To obtain such power, or as more commonly known, *medicine*, it was imperative that the potential recipient actually enter into the realm of the Other World albeit temporarily. This could only be achieved by undergoing a period of prolonged fasting or some other form of self-denial, in addition to - in many cases - a more tangible sacrifice, such as self-mutilation of the body in order to show sincerity and a serious commitment to one's endeavour. When during such an undertaking, a state of incognizance had been attained, then in a vision or dream one could communicate with the Other World, and obtain the benevolence of a particular Spirit-helper along with harnessing for his own use, the specific attributes associated with it, and upon which, thereafter, the recipient could not only depend when in time of need, but be blessed with the ability to emulate that Spirit-helper's specialities peculiar to itself. Not least, such would then insure self-preservation in the hostile world in which one struggled to survive. In many cases, it also gave the recipient the necessary power to either cure sickness, heal wounds, prophesy forthcoming events, locate missing persons and belongings and bring forth the buffalo and other game when needed, along with other attributes too numerous to mention, but each of which were regarded as mystical properties outside the Indian's natural environment and psyche. Thus, when an Indian proclaimed that his personal Spirit-helper which had previously proved its efficacy was dictating his actions, there was no room for indifference among his peers. All Crows believed without reserve in the potency of such *medicine* which was not to be ignored and certainly, not to be dismissed out of hand, which to do so would be to the dire detriment of all those involved.

For the above reasons, instances in the episodes which follow where examples of one's personal *medicine* power loom large, should not be regarded by the reader as historically incorrect or superfluous to the overall text. Such was a very real and overtly important part of Crow mentality in relation to their own perspective of reality during the old-time buffalo days. It was moreover, a part of their very existence in what was then a completely alien world, as compared to the non-Indian view of what is perceived as reality and considered more practical with regard to today's scientific knowledge and concepts. Certainly, without a Spirit-helper or mystic-protector, a Crow brave - supposedly - could not achieve success in war and, as a consequence, could not rise above that of lowly status within his community; lacking due honour and respect from one's fellows. For war, as previously noted, was a profound part of the Plains Indian's day to day existence. In truth, a state of being by which he was surrounded and consumed by in his every thought and action.

In due time therefore, Sore-Belly went out alone to the Crazy Mountains in order to fast and obtain a powerful Spirit-helper of his own. These mountains are so called owing to erratic weather conditions which occur around them, changing within a matter of minutes from glorious sunshine and warmth, to thunderous storms, freezing cold and snow.

Thus at a secluded place upon a craggy height, Sore-Belly fasted for several days and nights and did at length receive a vision. This, he later professed, was 'Thunder' itself in the guise of an eagle, which appeared to him in material form. When he came down from the mountain, he carried a piece of 'Thunder' with him and this became the most important sacred object among several others which he owned throughout his lifetime. It was this 'Thunder' *medicine*, Sore-Belly believed, which, thereafter, always guided him to where his enemies would be, while also causing him to be invincible in battle, protected from any metal weapon derived from the white man, such as leaden musket balls, iron-bladed lances, tomahawks and knives and of arrows tipped with iron. No others, it is said, were privy to gazing upon his 'Thunder' *medicine*, or knew exactly what it was. [1]

Sore-Belly was still a youth - not quite eighteen years old, but now with his newly acquired 'Thunder' *medicine*, he felt able, and was eager to go again to war. Not as novice in the capacity of a servant to older men, but as a warrior in his own right in search of enemy scalps and ponies. In addition, he had already decided upon the woman he would marry.

These two important episodes in the life of Sore-Belly became inter-related through the following circumstances, as imparted to the present Author by Winona Plenty-Hoops.

The story, she said, had been told her by her Grandmother Pretty-Medicine-Pipe, one of four daughters of old man Chips-The-Rock [born between 1828-29] who himself had been brought up by Sore-Belly as his son, although, in truth, there was no real blood tie between them, he being of mixed white-Indian parentage whose mother was but one of Sore-Belly's wives.

Chips-The-Rock's mother before she married Sore-Belly, was a member of the Greasy-Mouth clan, and already had a small daughter from an earlier liaison. At a time when the daughter was very young, both she and the mother had been captured by a Pikuni war-party during a spring raid on a Crow camp, and then carried north across the Missouri into what is now the province of Alberta, Canada. Their Pikuni captor, it transpired, treated the mother harshly; working her constantly so that she endured a miserable and painful existence.

Now in the same Pikuni camp there resided a middle-aged couple who had no children of their own. They asked if they might adopt the Crow woman and her daughter, to which the man - who currently owned the captives – agreed, and received many presents in return.

Sometime later near the end of autumn, the Pikuni decided to move further north to winter camping grounds on the far side of Bow River, along the course of which grew an abundance of trees and where warm Chinook winds blew from the west.

He who had since adopted the Crow woman proved to be a kind man. He took pity upon her plight and told her he would arrange her escape just before the Pikuni attempted to cross the river. This was a treacherous stream, he said, and once across, his people would be unlikely to re-cross it merely to recapture a runaway captive. In the meantime, the man told the Crow woman to make extra pairs of moccasins and packs of pemmican to sustain her and her daughter on their long journey south. These things, he said, she should hide under the lodge fire's ashes to prevent anyone discovering their plan.

At length, the Pikuni reached the Bow River and camped along its southern bank the night before their intended crossing. When all was quiet, the man awoke the Crow woman and bade her get ready to leave. He then called into the lodge a `bishka,` i.e., a dog, large and shaggy-haired, and to which the man spoke for some time. The dog then went out of the lodge, but soon came back on its own accord with its tail wagging furiously. The Pikuni man said to the woman,

> "All is well for this dog is my sacred *medicine* helper. The dog shall
> go with you. It will guide and protect you until you find your own
> people, who at this time of year, are sure to be encamped far up Big
> Horn River." [2]

The Crow woman did as instructed and with her daughter in tow, followed the dog out of the lodge. Together they then crept silently from the camp and started their long trek south.

After many days, perhaps weeks of hard traveling, the woman, her daughter and the dog at last reached the Big Horn River, and following its winding course upstream, they came to the mouth of what was once known as War-Man Creek but now called Two-Legging's Creek. Crossing the main river at a place where a rock shelf made it easy to do so, they then continued up War-Man Creek which at that time, was reduced to a dried up bed. When they had gone only a short distance, the woman's young daughter complained she was very thirsty and needed a drink. The mother placed the girl under an overhanging bank and went back to the main river [the Big Horn?] to get some water. When she returned, she found that her daughter had been killed and scalped, so she wrapped the body in a bundle and carrying it on her back, continued her journey. Several days later the dead child spoke to the mother, telling her not to get married until She, the daughter, told her it would be right to do so.

Not long after this strange occurrence, the woman was traveling through the Big Horn Canyon when she heard voices, and could see a man on the west side of the canyon and another on its east side, hunting Big Horn sheep. One of these men called out to his friend saying,

*"Stays-In-The-Pines, there are sheep right below you, why are you not trying to kill some of them?"* [3]

This man named Stays-In-The-Pines answered thus,

*"Yes, I see them, but I am listening to the voice of a woman crying."* [4]

The two hunters then came together and whilst discussing what to do, the woman showed herself, and behold, they recognized her as their sister who many moons before, had been carried off by the Pikuni. All three were overjoyed at their reunion and together, they travelled on to the Crow camp then located on Rotten Grass Creek only a few miles distant.

No one, it seems, in Winona's version of the tale, ever queried as to what had actually happened to the daughter. The story merely continues by saying that when rehabilitated among her own people, the woman had many able suitors seeking her hand in marriage. But abiding to her dead daughter's request, she refused them all. Then one day the deceased child, or rather the deceased child's spirit, apparently spoke to her again, saying it was now time for the woman to marry and that her husband should be none other than the young man named Sore-Belly.

At the same time, unbeknown to the woman, Sore-Belly himself had decided that the woman in question would be his wife. But on his own, he was finding it impossible to make a good impression upon the woman's kinfolk in order to show them that he was worthy of being her suitor. Fortunately, there was a man in the camp whose name was Hanging-Raven, then recognized as a great warrior. He had often taken Sore-Belly into his lodge and had become his mentor in many things. He therefore instructed his two sons to assist Sore-Belly in hunting buffalo, the meat of which Sore-Belly then took to the lodges of the woman's brothers as a gift. He did this four times and on the fourth time the brothers asked Sore-Belly why he had been bringing them such large quantities of meat. Without hesitation, Sore-Belly replied that he wished to marry their sister. The brothers were pleased with what he said. At once they invited Sore-Belly into their lodge and called him "Brother-in-law."

Sore-Belly at that time, it is said, was unkempt in appearance and his clothes ragged. The woman he had chosen to marry, however, who herself had been told to accept his proposal by the spirit voice of her dead daughter, cleaned him up and made fine clothes for him to wear and anon, the two were married as had been intended.

In due time, Sore-Belly sired four sons, each of whom his wife named in memory of her Pikuni captor's sacred dog helper. These four sons became known in later years respectively as, Old-Dog, Flat-Dog, Yellow-Dog [aka Old Coyote] and Hermaphrodite-Dog.

It was soon after his marriage that Sore-Belly, then around eighteen years of age, went on the war-path yet again as a fully-fledged warrior. The war-party was led by the same man Hanging-Raven who had ordered his sons to assist Sore-Belly in killing buffalo. [2] During the resulting fight with the enemy Sore-Belly counted his first *dakshey* [coup], the first of many more to come.

As was customary for young men of his age, Sore-Belly was then invited to join one of the several Warrior Societies among the tribe, and he selected that of the Half-Shaved-Heads as his society of choice. This Society was one of the oldest among the Crows, and in pre-horse days its members had shaved their heads but for a narrow strip as did their long-estranged Winnebago, Iowa and Oto cousins in the east. The custom, but for one or two individual members, was no longer extant in Sore-Belly`s day, although the name had been retained. As a young member of the fraternity, Sore-Belly became the brother friend of a fellow young warrior named Little-White-Bear, who was to prove himself a loyal and constant companion to Sore-Belly, often at the chief`s side during many a conflict against enemy tribes. Certainly after joining the Half-Shaved-Heads, Sore-Belly went on many a war-trail, while his wife during his absences, invoked her own strong *medicine* to assist him in his ventures.

During these early hostile escapades, in one fight alone he earned each of the four war deeds necessary to become a chief, and then repeated these accomplishments on each of his next three war-trips. This had not been done before, certainly not within living memory, and thus in a very short while he was being hailed as one of the tribe's great warriors, and while still regarded as a comparatively young man he had already become *"Aduxikuchka,"* a Pipe-Holder,` [i.e., leader of war-parties], and in which ventures, it is said, he was always successful, bringing home scores of captured ponies; women and children prisoners and a number of enemy scalps, shields and weapons as booty. Subsequently, when only around twenty-five years of age, he was elected as a member of the council of seventeen chiefs, which rank entitled him to speak upon all important issues concerning the welfare of the whole Crow Nation.

Still, though, Sore-Belly continued to go out on lonely vigils and vision quests even after becoming a pipe-holder, and, it is said, in one year alone he fasted at different times at various places all summer long.

On one such vigil he acquired a certain power enabling him to prophcsy forthcoming events, and many times during succeeding years, he proved his ability to do so. It is recalled that once he had a dream in which he had seen two horses in a Pikuni village. One was a pinto with red ears and a black spot on each flank along with some other peculiar markings, though now forgotten. The other animal, he said, was a grey, also with specific markings and he set out one day with a small party in order to steal both animals. Reaching the aforesaid Pikuni village, Sore-Belly and his companions entered among the lodges under cover of darkness and stole a number of horses. The next morning after the sun came up, it was seen that two of the captured ponies were marked exactly as had been seen in Sore-Belly`s dream.

Another story relates how Sore-Belly once told some companions that there was a particular mare in another Pikuni camp, which would soon give birth to twin colts. A fact not known to have been possible or indeed, so rare an

71

occurrence that none of his associates believed him. However, the great chief assured them it would be so, for his *medicine* helper had told him this thing. Sore-Belly was so persuasive that finally a few warriors decided to accompany him on his war trip. They found the Pikuni village where Sore-Belly had predicted it would be; captured a mare along with a number of other horses and returned safely to their home camp without mishap. Sure enough, not long after their return, the captured Pikuni mare gave birth to twin colts proving the power of Sore-Belly's *medicine* yet again.

Before this, however, and returning to Sore-Belly's eighteenth year, the more northern Crow bands – those known as Paunch Indians; and at a later date, as River Crow, - were continually suffering attacks and trespass into their hunting grounds abutting the Yellowstone River by marauding bands of Blackfoot and Atsina, while according to Alexander Henry's journal, in the moon of May, 1810, a grand host of combined Assiniboine and Cree was already assembling at the Eagle Hills, preparatory to launching a grand crusade against all the *"Gens de Corbeau"* [Crow] that coming summer.

What the outcome was we are not informed, but in June that year, a party of white beaver hunters led by the intrepid explorer come fur trapper Thomas James, when traveling downstream along Clark's Fork which enters the Yellowstone on its south side east of the Missouri's Three Forks district, they found near the mouth of the Clark, *"An army of the Crow Nation encamped."* [5]

James further reported that the Crows were then at war with the Blackfoot who they were then seeking to give battle, and that this meeting between white men and Crows was amicable. The two parties remained together a few days before the Crows continued on their way in a southerly direction. That same evening a white trapper who had been out hunting, came into camp. He reported that another much larger force of Indians was ensconced behind a breastwork of stones and earth near a cliff some four miles to the north. The white men supposed these Indians to be Blackfoot, and the following dawn with their numbers increased by another party of trappers, they went out in a body to attack the enemy and avenge themselves for past grievances suffered from that people.

When the trappers came close to the Indian position, they discovered it contained another party of around one-hundred Crows, and among whom was the fast-rising war-chief, Sore-Belly. The Crows were on their return journey from a raid on the Blackfoot, they said, and belonged to the same band with which the white men had only recently been encamped. The members of this war-party greeted the white men as friends and showing that they had been victorious in their recent venture, they paraded on horseback two abreast through the trapper's camp to the enjoyment of all present. After being told that the main body of Crows had left the white men's camp only one day earlier, the Crow war-party bade farewell and crossed the river in order to catch up with their people. The white men were impressed by the manner in which their Crow visitors crossed the river, as their leader Thomas James reported,

> "…Their manner of crossing the river was singular, and reminded
> me of the roving Tartars. They stripped themselves entirely naked,
> and every ten piled their accoutrements together, blankets, saddles,

weapons etc.;, on a tent of skin made of buffalo robes, and tying it up in a large round bundle, threw it into the river and plunged after, some swimming with these huge heaps, floating like corks, and others riding the horses or holding by the tails till they had all crossed the river. Arrived on the opposite bank, which they reached in little less time than I have taken to describe their passage, they dressed, mounted their horses, and marched off two and two, as before, and were quickly out of our sight." [6]

As noted previously, at the date in question the country embracing the Three Forks area of the Upper Missouri, was a bloody war-ground between the Crows, Blackfoot, Atsina, Flathead and Shoshoni, and, of course, for any white trappers and traders brave or formidable enough both in number and firearms who dare enter the region. Indeed, during this same year of 1810, another large war-band, this time of mixed Bloods and Atsina came down from the north intending to raid in the Big Horn country. Near the confluence of the Yellowstone and Big Horn Rivers they fell upon a party of white trappers, killed several and escaped with considerable booty which included furs and equipment. The Crows, although having escaped an assault upon their own people, were nonetheless incensed that *Billebaachii* [i. e. white men], - from whom the Crows obtained goods necessary to safeguard their very existence - should be attacked in the heart of the Crow domain. Such an event if allowed to continue unchecked, would threaten the very presence of Lisa's post and of white traders coming in person to Crow camps. It was for this reason that a large force led by Sore-Belly immediately set out to chastise the Blood and Atsina party.

Neither is the outcome of this particular episode specifically recorded, although it appears to be compatible with a similar contemporary event of an Atsina war-party fighting a pitched battle with Crows close to the Yellowstone River around that same time. The Atsina later reported the outcome of the fight to their Pikuni friends, who in turn, relayed the same to traders at the Northwest Fur Company post Fort Augustus on the South Saskatchewan. The Atsina said they had seen a white man's fort on the Yellowstone during their trip, and which they supposed, was occupied by the Long-Knives, e.g. Americans. They further said that one of the Atsina chiefs had been killed in the conflict along with several warriors wounded. The Atsina did not know how many if any Crows had been killed, although the Atsina had escaped with a number of Crow prisoners, thus suggesting a Crow camp had actually been attacked. The Atsina force, though, had been obliged to retreat, and as they retired from the battle ground, the Crows had shouted after them that in the future they would save the Atsina the trouble of coming so far south to war, as come summer the Crows themselves in company with their white friends, would invade the Atsina country and destroy the latter's camps along the Saskatchewan.

Such words had the desired effect and the Atsina took fright. Fearing a Crow invasion which they could ill resist, the Atsina planned to gain entry into several Northwest Fur Company posts in Canada, and under the pretence of trade, slaughter the white occupants and plunder the Company's stores to obtain firearms and other weapons with which to defend themselves against the Crows. As it was, the Atsina told their plans to their friends the Pikuni. But they, fearing that white traders would be driven away, preventing the Pikuni themselves from obtaining necessary goods deemed essential for pursuing their own intertribal wars, not only informed the white traders of the plan, but also threatened the Atsina with war if the latter dared carry out their design.

The Company posts, subsequently, were saved from destruction and the following summer, 1811, the Crows fulfilled their promise and invaded the Atsina country. The result was that a fierce and bloody battle was fought in which the Crows were victorious, and - to their way of thinking - they successfully evened up the score for those white trappers slain in Crow country by Bloods and Atsina the previous year.

Earlier, however, a large Pikuni war band had also gone south across the Missouri against the Crows. These Pikuni, too, noted the existence of a white man`s fort, thus indicating that they had travelled as far south as the mouth of the Big Horn in order to reach their quarry. In the event the Pikuni had assaulted a Crow camp, but according to their own account, although having driven the Crow defenders from the field, they obtained no scalps. They had found a small amount of artefacts worth plundering from the abandoned lodges, although the Crows had carried with them most things of value during their retreat. None of the attacking Pikuni had been killed, and only one of their number had been wounded by a musket ball which had broken the victim`s wrist and torn the flesh. The trader Alexander Henry the Younger - who later inspected the wound - deemed it would heal satisfactorily with only a little attendance. [7]

- 0 - 0 - 0 - 0 - 0 - 0 - 0 - 0 - 0 - 0 - 0 - 0 - 0 - 0 - 0 - 0 -

## CHAPTER. 7.

### SORE-BELLY WITH ARROW-HEAD`S BAND and RETURN OF EDWARD ROSE.

There were other events affecting the Crows in 1811, one of which involved members of John Jacob Astor`s "Astoria" expedition on behalf of the Fur Company of that name. In June, whilst on its way up the Missouri, the expedition stopped at the Arickara villages on the west bank of that river. There the party met the notorious Edward Rose, and the expedition`s leader William Price Hunt, persuaded Rose to accompany his party overland to the Rocky Mountains in the capacity of hunter, guide and interpreter. The mulatto agreed, but as was the case with his earlier employer Lisa, the contract in due time proved non-conducive to Hunt's expectations. As a result, when finally arriving at a Crow village near the Big Horn Mountains in September that year, Rose was duly dismissed. Thus Rose again returned to his beloved Crow people for a third time, although, as will be seen, he did not remain long.

Meanwhile, a few months earlier on June 29th albeit on the west side of the Rockies, Robert Stuart who also was a member of the John Jacob Astor enterprise [which the previous year had founded a post at the mouth of Columbia River on the North Pacific Seaboard], had started overland from the west with a party of trappers, carrying dispatches to be delivered to Astor himself in New York City, some three thousand miles east across the Continent.

By the time Stuart and his party reached Bear River on the east side of the Wind River Mountains, his retinue had been reduced to seven persons including himself and twenty horses. A small party indeed, to traverse such a hostile country due to its environment and unpredictable native inhabitants, not least among whom, was now included a wandering band of Crows. These last comprised a Crow faction known as "Arrow-Head's Band" and among which at this time, was the later-day chief, Twines-His-Horses-Tail [Rotten-Tail], along with young Sore-Belly then eighteen years old, and both of whom had temporarily joined Arrow-Head's Dried-Out-Furs' people merely for the thrill of adventure. [1] This particular band was apt to roam far south of the Yellowstone and Big Horn country in its raiding for horses and scalps, and was apt to prove unfriendly to small parties of white trappers when it was their fancy to do so. It was, however, due to the following episode that Sore-Belly came to understand the strengths and vulnerability of the white man, and which in future years would influence his dealings with them, by his employing either aggression or diplomacy as might benefit his purpose.

It had happened that while Stuart and his party were away catching fish, a number of Crows entered the white men's camp and when the trappers returned, a powerfully built Indian 6ft 4inches tall, who was probably Chief Arrow-Head himself, walked up to Stuart in a seemingly friendly manner, and professed he and his warriors were on their way to trade with the Shoshoni on the west side of the mountains. The white men were suspicious of the Indian's true intentions and as mid-night drew close, more Crows appeared until there were twenty-one warriors within the camp, as opposed to only seven white men. Throughout the rest of the night, the Crows became ever more obnoxious and intimidating, and the whites were obliged to remain doubly vigilant to prevent their horses and equipment being stolen by the wily Crows. The whites did trade an amount of buffalo meat from the Indians in exchange for a quantity of powder and ball, but come dawn the Crows made it clear they wished the trade to continue for which they now offered horses in return. However, the trapper's leader Robert Stuart was adamant that his men had finished trading for the time being. In response, the 6ft 4inch Indian rose up to his full height; slapped his chest and told Stuart that he was a great chief among the Crows; a man of power and importance and that Stuart should make him a worthy gift as was the custom among his people. The chief further requested that the fine horse upon which Stuart was then sitting would make a fitting present. To this Stuart refused, whereupon the chief placed his large hands on each side of Stuart and moved him to and fro in the saddle, as an indication of how powerless was the captain and the small band of white men compared to the Indians confronting them.

Still Stuart refused to surrender his horse and when the chief violently shook the horse's bridal, nearly toppling the rider from the saddle, Stuart drew forth his pistol and threatened to shoot the chief dead. Somewhat dismayed, the chief dodged behind his own horse to avoid the expected shot while the rest of the whites levelled their guns at the Crows, who quickly disappeared into the surrounding bush. Suddenly, the Crow chief was on his own surrounded by angry trappers. Almost at once his demeanour changed. He became jovial and laughed aloud at what he now professed was his big joke on the white men. Stuart, of course, was not fooled by the chief`s turn of expression, but not wishing to create further tension which might well result in bloodshed and in turn, incite the whole Crow tribe in seeking revenge upon his small party, Stuart also raised a laugh and presented the chief with twenty charges of powder, as compensation for not having secured Stuart`s horse in trade. Soon after this and in supposed good humour, the chief departed, and for the following six days the small party of whites continued their way east, although often changing direction to avoid running into other war bands traversing the region.

On September 19th, a lone Crow Indian appeared galloping on horseback a short distance away. He carried a red banner attached to the end of a lance and galloped past the white men. His passing was immediately followed by a tremendous whooping from Indian throats, and a number of mounted Crows suddenly appeared charging towards the trapper`s horse herd grazing outside the perimeter of the camp. This sudden charge caused the animals to take fright and race off in the direction of the red banner being waved on high by the lone warrior, who had since halted his pony atop the crest of a distant knoll. As the loose horses raced towards him, the Crow with the banner suddenly galloped off and the stampeding animals followed in his wake.

Meanwhile, the white men had run from their camp trying to get between the stampeding horses and pursuing Indians. They had levelled their muskets in an effort to turn the Indians away, but then another mounted Crow force appeared from a different direction, seemingly, intent on securing the camp baggage left unattended by the white men. Strange it was that this second party of charging Crows seemed merely to be playing with the whites. They rode right past the camp and included in their number bringing up the rear, was the same 6ft 4 inch chief who previously had been disparaged by Stuart six days before. Now, as the chief was in the act of galloping past the camp, he reined in his steed, raised himself from his animal`s back and grabbing his crotch in a vulgar manner, shouted some equally vulgar words at the white man Stuart.

One of Stuart`s men took aim at the chief with his musket, and was about to bring him down, when Stuart prevented him doing so with the words,

*"...you will bring destruction to us all."* [2]

Thus the chief and the rest of the Crows along with all the white men`s horses were allowed to escape and after the Indians had left, Stuart`s party was forced to continue its perilous journey on foot. Stuart, nevertheless, had been impressed by the audacity of the thieves who no more than twenty in number, had pitted their wits and daring against the muskets and dead-eyed marksmanship of the whites, should the latter have seen fit to show the Indians their worth on that occasion.

The small number of Arrow-Head`s Crow marauders harassing Stuart`s party, actually belonged to a much larger band comprising one-hundred tepees or more, and were roaming the Wind River region, generally creating havoc among other tribal peoples and with all white men they met. This is evident by the fact that later during Stuart`s travels while his party was still on foot, they came upon a forty lodge camp of poverty-stricken Shoshoni only recently plundered by the same Crow band mentioned above. The Crows, the white men were told, had stripped the Shoshoni of all but one of their horses; had taken all their knives, guns and even the lodge covers along with a number of women, leaving their victims destitute to face the oncoming winter as best they could. Thus the current Crow relationship with the Shoshoni was still that of alternative trading with one another and of outright hostility, and such was the precarious situation then existing across the Upper Missouri region.

It was, no doubt, warriors belonging to the same band of marauding Crows who, with the then young warrior Sore-Belly among them, were committing depredations also upon their one-time allies the Arapaho. Indeed, the report of Robert Stuart further tells us that whilst in winter quarters along Bear River east of the mountains, twenty Arapaho warriors all on foot visited his camp. They informed Stuart they were a war-party, following the trail of Crows who earlier, had assaulted an Arapaho village while most of its men-folk had been out hunting and escaped with several Arapaho women and most of their horses.

The Arapaho party was on a revenge raid, their leader said, and had been pursuing the Crows for sixteen days. They had no powder or ball for the few guns among them and were almost starved, as all the game, it seemed, had fled the country through which they were travelling. Stuart`s men accordingly fed their Arapaho guests, and the latter then left the white men after saying they had six more days to travel north to a river where they expected to find the Crow village. After unsuccessfully requesting a quantity of powder and ball from the white men, the Arapaho chief then remarked,

> "...We are poor now and are obliged to go on foot, but we shall
> come back laden with booty and all mounted horseback with scalps
> hanging at our bridles. We shall then give each of you a horse to
> keep you from being tired on your journey." [3]

Stuart, however, still refused to supply them with their ammunition needs and at length, the Arapahos continued on their way, promising to be back within two weeks. After the Arapaho party left, Stuart`s men vacated their winter quarters, lest they be molested by other wandering war bands and finally, in spring the following year [1812], after travelling down the Platte and Missouri Rivers and then overland to the cities in the East, they finally reached their objective of New York City. We have no way of knowing what the outcome was regarding the aforesaid Arapaho venture against the Crows, but from Stuart`s account we do know that Crows, yet again, were then at war with both their Shoshoni and Arapaho neighbours.

Sore-Belly meanwhile, soon after the affair with Stuart`s party, left Arrow-Head`s band and returned north to the Yellowstone, to be again among his own people of the Sore-Lip clan.

In late spring, 1812, Lisa again came up the Missouri in a keelboat. En route he stopped at the Arickara towns and willingly or not, again made contact with his one-time adversary Edward Rose, who since his sojourn among the Crows after being dismissed by Hunt, was once more far down the Missouri ensconced among the Arickara at the mouth of the Grand. The past altercation between Lisa and Rose was somehow smoothed over, and Rose entered into another contract with his old employer, which; as before, required Rose to trap and hunt as an employee in Lisa's brigade.

Circumstances, however, deterred Lisa from ascending the Missouri any further upstream than the Mandan villages, and at which point Rose lapsed into his now customary behaviour. This time he cajoled several thousand dollars' worth of trade goods from Lisa`s stores through a series of spurious claims, and returned for yet a fourth time to his adopted people the Crows. After distributing large quantities of trade goods among certain tribal members, who now believed he had since become a chief among the white men owing to his perceived wealth, Rose again took up a life of prestigious grandeur as far as Indian values were perceived at that time. It is said that Sore-Belly, now a proven warrior and war-chief of some standing, sheltered the mulatto in his own lodge and became his constant companion and confident. The later-day chronicler Captain Rueben Holmes of the United States Army met Rose in 1825, and obtaining his story first hand, wrote the following from personal observation,

> "...He [Rose] was truly great among these men [Crows]. They would hold up their hands to the full stretch of their arms, when they wished to express his grade, signifying that he was as high as it was possible for a man to be. All great men have whims. His whim was dress. He was covered with Indian finery. Plumes, beads, and bells nodded, glistened and jingled when he moved. He became "the lion" of the Nation. No white man or men could trade [with the Crows] but by his permission, and he was seen to exact a `douceur` as the price of his influence. His name was in every one's mouth, and his walk and dress was imitated by all in a greater or less degree." [4]

In another passage, the same chronicler recorded,

> "...I once had the opportunity of witnessing the manner in which he was received by them [Crows] after an absence of several years. The whole village turned out to greet him. The old chiefs uttered an exclamation of surprise; the braves advanced and invited him to the feast. The young men, whom he had left as boys, crowded around him...The children ran and shouted, until all were collected near him. Fear was the predominant effect that his presence had upon them; their curiosity could not overcome it, for, if by chance, he made a step towards them, they would scatter, run, and conceal themselves. The women, bless their sweet souls, ever kind, and gentle, and tender [sic] always love a brave man... He had a word for everyone, and every one a smile for him. Among them all one could easily see that he was a general favourite; but among the young girls, those just budding into womanhood, I thought I could

perceive the workings of a feeling different from the ordinary display of mere good will and friendship." [5]

Truly, Rose was a prominent and singular figure among the Crows, although it does appear that by late 1812 he had again left his adopted people and after some further adventures of a life-threatening nature, was to be found living among the Omaha near the mouth of the Niobrara far down the Missouri. He did not, apparently, see the Crows again until the summer of 1825, an event of which we will speak where appropriate.

- 0 - 0 - 0 - 0 - 0 - 0 - 0 - 0 - 0 - 0 - 0 - 0 - 0 - 0 - 0 - 0 –

## CHAPTER 8.

## BIG VICTORY OVER THE ASSINIBOINE.

The trader Lisa, meanwhile, had maintained his post at the mouth of the Big Horn only until the winter of 1812 / 1813, when; owing to the already expired date of his original three-year contract coupled with increased Indian hostility against his trappers, including being constantly robbed by Crows, the Big Horn post was finally abandoned and the Missouri Fur Company wound down.

Lisa`s new Missouri Fur Company which immediately followed, did open posts lower down the Missouri, but the closure of Fort Raymond meant that Crows no longer had regular and direct access to the white man's trade goods. As a consequence, they were obliged once more to look to their Hidatsa kinfolk and Mandan friends to supply them with much needed merchandise such as guns and ammunition. Expediently, the Crows patched up their quarrel with the Hidatsa, but at the same time, began suffering large-scale attacks upon their villages and hunting parties by Blackfoot, Atsina, Lakota and Assiniboine war-bands, each of which at once took full advantage of the Crow's weakened state, now that Lisa had forsaken the Big Horn country.

Of course, the Crows had continued to retaliate in kind and in 1812, a large Crow party had attacked a Lakota camp in or near the Black Hills, but was beaten off after having killed one Lakota. In another encounter soon after with the same tribal enemy, a war-party of ten Crows was caught out by the Lakota, who surrounded the Crow position and managed to kill eight so that only two Crows escaped. In yet a third event that same year, according to the Hunkpapa Lakota Long-Soldier`s winter-count, fifteen Crows had been discovered heading towards a Lakota camp. The Lakota attacked the Crows who dug trenches from which to fight behind, but in the event, all fifteen Crows were killed.

The following year [1813], a Lakota chief named Little-Bear was killed in a fight with Crows during which three were killed on each side, and in the same year, a large party of Bloods raided a Crow camp on the Big Horn River. The

Bloods were driven off with much slaughter and in 1814, a renowned Blood chief by the name of Topknot was killed in yet another big fight with Crows again in the heart of the latter's own domain, only this time on the Little Big Horn River.

Raids from the several Blackfoot-speaking tribes and Atsina against the Crows were, during this period, constant and destructive, although the Crows still managed to knock up a few successful raids themselves. Several present-day Crow informants stated, it was the year 1815 when a large Crow war-band successfully raided an Atsina camp and took several captives. One among the latter was a young Atsina girl then about ten years old, and after being adopted into the family of her captor she not only remained among the Crows, but earned fame in adult life as a fighter in numerous battles with her adopted people's enemies, and was actually elected to serve among the seventeen council chiefs of the Crow Nation. It seems that throughout her life she was variously known as Pine-Leaf, and at other times as either White-Flower or Cherry-Blossom, although she has come down to us in history by the more famous name of *Bia-wacheeitchish,* i.e., Woman-Chief.


As a result of having to constantly defend their camps and hunting grounds against more northern foes, the Crows were obliged to reduce somewhat their own raiding of Lakota and Cheyenne enemies east of the Powder. Perhaps, it was due to a temporary reduction in Crow - Lakota conflicts at this time, which ultimately paved the way for the red-stone calumet of peace to be temporarily smoked between them, or at least, between certain bands of both Nations.

According to an entry in the Oglala Lakota winter-count of American-Horse, it was in 1815 / `16 that the Lakota made a peace with the Crows at a place called Pine Bluff. This pact - although evidently of brief duration – actually applied only to the Oglala Lakota and did not involve the Teton as a whole. This is apparent by references in other Teton and Dakota `counts,` which continue to mention Crow - Lakota conflicts during and immediately following 1815 / `16. The American-Horse entry gives no further information regarding the peace-making event, although it is possible, indeed most likely, that it corresponds to a well-remembered episode in Crow oral history that tells of a time during the early years of the nineteenth century when a particular short period of peace was affected between the Crows and Lakota, a brief account of which is as follows.

It is told that some years earlier, a small Crow village had been destroyed by the Lakota and most of its fighting men killed. In the event the Lakota had carried away a number of captives among whom were included the wife of the Crow chief of the vanquished village, along with her two sons and a young nephew. The woman was made the wife of the leader of the Lakota war-party and both she and the young boys remained among their captors, the latter being brought up as Lakota warriors. Not until many years had passed, did the boys who had since grown to manhood, discover their true tribal identity and from that time on, the two brothers were determined to visit the Crows to see if any of their blood relatives were still living. So it was that when an appropriate opportunity arose, the two young men set out together on horseback for the Crow country. Suffice to say, when eventually they reached the Crows and made themselves known, they were received with much joy and friendship as befitted kinfolk long thought dead, who had returned to their own people unharmed.

The brothers met with their real father among the Crows and told him that their mother who had been the Crow chief's wife, was still alive and living among the Lakota, although she had since become the wife of another. For almost a year the brothers remained with the Crows, but then declared they were going back to the Lakota to visit their mother. Whilst on their visit, they said, they would attempt to induce the Lakota to lay aside the bloodied tomahawk of war and instead, meet with the Crows so that their two peoples could come together and smoke the calumet of peace.

Thus the brothers, now dressed completely in Crow attire including horse hair and pine gum extensions to their hair which was a particular fashion of the Crows, returned to the Lakota camp from whence they came. After a few days among the Lakota, they managed to persuade the latter's chiefs to meet with the Crows in the hopes of affecting a mutual truce between their peoples. And so it was, not long after, that this particular Lakota band and that of the Crows did come together on a large open stretch of grassland near the sandstone rock formation now known as Pompey's Pillar close to the south bank of the Yellowstone. Here they pitched their tepees alongside each other and for a period, resided in perfect harmony.

There was much celebration and socializing between members of the different bands, during which the Lakota chief returned the captive Crow woman to her rightful husband, while at the same time, both Crows and Lakota took wives and husbands from among each other's people and adopted each other's children.

After a period of about ten days, the double camp finally disbanded and with professions of undying friendship, the Crows went south towards the Big Horn River, while the Lakota returned to their own country east of the Black Hills.

So in essence runs Crow tradition of their people making a pact with the Lakota, although we cannot deduce from the account alone, which event is implied among several other occasions when, in the aftermath of a Crow - Lakota conflict, a brief period of peace was later affected between them. Neither are we told which Lakota band or bands were specifically involved in the pact. We do know that one or another band of Crows and one or another band of Teton Lakota did make peace with each other in 1851, a truce which lasted until 1855 or thereabouts, and again in 1858 between the Kicked-In-The-Belly Crow band and Miniconjou Lakota, and yet again in 1866. Without doubt, there had existed other temporary periods of amicability between their peoples at various times in earlier years, as indeed my Crow informant Joe Medicine Crow asserted when he said,

> "Sometimes the Siouxs [sic] and Crows would make a short truce and camp together for a few weeks. At such times they would trade with each other; discuss past conflicts, and meet with relatives who had been captured by one tribe or the other and had since married among their captor's tribe; raised a family and wished to remain where they were instead of returning to their own people." [1]

## BIG VICTORY OVER THE ASSINIBOINE

The tribal tradition recounted above, merely then applies to but one such episode of peace-making between Crows and the Oglala Lakota, and this being so, if the Lakota winter-count entry of American-Horse is correct, then after allowing a certain number of years to have elapsed before the two captive Crow boys - perhaps five years of age when taken - to become mature warriors of perhaps twenty years old, then they and the Crow woman in question may well have been captured during the destruction of the Crow village in 1801, as recorded in an earlier chapter and noted in the American-Horse winter-count for that year. It is indicative also that during the same year of 1815, the then Head chief of the whole Apsaalooka Nation, Paints-His-Face-Red, met his demise, although by what cause neither document sources nor tribal tradition can say. In his stead, the renowned Mountain Crow Chief Long-Hair who only recently had married a Lakota woman, filled the vacant position, and it was probably during the same aforementioned Crow – Lakota peace council, that Long-Hair had actually taken the Lakota woman for his wife.

Whatever the case, if one or another Teton band now harboured feelings of peace and goodwill towards the Crows, albeit on a temporary basis, the more remote Teton Lakota bands continued in their hostility. According to certain other Lakota winter-counts, in the same year of 1815 after having driven off a mounted attack from the Crows, a particular Lakota band celebrated the fact that one of their number had killed two horse-riding Crows with only a club, and in the following year of 1816, the Lakota again were holding a big celebration over their taking a number of scalps in yet another Lakota–Crow engagement.

Likewise, the Lakotas' linguistic cousins the Assiniboine had no such thoughts of friendship with the Crows. On the contrary, the Assiniboine were a populous and aggressive people whose warriors continued to replenish their pony herds from Crow stock. In recent years, they had actually stepped up their raiding of Crow camps and hunting parties, in an attempt to gain a foothold in that part of Crow country bordering the south side of the Missouri east of the Yellowstone.

The Assiniboine bands predominantly involved, were those roaming between the south branch of the Saskatchewan and the Missouri and about the head of the Assiniboine River. These bands were well supplied with guns and ammunition owing to regular contact with several Hudson's Bay posts in Canada and so, generally speaking, were always better armed than the Crows. However, they did suffer one important disadvantage which was apparent by their chronic lack of horses, as their own northern country was not conducive to raising such animals in suficient quantity. As a consequence, their war-parties invariably conducted forays on foot even when intent on securing enemy scalps and captives, and if met on the open Plains by the cavalry of their enemies, the Assiniboine marauders offered themselves as easy prey. Thus many of their smaller parties were defeated and oft' times, rubbed out when far from home.

In the early part of 1816, the Crows surprised just such an Assiniboine war-party and slaughtered them all. My informant Joe Medicine Crow narrated the details as he had heard them in his youth concerning this and the subsequent event, and in which, so it is said in tribal tradition, Chief Sore-Belly was one of the principle participants on the side of the Crows.

82

# BIG VICTORY OVER THE ASSINIBOINE

It had happened that the Paunch Crow band was traveling along the east bank of what was then the frozen course of the stream known today as Clark's Fork, this being one of the headwater tributaries feeding the Yellowstone from the south. The Crows as was their habit, had scouts out on each flank and to the fore reconnoitring the way ahead. It was this last mentioned group of scouts moving ahead of the band, which first discerned thirty "Yellow-legs," i.e. Assiniboine, in the very act of crossing Clark's Fork on the ice.

Needless to say the Assiniboine were *Awala-diile*, which was also the reason, perhaps, why they had chosen this particular time of year to undertake their venture, supposing that the deep snow and slippery ground of the season would prevent their intended quarry from using horses to any great effect, and that their own warriors if confronted, would be able to defend themselves on more equal terms. In this instance, the Crows had the element of surprise on their side and could easily have waited a more opportune time and place to attack their foes without risking undue loss among themselves. But any such idea was quickly thwarted when one of the Crow scouts riding in advance of his comrades, showed himself overeager to initiate the conflict.

Almost as soon as the Assiniboine were sighted, the Crow scout raised the war-cry "Koo-Koo-Hey," and alone spurred his pony forward; charging headlong towards the enemy. The Assiniboine were quick to respond. At once they shouldered their already-primed short-barrelled trade guns and fired a volley of leaden balls at the on-coming Crow. Several balls hit the scout's horse, causing it to stumble and roll over the ground throwing its rider in the process. But the lone Crow was unscathed. At once he regained his feet and knee-deep in snow, he stood his ground; presenting an imposing target for the Assiniboine, who hurriedly reloaded their pieces eager to bring him down.

The rest of the Crow warriors, meanwhile, not far in the rear of their comrade had heard the sound of gunfire. Immediately they raced forward in sizable number and thus saved the life of the lone scout who, but a moment later, would have been lying stiff and lifeless in the snow.

The sudden appearance of a mass of enemies to their front caused the Assiniboine to take fright. All at once they attempted to flee into a nearby timber where they hoped to make a stand. But the Crows in their excitement, charged right in amongst them. They scattered the foe in every direction, and although many of the Assiniboine fought desperately, it was only a matter of time before the Crows had killed them all.

Not one of the thirty man Assiniboine party escaped to tell the tale. Indeed, it was only after many weeks had passed and still the above mentioned party had not returned home, that the Assiniboine themselves accepted that their kinfolk must have met with disaster. Perhaps it was visiting Cree having heard of the fight from friendly Flatheads and Shoshoni who, at that time, were allied to the Crows, who finally brought the Assiniboine details of the war-party's fate. Either way, no sooner had the news been confirmed that Crows had rubbed out their tribesmen, a great clamouring for revenge erupted among the grieving Assiniboine kinfolk. Anon, the latter's headmen agreed to send a war-pipe to each of the scattered Assiniboine bands, with a request that they assemble a grand host of warriors, not only to wreak vengeance upon the perpetrators of the deed, but to wipe the Crow people from the earth.

As was the usual custom among the Assiniboine, not until the following summer did the grand war-party finally start forth in search of the Crows, and it is said that the number of warriors in the party was in excess of one-thousand. They travelled on foot, for they lacked horses enough to carry them to their objective.

It was late August, *"The moon when cherries are ripe"* [1817], before the Assiniboine host eventually reached the same Clark's Fork on the north-western border of Crow territory, and whereabouts, their thirty kinfolk had forfeited their lives the previous winter. The bones and skulls of those slaughtered still lay scattered on the ground, the sight of which only made the Assiniboine more eager for revenge. Many oaths were uttered and prayers raised up to the Great Spirit beseeching vengeance upon the slayers of their people. At the same time, an important chief among them made *medicine,* in order to determine if his own powerful `Spirit Helper` was on the side of the Assiniboine to give them success on their expedition. With this object in mind the chief placed what appeared to be a large rock on the ground, then addressed the gathering around him with words to the effect,

> "Until this time our sacred spirit helpers have been with us. But now
> we are almost come upon the enemy. We must seek a sign from the
> Great Spirit, as it will show us if we have offended the above powers
> in any way. If we have not, then a great victory shall be ours." [2]

The on-looking warriors were silent. They stood around filled with apprehension, mingled with a certain amount of reverential awe as they wondered what their chief would do next. At length, the Assiniboine chief drew his knife from its scabbard and drawing it across the aforementioned stone, actually cut it in two as if it was formed of soft clay. This, so the chief told the assembled host, was a sign that his *medicine* power was strong and that the Great Spirit was on the side of the Assiniboine, enabling them to take many Crow scalps and captives. Such words were just what the warriors wished to hear. In response they whooped and howled their satisfaction.

The Assiniboine Head chief on this occasion, seems likely to have been a well-known personage during the period in question known variously by the names *Le Gauche* [Left-handed] and *Tchatka* ["He-Who-Holds-The-Knife"]. This man certainly, would have fitted the role of head chief and medicine man as was the Assiniboine leader in the present account, and at a later date, was a well-known visitor among white traders at both English and American Fur Company posts. Indeed, he is known to have led formidable war-parties of between five-hundred and one-thousand warriors, but seems to have suffered as many catastrophic defeats as when; on other occasions, he was apt to gain brilliant victories.

From where the Assiniboine party had assembled on the south bank of Clark's Fork, a broad trail recently made by many pony-drags and horses was discovered leading in a southeast direction toward the Big Horn River and into the very heart of Crow country. The trail was comparatively fresh and after gathering up the remains of their ill-fated kindred which they deposited among nearby rocks in order to save them further despoilment from man and beast, the entire party again set forth now following the broad trail in a southeast direction, which they knew, must lead them to their quarry.

Unfortunately for the Assiniboine, this was the time of year when all the various Crow bands and clans came together as a united people, in order to hold their annual religious ceremonies which included the planting of the Sacred Tobacco Seeds. Thus between seven and eight-hundred lodges, comprising both the Mountain and Paunch Crow bands, were then pitched along the banks of the Little Big Horn River; close to where the 'Reno fight' took place many years later in June 1876.

Together, there was probably little short of fourteen-hundred males of fighting age in the Crow camps at this time, although according to Crow oral tradition, the villagers themselves had no idea that such a formidable force of enemies was then coming against them. It was only when a small party of Crow hunters accidentally espied their enemies from a distance near the mouth of the Little Big Horn that the alarm was given, but still the Crows had time to rally their warriors and prepare for a big fight. Sore-Belly at 24 or 25 years of age, and back in the North Country after abandoning Arrow-Head's band, was now a leading war-chief within the combined Crow camps. It was his suggestion that the non-combatants of whom they were several thousand, should take down their lodges and seek safety in the nearby Big Horn Mountains, rather than be endangered by being in the thick of battle if fighting should take place around the camp itself. He also decreed that as their own warriors appeared to outnumber those of the enemy and had the advantage of being mounted, two-thirds of the Crow fighting force should go out and meet the foe head on when the latter were still some distance from the camps, whilst those several hundred warriors remaining, should stay behind to protect the women, children and old-folk in their flight towards the Mountains. Such accordingly was done and very soon, some twelve-hundred and more Crow warriors were racing their war-ponies pell-mell, in the direction where the Assiniboine host had last been sighted.

Riding in the van of the Crows were the up and coming warriors Bear's-Head and Twines-His-Horses-Tail, along with young Chief Sore-Belly himself. Sore-Belly's upper body was stripped to the waist and on his head, he wore a long-tailed feathered bonnet. In his right hand held high, was a twelve-foot be feathered staff wrapped in otter fur and bent over at one end like a shepherd's crook, as were carried only by the two bravest men among the Half-Shaved-Heads Society.

The day was hot and the soil exceedingly dry, so when still two or three miles distant, the Assiniboine could see a great dust got up by thousands of hooves, as the Crows galloped their ponies across the prairie, whooping and singing as they rode.

When the Crows came into view, the Assiniboine at first stood their ground ready and eager to engage in battle. But very soon, as they realized the formidable number of enemies charging towards them, they all at once turned on their heels and endeavoured to gain the cover of trees and bushes growing thick along the river bank. But the Crows were upon them in an instant. Soon they had the Assiniboine almost completely surrounded and a desperate fight ensued much of which was hand to hand, and utmost bravery was displayed on both sides.

The Crows by sheer weight of numbers and momentum, slowly pushed ever forward and great was the slaughter of Assiniboine that day. But still the battle raged on as small pockets of Assiniboine warriors managed to keep the Crows at bay with their Hudson's Bay guns. Several Crows were killed and many wounded, along with a countless number of horses having been brought down by the enemy's deadly fire.

Sore-Belly, however, appeared to bear a charmed life. Oft-times he charged the enemy alone, utterly fearless of the danger he was in, and several times, it is said, he counted *dakshey* and struck down a number of Assiniboine warriors after running them down horseback and lancing them through. His singular bravery and recklessness stood out among the Crows on this occasion and he alone, it was thought, made it possible for the Crows to achieve a complete victory. Such was due, moreover, to his encouraging words in the heat of battle, and his superior strategy which helped destroy several pockets of Assiniboine resistance – one after the other – without excessive loss to the Crows themselves.

Only when the sun began to sink behind the western hills did the fighting cease, and only under cover of darkness could the surviving Assiniboine then extricate themselves from the scene. They afterwards commenced their long and hazardous return journey north, from where only several weeks earlier, they had started out in such high spirits; confident of success.

How many Assiniboine warriors were lost that day along the banks of the Little Big Horn, neither Assiniboine nor Crow tradition recalls? Neither is the number of Crow casualties remembered. Although the latter do say that as a result of this battle, never again did the Assiniboine come against them in force. Instead, they thereafter, only conducted small party raids upon the Crows in order to obtain a few animals from the latter's extensive pony herds.

So was gained a great and decisive victory by the Crows over the very people who, for several decades - nay! Many generations, had once brought much woe and grief upon Apsaalooka lodges when, in olden-days, the Crows had roamed as pedestrians in the Saskatchewan country of the north during their grandfathers' time.

Lieutenant James Bradley [previously cited], also obtained an account of this fight, probably from his Crow informant Little-Face in 1876. In Bradley's version, it is mentioned in addition that two Assiniboine were taken captive at that time, and conducted to the Crow head chief to be questioned as to the object of the Assiniboine expedition. The captives are said to have stated outright that it had been intended to cause a great destruction upon the Crows and then asked if any of their Assiniboine comrades had escaped. Upon being told that some had indeed escaped, the captives further asked that they themselves be set free in order that they could catch up with their comrades before they reached their home country. But the Crow chief replied to the effect that as the Assiniboine would not have shown such mercy to the Crows had they succeeded in their original design, then the Crows would not show mercy to them, and so saying, the two Assiniboine prisoners were taken to the edge of the valley and killed. Here, one might suppose, the captives in question were either young teenagers who had accompanied the grand war-party as servants, or if they be adults which is more likely as they were not adopted into the Crow tribe, then perhaps they had offered to carry terms of peace to their Assiniboine people. If this last had been the case, then obviously the Crows had not felt inclined to countenance such a proposal at that time.

We can be sure that this victory over such a formidable host of Assiniboine was, most certainly, soon made known to the Blackfoot, Cheyennes and Lakota, and may have deterred those three tribes - for the time being at least - from attempting a similar invasion into Crow country. This is not to say that raids upon Crow pony-herds abated to any significant degree, and the Crows still had constantly to be on their guard; always ready to give immediate pursuit to thieves. Likewise, in order to replenish their own dwindling herds with fresh animals, the Crows themselves were obliged to continue raiding other tribes. And so, it seemed, their war-parties were still constantly in the process of either going out or coming in; sometimes returning in a secretive and dejected manner when `bad medicine` had come their way. But, more often, the warriors came home on galloping war-ponies, singing songs of victory along with scalps and captured animals in abundance.

Such episodes of conflict were generally of a similar nature and would prove repetitious if repeated, although every so often a particular occurrence might cause an event, albeit seemingly trivial, to be remembered for all time, and would mark a specific year in a tribal calendar.

Just such an event occurred in 1819 / 20 and was used to commemorate that period in the Oglala `winter count` of Cloud-Shield. In this case it is recorded that a fight took place between two war-parties, one of Oglala Lakota, the other Crow. Both sides had expended their arrows and musket balls and threw dirt at each other instead, and as a consequence, the year has been remembered for that occurrence alone.

So here we see that the aforementioned peace between the Oglala and Crows had not, apparently, survived for any significant period, and withal, Crow feuding with the Blackfoot, Atsina and Cheyenne among other tribes, also continued in earnest.

As a result, the young Sore-Belly, it is said, was forever rallying his warriors in defence of Crow hunting grounds and at twenty-seven years of age, he was involved in more than just leading war-parties in pursuit of stolen ponies. Rather, he often organized large-scale crusades which forayed deep into enemy territory in order to "clean up," as the Crows would say, upon one or another enemy village in revenge for some earlier assault upon his people. Without doubt - as many present-day Crows assert - it was Sore-Belly at this period who instilled a sense of prowess and tribal pride into all his people, and he alone who created a united front to protect the land of *Echeta Casha* from their numerous and formidable foes.

- 0 - 0 - 0 - 0 - 0 - 0 - 0 - 0 - 0 - 0 - 0 - 0 - 0 - 0 - 0 - 0 –

## CHAPTER 9.

## THIRTY-TWO IN THE HANDS.

It has previously been noted that in or around the year 1815, Paints-His-Face-Red; Head chief of the Paunch band of Crows and titular head of the entire Crow Nation passed away, and Long-Hair had stepped into the vacant position. Perhaps this was due to Long-Hair`s exceptional *medicine* powers, rather than in recognition of his military achievements alone. His inauguration, however, as Head chief at that time when around fifty years of age, must include him as a prominent figure in earlier conflicts with his people's enemies. Be this as it may, from then on as paramount chief, he gave up the war-trail and put aside the tomahawk and lance other than defending his camp when attacked, or when in transit on the trail. Instead, he embraced the duties of a civil Head chief wholesale, which position decreed he always look to the benefit of the tribe as opposed to any personal desire for self-aggrandizement and renown. As such, he became beloved and ever-more respected among the Apsaalooka and to such degree, that his character was often pointed out to aspiring young warriors as a prime example of how a Crow should act and think; always holding the welfare of the people foremost and caring for the young, the old and infirm. [1]

Of the special attributes accredited to Long-Hair, that which appeared profound, so most white men who knew him agreed, was his extraordinary length of hair, variously recorded as being anywhere between nine and twelve feet long. On the other hand, as far as his own Crow people were concerned, his singular ability to prophesy correctly forthcoming events was an even greater attribute, by which they held him in awe and as one chosen by *Akbaa-tadia* itself. Such was the foresight of Long-Hair, that a number of his predictions were not actually fulfilled until one and even two generations after his death. This phenomenon has only served to add to the reverential adulation in which his memory has ever since been held among his descendants. Certainly, during the first five years of Long-Hair becoming paramount chief among his people, the Crows achieved ascendency in the endemic warfare of which they were constantly engaged. It was then said among the Crows that *Akbaa-tadia* was smiling upon his children and truly, the Star of the Apsaalooka shone bright.

Prominent among Crow enemies at this time were Cheyennes along with their confederates the Suhtaio, whose less-populous bands at this date, comprised an independent element variously known to other tribes as either, Staihitans, Skutani or `Flyers.` More often, they were apt to come off worse in their conflicts with the Crow, but notwithstanding their inferiority in numbers and some recent reversals, the Suhtaio were determined still to claim the Lower Powder and Tongue River country for themselves. Thus, they continued to engage in persistent warfare with the Crows, and seldom did a week pass which did not witness some bloody confrontation between the two. At times, one side or the other would get together a large war-party and move deep into their opponent's country, either to exact revenge for some recent defeat, or more simply, to antagonize the other in return for some lesser slight upon their honour.

Each victory nonetheless, as earlier noted, generally had its price to pay and the following episode is yet another case in point.

Due to a typical yet unsuccessful raid by a war-party of Cheyennes of the Suhtaio band, which had merely intended to steal horses from a Crow village, the Mountain Crows under the strategic direction of their Paramount Chief, Long-Hair, and executed by the now famed young war-chief Sore-Belly, wiped out thirty or more Cheyenne-Suhtaio Crooked-Lance Society warriors. Only one of the vanquished party survived, and he took news of the slaughter back to his people.

According to present-day Crow oral tradition, it had been late summer of 1819, that the combined camps of the Crow Nation were gathered together on the west bank of Tongue River holding their annual religious ceremonies. It was then that Long-Hair summoned the seventeen-strong council of head men to his large red and black-painted lodge, for, he said, he had something of great importance to tell them.

When all were gathered, including young Sore-Belly seated cross-legged around a central fire, Long-Hair took up several handfuls of dirt collected from a mole hill and fashioned a small mound on the ground before him. Then with a burning ember, he lit the contents of a long red-bowled pipe and drew a few puffs from the stem. In between puffs he mumbled incoherent phrases in a low voice, then passed the pipe from left to right around the circle of chiefs who each puffed on the stem in turn. At length, after all had smoked, Long-Hair addressed the assembly thus,

> "Aho my chiefs, this day I received a great and powerful vision in which my protectors Morning Star and Bear Spirit appeared and opened my eyes, enabling me to see things which, most surely, will come to pass. I saw enemies coming towards our camps and white powder smoke bursting from our thunder sticks. Anon, after the smoke had cleared, many warriors lay scalped and bloody all around. But they were not the warriors of the Apsaalooka. They were the bodies of our enemies the *Isaashupshe* – "Stripped Arrow People" [i.e. Cheyennes], not one remained alive." [2]

All those within the lodge had listened to their chief attentively, but now they whispered to one another as they deliberated on his words.

After a while Long-Hair held forth his clenched fists with arms outstretched and said,

"In these hands I hold the enemy. Tell me my chiefs, how many heads [scalps] you would have?

In response, one of the chiefs leaned forward on his haunches and replied, "Give us all that you hold."

Long-Hair then opened his fists and there, exposed for all to see, were eight small bones of a prairie dog owl, four in each palm. "I give you this many" Long-Hair said, as he scattered the bones over the mole-dirt mound before him.

The assembled chiefs cried "Aho" in unison, and then another among them said, "Give us more that we might sing our victory songs for many moons to come."

For a while Long-Hair sat silent; hands concealed behind his back. Then for a second time he held forth clenched fists with outstretched arms and said, "Again I ask, how many heads you would have?

"Give us all that you hold" was once more the reply.

Long-Hair opened his fists exposing another eight small bones of the prairie dog owl, and these, too, he spread out on the mole-dirt mound before him.

All those gathered now clapped a hand over their mouth in an expression of wonder, not knowing how or from where the bones had appeared when, but a moment before, they had observed for themselves the chief's empty hands.

Twice more those assembled clamoured for the heads of their enemies and twice more, Long-Hair repeated his actions, bringing the total times to the sacred number four, so that thirty-two small bones then lay scattered on the dirt mound before him. This, he said, was the number of enemies his spirit protectors had promised in his vision, "Thirty-Two in the hands."

Long-Hair then concluded the meeting by saying,

"My chiefs be patient ere my vision be fulfilled. Truly I say unto you it is forthcoming, by the time the next moon is born." [3]

The great Medicine Lodge camp soon after disbanded, and the ensuing days dragged by. On the fourth morning scouts came running into Long-Hair's camp with word that a war-party of Blood Blackfoot had been sighted not far from the lodges. At once a horde of Crow warriors mounted war-ponies; took up weapons and raced off to confront the foe. Suffice to say, the Blood party was dispersed with much loss, and the Crows returned waving a number of bloody top-knots in the air. Many among the victorious warriors assumed this indeed, was the victory earlier predicted by Long-Hair, although many scalps less had been taken than *"thirty-two in the hands."* The great chief, for his part, merely sat in his lodge, indicating by his lack of enthusiasm that the time was not yet come for the fulfilment of his prophecy, as the new moon had not appeared. But in truth, the wheels of fate had already been set in motion, to fulfil the prophetic words of Long-Hair.

Now some four days earlier in a Suhtaio-Cheyenne village nestling along the Belle Fourche branch of the Big Cheyenne River, it had happened the very same time as the Crow Chief Long-Hair had been explaining his vision to his headmen, that thirty-two Suhtaio braves had assembled in the warrior lodge of the Crooked-Lance Society, and made a road to make war on the Crows.

Early next morning before the sun came up, the party had started on foot towards the west. They were after Crow horses and were led by a man named One-Eyed-Antelope who carried the only gun among them.

It seemed as the Crooked-lance party travelled at a leisurely dog-trot, that the powers of the Suhtaio holy-men who had previously given prayers and blessings for the party's success, were strong, for they managed to reach the enemy country without miss-hap and everything was going to plan. The entire party was in high spirits and confident of success.

In an account of this affair recorded by the Northern Cheyenne historian John Stands-In-Timber, which he put together from recollections of old Crow and Cheyenne story-tellers early in the 1920s, it is stated that the Cheyenne [i.e. Suhtaio] party was traveling along Tongue River upstream with a scout out on both flanks. These scouts came in and reported that the Crows must also be on a war-trail, for they had seen a lot of sign, although they themselves had no idea where the enemy would be. Stands-in-Timber added that the Crows had in fact already discovered the Cheyennes, and intended to ambush them at the forks of a tributary of the Tongue now known as Prairie Dog Creek. The two scouts went out for a second time, but in a short while one returned saying again he had seen plenty of sign but not the enemy themselves. The other scout meanwhile, a man named Two-Bulls, remained ahead of the party on the east side of the creek and as it transpired, viewed the ensuing events from a concealed position some distance from where they occurred.

The rest of the party thus continued up Prairie Dog Creek to its fork, then travelled along the crest of a wide but low ridge separating the two streams. It was at this point that the party was suddenly attacked by Crows; quickly surrounded and forced into a desperate fight for their lives.

In yet another version obtained by George Grinnell from several Cheyenne and Crow informants, it is asserted that as the Cheyenne party was traveling through the hilly country over by Tongue River with scouts reconnoitring the area, they came upon a lone Indian also on foot, and immediately gave chase. Being hotly pursued by the Cheyennes, the Indian was soon overtaken and killed. Joe Medicine Crow added that upon examining their victim, the Cheyennes knew at once he was Crow by his fashion of jewellery and pompadour hair-style, but whether he had been scouting for a larger force in hiding, they could not determine. However, no sooner had his scalp been lifted, a great body of Crow warriors appeared; some on horseback, many on foot, and the Cheyennes themselves were obliged to flee. All accounts agree, however, it was after the Cheyennes had continued their trek between the forks of the creek and reached an area of flat land 200 yards by 300, that the Crows suddenly appeared; whooping and singing, and at first merely sat their ponies in a static position in full view of the Cheyennes before launching their attack.

In the meantime, the Cheyennes had at once taken to their heels. They ran towards a nearby hill and where, on its shale-strewn summit overlooking Prairie Dog Creek, they prepared to make their stand.

Seeing their quarry in flight before them, a large body of Crows charged headlong in pursuit in an effort to cut off their enemy's retreat. Their feathered bonnets streamed out behind them in the wind, as half-naked bodies; daubed with red and yellow ochre, strained forward in the saddle in their eagerness to reach the foe. But the Crow response had come too late. By the time they attempted to actually charge up the hill, the Cheyennes were ready to meet them from behind hastily built, but as to prove effective breastworks, and had dug-in, anticipating a long and determined contest.

The hill itself was a kind of natural fortress easy to defend. Most of the way around its base was very steep, but in one place it slopped gently from the summit down to the valley floor, and here horses could be ridden up to the crest without difficulty. The Cheyenne defenders entrenched along the top paid particular attention to this slope, and the Crows for all their endeavours, could not gain the height and over-run the position with their cavalry. As the Crow horsemen thundered up the slope, a barrage of well-aimed Cheyenne arrows broke the charge and forced the enemy back down into the valley below.

The failure of their first charge brought the Crows to their senses. They foresaw the folly of continuing a direct assault upon the hill, for other than the loss of many Crow warriors which such an action would undoubtedly incur, it would almost certainly be in vain. All the while, that is, the Cheyennes remained behind their defences and had a plentiful supply of ammunition. Instead, the Crows surrounded the position and sniped at the defenders from cover with their smooth-bore trade muskets, which the Crows just happened to have in abundance due to a recent trading excursion to their Hidatsa relatives. In this manner they kept the Cheyennes pinned down preventing their escape, and in the meantime, gallopers were dispatched back to the Crow camp with a request that more warriors should come out and assist them.

Chiefs Long-Hair and Sore-Belly both of the Sore-Lip clan were in the same Crow village at this time. When messengers came galloping in proclaiming aloud that Cheyennes were holed-up nearby, the two chiefs immediately took charge of the situation. Said Long-Hair to those around him, *"This is my prophecy about to be fulfilled."* [4] He then called all the fighting men to arms and bade them go out and confront the foe.

Other Crow camps since leaving the Medicine Lodge gathering were still in the vicinity, and Long-Hair sent runners to inform them what had happened. The entire Mountain Crow division was thus aroused. War clothes were hastily donned; faces and bodies painted and soon, hundreds of warriors, whooping and yelling, were racing their ponies pell-mell to the scene of conflict. Following behind came the Crow women and children and old ones, all eager to watch the fight and witness the annihilation of their mortal foes.

When finally arrived at the scene, Long-Hair held a council of war and spoke to those around him as follows,

> "Now is the time Morning Star and Bear Spirit shall fulfil the promise they gave me. Behold, they have given into our hands this day thirty-two of our Stripped-Arrow enemies. Now, I say unto you, before the sun goes down none of these people shall have escaped the scalping knives of the valiant Apsaalooka." [5]

In response, all those assembled let out a series of wild horrific war-whoops, and appeared much excited at the prospect of so certain and easy a victory. Long-Hair then continued,

"We ourselves have plenty of time. We need not sacrifice our brave men by engaging in rash actions to finish off the enemy too quickly. Let us instead say to our women, return to your camps, take down the lodges and bring them hither, and set them up on the flat land which surrounds this hill where sits the enemy supposing themselves secure. We shall remain in camp at this place until the battle is done, and these Stripped-Arrow People are no more." [6]

The Chief's suggestion was met with unanimous approval, and the tribal crier told the women to do as Long-Hair requested. The women obeyed and within an hour returned, bringing with them pack-horses and travois loaded down with tepee covers, lodge poles and all other domestic paraphernalia. The chief then instructed the lodges be pitched evenly around the base of the hill, thus cutting off all avenues of retreat for the besieged Cheyennes.

The Cheyennes meanwhile, viewed these goings on with apprehension from atop their rocky refuge, mingled, no doubt, with a degree of curiosity, but could only wait and ponder what might happen next.

Once the tepees had been erected the Crows began treating the affair like a festive occasion. Old men beat drums and blew on eagle-bone whistles, while the women sang Brave-Heart songs in praise of their husbands and sons to give them courage in the coming fight. Cooking pots were put to boil, and many non-combatants took up favourable positions to get a better view of the impending conflict in order to satisfy their morbid interest.

Having thus taken time in preparation, it was not until past mid-day before the Crows eventually resumed the fight. It was Sore-Belly who then directed the warriors to let lose a barrage of arrows and musket balls from all sides facing the defender's position, and soon, it seemed, every surrounding rock and bush concealed a Crow warrior.

Throughout the afternoon the barrage continued, and the Cheyennes responded in kind. They also shot back arrows fired by the Crows to supplement their own dwindling supply. Every so often a single musket shot would explode from the gun of the Cheyenne partisan One-Eyed-Antelope, but the Cheyenne response appeared to have little or no effect on the Crows. As one Crow musket was silenced, there was another to take its place. Several Cheyennes were wounded, some mortally, and their comrades knew well that their own demise was assured.

The Crows must have known this also. But as the day wore on the Crows themselves also suffered a number of casualties killed and seriously injured, one among whom was Sore-Belly's brother friend Little-White-Bear. This man suffered a musket ball in his groin, but was carried away by comrades back to the safety of the Crow non-combatants, and eventually recovered to fight another day.[7] Still, however, Sore-Belly was reluctant to order another direct assault upon the hillside, and at length, the sun began to sink over the western horizon.

As the light diminished, so did the firing of guns and arrows until it ceased completely and most of the Crows retired to their lodges. Crow guards kept watch on the hill throughout the night in case the enemy should try to escape, while at the same time, the beating of drums and singing of war and victory songs reverberated over the hills emanating from the valley below. Some Crows including men and women, hurled obscenities at the besieged and the latter in turn, sang loud their own Brave-Heart songs and retorted in defiance that when their fellow tribesmen heard of their deaths, they would send a great force into Crow country and rub out the entire Crow Nation.

So the night passed, and early next morning not long after the sun came up, the battle was resumed.

Periodically, lone Crows would make brazen dashes up the hillside in endeavours to reach the defenders and count *dakshey,* but few ran down again, and by mid-day, the Cheyennes were still holding their own and could not be budged.

It was about this time that a Cheyenne in full regalia of scalp-shirt, beaded leggings and eagle-feathered bonnet, jumped over the low breastworks and commenced running back and forth inviting the Crows to kill him. He was making a "caw-caw" sound and flapped his arms in imitation of a bird in order to ridicule the foe. The noise was deafening as every Crow musket, it seemed, was discharged almost simultaneously at him, and a cloud of arrows whistled through the air. By some miracle the lone Cheyenne was not hit, and he went back behind the breastworks to the welcoming cheers of bravado from his comrades. Soon after his return, he again leapt over the breastworks and repeated his actions in an expression of contempt for his enemies. Three times he did this thing, but on the third time he was cut down by another blanket volley of Crow missiles and killed.

It was not long after the death of this brave Cheyenne that the showers of arrows coming from the breastworks became more sporadic. Eventually the last Cheyenne arrow was spent, and only the partisan One-Eyed-Antelope was occasionally still shooting with his gun.

There was a Crow sniper lodged in a crevice between two rocks close to the Cheyenne position. His deadly aim had created some havoc within the breastworks, causing the Cheyennes to lose several of their number to his marksmanship alone.

The position of this Crow was pointed out to One-Eyed-Antelope and the next time the Crow exposed himself to view, the Cheyenne chief fired and blew the sniper's brains out. With cheers of adulation around him, One-Eyed-Antelope reloaded his gun, raised it to the sun and sang a *medicine* song. He then struck the butt on the ground [moreover to seat the ball rather than an assurance of success] and singling out another of the enemy, he fired again and killed a second Crow outright. Twice more One-Eyed-Antelope repeated the procedure, and each time he killed a Crow. But after the fourth shot there was silence from within the breastworks, for this was the last of the ammunition among them.

The Crows soon realized the predicament of the Cheyennes, and were determined to finish them off completely before day-light should fade again. Sore-Belly thus regrouped his forces and prepared at last to make another charge up the hillside, supposing only a few defenders were still alive.

Before such was done, however, a mournful wail suddenly emanated from the hilltop, and the Crows knew well its meaning. Their opponents were getting ready to die, for this was a Crooked-Lance death-song.

Not desiring to tarry longer, Sore-Belly raised the solitary war-cry "Koo-Koo-Hey," and in response a mass of Crow braves, most of whom were on foot and led by Sore-Belly also on foot, assaulted the height from all directions, scrambling over the rocks and over each other in their eagerness to get at the foe.

A popular Crow medicine man [whose name has been forgotten] wearing a buffalo-horned headdress and mounted on a fine steed, rode out in front of his comrades, and galloping up the slope of the hill was first to reach the Cheyenne position. Bravely he leapt his mount over the stone barricade and landed in the midst of the defenders. All at once the Cheyennes ran up to him and began flaying about him with tomahawks and slashing with their knives. One Cheyenne jumped up on the Crow's horse behind him and tussled for supremacy of the seat, and with the aid of his fellows, managed to topple the rider from the saddle. The Crow medicine man was dead before he touched the ground, and such was the unbridled frenzy of the Cheyennes, they dragged his body over the rocks and literally hacked it into pieces.

The next instant the rest of the Crows including Sore-Belly, were on the crest, tearing down the stone breastwork and screaming vengeance for the death of their medicine man.

In response, the remaining Cheyennes bunched themselves together and with knife or tomahawk in hand, prepared for the end. Suddenly they let out a series of wild ear-piercing war-cries and in unison, threw themselves headlong into the mass of Crows around them, stabbing and slashing blindly as they grappled with their enemies in a number of desperate hand to hand struggles. But one by one the remaining Cheyennes were dropped to the ground, either dead or dying, until all at last lay low.

Two Cheyenne brothers were in this fight standing side by side, and at the end they lay together in death on the blood-soaked ground, as once they had been together in life. [8]

The last Cheyenne to fall, it is said, fought most valiantly. He slew and disabled several Crows before he himself was over-powered by sheer weight of numbers and killed. His body was later found by Cheyennes nearly at the base of the hill. Apparently he had broken right through the Crow ranks, but finding no further place to run, had made his stand, and there he stayed, fighting unto death.

The jubilant Crows, including a great number of women and children who had been watching the contest from safe vantage points, then flooded onto the hilltop, and began dispatching the Crooked-Lance warriors who were still alive and stabbing those already dead. They stripped the clothing from the corpses, and gleefully hacked off the heads and limbs of their victims. These grisly trophies were then attached to the ends of lances and musket barrels to be paraded around the tepees during the victory celebrations to come.

A famous Mountain Crow warrior of a later date named Bull-Goes-Hunting [also known as Sees-the-Living-Bull], once told Joe Medicine Crow's informant Plain-Feather, that he – Bull-Goes-Hunting – was around three or four years old when the fight took place. At that time after the fighting had ceased, an uncle of Bull-Goes-Hunting took him over the battlefield where the dead and mutilated Cheyenne warriors lay all around, and encouraged his young nephew to touch several of the bloodied corpses with his hand in the act of counting *dakshey*. Bull-Goes-Hunting could remember but little of the event, he said, but had been teased about it many times as he grew older, being told he had been the youngest warrior in the fight on that occasion. [9]

All this activity on the hillside had been viewed by the surviving Crooked-Lance scout Two-Bulls, who had remained in a concealed position on a height not far north from the forks of Prairie Dog Creek.

Sometime later after darkness had fallen, Two-Bulls crept away unobserved by the Crows, and started his long and hazardous journey home.

When finally the scout did reach his home village and burst out news of his party`s slaughter, the whole population lapsed into a prolonged and excessive period of mourning. Arms and thighs were gashed; hair cut short and covered with ashes or torn out in hanks. Clothing and tepee covers were ripped and shredded and heart-rending lamentations filled the air. At once promises were made among the grieving kinfolk to mount a grand crusade against the Crows to avenge their loss. But in the meantime, there would be much sorrow within many Stripped Arrow lodges throughout the coming snows of winter.

During the immediate aftermath of the fight, the Crows had been ecstatic. In total thirty-one Cheyenne scalps then dangled from Apsaalooka waist-belts, albeit the victors had taken a heavy toll themselves to obtain them. Years later Crows told the Cheyennes that of the casualties they themselves had suffered, most sustained wounds of but slight degree and very few of their number had actually been killed in the affair. However, Some Crow informants today now say the true number of Crow dead on that occasion was really much higher, perhaps as many as twenty-five or more, if that is, one counts those who died later from their injuries.

Thus, if the Crows had lost a good many warriors in the engagement, then the prophecy of Chief Long-Hair had not entirely been fulfilled. But whatever the case, both Long-Hair and his subordinate Sore-Belly were elevated even higher in the people`s esteem. The Cheyennes on the other hand, considered the event of such importance, they prepared to mount a punitive expedition against the Crow perpetrators with the sole intent of inflicting severe damage upon that people's population and their pride. This the Crows must have expected, but it was not long before they gained yet another celebrated victory when Crows destroyed a twenty-man war-party of horse stealing Pikuni. These enemies, like the Cheyenne Crooked-Lance warriors preceding them, were likewise discovered before they even reached the camp they intended to raid. The Crows in over-whelming number lay in ambush and wiped out the Pikuni to a man. Suddenly, it seemed, the Crows were gaining victory after victory; their jubilant warriors - faces blackened with a mixture of grease and charcoal as a sign of success - returning home driving stolen horses before them and carrying plunder, such as the weapons and clothing of their victims, along with trailing scalps attached to the ends of lances, willow wands and musket barrels, and withal, a number of captured women and children to be raised in the Apsaalooka country as adopted members of the tribe.

Such was the fervour for war following these recent successes, that Long-Hair often remonstrated with his warriors for leaving the women and children unprotected while they pursued their bellicose endeavours. But Long-Hair`s words appeared to have little or no effect As war-parties continued to return victorious, more were those who wished to emulate their mentor's deeds and follow in their wake. The Cheyenne affair was thus considered but one memorable accomplishment among a spate of Crow successes, and far from their minds was any thought of Cheyennes seeking immediate retribution for the Crooked-Lance scalps so mercilessly obtained. Surely, thought the Crows, the Gods and Spirit ancestors of the Apsaalooka were smiling on their children, for were not the Crows the bravest and fiercest warriors on the Plains?  Not even Long-Hair and Sore-Belly could foresee the great calamity, which as a consequence, was now destined to befall their people.

- 0 - 0 - 0 - 0 - 0 - 0 - 0 - 0 - 0 - 0 - 0 - 0 - 0 - 0 - 0 - 0 - 0 -

## CHAPTER 10.

## WHEN EIGHT-HUNDRED WERE STOLEN.

With the passing of winter 1819 /`20 and spring sunshine melting the last snow on the hillsides, to the east of Crow country along timbered streams flowing through the Black Hills, the occupants of the scattered Cheyenne and Suhtaio villages began to stir from their inertia during the winter season.

Throughout those snow-bound moons whilst sat around flickering fires, there had been much Kill-Talk voiced against the Crows. At the same time High-Backed-Wolf - the Suhtaio Head Chief – had carried a war-pipe to the various Cheyenne bands and their Lakota allies, requesting the chiefs smoke and pledge themselves to join a grand crusade for revenge. The leading warriors and chiefs of the Cheyennes and Suhtaio accepted the pipe, while among the Lakota a number of Oglala puffed on the stem. Some Brule Lakota also took it up, along with a few Miniconjou from the lower Cheyenne River.

The fact that all Cheyenne and Suhtaio band chiefs along with some of their Lakota allies had accepted the pipe, and a very large number of warriors promising to join the venture, set the whole Nation buzzing with excitement.

Such was the people's enthusiasm, it was decided that the two most sacred talismans among the Cheyennes and Suhtaio consisting of four Sacred Arrows and a Sacred Buffalo-Horned Hat respectively, would be carried in front of the grand war-party to ensure its success. In addition, the whole tribe; women and children included, would actually join the march into the very heart of Crow country. Truly, the Cheyennes were determined that on this occasion, the Crows would pay dearly for their exultant scalp-dances the previous summer over thirty and more Crooked-Lance topknots.

Thus, when came *"The Moon when buffalo are fat;"* the beginning of June, 1820, the entire Cheyenne and Suhtaio-speaking Nation led by High-Backed-Wolf, along with a sizable contingent of Lakota allies under renowned

Oglala chiefs, Bull-Bear and Old-Smoke, started on their bellicose venture against the Crows.

After several weeks journey, the allied cavalcade reached a point along the Lower Powder not far from its junction with the Yellowstone. Here the allies set their base camps; the Cheyennes and Suhtaio on the west side of the river, the Lakota on the east side about one mile distant.

Even before the allies had erected their hundreds of tepees, the Crows, then in camp along Tongue River not far west, must have known of their coming. They could not, though, have known then if their enemies were coming merely to hunt or with hostile intent. The presence of women and children among the allies would usually have signalled peaceful motives, as very seldom did Indians put their families at risk by including non-combatants as part of an invading force. Nevertheless, as the Crows were resolved to stay their ground, they, too, began preparing for a fight.

This was the village of the *Ashalaho* [i.e. Many Lodges], the band of the Head Chief, Long-Hair, and which only recently had played host to the entire Crow population, comprising at this date somewhere in the region of one-thousand lodges. The respective Crow bands had been together holding their annual religious ceremonies, but had since split again into at least three separate bodies, each of which had gone off in a different direction to conduct its mid-summer hunt. As a consequence, this same Many Lodge village on the Tongue; being that nearest the allies, was now reduced to between two-hundred and two-hundred and fifty lodges which included members from each of the thirteen Crow clans, and contained around fifteen-hundred persons, including between four to five-hundred males of fighting age. [1]

Being aware of the presence of a large enemy force within striking distance of his village, Long Hair called together his subordinate chiefs and at once held a council of war. Among this illustrious gathering were several famous fighting men, such as Plays-With-His-Face, High-Bull, He-Who-Ties-His-Hair-Before, Wolf's-Paunch [Wolf-Belly], Little-White-Bull, Two-Face [Double-Face], Wooden-Bowl [Big-Bowl], Dog-That-Eats [Eats-With-Dog], The-Rain [Big-Rain], Little-White-Bear, and including, of course, the up and coming war-chief, Sore-Belly.

Long-Hair told those assembled to send out scouts in a specific direction, and at a certain place which he then described, they would find the enemy camps. His personal *medicine* helpers "Bear Spirit" and "Morning Star," he said, had told him this, and would also prevent the invaders moving away until the scouts had gathered whatever intelligence they wished to obtain.

The scouts duly set off to reconnoitre the allied camps, the result being they were discovered by the enemy and forced to make a precipitous retreat, leaving one of their number dead in the process. The Cheyenne High-Backed-Wolf, now fearing the allies would lose the initiative, immediately called together the headmen of the Cheyennes and Suhtaio along with their Lakota allies, in order to hold their own council of war.

During the course of deliberations, it was unanimously agreed they should attack the Crow village as soon as possible, before, that is, the Crows had time to react to their scout's report of the size and location of the allied camps, and take appropriate evasive action.

So it was only a few hours before midnight that the great allied war-party, numbering at least one thousand warriors all be-feathered and painted and mounted on wiry ponies decorated in a similar manner, started from their two camps along the Powder in search of the Crow village. In addition, a host of women and other non-combatants followed some distance behind, in order to watch the contest from safe vantage points, and in the expectation of carrying off much plunder from the camp they hoped to see destroyed

Meanwhile, in the Crow village, the surviving scouts had come loping in on their exhausted mounts. At the same time, a small pile of dried buffalo chips was hastily erected in the centre of the camp, and the leader of scouts had first to kick over the pile before reporting to the chiefs. Such an act was tantamount to making a vow that what he was about to relate would be the truth, and after complying with custom, the scout leader burst out the news of he and his comrade's ill-fated brush with the Cheyennes. He also mentioned the great size of the allied camps, along with added intelligence that the number of ponies belonging to the enemy scattered along both banks of the Powder could be counted in their thousands. Long-Hair was alarmed. Again he called his chiefs together and held a second council of war. The Crows could still not have known for sure if the Cheyennes and Lakota had come into the country specifically to fight or to hunt. Nevertheless, so the Crow chiefs reasoned, the Lakota and Cheyennes had now drawn first blood, and the chance of raiders sallying forth to harass their camp, was now a more certain threat to contend with.

Expediently, Long-Hair dispatched runners to take word of the great allied presence to the other Crow camps, with an urgent request to organize large war-parties and join the warriors of his own village, whereupon, they could go forth and attack the foe together. However, as an afterthought, thinking that the allies might even then be preparing to march against them, the subordinate chiefs decided not to await the arrival of their kinsmen. Instead, this time they countermanded Long-Hair`s directive and ignoring his advice, sent word to the various Crow camps that their respective war-bands should set out directly against the foe on their own initiatives. The chiefs further decided to move their village to Otter Creek [known to the Crows as Badger Creek], an eastern tributary of the Tongue, and at the same time, would send out their own warrior force to attack the allied camps before the enemy could start.

To this last proposal the other Crow camps did as suggested, and each of the warrior societies in eight large war-bands led by their respective Pipe-holders, started out in separate bodies against the foe. They set off independently of each other, although all travelling the same general direction. Among these several war-bands the largest belonged to the Half–Shaved-Heads Society led by Sore-Belly, and he, perhaps more than any other, was confident of achieving a great victory over his people's mortal foes. Long-Hair on the other hand, had previously advised caution. After hearing that nearly the entire fighting force of the Nation had been

99

instructed to go out at the same time, he berated the council for not leaving behind an adequate force to protect the camp, lest it be attacked while the warriors were away. But his warnings yet again, fell on deaf ears, and the war-bands were soon far distant in the blackness of the night.

It was intended that a number of formidable Crow war-parties would assault the allied camps from different directions, if, that is, their forces did not unite before reaching their objective. Either way, by so doing the Crows might gain the advantage of surprise. Their plan was to kill as many allied warriors as possible; capture a large number of women and children along with the horses, and drive the rest of the invaders back across the Powder, expelling them from Crow country once and for all.

Now, however, in the opposing camps of Crow, Lakota and Cheyenne, there were only women, children and old men and their civil chiefs [whose duty it was to stay with the non-combatants] left behind to defend the tepees if they themselves should be attacked. But, ironically, neither side`s rank and file imagined for one moment that their own villages were under immediate threat. All were certain that their respective war-parties could successfully deal with any eventuality.

It was not long after the several Crow parties had started from their separate villages that a young Crow warrior named Red-Owl, having been away at the time, came into the relocated camp on Otter Creek. Learning of the departure of the war-parties, he at once took up bow and quiver; mounted his war-pony and rode off into the night in an endeavour to catch up with the warriors. He was obliged to ride slowly as he tried to figure out the trail made by his kinsmen, with only a pale moon to give light.

At this time a young Suhtai named Whistling-Elk [later known as Spotted-Wolf] out scouting far ahead of the allied force, saw the lone Crow riding slowly along looking hard at the ground. For some reason Red-Owl dismounted from his horse, probably to inspect the trail more closely, and it was then that Whistling-Elk charged upon him. Before the Crow could reach for his bow and arrows carried in the quiver slung across his back, the Suhtai had knocked him twice on the head with his war club. Red-Owl fell to the ground and was lying quite still, apparently dead, so Whistling-Elk took the Crow's weapons and horse and rode back to the allied war-party to report what he had done.

When the allies heard of Whistling-Elk`s deed they were in high spirits, thinking that yet another of the enemy had been killed and supposing the man was likely a scout from the Crow village, they thought their own passage toward it would now go undetected and they themselves might take the enemy by surprise. As it transpired, the lone Crow who Whistling-Elk attacked was only stunned. After his assailant had ridden off, Red-Owl soon regained consciousness, whereupon, he headed straight back to the village he had recently left. Even as Red-Owl was returning to the village, he could hear the sound of many horses - like the rumbling noise of buffalo on the move - and he knew there must be a very large enemy war-party nearby heading in the same direction as himself.

100

It was shortly past midnight when Red-Owl came running, almost breathless into the Mountain Crow village in which were now only old men, women and children, all the warriors having gone in search of the allied camps. Red-Owl was still bleeding profusely from the head where he had been hit by the Suhtai Whistling-Elk, although he told the camp occupants he had been set upon by a number of enemy warriors who had counted coup upon him and stolen his weapons and horse. He also told of the many horses he had heard coming towards the village and advised the people to flee at once because of the imminent danger they were in.

Now it happened that Red-Owl had only recently stolen another man's wife and had eloped with her in order to escape the husband's wrath. This was the reason he had been absent from the village when the several Crow war-parties first started out. Because of this, Long-Hair and most of the people were not convinced by his story. Knowing of Red-Owl`s adultery, they agreed among themselves that the man whose wife he had stolen had come across him in the dark and beat him about the head with a pony quirt, as indeed, would not have been uncommon in such instances among the Crows, when a man's wife had been stolen or compromised and the injured party sought satisfaction.

Surely, the people said, if the enemy had in truth attacked him, they would have killed him and taken his scalp, and besides, if there were any Cheyennes or Lakota nearby, then their own Crow war-parties would have found them. The people made the decision, therefore, to remain where they were, although just in case there was an element of truth in Red-Owl`s words, Long-Hair commanded that a barricade of logs and brush be placed around the camp. This was duly done, `though in a haphazard manner and of somewhat flimsy nature as a half-hearted precaution against attack. Red-Owl did not bother to argue. Instead, he went immediately to the lodges of his friends and clan relatives and told them to quickly get their most prized possessions together and move away as soon as possible, for the whole village was doomed to disaster.

Altogether around fifty families were persuaded to leave the camp. They left their lodges standing, abandoning everything that was too heavy to carry or deemed of little value. They mounted their ponies and leading pack horses behind them, went out into the night with Red-Owl to seek a place of safety in the hills.

In the meantime, the allied war-party was making good progress and drawing ever closer to its objective, even though their actual route of travel was slightly off course from the exact location of the Crow village. On the other hand, the Crow forces had lost their bearings completely, and seemed to be heading away from the allied camps rather than toward them.

It was now but a few hours before dawn. Each of the two great war-bands, one composed of eight separate parties of Crows; the other of allied Cheyennes and Lakota, were travelling in opposite directions and actually passed one another without the least inclination of their doing so. Only many years later, when Crows discussed the affair with the Cheyennes and Lakota and compared the different routes of their respective war-bands during the night in question, did they realize how close they had come to actually bumping into each other in the dark.

By a stroke of providence on the part of the Lakota and Cheyennes, the Crow forces failed to find the allied camps, although the latter by then may have moved to a different location from where the first body of Crow scouts had initially found them. The allied warriors for their part, found their objective, but had some difficulty doing so, and the sun was already up before the Crow tepees along Otter Creek were sighted.

This, of course, was the same village of Long-Hair, the occupants of which due to the episode with Red-Owl the previous night, were still curled up on their pallets deep in slumber.

The allied warriors reined in their ponies among a surrounding stand of trees about one hundred yards distant from the outer perimeter of lodges, and thus positioned in many tight mounted groups, they faced the camp on three sides. Suddenly, there appeared on the far side of the village a procession of Crow women and children, along with a few old and middle-aged men coming leisurely towards the tepees. Some were horseback and others on foot leading pack animals, but all oblivious to the presence of their enemies. These were, in fact, a body of those who had gone out with Red-Owl during the night and now thought it safe to return.

Apparently, Red-Owl and his followers had gone just so far into the hills when they started quarrelling among themselves. Several of their number had been moaning it was too cold to stay out and when the sun came up and they could hear no sound of battle, they said that perhaps Red-Owl had been lying after all and nothing was going to happen to the village. As a result, about half these people; some twenty-five families in total, had left their more cautious companions and started back towards the camp.

The Cheyennes and Lakota saw them coming, and remaining hidden from view among the trees, they allowed them to enter the village before making their presence known.

A young Crow girl then between ten and twelve years of age, who was taken captive that day by Cheyennes and later known by the name of White-Haired-Killer, was a member of this Crow party returning from the hills. She always said they had no sooner got back to the village and were unloading their horses when the Cheyennes suddenly charged, taking them completely by surprise.

Having said this, according to the Cheyenne version the allies themselves had only just arrived on the scene, at virtually the same time as the returning non-combatants were approaching from the far side of the open ground surrounding the camp. The sun had been up some short while, but there seemed to be no activity within the camp itself. The Cheyennes also say they had been surprised that no Crow warriors had come out to meet them.

On this occasion, there appeared to be no determined opposition to the allied force and the latter were confident of an easy victory now they had the Crows at their mercy. Consequently, the allied host watched and waited in silence until the last of the returning Crows had entered the sleeping village and began unloading the packs from their horses.

One important man among the allied host on this occasion, was a Suhtaio warrior named Ice. He belonged to the Contrary Warrior Society, whose members were apt to speak and do things backward and had pledged never to retreat in battle, even if it meant certain death. This man was positioned on his war-pony a little in advance of the Cheyennes, looking conspicuous by the stuffed skin of a prairie-dog owl tied to his forehead, and the red paint of his society order covering his entire body which was naked, but for breech-clout and moccasins made from remnants of old lodge skins. In his left hand he held striped of its wolf-fur covering, a `holy` Thunder-Bow lance, thought to embody the power of `Thunder` itself, and it was this man who, by passing the lance behind his neck from left hand to right, actually gave the signal for the allied host to charge.

In response, the allies in a long colourful line, all at once charged from the timber and into the open, almost completely surrounding the camp. The allies, however, stopped some fifty yards from the camp perimeter, whereupon at first, whilst sat upon their painted ponies, they began singing and whooping, but which soon gave way to the fricative cry *"Shi, shi, shi,"* [2] which was to indicate that their hearts were very bad towards the Crows. At the same time, others beat quirts on hide-covered shields to arouse the sleeping occupants of the camp.

This sudden commotion did arouse the camp. It brought the Crows running from the lodges and the sight which met their eyes threw many into a panic. Some stood for an instant gazing with a fixed stare as if dumbstruck at the sight of the enemy host around them, and clapped a hand over their mouth in the customary expression of horror. Their chief Long Hair assisted by some of the old men, tried desperately to calm the people and restore some sense of order within the camp and they did, at length, manage to get the people in a defensive frame of mind. The flimsy barricade of logs and brush erected during the night was hastily re-enforced, and the gaps between the tepees filled with camp baggage and anything else the occupants could lay their hands on. All those who could use or hold a weapon took up positions facing the enemy, ready to defend themselves as best they could against the expected onslaught, whilst mothers with small children in their arms prepared to make their escape; if chance allowed, into the surrounding countryside.

The allies waited, meanwhile, for certain rites pertaining to their `Sacred Arrows` and `Sacred Hat` to be duly performed, and after the rites had been concluded, a champion among the Suhtaio named Two-Twists charged alone towards the village. This man had previously made a vow to do just that, in order to make way for his tribesmen who would follow in his wake and *"...redden the earth with Crow blood."* [3] Two-Twists leapt his pony over the barricades and with a white man`s sabre in one hand, slashed and stabbed at as many Crows as he could reach, be they old men, women or children. Two-Twists then returned to his own lines, but soon for a second time, he was urging his mount forward, and whilst again battling with Crows actually within the village, the rest of the allies charged the camp on three sides. Moments later the host of allies were themselves jumping their ponies over and through all obstacles before them; smashing into hide lodges and riding down everyone in their path, trampling them under hoof. Breaches appeared in every part of the breastworks, and as more and more allied warriors and horses crowded through them, the gaps grew even wider until nothing blocked their way.

Careering their ponies around within the inner circle of tepees, the allies bludgeoned their way through huddled groups of Crows; war-clubs and arrows flying; their lances dealing death to any who resisted their wrath. The scene within the camp was one of utmost confusion, as the occupants first ran this way then that in desperate endeavours to extricate themselves from the trap.

Some of the defenders did manage to mount horses and succeed in breaking through the enemy line, only minutes before the bulk of the latter came pouring through the breastworks and completely infested the camp. Others were not so lucky. White-Haired-Killer, the Crow girl taken captive that day, told her daughter Standing-In-The-Lodge many years later, that just before the Cheyennes and Lakota broke through into the camp, her mother had put her and her sister on a horse ready to flee into the hills. As mentioned earlier, White-Haired-Killer was then between ten and twelve years old, but her sister was a lot younger, perhaps only three or four and White-Haired-Killer was accustomed to looking after her, especially when travelling from one place to another. At such times the younger sister was always tied onto the horse to prevent her falling off. Unfortunately at this particular time, she did fall off and White-Haired-Killer was obliged to dismount in order to pick her up. Whilst in the act of doing so the allies came charging through the camp making a great hullabaloo. The Crow horses took fright which was probably the allies' purpose in the first place, and that belonging to White-Haired-Killer became unmanageable. It reared up on its hind legs then took off to join the rest of the animals which together, were then stampeding around the camp interior searching for an exit. White-Haired-Killer was suddenly left on her own and on foot, and was taken captive by a Cheyenne warrior even before she had a chance to run.

Of those who did manage to get out of the camp before all avenues of escape were cut off, most were women and children, although a few Crow men including Chief Long Hair, were among them.

These men were not cowards, but after defending their ground for a while, they had realized that they alone could not resist the overwhelming onslaught from such a vastly superior force, and as an act of expediency they joined the stream of fugitives as the latter raced both on foot and on horseback for the safety of distant hills.

In reality these men with Long-Hair at their head, had at first fought a desperate rear-guard action in order to give the fleeing fugitives a better chance to escape. A number of Cheyennes and Lakota saw these Crows racing for the hills, and pulling themselves away from what was going on in the camp, took off in hot pursuit.

Long-Hair was lagging behind. Seeing that a few of the allies were drawing close he suddenly reined in his horse; jumped unhesitant from its back and stood alone facing his oncoming attackers who he threatened to shoot with his short-barrelled trade gun. Almost at once his pursuers also reined up, not daring to venture near and instead, though still mounted, they hovered tentatively around whilst shouting abuse at the lone Crow and challenging him to come forward and fight. Long-Hair stayed his ground and returned the verbal challenges, but after a short while he vaulted onto his waiting horse and galloped off again, following the path of the fugitives.

The Cheyennes and Lakota immediately resumed the chase and being mounted on war-ponies, whereas the Crow chief rode nothing more than a pack horse, the allies were soon again at his heels and pressing him hard. It was a desperate race that followed, but it was not long before two Lakota warriors caught up, and riding alongside the Crow chief on either side, tried to pull him from the saddle. In the ensuing tussle Long-Hair was eventually thrown to the ground, but in an instant he was on his feet and braced again to defend himself with gun at the ready. Long-Hair's aggressive stance and look of determined resolution on his grim visage, caused his two nearest antagonists to draw back and await their comrades to come up and join them. Meanwhile, several Crows following in the rear of the fugitives, but ahead of Long-Hair, happened to glance behind them, and seeing the imminent danger their chief was in, they turned their horses around and yelling the Crow war-cry, raced back to give their assistance.

This small group of Crows composed of old and middle-aged men, and armed with only the basic of weapons such as stone headed war-clubs and lances, reached their chief just as the rest of the pursuing allies came into view.

Fortunately for Long-Hair his enemies had no chance to finish him off. The returning Crows quickly surrounded him and by their belligerent behaviour, indicated to the Cheyennes and Lakota that they were resolved to protect the person of their chief, no matter what the cost. The number of allies in this opposing group was not large, although they evidently had the advantage in age and weaponry. Even so, they decided that on this occasion discretion was the better part of valour and merely hurled a barrage of insults at the Crows, telling them they were going to take their women captive and describing in minute and lurid detail what sexual treats they had in store for them. They then rode back the way they had come and allowed the chief and his loyal followers to escape.

Another bunch of Crows had also managed to escape the camp and were fleeing toward the hills, but in a different direction to Long-Hair's group. These people were passing around the foot of a nearby butte when a mixed band of Cheyennes and Lakota got after them, and in the running fight which ensued, the allies killed them all including the old men, women and even some children. The Lakota later recalled the fight as *"When they* [Crows] *fled around it,"* [3] referring to the slaughter of fugitives around the butte in question. Only one small boy survived this particular episode and being on the back of a fast pony, he raced off in search of the Crow warriors whose several war-parties were still looking for the allied camps on both sides of the Powder.

Meantime, in the beleaguered Crow village the fight was in full swing, although all was now mayhem and confusion. The mass of horses and bodies seemed never ending, as the allies continued to career around the interior of the camp, striking down without mercy all the old and middle-aged men and scalping them. Dead Crows lay on top of one another and very soon their corpses littered the ground. The victors rounded up the surviving women and children in great bunches, whilst clouds of choking dust churned up by the galloping horse's hooves further impeded the Crows from offering any practical resistance. It is said that not a few of the Crow non-combatants simply resigned themselves to their fate and offered no resistance whatsoever. The allies ushered them this way and that and the Crows obeyed without complaint [which to do so would likely have meant instant death], going along with whomsoever claimed them as their captive.

Winona Plenty-Hoops remembered that when a small girl, some very old Crow persons whose mothers or fathers had been children at the time of the fight, would repeat what they had been told. They would emphasize the great number of horses charging around the interior of the camp,

> "... 'Iichilaa, Iichilaa, Iichilaa;' [horses, horses, horses], bumping into one another, knocking down people and lodges and raising great clouds of dust that the defenders found it hard to see before them. At the same time, they were constantly being showered with stones and clods of earth thrown up by the thousands of flying hooves." [4]

A number of Suhtaio and Cheyenne women accompanying the allied party were actively engaged in the carnage, and it were they who first began plundering the lodges and destroying them. They ripped the tepee coverings to shreds with their knives and broke the lodge poles into pieces so they could not be reused. They even smashed the clay cooking pots such was their hatred of the Crows. And when the majority of fighting was over, the rest of the Cheyenne and Suhtaio women who had been watching the unequal contest from a safe distance, ran into the camp on foot wielding knives, clubs and axes. They screamed with savage glee as they pounded and stabbed those of the foe lying wounded and even those already dead. They stripped the bodies naked then hacked them to pieces limb by limb, some parts of which they paraded on high attached to the end of their husband's lance points as grisly trophies of their victory.

While all this was going on, there was one particularly prominent figure among the Cheyennes. This man paraded around the ruined lodges wearing a strange shirt covered with small metal discs and wore an iron helmet to match. Years later, Crow survivors recalled that they had been much afraid of this man, and wondered if he was Human or a Spirit Person sent to aid their enemies. They further recalled; he was mounted on a big Spanish pacing mule and created an imposing spectacle a sight to behold. He sat so upright in the saddle, they said, that they, the Crows, thought he must have had some kind of wooden frame or brace strapped to his back in order to keep him so ridged.

In one part of the invested village a group of Crows, predominantly old women and children but with a few old men among them, stood huddled in a bunch cowering in the midst of the carnage going on around them. For some unknown reason the allied warriors left them alone and seemed to take no notice of them. Perhaps, though, they had already been claimed as captives by others among the allies, or were considered too old and decrepit to even be bothered with. The Cheyennes themselves did say later that they had not wanted the old Crow women

106

for they were thought to be of little use. They thus set them free, telling them to go find the rest of their people and inform them what the allies had done.

The battle over, the Cheyennes and Lakota asked the Crow women why there were hardly any Crow warriors in the village, and were told that several big war-parties had gone out the night before to attack the allied camps along the Powder. Apparently the allies still did not think their own camps were in immediate danger, probably because their villages had since been moved from their earlier location. Nevertheless, they quickly packed their plunder on spare horses captured from the Crows and prepared to leave the scene, lest the Crow war-parties should return in force. It was thus, around midday when the triumphant allies finally set off heading back to their base camps, driving a great herd of captured ponies before them along with all their Crow prisoners. Most of these latter were on foot, and were hurried along even though forced to carry heavy loads of plunder on their backs.

The allies left behind a scene of utter ruin. Not a few lodges had been set ablaze and amid the scattered debris of the camp, lay countless mutilated and mangled corpses some pin-cushioned with arrows, while a trail of dead bodies lay scattered along the several routes which groups of Crow fugitives had taken in their efforts to escape.

A sizable number of camp occupants notwithstanding, had managed to escape into the hills, but the victorious allies still took a very large number of prisoners. George Bent the half-White half-Cheyenne informant, asserted that the Cheyennes alone had captured well over two-hundred and fifty of the enemy - all young women and children - and that the Lakota had taken many more captives again. My own Crow informants agree that the number of Crow captives and deaths together amounted to around one-thousand persons in total, eight hundred of that number having been taken captive, and hence, why the event has ever since been remembered among the Crows as *"When the eight-hundred were stolen.* [5]

This last number is verified in the Hudson's Bay journal which pertains to the post at Lake Traverse for the date November 9th 1820, wherein it is recorded,

"...the Tetons went last Fall to war and returned a few days ago with 1100 horses and 800 prisoners of the Crow Indians." [6]

## AFTERMATH

According to the Cheyennes, it was not long past mid-day whilst the allies were on their way back to their base camps, that Cheyenne scouts riding ahead of the column looking for sign of the Crow war-parties, suddenly came galloping back at great speed and reported that a small band of Crows was heading towards them from the hills.

These people appear to have been the rest of the Crows who, the night before, had gone out with the aforementioned Red-Owl, for the party comprised only women and children and a few old men. They were on horseback and like their predecessors earlier in the day, were leading pack ponies loaded down with personal belongings. Evidently, they, too, now thought it safe to return, having no idea that their village had already been taken and destroyed.

A large body of Cheyennes quickly hid among the trees and bushes lining both sides of the path the Crows were traveling, and when the unsuspecting party came abreast of the hidden warriors the trap was sprung. Yelling their fearsome war-cries a horde of mounted Cheyennes converged on the Crows from both sides, taking their quarry by surprise. The Crow men-folk were killed outright and the women and children along with the pack-ponies taken captive. Some Crow children taken at that time and who remained thereafter with their captors, marrying into a Cheyenne or Lakota band and raising families of their own, later said,

"The Cheyennes and Siouxs [sic] swept down upon us and drove all our returning ones before them. We had not time to dismount, but were driven along like a herd of wild horses to their camps." [7]

The victorious allies then continued their journey home, now with these extra captives in tow.

Whilst en route, a single Crow brave appeared atop the crest of a hill overlooking the allied column below. He shouted down to the allies and using signs, asked if they had harmed the Crow village on Otter Creek. Now among the Cheyennes at this time was a young man who had been captured during an earlier attack, ostensibly during the allied Cheyenne and Lakota assault in 1801. This particular Crow who the Cheyennes had named Big-Prisoner, had since been fully adopted into the Cheyenne tribe and spoke both his captor's and his mother's tongue fluently. So it was that when the lone Crow called down from the hill-top, it was Big-Prisoner who turned off from the column and conversed with his fellow tribesman. The lone Crow hollered down saying that his name was Long-Jaw, and then asked if the allies had also killed the women and children in the village assaulted. Big-Prisoner replied that most of the women and children had been spared, although now captives of the Cheyennes and Lakota. Upon hearing this, the lone Crow turned his horse around and disappeared from the crest, and the Cheyennes later said they could hear him crying and bewailing the fate of his people as he rode away.

During all this time, the Crow boy also mentioned earlier, who had escaped the beleaguered village and survived the massacre of the fugitives, had been following up the trail of one of the Crow war-parties which had gone out the night before in search of the allied camps. We have noted that for some reason the Crow warriors had failed to locate their target and when the boy finally caught up with one of the parties and burst out the news that their own village had been attacked, the warriors became distraught. Riders were dispatched to locate and inform the other Crow parties the terrible news, and they in turn were distraught. They thought at once of their wives and families left to the dubious mercy of their mortal foes. They cried aloud to *Akbaa-tadia* and to their personal totems - begging them to preserve their kinfolk.

The Crow Pipe-holders could not keep the war-parties together. Groups of warriors and even lone individuals, all at once raced off at high speed back

108

towards Long-Hair's village in an effort to save their people. Thus, the Crow force which only moments before had been a match for any foe, broke up into two dozen or more separate bands, each warrior heeding only his personal fears and commitment to his loved ones. They completely disregarded the strength of their unity, the one real hope of achieving anything against their enemies. Sore-Belly, it is true, did exert all his powers of persuasion in order to keep the warriors in a cohesive body. But even his own great standing could not deter them from pursuing their individual designs.

Unfortunately the horses of the Crows were already tired, having been ridden all night in search of the allied camps. Now, racing at breakneck speed back toward the village, their animals quickly became exhausted, and it was long after the allied host had left before Crow warriors in one group after another began arriving at the scene; a smouldering, corpse-littered ruin. As each of the exhausted groups of warriors came in and beheld the carnage before them, they screamed aloud their grief and swore oaths of vengeance over the bodies of their dead and mutilated kinfolk. The whole atmosphere was a mixture of abject despair and anger.

When at last all the Crow warriors had returned and it was clear the allies had definitely left the vicinity, the surviving fugitives who had been lucky enough to escape into the hills, came treading gingerly back to the dilapidated camp. For many there was heart-rending sorrow as the men-folk searched among the ruins, discovering the dismembered corpses of close relatives, or alternatively, the realization dawned that a missing child, mother or wife had been led into captivity to suffer a fate they knew not what. Death Songs and hideous screams of anguish filled the air as blood flowed freely from gashed arms, legs and breasts. Others stabbed foreheads with knives or sharp stones and pulled the hair from their heads in great hanks, all in expressions of grief.

As the afternoon wore on, it became oppressively hot. The corpses of both man and beast lying in heaps and scattered around, quickly became flyblown and bloated. A great stench enveloped the scene and withal, the ghosts of the dead, it seemed, were everywhere. It was not a good place to stay. The Crow chiefs agreed they should leave as soon as possible and thus, Chief Long-Hair gathered together the remnants of his people and by nightfall, all had vacated the scene having left most everything behind. Some were those who endeavoured to hastily conceal their dead relatives in secluded spots among the surrounding brush and rocks, although many of the corpses were left where they had fallen, to become the prey of prairie beasts and their winged compatriots of the sky. The survivors in their extreme state of despondency could not bring themselves to adhere to custom, or even judge what was right or wrong. The world of the Apsaalooka had been shattered; the spirit power of *Echeta Casha* nullified and the people's pride and rational extinguished. What use to honour the dead, they thought, when the bonds which had kept the people together were rubbed out? The sacred blood ties of the Nation broken; torn asunder, and the people themselves dispersed. With heavy hearts the survivors headed southwest in a morbid, huddled band into the Big Horn Mountains. There to lick their wounds and take stock of the situation.

In the meantime, the cavalcade of Cheyennes and Lakota driving their Human captives and great herd of captured ponies before them, continued wending its way across country back from whence they came. When arriving at the camps, the women took down the lodges and the whole ensemble moved further upriver to a small tributary of the Powder, and it was here, the second night after the battle, that the allies held a grand victory dance which, Cheyenne veterans of the intertribal wars used to say, was the biggest dance of its kind ever held by their tribe. Such was the excitement of the occasion that the Cheyenne women, it is said, appeared to go crazy, offering sexual favours to any of their choosing. Hence, the tributary along which the allied camps were then pitched, has ever since been known among both Cheyennes and Sioux as "Crazy Woman Creek." [8]

Throughout all, the captive Crow women huddled in darkened lodges, wailed their mourning dirges and cried aloud over their slaughtered loved ones, whose grizzled remains were being abused before their eyes. The captured children of which there were many, sat together in bunches bewildered by all that was going on around them. The Cheyennes and Lakota traded off their booty with one another, haggling over every transaction, as they exchanged a captive for a horse or some other item of plunder obtained from the vanquished village.

At the same time, a Lakota warrior who had suffered serious wounds during the actual attack, finally succumbed to his injuries. As an act of vengeance his relatives set upon one of the female Crow prisoners with their knives; threw her still breathing body onto the camp fire, and whooped with fiendish delight as she slowly roasted to death.

At first the Cheyennes and Lakota had been united in their victory celebrations. But as often when Indian groups came into close proximity with one another for a prolonged period, congenial relations soon became strained. Arguments increased over the distribution of captives, as the informant George Bent averred, and the situation became decidedly heated, to the extent that warriors on both sides grabbed weapons and opposed each other in battle array, ready to clash in deadly combat as if facing mortal foes. Fortunately, the chiefs and headmen of the two camps intervened and after much difficult persuasion, managed to calm the situation and prevent a full scale conflict erupting among the lodges. As it was, one or two Cheyenne and Lakota warriors had already been either killed or seriously injured during the brief, but heated melee, ironically, by their own tribesmen, and certainly, several Crow captives had also lost their lives, being murdered out of hand through spite by one side or the other.

It was because of this dissension that the very next morning, the women of both camps again took down their lodges; packed the covers along with their domestic belongings on pony-drags, and in separate bodies began moving off in different directions.

And so it was that the grand allied expedition to punish the Crows came to an end. An end of the matter, that is, as far as the allies were concerned - but not so for the Crows.

There were those who believed their dire defeat had been brought on by their own people having become somewhat complacent due to a spate of recent victories and, thereby, neglectful in their devotion to *Akbaa-tadia*, and had not fully kept their part of the covenant with Old-Man-Coyote, who had promised to always protect and preserve the people.

Others blamed Chief Long-Hair himself for their great misfortune. Was it not his responsibility alone, they said, to propitiate and commune with the great unseen powers on behalf of the people? Why then had his *medicine* failed them? Surely, he must have angered the aforesaid powers in some way and; as a consequence, his once omnipotent protective *medicine,* made manifest by his miraculous growth of hair, had become nullified and impotent. Still others, meanwhile, cursed the young warriors and some each other for not having heeded Long-Hair's warnings, - riding off instead to seek personal acclaim and riches, rather than protecting the camp and its defenceless occupants. There had been members from all Crow clans in the village lately destroyed, and this caused much dissension among the people, as recriminations flew hot and all around.

Filled with grief and a temporary lack of tolerance, personal rivalries again came to the fore and threatened internal strife. None appeared to listen to the counselling of the chiefs, who tried in vain to calm the situation and allay the people's fears. In their respective opposing groups the entire Crow population scattered into numerous, small, individual camps. They ignored even the blood-ties of the clan and dispersed themselves throughout the Big Horn Mountains and beyond. There they spent the autumn and coming winter in seclusion; wallowing in their sorrow. Indeed, the coming winter was particularly severe and not a few of those in mourning actually froze to death in their isolation. Many were those now without mother, wife and children, whilst the old and decrepit, alone and bereft, with none to give them succour and entice them back into the fold, fended for themselves as best they could, - if they could - until such time the people would finally regain their senses and reunite as a tribe.

But for the time being the Apsaalooka remained fragmented and irreparably divided. Truly, it would take the persuasion of a great chief to instil again into the people that pride and confidence which had marked them high above their neighbours, both friend and foe alike. Yet none at present could foresee the rise of such a man, who alone could heal the great wound now tearing the Nation apart? Surely, thought the Crows, the Gods of the Apsaalooka had forsaken them. The star of their ancestors which once shone bright, was dimmed.

The afore recounted attack by Cheyennes and Lakota, proved to be the worst calamity ever to attend the Crows regarding their inter-tribal conflicts, and the largest number of Crow captives ever taken at one time by the enemy.

- 0 - 0 - 0 - 0 - 0 - 0 - 0 - 0 - 0 - 0 - 0 - 0 - 0 - 0 - 0 - 0 –

## CHAPTER 11.

### REGAINING THE INITIATIVE
### and
### VENGEANCE ON THE CHEYENNES.

Throughout the autumn and winter following the destruction of Long-Hair's village, many Crows grieving lost relatives, coupled with those who through personal guilt or having been driven from camp by the recriminations of others, stayed out alone, sad and dejected, - scattered here and there in individual bivouacs fashioned from brush and deer hides. In such a condition they spent their time lamenting and fasting to obtain forgiveness for their neglect of responsibility, which, they believed, had led directly to the death and enslavement of so many of their kinsmen.

In the meantime, the survivors sent messages by one means and another to several Lakota and Cheyenne camps, in the hopes of securing the release of the captives through trade, or simply, by the good will of the Lakota and Cheyennes themselves. In this way, albeit a very small number of women and children were actually allowed to return to the Crows, although a large number stayed among their captors, whose hearts for a long time were bad towards the Crows, and could not be persuaded to give them up.[1]

Thus those still grieving continued in their self-harming isolation, and not until spring the following year [1821], did they begin returning to the tribal fold. At first with a feeling of trepidation not knowing how they would be received. But their fears proved to be unfounded. Their fellow tribe's people welcomed their return. Indeed, they took pity upon their emaciated appearance, and showed much sympathy and appreciation for the sufferings they had endured; both in spirit and in body, made evident by the mutilations inflicted upon themselves during the process of their penances.

Chief Sore-Belly, so Crow oral tradition tells us, was the one who by his personal cajoling and good sense, finally persuaded the various clans to lay aside their age-old rivalries towards each other. Instead, he urged them to join together again for the mutual benefit and protection of all.

He it was who had travelled around the country during the cold, storm-filled moons while snow and ice lay thick on the land; searching out each and every small group of Crows then ostracized from the main body of the people. He told them they had grieved long enough and should now cease blaming each other and themselves for their tribe's misfortune. He spoke to them thus,

> "...Never again will such a calamity befall the Apsaalooka if now
> we come together and act as one. In our unity we shall re-populate
> our numbers and be strong, if not stronger than our enemies." [2]

The chief's words were listened to and the people acted upon them. Signal smokes called in the scattered camps from far and wide, and so it was when summer again rejuvenated the land, all the Crow clans came together again in one great tepee encampment situated at the base of "Long Mountain." This being a part of the Big Horn range immediately west from where stands the present-day town of Sheridan, Wyoming.

Now, with the whole Nation congregated in one large camp, it was plain to see that a great anomaly existed among the people regarding their current population.

The recent defeat had created a ratio of at least three males to every female. Many were the men-folk who had lost wives, while for those who wished to marry and raise children, there were not enough women of child-bearing age to go around.

It was in order to alleviate this situation that Sore-Belly with Chief Long-Hair`s approval, now showed himself an astute and far-sighted leader and not just a warrior of indomitable fighting spirit as he was purported to be, living solely for the thrill and dubious rewards of the warpath. Certainly, he was not preoccupied in personal indulgences to distract him from looking to the welfare of the people, and to the destruction of their enemies.

Having called together in council all the chiefs and prominent warriors, Sore-Belly, although a comparatively young man of twenty-eight years, but with much influence and an engaging personality and now regarded as the foremost war-chief among them, stood tall and erect in the forefront of those assembled. With sweeping gesticulations he addressed the council with words to the effect,

"Thou know it Crows, in the long-ago time *Akbaa-tadia* and *Isaah-ka-wauta* [Old-Man-Coyote] gave this land to our "Ancient ones." How red then was the blood of our fathers? Is it not their blood which gives life to this land? Let us then tread the path they trod and show our enemies we are *"hisshi baache"* [red men] like themselves. Let them know it is Apsaalooka blood which is ready to be spilt again on this land. Now, I say unto thee, from where the sun stands, when we fight our enemies we shall take as many captives as possible, even at the expense of counting *dakshey* and taking horses. These captives we shall raise as Crows and in this way, the Apsaalooka will increase in number and supply wives and warriors to enable us to match all who come against us. Each time we are attacked, our warriors shall go at once in pursuit, even if it leads our brave men into the very heart of the enemy's domain. By so doing, we shall deter our foes from collecting their scalps and increasing their pony herds from stock in the Crow country. These things if acted upon will make our people strong and respected among our neighbours, as were our forefathers in days gone by. This one who speaks says unto you; let us relax our tribal laws which forbid members of the same clan speaking to each other of their choice [i.e. a procreating liaison]. Let us instead, temporarily allow clan men-folk and women-folk to speak freely among themselves, and we shall repopulate our depleted Nation and `eat up` our enemies as did our fathers of old." [3]

This last suggestion was viewed as a radical idea and entailed long debate among those in council. At length, purely for practical purposes, all those assembled agreed to Sore-Belly`s proposals and hereafter, all enemy women and children who fell into Crow hands would be taken alive - if possible - and adopted into the tribe. At the same time, age-old taboos relating to the clan system were relaxed - albeit temporarily - and within only a few years, the Crows did increase their population to a number compatible to that existing prior to the catastrophic defeat on Otter Creek. This is not to say that sexual union between brother and sister or even between first cousins was countenanced, or indeed, ever suggested. Only that second and third cousins and, of course, non-blood kin such as adopted members into the clan, were now allowed free sexual expression among themselves.

The Crows for the most part, owing to the eloquence of Sore-Belly and added persuasions from Long-Hair and a subordinate chief named Big-Bowl, actually welcomed these new proposals. Although one can well imagine there remained not a few dissidents who were not about to accept even the thought of allowing sexual intercourse within the clan. This they would always regard as an act of incest, including that practiced between non-blood relatives who were clan members only in the adoptive sense and no more. Notwithstanding, however, any dissension regarding this point, Sore-Belly was looked up to by the vast majority of the people even more so than before, now being regarded not only as their mentor and protector, but as the great saviour of the Nation.

Today, Sore-Belly is given full credit in Crow oral tradition for introducing these revolutionary changes among his people. It is true to say, though, that an earlier precedent had occurred during the aftermath of several virulent epidemics which had struck the Crows between 1781 and 1802. In the wake of those recurring contagions, it had been found that more than one half of the entire Crow population had been wiped out. As a consequence, similar proposals such as Sore-Belly now instituted had been temporarily introduced, ostensibly by Chief Paints-His-Face-Red; who had then relaxed certain clan taboos in order to more quickly repopulate the tribe. It was then, perhaps, this earlier precedent which incited Sore-Belly to make his own proposals at this time.

Prior to 1820 each of the various "paired" Crow clans, generally speaking, had roamed as separate and to a large degree, independent bands. They had come together only during the time of annual tribal gatherings when the Nation's communal religious ceremonies were held, or merely by accident during the respective wanderings of each. At such times several paired clans might have joined together for a few months in order to hunt and socialize with one another. But from hereon as an act of expediency, and in order to counter any future disaster as had recently befallen Long-Hair's people, four and sometimes more clans would unite their populations to form a much larger band for mutual protection.

There was, of course, a limitation as to how long combined clans could stay together in any given area, owing to the amount of game needed to accommodate the people. For this reason, the Nation organized itself into three main tribal bodies each with its respective hunting territory. These three comprised the Mountain, Paunch, and Kicked-in-the-Belly bands, the largest of which even after the attack on Otter Creek, was the Mountain division led by Long-Hair, which boasting some 350 tepees, was still known as the "Many Lodge" band. On the other hand, the Paunch people comprised little short of three-hundred tepees, whilst the Kicked-in-the-Bellies, being offshoots from the Mountain band and composed predominantly of Whistling-Waters and an adopted people of

Athapaskan stock known as the Poor-War-Deeds clan, rarely exceeded more than 150 lodges, and often considerably less.

Returning to the above mentioned summer gathering of 1821, it was while all the Crow bands as a Nation were still encamped near "Long Mountain" in the shadow of the Big Horns, that an old and respected shaman named No-Rain called together all the young men present. He bade them go fast upon the aforesaid mountain in order to seek visions, so that each might acquire a strong Spirit-helper to enable the Apsaalooka to again achieve victory and power over their foes. A significant number of young males did as No-Rain requested. These men went out, each to some secluded place on the mountain and there, exposed to the elements, they prayed and fasted in the prospect of receiving a vision. Whether a vision was forthcoming or not, after a period of three or four days they returned to the camp exhausted; often more dead than alive.

An example of the intense devotion and attendant suffering their ordeals entailed, has been aptly described by a Crow warrior named Foolish-Man. As an informant to William Wildschut early in the twentieth century, he narrated the experience of a young Crow brave named Blows-Down.[4] This man Blows-Down had lost a brother killed in the earlier attack on Long-Hair`s village, and even though he had already several times sought a vision and Spirit-helper, he had not yet been successful. At the behest of No-Rain, Blows-Down was one of those who now went out alone onto the mountain.

Blows-Down selected a spot where he built a low platform of stones covered with pounded cedar, and which was just long enough and wide enough to accommodate his body. Upon this platform he intended to repose whilst awaiting his vision to appear. Before he did so, he stood for a while facing the sun and pointing a finger in its direction, cried aloud in supplication to *Akbaa-tadia* with the words,

> "Father I am offering you a piece of my flesh and for your sake, will I shed my blood. May the "Without Fires" [i.e. animals and the birds of the air] eat it and drink it. I pray to you Father, that you may favour me with a strong vision. I am poor and humble before you. Father, I have sought your help before but for some reason you gave me no dream. Now, once more I pray to you to give me a vision, Let the "Without Fires" come to me. I have lost a brother and I feel grieved over his loss. I implore your aid. I seek strong *medicine* so that I can avenge the death of my brother. I place my whole being in your care. Father, do not let me suffer long." [4]

Blows-Down then placed his left hand on a cedar twig; took up an iron-bladed knife and chopped off the end joint of his middle finger. He held up the severed digit toward the sun as a sacrifice to the Great Spirit, and with a second short prayer, placed the digit upon an exposed rock nearby. He was shedding much blood which sprinkled the ground as he walked around the rock, and after becoming weak, he lay down on his prepared platform and quickly fell into a state of unconsciousness.

When Blows-Down awoke the sun was already far above the horizon. But in spite of the sun's heat and he being covered with a thick buffalo robe painted for the occasion with white clay, he felt very cold and was shivering. He arose from his platform and began to cry. He prayed and pleaded to the sun and to the "Without Fires" to give him a powerful vision, and when he could again no longer stand, he sat down; lit a pipe, and offered a smoke to his Father the sun, and to his Mother, the earth. And thus the day passed.

That night and the following day and night, still no vision came. But during the third night just before dawn, he awoke, and in the words of Foolish-Man to Wildschut,

"He was wide awake and gazing toward the east when the first streaks of dawn began to colour the horizon. Then suddenly, in the clouds overhanging the sky, a man appeared. He came nearer and nearer. Finally he appeared to step out of a cloud upon the toes of Blows-Down. Yet Blows-Down did not feel any weight. The man then stepped down beside his couch. As his feet touched the ground, a blaze of light issued from the points of contact. The earth seemed to be aflame and a column of smoke ascended skyward. `Then the man spoke. "My child, arise from your bed of torture. I have come to adopt you as my son." He grasped Blows-Down by the hand and said, "On you I will bestow my power. `` [5]

Apparently from nowhere, the Spirit Being produced a hoop. Holding it in front of Blows-Down, the spirit told him to look through it. When Blows-Down did so, he saw all the enemy tribes just as if they were close to him. The spirit then told Blows-Down that he, the spirit, was the Morning Star; that he had pitied Blows-Down for a long time and had finally decided to come to him; to adopt him, and give him his personal *medicine*.

The Morning Star told Blows-Down to fashion such a hoop for himself and that he might make three copies of this *medicine*, although no more than four should ever be made. He then said that whenever an enemy war-party approached the camp in which Blows-Down was staying, the said *medicine* hoop would warn him of its coming. Finally, the Morning Star told Blows-Down,

*"If you pray to me, your people [Crows] shall increase in number."* [6]

When Blows-Down came down from the mountain, he told his friends all that had occurred during his vigil, and it is said that his friends were happy because they knew he must have received a powerful vision, and especially so when Blows-Down told them, *"Never again shall the enemy surprise us, for I shall know of their coming."* [7]

Some few weeks later during the middle days of summer, and after the Crows had moved to the vicinity of the present-day town of Big Timber, Blows-Down invited fifteen warriors to join him on a war trip. Among his companions on this occasion were Sits-In-The-Middle-Of-The-Land, Wolf-Carrier, Crow-Head, and a man called, He-Drank-Himself.

116

On the east side of the Wolf Teeth Mountains, the party led by Blows-Down discovered a Lakota camp. The Crows waited for nightfall then drove off a large herd of Lakota ponies and made their escape. The Lakota gave chase and early next morning, they came within sight of the thieves as the latter were in the act of crossing the Big Horn River. Blows-Down now invoked his *medicine* and in this way, caused a big storm to come up in the guise of a howling blizzard which struck with great violence between the Crows and their pursuers. With loose snow tossing about in great billowing clouds, it was impossible for the Lakota to see the way ahead. At length, it forced them to abandon the chase and return empty handed from whence they came.

Suffice to say, the Crow party safely reached home with a large number of captured ponies in tow. The people were overjoyed, for to bring on a snow-storm in the middle of summer surely indicated that the Apsaalooka Gods were again protecting the people. In addition, this was the first success their warriors had achieved over any of their enemies, since the calamity attending Long-Hair`s village on Otter Creek.

The success of Blows-Down`s war trip instilled renewed confidence in many Crow warriors, as since the disaster of 1820 they had been reluctant to go to war, supposing bad luck would befall them all the while the *medicine* power of their enemies, they believed, remained stronger than their own.

So it was after the return of Blows-Down, two or three Crow parties also went out against the foe. These raids, primarily, were horse stealing ventures which by themselves, did not inflict any serious damage upon the enemy. Thus, still the Cheyennes and Lakota went unpunished for the carnage they had wrought the previous summer.

It was not until some weeks later, after the combined Mountain and Paunch Crow bands had moved again and encamped along the Yellowstone across from the present-day town of Billings, that Sore-Belly himself declared, he personally was at last ready to lead a revenge raid against the killers of Long-Hair`s people; if, that is, any warriors were now brave enough to join him.

In response many flocked to his call and preparations were made before starting south to, "clean up" on the Cheyennes.

This must refer to the same episode of which Lieutenant James H. Bradley was told in 1876, and what Joe Medicine Crow later heard from old-time Crow historians in his youth [1930s], that about one year after the attack on the Otter Creek village, Sore-Belly and a large Crow war-party went into Cheyenne country and killed many of the enemy. It was Chief Sore-Belly who had organized the expedition on that occasion and he alone, who planned the strategy employed.

It is said also that the day before the grand party`s departure, Sore-Belly requested all those wishing to join the expedition to parade in their best regalia before him, and those wishing to take vows of vengeance, would then be allowed to do so in a ceremonial manner.

It was to be a crusade which Sore-Belly had previously planned and meditated upon for many moons. To the extent that he had become somewhat obsessed as regards its successful conclusion. Often he had proclaimed to those around him of his profound hatred for the Cheyennes, and especially his disdain for the particular Cheyenne Chief High-Backed-Wolf who was known to the Crows as Striped-Elk, and of whom Sore-Belly said,

> "...Now the man with stench in his hair is forcing our people to be miserable and makes them grieve and cry. Over there, the Cheyennes think they alone are brave. He makes my poor people sit in the lodges in places where the water drips on them. He beats them and kills them at will. Now it will come to an end. We shall meet with the enemy and have a decision be it that the enemy is killed or we Crows are killed. Now is the time we shall have a decision, one way or the other." [8]

This then, was to be a venture dear to Sore-Belly's heart, and would be governed by his personal plan of attack. His strategy was to send a decoy force to the enemy camp, which would entice the Cheyennes into a trap to be executed by the main Crow body positioned in hiding further along the trail. The success of the expedition would, at last, Sore-Belly thought, exact retribution upon those who earlier had wrought so much woe and grief upon his people.

Thus that same day around mid-afternoon, the occupants of the combined Mountain and Paunch villages, including all the warriors, old men and women, assembled in the large open space within the camp circle. They readied themselves to honour the leading men and chiefs among them and to pay homage to the great Sore-Belly himself when he condescended to appear before them. At length, Sore-Belly did appear, bedecked in a long double-tailed eagle feathered bonnet; beaded and scalp-fringed war-shirt and leggings, and beaded moccasins with wolf tails attached at the heels. He was mounted on a magnificent black pony with a prominent white blaze on its forehead, and positioning himself at the south entrance of the tepee circle, he presented a formidable and imposing sight.

Then followed the steady throb of war drums beating, as into the centre of the circle the tribal herald who was on foot, led the war-pony of a popular and distinguished fighter and council chief named Little-White-Bull, sitting proud and erect astride the animal's back. The herald proclaimed aloud to the spectators how brave this warrior would be in the coming fight, while Little-White-Bull himself responded by vowing vengeance on the enemy and thereby, would allow those who had lost kinfolk the year before to cease their mourning. The warriors whooped their war-cries in unison, while the women raised the tremolo and sang praise songs in recognition of their champion parading before them. After this, another mounted warrior named Small-Back was also led into the circle by the camp herald, and the same or similar speeches were made by both. Following Small-Back came several more great fighters, among whom were included Passes-Women, Wants-To-Die, High-Backbone, Two-Face and High-Lance. Each of these men was well known as being formidable in battle, and after each had virtually reiterated words that had been said before, they, too, were honoured by the people.

Also prominent among the eminent warriors at this time, was a middle-aged man named Plays-With-His-Face. He had lost most of his immediate relatives during the attack on Long-Hair's village apart from his mother and a brother [who was the same Two-Face noted above], and now had little regard for his own safty, as he no longer cared to live. Plays-With-His-Face was a Sore-Lip clan member of the Lump-Wood society, and recognized as a brave fighter who knew not the meaning of fear. Often he wore a long-tailed buffalo horned war-bonnet and was regarded as one reckless in battle, likely to be killed at any time. Some declared it was the intervention of divine providence alone why he had escaped earlier situations which had seemed like certain death, and were not surprised when he asked Sore-Belly to let him be among the proposed decoy party. This would be a dangerous undertaking especially for a person already past his prime. But knowing the dare-devil potential of Plays-With-His-Face, Sore-Belly agreed to the request.

When this part of the ceremony was over, Sore-Belly invoked his personal *medicine* which was the 'Thunder,' and this time he actually did so in full view of the people. He thereafter commanded that while on the march, no birds, even of small size and seemingly insignificant, which, it was believed, were connected to 'Thunder' itself, should be killed. For such, he said, would break the potency of his *medicine* and lead to the death of some among the Crows.

Soon after this the warriors prepared themselves for war, and that same night, a grand Crow host of some two-hundred warriors along with a number of women tending to the needs of their men-folk, started out in search of the Cheyennes, all believing the omens were auspicious for the party's success.

The following morning after travelling only a short distance, a young female named Likes-the-Old-Women made a swipe at a meadowlark flying too close to her face. The bird was accidently killed and she told Sore-Belly what she had done. The chief rebuked her for her carelessness saying he could do nothing about it now, but surely, one of their number if not more would subsequently be killed in the coming fight. Still, however, Sore-Belly was resolved to continue on the war-trail and meet the foe in combat. So the grand party travelled on, notwithstanding that the great chief's *medicine* had already been undermined.

After a few more days of hard traveling, the grand party came near a large Cheyenne village on Horse Creek, a tributary running into the south side of the North Fork of the Platte. Here Sore-Belly told his warriors to site their base camp, for this was as far as they should go, and when darkness covered the land, six Crow warriors who had been selected as the aforementioned decoys and among whom was Plays-With-His-Face and the council chief Little-White-Bull acting as their leader, started out on horseback towards the Cheyenne village. The main body of Crows meanwhile, positioned themselves some miles distant in two gullies running parallel to each other either side of a narrow stretch of open ground semi-obscured by stands of cottonwood trees. Here they would wait for the Cheyenne force which was expected to give chase to the decoys, who would lead the Cheyennes into the trap waiting to be sprung by hidden Crows.

It was just before dawn when the Crow decoys came close to their objective, whereupon they dismounted and walked their ponies at a slow pace.

This was to allow the animals to get their second wind before charging the enemy camp, and as they continued on, they entered a sunken defile along which they travelled to obscure themselves from view. It was then that Plays-With-His-Face became angry and impatient. He berated his companions for what he thought was their over caution and timidity saying,

> "We are not dogs skulking around, afraid to get to grips with the enemy. Let us go to them in the open and kill them face to face. That will cause them to make a charge upon us. We were not told to creep along hidden from view." [9]

By his words Plays-With-His-Face meant they should bring the Cheyennes as quickly as possible to the place where Sore-Belly and the rest of the Crows were waiting. His blood was hot, he said, and he could no longer wait to carry destruction to the enemy. Little-White-Bull, even though having himself the reputation of a somewhat impetuous and reckless character, this time showed a degree of caution. He refused to do as Plays-With-His-Face suggested, which caused the latter to ride off towards the Cheyenne village intending to confront the enemy alone. In his wake, one of Little-White-Bull's companions, a slightly younger man named Hanging-Raven, the same who had been a mentor to Sore-Belly in the chief's childhood days, raced his pony after Plays-With-His-Face ready to join him in his reckless endeavour, and when coming to the crest of a ridge over-looking the village, both Plays-With-His-Face and Hanging-Raven halted their mounts and surveyed the scene below. *

It being mid-summer, the whole Cheyenne Nation had earlier come together adjacent to Horse Creek, and had just finished conducting their Medicine Lodge ceremonies. Their tepees had been positioned in the shape of a large horse shoe several ranks deep. In this camp were many Crow persons taken during the attack on Long-Hair's village and some lodges, it is said, contained four or five captives each. Now, as the two Crow decoys arrived on the scene, the morning sun was just coming up, and some Cheyennes were already taking down their tepees and preparing to move. Others had previously moved off, and were meandering slowly over the prairie with pole-drags and loose ponies in tow.

According to the Cheyenne version, a woman in camp out early collecting firewood, heard the faint sound of a human voice, and casting her gaze towards a ridge-top, she spied a lone horseman positioned on its crest. The horseman then began ridding back and forth along the ridge at a slow gait, evidently hoping to be seen more clearly by the camp occupants, whereupon, the woman ran back into camp and called her people to come and look at this strange sight. Many Cheyennes responded and went over to where the old woman had been standing in order to determine what or who it might be. The lone rider then began making a kind of wailing noise. But the Cheyennes could not decide if he

*In another account, the companion of Plays-With-His-Face was a teenager then named, Creeps-Through-the-Lodges, albeit later known as Four-Dances. [Plain-Feather to Barney Old-Coyote, LBHC Archives, 1959].

was one of their own people or an enemy, and if he was singing a song or crying Some said one thing, some another, while those of a more impetuous nature urged others to mount their ponies and ride out to get a closer look.

The Crow version, however, continues by stating that from their position overlooking the Cheyenne camp, Plays-With-His-Face and Hanging-Raven spied a man easing himself in the brush some way from the lodges still standing, and at once the two Crows galloped their ponies down the ridge slope in an attempt to strike this lone Cheyenne and claim the highest honour by counting the first *dakshey* of the impending conflict. As they careered towards this man, some village occupants saw what was happening and called to their comrade to run. Hanging-Raven was racing far ahead of Plays-With-His-Face, and by following close on the heels of the Cheyenne, allowed himself to be carried into the enemy camp before striking his fleeing foe. Hanging-Raven did manage to return safely and unharmed to the side of his companion, who by then, had already returned to the ridge top. Plays-With-His-Face before this, had himself struck a second Cheyenne discovered outside the camp, but not seen by Hanging-Raven, and so it was Plays-With-His-Face who earned the right to claim the first *dakshey* of the expedition.

After this, Plays-With-His-Face continued to sit his pony on the ridge top in clear view of the Cheyennes, while his companion Hanging-Raven being satisfied with his deed, rode back to where Little-White-Bull and the other decoys were still positioned some distance away. The Cheyennes by then had discerned by the hairstyle and costume of Plays-With-His-Face that he was Crow, and this intelligence was quickly passed from mouth to mouth among the villagers. An excited howl issued from the throats of the young warriors as they psyched themselves up for battle, believing there would be more Crows nearby.

Now among the Cheyennes at this time was a visiting Hidatsa. This man who was fluent in the Crow language, was asked by the Cheyennes to find out from the lone Crow who he was and why he had come to their camp in such a fashion. The Hidatsa thus rode out to the base of the ridge and when within hearing distance, repeated aloud what the Cheyennes wished to know, and to which Plays-With-His-Face replied,

> "…Ho, Striped-Feather-People, when I was away hunting you came to my village with a cloud of warriors and killed my kin-folk and took away my wife making me alone and saddened. I came to your camp to get back my wife, or be killed. But I became afraid and fled, so now I ask you ride after me and kill me, I do not want to live." [10]

When the Hidatsa interpreter relayed these words back to the Cheyennes, a number of warriors were ready to go after Plays-With-His-Face and satisfy his request. But the Hidatsa advised caution, saying that the Crow may not be alone, and it was highly likely there were many Crow enemies waiting out of sight and ready to strike. Such a warning did deter most Cheyennes from going out after the lone Crow, who by then, however, had himself vacated the ridge-top and was no longer in view.

In the meantime, while the Cheyennes dithered among themselves whether to go out or not, the rest of the Crow decoy group led by Little-White-Bull, having moved closer to the Cheyenne village, met up with Plays-With-His-Face whilst in the process of returning to his comrades where he had left them. Having come together again, three of their number continued on towards the enemy camp, while the rest including Plays-With-His-Face, Hanging-Raven and Little-White-Bull remained where they were, and instead waited for their three comrades to bring the Cheyennes in a body towards them.

Also in the Cheyenne camp at this time was the keeper of that tribe's Sacred Medicine Arrows. His name was War-Path-Bear [also known as Feathered-Bear], [11] a wise and respected patriarch among his people. A group of young men, all Cheyenne Bowstring Society warriors who were guardians of the Sacred Arrow lodge and its keeper, after spying the arrival of the three Crows on the crest of another small knoll over-looking the camp, mounted their war-ponies and took up arms, and were about to charge out to see if they could capture the three by themselves. Like the Hidatsa before him, War-Path-Bear, too, advised caution. He urged these young men not to go on their own, but to wait until a large party was assembled and all go out together. Perhaps the three Crows were also decoys, he said, as their Hidatsa friend likewise suspected, and that a formidable Crow force might be in hiding waiting to ambush them in the hills.

Some took heed of the "Arrow" Keeper's words, but twelve young men of the Bowstring Society refused to listen. They whipped up their ponies and rode out to confront the Crows, eager to count their coups upon them.

Seeing these Cheyennes riding towards them, the three Crows vacated the ridge top and were soon racing back to their comrades with the twelve Cheyennes in hot pursuit. When joining again with the rest of their party, all six Crows galloped off together in the direction of the distant gullies, where Sore-Belly and his warriors were waiting.

While the decoys were racing ahead, Plays-With-His-Face who was bringing up the rear, suddenly reined in his pony and turned to face the foe alone. Again Plays-With-His-Face began singing and wailing and at first did not move from his static position. Calmly he sat his horse until the twelve Cheyenne Bowstrings were no more than twenty-five yards distant. Then he suddenly turned his mount around and drumming his heels smartly into its flanks, sped away across the Plain following in the wake of his comrades. The Cheyennes did not stop. Immediately they spurred their own ponies on faster as they continued their pursuit.

Before Plays-With-His-Face had gone much further, it seemed that his horse was tiring and soon the Cheyennes were rapidly gaining ground. When, however the twelve Cheyennes were almost upon him, the Crow's horse found a new spurt of energy and pulled away, leaving them far behind. Thus the chase continued and soon the distance between pursued and pursuers began to shrink yet again. But once more, just as the Cheyennes thought themselves near enough to strike, the Crow's horse again spurted forward and drew ahead, its rider now appearing to lash the animal ferociously across both flanks with his quirt. By this time it was obvious to the pursuers that the lone Crow indeed, was acting as a

122

decoy, endeavouring to lure them into a trap. But thinking they would overtake him in another moment, they refused to relax their speed or give up the chase. The Cheyennes urged their mounts on even faster and were concentrating so much upon their quarry that they paid little attention to where he was leading them, or to what might lay ahead.

As Plays-With-His-Face continued to race across the grasslands, he suddenly jumped from his pony's back and began running alongside the animal with one arm resting on its neck. This caused the Cheyennes to believe that the horse Plays-With-His-Face was riding was now very tired and might soon give out through exhaustion.

By now the open prairie was far behind, as the lone Crow still on foot and only just ahead, led his pursuers through a narrow passage between the two gullies obscured by stands of cottonwood trees on either side.

The Cheyennes were gaining fast. They were almost alongside Plays-With-His-Face when suddenly, up and out of both gullies there simultaneously appeared hundreds of mounted Crows. They shouted "Koo-Koo-Hay" at the tops of their voices, and in an instant, a cloud of Crow missiles had dropped several among the twelve Cheyennes from their saddles. The remaining Cheyennes, still on horseback, bunched themselves together and began battling furiously with those Crows brave enough to charge in amongst them, and for a while, they held the Crows at bay.

In the meantime, a great number of Cheyennes had by then left their camp and were following up their twelve kinsmen for fear of what had already happened. Unfortunately, they were still some distance in the rear, but as they rode they could see rising in the distance to their front a great cloud of dust, and as the Cheyennes later described it,

*"A dark shadow lay over the prairie, indicating that a fierce battle was taking place."* [12]

During the furious melee then going on, several more Cheyennes were killed before the few survivors made a sudden bold dash through the Crow lines, and began racing back the way they had come. The Crows, after scalping and cutting up the dead Cheyennes, took up the pursuit as they could see that the horses of the Cheyenne survivors were quickly tiring. The Crows would have overtaken and killed them all, had it not been that just when the fleeing fugitives were on the verge of annihilation, the main body of Cheyennes from the village finally came up. They immediately went smashing into the charging Crow ranks and a fierce hand to hand tussle ensued. Lance points and iron-bladed tomahawks flashed in the sunlight; bows twanged and the very ground soon became soggy with the blood of those wounded and dying; both of horses and of men.

Sore-Belly was in the forefront of the Crows. He was wearing this day a double-tailed feathered bonnet and as usual, carried a lance which he wielded with deadly effect, toppling several Cheyennes from their saddles. However, being bunched up in the narrow strip of land between the gullies, neither body could manoeuvre effectively. They were severely hampered by a lack of space and in the close fighting, a number of warriors on each side were killed and others severely wounded, and as more Cheyennes came up allowing an additional number of reinforcements to enter the fray, the Crows were halted in their tracks. They were obliged to fall back in order to put some little distance between themselves and the enemy.

It was then that the Crow champion Two-Face reined in his steed. He dismounted and confronted the oncoming Cheyennes alone and on foot, crying aloud that he for one would not flee in face of the foe. This was a suicidal action on Two-Face's part, and the rest of the Crows seeing him thus, all at once turned their ponies around and in a body, charged back into the fight in order to protect their comrade. But the Cheyenne force was too strong to overcome, and although Two-Face survived, the momentum of the Crow onslaught was checked. A great melee again ensued with both horses and riders mixed up together and during which, the warrior Wants-to-Die, who also had paraded around the lodges before starting from the Crow village, now attempted to fulfil his vow of bringing destruction to the Cheyennes so the survivors of Long-Hair's people might cease their grieving. This man lashed his pony with his quirt and galloped unhesitant right in amongst a thick bunch of the enemy, and such was his fury that he alone succeeded in forcing the Cheyennes back, after which he returned to his own ranks, escaping from what had seemed like certain death.

Following this, the Crow Passes-Women then charged into the midst of the enemy, and after him the indomitable Plays-With-His-Face followed suit, whereupon, they were immediately followed by Little-White-Bear, Bear's-Head, Twines-His-Horses-Tail and Sore-Belly, who together led the rest of the Crows in yet another determined charge. This time the Crows did not falter. They turned the Cheyennes and forced them to flee in such a disorganized manner, that the latter's retreat quickly became a rout. The Crows harried them relentlessly, killing and wounding an additional number of Cheyennes in the process. The Crows later said,

> "...The battle was like a whirlwind. There was dust everywhere and the sound of gunfire was heard even after the fight was over and the great dust settled, as our victorious Crows continued to swarm over the battlefield, shooting those of the enemy who were wounded and even those already dead." [13]

One among the fleeing enemy was the same Hidatsa who, earlier that day, had conversed with Plays-With-His-Face when on the ridge top over-looking the Cheyenne camp. This man was mounted on a near-exhausted pony, and was overtaken by a number of Crows who surrounded him and had him at their mercy. In his desperate situation the Hidatsa began pleading with the Crows, calling them friends and cousins in the hope they would spare his life. The Crows asked him why he had been riding with their mortal foes, to which the Hidatsa replied that he was a poor man and not even worthy of killing. For some reason the Crows did not kill him, but showed their utmost contempt by urinating over him and then copulating with him anally to his great humiliation, and when they had finished, they beat him about the buttocks with the flats of their bows before sending him away disgraced, saying that next time there was a fight, he should remain among the women where he belonged. At length, however, the Crows grew tired and gave up the fight, whereupon they made a strategic but organized departure from the scene. In total the Crows had sustained the loss of six warriors dead along with several wounded, and these they carried with them on their journey home. A small number among the discomfited Cheyennes followed at a distance for a few miles before they themselves grew tired; gave up their trek, and returned to their village.

It had not been an over-whelming victory for the Crows, even though they had inflicted more casualties upon the foe than they themselves sustained. Many blamed the earlier killing of the meadow lark by the Crow woman as the reason their great chief's *medicine* had not been fully potent. Nevertheless, after the warriors arrived at their home camp, the event was celebrated with gusto. It was considered their people's first great feat of arms since the disaster attending Long-Hair's village the previous summer.

As for the Cheyennes, after returning to their own camp from whence they came, the women relatives of those who had not returned, went out to the site of the battle with pony-drags and collected together the remains of their dead. Eight of the original party of Bowstring Cheyennes were among those killed and had been cut up in a most horrible manner. Some were missing their head, whilst others were without arms, legs, hands and feet. The body parts were scattered over a wide area and the women spent many hours searching for all the pieces in order to carry them home. All eight had been servants of the Cheyenne's Sacred Arrow lodge, and it was to that place that their body parts were first taken. There the limbs were put together as best could be, after which each corpse was wrapped in a robe and placed on a raised pallet within a specially enlarged tepee erected specifically for the repose of the dead.

The Cheyennes today admit they then did a terrible thing in the eyes of Cheyenne law. But the relatives of those killed, they say, were wrought with anger and grief which knew no bounds. Some relatives of the eight dead Cheyennes had Crow captives taken during the attack on Long-Hair's village. These captives had since been living in their lodges as adopted members of the tribe. But notwithstanding this, a number of Cheyennes dragged eight of the captives over to the burial tepee, and slew them without mercy by clubbing them to death. They then lay the Crow corpses around the base of the lodge, stacking them one upon the other as if they were logs, commonly used to keep tepee covers down in the advent of strong winds. Not long after this the Cheyennes moved away from the region, as was their custom when blood had been spilt roundabout. They thus left the Crow bodies to the mercy of the elements and to tooth and claw of the prairie creatures.

It must be said that many among the Cheyennes even then, condemned the slaughter of the captives, as it was the custom after a prisoner had been taken into a lodge and nourished, that he or she was then accepted into Cheyenne society as a family member. To kill such a person thereafter, was considered an act of homicide within the tribe, and it is further said that the next time the Sacred Arrow bundle was opened in order to renew its contents, specks of blood were found on the Sacred Arrow flights themselves. The blood, it was believed, of the murdered Crow captives.

125

Many years later during the so-called Fitzpatrick Treaty gathering of 1851, when Crows and Cheyennes among other tribes, came together at the behest of the American Government and made formal pacts with each other, which in some cases, lasted at least five years, the Crows and Cheyennes discussed past battles between them. It was then that the Crow chief Big-Shadow pointed out to the Cheyennes the Crow warrior Hanging-Raven, the same who had been the companion of Plays-With-His-Face, and one of those who had led the twelve young Cheyenne warriors into the trap at the time of the fight in question. The Cheyennes were surprised to see a very old man, his body painted red all over and wearing a necklace of raven feathers with their tips cut off, signifying he had cut the throats of his enemies. The Cheyennes welcomed him among them, saying they had waited many years to speak with him. They asked whether the lone Crow on the ridge top had been singing or crying, as it had caused much debate among the Cheyennes, some declaring that he sang and others that he cried, and since then, they had craved a true answer to the question.

The old Crow warrior replied freely, saying the man they were referring to was Plays-With-His-Face and he had been doing both things. He had been crying, Hanging-Raven said, for those of his people killed by Cheyennes and Lakota during the attack on Long-Hair's village, but had also been singing a war song for revenge. Plays-With-His-Face himself by that date had long since died, having committed suicide after contracting smallpox in 1833, and of which we will speak where appropriate.

All being said, this 1821 Sore-Belly inspired attack on the Cheyennes had, primarily, been conducted for revenge and, certainly, it showed the Crows had not been cowed by their tribe's earlier defeat at Cheyenne hands. Indeed, Sore-Belly had made it known that the Crows were still a force to be reckoned with, whose warriors could and would take the offensive against any and all their foes, even deep into the enemy's own domain.

$$- 0 - 0 - 0 - 0 - 0 - 0 - 0 - 0 - 0 - 0 - 0 - 0 - 0 -$$

## CHAPTER 12.

## "CLEANING UP" ON THE LAKOTA and ARROW-HEAD'S BAND.

When Sore-Belly returned from the aforementioned fight with the Cheyenne, many Crow warriors were still clamouring for war. They requested him to lead them yet again into the very country of their foes, and thus, soon after his triumphant return, the great chief capitulated to their pleas and turned his attention east, intending to exact overdue vengeance upon the Lakota for their part in the carnage wrought upon Long-Hair's people on Otter Creek.

So it happened near the end of summer 1821, Sore-Belly set out once again at the head of a large force of warriors, now to attack the Lakota in their own domain. This time, however, the expedition would not only seek revenge, but, additionally, would endeavour to take as many women and children captive as possible, with a view to their being adopted into the Apsaalooka Nation.

It is said that Sore-Belly led his warriors deep into Lakota country, which then embraced the area between the lower Cheyenne and Bad [Teton] Rivers east of the Black Hills and west of the middle course of the Missouri.

Unfortunately, few details concerning the actual fight are recalled in Crow oral tradition or in the written sources. We are told only that Sore-Belly`s party, then including a sub-chief named Grizzly-Bear, surprised an Oglala village; utterly destroyed it; killed a good number of Lakota men-folk and took many women and children captive. In addition, the Crows obtained hundreds of Lakota ponies, along with all the tepees and personal belongings and other paraphernalia which they carried away as booty. More important, perhaps, was that the victors set free a number of Crow captives found in the camp and who were joyfully reunited with their kinfolk. One account states further, that several hundred Lakota prisoners were taken, which may indeed have been the case. [1]

Certainly, there was much excitement when the victorious party returned home. The Crows themselves had again suffered only few casualties, and victory dances were held for many weeks thereafter.

There was at this time, one Crow warrior whose mother it was had been burned to death in the allied camp in the aftermath of the destruction of Long-Hair`s people; and still he craved for vengeance. This man had learned the fate of his mother from Crow captives recently rescued. In response, he singled out a young Lakota maiden and declared he would torture her to death to appease the spirit of his mother. The torture of prisoners was not usual among Crows, who always preferred to adopt a captive into the tribe. But on this occasion as the warrior in question had the backing of a large body of friends and family, the chiefs only tried to dissuade him with words, lest civil strife broke out in camp and Crow blood was spilt by fellow Crows.

Try as the chiefs did, the bereaved man would not be turned from his resolve. He took hold of the victim, and after calmly leading her to where a crowd of toothless old Crow women were huddled, hurled her into their midst. In their cruel and unbridled frenzy the old women - whose fingers on both hands were missing many joints lopped off over the years as one by one, close relatives had fallen under the scalping knives of their enemies - now vented their vengeful emotions without respite. They tore the clothes from the captive's body; beat her with sticks and pricked her with the tips of their knives. They then heaped filth and human excrement upon her as she stood naked and shamed; frozen to the spot with fear. The man at length stepped up to her; drew his knife from its scabbard and began stabbing the poor unfortunate about the body until his lust for vengeance was sated. The poor woman, though, was yet alive and as the man departed, the old hags resumed their torments, by cutting strips of skin and flesh from the unfortunate's limbs until, *"...death came to her relief."* [2] This regrettable episode, say the Crows, was one of the few times they had ever tortured a captive once he or she had been brought into the village, and was merely an overt expression of revenge by those who themselves, had lost close relatives to the Lakota. The success of the expedition had, however, achieved an additional degree of revenge for the destruction of Long-Hair`s village the previous summer.

At this date, even though all Crow clans again appeared to be united, there still remained the aforementioned dissident group known as the "Dried-Out-Furs," or simply, "Arrow-Head`s Band" after the name of the chief who led them.

Some years previously Arrow-Head, when a leading chief of the Treacherous Lodge clan, had been in serious rivalry with Chief One-Heart of the Whistling-Waters clan. Several years prior to the destruction of Long-Hair`s village, the long-term antagonism between the two chiefs had reached a climax and as a result of continuing disagreements, the followers of both had taken up weapons and faced each other in battle array ready to engage in mortal combat. Fortunately, the headmen of the other clans present intervened, and after much persuasion, managed to avert civil bloodshed between them. But hereafter there grew an even greater schism which split the two chiefs and their respective adherents asunder, and Arrow-Head and One-Heart would never again be reconciled. It was not long after this altercation that Chief Arrow-Head, along with eighty-eight lodges of clan followers, actually moved away from the main body of the tribe and were referred to as the Dried-Out-Furs band, owing to their preferred location far south from traditional Crow country where beaver skins and other prime pelts were kept moist and supple, not drying out too quickly as they did in the heat of the southern country. For a number of years Arrow-Head`s band roamed and hunted as a separate body between the North and South Forks of the Platte River and even further south throughout present-day Colorado and Arkansas. During this time, Arrow-Head and his people experienced ills and fortunes peculiar to themselves, and only occasionally did they return north to pay brief visits to their kinfolk in the Yellowstone and Big Horn country.

As time passed, Arrow-Head`s secessionists had very few women among them, having since been joined by a significant number of warriors who had lost wives and children during the catastrophe attending Long-Hair`s people. Indeed, it is recalled in Crow oral tradition that after being joined by these new arrivals, Arrow-Head had held council with his followers, and during which it was decided that from then on, they would fight with all peoples they met and either become rich in war honours, stolen ponies and captives, or; if fate decreed otherwise, then be completely "rubbed out" in the process.

As noted previously, Sore-Belly when a younger man, had for a short while rode with this band, although no account of the battles Arrow-Head`s people fought are today recalled in Crow oral tradition. What is remembered is that during their absence from the North Country, they were accustomed to loiter about the upper courses of the Arkansas, Red and Canadian rivers of north-western Texas and Oklahoma. At times they traded with and raided the Spanish and Pueblo settlements in what now are the states of Arizona and New Mexico, and it is likely that at least a part of this band, were those responsible for hostile acts upon one and another party of white men prior to the early 1830s. We do know, however, from contemporary documented sources, that Arrow-Head`s people were particularly active in raiding a conglomerate of tribal bands commonly known as the "Trading Indians." These last under the titular head of an Arapaho chief named Bear`s-Tooth, comprised an admixture of peoples including Arapaho, Kiowa, Kiowa-Apache [Gattacka], Comanche, Oto and Cheyenne. They, too, generally roamed the country about the headwaters of the Arkansas and Red River close to the eastern foothills of the Rocky Mountains. They owned vast herds of ponies and mules, being alternatively in friendly and hostile contact with the Pueblo towns and Spanish settlements further south, and from where most of their stock was obtained either by trade or by theft.

In their turn Arrow-Head`s Crows after raiding the Trading Indians, passed their surplus stock on to either the Shoshoni and others at the latter`s trading fairs on Green River, and also to companies of white men on the headwaters of the North Platte near South Pass. On the other hand, Arrow-Head`s band itself lost many animals to raiding Blackfoot-speaking tribes and to the Atsina, Assiniboine, Cheyenne and Lakota, and, moreover, to the Pawnee, who were then closer in proximity to the North and South Platte regions. What surplus animals Arrow-Head`s band did manage to retain, they bartered to the Mandan and Hidatsa on the Missouri in exchange for guns and ammunition [commodities unobtainable from the Mexicans], along with luxury goods such as corn and vegetables and the like. It was then, probably Arrow-Head`s Crow band of dissidents which in the winter of 1821 /`22, was encamped somewhere along the North Platte River close to the Rocky Mountains at South Pass. From there they sent out raiding parties against the camps of the above mentioned Trading Indians.

At the time of which we speak, a party of white men led by Colonel Hugh Glen and Major Jacob Fowler were in the process of exploring the Upper Arkansas River country. These white men had made friendly contact with the Trading Indians and among whom they had chosen to reside for several weeks. Major Fowler kept a journal of the party`s day to day progress and recorded that it was November 19th, 1821, that his party first arrived at the Trading Indian`s camp, then situated on the north side of the Arkansas not far from present-day Nepesta in Pueblo County, Colorado. Only five days prior to the white men`s arrival, Fowler noted, the Trading Indians had a big fight with Crows near the mountains and in the event, the Arapaho and their allies had lost nine men killed and the Crows fifteen. While still with the Indians on December 12th, the report continues, a war-party of Iatans [Comanche or Ute?] came in, returning from a raid on a Crow village then located on the Platte below the mountains, some five nights travel from the Arkansas. [3]

The following day [December 13th] three men from Fowler`s party whilst hunting buffalo near the mountains, met thirteen Crow Indians driving two-hundred horses before them recently stolen from the Trading Indian`s camp. The Crows took the white men prisoners, but only, they said, to prevent them giving information to the Trading Indians of their whereabouts. They thereafter escorted the white men back to the river [Arkansas?] which was then frozen over, and told them that the rest of their Nation [e.g. Arrow-Head`s band?] was on the Platte with another group of white men about thirty-five in number, and with whom the Crows were on very good terms. They added that they themselves had left their own village on the aforesaid river about ten nights earlier, and that it would take them three nights to return there with their stolen herd. Before leaving, these Crows then took from the white men all their powder, ball and blankets, but gave them in return nine of their stolen horses. While this exchange was being made and the rest of the Crow party had already started north and were in the act of crossing the river on the ice driving the stolen herd before them, a war-party of Arapaho suddenly came up, evidently in pursuit of the thieves. Overtaking the Crows, a battle immediately ensued and during which, the Arapaho retrieved most of their horses. The Crows did manage to escape for the most part intact still with some of the stolen stock in tow, but the white men meanwhile, as soon as the fight started, had abandoned all their spare horses and; according to the Major`s report, fled in the opposite direction.

Glen and Fowler`s party at length, left the Trading Indian`s village and continued their travels. One month later on January 17th [1822], they were ensconced in winter quarters on the site where the town of Pueblo, Colorado was later built. That night a Crow war-party on foot with two pack horses in tow and thus on a horse-stealing raid, entered the white men`s camp.

The Indians appeared friendly and some among them recognized the three men they had made temporary prisoners the month before. These Crows told their hosts they had successfully extricated themselves from the fight with the Arapaho at that time, and, in fact, were on their way to war with the Trading Indians again. The Crows were fed by the whites and given tobacco, after which the Crows, *"sang a song before they all lay down to sleep."* [3]

Come morning, the Crow chief asked the whites for more tobacco and also powder and lead for his warriors, and receiving what he wanted, he presented a horse to the Major as payment. The Crow chief informed the whites that the Arapaho had left the country and gone south, and that his own party after their intended raid, would return to the river further north where another group of white men – now sixty-five in number - were again trading with his Nation [band?]. The Crows then began their departure from the camp, although as they went they attempted to pilfer anything they could lay their hands on. This infuriated the white men who snatched up their arms and stood ready for a fight. The tension was finally eased, and the Crows went on their way seemingly still in good humour. It was only after the Crows had left that the white men discovered several important things missing from the camp, but by then it was too late to retrieve them. Evidently the Glen and Fowler party gained some satisfaction for their losses when on January 28th, the very same Crow war-party returned to the white men`s camp. The Crows apparently had been unable to steal any horses on their venture, as they were still on foot and they informed the whites that in a recent fight with the Arapaho, the latter had lost five warriors and the Crows three. Again the Crow chief begged for powder, ball and tobacco, and received enough to his apparent appeasement. But once again as the Crows were making their departure, they attempted to pilfer all and sundry from the camp. This time, though, Major Fowler was most firm and managed to force the Indians to continue on their way empty handed.

Such then was the situation between Crows and white men in the southern country, although while Glen and Fowler had been associating with Bear Tooth`s conglomerate of Trading Indians on the Arkansas, other parties of white men had been accommodating Arrow-Head`s Crow band on the Platte, and additional groups of white men were trapping Crow country in the Snake River, Yellowstone and Big Horn districts of the Upper Missouri much further north. At the same time, raiders from each of the Blackfoot-speaking tribes and their allies the Atsina, were constantly harassing Crow camps and hunting parties. In early May 1822, a thirty-three strong Piegan war band led by a chief named Iron-Shirt, successfully raided a Crow camp on the Yellowstone some sixty miles east of present-day Billings, while in November, the Hudson`s Bay trader Donald Mackenzie when undertaking his so-called Bow River expedition, was told that Crow Indians had recently destroyed five Pikuni families on Belly River in central Alberta, Canada. In December following, an Atsina party returned home victorious from a hostile venture against Crows south of the Missouri, and in addition, the American-Horse winter-count records for the same year that a Lakota chief named The-Dog, stole seventy horses from the Crows. White men, too, were apt to suffer from the same hostile expeditions against the Crows. Such had been the case soon after the aforementioned Iron-Shirt episode, when a Blood Blackfoot war band comprising thirty-eight warriors out against Crows, stumbled across a party of white trappers of the Missouri Fur Company and killed fourteen of the latter, including their leaders Michael Immell and Robert Jones .

In spring the following year [1823], a number of deserters from a brigade of trappers employed by the Hudson`s Bay Company which had been ensconced among Long-Hair`s Mountain band the previous winter, were attacked and robbed by Crows, it is said, but who actually belonged to Chief Arrow-Head`s Dried-Out-Furs people, and later, the same trapper party on its way to Fort Atkinson on the lower Missouri was attacked by Cheyennes . Having said this, another two trapper brigades belonging to the Missouri Fur Company and led by William Ashley and Andrew Henry respectively, were themselves then in close contact with both Mountain and Paunch Crow bands in the Big Horn and Yellowstone country. Generally speaking, Ashley`s and Henry`s men got on well enough with the Crows, but were always at loggerheads with the Blackfoot. As a result, they were subject to clashing with Blackfoot and Atsina war-parties which infested those regions during the summer months in their quest for Crow scalps and horses.

In late June, 1823, Ashley`s trappers fought off an attack from a large Blackfoot war-party on its way to raid a Crow village ten miles distant on the Yellowstone and several white trappers were killed. In July, another Blackfoot war-party out looking for Crows, attacked eleven trappers belonging to Henry`s brigade and another four whites were killed. Both events had arisen due to the continuous warfare being waged between Crows and their neighbours, which encouraged bands of Blackfoot, Atsina, Assiniboine, Lakota and Cheyennes to cross the Upper Missouri country searching for their inveterate foes. Any white men unlucky enough to run afoul of such bands, were apt to suffer the consequences of their wrath. Sometimes a small band of Crows would remain close to one or other of the trapper brigades, as in summer this year when Crows, among whom was their adopted hero Edward Rose, hovered around Ashley`s men as additional protection from a host of Cheyenne enemies then roaming the region.

Thus the main Crow bands led by Sore-Belly and Long-Hair remained at peace with the white men, and were vigorously conducting their own hostile forays against each of the enemy tribes around them. A more successful venture than that recently conducted against the Lakota regarding the taking of captives by Sore-Belly`s followers after the destruction of Long-Hair`s village, was said by Lieutenant James H. Bradley to have occurred during this particular period, although in Bradley`s account precise details of the event are lacking.

We are informed merely by Bradley that a large Crow war-party assaulted a Blackfoot camp; killed a good number and took many women and children captive. After returning to their home base, the Crow chief - who Bradley does not name - attempted to count the number of captives taken, but when reaching seven-hundred he gave up the task in frustration. This account further states that among the Crows at that time foreign prisoners probably numbered one-thousand in total, although it is not made clear if this number should also include captives taken from the Cheyenne and Lakota during earlier battles with those tribes. Nevertheless, Bradley's version does confirm that many of the female captives - several hundred in number - were immediately wed to Crow men who were without wives, and in such a way the population of the Crow Nation was expanded at a single stroke. It seems, though, that this particular Crow fight with the Blackfoot as mentioned by Bradley, actually applies to a later engagement between the two tribes which took place in 1824, and will be spoken of where appropriate, although it has earlier been noted that in November, 1822, the trader Donald Mackenzie recorded that Crow Indians had wiped out a small camp of Pikuni lodges on Belly River, and, perhaps, this was the actual event later confused by Bradley with the fight of 1824.

It was due to this and other victories that Sore-Belly`s position as Head war-chief of the Apsaalooka was recognized and accepted by all. As a consequence, his personal following and popularity increased to such extent, that even the great Chief Long-Hair`s influence became somewhat curtailed. Certainly this was true as regards Long-Hair`s once unilateral decision making for the Nation as a whole. As a result of Sore-Belly`s newly acclaimed status, Long-Hair himself, although still recognized as *"Ashakee,"** was, henceforward, often over-ruled, and a dangerous degree of rivalry began to grow between the respective followers of both. This is not to say there was any serious friction between the two great chiefs themselves, although in order to subdue the people's propensity for indulging in civil strife, in 1823 Sore-Belly took his followers north into the Judith Basin district, and joining the Paunch Crow band, they and Sore-Belly`s people, became known among themselves and to others of their Nation as *"Binnesslipele,"* i. e. "Dung-on-the-Banks" due to their habitat on the north side of the Yellowstone, although more comonally they were known as River Crows, and the term "Paunch Indians" became obsolete.. From that time on this newly-formed band remained somewhat aloof from their Mountain cousins, in so much, as throughout most of the year they roamed as an independent division led by their own Head Chief Sore-Belly. They did come south at intervals, albeit for brief periods, either by accident or design, but usually in order to conduct certain religious rites with the rest of the

*Literally, "Owner of Camp," that is, `Chief of Chiefs.`

Nation, such as combined Sun-dances and the planting of the Nation's Sacred Tobacco Seeds, and at other times, simply to join their southern brethren in order to socialize with one another.

Rarely, though, did the River and Mountain Crows and the Kicked-in-the-Belly band, hereafter, conduct combined hostile expeditions against mutual foes, notwithstanding that certain members of all three bands might move back and forth between each other's camps as the fancy took them.

At regular intervals when north of the Yellowstone, Sore-Belly and his band would pay extended visits to their Hidatsa relatives on Knife River lower down the Missouri and sometimes, cross to the west side of the Rockies in order to visit Sore-Belly's Flathead relatives, and trade horses from the Nez-Perce when they were not at war with those peoples. As time went by, Sore-Belly became even more popular within the tribe so that by 1824; when around thirty-one years old, he was elected to serve as joint Head chief along with Long-Hair of the entire Apsaalooka Nation.

By then, it is said, his war deeds were so numerous that like the esteemed Long-Hair, they could not be counted. Neither did any one man command such singular influence over the Crow people both in times of peace and in war. Sore-Belly had achieved this by earning the unanimous respect of the Nation who had overall faith in his judgment. Always he took personal responsibility rather than delegate it to the tribal council alone, although it is true to say that he was mindful of the council's advice at all times.

Even his enemies knew well his fame and of those white men who made his acquaintance, although some thought him a disagreeable character; abrupt, pretentious and surly, most others with whom he met spoke of him as a friend; hospitable and accommodating, whilst acknowledging his ability as a brave and fearless fighter, possessing a natural gift of leadership comparable to any in what might be termed, perhaps, the more sophisticated world.

As regards Chief Long-Hair, he had always encouraged his people to keep on friendly terms with white men in order to trade with them, which he foresaw as necessary to enable his people to hold off the Lakota, Cheyennes and Blackfoot who were ever his people's antagonists. This involved many of the Crow men folk spending long uncomfortable periods in the pursuit of trapping beaver and other fur-bearing animals, solely for the white man's trade; and was an employment that went against the very grain of a Crow Indian's philosophy. Sore-Belly on the contrary was not so accommodating. He did not personally advocate open war with the white men as did the Arickara, Blackfoot and Atsina, but does seem to have often turned a blind eye when members of his band deliberately committed unfriendly acts upon individual parties of trappers. In the main these acts took the form of horse stealing raids, and when sometimes one or two Crows or white men were killed during such altercations, it invariably involved Chief Arrow-Head's band of dissidents who had no allegiance to any but themselves.

Sore-Belly overall, proved to be more of a `Iilapaache` i.e. 'friend' to the whites rather than their enemy, for like Long-Hair he knew, of course - even if his rank and file warriors did not - that with an adequate supply of firearms, powder and ball on hand, his people could always defend themselves when need be, and could carry offensive warfare deep into the enemy's own domain. Certainly under Sore-Belly`s warrior leadership, important Crow victories were not only gained in the very countries of the Blackfoot, Atsina and Assiniboine, but also in the Lakota and Cheyenne domains to the east, and when occasion arose, in both Arapaho and Shoshoni lands to the south and west respectively.

As a tactician and defender of his people Sore-Belly had no peer, and almost unique among Indians, he placed guards around his camp night and day to give immediate warning of approaching enemies. He personally organized and led grand hostile expeditions, taking whole villages by surprise and hitting them hard. His forces, as Joe Medicine Crow graphically described it,

> *"Cleaned up on the Cheyenne, Siouxs [sic] and Blackfoots [sic] several times."* [4]

At one time, Joe continued, a Crow war-party led by Sore-Belly, entirely wiped out a Piegan Blackfoot camp of eighty lodges, and at other times he and his warriors wreaked havoc upon the Atsina and Assiniboine, and even upon the Shoshoni and Nez-Perce west of the Rocky Mountains.

Indeed, it is said that unlike his contemporaries both friend and foe, Sore-Belly always took sole command of the more important military ventures undertaken by Crow war-parties. He saw to it also that his warriors were always well equipped with good mounts and weapons. These he would personally inspect from time to time, and would often actually exclude certain members whose accoutrements did not come up to standard.

He meticulously planned his military operations, taking adequate precautions in order to protect his warriors from counter attack and to minimize his own casualties. According to current Crow oral tradition, he was always victorious against his people's enemies and throughout the duration of his chieftainship, the Crows became the most formidable opponents on the Northern Plains. Whenever a Crow party suffered a significant defeat, it was Sore-Belly who sought revenge rather than the relatives of those slain as had been the Crow custom before his time, and he deliberately made it known across the Plains that any attack upon his people would not go un-avenged, but would be reciprocated in kind.

Again in the ilk of Long-Hair, Sore-Belly was quiet and reserved in his personal manner and demeanour. He spoke few words, but what he did say was with force and eloquence and invariably had the desired effect. He was not known to personally boast of his own achievements, neither, though, did he often join in the tribe`s communal religious rites, and only rarely did he invoke his personal "Spirit Helper" in public. Rather he retired alone into the hills whenever he felt the need to do so.

In stature he was once described as, *"...A fine, tall man with a pleasing countenance."* [5] While the Jesuit Missionary Father Pierre DeSmet when writing in 1854, said of Sore-Belly, who he termed Rotten-Belly from his Lakota name of *"Tezi-Goe,"*

"...He was as much renowned for his bravery in war as for his wisdom in council, and the patriotic love that he testified to the whole [Crow] Nation." [6]

Sore-Belly`s physique, it is said, was well proportioned and when arrayed in his war clothes he presented an imposing example of native splendour. His hair always hung loose but was clipped fairly short over the temples, whilst that over the forehead was in the form of a roach, stiffened with white or yellow clay, the rest left hanging down his back. When in battle, he wore a beautiful eagle-feathered bonnet which sported a double tail and touched the ground behind him as he walked. His war-shirt and leggings were fringed with the scalps of his enemies and even his buffalo robe, upon which were painted his war exploits in simple stick-like drawings, was edged with human hair; a singular mark of distinction indicating his great prowess in battle. When in camp, he carried with him a tame eagle usually perched on one shoulder or on his left arm and this, he professed, was the personification of his personal *medicine* helper, `Thunder` itself.

One sacred object which he did display and employ in public, usually as an aid to his prophesying abilities and to assure success in his ventures, was a certain buffalo hide *medicine* shield. Emblazoned upon its cover was depicted a human-like figure etched in red with a black outline. This figure has been said by some to represent the moon that had appeared in human-like form to Sore-Belly during one of his many vision quests and personally gave him the design on the shield. The figure itself which was crudely executed with exceptionally large ears, seems, moreover, to have represented either an androgynous or conversely, neuter personage, being neither male nor female and thus symbolizing creation itself [made manifest by the moon] and the continuity of Mother Nature's world. Some other Crow informants declare that the figure represented the personage of "Thrown-in-the-Spring," who indeed, is one of a pair of `twin` culture heroes in the mythology of both the Hidatsa and Crows, while yet another explanation states that the figure depicted the `Thunder Being,` which as previously noted, had also appeared to the chief during one of his numerous vision quests in material form and was his personal Spirit helper. Attached to the shield cover obscuring part of the left side of the painted figure, was the dried head and body of a crane in partial wrapping of red flannel, while tied to the upper right corner was a single eagle feather, and at the lower right corner a deer tail, these also partially wrapped in red flannel.

Before starting upon any large-scale or important hostile expedition, Sore-Belly would first climb to the top of a pile of buffalo chips, and from that position, would cast the aforesaid shield along the ground in such a way, that it would roll on its edge wobbling from side to side until it finally keeled over and lay flat. If the painted side of the shield then faced upwards, the success of the proposed venture was guaranteed, but if face down, it was an omen for failure and the venture would invariably be abandoned. This shield was still in use within the tribe long after Sore-Belly`s demise. Another personal accoutrement of the great chief was a particularly large mountain goat horn [Big Horn sheep], and this he was in the habit of blowing when in camp, in order to arouse the people whenever something of note was about to happen.

Winona Plenty-Hoops added that Sore-Belly's sole purpose in life, as head war chief of the Nation, was to protect the people and to make better their existence. At the same time, he made the people strong in order to survive and flourish in their own right whilst residing in a constantly hostile, always threatening environment, surrounded as they were by numerous powerful tribes whose sole vocation, it seemed, was to obliterate all Crows from the Earth. Winona also declared that as a symbolic gesture, the chief often wore his hair loose and unkempt, for, he said, he was constantly in mourning for his people.

The American Fur Company trader Edwin Denig, in a short biography of Sore-Belly whom he calls, Rotten-Belly, had this to say of the chief;

> "...Other things aided this man [Sore-Belly] on his road to the chieftainship. He had large and rich connections, was considered a prophet or medicine man, one who could obtain supernatural aid in his operations. He made no show of his *medicine*, no parade of sacrifices, or smokings [sic], no sign or ceremonies, but silently and alone he prayed to the thunder for assistance. In his general conduct he was not an agreeable man, but rather of a quiet, surly disposition. He spoke but little, but that in a tone of command. His great superiority over others consisted in decision, action, and an utter disregard for the safety of his own person..." [7]

A particular story as told to Colonel A. B. Welch by an old Hidatsa informant in 1923, has all the hall-marks of applying to another episode in the life of Sore-Belly. Likely the event had occurred in the early 1820s, although the Crows are not specifically mentioned. The story tells of a time when a large party of Chippewa went on foot to attack the Hidatsa and brought with them a number of women and children in order to carry off the plunder they expected to take from the Hidatsa village. The Hidatsa then had a great chief and medicine man among them who could do extraordinary things, and also apparently, they had prior word that enemies were coming against them. The aforesaid chief decided to go out and meet the enemy before they got too close to the village and at a certain place on the prairie, he secreted two-hundred of his warriors on one side of a draw, and another one-hundred among a stand of trees nearby. At that time the enemy were still some distance away, so at night the chief took up his *medicine* shield and standing on top of a pile of buffalo chips, he rolled the shield along the ground. As the shield rolled a line of fire appeared, and after chanting a few sacred songs, the chief rolled the shield again and once more, another line of fire was created. The chief told his warriors that no one should cross the line of fire, for if they did they would surely be slain in the forthcoming battle. There was one Hidatsa, however, who disregarded the chief's words and actually crossed the line of fire.

The next morning the Chippewa appeared in force. They spied the hundred warriors among the trees and charged in to attack them. At this point the chief with the Hidatsa rolled his shield, and thus again created a line of fire. He then said to those around him,

> "None of us shall be killed this day, except He who last night disobeyed my order and stepped across the flames." [8]

The chief then led the concealed two-hundred warriors forward into the thick of the enemy and in the great bloody melee which followed, the Hidatsa were victorious. Many of the enemy were killed and scalped, and a large number of Chippewa women and children were carried off by the victors. Only one Hidatsa was slain, and this was the same man who had defied the powerful *medicine* of the chief.

The mention of the *medicine* shield being rolled along the ground; the pile of buffalo chips; the singing of sacred songs along with the prophecy that only one man among them would be killed, are, of course, each compatible with the Crow chief Sore-Belly when invoking his own powerful *medicine* on other occasions. It is likely therefore, that Crows were included among the Hidatsa during the above mentioned fight and further, that the chief referred to was none other than Sore-Belly himself.

There are indeed, many instances to be found in Crow oral tradition and recorded in the written documents which attest to the strategic ability and warrior prowess of Sore-Belly, although it seems to be that it was only after the disastrous allied Lakota and Cheyenne attack on Long-Hair`s village in the summer of 1820, that Sore-Belly really begun his illustrious career as head war-chief of his Nation. In this role as earlier noted, his first act had been to bring the bulk of Crow people together again as a cohesive fighting body, and instil in them the martial capacity not only to match their foes, but to outdo them both in cunning and in valour when on the field of combat. True it is that all the Northern Plains Tribes came to know and fear the name of *"Alapooish;"* or Sore-Belly, –the great war-chief of the Apsaalooka.

– 0 – 0 – 0 – 0 – 0 – 0 – 0 – 0 – 0 – 0 – 0 – 0 – 0 – 0 –


## CHAPTER. 13.


## DESTROYING THE BLOOD AND PIKUNI COLUMN.


For many years past, Crow war-bands and hunting groups had sporadically roamed throughout the Judith Basin north of the Musselshell. But so also had various Blackfoot-speaking tribes along with the Atsina, Assiniboine, Flathead and Shoshoni. In truth, the area had been regarded as a kind of no-man`s land; a hunting ground and war ground, wherein all parties travelled at their peril. Now, though, the situation had changed. When any of the aforesaid tribes came into that country, they invariably found Sore-Belly`s River Crow band firmly entrenched and in formidable force.

Such a position understandably, brought Sore-Belly and his River Crows into more regular conflict with all the above mentioned peoples, each of whom were now within easier traveling distance to Crow camps. The Blackfoot especially, vehemently resented any permanent Crow presence in lands through which several Blackfoot tribes had previously roamed at will.

Numerically speaking, the overall population of the Blackfoot tribes combined, far outnumbered both the Mountain and River Crows together, so that never did the latter claim exclusive right to those hunting grounds between the Judith and Missouri Rivers. One must assume that even with the great war-chief Sore-Belly at their head, the River Crows still only warily entered the buffalo country north of the Musselshell, but rather, they remained further south between that river and the Yellowstone.

Having said this, and notwithstanding their being almost constantly engaged in deadly conflicts with the Blackfoot and other enemies to the north, west and south, when between the Yellowstone and Musselshell the *Binnesslipele,* i.e. River Crows, with little short of three-hundred lodges comprising between five-hundred and six-hundred fighting men, could still usually hold their own against all who came against them, and under the leadership of Sore-Belly, they did become the undisputed "Keepers" of that country.

Nevertheless, the Blackfoot continued raiding Crows without respite, and the following years are replete with references to hostile encounters between Crows and one or another band of Blackfoot-speaking enemies.

According to the memoirs of the Hudson's Bay trader, John E. Harriot, it had been during the winter of 1822 / 23 that a seven-hundred strong war-band of combined Atsina and Siksika [Blackfoot-Proper], had a big battle with a large body of Crows somewhere near the mouth of the Musselshell. As a result, the Atsina and Siksika were sorely defeated with the loss of many warriors.

In late summer the following year, 1824, according to another Hudson's Bay trader named John Rowand, an even larger war-band of Atsina this time in company with Blood Blackfoot, had an important fight with Crows and in the event, one-hundred and seventy Bloods and Atsina were lost. This last-named episode is likely the same referred to in Crow oral tradition when Chief Sore-Belly, at the head of a large mixed River and Mountain Crow war band along with a number of Shoshoni allies, severely defeated a large combined force of Pikunies, Small Robes and Bloods, of which the Crows killed many and took captive a great number of women and children.

The affair was certainly an important episode in Sore-Belly`s career, and consolidated Sore-Belly`s high standing among his people as paramount war-chief of the entire Apsaalooka Nation. The event is also compatible with the previously mentioned victory of Sore-Belly over the Blackfoot as noted by Lieutenant James Bradley, and likewise, with an account of a battle narrated by the `White Blackfoot` Hugh Munroe to his biographer James Willard Schultz late in the nineteenth century, only that Schultz wrongly dated the event as occurring in 1816. A composite account of this important episode in Crow history is as follows.

It had happened after the combined Crow bands had concluded their annual religious festivals somewhere along the middle course of the Big Horn, that

Sore-Belly led his entire River Crow band - along with a contingent of fifty lodges of Chief Long-Hair's Mountain people - north across the Yellowstone. They then continued further north into the Plains of the Judith River district above the Musselshell where they intended to procure buffalo meat and hides to sustain them through the winter. At that time of year, buffalo were numerous in the lush prairies of the north Montana country, and the Crows proposed to remain in the area several weeks.

For one or two years prior to the episode in question, the *Bikkaashe* – the Grass-Lodges, i.e. Shoshoni, specifically those known as Eastern or Sheep-eater bands, but who were buffalo hunting Plains dwellers part of the year, were then at peace with the Mountain Crows. The Shoshoni had also made another tentative agreement with the River Crows, which allowed both peoples to again hunt at will in the country embracing the Upper Missouri and adjacent to the Musselshell. The Shoshoni, though, usually kept close to the eastern foothills of the Rocky Mountains, while the River Crows remained further east.

Most likely, this latest Crow - Shoshoni pact had been brought about due to the persuasions of American Fur Company traders, who had considered it conducive to their own interests in bringing the River Crows and Shoshoni together in peace, and thereby relieve somewhat, pressure exerted upon that Company by warring Indian parties crisscrossing the country, which if not actually hostile towards white trappers, they often obstructed the latter in pursuing their chosen employment.

Invariably at this period when Crows and Shoshoni did come together, they organized combined war-parties to go in search of enemy camps from which they ran off droves of horses in a night or dawn-time raid. At the same time, however, any of their own war or hunting parties were at risk of being attacked by roving Blackfoot, perhaps to be cut off and annihilated if the opportunity presented itself to do so. For the Bloods, Pikuni, Siksika and their confederates the Atsina and Sarsi, had not made any such pact with either the Crows or Shoshoni, and continued to harass both peoples whenever the fancy took them.

So it was that when Sore-Belly's people arrived in the Judith Basin this summer of 1824, a certain Shoshoni band was already roaming the district for precisely the same reason as were the Crows in order to conduct their tribal hunt. In accordance with the recent pact between their peoples, these visitors from west of the Rockies had previously sent a present of tobacco to Sore-Belly with an invitation to meet together in order to consolidate their now amicable relationship. The two tribes would then trade and socialize with each other, while affording mutual protection against common foes by the uniting of their camps.

It was soon after Sore-Belly's Crows had set up their camp on the north side of the Musselshell, that a Crow war-party returned from yet another victory over the Lakota. Amid the ensuing celebrations in the aftermath of the party's triumphant return, many warriors became caught up in the fervour of the occasion and became themselves eager to go to war. They requested Sore-Belly to lead them north against the *Itshiipite* [Blackfoot], and the great war-chief was easily persuaded. He agreed to exact long-overdue vengeance upon the Pikuni specifically, for having made the Crows suffer when inactive in the aftermath of the destruction of Long-Hair's village. During that time, as already noted, war-parties predominantly of North Pikuni and Bloods, had taken advantage of the Crow's despondency, and had not ceased raiding the then scattered and vulnerable Crow camps; stealing horses and killing one or two persons without any serious reciprocal action having been launched against them.

Sore-Belly, however, decided that first his Crow followers should visit their Shoshoni allies as originally intended, for already the Shoshoni had come east through the mountain passes on their annual buffalo hunt, and their warriors could assist their Crow friends in a joint crusade against the common foe. Sore-Belly knew also that one or more Pikuni band would likely be coming south, as they invariably did at this time of year, to hunt buffalo in the Judith Basin for their own winter supply of meat and robes, and the Crows and Shoshoni had merely to bide their time and attack either the Pikuni camps or their hunters whenever it suited them to do so.

Subsequently, Sore-Belly set out at the head of a large force of warriors, intending to first unite with the Shoshoni and thereafter, make a punitive strike against any Blood, Pikuni or Siksika band they might happen to meet.

Now it had happened only a month or two earlier, that the Small Robe band of Pikuni along with a mixed band of Bloods and North Pikuni, had agreed to hold their summer Sun-Dance ceremonies together in late August on Badger Creek, a southern branch of the Marias River north of the Judith. Before reaching this trysting site, the Small Robes encamped on Cut Bank Creek and whilst Sore-Belly was en route to meet the Shoshoni, a party of Small Robes led by their war-chief Rising-Head, went out to scout the surrounding country lest enemies be in the area.

As fate would have it, the Small Robe war-party came upon a small bunch of Crows. The Small Robes immediately gave chase, and the Crows retreated to the top of a butte where they made a stand. The Small Robe party was in overwhelming number and in the ensuing contest, seven Crows were killed. Assuming that these Crow enemies had been a small horse-stealing party, the Small Robes supposed they had wiped them all out, and harboured no anxiety that their murderous deed would pose any immediate threat to the safety of their own people.

In reality, there had originally been eight Crows in the party, who being a part of the much larger force under Sore-Belly then on its way northwest to visit the Shoshoni, had been sent out from their main body to reconnoitre the way ahead. The surviving scout managed to escape the slaughter, having watched the slaying of his comrades from hiding, and after the killers left the scene, this man returned with all haste to his people and informed them what had happened.

Upon hearing the lone survivor's report, Sore-Belly became incensed. He at once abandoned his original plan of visiting the Shoshoni and called his headmen together for a hurried council of war. It was then unanimously agreed that instead, they should prepare to attack the Small Robes without delay and avenge their seven kinsmen. They did not know then that many more Pikuni and Bloods were also in the area.

It was decided therefore, merely to send a messenger to the Shoshoni camp requesting they join the Crows in their proposed attack. In addition, it was intended that the expedition this time would not only seek vengeance for past wrongs, but would endeavour to take as many women and children captive as possible with a view to their being adopted into Apsaalooka households, thereby increasing even further the tribe's depleted population.

In the meantime, the Small Robes, Bloods and Pikuni had held their Sun dances, whereupon, the Small Robes separated from the other Blackfoot bands and began moving south towards the Musselshell to conduct their late summer hunt. The remainder of the Pikuni in company with a part of the Bloods in two widely separated bands, followed slowly in the same direction some distance behind the Small Robes, whilst the rest of the Bloods comprising the majority of that people and who had since separated from the rest, moved northeast towards the Bear Paw Mountains intending to join their Atsina allies.

Whilst travelling north, the Crows were subsequently joined by around fifty lodges of Shoshoni in response to Sore-Belly`s request and that night, the Shoshoni set their camp adjacent to the Crows somewhere between the north bank of the Musselshell and the upper course of the Judith. In total this combined Crow and Shoshoni village now contained between three-hundred and fifty and four-hundred lodges and could muster over seven-hundred warriors. A formidable force, Sore-Belly thought, to combat any foreign war bands in the region.

Nevertheless, the ever pragmatic Sore-Belly did not immediately go against the foe. First he sent out two scouts to determine the exact location of the enemy camp and also its size, in order that the number of Blackfoot warriors on hand might be reasonably deduced.

The Crow scouts returned next morning saying the enemy were encamped about ten miles distant on Arrow Creek, a stream that rises in the Belt Mountains about sixty miles south of the Great Falls of the Missouri. This was, in fact, the same band of Small Robes which earlier, had separated from the main Pikuni and Blood body and whose village contained only half the number of lodges as comprised the allied Crow and Shoshoni camps in total. Thus, the Crow chief assumed there would only be around four-hundred enemy fighting-men to contend with, and the Crows with at least some seven-hundred braves, would have the advantage. As a rule among Indians, an attacking party would have been reluctant to assault the enemy if the attackers themselves were not numerically superior. But Sore-Belly actually divided his force on this occasion.

Contrary to what others may have done in his position, Sore-Belly decided to keep a protective guard around his two camps, lest the villages themselves be attacked whilst he and the Crow / Shoshoni war-party was out against the foe. He judged that around four-hundred warriors alone would be sufficient to defeat the enemy, if that is, the Crows retained the element of surprise and could catch their quarry strung out over the prairie in a moving column. He did not know that since the Crow scouts had first sighted the enemy, the other large conglomerate of Pikuni and Bloods had caught up with their Small Robe cousins, and had set their camps further along the same Arrow Creek and that together, the enemy could muster some one thousand warriors in total.

Sore-Belly was well known as one who would invariably take offensive action, rather than go on the defence. In this way he hoped to discourage his people's enemies from raiding into Crow country without fear of reprisal and its dire consequences. With this in mind, he now sent out another party of scouts in order to reconnoitre the enemy more closely and to ascertain their intended movements. In the interim, he collected together a large body of warriors and got ready to engage the foe at any given moment.

In due course the Crow scouts returned for a second time, and let it be known that the original Blackfoot camp had since been reinforced and now outnumbered that of the Crows by many more lodges. Sore-Belly, however, was unperturbed. He knew, of course, that the enemy would have their own scouts out watching the Crow and Shoshoni village, but he was determined to attack first and to this end, he endeavoured to lead the Pikuni and Bloods into a trap. By a skilful manoeuvre, he gave the impression to any Pikuni spies that might be in the area, that he was leading his people south across the Musselshell, out of the country, when in truth, he was actually positioning his warriors in a favourable location, wherefrom they could encircle the foe and launch their attack when the time was deemed right to ensure victory.

Accordingly, a third body of scouts was sent out having been instructed by Sore-Belly to report immediately if the enemy began dismantling their lodges as if getting ready to move.

It was the very next morning when the scouts came running into camp. They reported that the Pikuni, Small Robes and Bloods having taken down their lodges and packed them on pony-drags, were now actually moving across the open prairie heading south towards where the Crows and Shoshoni themselves were encamped. Obviously, the enemy host at this stage could not have known the precise location of the Crows, having, it would seem, fallen for Sore-Belly`s ruse. They must indeed, have harboured the belief that the Crows had left the country completely.

Upon hearing his scout's report, Sore-Belly at once ordered his warriors to mount their ponies and prepare to start out against the foe.

With at least four-hundred warriors at his back, each of whom was well-armed and mounted astride a spirited steed, the Crow chief led his be-feathered host north from the Musselshell to a high plateau overlooking the prairie below. Here he concealed his force below the rim, whilst he and his brother friend Little-White-Bear crawled on their stomachs to the lip of the plateau and spied the open country ahead. There in the distance was the long stretched-out snake-like column of their Pikuni enemies, coming slowly in three widely separated bands toward the Crow's hidden position. The Pikuni, apparently, had no idea that a formidable body of their most mortal foe was in the immediate vicinity, so that not only were the people in the column traveling casually and in a seemingly carefree and unsuspecting manner, but no scouts had been deployed to reconnoitre the way ahead in case enemies were nearby.

For a while Sore-Belly and Little-White-Bear watched their enemy's progress, whose column stretched out even further as the morning wore on. Wide gaps appeared between the groups of traveling people as they continued to move slowly and disconnectedly across the grasslands. In truth, almost the entire Pikuni tribe and a part of the Bloods were traveling in this column, which stretched over the Plain for a distance of fifteen miles and more, led by around eighty Pikuni families four or five miles in advance of the second group comprised of Pikuni and Small Robes. The third and largest group bringing up the rear, was at least ten miles behind the Small Robes, made up of mixed Pikuni and Bloods comprising some five-hundred warriors, although these second and third groups were out of sight from the Crows owing to a number of intervening ridges.

Patiently, Sore-Belly and Little-White-Bear waited until their prey came near. Not until those at the head of the column were within range of half a gunshot did they vacate the plateau and re-join their warriors. After mounting his war pony, Sore-Belly raised the Crow war-cry and with fifty of his best warriors beside him, suddenly charged out from concealment and headlong towards the foe. Immediately behind led by Little-White-Bear came the rest of the Crow and Shoshoni host, each warrior bedecked in feathers and paint and waving either a lance, musket, bow, or long-handled tomahawk in the air. At the same time they, too, screamed their war-whoops as they charged forward.

A Pikuni chief riding at the head of the column, at once pulled up his pony and for a moment stared at the sight before him. Even before he could turn his mount and flee or present any semblance of defence, he was cut down and scalped. His companions near him were knocked to the ground by the galloping Crow ponies and struck with pony quirts and fusee barrels as the Crow riders in the forefront of the charging host rode past, counting *dakshey* upon the enemy be they men, women or children, and killing the warriors as they went. Some other Crows coming behind the foremost body of attackers claimed a number of Pikuni women and children as captives, along with the horses the latter were riding as the spoils of war.

Even so, the majority of Pikuni non-combatants all mixed up together, did manage to turn their ponies around and flee. These were hotly pursued by the Crows who ran down the old men among them, cutting several off from the main body and killing them in small isolated bunches. They knocked the women from their horses and those on foot they knocked to the ground by bumping their own mounts into them, then took them captive. Even the Crows admitted later, that some of these Pikuni non-combatants did regrettably, suffer death in the process.

When first the Crows attacked, there had been comparatively few Pikuni warriors at the head of the column. But some of these were brave men and albeit not more than one-hundred strong, they stolidly stood their ground. However, Pikuni and Small Robes reinforcements from the centre of the column having seen what was happening, were by then already charging forward, and when these fresh fighters eventually joined their beleaguered comrades, they together formed a strong defensive line. In response, the Crows regrouped and charged several abreast in a long cavalcade. Riding across the enemy line at an angle, they shot arrows and fusee balls from under their pony's necks as they passed. When reaching the far end of the line, the Crows suddenly wheeled their ponies around and making a wide arc, returned to their previous position in order to charge again, and this manoeuvre they repeated many times.

Among the Pikuni fighters this day was a white man named Hugh Munroe, a trapper and trader in the employ of the Hudson's Bay Company and an adopted member of the Small-Robe Pikuni band. Hugh Munroe stated in essence that he with only twenty or thirty companions, had been riding a few miles back in the middle of the column composed of Small Robes and Pikuni when first the Crows launched their attack. Together, Munroe and his companions raced their ponies forward in an attempt to check the enemy so that the women and children could escape. Upon their coming to grips with the Crows, Munroe declared, there were then all together around two-hundred Small Robes and Pikuni warriors engaged in the fight, which was still a small force in comparison to the estimated four-hundred Crows opposing them. However, as additional Pikunni reinforcements continued to charge forward from the middle of the column, it caused Munroe to comment, *"...I looked behind and the sight of hundreds of our men coming on was encouraging."* [1]

Not many Crows carried firearms at this date, whereas the Blackfoot tribes owned a good number, and as their own warriors began to return fire with their short-barrelled smoothbore fusees, many Crow horses went down and several of their riders either killed or toppled from their wounded mounts. Gun wads flew all around, and it is true to say that the guns of the Blackfoot compared to the bows and arrows of the Crows, did go a long way in compensating for the disparity in numbers between the opposing forces.

During this part of the battle, a well-known Small Robe sub-chief named Lone-Walker, was in the van of the second group of Pikuni and Small-Robes reinforcements which had ridden forward from the middle of the column. A great cry went up among these fresh fighters, urging each other to save the women and children. It seemed all were determined to get to grips with the Crows and drive them from the field, rather than employing a holding action as their Pikuni comrades initially engaged, had been obliged to do owing to their inferiority in number.

This man Lone-Walker singled out one of the enemy who, he thought, was also a chief by the feathered bonnet and war-shirt he was wearing, and charged directly towards him. The Crow chief saw him coming and immediately, urged his own pony forward in order to meet the Small-Robe chief in single combat. Each man galloped his mount towards his opponent across the open prairie, while whipping them furiously with their quirts to elicit more speed. They actually forced their steeds to collide with each other, the impact of which sent both animals crashing to the ground. The riders themselves barely managed to jump clear from being trapped under the crushing weight of their horses. But quickly both contestants regained their feet, and throwing away their weapons; the Small-Robe his empty gun; the Crow his bow and now empty quiver, they ran forward to engage in a hand to hand fight to the death.

The Crow was first to draw his broad-bladed knife and was upon the Small-Robe chief before the latter could draw his. By this time, however, a large number of Crows, Pikuni and Small-Robes were themselves engaged in their own bloody hand to hand contests. Each side endeavouring to get close enough to assist their respective champions, who were fully engaged in grappling with each other in their life and death struggle.

The Small-Robe Lone-Walker was a well-built man and very strong. As the Crow chief lunged at him with knife raised in one hand, his opponent avoided the stroke; grabbed the Crow's wrist and twisted it in such a manner that the raised knife dropped harmlessly to the ground. The Crow managed to wrest free, but as he bent down to retrieve his blade, the Small-Robe chief drew his own knife and springing upon his adversary, stabbed him a vicious blow in the back which pierced the man's heart, and according to one account, killed the Crow chief outright.

As it was, the final result of Lone-Walker's single combat with the Crow chief, actually went hardly noticed by the rest of the Crows and their antagonists, who were too preoccupied in battling it out between themselves in a tightly packed melee.

Referring to the aftermath of Lone-Walker's knife fight with his Crow adversary, Hugh Munroe said,

> "... In the meantime we were in a terrible scrimmage; a thick mix up of riders. I had stuck my gun in under my belt, there was no time to reload it, and had fired one of my pistols, and now got out the other one. Red-Crow and I were side by side. He had shot away his handful of arrows and was reaching into his quiver for more when a Crow rode up beside him, reached out and grasped him by the arm, endeavouring to pull him over and knife him. I saw him just in time to poke my pistol over past Red-Crow and fire, and down he went from his horse! The sight of him falling, his awful stare of hate made me sick and sorry for him, enemy though he was!...I replaced the pistol and got out my gun to use as a club, as I saw others doing. But just then I saw a wounded woman stagger to her feet, and then with a cry throw up her hands and fall dead, and I shouted with joy that I had killed, ... The enemies of the Pi-kun-i were my enemies so long as they tried to do me harm." [2]

Meanwhile, those of the Pikuni noncombatants who had been in the forward part of the column, were still in full flight racing back the way they had come. Soon, however, the Pikuni and Bloods traveling with the third group some fifteen and more miles back, noticed the sudden appearance of a great dust cloud in the distance ahead, and seeing fugitives on horseback racing towards them, they realized that the front of the column must be under attack. In response a great host of horsemen including not only warriors of fighting age, but also old men and teenage boys led by their great chiefs Iron-Shield, Rising-Head, Big-Lake and Big-Snake, all at once galloped forward in a desperate endeavour to assist their comrades. With these additional reinforcements, the number of Pikuni and Bloods soon to be engaged in the fight would be many hundreds more than the four-hundred Crows, and the latter, seeing these fresh fighters coming towards them by the cloud of dust got up by the flying hooves of their ponies, assumed their enemies were in even greater strength than they really were.

Thus while a part of the Crow force continued battling the line of enemies to their front, others among them again took up the pursuit of the fugitives from where they had left off, in an endeavour to inflict as much damage upon the fleeing noncombatants as they could before the bulk of Pikuni and Blood reinforcements from the rear of the column actually entered the fray. These Crows began racing their ponies down the length of the scattered column, striking the women and old people with their coup sticks, whilst shooting others with arrows and musket balls or simply clubbing them to the ground. Many more of the younger noncombatants both women and children were taken up across the withers of Crow ponies and carried away as captives, or were ushered along on foot in front of Crow riders.

Although the third band of Pikuni and Blood reinforcements was coming up fast, they were still some way distant to enable them to give practical help, and the unequal contest continued unabated.

Soon, however, the Crows and Shoshoni at last tired of the melee and deciding to give way, began withdrawing across the prairie back the way they had come. Those who had been dismounted or wounded during the fight, were taken up behind comrades, while their dead were also carried away across the withers of their ponies.

Sore-Belly's protective *medicine* had remained strong, so that neither iron hatchet, metal-tipped arrow, lance-point or leaden ball had touched his person, and although Little-White-Bear, - ever at the great chief's side battling against the foe, - had suffered several wounds, albeit of superficial degree, he, too, survived to fight another day. [3]

The Small Robes and Pikuni had also had enough, and not yet being joined by the bulk of reinforcements from the rear of the column who were still five or more miles distant, they merely sat their exhausted ponies and watched as their enemies rode slowly out of sight.

A terse account of the affair penned by Edwin T. Denig when head clerk at the Upper Missouri post Fort Union during the 1850s, and probably obtained from the Pikuni or Bloods rather than Crows, seems in essence to concur with the Munroe account, the trader Denig stating,

> "Their [Blackfoot] long and weak line of March was literally rubbed out by their savage foes [Crows]. Whoever endeavoured to defend was killed, the women and children taken prisoners. Although they [Blackfoot)] fought bravely for some time they soon were obliged to leave their families and seek safety in flight. Others died defending their children." [4]

Crow oral tradition concerning the affair as related to the present Author by Joseph Medicine Crow, asserts it was only when the Crow and Shoshoni mounts had become tired and exhausted, that Sore-Belly himself put an end to the pursuit and called his warriors back. He bade them be satisfied with what they had

146

already accomplished in their taking many scalps, captives, horses and much booty in camp paraphernalia and personal belongings. He then led them south and returned to the Crow and Shoshoni villages on the Musselshell and their anxiously awaiting kinfolk, *"The triumphant warriors singing loud their victory songs as they rode."* [5]

Conversely, Hugh Munroe declared it was the Crows eventually driven from the field, although he did admit that the Blackfoot themselves did not pursue at that point. This appears strange if the Pikuni then had the advantage as he himself stated, and might therefore, have succeeded easily in rescuing their captured kinfolk from the hands of the enemy. In fairness to Munroe, however, he did also state that the Pikuni and Bloods were anxious to get back to their families, in order to determine whether they be alive or dead, and so had little heart to continue the fight. In addition, the Pikuni and Blood new arrivals when they finally came up from the rear of the column, had already overrun their horses, and so needed to wait a while for the animals to regain stamina before following up the foe.

Munroe further stated that after the Crows departed the scene, several parties of Pikuni and Small Robe men and women rummaged over the battleground gathering up their dead and wounded. They also retrieved whatever had been left of their abandoned packs and belongings, all of which now lay scattered along the trail over which the advance group of the Pikuni column had passed. Both dead and dying people and horses lay everywhere, and here and there exhausted ponies - some still attached to their travois poles - stood motionless either singularly or in bunches of threes and fours. These were rounded up; the dead and dying Pikuni bodies then draped across the animal's withers and led quietly away to where the vanquished survivors had set up their lodges. This time along a small stream not far north of the scene of conflict.

In case the Crows should return to finish the job they had started, a band of Pikuni warriors among who were included old men and teenage boys to augment their number, remained out on the prairie guarding those still searching among the battle carnage strewn around.

Finally, as the sun slowly dipped below the western horizon, even those searching for slain loved ones returned to their camp, which soon became a scene of great sadness and sorrow.

The relatives of those slain and dying screamed their mournful lamentations and mutilated themselves in overt expressions of grief. The corpses were wrapped in bundles and placed in branches of trees growing thick along the river bank. The Pikuni and Blood chiefs meanwhile, heaped recriminations upon themselves for not having had a strong warrior force out at the head of the column, along with parties of scouts both on the flanks and at the rear. Such should have been the customary procedure whenever an Indian village was on the move, spread out and vulnerable as it would be when traveling over open grasslands.

The aforementioned Hugh Munroe, did not report any captives being taken, but said in total eighty-nine Blackfoot had been killed, which included forty-one warriors during the actual battle along with thirty-two women and girls and nine children, and that seven more persons died later of their wounds. The Crows for their part, Munroe continued, lost sixty-one killed and a number of wounded, many of whom, he believed, were sure to have died later. A contemporary reference to the fight, however, as recorded in the journal of the Hudson's Bay Factor John Rowand at Fort Edmonton on the Saskatchewan, Canada, mentioned in October the same year of the fight,

> "...The Crows and 'Mountain' Indians [Shoshoni?], have slaughtered one-hundred and seventy Blackfoot in a pitched battle on the south side of the Missouri." [6]

Several accounts, nevertheless, agree that the Crow victors grew tired of scalping their fallen foes and were content to retire from the field. They carried away much booty consisting of lodge covers, animal skins and robes, household paraphernalia and provisions, an assortment of weapons, including guns and ammunition, along with parfleches packed with ceremonial clothing. In addition, they had captured at least five-hundred ponies along with more than one-hundred women and children prisoners, among whom were included a mother and daughter of mixed Iroquois and white parentage.

Whatever the exact number of their own casualties, the Crows knew they had achieved a great victory over their most virulent foes. But early that same afternoon having returned to their villages, a large force of Blackfoot suddenly appeared in the distance, and the Crows had been obliged to go out from their camps and again prepare for battle.

It seems that after the Crows and Shoshoni initially left the field of combat, the Pikuni and Small Robes rallied their scattered forces, which then included the additional fighting men of Pikuni and Bloods who had been at the rear of the column. These were those who had not got to grips with the foe during the morning's conflict, and comprised some five-hundred warriors still eager for battle. Several hours later after resting their horses, they actually followed the victor's trail in the hope of over-taking and forcing the Crows to abandon their captives, along with the booty taken which might prove too cumbersome to hold on to if forced into precipitous flight. Unfortunately for the Blackfoot, they did not expect to find two large villages in their path, having supposed that those who attacked them earlier had been no more than a wandering, albeit formidable war-party. Instead, the whole fighting force of the combined Crow and Shoshoni camps came out to meet them, and the latter were in such strength as compared to their opponents, that after a few ineffectual skirmishes, the Pikuni and Bloods realized there was little chance of victory or of rescuing their captured relatives. They thus gave up the fight; vacated the field and returned from whence they came, lamenting the loss of their stolen wives and children, their horses and their dead.

Before the sun disappeared completely over the western horizon, the grand Pikuni and Blood war-party after abandoning the fight outside the Crow and Shoshoni villages, rode sullenly and dejected into their home camps. Many of the warriors were very tired and sat slumped over on the backs of their exhausted ponies. They informed their chiefs that both the River and Mountain Crow along

148

with many Shoshoni, were encamped together along the north bank of the Musselshell and their number was such, that all the Pikuni alone would not be able to match them.

Because of this intelligence there arose some anxiety among the Pikuni. Many thought the Crows in more formidable number than seen that morning, might return to renew their attack and destroy the Pikuni tribe completely. Thus, the Pikuni chiefs hurriedly dispatched three messengers to the main body of Bloods which earlier had gone northeast to the Bear Paw region, with a request to come back and re-join their Pikuni cousins. Then their combined forces could pursue the Crows and exact vengeance for the recent slaughter, not to mention retrieving the captive women and children.

A few days after this; whilst awaiting the main band of Bloods to respond, the entire Pikuni host moved north to the Judith. After one or two nights stay they moved again, this time east to Armell`s Creek, and set up a more permanent camp not far from the pass that leads over the Snowy Mountains as a gateway to the south, and there they awaited the arrival of their allies.

It was some eight or nine days later when a number of Pikuni scouts came in. These had been sent out several days earlier to spy on the Crows, and bring word to their people the moment a large Crow war-party appeared to be starting north in the direction of the Pikuni camps. The scouts reported that some of the Crows had already left the main body and returned south, although there still remained two sizable camps, albeit now relocated on the south bank of the Musselshell. A position, in fact, almost directly due south of the pass through the Snowy Mountains.

At about the same time as the scouts were making their report, the three Pikuni messengers who had gone northeast in search of the Bloods, also returned, but now in the company of several hundred Blood warriors led by two of their great chiefs and fighters Eagle-Ribs and Bull-Trail. The Blood Chief Eagle-Ribs told the Pikuni that on the morrow, his whole tribe would arrive and true to his word, the Bloods came in the next day along with some thirty lodges of Atsina and even a number of Sarsi allies from the Bow River district of Alberta.

These new arrivals set their tepees in a circle next to those of the Pikuni and Small Robes and together, their lodges now numbered almost one-thousand, with an estimated total fighting force of close to two-thousand warriors.

In due course a council of war was held, to which all the Blood and Pikuni chiefs and leading warriors were invited, including the head chief of the Atsina contingent named Sitting-Woman [the first of that name]. It was agreed that they should start against the Crows the very next morning; a great host of warriors going ahead, while the rest of the people with all the tepees and spare horses would follow at their own pace. This was in case the Blackfoot villages themselves were attacked by any other enemy force which might be in the country whilst the men folk were on the war-trail, and in such an event, the non-combatants would still be close enough to enable them to seek protection from their warriors. In the meantime, another group of Blackfoot scouts was sent out in order to continue observing the Crows and their movements, while by a forced march the Pikuni,

149

Blood and Atsina would follow up the scouts, so as to reach the enemy camps in the afternoon of their second day out.

So it was the very next morning following their war council, that little short of two-thousand warriors including Bloods, Small Robes, Pikuni and Atsina, started south to raid the Crows and Shoshoni for vengeance.

Sure enough, before noon on their second day out the Blackfoot host came to the pass which led through the Snowy Mountains. At this point the grand war-party met the body of scouts delegated to watch the Crow villages, but who were now waiting at the north entrance of the pass in order to report to their chiefs. The scouts declared they had seen no movement that morning in or around the Crow villages, and neither had they seen the Crow pony herd. Previously, they said, there had been much activity on both sides of the Musselshell when the Crows had gone out to hunt, or to attend to their animals left grazing on the prairies abutting both sides of the river.

With this intelligence, it became obvious to many among the Blackfoot host and their Atsina allies that the Crows must have had their own scouts out, and being fully aware of the great number coming against them, they were already preparing to move. With this in mind the Blackfoot war-band quickly rode through the pass to the south side of the Snowy Mountains. They then raced their ponies across the open prairie on the far side towards the Musselshell some twenty miles distant, hoping to catch their Crow and Shoshoni enemies before they dismantled their camps completely and fled. When, however, the Blackfoot and Atsina warriors reined in their ponies atop the crest of a ridge overlooking the river valley below, only a few buffalo-hide lodges could be seen. Instead, countless sets of bare lodge poles standing in tripod fashion, showed clearly that the camp occupants had already left; in much haste apparently, to escape a confrontation with such a formidable force.

The combined Crow and Shoshoni camps had likely contained some three-hundred and fifty lodges in total, with a fighting strength of between seven-hundred and eight-hundred warriors. Thus they had obviously realized the danger of remaining where they were. They would be outnumbered by more than two to one, and they knew also from the earlier engagement, that many of those coming against them would be carrying guns of some description. These had been obtained in quantity on a regular basis from Hudson's Bay trading posts in Canada and gave all Blackfoot-speaking bands a great advantage over the Crows, who for the most part, were obliged to depend on the bow and arrow, lance and war-club since the recent refusal of white traders to supply them firearms. Not surprisingly then, the Crows and Shoshoni had expediently fled the area, leaving behind all they deemed cumbersome and unnecessary, lest it slowed them in their flight. Although their recently acquired captured ponies and Pikuni prisoners, they took with them.

Upon close inspection of the abandoned camps, the Blackfoot host and Atsina allies discovered that most of the occupants had actually left the previous night. Their own horses by this time were jaded and near exhaustion owing to their hectic twenty-mile race across the prairie, and the chiefs realized that their Crow enemies had too long a start to be overtaken before the latter crossed the Yellowstone. Once across that river and in their own country the Crows could make a stand in the abundant timber, or simply disperse in any direction and, perhaps, seriously damage their pursuers by launching counter attacks from ambush. The Blackfoot chiefs therefore, decided to abandon their original objective. After gathering up everything of value the fleeing Crows had left, they rode slowly northwards returning from whence they came, determined to even up the score at some future date.

The Blackfoot tribes and their allies supposed they themselves had now forced the River Crows out of the North Country, and a combined Blackfoot presence alone would, hereafter, be sufficient to keep the Crows south of the Musselshell. Thus, rather than recording the humiliating defeat of the column and the loss of so many killed and taken captive by the Crows, the year of this event is recorded in the Blood Blackfoot winter-count of Bad-Head as follows,

*"Winter 1824, "Crows; when we drove them away."* [7]

The Crows needless to say, safely reached their home country without mishap. The great chief, Sore-Belly, was hailed with many praises and received much honour as the paramount leader of the victorious expedition. Joe Medicine Crow added that several others among the Crow force also received acclaim for deeds of valour performed during the conflict. These included the then pipe-holder warriors Long-Horse, Grizzly-Bear and Bear`s-Head, each of whom at a later date, became leading chiefs in their own right.

On the other hand, the women and children prisoners were distributed as evenly as possible among the various Crow clans and together, the Crows and Shoshoni revelled in the riches they had acquired due to the abundance of booty captured. Scalp-dances and victory celebrations went on every night for many a week, and thus it seemed, at last, the gods of the Apsaalooka were yet again, smiling on their children.

$$- 0 - 0 - 0 - 0 - 0 - 0 - 0 - 0 - 0 - 0 - 0 - 0 - 0 - 0 -$$

## CHAPTER 14.

## ENTER THE AMERICAN EAGLE AND CHASTISING THE HIDATSA.

Among those taken captive by the victorious Crows during the attack on the Pikuni and Blood column, were a mother and daughter of mixed Iroquois and white parentage. They had previously been taken from the Flathead on Columbia River during a Blackfoot raid on a small village of that people, and somehow, word of their now being held by Crows reached the ears of the then United States Government appointed agent for the Upper Missouri tribes, Major Benjamin O`Fallon.

We are not told if the white husband of the female captive had personally requested the Major to secure her freedom, or if the fact that the woman and daughter had white blood was itself, reason enough to procure their release. Whatever the case, when during midsummer the following year of 1825, a Government expedition sailed up the Missouri in order to make peace treaties with

151

the western tribes and induce them to cease warring between themselves, the release of the above mentioned captives was also high on the agenda.

There was, though, a more paramount issue the expedition hoped to address, which was to curtail – if possible – the continuous harassment of white traders and trappers by Indians of the Great Plains and Upper Missouri regions. Such had culminated in an 1823 Government campaign against the Arickara, along with certain outrages committed upon individual parties of white men by belligerent Indians among whom Crows were included.

One significant instance of Crow hostility towards white men had occurred in August, 1824. It was then that a brigade of one-hundred and sixteen independent white trappers with three-hundred mules and seventeen horses under the command of Sylvester Pattie, had started from a rendezvous point on the lower course of the Platte on the first stage of a trading and trapping enterprise, which was intended to terminate at the town of Santa Fe in what was then the Spanish possession of New Mexico. [1]

On August 31st whilst ascending a southern tributary of the Smokey Hill River, Kansas, some distance southwest of the Skidi Pawnee villages on the Loup, the aforementioned party stumbled across the mangled corpses of two white men, lately killed and scalped by Indians. The ground round about was,
*"...torn and trampled by both horses and footmen and stuck full of arrows."* [2]

A few hundred yards away lay the bodies of five dead Indians; evidently casualties of the recent fight. Fresh Indian sign was very much apparent and after moving a few miles upstream, the trappers made camp for the night without fires, lest they attracted the attention of the Indians who – the trappers believed – were still in the area. The trappers decided to exact vengeance upon the slayers of the two white men and to this end, ten men were sent further up the creek in the hope of discovering the Indian's encampment by the glow of their fires.

After a night trek of some four miles or so, the ten scouts discerned at least twenty small fires in the distance indicating the whereabouts of the Indians, and with this intelligence they returned to their own camp to gather reinforcements. In response sixty trappers led by Sylvester Pattie himself, checked their firearms and other weapons then moved silently up stream. By three o. clock in the morning they had successfully surrounded the sleeping Indian camp and were waiting patiently for the night to pass before launching their attack. When at last dawn broke, the Indians began rising from their slumber and almost immediately, they spotted two of the trappers lying in wait. At once the Indians raised their war-cries and waving weapons in the air, raced towards them, *"...with great fury,"* it was said. [3]

The leader of the trappers commanded his men to open fire, and a barrage of musket and pistol shot stopped the charging Indians in their tracks. The latter, however, then stood their ground and returned the fire with arrows. But when the trappers charged upon them, the Indians fled in *"...confusion and disarray."* [4] Only one of the trappers had been wounded, and he died the following day.

Having returned to their own camp with prisoners in tow, the trappers asked the Indians to what tribe they belonged and were instantly answered they were Crows. When further asked why they had killed the two white men found the previous day, the Indians replied that having come across them accidently, the Crow chief had merely asked the whites to share their powder and ball with them. But this being refused, the Crows had then killed them both and taken it all. They further admitted that they themselves had lost four of their best young warriors in the process.

Surprisingly, the trapper's leader Pattie, then returned the Indian's bows and arrows and told them that it was not the white man's way to slaughter unarmed prisoners. Instead, the trappers set them free, telling them to inform their kinfolk what had happened and if they attacked any white men again, then the trappers themselves would slaughter all the Crows they found, as they were not afraid of any number the Crows might send against them.

One of the freed Crows; probably the partisan, then gave the trapper's leader an eagle feather and after referring to him as, *"A good man,"* [5] stated that never again would he kill another white man. Thus Crows and trappers on this occasion parted in good faith. But other Crow parties persisted in belligerent acts against the more vulnerable white men they were apt to meet on the trail.

In all fairness, considering the southern location of the particular Crow party encountered by Pattie's trappers, many hundreds of miles south from the Yellowstone and Big Horn country, they may have been a part of Chief Arrow-Head's Dried-Out-Furs band, who after the destruction of Long-Hair's village on Otter Creek, had made their split from their Apsaalooka kinfolk a more permanent move in favour of the Southern Country. This would explain why they apparently harboured no qualms of creating animosity between themselves and the white men, not being influenced by alternative circumstances in the North. Among Arrow-Head's band at this time was the then young Crow warrior Twines-His-Horses-Tail. This man, we know, was roaming the southern country during the period in question, and at a later date under the name of Rotten-Tail, he became head chief of the River Crow.

There was, though, albeit a minority of Crows even in the North Country, who certainly were culpable of hostile acts upon white men, as a report by General William Ashley of the American Fur Company to General Atkinson dated December 1st 1825, makes clear. The report states that earlier on April 2d, Ashley's trappers whilst roaming the Upper Missouri country lost seventeen horses to marauding Crows. The trappers unsuccessfully trailed the thieves, but the Crows escaped. Later on July 2d, Ashley's men had a hot fight with around sixty Blackfoot out looking for Crows near the Big Horn River. During this engagement the white men suffered the loss of all but two of their horses and had one man wounded. Three days later, however, around midnight after replenishing their stock from another party of Ashley's men, the trappers were attacked by Crows and in this event, one Crow was killed and another wounded through the body. The trappers suffered no injuries but immediately thereafter, Ashley's two parties joined forces and promptly left the country.

It was then, in an endeavour to halt this recent spate of troubles between Indians and whites, that a formidable detachment of infantry with two cannons under the command of General Henry Atkinson and the aforementioned Major

O'Fallon; with Edward Rose acting as scout and interpreter, sailed and propelled their way up the Missouri in nine 'wheel boats' in an attempt to impress the Indians by affording them a token idea of the white man's military strength, and to obtain agreements of peace from as many Missouri tribes as possible.

. This initiative became known as the "Atkinson O'Fallon Expedition" and the resulting pacts made with tribes contacted, were referred to as "Friendship Treaties."

In short, the expedition met and made pacts with the Omaha, Ponca, several bands of Teton [Lakota], Arickara and Cheyenne, and among the last-named with which the commissioners counselled, was the Suhtai chief, High-Backed-Wolf, the same who had played such a prominent role in the destruction of Long-Hair's Crow village five years earlier.

Upon arriving among the Mandan in mid-July 1825, O'Fallon at once dispatched the trader Toissaint Charboneau - then domiciled among the Hidatsa - to go in search of the Crows and invite them to the Mandan villages, so they, too, could conclude their own treaty of friendship with the Americans.

On July 27th before Charboneau returned, eight Crow Indians visited General Atkinson's military cantonment on their own volition and informed him that the main body of their people was about thirty miles distant [i.e. one or two days journey]. The Indian emissaries were given presents by the General and instructed to tell their people that the white men were eagerly waiting to welcome their whole band when it came in. The eight Crows then left to return to their people and the following day [July 28th], Charboneau himself returned, bringing word that the Crows would arrive in three or four days' time.

The Crows did not appear on the specified date, but on the morning of August I, two Crows came in with word that their main body was but fifteen miles away. The General now sent a Captain Riley with one of the visiting Crows along with a Major Gordon and four soldiers as escort, to inform the Crows that the commissioners were still eagerly awaiting their arrival.

It was not until August 3d before Captain Riley and his military escort finally returned to the cantonment, but now accompanying the soldiers was a large part of the Crow Nation led by their paramount chief, Long-Hair. The Indians were on horseback riding in column formation, the warriors some six-hundred strong, bedecked in all the ceremonial finery which they deemed befitted such an occasion. After parading past the cantonment in their native splendour, they set up their three-hundred or so tepees adjacent to the earth and timber lodges of the Mandan, and in total sixteen of the seventeen council chiefs of the Crow Nation were present. Only Sore-Belly with six lodges and forty warriors were absent, as they had earlier gone west across the mountains on a visit to Sore-Belly's relatives among the Flatheads.

The Indians, it seemed, appeared more excited at reuniting with their adopted brother, "Five-Scalps" [Edward Rose], than the presence of American soldiers and Government delegates in their midst. Needless to say, Rose immediately renewed his acquaintance with his old friends whose overt display of affection towards him did not go unnoticed by one, Reuben Holmes, a lieutenant in the sixth infantry then attached to General Atkinson`s military escort. Holmes recorded his observations as follows,

> "...He [Rose] had a word for everyone and every one a smile for him. Among them all one could easily see that he was a general favourite; but among the young girls, those just budding into womanhood, I thought I could perceive the workings of a feeling different from the ordinary display of mere good will and friendship. Before, and when he announced his intention to remain among them, I thought I could discover by the irregular rising and falling of their [the females] bosoms, an indefinable emotion stealing over their souls. There was something in their eyes, and a kind of hesitating, quivering intonation in their expression, that plainly spoke their hopes and fears, at one and the same moment. There was a half-advancing, half-retreating manner about them, that seemed inwardly to ask, will he like me, or will he not? From the oldest to the youngest, there was, in fact, a genuine burst of joy at his arrival, and as genuine and a general expression of pleasure, at his intention to remain with them." [6]

The next day following the arrival of the Crows, Long-Hair and his retinue of sub-chiefs sat in council with Agent O`Fallon and a like number of military personnel, which included General Atkinson and the mulatto Rose acting as interpreter between the parties.

After preliminary speeches of welcome had been made by each side, the articles of the proposed treaty were read out as follows,

ARTICLE 1. It is admitted by the Crow tribe of Indians, that they reside within the territorial limits of the United States, acknowledge their supremacy, and claim their protection.—The said tribe also admit the right of the United States to regulate all trade and intercourse with them.

ARTICLE 2. The United States agree to receive the Crow tribe of Indians into their friendship, and under their protection, and to extend to them, from time to time, such benefits and acts of kindness as may be convenient, and seem just and proper to the President of the United States.

ARTICLE 3. All trade and intercourse with the Crow tribe shall be transacted at such place or places as may be designated and pointed out by the President of the United States, through his agents; and none but American citizens, duly authorized by the United States, shall be admitted to trade or hold intercourse with said tribe of Indians.

ARTICLE 4. That the Crow tribe may be accommodated with such articles of merchandise, &c. as their necessities may demand, the United States agree to admit and license traders to hold intercourse with said tribe, under mild

155

and equitable regulations: in consideration of which, the Crow tribe bind themselves to extend protection to the persons and the property of the traders, and the persons legally employed under them, whilst they remain within the limits of their district of country…And they further agree to give safe conduct to all persons who may be legally authorized by the United States to pass through their country, and to protect in their persons and property all agents or other persons sent by the United States to reside temporarily among them; and that they will not, whilst on their distant excursions, molest or interrupt any American citizen or citizens, who may be passing from the United States to New Mexico, or returning from thence to the United States.

ARTICLE 5…It is hereby agreed, that for injuries done by individuals, no private revenge or retaliation shall take place, but instead thereof, complaints shall be made, by the party injured, to the superintendent or agent of Indian affairs, or other person appointed by the President; and it shall be the duty of said Chiefs, upon complaint being made as aforesaid, to deliver up the person or persons against whom the complaint is made, to the end that he or they may be punished, agreeably to the laws of the United States. And, in like manner, if any robbery, violence, or murder, shall be committed on any Indian or Indians belonging to the said tribe, the person or persons so offending shall be tried, and, if found guilty, shall be punished in like manner as if the injury had been done to a white man…And the United States hereby guaranty to any Indian or Indians of said tribe, a full indemnification for any horses or other property which may be stolen from them by any of their citizens: Provided, That the property stolen cannot be recovered, and that sufficient proof is produced that it was actually stolen by a citizen of the United States. And the said tribe engage, on the requisition or demand of the President of the United States, or of the agents, to deliver up any white man resident among them.

Edward Rose interpreted the above articles into Crow, doing his best to explain their full meaning to the Indians, and after which the said document was signed. First among the Crows to be registered was Chief Long-Hair. He touched his tongue with the tip of a knife, after which one of the white officials with a quill-pen entered a mark in the form of an `X` on the treaty paper itself. Each of Long-Hair's subordinate chiefs then followed suit in order of importance, and as their names were translated by Rose, they, too, with the mark of an `X` were also entered on the paper. The list of Crow tribal signatories was thus recorded as follows,

"E-she-huns-ska" --------------------Long-Hair.
"She-wo-cub-bish" --------------------One-That-Sings-Bad.
"Har-rar-shash" -------------------------One-That-Rains [Big-Rain].
"Chay-ta-pah-ha" -----------------------Wolf's-Paunch [Wolf-Belly].
"Huch-che-rach" ------------------------Little-Black-Dog.
"Mah-pitch"-----------------------------Bare-Shoulder.
"Esh-ca-ca-mah-hoo"--------------------Standing-Lance [High-Lance].

"Che-rep-con-nes-ta-chea"------------Little-White-Bull [He-Who-Looks-at-the-Albino-Buffalo].
Mah-shay-she-ra"-----------------------Yellow-Big-Belly [Yellow-Belly].
"Co-tah-bah-sah"-------------------------One-That-Runs.
"Bah-cha-na-mach"----------------------One-That-Sits-in-the-Pine [Lone-Pine].
"He-ran-dah-pah"----------------------- One-That-Ties-His-Hair-Before.
"Bas-ca-bah-ru-sha"---------------------.Dog-That-Eats [Eats-like-a-Dog].
"Nah-puch-kia"-------------------------Holds-The-Stick-in-His-Mouth.
"Bah-da-ah-chan-dah"----------------- One-That-Jumps-Over-Every-Person.
"Mash-pah-hashne."................... One-That-is-Not-Right. [7]

So it was that the great Mountain Crow Chief Long-Hair among others, accepted the treaty terms by promising undying friendship between their Apsaalooka people and the Government of the United States. Having completed the treaty signing, General Atkinson left the council tent in order to take his midday repast, supposing that the official part of the gathering had been concluded.

Only the distribution of gifts to Crow dignitaries remained on the agenda. Indeed, the chiefs were now waiting anxiously for the expected presents which they could see piled up before them, including blankets, beads, knives, iron tomahawks and trade muskets among other things. Before, however, the distribution began, Major O`Fallon first demanded that the Crows give up their recently acquired half-breed Iroquois captives [taken during Sore-Belly`s attack on the Pikuni and Blood column the previous year], so they, the captives, could be reunited with their proper kinfolk. The Crow response was that of surprise accompanied with an emphatic `No! They had taken them from their enemies, the chiefs said, and the captives now clearly belonged to the Crows. Again the Agent pressed the issue, whereupon the Crows offered to fight the whites there and then and settle the matter by the outcome of the conflict.

Expediently O`Fallon declined to fight at that precise time, but requested the Indians return the next day when he would be better prepared to give them battle. The Crow Chief Big-Rain then rose to his feet. With wide gesticulations he replied through the interpreter Rose, that the white men were not a match for the Crows and that his warriors could whip their whole army.

In response to Big-Rain`s words, O`Fallon, who was known for his hot temper, lost control. He drew forth his flintlock pistol and fired point blank at the chief's chest. Fortunately the piece only snapped harmlessly; failing to fire, upon which the Agent then struck Big-Rain a vicious blow on the head with the barrel, causing a severe gash that instantly subdued the chief in his tracks. All was now mayhem as the other chiefs in the confusion, attempted to help themselves to the presents stacked up before them. But even in this their plans were thwarted. The mulatto Rose was quick to react. Seizing a musket from the assorted gifts he placed one foot on the pile, and holding the musket in both hands by the barrel in a club-like manner, he stood poised ready to strike the very person of Chief Long-Hair, or indeed, of any other chief who came near.

There were many Indians milling around the council area and had not one or more white men called upon Rose to restrain himself, the entire Government party must surely have been "rubbed out." Rose, however, was still inclined to engage himself in the threatened debacle and replied he would heed none but Major O'Fallon's words. This being said, the Major immediately ordered him to desist and Rose reluctantly complied. The scene, though, remained ripe for potential bloodletting on a grand scale. Only the timely return of General Atkinson, who ordered his soldiers to stand to arms, quelled the volatile situation. It was too late, though, to have prevented the Crows spiking the touch holes of the General's cannon and filling the barrels with turf so as to put them out of action. It was probably at this time; according to Beckwourth [but who was not a party to the treaty gathering itself ], that Long-Hair spoke as follows,

"White chief, the Crows have never yet shed the blood of the white people; they have always treated them like brothers. You have now shed the first blood; my people are angry and we must fight."
To Long-Hair's words the General replied,
"Chief, I was told by my friend the great Red-haired chief [William Clark; then Superintendent of Indian Affairs] that the Crows were a good people; that they were our friends.
"The Red-haired chief," exclaimed Long-Hair in astonishment, "Are you his people?"
"Yes," replied the General.
"The Red-haired chief is a great chief," retorted Long-Hair, "and when he hears you have shed the blood of a Crow, he will be angry and punish you for it. Go home and tell the Red-haired chief that you have shed the blood of a Crow, and though our people were angry, we did not kill his people. Tell him that you saw Long-Hair, he Crow chief, to whom you gave the red plume many winters ago."
8

At length, after further discourse and persuasion, the Indians departed, albeit in a sullen mood. They had, however, agreed to visit the commissioners the next day to resolve the matter amicably to the satisfaction of all.

The next morning, August 5th, and true to their word, the Crow chiefs returned to the council tent. The scene was now somewhat friendly, and the chiefs received extra gifts, in order - as the Indians would say – "to cover" the great insults inflicted upon the head chief Long-Hair and his subordinate Big-Rain. The Crow chief then told the General,

*"Our wounds are now covered, and we will throw all that has passed behind us."* 9

Later that morning after the council concluded, the Crows returned to their camp. General Atkinson [presumably in the company of Rose] then visited Long-Hair in the lodge where the chief resided, and he and the chief enjoyed a further conversation together. Although after leaving the lodge, the General was still wary of the Indian's intentions; whether they be friendly or hostile, and ordered his soldiers to remain on a military footing with arms at the ready.

That same afternoon many Crows visited the cantonment in a very friendly manner, and soon the fears of the whites were dispelled. Again according to Beckwourth's version of events, the two half-blood Iroquois captives whose release had prompted the altercation in the first place, were duly given up to the commissioners, although no further mention is made in the official accounts of the expedition regarding if this was, or was not the case.

In yet another version, it is stated that the said captives were not then among those Crows in attendance. It is indicative, however, that a Flathead oral tradition states that in 1832 or early '33, a similar Government expedition consisting of seven 'wheel boats' ascended the Upper Missouri under the leadership of one, Colonel Clark, and among others on the expedition was an Iroquois trapper who's son by a Kutenai mother, along with a Flathead woman and child, had been taken captive by Crows some time earlier. The tradition further states that the expedition while on its way to the Yellowstone, eventually met with Crows and at which time, after the white men had threatened to destroy the Crow village with their howitzers, the Flathead woman and child were reluctantly returned by the Crow head chief himself, who had previousaly taken the woman as an extra wife. The Iroquois trapper's own son was not among the Crows at the meeting, but with another band [evidently Sore-Belly's forty absent lodges], and thus, was not given up at this time, and was not heard of again. [10]

The discrepency with this Flathead tradition is the dating. Wheel boats,' which were worked manually by their crews, were only first used with success by the Atkinson-O'Fallon expedition in 1825, but ceased to be used by the military *after* that expedition's return to St. Louis. The Flathead account, however, if one disregards the dating, does concur with Crow oral history, which states that it was during the Atkinson-O'Fallon council, that Chief Long-Hair was presented a red plume by an Iroquois trapper, which the latter had worn in his hair as his personal protective *medicine*. Hence, thereafter, Long-Hair was also known by the name, Red-Feather-On-The-Side-Of-The-Temple, and it would seem that the reason Long-Hair had been given the red plume, was as a token of thanks by the trapper for the return of the captives. [11]

This would mean, of course, that Beckwourth was wrong in his rendering of Long-Hair's speech, in which he mentioned the Crow chief, at an earlier date, having been given the red plume by the Red-haired chief William Clark. Furthermore, Long-Hair could not have met William Clark during the time of the Lewis and Clark expedition, as the explorers did not meet with, or have contact with Crows during the course of their travels. Having said this, if there is any truth in the Beckwourth account, then perhaps Long-Hair was actually referring to one or another prominent white man who also had red hair, but who both Long-Hair and Beckwourth confused with William Clark.

Whatever the case, the next morning, August 6th, the expedition members re-embarked on their wheel boats and continued up the Missouri toward the mouth of the Yellowstone. When only some six miles above the mouth of the Knife and the Hidatsa villages, the whites disembarked and set up camp for the night. With them remained a lone Crow Indian named Hair-Lip, of whom the official journal reported, *"...He is a dignified and well behaved man of a lying disposition as most Indians are."* [12]

The main Crow body had also left the council grounds that morning to make their way home, and these made camp further upriver three miles from the camp of the whites. A number of Crows visited the white men later that day, but left at dusk along with the Crow named Hair-Lip, and the following morning, both parties pursued their independent routes and were soon lost from each other's view. Thus came to an end the first officially sponsored meeting between the Crows and United States Government agents. An event which unbeknown to the Crows, would have far-reaching consequences regarding both people's relations with each other in future years.

Notwithstanding, however, the signing of the so-called "Friendship treaty" by all but one of the Crow chiefs, many of the rank and file tribal members still smarted over the humiliation suffered by their chief Long-Hair at the treaty ground, along with the wounding of Big-Rain. As a consequence, they continued to take advantage of the more vulnerable parties of white trappers accosted in Crow country, although there is no indication in existing records that after the signing of this treaty in 1825, white men were actually killed by Crows. On the other hand, horses, pelts, equipment and personal belongings were still taken from the whites on a regular basis. Likewise, the treaty in no way helped to create a reduction in Crow conflicts with their Indian enemies and for the Crows, intertribal warfare continued as vigorously as ever.

The truth of the matter is, that this particular Government initiative had not intended to undermine the independent autonomy of the tribes, or to cause any drastic change to their way of life and culture. Merely it was intended to obtain acknowledgment from the Indians of the supremacy of the United States, which in turn, promised to protect its Indian neighbours and enter into mutual agreements so that neither would assist the enemies of the other. Hereafter, the Indians would be expected to abide by the same laws of commerce as then in force by the said government among white Americans and thereby, allow the regulation of trade, in conjunction with white traders and trappers being allowed to cross tribal lands and ply their merchant boats up and down the Missouri without fear of harassment. In this particular the expedition was to prove partially successful, but as for tribes making pacts between themselves, even though the Cheyenne, Arickara, some bands of Lakota, Assiniboine, Mandan and Hidatsa did meet in friendship with each other in response to the expedition's requests, any inter-tribal pacts affected at this time, were merely of a temporary nature and were broken before the coming of winter.

The fact that the Crow Head Chief, Long-Hair, had suffered a degree of humiliation at the hands of white officials during the treaty signing, caused his high standing among the Apsaalooka to become even further diminished. The result being that although having been a renowned and successful war leader in his younger days, hereafter he was regarded only as a civic chief, and moreover, as a "holy" man, even though he still retained the title and position of *"Ashakee,"* i.e. `Chief of Chiefs. ` It was Sore-Belly who was now recognized as the paramount war-chief of the Nation, and oft-times, his authority was comparable to that of Long-Hair, even among the Mountain Crow band when making war or peace with one tribe or another. In the everyday activities of camp life, Sore-Belly`s authority and influence became such, that he it was who personally said yea or nay. He alone decided upon camping sites and organized the people's communal buffalo hunts, decisions once, customarily, left to the subordinate council of chiefs.

Sore-Belly, not having been personally present during the treaty signing, was therefore, was not technically obliged to adhere to its agreements. He was, though, astute enough to realize the benefits which peaceful relations with the white man could bestow upon his people, and he took pains to control the more incorrigible warriors among his band. He tried to prevent them from deliberately antagonizing white trappers and traders with whom his people came in contact and to this end, he was largely successful.

Not surprisingly, by 1826, after achieving the previously recounted victories over his people's enemies, Sore-Belly, albeit unofficially, actually superseded the position of Long-Hair to become himself in the eyes of many among both Mountain and River Crows, the recognized Head chief of the Nation, and regarded as an alternative to Long-Hair as "Chief of Chiefs" both in the military and civic capacity. As such he became somewhat arrogant and conceited. At least this was the impression harboured by certain white men of his acquaintance, particularly one Francis Chardon, chief trader at Fort Clark and later at Fort McKenzie during the eighteen-thirties and forties.

Sore-Belly, though, was in every way a product of his tribal upbringing and surroundings, in which all foreigners were potential enemies; threatening his people with subjugation or extermination. He could not deviate from his indoctrinated philosophy, in so much as compassion, mercy and humility could only be exercised sparingly, and, moreover, when beneficial to his people as a whole. As such, Sore-Belly was, to a degree, compassionate, compared to what was then general among Indians, but due to the hostile world which he and his people were endeavouring to survive in, he could not afford his own warrior status to be undermined, lest it be construed as weakness.

An example of this side of Sore-Belly`s character was made apparent when he exercised the full unbridled power of his protective *medicine* helper, the `Thunder,` and this in a spectacular manner which is still recounted today in Crow oral tradition. The reason for inciting his actions at this time would, perhaps, have appeared trivial if not common place to another in his position. But Sore-Belly took it as a personal affront to his perceived standing among his people and of his individual prowess, which resulted in the following episode.

Sore-Belly had often made friendly overtures to one or another tribe in order to broach more congenial relationships, be they friend or foe, and to this effect, during late summer, 1826, Sore-Belly and a large contingent of River Crows paid an unexpected visit to the Hidatsa, whose earth-lodge villages stood on both banks of the Knife near its junction with the Missouri.

After several weeks of congenial feasting, dancing and trading, Sore-Belly and his followers finally packed their tepee covers and belongings on pony drags, and prepared to leave their Hidatsa hosts to return to their own country north of the Yellowstone. Sore-Belly at that time owned a fine bay mare, a fast buffalo runner of which he was particularly proud. However, having gathered in their ponies from the previous night's grazing, it was discovered that Sore-Belly`s bay mare was nowhere to be found.

There was no reason to suppose that foreign raiders had come anywhere near the villages during the night and it was assumed by the Crows, that a Hidatsa had stolen the horse and very likely, had it secreted in some dark recess of one of the numerous earth-lodges where it would remain until after the Crows departed. Of this Sore-Belly was convinced, but to have forcibly entered any of the lodges without the owner's consent would undoubtedly have resulted in conflict, and the Crows being grossly outnumbered by their Hidatsa hosts would not have been in a favourable position to survive such a contest. Instead, the Crow chief in his anger at first demanded that the Hidatsa chief named Black-Moccasin, command the thief to return the horse; but the Hidatsa chief made no response. Sore-Belly then cried aloud to all the Hidatsa, saying,

"…Truly, the Hidatsa know the name of Alapooish, but still you do not fear his power which comes from "Thunder" itself. Know it then, that `Thunder` is his "*medicine*" father, who allows Alapooish to call upon him and do great things. Soon Alapooish will request his assistance that he might punish the Hidatsa for their perfidy. Know it well *Bikansahtahisshe-xawuhxawuua* [i.e. Carrot-Crunchers], ere long you shall witness his power and know what it is to incur his displeasure." [13]

Having berated the Hidatsa thus, Sore-Belly and his people then left their hosts and started on their long trek home. They travelled west at a slow pace until mid-afternoon, when for no apparent reason, Sore-Belly called a halt and bade his people set up their tepees on the open prairie, for here he intended they should camp for the night.

The day was still bright and warm; the sky azure blue without a cloud to be seen. But Sore-Belly now did a strange thing. He began securing the hide cover of his tepee with extra pegs which his several wives hammered into the ground and in addition, he bade them attach guide ropes in order to secure the lodge more firmly. He even had heavy stones placed around the edge of the tepee cover where it touched the ground, as one would do when anticipating an impending storm. His people watched him with curiosity. But when their chief bade them do likewise to their own tepees, they immediately followed suit. They trusted implicitly in his judgment and having done this, the people waited to see what would happen next.

The rest of the afternoon passed without event, and some of the people said to one another that this time their great chief's *medicine* had failed him, as nothing of note had occurred. Then, as the sun began to set over the western horizon, from the tepee of Sore-Belly came four loud blasts from his large mountain-goat horn, and all those in camp were immediately put on their guard.

Suddenly the sky darkened; a howling wind blew up and rapidly increased its ferocity to a degree not recalled among the Crows in living memory. All the tepees shook violently, but owing to the precautions taken by their owners as instructed by Sore-Belly, not one tepee was destroyed or even overturned by the great wind that swept all else before it across the open prairie. The very heavens next seemed to open wide and a great torrent of rain caused such a deluge that within a very short while, the once dry and dusty prairie ravines and gullies became filled with fast-flowing water. The ground about quickly turned to mud with large pools forming in every depression. Then, as if this was not enough, when the sudden downpour finally ceased, giant hailstones the size of a man's fist, it is said, rained down upon the land, beating and crashing against the hide tepee covers and in the words of Winona Plenty Hoops,

*"Went bouncing over the ground like hundreds of rubber balls."* [14]

Such was the fury of the storm's onslaught that none could stand against it, lest they literally be blown off their feet or knocked unconscious by the balls of ice hurtling from the sky. The Crows remained in their lodges which being doubly secured, withstood the tempest, and the people merely waited patiently for the storm to pass. Come morning, the sky again was clear and bright, but Sore-Belly commanded his people to remain where they were. Not only was the ground still too wet to travel, but he fully expected something more to happen before the day was done. Sore-Belly turned to his people and cried,

"Perhaps now the Hidatsa will repent their foolishness and return the horse they stole from Alapooish, having witnessed the power of his father, the 'Thunder.'" [15]

All those among the Crows had no doubt whatsoever, that the violent storm had been conjured up by the great chief himself. As the day wore on and the prairie sun shined bright and hot, the water-filled gullies and muddy pools quickly dried out and then; late in the afternoon, the Crows discerned in the distance a column of people on horseback and on foot coming slowly towards their camp. Some were singing a doleful song, while others raised repeated cries to the unseen spirits as if lamenting a great disaster.

These people were soon recognized as Hidatsa with their head chief Black-Moccasin riding in the van. He carried a peace pipe in the crook of his right arm, and in his left hand he held the halter rope of a fine bay mare trotting disconcertedly behind him. Close by came a number of pack-ponies loaded down with presents. These included beautifully tanned and embroidered leather shirts and leggings, blue and red trade blankets, tanned buffalo and elk-hide robes, along with other articles such as weapons and domestic items, all of which were to be presented to the Crow chief to appease his wrath.

Sore-Belly stood alone and silent in front of the door flap of his tepee ready to receive them; arms folded across his chest; his face impassive as the Hidatsa rode up. The chief Black-Moccasin and his headmen dismounted from their ponies while at the same time, several Hidatsa women started to unload the aforementioned gifts and stacked them up in a great pile on the ground before

Sore-Belly's tepee. The Hidatsa chief then addressed Sore-Belly with words to the effect,

> "We have done wrong and have been punished. Your horse was taken and we refused to return it. You left us in anger yesterday morning, and last night there came upon us a furious storm of rain and hail that soaked our houses so that many of them fell in and are destroyed. Others are filled with water and their occupants forced to seek shelter where they can. The hail beat down our corn and pumpkins, and our fields are now desolate. Where shall we look for food this coming winter? We now return your horse and bring you presents, and beg you turn your anger from us." [16]

The return of the bay horse along with many presents was welcomed by Sore-Belly, although the experience of seeing the Hidatsa humbling themselves before him and acknowledging his great standing, was that which gave the greatest satisfaction. At once his stern demeanour changed, and he answered the Hidatsa and their chief Black-Moccasin thus,

> "This one who you know as Alapooish bears the Hidatsa no ill will. Alapooish accepts your presents and shall injure you no more. But you did well to curb his displeasure, for this winter Alapooish should have caused such a storm of snow to come upon you as was never seen before. He would have heaped it over your villages so that you could not have escaped and must have perished. They are fools who incur the resentment of Alapooish." [17]

The episode over, both peoples went their separate ways, the Hidatsa returning to their dilapidated earthen lodges; the Crows towards their own hunting grounds in the Yellowstone country several hundred miles west. So it was that the Crows and Hidatsa continued in friendship with one another, albeit the latter now with a better understanding of the Crow chief's personal power and prestige.

$$- 0 - 0 - 0 - 0 - 0 - 0 - 0 - 0 - 0 - 0 - 0 - 0 -$$

CROWS, ONCE YOUNG WARRIORS WITH SORE-BELLY.
LEFT TO RIGHT; LONG-HORSE, SITS-IN-MIDDLE-OF-LAND AND WOLF-BELLY.
*[Smithsonian Institution, Washington D. C. 1873]*

**THE AUTHOR WITH JOE MEDICINE CROW. GARRYOWEN. MONTANA. 2011.**
*[Author`s collection]*

**THE AUTHOR WITH WINONA PLENTY-HOOPS. LODGE GRASS. MONTANA. 2011.**
*[Author`s collection]*

**CROW CHIEF, TWO CROWS,**
**A CONTEMPORARY OF SORE-BELLY.**
*[Painted from life by George Catlin in 1832]*

Crow chief, Big-Bowl.
[Painted by A. J. Miller in 1837]

Crow chief, Four-Wolves.
[Painted by George Catlin in 1832]

Crow chief, Bull-Goes-Hunting.
*[Photo by Edward S. Curtis, 1907]*

Cheyenne chief, High-Backed-Wolf.
*[Painted by George Catlin in 1832]*

**Chief Sore-Belly's personal Medicine pipe.**
*[Museum of Chicago, U.S.A.]*

Dance of the Half-Shaved-Heads Society, showing the Mandan equivalent.
*[Painted by Karl Bodmer. 1833. Joslyn Art Museum. Nebraska. U.S.A.]*

**Kenneth McKenzie.**
*[Missouri Historical Society]*

**Edwin T. Denig.**
*[Montana Historical Society]*

**Robert Stuart.**
*[Missouri Historical Society]*

**Captain Benjamin L. Bonneville.**
*[Montana Historical Society]*

**CROW CHIEF, TIES-HIS-HAIR-BEFORE,**
**A CONTEMPORARY OF SORE-BELLY.**
*[Painted from life by George Catlin in 1832]*

HUGH MUNROE IN OLD AGE WITH BLACKFOOT RELATIVES.
*[Photo from, "Rising Wolf, the White Blackfoot," by James Willard Schultz]*

**Lieutenant James H. Bradley**
*[Montana Historical Society]*

**Alexander Culbertson**
*[Missouri Historical Society]*

# PART 11.

## DENIZENS OF THE UPPER MISSOURI

**RIVER CROW CHIEFS BEAR`S-HEAD AND ROTTEN-TAIL**
[Warriors who rode with Sore-Belly. Photo taken in 1859. Yale University]

**CROW CHIEF, SACRED-RAVEN, i. e. MEDICINE-CROW 1ST.**

## CHAPTER 15.

## CAPTURED PONIES, COUPS AND SCALPS.

One should not suppose that the Atkinson - O`Fallon initiative of 1825, did in any way curtail the aggressive Indian spirit towards their long-term antagonists. Intertribal warfare persisted unabated, albeit in October that year under the influence of the Hudson`s Bay trader Peter Skene Ogden, the Bloods, Siksika, Piegan [Pikuni] and Atsina did make pacts with the Flathead, Kutenai, Shoshoni and Nez-Perce.[1] It was probably for this reason that the Crows were reported by Ogden as then being at war with the Shoshoni, because of the latter's supposed new alliance with the Blackfoot who were then still at war with the Crows. However, by the following year the Crows must have patched up their quarrel with the Shoshoni, if it existed, for they were then again at peace with one another and as regards the Shoshoni specifically, they were again allied with Crows against all Blackfoot-speaking tribes and the latter`s confederates. Thus even several of the Ogden inspired pacts of 1825 lasted only to the following winter. Certainly from early 1826 onward, intertribal war on the Crow front actually escalated, as the obtaining of beaver and other pelts to trade to the white man became more intense and competitive between the tribes, and subsequently, more aggressive in its pursuit.

Truly then, the upper country was still a bloody arena. But this did not deter white trappers from entering the region. Not only in expectation of monetary gain from the procurement of beaver pelts, but also, due to the appeal of adventure and freedom from the dictates and confines of urban society in the towns and cities of the East. A number of licensed fur companies did conduct their business with controls and commitments pertaining to both their employees and the Indians. But by far the majority of white men now flooding into the upper country were so-called "Free Trappers;" unregulated and unconstrained wandering through the Indian domains at will. They lacked allegiance or obligation to any but themselves and often ran afoul of Indian scalping parties. If fortunate, they were merely robbed of their furs and equipment by the Indians and left with their lives, albeit to make their way through the wilderness at the mercy of other Indian enemies, the mountains, wild animals and the extremes of nature. If lucky they might reach a point of safety, whether it be another group of white men; a friendly Indian village, or a trading post where their sufferings could at last be alleviated.

So it was during the same year of 1826, Blackfoot raiders stole a very large number of horses from Sore-Belly`s River Crows in a single raid near a butte known as "Goose Neck" in the Little Belt Mountains of north-central Montana, while according to the trapper Robert Campbell, four Crows, two each in separate engagements were killed by white men, which incensed a number of Crows into taking a temporary hostile stance against all white trappers and traders. There is, however, no documented record of Crows actually killing white men in retaliation during this period, although the possibility of their doing so managed to deter the trading companies for the time being, from re-occupying their posts in Crow country. For the next two years, many white men thought it wise to be extra wary if encountering Crows upon the trail. The majority of Crows nevertheless, did realize that not having direct access to the white man`s guns and ammunition, was a severe setback to their tribe`s survival in the hostile environment in which they lived. There was some degree of compensation, in so much as the Crows could still obtain certain white trade goods from their Hidatsa relatives lower down the Missouri. Not to mention the guns, metal knives, hatchets and ammunition which they continued to obtain as booty during the course of their intertribal conflicts. Paradoxically, though, certain small bands of `Free` white trappers continued sporadically, to team up with one or another of the more tolerant Crow groups in order to socialize together, and even to act as allies against mutual Blackfoot and Atsina antagonists.

A Hunkpapa Lakota winter-count entry for 1826, records that a famous Lakota chief named Corn-Stalk went to war against the Crows and returned with many scalps. Probably this refers to the well-known Miniconjou chief known at a later date simply as Corn, and, perhaps, the Crows suffered great loss on that occasion. However, good fortune did attend Sore-Belly`s River Crows when in October this year [1826], a party of Beaver Hills Cree from the north visited Sore-Belly`s camp in an attempt to make peace with their erstwhile foe.

Such an unprecedented move on the part of the Cree, was in response to their having recently suffered a severe defeat at the hands of a combined Siksika, Blood, Atsina and Sarsi force that had attacked the Beaver Hills Cree camp the previous month and killed ten occupants in the process. The raiders themselves also suffered a number killed in the affray, but rode off victorious with eighty buffalo-hide tents and all the camp booty besides. Thus for the time being, the Beaver Hills Cree dare not stay in the North Country for fear of the Blackfoot.

Expediently they came south; on the one hand to obtain horses and a temporary refuge among the Crows, on the other to make contact with American traders on the Yellowstone. These new arrivals were made welcome by Sore-Belly, who no longer having access to a trading post in his own country due to his people`s perceived hostility to white men the previous year, readily accepted the peace initiative from the Cree. He saw in them a source of goods from Canadian traders north of the International boundary, and as an ally against the Blackfoot and their confederates who were the inveterate enemies of the Crows and now, of the Beaver Hills Cree also.

As a consequence, in January 1827, Sore-Belly`s River Crows with Beaver Hills Cree allies, joined in a great battle against the Siksika in which fifteen of the latter were slain including three men of distinction, and one hundred and sixty-five Siksika horses driven off by the victors. Not only were the Crows and their Cree associates victorious on the field, but they drove the enemy north across the Missouri and even further, to the Hudson`s Bay post Fort Edmonton on the North Saskatchewan River. Then only did the victors halt their pursuit and return south from whence they came, while the discomfited Siksika sought refuge among the Hudson`s Bay employees at the fort. The result of this reversal on the part of the Siksika was that they and their kinfolk the Bloods, led by a well-known chief named Bulls-Back-Fat, immediately sent an offering of tobacco to the Carlton House Cree bands and Stony Assiniboine of that eastern district with a proposal of peace between their peoples. Hopefully, they thought, such would help patch up their recent quarrel with the Beaver Hills Cree and by increasing their combined strength, thereby break the latter`s new alliance with the Crow.

For a while the Cree band involved dithered over the proposal, while the Assiniboine made no response at all and in the following month of February [1827], the Crows again whipped the Blackfoot, this time in the guise of a Pikuni party which had gone south of the Missouri to hunt. In this engagement fourteen Pikuni were killed and may have been the same Pikuni war band that in the following moon near the head of the Jefferson Fork of the Missouri, battled with a mixed band of American and Hudson`s Bay trappers among whom were Robert Campbell and Peter Skene Ogden. During this event an Iroquois trapper known as "Old Pierre" was killed, in who`s memory the famous topographical feature of Pierre`s Hole, Idaho, has been subsequently named. Thus, it seems, Crows belonging to both the Mountain and River bands had, at this period, at last achieved the ascendency in the Upper Missouri country.

In late April or early May [1827], after the Siksika and Bloods had earnestly reiterated their desire for a reconciliation with the Cree and Assiniboine, a party of Bloods did meet a number of Beaver Hills Cree at Fort Edmonton and together, discussed the prospects of peace. Originally a Blood initiative, this proposed pact was meant to include the latter`s confederated tribes of Siksika, Pikuni, Atsina and Sarsi, and to facilitate unobstructed access to Hudson`s Bay posts without fear of Cree and Assiniboine harassment.

As previously mentioned, it would also increase their strength in their ongoing war with the Crows who were ever a threat to all Blackfoot tribes and their allies, each time these last named attempted to exploit the rich fur-trapping grounds in the Missouri Three Forks and Yellowstone regions. Indeed, the Bloods especially, wished it known that they intended to continue their war with the Crows in earnest. However, it was April the following year of 1828 before an official peace-making took place between the Bloods, Siksika and Sarsi on one side, and the Carlton House and Beaver Hills Cree along with the Stony Assiniboine on the other.

During the winter of 1827 /`28 and throughout the ensuing spring and summer, the Crows still held the upper hand and suffered no serious reversal from their many foes. They now appeared haughty and fickle, and even though Sore-Belly advocated strongly for the return of white traders to the Crow country, the continuing aggressive stance from rank and file warriors in the tribe – notwithstanding their sometimes camping in harmony with certain groups of "Free" white trappers when it suited them to do so, – still deterred most other white men from staying too long in the Crow domain.

Examples of the above scenario had occurred the previous summer of `27, when Crows near South Pass ran off most of the horses belonging to men of Joshua Pilcher`s fur company then en route with goods from the East to supply the annual `Trapper`s Rendezvous` for that year, and in yet another incident during the winter of 1827 /`28, a party of Crows returning from a visit to the Shoshoni in the Great Salt Lake district of Utah, stole four horses from Robert Campbell's trapper camp at a place called Cache Valley north of the Sweetwater River. Then in the new year [February 1828], a large River Crow war-party led by Sore-Belly went north; ambushed a small Atsina camp and in the event, killed at least twenty-five Atsina warriors and carried off a great amount of plunder including guns, powder and ball. In March, another or perhaps, the same war band of Sore- Belly's Crows scored a second victory, this time over a combined Siksika and Blood force during which a Blood chief by the name of Crowfoot was killed, while somewhere on the North Platte a band of trappers including Henry Vanderburgh, William Bent and Lucien Fontenelle among others, had *"...a set to with Crows"* [2] and during which the trappers lost two men. However, following this in late August or early September, another big fight took place between on the one side an allied party of Mountain Crow, Shoshoni and American trappers, and on the other, a large Pikuni war band. This fight was reported by the Hudson's Bay factor at Fort Edmonton on the 8th of October 1828, who merely stated,

"The Piegans have had a battle with the Crow Indians as well as the Snake, and that eighteen Americans have been killed." [3]

Quite likely this reference applies to a specific episode also mentioned by James Beckwourth in his "Life and Adventures" as occurring about this same period, wherein it is stated that a mixed band of white trappers and Indians had pitched their lodges on a jutting piece of land creating a horseshoe bend in a river flanked on both sides by thick stands of timber. Their lodges stood four rows deep in the narrow part of the horseshoe at the entrance of the bend, and in front of which the Indian and trapper defenders were positioned. Their women and children and spare horses were placed between the rear of the lodges and the river at the back of the horseshoe bend.

According to this account there were many Blackfoot [Piegans ?], two-thousand five-hundred, Beckwourth said, who made a series of furious charges upon the camp and twice succeeded in driving the defenders back, so that the lodges were then between the opposing forces as a protective barrier. For the most part, the Indian defenders relied on bows and arrows as only their white companions and a few others had guns of any description. But still they managed to keep from being overrun and at length, a large body of mounted Indian defenders rode undetected through the timber along one side of the bend, and manoeuvred in such a way as to charge the enemy's rear. At the same moment another large body of mounted Indians and white defenders – led by the trapper William Sublette – simultaneously charged the enemy from the front, and such was the double impact, that the entire Pikuni force was obliged to flee leaving their dead upon the field. The defender's loss, Beckwourth continued, was sixteen killed outright with fifty or sixty wounded including Beckwourth himself, whilst the Blackfoot attackers - again by Beckwourth's count - supposedly lost some one-hundred and sixty dead, which number can only be regarded as preposterous.

The fact that soon after the fight, a number of Shoshoni and Crow reinforcements joined with those in the defender's camp, indicates that Crows and

Shoshoni were indeed the trapper`s Indian allies on this occasion, and that Beckwourth`s account does refer to the same event as noted by the Hudson`s Bay Company factor at Edmonton House. It is also the same event referred to in the Bull-Plume Piegan winter-count for the year 1828, wherein it is stated,

"When the Piegans Lost the Battle," [4]

It was, perhaps, because of the involvement of white trappers in the above episode, that soon after the fight and notwithstanding a small number of incorrigibles on both sides, friendly relations were finally restored between white men and the majority of Crows. Certainly during the following winter of 1828 /`29, Robert Campbell and others including James Bridger after trapping along the Powder, Tongue and Big Horn Rivers, spent the winter in the camp of Chief Long-Hair`s Mountain Crows and among whom at that time, was Sore-Belly with his wife`s Greasy-Mouth clan, and it was in Sore-Belly`s lodge that Campbell was then residing.

Earlier, while ensconced near the Popo Agie River where it flows into Wind River, Campbell had cached one-hundred and fifty beaver pelts, but sometime during his stay in Sore-Belly`s lodge, a returning Crow war-party came in from the south with fresh scalps taken during a raid on the Cheyenne and Arapaho. As usual during the ensuing revelry celebrating the warrior`s victorious return, the war party members boasted of their deeds and it was also proclaimed aloud how they had robbed a cache of beaver skins, the same only recently buried by Campbell near the Popo Agie. When recounting the event some years later, Campbell himself stated that the Crow chief Long-Hair inquired from Campbell if he had cached any pelts which had since been stolen. Being answered in the affirmative, Long-Hair promised that he himself would neither eat nor sleep until all the skins were returned. The chief then mounted a horse and rode among the lodges, crying aloud that his people had been a long time without traders and they must not keep one skin back. Such was the people`s high esteem for the old chief and fear of his supposed magical powers, that every beaver skin was duly returned, at which point Long-Hair finally broke his fast and from that time on, all white men were again made welcome among the Crows.

Indeed, it was probably Robert Campbell whilst residing in Sore-Belly`s lodge during the winter in question, who had an intimate relationship with one of Sore-Belly`s wives or, more specifically, with the chief`s first wife who had once been a captive of the Pikuni. Certainly, it was the custom among the Crows – as among most other tribes – to offer one`s wife or wives to a guest as a token of hospitality, and to refuse such an offer was to offend. Campbell, undoubtedly, had been offered such a comfort, and likely had been obliged to accept. Perhaps then, this was how some appropriate months later, the said woman gave birth to a son with light complexion and blue eyes. Sore-Belly himself is said to have told those around him that the new arrival was, indeed, "an unusual boy," and predicted that when the boy grew older, he would be able to speak the white man`s language. In later years, after the boy had grown to manhood, he was known by the name of Chips-the-Rock, and when white men came to his camp, it was he who translated their words into Crow. Chips-The-Rock`s Grandfather on his mother`s side, often told the people that the reason his grandson looked like a white man, was because his mother had too often watched a particular white man who had resided in Sore-Belly`s tepee during the winter prior to his birth, and thus, one must conclude what one will. Chips-the-Rock himself sired four daughters, one of whom was named Pretty-Medicine-Pipe, born in 1858.

This woman first married a famous Crow warrior and chief named Old-Crow, and after his demise, she became the wife of White-Man-Runs-Him. Pretty-Medicine-Pipe, therefore, was the Grandmother of the present Author`s friend and informant, Winona Plenty-Hoops, and from whom the story is derived.

It was also during Campbell`s stay in Sore-Belly`s lodge this same winter of 1828, that Campbell heard the chief`s soliloquy pertaining to the Crow domain. Campbell noted down Sore-Belly`s words verbatim which were as follows,

"The Crow country is a good country. The Great Spirit has put it exactly in the right place; while you are in it you fare well; whenever you go out of it, which any way you travel you fare worse. If you go to the south, you have to wander over great barren Plains; the water is warm and bad and you meet with fever and ague. To the north it is cold; the winters are long and bitter and there is no grass; you cannot keep horses there but must travel with dogs. What is a country without horses? On the Columbia they are poor and dirty, paddle about in canoes and eat fish. Their teeth are worn out; they are always taking fish bones out of their mouths; fish is poor food. To the east they dwell in villages; they live well, but they drink the muddy waters of the Missouri – that is bad. A Crow`s dog would not drink such water…About the forks of the Missouri is a fine country; good water, good grass, plenty of buffalo. In summer it is almost as good as the Crow country, but in winter it is cold; the grass is gone and there is no salt weed for the horses. …The Crow country is exactly in the right place.

It has snowy mountains and sunny Plains, all kinds of climates and good things for every season. When the summer heats scorch the prairies, you can draw up under the mountains where the air is sweet and cool, the grass fresh, and the bright streams come tumbling out of the snow banks. There you can hunt the elk, the deer and the antelope, when their skins are fit for dressing, there you will find plenty of white bears and mountain sheep. In the autumn, when your horses are fat and strong from the mountain pastures, you can go down into the Plains and hunt the buffalo, or trap beaver on the streams. And when winter comes on, you can take shelter in the woody bottoms along the rivers; there you will find buffalo meat for yourselves, and cottonwood bark for your horses; or you may winter in the Wind River valley, where there is salt weed in abundance. The Crow country is in exactly the right place. Everything good is to be found there. There is no country like the Crow country." [5]

From the above extract, one can understand why Sore-Belly was so determined to protect his domain against all invaders who craved the Crow country for themselves, and why he always advocated friendship with the white man. This was to afford his people a strong ally in their constant intertribal wars, and to enable them to obtain the white trader`s guns and other commodities, without which the Crows would eventually be overwhelmed by their enemies if not destroyed utterly as a separate tribal entity. Certainly white trappers and traders hereafter, again regarded the majority of Crows as "friendlies," although neither side could be fully trusted. There were always rogue elements among both white men and Crows alike, who sometimes stole each other`s horses and belongings and even a scalp or two when there was little risk of being detected.

Exacerbating the situation and still threatening a serious breakdown in Crow - white relations, was Chief Arrow-Head`s Dried-Out-Furs Crow band of dissidents, members of which continued to sporadically harass white men when they saw fit to do so, and were even at loggerheads with their own tribal cousins of the Whistling-Waters Crow clan. However, yet another reason which continued to create Crow confrontations with white trappers and traders, was the intense rivalry existing between the different fur companies themselves, whose strategy it was to encourage one or another tribe to commit hostile acts upon the employees of a competitive company, and to prevent other Indians from accessing furs and pelts if they were suppliers to the opposition.

This also promoted intertribal warfare throughout the region, and the Indians were willing participants. It was in a tribe`s own interest to prevent enemies from trading with white men for guns and ammunition, the possession of which gave the advantage to one tribe over another.

It had been for this reason that Long-Hair had returned Campbell`s stolen pelts in order to instigate a renewal of trade between the white men and his people, while at the same time, Long-Hair and Sore-Belly persistently badgered both Campbell and Bridger to re-establish a permanent trading post in Crow country. Likewise, the nefarious Blackfoot, Atsina and Assiniboine also craved posts in their own domains, which would allow themselves convenient access to the white man`s goods, rather than the Indians having to traverse hostile regions through which they travelled at their peril.

So it was, come spring of 1829, after Campbell and his white companions had finally left Long Hair`s village to continue trapping through the country, they did so still wary of physical violence from parties of dissident Crows. Raiding bands of Blackfoot and Atsina, of course, continued to invest the region and always posed a significant threat to Crows and white trappers alike.

Indeed, a part of Campbell`s brigade soon after vacating Long-Hair`s village had all its horses stolen by a band of Blackfoot thieves, while in another event, the Crows lost both horses and a few scalps to the same Blackfoot marauders.

The Crows retaliated by constantly harassing the Blackfoot and the latter`s Sarsi and Atsina allies and it was in this same year of 1829, according to the Blood Indian Bad-Head`s winter count, that seven warriors of Sore Belly`s River Crows were annihilated by Bloods led by their famous chief, Spotted-Bear,

181

at a place known as Buffalo Horn Butte near present-day Chinook in north-western Montana.

The Crows were still at peace with the Shoshoni and, tentatively, with the Beaver Hills Cree and once again at peace with the Flatheads, but they were at war with every other Plains-dwelling tribe, among whom were included Cheyennes, Arapaho and Lakota. This very summer William Sublette`s brigade of trappers met a large war-party of combined Lakota, Cheyenne and Arapaho on Powder River. The Indians, Sublette later recorded, were on a hostile expedition against the Crows. It is not recorded or remembered what the outcome was regarding the expedition, although very soon after meeting Sublette, a memorable fight did take place, - ostensibly later that same summer of 1829, - when a formidable Northern Cheyenne and Suhtaio war-party also went searching for Crow scalps and women and children captives.

Earlier that year a Northern Cheyenne chief of some standing [whose name has been forgotten], had been killed by Crows. Perhaps this had occurred during the same Lakota, Cheyenne and Arapaho expedition met by Sublette, but whatever the case, in response, the Omissis and Suhtaio Cheyenne bands then generally roaming the Black Hills region of South Dakota decided to punish the Crows, and a large war-party comprising a little over one-hundred braves was organized to do just that. The warriors travelled on horseback as it was intended to take scalps rather than horses alone. Among their number was a well-known Suhtaio shaman named Old-Horn [in later years known as Blind-Bull], along with his son named Box-Elder [later known as Brave-Wolf]. The shaman Old-Horn was the owner of a powerful *medicine* that had been given him by the wolves, and this, it was believed, would protect both he and any with him from harm.

Now it happened that a mixed war-band consisting of a few Mountain Crows and a large number of Sore-Belly`s River Crows along with a contingent of Shoshoni allies, was at that same time traveling from the Wind River region towards the buffalo country east of the Big Horn Mountains. In total, not including non-combatants, this combined group numbered little short of one-hundred and fifty warriors, and having scouts out reconnoitring the route ahead, they discovered the aforesaid Cheyenne war-party and surrounded it, even before the enemy knew what was happening.

When the Cheyennes did realize their vulnerable situation, they all at once dismounted and hastily erected a kind of barricade with brush and dead timber, and behind which they prepared to defend themselves against what they thought, would be imminent attack.

The first action on the part of the Crows and Shoshoni, however, whose complement of fighting men was not much greater than the enemy, was to stampede the latter`s horses, after which they began sniping from cover at the enemy already entrenched behind their breastwork. The defenders returned the fire with arrows and musket balls, and throughout the daylight hours the conflict continued, incurring one or two casualties on both sides.

Come nightfall hostilities ceased, but the Cheyennes could not escape owing to the vigilance of the Crows and Shoshoni, who kept a close watch on the position and shot missiles at anyone and anything that moved.

As the sun came up the following morning, reciprocal shooting began again and in such a way for another three days and nights, the conflict continued. The Crows and Shoshoni would not give up; and the enemy could not be budged.

During all this time several Crows and Shoshoni had been wounded, whilst the latter had no way of knowing for sure how many – if any – casualties their besieged enemies may have suffered. The Crows and their allies knew too well what great loss to their own numbers would be incurred if they were to storm the position head on. Thus they merely carried on sniping at the foe, while shouting the customary epithets of abuse and insults in an attempt to lure the Cheyennes into the open.

By the fourth day the besieged Cheyennes were suffering greatly from thirst and fatigue, and had fully resigned themselves to being annihilated by the foe. It was at this stage in the siege that a pack of wolves in the vicinity – smelling blood and sensing the human carnage about to transpire - all at once set up a continuous howling, which was interpreted in different ways by the respective combatants at the scene. The Crows and Shoshoni were sure that the sudden gathering of wolves was a sign the enemy would soon all be killed, while among the Cheyennes the shaman Old-Horn actually welcomed what he heard.

The wolves, he said, were his sacred protectors and were talking to him in a way that only he could understand. He told his companions that the wolves were telling him to send his son Box-Elder outside the breastworks to make *medicine,* and by so doing, their whole party would be saved.

Whatever his personal misgivings, Box-Elder did as Old-Horn instructed and stepped outside the breastworks in full view of the enemy. He then began blowing on a high-pitched eagle bone whistle and performed a kind of rhythmic dance in front of the Cheyenne position. The Crows and Shoshoni were at first curious regarding the actions of this lone Cheyenne, and suspecting that some powerful *medicine* was being directed against them, they became apprehensive as to what would happen next. Then all at once the wolves ceased their howling and the lone Cheyenne still blowing his whistle, suddenly charged directly towards the enemy. At the same instant, the remaining Cheyennes leapt over the breastworks and followed in the wake of Box-Elder. The whole force of Crows and Shoshoni seemed to take fright and they retreated back a little, giving room to the charging Cheyennes rather than getting to grips with them in hand to hand conflicts, which would incur many more casualties than the Crows themselves deemed necessary. Thus the Crows and Shoshoni continued to hold back and subsequently, allowed the Cheyennes to make their escape, and albeit on foot, return safely to their own country.

The Crows and Shoshoni then retired from the scene, satisfied with the number of horses they had taken from the enemy.

Even so, while most of their warriors were moving away from the region, a number of Crows upon discovering a party of white trappers in the area, ran off nearly all their horses to help compensate for the recent humiliation suffered at the hands of the Cheyennes. This camp of trappers just happened to belong to chief's Long-Hair and Sore-Belly`s old friend Robert Campbell, although Campbell himself was not present at the time. [6]

$$- 0 - 0 - 0 - 0 - 0 - 0 - 0 - 0 - 0 - 0 - 0 - 0 - 0 - 0 -$$

## CHAPTER. 16.

## JAMES P. BECKWORTH and LITTLE-WHITE-BULL`S LAST STAND.

It was the same year of 1829 soon after the aforementioned episode with Cheyennes, that James Beckwourth the mulatto Mountain Man who had often been a member of Robert Campbell`s fur company brigade, was adopted into the Crow tribe. Beckwourth later dictated his life story to T.D. Bonner sometime between 1854 and 1855, which was published in 1856 under the title *"Life and Adventures of James P. Beckwourth."* [1]

According to Beckwourth who, it must be said, was well known for wild exaggeration even though the events he mentioned did, for the most part, actually take place, he was first introduced to the Crows by a fellow trapper named Caleb Greenwood [the *"Life and Adventures"* erroneously give the date as 1827]. This man Greenwood told the Crows that Beckwourth, although born a Crow, had been taken captive by Cheyennes when a child. The Crows were desirous to know how this could be, and according to Beckwourth`s account, Greenwood replied that so many winters earlier the Cheyennes had defeated the Crows, killing many Crow warriors and carrying off a large number of women and children. Greenwood then said that Beckwourth had been a *bar-cacha* [child] among the Crows at that time, and that Cheyennes had afterwards sold him to the Whites. Beckwourth`s account continues by stating that when the Crows returned to their village and relayed Greenwood`s words, all those mothers who had lost young sons during the defeat in question wondered if Beckwourth was not their own child, when; so Beckwourth stated, *"...the Crows had lost two thousand warriors and a host of women and children with the ensuing captivity,"* [2].

In a later passage, Beckwourth further stated that a crowd of women gathered around in order to inspect his person in detail. They were looking for any distinguishing marks on his body, whereby they might recognize their *"brave son."* [3] One Crow woman, being the wife of the council chief, Big-Bowl, whose three year old son had indeed been carried away during the destruction of a Crow village, professed that Beckwourth was, in fact, her long-lost offspring because of a mole on Beckwourth`s eyelid, and this - as far as the woman was concerned - proved beyond doubt Beckwourth`s true identity.

Beckwourth`s reference to the destruction of a Crow village, although completely false regarding his alleged connection and including the customary exaggeration of numbers killed found throughout his *"Life and Adventures,"* seems, however, to have confused the later-date destruction of Chief Long-Hair`s village in 1820 with that of 1801, but which does imply that the 1820 event was considered of such importance, it was still a topic of conversation many years later, and was an episode of common knowledge among both Indians and white men during Beckwourth`s time in the Far West.

Certainly, an important collection of historical data concerning both Crow and Cheyenne and Crow and Blackfoot-Atsina warfare during the eighteen-thirties is included in Beckwourth`s recollections, and his memory of the death of the Crow Little-White-Bull, correlates favourably with other contemporary and tribal traditional versions, and which in essence run as follows.

During the middle part of January, 1830, a combined group of Kicked-in-the-Belly and River Crows left their winter camps. They travelled some three-hundred miles east, following the twisting courses of the Yellowstone and Missouri downstream in order to visit Kipp`s post at the mouth of White Earth River and also, the resident Hidatsa and Mandan villages between Knife River and the Heart. Usually such excursions lasted no longer than six weeks, but in this case, owing to freezing weather and recurring storms, the month of March – *"The Moon when river ice breaks up"*- was waxing full, and still the Crow trading party was ensconced outside the Hidatsa villages, merely awaiting the sky to clear before setting out for home.

Whilst on their trip down the Missouri, a combined Arickara, Cheyenne and Lakota war-band had attacked the River Crow camp then on the north bank of the Yellowstone. This time there remained an adequate Crow force to defend the lodges, and after a fierce contest some of which was hand to hand, the defenders managed to drive their assailants off. The Allies gave up the fight and retreated, but the Cheyennes had captured a four-year old boy from the Crows, and he they carried with them back to the Cheyenne country.

Meanwhile, returning to the Crow trading party having gone to visit Kipp`s post and their Hidatsa relatives, a Lakota war-party scouring the countryside, spied the Crow horses dotted over the prairie outside one of the Hidatsa towns. Under cover of darkness the raiders rounded up the scattered herd and drove off one hundred and fifty head, being all the horses then belonging to the Crows after having traded their surplus stock to the Hidatsa.

Next morning upon discovering their loss, a large number of Crow warriors at once started out on foot following the trail of the thieves. The weather by then, had turned decidedly colder. It snowed and stormed and after several days of hard travelling, most of the pursuers returned to the Hidatsa villages empty handed. All that is, but a small band comprised of twenty-three Crows.

These were led by the sub-chief Little White Bull clad in a bright red blanket coat. He and his companions with a number of pack dogs in tow, continued to follow the trail, determined to retrieve the stolen stock.

This man Little-White-Bull who`s proper name was "Keeps-Looking-At-the-Albino-Buffalo," was a member of the Whistling Waters Crow band. He was a well-respected but somewhat reckless leader of the Big Dog warrior society, and had been a member of the decoys which, along with Plays-With-His-face and others, had led Cheyennes into the Crow trap nine summers earlier, Also, he had been a signer of the Atkinson-O`Fallon Friendship Treaty of 1825.

Little-White-Bull`s party trekked on foot for several days and nights, but owing to the severity of weather and believing they had lost the trail, they, too, decided to give up the chase. They therefore made a night camp intending to make their way home to the Yellowstone next morning. Unfortunately, they unwittingly set up their bivouacs on the east bank of the lower course of the Powder, actually between two camps of their Lakota and Cheyenne enemies, and among whom was included the Jediah Smith and David Jackson party of white trappers. The allied camps at that time were obscured from view by a heavy mist and snow-covered foliage of the surrounding region.

Regarding the Lakota and Cheyennes, it was not long before they discovered the Crow presence. During the night, a number of their warriors silently surrounded the Crow position and at dawn, made their presence known.

The Crows were taken by surprise. In response they fled to a nearby slush-filled hollow crossed by a fallen log. Over the log they draped their buffalo robes to obscure themselves from their enemies aim, and prepared to defend themselves as best they could. However, before the fight commenced, a Lakota chief stepped forward and addressed the Crows in their own language supplemented with signs. He told them he was sorry to keep them waiting, but his warriors were frozen to the bone, having spent the night without fire so not to give their presence away. First they would warm themselves, he said, and after which, *"...You Raven Men shall be no more, unless as is your name you fly away, or like the prairie-dog, can burrow in the ground."* [4]

At length, after the Lakota and Cheyennes were sufficiently thawed they did charge forward. But the Crows had a number of muskets between them and a volley from the hollow dropped several of the enemy, obliging the rest to flee and seek cover from the deadly missiles.

Now in the Cheyenne village at this time was a man named Medicine-Water. He was the recent possessor of a so-called iron shirt, the same worn by one of the allies during the attack on Long-Hair`s people ten years earlier. This man`s brother-in-law requested he be allowed to wear the shirt in the fight then going on, to which Medicine-Water agreed, and his brother-in-law hastily doned the shirt. He next mounted his war-pony and rode alone into the open space between his people and the hollow. Slowly he paraded back and forth in front of the allied lines, enabling all present to marvel at his splendour. Then, after proclaiming his prowess, he let out an ear-splitting war cry; kicked his pony`s flanks with his heels and rode at a gallop towards the hollow, wherein the luckless Crows were crouched.

As their iron-clad nemesis urged his pony forward, a barrage of musket fire again burst from the Crow position, and the Cheyenne`s horse suddenly buckled; keeled over, throwing its rider in the process. Quickly the Cheyenne regained his feet, and so sure of his invulnerability in his iron shirt which could turn musket balls and iron-headed arrows, he continued on foot towards the hollow under the very muzzles of Crow guns.

A great cheer of bravado resounded from the throats of the on-looking Allies. Yet before he had gone a few steps more, a single shot rang out and a well-aimed Crow musket ball struck the Cheyenne in the forehead, killing him instantly. His over-weighted body went crashing to the ground, his life`s blood staining the snow around him.

Seeing their champion fall, the Cheyennes and Lakota raised a tremendous hissing cry of *"Shi, shi, shi,"* [5] which was an expression of extreme hate, and in a frenzied mob, rushed forward in an endeavour to retrieve the body before the Crows could wreak vengeance upon it. But again the fire from the hollow beat them back, and they were obliged to leave their hero to the mercy of the foe.

The Crow chief Little-White-Bull in his red blanket coat and holding his musket in one hand, climbed out from the hollow. Rushing over the snow to the prostrate form, he threw his gun to the ground and drawing forth a large `Green-River` knife from its scabbard, began stabbing the dead Cheyenne about the body, screaming oaths of vengeance as he did so. The iron shirt encasing his fallen foe prevented his knife piercing the flesh and in his continued frenzy; he proceeded to cut off the hands and feet of his victim and to sever the head from the shoulders. The Cheyennes and Lakota howled with anger as they watched their comrade being thus abused and at the same time, unleashed a shower of missiles at the Crow chief as he calmly went about his grisly work. Try as they might, the Allies failed to bring him down, and the Crow remained undaunted as arrows and balls flew thick about him. Finally, Little-White-Bull rose to his feet and cradling his musket in the crook of his right arm, he turned and faced the Allies. In his other hand he held aloft the bloodied severed head and cried aloud to his enemies in broken Lakota,

> "See now Stripped-feathered dogs and Cut-Heads, here is your champion. It is this one, He-That-Keeps-Looking-At-the-Albino-Buffalo who has done this terrible thing." [6]

Next he took hold of the trophy by the braids and swung it around in the air above him, then shook it in the faces of the enemy and taunted them to,
*"Come on and fight."* [7]
But none of the Allies went forth to meet him, and the Crow chief returned to the hollow from whence he came.

Throughout the rest of the morning the fight continued, both sides shooting sporadically at each other from cover, while every now and then, single combats would take place between champions from each side in the no-man`s land between the two. In such combats, it is said, the Crow chief in his red coat was very brave, and each time victorious.

It is also said that as the contest dragged on and the cold increased, only three of the Crow defenders resisted manfully, while their comrades became so benumbed with cold, they could make but little effort. It is more likely, however, that there was a shortage of ammunition among them, if indeed, all the Crows had

187

possessed guns in the first place. But whatever the case, as the contest progressed, the defence rested almost entirely upon the actions of these three, albeit opposed by odds of at least fifty to one.

At the same time, those among the Crows who did have guns were conserving what powder and ball they had left. But still their courage did not falter. Their Death-songs rang out clear above the war-whoops and victory chants of their enemies, who continued shooting every time a Crow exposed himself to view, and withal, they shouted across the field,

*"We shall rub you out and feed your carcasses to our dogs."* [8]

And so painfully and slowly the hours dragged by. The icy chill became more intense and blood froze solid in the wounds.

At length, the sun reached its highest point in the sky and thereafter, there came no more shots from the hollow. Only the Crow partisan Little-White-Bull remained alive among his comrades. The Allies had also ceased shooting, and an eerie silence enveloped the scene.

Then, like a ghost arising from its slumber, Little-White-Bull suddenly re-emerged from the hollow. With musket cradled in one arm, he walked deliberately towards his besiegers who themselves having also risen from cover, stood motionless with mouths agape.

The lone Crow; prominent in his red blanket-coat and completely fearless, came boldly on. After a few steps more he stopped, and standing in full view, he gesticulated in signs interspersed with a smattering of Lakota as he showered a series of profane oaths upon his antagonists.

He then cried aloud that he had taken so many of their scalps his lodge was dark with hair, and had ridden their horses, he said, until he was tired of riding. He next pointed to the noon-day sun directly above and continued,

*"This one is like the sun. You shall kill him, but he will not die until Sun, his father, hangs low in the sky."* [9]

The lone Crow then repeatedly beckoned the enemy, inviting them to, *"come close and give me combat."* [10]

But the Allies drew back, wondering at his bravery, and none would dare go near him.

After a while, in a fit of disgust at the refusal of the enemy to accommodate his wish, the Crow chief gave up his pleadings and returned to the hollow now filled with the frozen corpses of his comrades.

Several times throughout the afternoon, Little-White-Bull again climbed out of the hollow and advanced towards the enemy. Each time he called to them saying, *"Come on and kill me"* [11] for he was eager and ready to die. But the enemy still would not go near. They told him in signs they would let him live and go home safely to his people, as he was too brave a warrior to kill. But Little-White-Bull refused their offers and continued calling to the enemy, begging them to finish him off and send him to his ancestors where he could join the spirits of his companions, now lying stiff and contorted around him.

The hours again dragged by. The sun began sinking in the west and twilight was descending, and still the lone Crow refused to escape.

At last, one among the party of white trappers crept close to the hollow. Seeing the lone Crow sitting on his haunches looking hard at the ground with elbows on his knees supporting his chin with his fists, the trapper took aim with his musket, then shot the Crow chief in the forehead, killing him outright.

Still, however, the Lakota and Cheyennes were reluctant to go forward until convinced that all resistance had ceased. It was some time later after crawling on their bellies to the lip of the hollow; expecting every moment that Little-White-Bull would reappear, before they finally stood up and looking down on the frozen corpses, examined their gory work.

Cautiously, they approached the body of Little-White-Bull with raised axes, and when close enough, they smashed in his head to be sure he was truly dead. Even then, it is said, the backside of the chief reared up and the body began turning somersaults head over heels around the hollow. The Allies could not stop the carcass moving, although striking it many times with axes and shooting arrows into it up to the flights. Anon they built a fire upon which they threw the chief's body, and burned it up until nothing was left save the charred bones and ashes.

Rummaging around the hollow, the Allies soon found huddled under the frozen corpses, two boy servants of the Crows, shaming death. For the moment the Allies had sated their thirst for blood. They took pity on the boys and took them captive with a view to adopting them among their own. The two servants, though, had other ideas. Either fearing torture at the hands of their captors, or simply abhorrent at the thought of spending the rest of their lives among the slayers of their comrades, the youths drew concealed knives from about their persons and simultaneously, stabbed those of the enemy standing nearest them. Immediately they were set upon by their enraged captors and within minutes, had been hacked to pieces.

The Allies now lost all self-control. They screamed for vengeance and in a frenzy of blood-lust, they hauled the Crow bodies from the hollow and butchered them in a most blood-thirsty manner. They tore off the scalps and stripped them of clothing, then cut off the heads and amputated the frozen limbs before using dogs to drag the mangled torsos to their camps.

The victors then danced and sang as they waved the grisly trophies triumphantly in the air. The Crow heads were raised on poles and paraded among the people, who prodded them with sticks and poked the eyes from the sockets. And when the adults had mocked them enough, the children played ball with the skulls, kicking them to and fro among the tepees. It is said that even a number of white trappers joined in the victory celebrations, and they, too, danced and howled as enthusiastically as any Indian. [12]

It was many days after the return to the Hidatsa village of the main Crow party, which, initially, had gone in pursuit of the thieves, that pack dogs having accompanied the ill-fated warriors with Little-White-Bull came limping into camp. The animals were dilapidated and footsore; the loads missing from their backs. This was the second inclination the Crows had of their champion's misfortune, for a blood-red moon had recently appeared in the night sky, and this; being a portent of disaster, had caused many to already suspect the worst.

So it was with heavy hearts, the Crows prepared to return to the Yellowstone and home.

Before they could start, the Crows were obliged to buy back a significant number of ponies which earlier, they had sold to their hosts. For although a number of horse-stealing raids to replenish the stolen stock had been conducted in the interim against the Hunkpapa and Yanktonais and also against the Arickara, such escapades had not supplied enough animals to transport the whole Crow party home. Without Little-White-Bull having retrieved their lost stock, they were obliged to turn to their Hidatsa cousins in order to make up the required number of animals needed, and the Hidatsa took full advantage of the situation. Not for a moment ignoring the opportunity to make a lucrative profit; even from those considered cousins and friends, the Hidatsa virtually cleaned out the Crows of all the white man`s goods which included an assortment of trinkets and domestic items which the Crows had earlier amassed. The Hidatsa left them only their guns, powder and ball, the result being, it was a despondent not to say impoverished Crow group which finally set out for home.

Once back in *Echeta Casha*, by which time the snows had cleared and long-awaited spring sunshine warmed the land, Sore-Belly and his headmen convened a council to discuss the possibilities of Little-White Bull`s fate. After a period of deliberation, it was decided to send out a group of warriors in search of the missing party, to determine once and for all if its members be alive or dead. It was known that Little-White-Bull had intended to raid the Cheyenne winter camps, and the Crows were aware that certain bands of that people were accustomed to spending the winter months somewhere along the course of the Lower Powder or one of that river`s connecting streams.

Consequently, it was in that direction in the early part of April that the Crow search party travelled.

It was a strong force of around fifty warriors, each of whom was well mounted and armed; several carrying smoothbore trade guns or old muskets with the barrels cut down so as to be handled more easily from horseback. Their Pipe-holder was the sub-chief Little-White-Bear, a close friend and confident of Sore-Belly with many successful war deeds to his credit.

As they travelled the warriors were ever on the alert, lest they run afoul of one or another roving enemy war-band which, during this time of year, invested the country through which they intended to pass, and the Crows were resolved to give good account of themselves if attacked.

In the meantime, owing to yet another period of severe stormy weather following the Little-White-Bull slaughter, the allied camps at the mouth of the Powder had been prevented from moving. This had given rise to a certain amount of anxiety among the camp occupants, ere the ghosts of the slain Crow warriors should haunt their killers, or in some other supernatural way bring calamity upon them. But notwithstanding their fears, it was not until the beginning of April, *"The Moon when rivers begin to rise,"* before the allied bands finally vacated their winter quarters and went their separate ways.

Thus it was only a day or two after the last of the allied bands had left their winter camps, that Little-White-Bear and his fifty-strong group of Crows searching for sign of Little-White-Bull`s party, arrived on the scene.

Casually, the Crows rummaged among the abandoned campsites, and it was not long before one of their number stumbled across the scattered remains of their missing kinfolk. These were recognised by hair and ear ornaments and personal amulets, still attached to some of the severed heads and mangled limbs left lying amid the debris of the camps. The Crows were overcome with grief when they realised the whole party belonging to Little-White-Bull had been destroyed. As was their custom the searchers shed copious tears, while at the same time they swore aloud oaths of vengeance upon the slayers and cried to *Akbaa-tadia* to assist them in avenging their loss.

Now if at first this party of Crows had only intended to discover the whereabouts of their missing kinsmen, and report their findings to Sore-Belly in camp along the Yellowstone, the grisly sight which met their eyes incensed their passions to such extent, that the partisan Little-White-Bear decided then and there, they should hunt down the culprits and exact some measure of retribution before returning home with news of the disaster.

As it was, several trails led from the abandoned campsites in different directions. One of these appeared comparatively fresh, being only a few days old and was less broad than the others, indicating it had been made by a smaller number of people. The Crows wasted no time following up this particular trail in the hopes of catching their enemies on the move. In such an event, being encumbered with pony drags and camp equipment, the enemy would be at a disadvantage and at the mercy of the Crows.

The trail proved easy to follow and the searchers had not gone more than six miles upon it, before they discerned a small Cheyenne camp of nine lodges nestling peaceably on the open Plain. Surrounding the camp were many loose ponies milling around seemingly unattended.

Little-White-Bear decided to attack the camp head on without the usual delay, which would have involved parading in front of the foe, in order to show off their paint and feathers and prancing ponies before battle commenced. This time it was the intention to do as much damage as possible by not allowing the enemy to prepare a satisfactory defence. The Crows would kill as many Cheyennes as they could; drive off the ponies and escape before the alarm could be raised to bring reinforcements from other Cheyenne camps likely in the region. So it was that without warning, the fifty Crows let out their blood-chilling war-cries and charged headlong towards the camp.

While most of the Crows were engaged in slaughtering the men-folk, others concentrated on rounding up the abandoned ponies, whilst still others collected together the women and children and ransacked the ruined tepees, taking weapons, animal skins and an assortment of personal belongings as booty.

It was, though, the victorious Crows who were then in a vulnerable position. Here they were deep in hostile country, in danger that an unknown number of enemy warriors might, at that very moment, be preparing to come against them. It was expedient, Little-White-Bear said, that they remove themselves as quickly as possible into a more favourable location, before their own party was surrounded by the full fighting force of the enemy and destroyed. As it transpired, the enemy did not appear and the Crows were not overtaken. They made good their escape, and having avenged Little-White-Bull and his comrades, it was a jubilant party that re-entered Sore Belly`s village on the Yellowstone.

Nonetheless, in truth, this particular Crow victory even though welcomed by the tribe and celebrated accordingly, was but a brief respite in a current spate of misfortune suffered by some smaller Crow parties when engaged against one or another enemy force. Certainly, during the latter part of spring this year of 1830, Cheyennes were particularly active on the Crow front, taking a number of scalps and driving off droves of horses from Apsaalooka camps, without any significant acts of retaliation from the Crows themselves.

Around this date the Crows possessed more horses per head of population than any other tribe on the Northern Plains. It was estimated by a contemporary observer that the average number of animals then among them was fifteen horses per lodge, although some tribal members alone, owned in excess of one hundred. As a consequence, the Crows were almost constantly beset by raiding parties from neighbouring Blackfoot and Atsina and even from more distant peoples such as Assiniboine and Cree, who having heard through the moccasin grapevine of the abundant number of fine ponies in Crow country, had made it their vocation in life to redistribute Crow wealth across the Plains on what they saw as a more egalitarian basis. Against the Blackfoot and Atsina the Crows defended their property with vigour and often retaliated in kind, either to retrieve stolen stock or to increase their own herds, if not indeed, merely for the sheer excitement of travelling the warpath which, in reality, was usually far greater an incentive than economic necessity alone. The Cheyennes, it may be added, always admitted it were the Crows who stole the greater number of their horses, and were one of the tribes against whom the Cheyenne had to fight the hardest.

Overall the Crows could hold their own against their various enemies and at this date, they were slightly superior to the Cheyennes and Suhtaio regarding the number of warriors they could throw into the field. It is also certain that during this particular period between 1830 and 1840, the Cheyennes and Suhtaio lost as many warriors killed and women and children taken captive at Crow hands, as did the Crows at the hands of the Cheyennes and Suhtaio.

Generally speaking then, it was an equal contest between the two; before that is the late 1850s, by which time the Cheyennes had acquired the full weight of the Lakota population to assist them as allies in their hostile endeavours.

However, during the time in question in the early 1830s, the Crows had the great war-chief Sore-Belly among them, who not only brought his people many victories, but had moulded the Crow warriors into a formidable fighting force, to be respected and feared by all.

Having said this, in the latter part of spring, another Crow party was surprised on the open Plains by a Cheyenne / Suhtaio war-band and completely routed. The survivors reached home badly mauled with several dead and wounded comrades in tow. In response the warriors harangued their Pipe-holders, inciting them to get up a grand war-party and strike yet another decisive blow against the "Striped Arrow People," and thereby, dissuade that people's warriors from counting their coups in Crow country.

So it was in the early part of June, a formidable Crow war-party; ostensibly led by Sore-Belly, started forth to wreak vengeance yet again on the Cheyennes.

A more detailed account of the resulting confrontation on this occasion, has been given elsewhere by the present Author so will not be repeated here. [13]

It may merely be said that the Crows found a Cheyenne camp of some thirty-seven lodges situated at the end of a canyon bordering a stream known as Antelope Creek flowing into the North Platte. The Cheyennes were already aware that a large war band of Crows was in the vicinity and in response, had barricaded their village and were prepared to offer a determined defence when Sore-Bely and his warriors arrived on the scene. The ensuing confrontation ended in stalemate, although victory was accredited to the Crows who`s number suffered no casualties, whereby the Cheyennes lost two men killed and their scalps taken, along with a number of ponies rounded up by the Crows who found them grazing outside the camp`s perimeter. The trip was thus considered worthwhile to the Crows, and they returned to their home camp triumphant with Sore-Belly at their head.

It would appear that the Cheyenne occupants of the village along Antelope Creek, had been in the process of moving towards a prearranged rendezvous site on the South Fork of the Platte, where they intended to join the rest of their Nation in preparation for a grand tribal crusade against the Pawnee.

It could only have been an act of providence therefore, which had prevented the aforesaid Crow war-party from stumbling across the main Cheyenne camp, and in which event the tables would have been turned, and not many Crows would have escaped with their scalps.

In corroboration of the aforementioned fight along Antelope Creek, it had been only a few days after the event that a small party of white trappers was moving along the North Fork of the Platte towards the rich beaver grounds west of the Laramie Mountains. According to W. A. Ferris who was a member of the trapper party, on June 13th, they came across a lone tepee left standing by Cheyennes, who only recently had vacated the site.

Inside the tepee the trappers observed two raised platforms, on each of which lay the scalped corpse of an adult male. The implements of war and the chase had been laid out beside them, although both bodies, Ferris remarked,
*"...had been hacked and mangled in a manner truly savage and revolting."* [14]

A Cheyenne who had attached himself to the trapper`s party explained the circumstances of the burial tepee at this place. The corpses were Cheyennes, the trappers were told, killed in battle with Crows only five days earlier, and Ferris went on to describe the scene,

"Lying upon the ground a few paces from the tepee, exposed to all the elements, was the body of a dead male child no more than four years old. The poor innocent had been deliberately and horribly

193

maimed and disfigured, evidently by repeated blows from a war club, and there was the mark of a deep stab wound in his side." [15]

The said child had been a prisoner among the Cheyennes, taken from Crows the previous winter, and now murdered in retaliation for the deaths of the two Cheyennes reposing on their funeral scaffolds. The tepee apparently, actually housed the bodies of the two Cheyennes slain by Sore-Belly`s Crows outside the latter`s village. Thus we have corroboration for Beckwourth`s accounts of both the child taken earlier during the combined attack on the Crows by Arickara and Cheyennes, and also, of the fight on Antelope Creek.

As regards the aforesaid proposed crusade by the entire Cheyenne Nation against the Pawnee, such did eventually take place later that summer of 1830. It proved a disaster for the Cheyennes and subsequently, was considered beneficial to the Crows.

The result of the Cheyenne - Pawnee confrontation was that the former lost their Sacred Medicine Arrows to the enemy. These were the Cheyenne`s most revered holy objects thought to guarantee the overall welfare of the people and; more particularly, to bring them success in war. The loss of these talismans [having actually been captured by the Pawnee], filled the Cheyennes with despondency and forebodings of doom for their people's future.

As it was, the proverbial moccasin grapevine carried word of the Cheyenne`s great misfortune across the Plains and to the country of the Crows. They, of course, showed no sympathy, but actually stepped up their offensives against Cheyenne camps, now supposing the occupants to be in disarray and likely reluctant to conduct large-scale reciprocal operations.

Thus, throughout the end days of summer, several Crow war-parties went out crisscrossing the Plains, looking specifically for Cheyennes to attack.

One such Crow party comprising around thirty braves, again with Sore-Belly as its pipe-holder, was on horseback scouring the countryside looking for enemies to fight. They soon stumbled across a group of Cheyenne warriors eighteen in number, who also being on horseback, were themselves a war-party heading for the Crow country. Indeed, it seems the Crows had misjudged their enemies` state of mind on this occasion. Horse-stealing parties generally went on foot so as to ride home on captured ponies, but this particular Cheyenne group, although supposedly still grieving the loss of their sacred talismans, were after scalps, being eager to regain lost prestige which only enemy hair, no matter to which tribe it belonged, could compensate for their recent misfortune.

Both parties had been travelling casually across an open stretch of prairie when they spied each other at the same time. The Crows having the advantage in number did not hesitate. All at once they raised the Apsaalooka war cry; whipped up their ponies and charged straight towards the foe. But the Cheyennes, ignoring their own disparity in number, made no attempt to flee. Instead they boldly stood their ground and braced themselves to receive the attack.

The leader of the Cheyennes calmly sat his horse watching the Crows as they galloped towards his party. Casually, he opened the priming pan of his flintlock to check the powder, closed it and slapped the breech to settle the ball in the barrel, and appeared to take little heed of two mounted Crows racing side by side directly in his path. As these two men bore down upon him, the Cheyenne chief slowly raised the musket to one shoulder with the barrel pointing towards his attackers. Then, just as he was about to squeeze the trigger, the two Crows veered off, one to the right; the other to the left and the Cheyenne swung his piece around, threatening to shoot the foremost of his antagonists. This foremost Crow was armed with an iron-headed tomahawk and being close enough to strike, was deemed the more dangerous of the two. The Crow was riding up on the Cheyenne`s right side and owing to the awkward posture the Cheyenne chief had to contrive in order to shoot across at his opponent, the Crow was upon him before the chief could discharge his piece. The Crow rode right up to his adversary; grabbed the very muzzle of the gun with one hand and jerked it upwards. At that instant the Cheyenne did squeeze the trigger, but the ball sped harmlessly past his attacker who was so close, that the powder from the explosion burned deep into the man`s left cheek, scarring him for life. Almost at the same time, this same Crow struck the Cheyenne a terrible blow with his axe, splitting his opponent`s head wide open. This caused the latter to fall from his horse and lay quite still on the prairie, apparently dead.

Others among the Crows went crashing into the rest of the opposing party, and it was a short fight before the remaining Cheyennes were routed. James Beckwourth declared that all eighteen Cheyennes were slain in the melee, while none of the Crows were killed and only four slightly wounded. It is unlikely, however, that the entire Cheyenne party was slaughtered at this time, or surely, the Cheyennes themselves would then have had some recollection of the affair. Beckwourth - from whom the only account of the battle comes – did not mention scalps, horses or captured equipment and weapons that the Crows would have taken as booty, even though in his memoirs, he usually went to great pains to enumerate such details. This suggests by its omission, that few Cheyennes were actually killed that day and further, that the fight was most probably a stand-off. Both sides breaking off hostilities after an appropriate period had elapsed, the Cheyennes then withdrawing from the field taking their dead and wounded with them. Often the mere striking of an enemy in the act of counting coup, was considered an achievement sufficient to satisfy one or the other party. It is indicative to note, that if the destruction of the enemy was likely to incur more injuries to the potential victors than what was usually regarded acceptable, then the fight would invariably have been called off without a decisive conclusion for either side.

Beckwourth actually stated that he himself was the man who killed the Cheyenne chief on this occasion, and in truth, he did carry an old powder-burn on his left cheek when interviewed by T. D. Bonner during the winter of 1854/`55. Beckwourth added that the Cheyenne chief was a man well known across the Plains, but did not give his name. He had singled him out as the Cheyenne leader, Beckwourth said, having recognized him as a chief by his headdress and peculiar hair-style which distinguished him as such. From this it might be inferred that the chief was wearing the old-time Cheyenne hair fashion which took the form of a coil of hair surmounting the forehead. This was an old-time style, although still sported by great warriors and other high-standing personages among several Plains Tribes at that time in order to show both rank and prestige. Regarding the name of the Cheyenne chief in question, in the mid eighteen-forties, Beckwourth was a regular visitor among his erstwhile foes the Cheyennes and during which times, he often discussed past conflicts that had occurred between them and his adopted people the Crows. On one such visit a Cheyenne chief named Old-Bark [Aka Bear-With-Feathers], then the Head man of the Cheyenne Watapio band, stepped forward and said,

> "Warrior, you killed me once, look here," and then withdrew the hair from his right temple showing that his cheek had been badly torn and his ear entirely missing. "But," he added, "I did not die. You fought bravely that day." [16]

Beckwourth did not say specifically, but, perhaps, it was during the afore-mentioned fight when eighteen Cheyennes had been defeated, that Old-Bark was struck such a vicious blow with an axe. All being said, Beckwourth's account of the actual fight, once again, seems to concur with his propensity for exaggeration when referring to the number of enemies slain and which in the above case, he utilized to the full.

$$- 0 - 0 - 0 - 0 - 0 - 0 - 0 - 0 - 0 - 0 - 0 - 0 - 0 - 0 -$$

## CHAPTER. 17.

### DEFENDING THE PACKHORSE COLUMN.

The summer of 1830 faded from the Plains and the month of October, *"The Moon when geese fly south,"* heralded the opening days of autumn. There was now a chill in the morning air, and it would not be long before the first flurries of snow beckoned in the winter season.

Before this, there came the sudden return of balmy weather as is peculiar to the North American Continent, and commonly known as "Indian Summer."

This was the sign the Crows and Sore-Belly had been awaiting. Now was the time to start their annual trip down the Missouri in order to visit James Kipp's trading post Fort Floyd and their Hidatsa relatives further down river, and where as in previous seasons, the Crows would exchange their surplus furs and buffalo robes for the white man's trade goods. It was imperative that the Crows replenish their dwindling supplies of guns, powder and ball, metal axes, knives and other accoutrements upon which they now depended so heavily, and without which, the Crows could not hope to defend themselves effectively against their numerous foes.

Rarely did the Hidatsa themselves risk the long trip through hostile Cheyenne and Lakota country in order to visit the Crows. If, however, they had adopted the role as middlemen between their Crow relatives and the white man, then they would have become affluent in grand Indian style and exercised a high degree of influence over various Plains Tribes, as indeed, their Mandan neighbours had done in bygone years. My Crow informant Joseph Medicine-Crow graphically summed up the situation when he said,

> "The Crows were good horseback fighters. They had many fine horses to carry their packs and could go anywhere in formidable numbers. The Hidatsa had few horses and could not mount large parties, or go too far on the Plains without military support. The Hidatsa country was not a good country for raising horses, and were afraid to go to the Crows because of the Cheyenne and Siouxs [sic]."
> [1]

As regards the Crows, they had not good fortune when it came to the locating of trading posts in their own country. Notwithstanding that between 1807 and 1812, Manuel Lisa's small establishment Fort Raymond operating near the confluence of the Bighorn and the Yellowstone had proved a successful commercial interaction for both Lisa and Crows, when Lisa dissolved his company in the winter of 1812 / '13, the post had been abandoned and soon fell into disrepair. After this, in late 1821 or early '22, the trappers Michelle Immell and Robert Jones of Joseph Pilcher's newly formed "Missouri Fur Company," erected a small post named Fort Benton on the Yellowstone about three miles east of the mouth of the Big Horn. But this post which also had been convenient for Crow trade was abandoned the following year of 1823.

In late summer 1822, partners William Ashley and Andrew Henry of the same reformed Missouri Fur Company, had built their own trading post named Fort Henry on the south side of the Missouri near the mouth of the Yellowstone, although this establishment, likewise, was short-lived and vacated the same year before the Crows could reap benefit from it. In its stead in late autumn 1823, a second Fort Henry was erected by the same partners at the mouth of the Big Horn close to the site of the then already dilapidated Fort Benton. However, unfortunately for the Crows, this second Fort Henry and its white personnel were subject to much harassment, particularly from the Pikuni, Blood and Siksika along with the latter's Atsina confederates, and this post, too, was abandoned the following summer of 1824 after only one or two seasons duration. Since that time the Crows had been left without practical access to any trading post in the Upper Missouri country.

The Crows needed a regular supply of goods from the white man either on a direct or indirect basis. Indeed, since the closure of the second Fort Henry, their chiefs had consistently begged those white men with whom they came in contact, to re-establish a permanent post in Crow country, or at least, supply them with a resident trader who could act as a middle man. Beckwourth prior to 1831 had not been a leading light in any trading concern, being merely an employee and sometimes "Free trapper" selling his furs to whomever he chose. Later, as an employee of the American Fur Company, he did persuade the Crows on behalf of his boss Kenneth McKenzie to carry their pelts and buffalo robes to Fort Union on the Missouri near the mouth of the Yellowstone, rather than continue their sporadic and unreliable commerce with itinerant traders and trappers of the rival Rocky Mountain Fur Company, with whom the Crows previously had been obliged to deal. Fort Union, it is true, had been built in the autumn of 1829, but had soon after burned down and although rebuilt and fully operational again before the end of 1830, it often played host to formidable parties of Blackfoot, Assiniboine and Atsina, all of whom were then the inveterate antagonists of the Crow. This fact to date [late autumn 1830], had deterred the Crows from visiting the fort, lest they be attacked and overwhelmed by foreign war-bands.

On the other hand, the small subsidiary American Fur Company post Fort Floyd administered by James Kipp, [established in 1826 on the Missouri close to White Earth River three miles from the Knife, and replaced one year later by a superior structure], remained operational until late 1830, when an expansion of trade at the above mentioned Fort Union, finally caused Fort Floyd to become obsolete and subsequently abandoned and burned. Kipp`s more famous post of Fort Clark, overlooking the Missouri adjacent to the Mandan towns eight miles downstream from the Hidatsa, was not built until spring or early summer of 1831, and thus; before that date, the Crows were obliged to visit Fort Floyd. At such times, the Crows, thereafter, would proceed further downstream to the Hidatsa and Mandan towns, whose occupants, customarily, welcomed their arrival. On the one hand as relatives to the Hidatsa and on the other, as friends and allies to the Mandan against mutual foes.

In order to reach Fort Floyd, the Crows had to travel a long distance from the Big Horn country. Their route followed the courses of the Yellowstone and Missouri Rivers downstream as far as White Earth River, and by so doing, were obliged to traverse an extensive hostile region, often infested by Cheyenne and Suhtaio enemies who roamed the intervening country at will.

Having said this, in late summer and early autumn it was not such a daunting prospect. During that short period both the Suhtaio and Cheyennes were usually further south, having congregated their numbers along the South Fork of the Big Cheyenne River in order to hold their annual Medicine Lodge ceremonies. As a result, these latter peoples were often far distant from the country through which the Crows were apt to travel when on their trips to Kipp`s post. If a Crow trading party was attacked, it would invariably be during its return journey to the Crow homeland. At such times the Cheyennes and Suhtaio would have re-entered the North Country and were on the lookout for just such a Crow column; hampered with women and children, travois and pack-ponies. These last loaded down with domestic belongings and recently obtained trade goods from Fort Floyd and the Hidatsa and Mandan villages. A tempting prize for any enemy force out searching for plunder and scalps.

So it was that the aforementioned Crow trading party led by Sore-Belly and his brother friend Little-White-Bear, left the Yellowstone country in early autumn 1830, and travelling east; crossed the Northern Plains within sight of the south bank of the Missouri. They intended to first visit Kipp`s post at the mouth of White Earth River, and then the earth-lodge towns of the Hidatsa and Mandan further downstream.

In total, the Crow party in column formation comprised around two-hundred warriors with at least double that number of non-combatants, including old folk and women and children. They then had many spare ponies in tow, some of which to trade to the Hidatsa and Mandan, whilst others were over-laden with pelts, hides and tanned buffalo robes to be traded at the fort. Thus hundreds of horses brought up the rear of the column, raising a great cloud of dust as they were herded along by young boys in the band. A number of travois were also included, these being attached to other horses carrying lodge poles; tepee covers and domestic belongings, and in addition, each warrior was mounted and in case of attack, had his war-pony - with *medicine* shield and lance tied to the saddle pommel - tethered by his side, ready to be ridden into combat at a moment's notice. In such a manner the Crows travelled, stretched out in a long twisting column as they wended their way across the open grasslands.

During their downriver trek no enemies were sighted and the Crows managed to reach each of their destinations without mishap.

At length, having concluded their trade at Kipp's post and a two week visit among their Hidatsa kinfolk and Mandan friends, which had involved a hectic period of socializing, courting, horse racing and exchanging general news and family gossip, the entire Crow party after repacking tepee covers and other paraphernalia including recently acquired trade goods of beads, calico, red and blue strouding and, most importantly, muskets, powder and ball, started west for the Yellowstone country and home, traveling the same route by which they had come.

It was about this time that a formidable body of Cheyennes composed of two or more bands, one of which included Suhtaio confederates, had recently left the country of the South Fork of the Big Cheyenne, and were now roaming north of the Black Hills along the Belle Fourch branch of that stream. They were hunting deer and buffalo before moving northwest to their winter camping grounds along the lower Powder. The Cheyennes were still smarting over their recent defeat at Pawnee hands which had incurred the loss of their Sacred Medicine Arrows, and were eager to gain compensation by obtaining a victory over any Indian foe they might encounter. Thus a large Cheyenne war-band consisting of around two-hundred and fifty warriors, happened to be roaming the same region when their scouts discerned in the distance the aforesaid Crow column, moving slowly west across the open Plain.

Upon being informed that Crows were in the vicinity, the Cheyenne chiefs decided to attack the column while it was strung out and vulnerable. But first they would endeavour to get closer without being detected, so to make their assault more effective.

Fortunately the Crows had their own scouts out to the fore of their main body and on its flanks, and it was one of these scouts riding ahead of his companions, who accidentally came face to face with the whole Cheyenne force. Quickly he turned his horse around and raced back to his people, frantically screaming that a great war-party of "Striped-Arrow-People" was coming towards them. The Cheyennes upon being discovered, immediately raised their war-cries and galloped after the fleeing Crow, so that within minutes they came in sight of the column.

Seeing the mass of Cheyenne warriors charging forward, Sore-Belly began shouting commands to his people. He told them to prepare for instant battle and instinctively, the womenfolk made a circle with their pony-drags and hurriedly filled the gaps between them with camp baggage and packs. The remuda and pack horses were herded into the centre of the circle to prevent their being stampeded, while the Crow warriors who had decided to fight on foot so as to handle their guns more effectively, quickly formed themselves in line, all armed and ready for combat. With their smoothbore fusees they faced the oncoming enemy, and having a liberal supply of powder and ball obtained during their recent visit to Kipp`s Fort, were well-equipped to defend themselves and their families.

This positive stance on the part of the Crows, showing they were prepared to fight rather than flee, surprised the Cheyennes to some extent, who in turn, had expected the column to be seized with panic and scatter in confusion. Such an action would have ensured a running fight in which firearms could not be used adequately from the backs of galloping horses, and the Cheyennes themselves could have knocked the fleeing Crows on the head with their war-clubs, or lanced them through from behind.

As it was, the mass of Cheyennes in unregimented order and with only a few guns and little ammunition between them, charged headlong into a solid wall of resistance. Gun wads were flying, it is said, as the Crows discharged their pieces in a volley and a shower of leaden balls went smashing into the Cheyenne ranks, toppling warriors from their saddles and causing many a horse to stumble and fall. But this first charge was a feint and before the riders actually reached the Crow line, they suddenly veered their ponies off to one side, which was to make room for a second wave of charging Cheyennes coming immediately behind. The attackers now expected to catch the defenders with ramrods stuck half-way down their gun barrels as they attempted to reload, and thought they would ride over the defenders before they had time to recharge their pieces.

Sore-Belly, though, grand strategist that he was, was too wary and able a tactician to be caught in such a predicament. Previous to the commencement of battle, he had instructed his warriors to fire only half their guns at one time and now, as the second wave of galloping Cheyennes came close, the remaining Crow guns were also discharged in a volley. The attackers were showered again with a barrage of leaden balls, and more of their number went crashing to the ground along with many of their horses being either killed or wounded. The charge was completely broken only yards from its objective, and the surviving Cheyennes scattered out of range in all directions.

The Crows were elated. At once they became filled with delusions of their own superiority. Seeing the enemy in disarray, they mounted their war ponies; took up shields and lances and in a compact body with Little-White-Bear at their head, they broke their defensive formation and raced their ponies across the Plain in a counter charge against the foe.

Meanwhile, the Cheyennes had regrouped and once again were racing forward. They met the Crow onslaught with a determined resolution not to cede their ground. But the momentum of the Crow charge led by Little-White-Bear, bedecked in an eagle-feathered bonnet, carried all before it and many Cheyennes were either killed or injured. The opposing forces then withdrew a short way and halted. They formed two long lines, and for a while faced each other across the prairie before coming together again in another general affray.

At this point much of the fighting was hand to hand as groups of warriors on one side battled it out with those on the other. Sore-Belly, though, had pre-planned for this eventuality also. Whenever a Crow warrior's horse was killed or maimed so as to be rendered out of action, or simply showed signs of exhaustion, the Crow women having been previously instructed by their chief, were right there in the midst of the melee with fresh mounts for those of their fighting men who were unhorsed, and in such a way they kept all their own warriors in the fight at one time.

The result was that the Cheyennes could not make any headway against their opponents. Eventually they lost heart; broke ranks and retreated in some confusion back the way they had come, taking their dead and wounded with them. The Crow warriors did not attempt to follow. Instead they returned jubilantly to their circle of pony-drags and braced themselves to receive another assault, expecting the foe to regroup and charge again.

The Cheyennes did re-consolidate their force, and for a third time made a charge upon the circle of pony-drags. But as before, they were met with such a hot reception from the defender's muskets that they very soon gave up the fight, and this time, fled the field completely.

Notwithstanding that the Crows themselves had sustained a number of casualties, along with the loss of several pack-ponies laden with trade goods, upon seeing the foe in flight, a host of warriors ignored Sore-Belly`s pleas to remain within the protection of the circle and raced after the fleeing Cheyennes, obliging the latter to take refuge in a nearby timber into which the Crows were reluctant to follow. Instead, they milled around on their ponies at the edge of the timber, shouting insults and taunting the Cheyennes to come out into the open and fight. But the beleaguered Cheyennes had no intention of being lured into forsaking their safe refuge and after a while, the Crow warriors returned again to their circle of pony-drags. After assisting the women-folk in re-packing their belongings, their whole force then continued west, moving slowly and more cautiously towards the Yellowstone and home.

Our old friend James Beckwourth declared in his memoirs, that he had been in this fight on the side of the Crows. He personally, he said, had received an arrow wound in the head,

*".....but not so serious to prevent me doing duty."* [2]

He further stated that the Crows lost nine dead and thirteen wounded in the fight, along with one packhorse loaded down with trade goods. The Cheyennes on the other hand, again according to Beckwourth, did not succeed in scalping any of the Crow dead, while the Crows had taken eleven scalps, although Beckwourth added that the Cheyennes admitted at a later date, that their own losses killed that day was as many as fifty-six warriors in total.

My friend Joe Medicine-Crow, who himself had heard a brief account of the affair from his old Crow informant Plain-Feather, agreed that the Crows had lost some good warriors in the fight and that a large quantity of much needed merchandise recently traded from Kipp's post, had fallen into the hands of the Cheyennes. He could not comment on the Cheyenne losses, he said, but suggested that the number of fifty-six Cheyennes killed as given by Beckwourth, most likely included also those of the latter who had been wounded, but among whom, many would have recovered from their injuries. Joe further suggested that the Cheyennes gained some solace in their defeat by the large quantity of trade goods they captured, which included a number of much needed guns and ammunition.

The Crow column, meanwhile, travelled on without further incident. They carried the bodies of their own kinsmen killed more than two-hundred miles home to the Yellowstone, rather than leave them in the land of the enemy where the corpses, if discovered in their resting places, would have been abused and mutilated by the vengeful Cheyennes.

When finally ensconced back in their own country, a grand celebration was held, as the fight was considered a great victory by the Crows. The women-folk sang praise songs in honour of their brave men, whilst the latter themselves stomped out the victory dance and paraded aloft the bloodied scalps, along with captured weapons and shields taken from the vanquished foe.

It was soon after the above mentioned trading party's return to the Yellowstone and before the first fall of snow, that Sore-Belly's River Crow people moved south, having previously agreed to spend the coming winter with their cousins the Mountain Crow.

Whilst en route south, Sore-Belly's people made a detour into the Tongue River and Rosebud area in order to drive the buffalo before them. These animals were then driven southwest into the Big Horn Basin where there was sufficient pasture year round and was a procedure known as 'holding the buffalo.' Such was the custom of the Crows especially of the *Eelalapito* – the Kicked-in-the-Belly band, so to have a plentiful supply of meat readily on hand to sustain the people in winter quarters. This being done, both the River and Mountain Crows [including the Kicked-in-the-Bellies], thereafter travelled further west, and set their camps adjacent to each other in the Lower Wind River valley southwest of the Big Horn Mountains.

It was early in the New Year [1831], that two separate bodies of Crows representing two rival warrior societies, started out on foot at the same time from their winter villages along Wind River, intent on going deep into the Cheyenne domain in search of horses and scalps. Both parties were small in number as befitted horse-stealing expeditions and they took alternative routes towards the enemy country. One party comprised nineteen warriors led by a man named Red-Eyes. The other, consisting of sixteen warriors was led by the well-known sub-chief, Yellow-Belly, who was a close friend of Sore-Belly and had also been a signer of the Friendship Treaty of 1825.

202

The weather was severe and both parties on foot, each brave wrapped in a thick buffalo robe as protection against the cold. It is said that the respective pipe-holders on this occasion, had started upon their separate undertakings in order to show between themselves, who was the most competent War-leader of the two.

After travelling twenty days, the party led by Yellow-Belly came to a halt upon the summit of a high eminence, from the top of which one could see far across the country. Below them in a small valley, they beheld a group of around thirty mounted Cheyennes engaged in running buffalo, while in the opposite direction some few miles distant, the outline of a small Cheyenne village could faintly be discerned.

Leading from the base of a nearby rocky height and in the direction of the Cheyenne village, were three dry gullies running parallel to one another across the valley floor. The centre gully showed by a fresh trail running through it, that this was being used by the Cheyennes as a common route to and from their village. The Crows realized that the hunters were sure to use this same trail when returning to the camp after completing their hunt, and Yellow-Belly decided to secrete his warriors in ambush at that place.

The Crows - each of whom carried a gun of some description as well as a bow and arrows and war-club - first turned their robes inside out with the fleece on show, so that if seen by the Cheyennes from a distance, they might be mistaken for buffalo. They then moved down from the hilltop, and dividing their number into two groups, carefully positioned themselves along the two outer gullies, an equal number of men on each sides. One of the groups stationed itself a little ahead of the other, so that when firing their guns towards the centre gully, they would not be firing directly across with the risk of hitting their own men.

Patiently the hidden Crows waited for the hunters to finish their kill and return along the centre trail, whereupon they would spring their trap and have their enemies in a crossfire.

It was not long before the Cheyennes in small separate groups, came ambling along the centre gully just as the Crows had anticipated. There were a number of women and children among them who had been out butchering the carcasses, and these were now walking slowly along the trail leading pack ponies loaded down with meat. The Crows remained concealed behind the banks of the outer gullies and allowed several of the enemy in small groups of twos and threes, to pass by unmolested.

Then came a group of a dozen or more both male and female, the men astride their running horses; the women leading animals with packs. When this group of Cheyennes which was just ahead of their main body came abreast of the furthermost line of hidden Crows, a sudden volley of gunfire exploded from each side of the centre gully. Nine Cheyennes were dropped in this first discharge alone and then eight more, as the rest of the Crow fusees found their marks on the main body of Cheyennes coming behind. The Cheyennes had been taken by surprise, but some few on horseback did manage to escape, and racing their ponies across the open grasslands, reached their village and raised the alarm among their tribesmen. Within a matter of minutes a great number of Cheyenne warriors had grabbed their weapons; mounted war-ponies and were racing to the scene of conflict to give assistance to their kinfolk.

In the meantime, three more Cheyennes had been brought down by the Crows. These three had actually been ahead of the main group after being allowed by the Crows to pass unmolested, but had turned back to give their assistance when first the sound of gunfire was heard. The Crows by then were jumping over the gully walls and while some of their number held off the remaining hunters by threatening to shoot with their empty guns, others ripped the scalps from the heads of those that had fallen and cut off their arms and legs. They then cut the loads from the backs of the ponies, after which they herded together the captured animals; mounted the fleetest in the bunch, and crashing through the rest of the Cheyennes, raced along the centre gully back from where they had come, reloading their pieces as they rode.

Meanwhile, Cheyenne warriors from the village were coming up fast, some on horseback and many on foot.

When the Cheyennes from the village reached the prostrate bodies of the scalped and mutilated hunters, including men, women and children lying in pools of their own blood, they howled with rage and screamed various oaths of vengeance. Those who were mounted immediately galloped after the killers, whilst those on foot ran back to their village; mounted war-ponies and called all the Cheyenne fighting men to arms.

Now Cheyenne blood was up and they pursued the fleeing Crows at a rapid gait.

The captured mounts the Crows were riding were already tired, having been ridden hard during that morning's hunt. They proved no match for the fresh animals being ridden by the pursuing Cheyennes and soon the Crows were being hard pressed. They fled through a small timber towards the rocky height wherefrom they had started, and at which place they hoped to make a stand.

The height, although a welcome refuge, proved difficult to scale and the captured pack ponies stumbled and fell as well as the horses the Crows themselves were riding. However, rather than discard their captured stock, the Crows dismounted and drove the animals before them up the rocky slope. When at last reaching the summit, they took up defensive positions and prepared to defend themselves as best they could.

Before the Cheyennes arrived, the Crows had hastily erected a low barricade of loose rocks and stones, and were satisfied they were in a reasonably secure position to hold off the impending attack.

Their rocky refuge was somewhat of a natural fortress. In order for the Cheyennes to storm the barricade from the front, they would have to face the full fire power of Crow guns. To take the position from the rear was equally precarious. For notwithstanding that the Cheyennes would have to make a long circuitous movement of several miles around the base of the height, they would still be fully exposed if they attempted to make an ascent from that side.

When at last, however, the bulk of Cheyennes did arrive, they at once stormed the Crow defences in a brave but futile effort to get among their foes.

Needless to say, their first attempt up the slope was repulsed and they were driven back with a number of casualties.

The Cheyennes thereafter, showered the besieged with fusee balls, arrows and lances, while every now and then, one and another Cheyenne warrior would scramble on foot up the rocky slope under the very muzzles of the defender's guns in rash and often costly outbursts of bravado, simply in an endeavour to count coup. The Crows themselves hardly suffered at all from such sporadic assaults, neither were they seriously affected by the indiscriminate Cheyenne fire. And so the fight dragged on without apparent gain to either side.

There was one particularly brave Cheyenne who Beckwourth calls Leg-In-The-Water, and of whom Joe Medicine Crow added, was mounted on a fine appaloosa pony and carried a be-feathered lance. He alone did manage to ride up the slope and leaping his mount over the barricade, landed in the midst of the Crows. The Cheyenne thrust at his nearest antagonist with his lance and then another, and in this way, counted several coups upon the enemy. One of the Crows then parried the lance by employing a blocking action with his tomahawk and swinging his weapon again, struck the Cheyenne a terrible blow on the upper part of his body, almost severing the Cheyenne`s arm from the shoulder. Leg-In-The-Water dropped the lance and fell from his horse. But before his opponent could finish him off, he had picked himself up and leaving his horse among the enemy, he jumped back over the breastworks and ran down the slope into the arms of his waiting comrades. As he ran, the Crows took pot-shots with their fusees, the balls kicking up dirt between his feet, while at the same time the very rocks, it is said, echoed to peals of mocking Crow laughter as they tried their best to shame him among his Cheyenne comrades. [3]

Again the Cheyenne besiegers began pouring a stream of missiles into the Crow position and this time several Crows were hit, although none too seriously, including their leader Yellow-Belly who received a musket ball in one arm.

So the fight dragged on, although on no account could the Cheyennes dislodge their foes, and as dusk began to fall, the weather turned decidedly colder.

The besiegers thus ceased their barrages and one by one, began slipping back to their village, to the warmth of their lodges and the comforts of their women. Only a handful of Cheyennes were left to keep watch on the hill, lest the Crows should escape in the night.

Evidently, the Cheyennes were confident that the enemy was trapped in their own chosen fortress and come morning, when the whole Cheyenne force again joined the fray, then in one determined effort they would be sure to carry all before them, rubbing out the Crow party one and all.

In the meantime, although having suffered few casualties with what might be termed minor wounds, the Crows knew they were in a serious predicament. They fully realized that their ammunition would not last long once the fighting resumed come morning, and that a full-scale assault by the Cheyennes would undoubtedly prove the end of them all. Their only hope of salvation lay in their ability to vacate their position; before the sun rose again at dawn.

To this end in the stillness of the night, the Crows explored more closely their rocky retreat, anxiously searching for a means of escape. Fortunately the moon was up and after a while they discovered what they were looking for.

Twisting in and out among the rocks was a narrow defile leading down from the summit of the height to its base. It then ran out through the grasslands on the far side of where the Cheyenne watchers were ensconced. At the base of the hill the defile was obscured from view by a heavy growth of brush and timber, and it was this that had prevented the Cheyennes from discovering it earlier. Indeed, the latter were under the impression there was no other way up or down, except the route the fleeing Crows had taken when first they had scaled the height.

The Crows now desperate, were quick to take advantage of their discovery. Immediately they sent a scout on ahead down the ravine to see that the way was clear, then in single file and leaving their horses behind, the rest of the party followed their lone comrade's descent, ever cautious - ever watchful.

Upon reaching the base of the hill they continued along the ravine, and when far enough away not to be seen by their enemies, they climbed out onto the prairie itself. Then, following the North Star, they ran on foot as fast as they could across the broken ground in the direction of home, and thus melted away in the blackness of the night.

One can imagine the look of surprise on Cheyenne faces when, next morning, having again gathered at the scene and after scaling the height, albeit in the absence of opposition, they found that the summit had been abandoned but for the horses – and the wily Crows nowhere to be found.

The Cheyennes themselves had suffered a number of casualties during the battle, twenty by Beckwourth's count, and as far as they knew, they had not been able to kill even one of the enemy. They must have been livid with rage and frustration, for by then the Crows had too much of a start to make pursuit a viable prospect. The Cheyennes fully realized also that a small party on foot could conceal itself easily in any number of obscure hiding places and more adequately cover their trail than a party on horseback, and this last especially so, in such rugged country through which the Crows would be travelling. The deluded Cheyennes could only seethe at their own impotence, and wait patiently for the day when revenge for loved ones lost might be gained in full.

The Crows for their part, safely reached their home camp and soon after, Yellow-Belly's rival Red-Eyes and his party came in. They also had incurred a brush with Cheyennes and during which, their party had taken a number of scalps in the process. Thus it still was not proven who the most competent leader might be; Yellow-Belly or Red-Eyes? But needless to say, there was much singing and dancing among the Crows throughout the following weeks. However, it was not long after these two episodes that a number of Crow warriors did meet disaster, although not by human hand.

– 0 – 0 – 0 – 0 – 0 – 0 – 0 – 0 – 0 – 0 – 0 – 0 – 0 – 0 –

## CHAPTER 18.

## THE BATTLE AT GRAPEVINE CREEK AND THE BIG-PRISONER AFFAIR.

The winter of 1830 /`31 like that of the preceding year was particularly severe. Many potential raiders among the warring tribes preferred to stay home in their comfortable lodges, rather than brave excessive inclement weather on the war-trail. There were those, however, especially among the Crows compared to other tribes, who actually preferred to undertake their bellicose ventures during a snow fall, suspecting the enemy to be ensconced in warm lodges; reluctant to keep close watch over their horses, let alone go in pursuit of thieves.

Just such a man was the Crow chief, Heap-of-Dogs, who notwithstanding the severe elements and along with fifty fellow braves, started out one icy morning from the combined Crow camp then still located on the south side of the lower course of Wind River. They travelled southeast, *Awala-diile,* intending to raid one or more Cheyenne village on the Laramie Fork of the North Platte.

On their second day out, the party came to Stillwater River and made camp for the night. The following morning they crossed the river and continuing southeast, entered the Bear Tooth Mountain region where they began traversing an open plateau some twenty miles wide, devoid of cover of any kind. Their leader Heap-of-Dogs was endeavouring to reach some high hills in the distance, beyond which lay a direct route to the Cheyenne camps on the Laramie. Suddenly, when the party was only half way across the plateau, a violent wind blew up immediately followed by a howling blizzard, and before long, most of the warriors were floundering knee-deep in snow. Others doubled up and stood motionless owing to the intense cold and slicing wind.

Said Winona Plenty-Hoops, *"Chilia, chilia, kaashi kaashi chilia,"* [i. e., `Cold, cold, much much cold`], and it soon became obvious they could not continue without disastrous consequences befalling them all. Several had already succumbed to frost-bite and others; having fallen in the snow, actually froze to death where they lay. Heap-of-Dogs finally decided to abandon the party`s original objective and by utilizing the robes of their dead comrades for added warmth, those left on their feet turned about and trudged back the way they had come. Of the fifty warriors which initially had started out with Heap-of-Dogs, less than half returned to their home camp alive. Ever since that time, the Crows have known the area where occurred the disastrous episode as *"Where they froze to death,"* and a nearby creek flowing north into the Yellowstone as, *"Froze to death Creek."*

Such then was an unexpected blow to Crow moral, but fortune once again, was about to bode well for the Nation as a whole. [1]

The earlier mentioned American Fur Company post Fort Union at the mouth of the Yellowstone, had been built primarily for the Assiniboine trade, along with the latter`s Plains Cree confederates, and initially, the post had been viewed with some trepidation by the Crows. It did, however, eventually prove beneficial to Sore-Belly and his people.

# BATTLE AT GRAPEVINE CREEK and the BIG-PRISONER AFFAIR.

The fort's proprietor Kenneth McKenzie had sent word at the onset of winter 1830 /'31, inviting the chief and his followers to bring their furs and buffalo robes to the post where they could obtain all the white man's trade goods they required. McKenzie had also given assurances that the Crows would be safe from harm, being under the protection of the white men, and would be included in a general truce which prevailed among the different tribes when actually trading at the fort, notwithstanding they be the mortal enemies of the Crows and of each other.

So it was that any fears Sore-Belly and his followers may earlier have harboured regarding visiting the post, because of numerous formidable war bands which might be encountered, they had now been somewhat dispelled by McKenzie's invite, and Sore-Belly could not afford to refuse.

Accordingly, before the end of winter 1831, a strong body of River Crows did respond to McKenzie's request, to see for themselves if his words were true.

Indeed, McKenzie's assurances were not idle words and from that time on, Sore-Belly and his River Crow band became frequent visitors to Fort Union, and a mutual bond thereafter, was forged between River Crows and American Fur Company employees. There was, though, as earlier noted, intense rivalry between the different fur companies operating in the Upper Missouri country.

Certainly, some of Sore-Belly's River Crows were cajoled by McKenzie's agents such as James Beckwourth and Robert Meldrum, into perpetrating a number of nefarious deeds in order to disadvantage the American Fur Company's competitors. This usually took the form of Crow harassment of rival company employees, by robbing the latter of their horses and pelts and sometimes, by acts of physical violence towards the rival trappers themselves.

An example of this occurred in early March 1831 while snow still lay thick on the ground. It was then that a sixty-strong war-party of River Crows raided the winter camp of the rival Rocky Mountain Fur Company and escaped with a large number of horses. The trappers were left in a serious predicament and sorely needed to retrieve the stolen animals before they could move any further. In response, a large band of trappers which included among their number such notables as Joe Meek, Antoine Godin and Robert 'Doc' Newell, set out as soon as possible, endeavouring to trail the thieves and retrieve the stolen stock.

For two days and nights the trappers followed the trail on snow-shoes, and on the third day came up with the thieves, who had stopped to rest in a flimsy log war-camp somewhere along a small tributary of the Little Big Horn. The Crows had obviously thought the trappers would not have followed in such bad weather, so had relaxed their vigilance once they were in familiar home territory.

The trappers, though, were in a determined mood. That night they secreted the larger part of their force atop the crest of a ridge overlooking the Crow camp on the far side of the river, and when at last all the Crows were wrapped in their warm robes and deep in slumber, two of the trappers, Robert Newell and Antoine Godin, crept up to the log fort, untied some of the horses left around the perimeter and drove them back across the river.

The Crows were awakened by the noise of trampling hooves. They grabbed their weapons and rushed out of their fort, only to be met with a thunderous volley of musket and small arms fire from the ridge top, and seven of their number were felled in this first discharge alone. The rest of the trappers swung onto the bare backs of other loose horses and driving the remainder of the herd before them, made a hasty retreat back to the far distant camp from whence they came. It was then the Crow's turn to continue their trek on foot. [2]

Sore-Belly had not himself been a party to the event. But he had not actually tried to prevent his followers from such an action. He, of course, like most Indians, believed that all horses, notwithstanding to whom they might belong, were fair game, so to speak, and thus for the taking by whomsoever could successfully steal them.

There were other events, however, due to Crow friendship with the American Fur Company which were to prove more beneficial to Sore-Belly and his people. McKenzie had a mind to put an end to the incessant intertribal warfare then raging across the entire Upper Missouri country and to bring the respective warring tribes together in peace. Not, though, due to any paramount moral conviction on McKenzie's part, but in order that intertribal trade beneficial to *his* Company, be conducted without hindrance from Indian war-parties crisscrossing the region. McKenzie was successful in a number of his peace-making endeavours. In the spring, he had managed to effect pacts between the Crows and Atsina [which included the latter's Arapaho cousins], and later, between the Assiniboine and Blackfoot.

Even earlier, during the previous winter [1830 /'31], Sore-Belly had been induced by McKenzie to again hold out the hand of friendship to those Beaver Hills Cree in the vicinity of the North Branch of the Saskatchewan. These were the same people who, along with their Assiniboine allies, had once been Crow enemies from a time immemorial, and after a short period of peace with the Crows in 1827, had since re-joined the Blackfoot as allies and confederates, although in truth, they had not as yet personally resumed hostilities against the Crow. McKenzie for his part, merely wished to poach the Cree and Assiniboine trade from the rival Hudson's Bay Company, in order to obtain Canadian pelts now that the supply of beaver below the International Border was already dwindling, and thought a Crow peace with the Cree could only enhance his designs.

Thus McKenzie persuaded Sore-Belly to send *"pressing messages"* [3] to the Beaver Hills Cree, requesting that their chief La Quartre and his people again come south and meet the Crows in friendship. The Crow invite further promised to provide a strong party of warriors to escort their guests back to the North Country and would supply them with Crow horses, *"At very moderate prices."* [4]

As regards the Cree, they were somewhat undecided whether to continue their peaceful relations with the Crows, and throughout the rest of that winter of 1830 /'31, the Cree chief La Quartre and his headmen had sat in numerous councils discussing the matter among themselves.

The Cree-speaking bands constituted a very populous and widely scattered people, but rarely if ever did more than one Cree group act in concert, having no real hard and fast central government or national unifying structure between them. Each group was an autonomous entity adhering to its own whims and fortunes whichever way it chose, be it in a completely contrary manner to that which other Cree-speaking groups might have pursued.

During that same winter both Beaver Hills Cree and Blackfoot had been camped together throughout the season's duration, so it was not surprising come spring 1831, the Beaver Hills Cree at first decided to shrug off their temporary truce with the Crows, and prepared to undertake a joint hostile venture with their Siksika and Sarsi friends against the Mountain Crows in the Big Horn country. As it was, the undertaking fizzled out before hostile contact could be made, owing to Sarsi allies of the Siksika having had a heated dispute with the accompanying Cree over missing horses.

This dissention in the ranks served to break up the Cree / Siksika venture, to the relief one assumes of the Mountain Crows, although the reason for the aforesaid crusade in the first place, had probably been in response to a recent disaster only one moon earlier, suffered by a large Pikuni party from Pigeon Lake [Alberta] at Crow hands This latter occurrence was noted in the Hudson's Bay Company records for that season and later, by one, Henry Stelfox.

The Crows themselves have an account of the same event in their oral histories, and it shows that Crows; notwithstanding McKenzie's efforts, were apt to be just as fickle as any among their enemies.

On the south side of the Yellowstone between the Big Horn River and Pryor Creek, there runs a small stream known as Grapevine Creek. Close to this stream is a rocky cliff once used as an old-time buffalo Jump site by the Crows, and thus the area around is known to that people as, *"Where we pack meat."* [5] It was after just such a buffalo drive at this place in the latter part of March, 1831, that the Mountain Crows along with twenty lodges of River Crows led by Sore-Belly, were encamped along a stream since known as Hoodoo Creek where the town of Livingston, Montana now stands. The camp shined red, with countless strips of glistening bloody meat hanging on racks in the noon-day sun.

It happened that a war-band of Pikuni some sixty warriors strong, was wandering around on the south side of the Yellowstone in the vicinity of Muddy Creek not far north of the Grapevine. They had been trapping furs to trade at the Hudson's Bay Company post Rocky Mountain House, which stood in the Blackfoot country on Bow River in southern Alberta across the International Border. The Pikuni were *Awala-diile* and were also looking to raid Crow pony herds, as they knew the Mountain Crows were apt to frequent the Grapevine area at this time of year.

The Crow version states that their own village had only recently moved from Grapevine Creek to Hoodoo Creek some five miles away, and it was probably their trail of lodge poles, horses and people which the Pikuni party had been following.

The Pikuni must have realized from the size of the trail that it was a large body of Crows ahead. But undaunted, the party travelled on and soon spied two Crows engaged in butchering a buffalo at the foot of the aforesaid cliff. At the same instant the two Crows saw the Pikuni, and being grossly outnumbered, they at once jumped on their ponies and raced away to raise the alarm at their village on Hoodoo Creek. Realizing they had been discovered and that a large body of

Crows on horseback was sure to come against them, the Pikuni singled out a nearby knoll strewn with rocks of various size and ran towards it. There with the surrounding stones and rocks, they hastily constructed many small circular breastworks – twenty-three in total – and prepared to defend themselves in the event of being attacked.

As the Pikuni suspected, a great number of Crows did soon appear, and arrayed themselves along the crest of an adjacent rise some one-hundred yards distant in full view of the enemy.

At this particular time the Crows had few firearms among them and little powder and ball for those pieces they did possess, as they had not yet made their customary visits to the trading posts or to their Hidatsa and Mandan friends to replenish their stocks. A lack of such weapons seems to have been the case also with the Pikuni, who either had few guns between them, or had used up most of their powder and ball during their previous wandering. Certainly, several systematic searches of the battleground since the time of the fight, have failed to disclose any sign of pre-cartridge day ammunition such as musket or fusee balls, whereas, stone arrow heads and spear points; one of a transparent obsidian-type glass, have been retrieved in some quantity. But whatever the case, when the Crows did finally charge the knoll, the Pikuni easily repulsed the assault with bows and arrows and the few serviceable firearms, if any, in their possession, and when the Crows charged the position a second time, they were again obliged to retreat with several of their number wounded.

After this the Crows held back while discussing among themselves how best they could dislodge the enemy, without, that is, incurring further casualties among themselves.

It was during this lull in the fighting that a Crow brave named Stump-Horn belatedly joined his tribesmen. This man was large in stature with a darker skin than usual among the Crows. Some present-day informants believe he had been captured by Crows when young from some enemy tribe, probably the Ute, who were sometimes referred to as `Black Men` owing to their darker complexion. He was also known to possess strong *medicine*, which he said, would give the attacking force a great victory on this occasion. His *medicine* emanated from a young bull-elk and he wore a robe with that animal depicted on it. For a weapon, he carried a peculiar shaped tomahawk or club with a double elk-horn head, which, supposedly, contained the actual power of the bull-elk itself. He told the Crows hovering around, that he alone would charge on foot up the slope of the knoll on its southwest side, and would draw the enemy`s fire. Then, when the rest of the Crows saw him engaging the enemy hand to hand, they, too, should charge up the slope and overrun the Pikuni defences.

Sore-Belly and his subordinate chiefs agreed to the plan and soon after, Stump-Horn; with only a shield and his elk-horn club, was racing on foot up the slope towards the foe. The entrenched Pikuni shot a torrent of missiles at him, but he was not hit, and the next moment he was actually inside one of the rocky entrenchments, battling furiously with its two occupants who had not time to fix more arrows to their bows. Stump-Horn seemed to bare a charmed life. He quickly dispatched both enemies with his war-club before being set upon by other Pikuni

211

nearby. However, before the enemy could bring him down, the rest of the Crow warriors with Sore-belly at their head, were already on top of the slope, both on horseback and on foot, and a bloody hand to hand melee ensued.

From their small rocky enclosures, the Pikuni, some alone and others in twos and threes, fought bravely and desperately against the over-whelming odds assaulting them. However, a little less than half the Pikuni force did manage to vacate their breastworks, and these ran down the steep slope of the knoll on its north side in their effort to escape. Many Crows meanwhile, had already circled around the base of the knoll and so blocked the route of retreat. Thus, while thirty-one or thirty-three Pikuni were butchered on top of the knoll, most of the remainder were cut down at its base on the north side. In total fifty-seven Pikuni lay dead or mortally wounded, both within and away from their respective breastworks.

Three Pikuni survived the slaughter, and these made their escape across the open Plain to the north of the knoll and back towards Muddy Creek from whence they came. One of these escapees had been seriously injured during the fight and he died of his wounds before reaching home. Another had the misfortune to run into a Grizzly Bear and was torn to pieces, and only one of the original sixty-strong Pikuni party actually reached his home camp north of the Missouri.

The Crow victors were jubilant. They had suffered only a few wounded, and in addition to the scalps and weapons which they took, they acquired a large stock of furs and pelts – supposedly 2,000 in number - which the Pikuni had in their possession at the time.

It was for this reason that the Pikuni did not go to Rocky Mountain House to trade that spring and summer, as they then had few if any furs to trade. As a result, that post did not open the following year as there was thought to be little profit for the Company to make it viable. Indeed, it is recorded in a Hudson's Bay Company journal for the winter of 1830 /`31,

> "The Crows attacked a group of Piegans, killing 57 warriors and stealing their furs." [6]

The captured pelts in question were later traded by the Crows to Kenneth McKenzie at Fort Union in exchange for much needed guns and powder and ball among other things, deemed necessary for the Crows own continued survival.

So it was that the Crow - Pikuni war raged on unabated, while at the same time the Beaver Hills Cree as new found allies of the Siksika, Bloods and Atsina, continued to discuss between themselves whether to accept the peace proposal from Chief Sore-Belly's River Crows and thereby, abandon the Hudson's Bay Company in favour of carrying their trade south to the Americans.

It was a situation, strange as it seems, which in no way deterred Sore-Belly from continuing to woo the confidence of the Cree to his side.

As regards the Beaver Hills Cree, things then took a turn for the worse. Their dispute with the Sarsi over missing ponies at the close of the previous winter, had resulted in war not only between the last named two peoples, but had created hostilities between the Sarsi and Siksika also. However, before the end of spring the Sarsi and Siksika had patched up their quarrel and together, they then turned upon the Cree.

Meanwhile, having been made aware of the Crow overtures to the Cree, Hudson's Bay Company officials had became concerned that they might lose their Cree customers to the Americans south of the line. Perhaps they had attempted to dissuade the Cree from responding to the Crow chief's invitation, but if so, it was to no avail. The Cree finally made up their minds to accept Sore-Belly's offer due to the recent hostilities with the Sarsi and Siksika, and also, to visit Fort Union on the Yellowstone, to see for themselves how the Americans treated their Indian customers.

Be this as it may, it was not until June 10th before a strong party of Cree along with a number of Plains Ojibwa [Chippewa] associates, started out on the long journey south to visit Sore-Belly and the River Crows.

It seems, though, that the expedition had been a half-hearted affair, as many among the Cree were still sceptical of Crow motives and feared some kind of treachery on the part of the latter. Before contact could be made, the Cree expedition was assaulted by a strong Mandan force on the north side of the Missouri. The Mandan, of course, were closely associated with the Crows and had likely been fully aware of the latter's peaceful intentions towards the Cree. Perhaps the Mandan feared losing their own role as middle men in both the Crow and Cree trade, but whatever the case, a desperate fight ensued before the Cree finally drove their Mandan attackers off.

Whether the Cree thereafter continued on to meet with Sore-Belly, or gave up the enterprise altogether and returned home, we are not told. But before the year was out, another initiative from McKenzie did broach an official peace between Sore-Belly's River Crows and the Beaver Hills Cree, albeit for a short period of time, of which we will speak later.

Certainly, the bringing together of tribal enemies to smoke the pipe of peace when visiting Fort Union, was no mean achievement on the part of its proprietor McKenzie. But unfortunately, most of these pacts as were periodically effected, lasted little longer than the return of the respective parties to their home countries.

During mid-summer [1831], just such a temporary pact had been made between a small band of Crows and a band of Lakota which happened to be visiting Fort Union at the same time. Only a few days later after the Lakota trading party had left, and the Crows still camped outside the walls of the fort, the same band of Lakota suddenly re-appeared and charged the Crow camp.

The Crow warriors present were much inferior in number to their attackers. Expediently they raced for the fort, men, women and children, in order to seek protection among the white men within the palisade walls.

The fort employees did accommodate the fleeing Crows and immediately barred the gate shut against the Lakota. The Lakota plan was thus thwarted. They dare not assault the fort itself as the white men were known to be excellent shots, not to mention severe damage that canon mounted in both bastions of the fort would do to any attacking body. The Lakota halted their assault. Instead, they sent forward several peace emissaries with requests to speak with those inside. None at first among the occupants in the fort were brave enough, or perhaps foolhardy enough to go out and meet with the emissaries. But at length, the Crow female fighter Woman-Chief mounted her pony, and alone, she rode through the gates and towards the foe. As she did so, several among the Lakota at once threw off their peaceful pretence and shot arrows at her. But rather than flee back inside the fort, Woman-Chief actually fitted an arrow to her bowstring and shot back at the enemy. Her first missile found its mark and repeating her action, she actually brought down another Lakota, after which she did return inside the fort to loud adulation from both the Crows and white men therein. The rest of the Lakota war-band having been somewhat humiliated, picked up their two fallen tribesmen and sullenly left the scene. The Crows concluded their trade, and after holding a victory dance to the delight of the fort employees, they eventually left the vicinity and returned to their home camp safely. [7]

Some such truces as initiated by McKenzie did survive slightly longer. As was the case when the Atsina had entered into their aforementioned pact with Crows in early 1831, but as had happened in previous decades, ensuing circumstances precluded any long-term amiable interaction between the two, of which the following episode is a case in point.

Due to conversations between Crows and their new-found Atsina friends at Fort Union, the Kicked-in-the-Bellies Crow chief, Big-Bowl, [Beckwourth's adopted father and who's portrait was painted by Alfred Jacob Miller in 1837], learned that his real son who had previously been taken captive by Cheyennes, and by Beckwourth's adoption Big-Bowl had meant to replace, was still alive and among a particular Cheyenne band known as the Watapio then roaming the South Platte region.

The son in question was known among the Cheyennes by the name of Big-Prisoner. He had last been seen when, in the aftermath of the allied Lakota and Cheyenne attack on the Mountain Crow camp of Long-Hair in 1820, he had been among the victorious allies, and it was he who had conversed with the lone Crow appearing on the bluff top above the allied column as it made its way back to the allied camps.

Upon hearing of his son's present whereabouts, Big-Bowl immediately sent runners with a gift of tobacco via the Atsina to the latter's Arapaho cousins, along with a message saying that he, Big-Bowl, was coming south with his Crow band on a peace mission to the Arapaho and Cheyennes.

Now it had happened that a band of Atsina led by a chief known as Old Bald Eagle had already gone south two years earlier, and having joined with an Arapaho band, was often in the company of fifty lodges of the aforesaid Watapio Cheyennes. The Atsina and Arapaho chiefs received the Crow emissaries in friendship and accepted the tobacco offering from Big-Bowl. They promised to relay the Crow chief's message of peace when next they met the Cheyennes, not for a moment thinking it would be accepted, owing to the bloody conflicts still taking place on a regular basis between that people and Crows.

The Watapio Cheyenne chief, Old-Bark, did nonetheless, agree to meet with his mortal foes and in late summer the same year [1831], along with a small

Arapaho band and the latter's Atsina confederates, Old-Bark moved his village north to the mouth of Crow Creek near where the town of Cheyenne, Wyoming now stands. Here the three allied bands pitched their tepees in their separate camps and awaited the arrival of the Crows.

It was only a few days later when travelling in a long column, the Crows came snaking down from a high point on the prairie north of the allied camps. The Crows comprised some two-hundred lodges, with an additional small visiting band of Kiowa some forty lodges strong led by the latter's famous chief of a later date named "Dohausan," although better known as "Little-Bluff "or "Little-Mountain." When arrived along the creek, the Crows and Kiowa pitched their lodges a little way from the Arapaho and Atsina, but some respectable distance from the Cheyennes. Within the hour the tepees of these new arrivals had been erected and cooking pots were on the boil. The Crow Big-Bowl then sent word to each of the three allied bands of Arapaho, Atsina and Cheyenne, inviting their chiefs and headmen to a grand feast in the Crow camp. For such was the custom whenever warring tribes came together for peaceful motives.

The Arapaho and Atsina having previously made their pacts with the Crows due to the aforesaid initiative from Kenneth McKenzie, accepted the invitation. But the Cheyennes not having been a party to any such peace-making, were suspicious and stayed away. Thus the Arapaho and Atsina chiefs alone visited the Crow camp, and after the feast was over, Big-Bowl arose and addressed his guests. He told the Arapaho that his only wish was to get his son back from the Cheyennes, but if the Cheyennes wanted to resume the war between them, then it was alright with the Crows. Big-Bowl then asked the Arapaho chief to relay his words to the Cheyennes, to which the Arapaho chief agreed, and thereafter the Arapaho and Atsina guests returned to their respective camps.

When the Cheyenne Old-Bark received the Crow message via the Arapahos, he summoned the captive Big-Prisoner to his lodge. After informing him what the Crow chief had said, Old-Bark left the decision to the captive, whether to return to his blood relatives the Crows, or stay among his adopted people the Cheyennes. It was not too hard a decision for Big-Prisoner to make. He had been with the Cheyennes for many years; had since married a Cheyenne woman and now had a family and children of his own. His adopted tribe had treated him well over the years, and so he declined to go back to the Crows. Instead, he sent word to the Crow chief informing him that he intended to remain with the Cheyennes ever more.

The number of Crow warriors with Big-Bowl out-numbered the Cheyennes at least four to one, and were much better armed with firearms at this time than were the latter. Certainly, it would have been a simple matter to attack the Cheyenne camp and recapture not only Big-Prisoner, but any other captives of Crow blood who might be in the camp, along with the Cheyenne pony herd and whatever was deemed worthy of carrying away as booty. Such a plan, however, could only succeed if the Arapaho and Atsina stayed neutral and did not involve their own warriors in the affair. The Crow chief knew this and the next day, he and his headmen again held a feast for the Arapaho and Atsina. This time Big-Bowl asked them to assist the Crows in annihilating the Cheyennes and to help in retrieving his stolen son. Said the Crow chief with words to the effect,

> "We Crows, Atsina and Arapaho for generations have often been friends. In the long-ago time, we hunted and fought as one in the snow country of the north. These Striped-Arrow-People are always making trouble. It is time they were whipped like dogs and suffered the wrath of those whose relatives they have butchered these many winters past." [8]

After the Crow chief had uttered these words, a warrior present named Small-Man, who was Atsina by birth but now recognized as a sub-chief among the Arapaho, stood up and replied to the Crow chief saying,

> "Yes, the days of which you speak were in the long-ago time. For many winters we Arapaho, Atsina and Cheyennes have been living and dying together as brothers. If the Crows wish to make the ground muddy with Cheyenne blood, then they must fight the Arapaho and Atsina also." [9]

In response to this brash reply, one after another of the respective Arapaho and Atsina headmen also stood up, and repeated the same sentiments as expressed by Small-Man.

Big-Bowl was despondent to say the least. He conveyed his deep-felt disappointment to think that those before him were not the good friends he had supposed them to be, and how aggrieved he was, knowing he was to lose his beloved son forever. The chief concluded by declaring that the Crows and Kiowa would leave the next day. But, he continued, before they did so, his people would visit the Arapaho and Atsina camp and perform a grand dance in their honour, and so saying, he declared the council over.

Later that day in the Crow chief's lodge, it was decided that during the coming dance, the Crows and their Kiowa friends would surprise the Arapaho, Atsina and Cheyennes and slaughter them all. In addition, two strong-armed Crow warriors were selected to race their ponies along each side of Big-Prisoner himself, and carry him off in a 'prairie rescue' routine.

Now at this time, there was a young man in the Crow camp who had relatives among the Arapaho, and did not wish them harmed. Without the knowledge of Big-Bowl and his fellow tribesmen, this man slipped out of the village that night, and went over to the Arapaho camp to warn them of the Crow intentions. Once informed of the plan, the Arapahos immediately sent word to the nearby Cheyennes, and hurriedly the allied chiefs held their own council of war to discuss the matter further. The allies, thereafter, stationed guards around their camps and ordered scouts to spy on activities going on in the Crow and Kiowa village, and those who slept that night did so fully clothed with weapons at their side.

During the night the Crows and Kiowa as a matter of course, sent their own scouts out and when these clashed with some of those from the Arapaho and Cheyenne camps, the Crows fully suspected their plan had been betrayed.

The next morning the Crows did not go to the Arapaho camp to dance as promised. Instead they waited for the Arapaho, Atsina and Cheyennes to make their move. Throughout the morning selected warriors from each side rode back and forth over the prairie; ready to raise the alarm if the other side should appear to be preparing to attack.

Around mid-day, several of the opposing riders did clash and a brief skirmish ensued. At once the Crow and Kiowa warriors and those among the allied bands mounted their war-ponies and forming up in two long opposing lines, faced each other across the intervening open ground between the camps.

At the same time the women among the Arapaho, Atsina and Cheyenne camps hastily took down their lodges, and after loading the tepee covers and belongings on pony drags, began fleeing towards some nearby hills so to be out of range during the bloody conflict which, they believed, was about to commence.

Strange it was, however, that none appeared over anxious to begin an all-out melee, as no specific move was made to engage the foe by either side. As it transpired, several lone warriors from the respective forces, would gallop back and forth across the no-man's land between the lines and challenge a champion from among their opponents to meet them in single combat.

Thus was the order of battle throughout the day and during which, the Atsina-Arapaho Chief Small-Man showed outstanding bravery, bringing much honour to his people. The Kiowa Chief Dohausan on the other hand, fighting alongside the Crows, also, it is said, lived up to his reputation as a fearless fighter.

At length, the Crow and Kiowa women and other non-combatants also began dismantling their lodges and soon after, were heading north, back towards their own country on the far side of the Yellowstone. The Crow and Kiowa warriors, too, after initially acting as a rear guard then withdrew from the battle ground, albeit still presenting a strong defending body as they followed in the wake of their non-combatanta and likewise, slowly disappeared from view. The allies did not attempt to follow, and the conflict came to an end.

The fight is remembered among the Cheyennes and Arapaho as, *"When the Crows came down,"* i.e., came south, [10] and among the Crows as, *"When the Kiowa helped the Crows."* [11]

Meanwhile, Big-Bowl would bide his time, and true enough under the leadership of the great Sore-Belly, full vengeance would be exacted upon the perfidious Atsina before the end of summer the following year.

So much then for the recent McKenzie inspired pact between the Crow, Atsina and Arapaho, and little hope, - for the time being - that Sore-Belly's overtures of peace to the Cheyennes would ever be accepted.

Notwithstanding, however, this temporary setback for the Crows due to the Cheyenne, Arapaho and Atsina stand against them, at this period in the early eighteen-thirties, now having direct access to a regular supply of guns and ammunition at Fort Union, the Crows regarded themselves as formidable opponents and as true denizens of the Yellowstone and Big Horn regions. There can be little doubt that such a situation had come about solely through the determination, ability and influence of their great war-chief Sore-Belly. He it was who had shown on countless occasions that not only were the Crows more than able to hold their hunting grounds against any and all comers, but could match their foes in both valour and in spirit; often surpassing them on the field of conflict. Not to mention hitting them hard in their own domains which, in previous decades, had rarely suffered any concerted Crow invasion.

More important, perhaps, was Sore-Belly`s personal foresight in courting the friendship of the whites, who subsequently helped in no small way to protect Crow lands and Crow welfare in the Upper Missouri country.

Be this as it may, incessant unrelenting warfare between the tribes, necessarily incurred huge dents in their respective populations. Peoples such as the Cheyennes and Suhtaio could not have sustained such losses without dire consequences to their very existence, were it not that they were allied to the populous Lakota and Arapaho, who`s own numbers when augmenting those of the Cheyennes, allowed the latter to more than equal the Crows and other enemies in numerical strength. The Crows for their part, although able to boast nearly twice the population of the Cheyennes and Suhtaio combined, had many more foes to contend with and fewer allies upon which they could depend.

Other than the vast number of horses owned by the Crows, which was usually enough reason for foreign war-bands to raid their camps, they also resided in a most vulnerable position, claiming as they did some of the finest hunting territory west of the Mississippi. Crow country, as previously noted, was a land of prairies, mountains and rivers, well-stocked year round with an abundance of buffalo, deer, elk, antelope and big-horn sheep. Its pine-covered hills and mountains offered cool breezes during the sweltering heat of summer, along with thick cotton-wood groves through which ambled clear crystal streams filled with fish. The cottonwoods themselves gave shelter from the snows and icy winds of winter, whilst providing nourishment for Crow ponies during those snow-bound moons. No wonder Crow country was coveted by all the surrounding tribes, among which the Lakota were fast becoming the most persistent interlopers into the Crow domain, and it was fully realized that the Lakota; being populous and aggressive, might prove more of a threat to Crow occupation and the latter`s very existence than the Cheyennes and Suhtaio, with whom at present, the Crows were already engaged in bloody confrontations for control of the Powder and Tongue River regions.

There was, though, a warrior`s mutual respect between the Crows and Lakota. Often short truces were affected between them, during which brief interludes members of one tribe would visit those of the other in order to trade or merely to discuss past battles between their respective peoples along with general gossip of the day. Relatives of those taken captive in previous engagements would be visited in their captor`s own village, at which time family news would be exchanged. These captives had invariably been abducted when young and having grown up and married into the captor`s tribe, had since raised a family of their own and thereafter, opted to remain where they were. With regard to the male offspring of these mixed marriages, both the Crows and Lakota had plenty of other enemies to contend with, without one having to fight against one`s own blood kin, unless it became absolutely necessary to do so in order to protect themselves and their new family and friends when attacked.

The Cheyennes and Suhtaio on the other hand, not having been at peace with the Crows for at least a generation, did have one thing in common with them. In so much that the Lakota – being numerically stronger - were also pressing on the Cheyennes as they, the Lakota, continued their expansion into the western buffalo country. They had already filled up the Black Hills region of southwestern South Dakota, which for many years past, had once been occupied by Cheyennes and Suhtaio alone. It had been similar pressure at an earlier date from a host of Lakota migrants, which had induced the Cheyennes and Suhtaio to move west from the Missouri and into the Black Hills area in the first place.

The Crows knew this only too well and for that reason, Sore-Belly declared he and the Crows would still welcome a permanent peace with the Cheyennes. Such was sure to prove beneficial to both, for then their two peoples together could resist the steady encroachment of the Lakota. Sore-Belly even went further by making it known that he was finally prepared to acknowledge the Suhtaio as permanent residents of the Tongue River country which, as yet, was still regarded as Crow hunting ground, even though certain other Cheyenne-speaking bands had, for some time past, been treating it as their own.

Unfortunately for the Crows, the Suhtaio and most other Cheyenne bands, were not then of a mind to entreat for a foothold in the disputed country.

All the while, that is, the prospect remained whereby, they might take as much land as they wanted by force of arms, and especially so, with the powerful and belligerent Lakota as their allies. Thus, to the Cheyennes and Suhtaio way of thinking, there appeared no reason to ease their current warfare with any of their enemies; least of all the Crows, and their war-parties continued to raid Crow villages and pony herds whenever the fancy took them. At other times, both the Cheyennes and Suhtaio endeavoured to regain prestige by lifting a few Crow scalps, and after a whipping from some other tribe were inclined to seek compensation from any foe that happened to be on hand.

Sore-Belly himself harboured a more compromising attitude. He continued to believe that the Cheyennes would still listen to his proposal of peace, more especially, perhaps, now that the Cheyennes did not have the power of their Sacred Medicine Arrows to protect them. But for the time being this was not to be, and unabated warfare continued between that people and Crows in all its unbridled fury.

- 0 - 0 - 0 - 0 - 0 - 0 - 0 - 0 - 0 - 0 - 0 - 0 - 0 - 0 - 0 - 0 - 0 -

## CHAPTER. 19.

## SORE-BELLY SAVES HIS SON FROM THE ENEMY.

By the early days of autumn [1831], both the Cheyennes and Suhtaio - albeit still smarting over the loss of their Sacred Arrows to the Pawnees, - had become extremely vexed due to a sudden upsurge of Crow reciprocal attacks upon their pony herds and hunting parties. Now the Cheyennes resolved to send a formidable host into Crow country. In part to help compensate for their own recent defeat at Pawnne hands, but also, in an attempt to even up old scores and curb somewhat, the Crow enthusiasm for war. [1]

One account states that the resulting Cheyenne war-party consisted of no less than three thousand warriors, [2] but, of course, even if the whole Cheyenne-speaking Nation had been members of the foray, the actual warrior strength would still not have exceeded some eight-hundred fighting men at most. What is known, is that the Cheyennes and Suhtaio war-party was certainly a formidable one and had started out from a large Cheyenne-Suhtaio village then situated somewhere along the North Platte River. The party was led by the great war-chief High-Backed-Wolf, the same who had led the allied force against Long-Hair's Crow village destroyed in 1820, when many captives were taken.

The Cheyenne party on this occasion, at first travelled along a similar route as taken during the 1820 event, and then headed northwest to Tongue River in two separate bodies.

The Cheyenne chief's strategy at this time was that whilst a decoy force attacked the Crow village and ran off the pony herd, the main body of Cheyennes would position itself in the path they expected the pursuing Crows to take when chasing the thieves. There they would wait in hiding until the Crows came up and then, having the advantage of surprise, the Cheyennes would be able to inflict a severe drubbing upon the enemy.

Thus on the west bank of Powder River the Cheyennes set up their war camp and that same night, the decoy party started west towards the Tongue. They intended to reach the unsuspecting enemy at dawn, which happened to be the River Crow village in which Sore-Belly was then residing.

Come sun-up, more than one-hundred Cheyenne warriors were already positioned along one side of the Crow village, between themselves and which grazed the Crow pony herd.

Suddenly, as the first of the sun's morning rays lit up the scene, a lone Cheyenne war-cry split the silence, and beating quirts, tomahawks and musket barrels on bull-hide shields, the entire Cheyenne line raced their mounts forward. They went careering into the herd which took up en masse and stampeded before the charging warriors. Two Crow boy herders being caught between the flying hooves of their animals, proved easy targets for the Cheyennes and were set upon by a score of painted horsemen, who lanced them through, then sent iron-headed arrows into them before tearing off their scalps and trampling the prostrate corpses under hoof.

As the majority of Crows came stumbling from their lodges, a large number of Cheyennes turned and faced them. They hurled insults and abuse at the Crows and called to them that if they wanted their animals back, they would have to match the Cheyennes in the chase and take them if they dare. The Crows were sorely tempted to do just that, there being more than enough ponies left in the village for the Crow warriors to give a spirited pursuit. However, although the Crows could match the enemy in the number of warriors present, their wise Chief Sore-Belly, fearing the attack to be a ruse to draw his warriors into a trap, quelled their enthusiasm and excitement. He prevented the Crows from pursuing the foe and their being lured into a disastrous confrontation. Thus, as none among the Crows took up the challenge, the Cheyennes realized their ruse had failed.

After a short while they rode off to join their comrades in ambush, albeit driving a vast number of Crow ponies before them. But even this could not induce the Crows to follow.

When the two Cheyenne forces came together again, they agreed among themselves that as none of their own number had been killed, they should be content with the captured herd and two Crow scalps. The Cheyenne-Suhtaio Pipe-holder High-Backed-Wolf, felt the war-party had fulfilled its obligations and subsequently, he called an end to the expedition and he and his warriors started for home.

Of the captured herd, it is said that many ran off on their own accord or were recaptured by small parties of Crows, who trailed the Cheyennes on the latter's homeward journey from their war-camp on the Powder. During this event, small groups of Crows conducted numerous lighting sorties upon the Cheyenne column, each time retrieving a large bunch of animals when they did so. By the time the grand enemy host reached its home camp on the North Platte, less than a third of the original number of animals driven off from the Crow village, still remained in Cheyenne hands. [3]

The Crows themselves deemed they had come off comparatively light compared to what might have transpired. They still had ponies in abundance and would soon make up their loss by raiding stock from other tribes. The Crows, therefore, continued their usual routine; visiting the trading post of Fort Union, and conducting their seasonal buffalo hunts. They also sent out their own war-parties to raid the camps and pony herds of their enemies, among whom not least, were always the Cheyennes and Suhtaio.

Some few moons after the last-mentioned event, two bands of Cheyenne, comprising the Hevietanio of Chief Yellow-Wolf and the Ovimimana of Blue-Horse, were roaming the lower Powder River country together. The two bands wandered up and down both banks and along one and another of its connecting streams hunting deer and buffalo at their leisure. They were amassing a store of meat and hides to see them through the coming winter. [4]

During the course of their circuitous movements, the Cheyennes made camp one time on the west side of the middle course of the Powder. Here they were joined by a large Suhtaio band which just happened to be passing through that district en route to their own wintering ground lower down that same river near its confluence with the Yellowstone.

Earlier throughout the summer months, the whole region would have been swarming with Crows. But by the end of *"The Moon when leaves turn yellow"* [autumn], each Crow band, customarily, was already traveling towards its own wintering ground, either near the Big Horn Mountains or in the Wind River Valley west and southwest respectively.

It seems that the Kicked-in-the-Belly band under their Head chief, High-Squirrel, was late moving that year. When the first flurries of snow began settling on the hillsides, their village was still positioned in their autumn hunting ground, along a branch of the Mitzpah River which flows from the west into the lower course of the Powder.

At the same time, the aforementioned Cheyenne bands and Suhtaio were setting up their tepees only two days traveling distance east of the Mitzpah, and it was not long before they and the Crows became aware of each other's presence. The inevitable consequence was that very soon, both Crow and Cheyenne warriors were raiding each other's pony herds; harassing each other's hunting parties and taking the odd scalp here and there. And so it went on, practically day after day without respite.

During this period of almost constant strife, a large Cheyenne / Suhtaio war-party went over to attack the Crow village, at which time the taking of scalps was the intended prize rather than the stealing of horses. In short, the Cheyenne force attacked the Crow camp and did manage to invest the outer lodges before finally being driven off. In the event, the Cheyennes escaped with five Crow women and one boy around ten years old. We are not told how many casualties were incurred either among the Cheyennes or Crows, although the six captives remained permanently thereafter with the Cheyennes.

Being disadvantaged in numbers as compared to the combined strength of the Cheyennes and Suhtaio, it was soon after this that the Kicked-in-the-Bellies decided to strike their lodges and move some distance west to the Little Big Horn River. Here they joined Long-Hair`s people already encamped, and among which band at this time was Sore-Belly with around fifty lodges of River Crows on an extended visit to their Mountain Crow cousins. Thus the Kicked-in-the-Bellies again set up their tepees, now confident of opposing the Cheyennes and Suhtaio on more equal terms.

The Cheyennes and Suhtaio, meanwhile, also struck their lodges and followed in the wake of their enemies. After crossing the Tongue, they, too, again set up their camps, this time along one of the headwater branches of Rosebud Creek only some twelve miles distant from where the Crows were positioned.

Once again war-parties from both sides began going out against each other's camps; stealing horses and scalps as before, and after three weeks of tit-for-tat raiding, the situation finally reached a climax.

A party of four Crows led by the famous sub-chief Yellow-Belly and including James Beckwourth the mulatto mountain man, set out one night on a horse stealing expedition against the Cheyenne village. It was a little before dawn when the party reached its objective while the camp occupants were still asleep on their pallets. The Crows proceeded to creep stealthily around the slumbering camp, whilst untying the best ponies from their picket ropes outside the very door flaps of the owner's lodges.

Suddenly, out of the murky gloom, a solitary Cheyenne on horseback appeared. He was nearly upon the raiders before he could discern what they were doing, and seeing also that the latter's bows were already strung and fitted with arrows, the Cheyenne immediately turned his horse around and endeavoured to escape out of range. At the same time he cried aloud his discovery and called his tribesmen to arms. In a matter of seconds, it seemed, the lone Cheyenne was crumpling up over his horse's neck, then falling to the ground with a Crow arrow quivering in his back.

Already tepee flaps were being drawn back and drowsy Cheyennes, blinking in the dim light of dawn, grabbed their weapons and ran towards the trespassers.

Beckwourth and two of the raiders now mounted on Cheyenne steeds with other stolen animals in tow, were about to leave the village in haste. The fourth Crow was still dismounted and was actually engaged in scalping the prostrate Cheyenne. He had carelessly let go of his horse's reins and did not notice the animal wandering off among the tepees. The howling Cheyennes ran towards him intent on getting one scalp at least, even if the rest of the Crow raiders did manage to escape, and the lone Crow was suddenly aware of what appeared to be his imminent doom.

Seeing the crowd of Cheyennes coming towards him with tomahawks and hatchets raised, the Crow looked around frantically for his mount. Desperately he cried to his companions for help, but they were reluctant to risk what appeared to be a futile rescue attempt, likely to result in their own lives becoming forfeit in the process.

The Cheyennes were almost upon the unhorsed Crow when Beckwourth, having taken pity on his comrade's plight, all at once dropped the jaw rope attached to the lead animal of his string of stolen ponies, and spurring his own mount back into the enemy village now alive with angry Cheyennes, he rode over to the terrified Crow. Quickly he pulled him up on his horse behind him, and raced out of the village away from the very jaws of death.

The Crows collected an additional seven Cheyenne horses as they fled, whilst at the same time dodging a cloud of arrows whistling past their ears. A volley of musket shot also rang out behind them amid curses and cries of anger from the Cheyennes.

It must be said that both the Cheyennes and Suhtaio, in truth, admired such a show of bravery even from their enemies. But still they were livid at the sheer audacity of the Crows in making their raid in almost broad daylight, and more so, for their getting away with a number of horses and a scalp.

Almost at once a large body of Cheyenne and Suhtaio warriors started out after the thieves, but they could not overtake them before the latter reached the safety of their own village on the Little Big Horn.

The Cheyenne war-party nonetheless, continued right up to the Crow camp, whereupon they began shooting arrows and musket balls into the lodges and in total [according to Beckwourth], six Crows were killed. Fortunately for the village occupants, the Cheyenne war-party was too small to attempt a direct assault, and after a few hours they gave up the fight and returned to their own camp on the Rosebud.

That same night in the Cheyenne / Suhtaio village, the chiefs and headmen held a council of war. They decided to attack the Crow camp with their whole fighting force the following morning, and attempt to drive the Crows away from that part of the Big Horn country.

This the Crows had already anticipated and before sunup next day, a large number of Crow warriors led by chiefs High-Squirrel and Yellow-Belly, and including the female fighter Woman-Chief, who many times had fought Crow enemies alongside the men-folk, rode out some distance from the camp. [5]

They secreted themselves in ambush among the thick brush and timber bordering both sides of a trail, which they suspected the Cheyenne war-party would take on its way to the Crow camp.

As it was the Cheyenne war-party comprising over two-hundred warriors, passed only a few yards from the place the Crows had picked for their surprise attack before the Crows themselves had a chance to get into position.

Thus the Cheyennes continued towards their objective without being molested by the Crows.

In the meantime, the occupants in the Crow village had not been idle.

During the night Sore-Belly had commanded that the tepees be taken down and re-erected in a defensive circle. The gaps between the lodges were then filled with brush and logs and camp baggage stacked as high as a man's chest. All the horses were driven into the centre of the lodge circle and behind these defences, stood at least one-hundred able-bodied warriors along with twice that number of old men and teenage boys, all prepared to repel the expected attack. Many Crow warriors carried muskets with a plentiful supply of powder and ball, while the rest were armed with lances, bows and arrows and tomahawks of every description. The majority of warriors led by High-Squirrel and Yellow-Belly who had gone out earlier to prepare the ambush, were unperturbed at missing the enemy force. They were confident that the Cheyennes would not be able to break through the camp defences and they decided therefore, to remain where they were in concealment, ready to attack the enemy force when on its way back to its own village on the Rosebud.

When the Cheyenne war-party did reach the Crow village, they could plainly see there would be little hope of getting through the barricades and in amongst the lodges as they had back in 1820. This time the defences were far more formidable, with many well-armed and determined opponents standing resolutely behind them.

Nevertheless, the Cheyennes and Suhtaio not to lose face, made one or two assaults upon the barricades. But these were at best half-hearted attempts and if anything, such rash actions had little effect upon the defenders. It was not long before the attackers after suffering four warriors wounded, gave up the fight and set off for home leaving the camp occupants to themselves. Subsequently, the enemy war-party blundered headlong into the Crow ambush along their return trail, and a much bloodier contest ensued.

The Cheyennes, although taken by surprise were quick to rally, and fought with much bravery and determination. But being hard pressed and outnumbered, they soon began falling to the war-clubs and missiles of the Crows. Woman-Chief, it is said, was in among the thickest of the fighting much of which was hand to hand. She herself is credited with knocking three Cheyennes from their horses and lancing them through.

In spite of their determined resistance, the Cheyennes and Suhtaio found it hard to manoeuvre, as their horses were very tired having been ridden throughout the night and most of that morning. On the other hand the mounts belonging to the Crows were fresh and fleet, and in addition, the defenders from the Crow village led by the great Sore-Belly, were now also coming up in formidable number to join in the fray. It appeared for a moment that the Cheyennes would be surrounded and their entire force annihilated.

However, before the trap could be executed, the Cheyennes and Suhtaio made a last concerted effort and did manage to break through the Crow lines and make their escape. Needless to say their retreat turned into a rout as the Cheyennes scattered in several directions leaving sixteen of their number dead on the field. They did not have time or perhaps, the inclination to retrieve the bodies of their prostrate comrades and carry them off.

The victorious Crows whooped in savage jubilation, although they did not attempt to follow the enemy further. Instead they stripped the corpses of the fallen Cheyennes; took their scalps and equipment and returned to the Crow camp in triumph. For many days and nights thereafter, the Crows stomped out the victory dance whilst their womenfolk sang praises to their deeds.

It was a sorry and dejected party of Cheyennes and Suhtaio that returned in silence to their home village. Later that day, as for many days and nights to come, there was much mourning and sorrow among their people.

Soon after this the Cheyennes and Suhtaio took down their lodges; packed them on pony drags and moved east back across the Powder from whence they came. There they lingered for a while licking their wounds, after which they began moving slowly downstream towards that river's mouth and their winter camping grounds. Perhaps, thought the Cheyenne and Suhtaio chiefs, in the near future they would get together another grand force to again invade the Crow country and exact revenge.

Of the six prisoners taken during the initial Cheyenne / Suhtaio attack upon the Crow village on the Mitzpah, all subsequently remained with their captors. Of these six, the young Crow boy then about ten years old, later became a great medicine man and warrior among his adopted Suhtaio people. He grew up in the Suhtaio camp and whilst still a young boy, became the close friend of a Cheyenne girl named, Eagle-Feather-on-the-Forehead only a little older than himself. The girl later adopted the Crow captive as her brother and in compliance with Cheyenne custom, he became a member of her family and thus an accepted member of the tribe. As he grew to manhood he was noted for his physical stamina and athletic prowess. He was tall in stature and strong in limb and could out walk and out run all the young men of his age group. Because of this the Cheyennes dubbed him *"Kam-xe-veox-ta,"* meaning Wooden-Leg, implying that his legs never tired owing to their being made of wood. [6]

Beckwourth who, supposedly, was among the Crows throughout the three weeks of continuous strife, mentioned in his memoirs the Crow movement west of the Mitzpah to the Little Big Horn. He further stated that during the initial Cheyenne assault on the Crow village, a total of six Crows had been killed. [7] The Cheyenne account on the other hand as narrated by a nephew of Wooden-Leg [who was known by the same name], does not mention how many Crows and Cheyennes had been slain, but stated six Crows had been carried into captivity.

The discrepancy here is academic. As far as the Crows themselves were concerned, if the captives were not afterwards murdered by the Cheyennes as sometimes would have been the case, or as the Crows were unlikely to see their captured relatives again, then to all intent and purpose they may as well have been considered dead. The important thing is that Beckwourth's account and that given by Wooden-Leg's nephew in his narration to Thomas B. Marquis, appear to refer to the same episode. Each version corroborates the other and concur as to the date implied for the event. All being said, if Beckwourth's number of Cheyennes killed during the affray is anything near the truth, then considering those who in addition, had been seriously wounded and may well have died later as a result, not to mention a number of Cheyenne dead which may have been carried from the field by their tribesmen unbeknown to the Crows, then the Cheyenne and Suhtaio force on this occasion must have suffered a severe defeat by any standard.

Soon after this event, ostensibly during early winter [1831/'32], Sore-Belly and his fifty lodges returned north to the Yellowstone and reunited with the rest of the River Crow band. They were then ensconced in winter quarters close to the curious natural rock formation known as "Pompey's Pillar," some twenty miles east of where the town of Huntley is now sited. It was from this Crow village on the south bank of the Yellowstone that Sore-Belly, soon after his arrival, started south one morning with a body of fifty or more warriors against yet another village of Cheyennes, thought to be situated some two-hundred miles distant on the North Platte.

The weather was unusually mild for the season, and the party went *Awala diile,* so to ride stolen ponies home. A number of teenage boys were also included to help tend to the warrior's needs whilst on the trail, and for several weeks the party travelled in a south-easterly direction.

Coming at length into country frequented by Cheyennes, Sore-Belly dispatched a body of scouts to reconnoitre the way ahead. As usual on such ventures, the scouts had been instructed not to engage the Cheyennes themselves, or to make their presence known. They had been told merely to locate the exact whereabouts of the enemy; assess the latter's strength and report back to Sore-Belly. Then the whole Crow party might attack the foe together without losing the element of surprise.

On this occasion the scouts did not adhere to their instructions. After stumbling across a small number of Cheyennes engaged in butchering buffalo, the scouts decided to attack and kill them all.

There were five Crow scouts and five Cheyennes and the opportunity presented, was too much a temptation for the scouts to pass. Creeping silently to within close gunshot range of the unsuspecting hunters, each of the scouts singled out a specific target and fired their guns simultaneously. Four of the hunters were dropped in the initial discharge, whereupon the surviving hunter vaulted astride a pony tethered nearby, and galloped off to gain the safety of his village, and where he raised the alarm that enemies were in the vicinity.

The Crow scouts meanwhile, scalped and robbed their dead victims. They realized they themselves would not be able to overtake the fleeing Cheyenne before he reached his camp. They thus mounted the ponies of the dead hunters including a packhorse, on which the latter had intended to carry home meat from their kill, and rode back to the main body of Crows to report what they had done.

Upon hearing the scouts` report, Sore-Belly was alarmed. The scouts told him it were they who had first been discovered by the Cheyennes, and had been obliged to mount an attack to prevent the hunters getting away and giving intelligence to their people that a Crow war-party was nearby. The fact, however, that one of the hunters had managed to escape, would mean that Cheyennes in great force would soon come looking for the Crows, eager for their scalps.

Knowing this to be the case, Sore-Belly decided to abort the original mission now the element of surprise was lost. The scouts had taken four scalps and captured several Cheyenne ponies and as no Crow casualties had yet been sustained, the venture could still be considered a success incurring no shame or dishonour if the party returned home. In addition, the Crow chief also realized that being on foot [but for the five captured ponies], his warriors would be no match against cavalry if the Cheyennes should catch them on the open prairie.

The whole party therefore, turned around and began retracing their steps northwest towards the Yellowstone and home.

By this time, however, a freak turn in the weather caused the temperature to drop rapidly, and a sudden ceasation of snowfall made it impossible to hide their tracks. For this reason the Crows travelled the rest of that day and through the coming night, endeavouring to put distance between themselves and any Cheyenne force which, even then, might be following their trail.

Come morning the Crow party rested. They kindled small fires to roast meat and thaw themselves a little before continuing their trek north, and when again they started off, they left one of their number behind to look out for the enemy if in pursuit. Before the rest of the Crows had gone far, this man caught them up and burst out the news that a horde of Stripped-Arrow-People was close on their trail, and being on horseback, they were likely to reach them in a short while. In response, Sore-Belly sent a group of warriors ahead in order to find a suitable place from where his party could make a stand. Fortunately, the Crows soon spied a gully cutting across the prairie floor and deeming this as good a place as any for defence, Sore-Belly secreted the boy members of his party and the captured ponies in the depth of the gully, while the Crow fighting men formed a line in front of its edge and with guns at the ready, prepared to defend themselves against the oncoming Cheyennes.

It was not long before the Cheyennes; a-whooping and a-hollering, arrived on the scene. They outnumbered the Crows by at least two to one and at once, they urged their ponies forward in an attempt to overrun the Crow position. When the charging Cheyennes drew within close musket range, a barrage of lead shot exploded from the Crows and several Cheyenne horses and riders were sent crashing to the ground. The Cheyenne charge broke and dispersed, whereupon the Crows jumped into the gully itself and took up defensive postures behind its bank. They hastily reloaded their pieces and levelled them again, ready to repel the next expected onslaught from the foe.

The Cheyennes, though, could plainly see that the Crows were in a strong position. Neither had they expected so many guns among the enemy, whilst the Cheyennes themselves had few firearms of any description, being armed moreover with tomahawks, lances and bows and arrows. Thus they were reluctant to make another direct assault and instead, began shooting arrows at their opponents by pointing their bows upwards and firing their shafts into the air, so that they arched and fell at random into the gully below.

There were some among the Cheyennes, however, who were braver than their fellows on this occasion, and every so often a lone Cheyenne would make a reckless dash towards the gully. If lucky enough to actually reach the bank unscathed, the lone attacker would simply touch the gully bank with a lance or stick of some kind in the act of counting coup, although some others did shoot arrows or hurl a be-feathered lance in amongst the defenders, and in this way, they succeeded in wounding a number of Crows.

It is said that the marksmanship of the defenders was deadly, and several Cheyennes were felled during their sometimes foolhardy attempts to count coup. But still the Cheyennes would not risk another full-scale assault and the fight appeared to be a stand-off. At length, owing to the superior number of Cheyennes engaged compared to that of the Crows, and notwithstanding that the Cheyennes had already suffered more casualties than the besieged, it still appeared to many of the Crows that their own party would inevitably be annihilated. It would only be a matter of time before the Crows expended the last of their ammunition, and at which point the Cheyennes would certainly charge the gully in force; overwhelm the position and put all the Crows to a gory if not torturous end.

Even Sore-Belly who, to date, had never suffered a wound in his many conflicts, due to his personal *medicine* power which protected him from iron-bladed weapons and leaden balls, was now convinced of the imminent demise of his entire party. Accordingly, he did an unusual and seemingly heartless thing.

He called to his side a lad around sixteen years old who, it is alleged, was Sore-Belly's son, and to this boy the chief said,

> "My son we shall all be killed this day. The Cheyennes are brave
> and have a cloud of warriors before us. It must not be said that his
> son was killed by the enemy before this one, who is bound to protect

him with his life. Therefore, this one must kill you before he too dies." [8]

The chief then stabbed the boy to death.

According to the Beckwourth account, the great chief appeared to be much agitated by all that was going on around him and having slain the young boy at his side, the chief then jumped upon the gully bank and in full view of the enemy, addressed the Cheyennes with words to the effect;

> "Ho, Cheyennes, I am here; come and kill me if you dare. Only then can you slay my warriors when I am no longer able to protect them. I have killed your braves these many years past, many by my own hand and the many Cheyenne scalps I have taken darken my lodge. Come my friends, come on and kill me if you dare." [9]

And then a second strange thing happened.

Rather than shoot at the Crow chief whose prominent stance presented an imposing and clear target for their missiles, the Cheyennes merely stood around in silence and made no further hostile response.

If the Cheyennes had actually witnessed Sore-Belly`s slaying of the boy, then perhaps they were reluctant to engage the enemy further, supposing that the man before them was *"touched"* by the Great Spirit, i.e. a crazy person. Although it is more likely that having already sustained a number of dead and wounded, and now being suddenly aware it was the renowned Sore-Belly himself against whom they were pitted, the Cheyennes were loath to suffer more casualties. Such would surely be the case if they attempted to wipe out the Crow party which, they believed, still had a plentiful supply of ammunition and having been encouraged by their chief, would sell their lives dearly in the event.

The result was that the Cheyennes withdrew out of range. They soon after vacated the field completely and returned to the village from whence they came, taking their dead and wounded with them. When some time later the Crows thought it safe to come out from behind their protective gully and looked around, their enemies were nowhere to be seen.

Sore-Belly was now full of remorse. He sat down on his own and lit a pipe, and as he quietly smoked he contemplated the bloody deed he had done. But whatever regrets he may have harboured, he consoled himself by believing that by sacrificing the boy he had, in reality, elicited the Great Spirit's protection for the rest of the Crow party and thereby, prevented them from being rubbed out. As it was the Crows returned to the gully and remained in the safety of its refuge until nightfall. Then, under the pale light of a hoary moon, they started once again on their long journey north towards the Yellowstone and home.

According to Beckwourth`s account of the affair, the Crows had in total slain eighteen Cheyennes since starting out on the war-trail from the Yellowstone. But they themselves had suffered eight dead and around one dozen injured with wounds of varying degree. It was not then a victorious party that returned to the

River Crow village. Instead, there was the customary period of mourning before any scalp or victory dances could be held.

The mention of the killing of the Crow boy comes solely from Beckwourth's *"Life and Adventures"* and one must, therefore, merely take it as it stands or dismiss its authenticity completely. However, there seems no tangible reason why Beckwourth should deliberately have lied on this occasion, other than embellishing the account with his usual exaggeration of numbers slain. The actual words he purports to have been spoken by the Crow chief are certainly rendered in the Indian idiom, such as the expression, *"...a cloud of warriors."*

There can be little doubt that the leader of the Crow war-party was meant by Beckwourth to refer to the great chief Sore-Belly himself. Beckwourth states correctly that there were only two head chiefs among the Crows, and that one of these head chiefs was the pipe-holder during the fight in question. The additional assertion that the Crow village was then sited near Pompey's Pillar adjacent to the Yellowstone, implies also that the said chief belonged to the River Crow band, who's winter camping ground, we know, was in that region. Chief Long-Hair's Mountain band invariably wintered in the Wind River district southwest of the Big Horn Mountains, and by this date [1831/'32], Long-Hair, of course, was far too old to undertake such a long and arduous expedition himself. Sore-Belly on the other hand, was ever active at this period, and noted for travelling long distances in order to raid the enemy deep in the latter's own country.

Having said this, it is unlikely that Sore-Belly, or indeed any other Crow chief would have deliberately slain his own son for the reason Beckwourth asserts. Sore-Belly himself, according to several white men who knew him personally and from reputation, was considered *"a compassionate man"* [10] and ever vicarious as regards his fellow Crows. *

In addition, of the four blood sons who Sore-Belly is said to have sired along with his foster-son named Chips-the-Rock, all are known to have lived long after this period of the early eighteen-thirties.

Sore-Belly, though, did own a number of captives from enemy tribes who he employed as personal servants and the like. This being so, it is certainly feasible that if the Crow chief had slain a captive at this time, then the captive was probably Cheyenne, and that the murder of the boy was to prevent his being reunited with his own people after Sore-Belly and his warriors had been killed, and so grow up as yet another enemy who would kill more Crows in the future.

- 0 - 0 - 0 - 0 - 0 - 0 - 0 - 0 - 0 - 0 - 0 - 0 - 0 - 0 - 0 - 0 -


**\*There are, however, other examples in Plains Indian history when close relatives had been killed by kinfolk in a similar circumstance. Such was the case regarding the Cheyenne Chief Tall-Bull, who is reported to have first killed his wife before he himself was killed during the battle of Summit Springs in 1869.**

## CHAPTER 20.

## THE FIGHT AT LARAMIE FORK and SUNKEN TRADE GOODS.


Since the "Friendship Treaty" of 1825, unremitting intertribal warfare, along with continued Indian harassment of white trappers and traders in the Upper Missouri region, was still proving a setback to the fur-trading economy of the United States. In order to bring again some semblance of peace between Indians and whites and between the warring tribes themselves, in late autumn 1831, Major John F. A. Sanford – one-time trader now in the role of Government Agent for the Upper Missouri Nations – had set out from Washington DC., to Fort Union on the Yellowstone. It was intended that Sanford after meeting with tribal chiefs, would return with a number of delegates to the United States' Capital. There the Indians could witness the strength and resources of the white man first hand, and be overawed to the extent that they would desist from harassing white men in the fur country, by affording them a healthy respect for and fear of chastisement from, the armed forces of the American Government. [1]

Pre-empting Sanford`s initiative, the Fort Union boss Kenneth McKenzie had previously obtained his own, albeit, temporary agreements of peace between the different tribes visiting his trading establishments. But these pacts primarily, as previously noted, were for the benefit of the American Fur Company alone, and not for the general well-being of other entrepreneurs in the Upper Missouri country. Major Sanford on the other hand, attempted to persuade not only as many tribes as he could, but also all white men in the Indian country into accepting his Government`s peace proposals, and to this end albeit with McKenzie's assistance, the Major himself met with chiefs of the Assiniboine, Plains Cree, Chippewa, Cheyenne, Atsina and the several Blackfoot-speaking tribes, and cajoled their head men into again smoking the calumet of peace with each other in the expectation of much longer-lasting pacts being effected between them. A number of tribal delegates thereafter agreed to accompany the Major to Washington and meet the Great White Father, President Andrew Jackson. Of these last, the Blackfoot and Cheyenne emissaries dropped out somewhere en route between Fort Union and St. Louis, and only the Assiniboine, Cree and Chippewa chiefs actually arrived at the Capital. It had originally been intended to include one or more Crows among the delegates, but for some unspecified reason the Crows were not contacted by the Major, who had merely met with deputations from the various tribes as they came to Fort Union to trade, and runners sent to locate the distant Crow villages had failed to find their quarry. Nonetheless, the Crows; or rather Sore-Belly`s River band as opposed to the Mountain Crows, were included in their absence as partners to the resulting pacts between the tribes. [2]

Regarding the Cheyenne–Crow pact specifically, it seems that only a part of the Cheyenne-proper, albeit temporarily, held to the agreement, due, moreover, to hostilities occurring between other Cheyennes and certain bands of Lakota, which persisted for nearly five years before coming together again in peace. The

231

Suhtaio, who were also known as `Staihitans` and `Flyers` in these early days, had at first also made a corresponding pact with the Crows, but owing to the Suhtaio`s autonomous situation at that time, their truce did not last longer than the following spring.

Even so, throughout the winter of 1831 / `32, only a few moons after Sore-Belly`s most recent conflict with Cheyennes on the North Platte, a tentative period of peace; in theory at least, did exist between the River Crows, Assiniboine, Atsina, Plains Cree, some Cheyenne bands, and the Pikuni and Bloods. However, as in the case of the Crow–Suhtaio pact, before the ensuing summer the situation between most of the aforesaid tribes had again deteriorated sufficiently, for their bellicose propensities to have regenerated the old routine.

We are not told why these intertribal pacts with the Crows did not last. Although from the beginning they had been of a precarious nature. The Indian`s over-riding need for members of one tribe to steal horses from another, which often involved the killing of one or more tribal members, had probably in itself been reason enough to break the Suhtaio – Crow peace. In addition, the fact that the Assiniboine were then at peace with the Blackfoot, and that the Beaver Hills Cree were again at war with all Blackfoot-speaking peoples while at peace with the Crows, undoubtedly had a significant effect for the Assiniboine, Pikuni and Bloods to break their own truces with the Crows, and regard them again as the common foe. In all events by spring 1832, any pacts between the above mentioned tribes and Crows - excluding that with the Beaver Hills Cree which Head chiefs Sore-Belly and La Quartre continued to prop up – were considered as already broken by the rank and file warriors, and intertribal warfare was soon regenerated to continue as fervently as before.

So it was, as the short days of winter slowly lengthened into spring and ponies grew fit and fleet on new grass, veterans of the warpath yearned again to catch the scent of battle in their nostrils. Young men as yet untested in the field, became eager to emulate their fathers and mentors and thereby, prove worthy among their peers. Then how the womenfolk would raise the tremolo in their honour and dance in celebration of their victorious deeds. Old men would sing their praises, while for those displaying a captured pony, scalp or weapon, old names would be "thrown away" and new ones given in their stead. Then could a young bride be purchased for the price of so many horses; and "Yes," it was said,

"He who travelled the red road would achieve much social standing, and perhaps, glorious honour in a warrior's death." [3]

Thus, as for generations past, numerous bands of eager braves started forth from one Crow village and another; in one direction and another, but all with one purpose in mind. To steal the horses of their enemies; take their enemy`s heads [scalps] and their women and children captive, along with plunder from the lodges they would hopefully destroy.

Crow war-parties once again were blazing their bloody trails. East against the Cut-Heads [Lakota] and the Striped-Arrow-People [Cheyenne]. South against the Black-Men [Utes]. West against the Pierced-Noses [Nez-Perce]. Northeast against the Yellow-Legs [Assiniboine] and North against the Pikuni, Blood and Siksika [Blackfoot], and among whom were included the latter's allies and confederates, the Hairy-Nostrils [Atsina] and Sarsi.

It was around this time that a formidable Crow war-band attacked and destroyed thirty lodges of Assiniboine on the banks of the Yellowstone, although strange to say, other bands of Assiniboine in the Beaver Hills district further north, still remained tentatively at peace with the Crows.

Additionally, during this same period, a number of renegade Crow war parties still roamed indiscriminately across the Plains; merely looking for unsuspecting persons - be they Indian or white - who could be robbed and plundered at ease, or indeed, for any foreign camp left vulnerable as an invitation to be attacked.

Not least among these itinerant renegade Crow groups was Arrow-Head's band, generally known as the Dried-Out-Furs, the same whose members had disassociated from the main Treacherous Lodge clan after the destruction of Long-Hair's village some dozen years earlier. Since then they had continued to roam towards the south as an independent body, enemies to all and friends to no one, and only sporadically did they revisit their Crow kinfolk in the north.

Both the Mountain and River Crows as a rule, left Arrow-Head's band to their own devices, although there was often a degree of hostile contact between Arrow-Head's Treacherous Lodges and the Whistling-Waters clan whenever they were apt to meet. For their own part, Chiefs Long-Hair and Sore-Belly ignored Arrow-Head's band and instead, continued to concentrate on their own issues and upon enemies closer to their own domain. Such enemies threatened the Crow people's immediate safety and survival, and included Cheyennes who, yet again, were now regularly raiding into Crow country with a vengeance.

On May 24th, 1832, a number of white trappers led by a Captain Benjamin Louis Bonneville were following the course of the Platte River upstream. En route they came face to face with a Crow war-party of around sixty warriors, ostensibly led by Sore-Belly. The Indians, *"a-yelling and a-screaming,"* came careering on their ponies towards the trappers. But just as suddenly as they had charged, they split into two groups; veered off to the left and right and circled the white men several times. This was the customary procedure of Indians when greeting friends and after a short while, the Crow war-chief reined in his horse; dismounted, and going up to Bonneville, shook him by the hand. After this the chief produced a pipe and both he and the captain sat down on the prairie grass and smoked. The chief informed the trappers they were Crows in pursuit of a war-band of Cheyennes [i.e. Suhtaio] which previously, had attacked a Crow village in the night and escaped after killing a Crow. His party, the chief added, had been trailing the attackers for a number of days and were not of a mind to return home until their slain tribesman had been avenged. This was the reason this particular Crow war-party led by Sore-Belly had started forth against the Cheyennes. After assuring the white men of their friendship, the Indians took leave and continued along their route, which it transpired, according to present-day Crow oral history, eventually led to a small camp of Suhtaio-speaking Cheyennes ensconced along a fork of the Laramie River in what is now north-eastern Wyoming.

As previously noted, the Crow party in question then comprised some sixty warriors and after sighting the enemy in the distance, they first attacked a small group of Suhtaio which had started on a buffalo hunt and was only a few miles from the village it had recently left. Not suprisingly, the sudden sound of gunfire aroused the occupants of the Suhtaio camp. At once Suhtaio warriors grabbed weapons and jumped astride their war-ponies, then raced out of the village to give assistance to the beleaguered hunters. Some of the Suhtaio women-folk began singing Strong-Heart songs to encourage their menfolk. But soon the same Suhtaio warriors were racing their ponies back towards the village hotly pursued by Crows, which caused the Suhtaio women to take fright. In a moment of panic, they gathered their young children around them and ran from the village to the Laramie River which they attempted to cross, in order to escape to a larger village of Cheyenne confederates some distance away.

Throughout most of the year the Laramie River is only knee deep, but at this particular time it was high-flowing due to spring melt waters issuing down from distant mountains. As the fleeing non-combatants leapt into the river, the water came up to their chests, and it was with much difficulty that the refugees managed to reach the far bank and safety.

Meanwhile, the Crows were continuing to press home their attack in an endeavour to reach the Suhtaio lodges. But the buffalo hunters, although in retreat, kept turning back to face and engage their pursuers and in such a way, succeeded in retarding the Crow advance.

During this part of the melee, an important man among the Suhtaio who was probably a chief, was toppled from his horse by a Crow missile. A number of Crows tried to reach his body in order to count coup and take the scalp. The event caused the fleeing Suhtaio to rally their force. They raced back to the prostrate form of their fallen comrade, and managed to prevent the Crows from getting close enough to achieve their objective.

While all this was going on and the Crows, it seemed, by their superior numbers, were about to rub out the Suhtaio before them, fresh war-cries suddenly reverberated across the prairie, and a much larger body of Cheyenne warriors came charging on horseback into the fray. These had previously heard the sound of battle carried on the wind and having realized what was happening, they had set out from the larger distant Cheyenne village, even before those of their kinfolk who had swam the Laramie River brought word of the attack.

When Sore-Belly spied this fresh body of Cheyennes charging towards his party, and whose number far exceeded his own, he ordered a retreat and the Crows gave up the fight and raced away. They were satisfied with having taken a number of Suhtaio scalps while none of their own warriors had yet been killed, and only a few had suffered wounds, though of minor degree.

Such was the outcome of this Crow venture, and it was this same war party with Sore-Belly as its Pipe-holder, which on June 1st whilst on its return journey north to the Big Horn, again met Captain Bonneville's brigade of white trappers, the latter still following the course of the North Platte westward before detouring south towards the Green River trapping grounds. Captain Bonneville later reported that the Crows,

"…Came in [a] vaunting and [in] vainglorious style; displaying five Cheyenne scalps, the trophies of their vengeance." [4]

Accordingly, the Crows accredited yet another victory to their great war-chief Sore-Belly, even though, in truth, the enemy had actually driven the Crows from the field on this occasion.

Only a few weeks after the aforementioned fight with Suhtaio and Cheyennes, the entire band of Sore-Belly's River Crows re-entered the North Country, and set their camp on the south bank of the Missouri between the Marias and the Musselshell.

In the early part of June, the American Fur Company trader David D. Mitchell with a retinue of French Canadian employees, was poleing the keel boat *Beaver* upstream along the Missouri to the newly erected Fort Piegan near the mouth of the Marias [the precursor of the subsequent Fort McKenzie]. En route, Mitchell had ordered the boat to be moored for the night, intending to continue his journey next morning.

Uncustomary at that time, the Missouri was still in full flood, and just before dawn a violent storm blew up, with a wind so strong that the boat broke from its lines and was dashed against a *barras*, smashing the boat's hull in the process Within minutes the boat sank, taking two of Mitchell's employees and thirty-thousand dollars' worth of trade goods destined for the Blackfoot to the bottom of the river. Mitchell then returned to Fort Union to outfit another expedition, having given up the first enterprise as completely lost.

Sore-Belly and his River Crows then encamped on the south bank of the Missouri were not far, in fact, from where the wreck took place and were fully aware of what had happened. As soon as the storm had passed and the trader Mitchell and his retinue departed downstream, a horde of Crows including men, women and teenagers of both sexes, gathered at the wreck site. They immediately began diving into the river and swimming under water, endeavouring to salvage what they could from the sunken goods.

In this way they brought up from the river bed a large quantity of goods, including coffee, flour, sugar, calico, strouding, knives, hatchets and iron cooking pots among other things. One Crow woman having dived down to the wreck, emerged with a large sack of beads. This, say the Crows, was the first time they had seen multi-coloured beads, and was the first time they began decorating their clothes and footwear in gaily multi-coloured floral patterns, as opposed to the large blue and white so-called 'pony' beads previously used for the same purpose. However, whilst the majority of Crows were busily engaged and totally immersed in the general excitement of their occupation, they relaxed their usual vigilance as to what was happening elsewhere in the region.

Unnoticed by the Crows, a large Assiniboine war-party was then in the area. The party was on foot and again led by their infamous chief, *"Tchatka,"* also known as "The-Left-Hand" or *"La Gauche."* They were out on a hostile

235

expedition intending to steal horses from any foreign camp they might encounter, as the Assiniboine, it seemed, were forever in need of horses, although enemy scalps were always considered a much welcome bonus.

It has already been noted that the McKenzie inspired pact between the Crows and more eastern Assiniboine bands had been short-lived. Not surprisingly because those particular Assiniboine were then in league with the Pikuni and thus, had continued to regard Crows as the common enemy. It was, of course, the eastern Assiniboine who had suffered the massacre of their thirty lodges the previous year by Sore-Belly's warriors, and it was probably in order to avenge that deed moreover, why their chief *Tchatka* had undertaken this hostile expedition into Crow country south of the Missouri.

So it was while the Crows were engrossed in salvaging the above mentioned trade goods, that this host of Assiniboine led by *Tchatka,* discovered the Crow village, and even though the Assiniboine were on foot, they decided to launch a sudden attack on the now sparsely occupied camp.

The majority of Crow fighting men were scattered along the bank of the Missouri, preoccupied in their work around the wreck site. The Assiniboine thus had the clear advantage of surprise and being superior in number, they immediately assaulted the camp.

Upon hearing the distant sound of gunfire, Sore-Belly was quick to rally his warriors. After consolidating his force, he led them both on horseback and on foot in a frantic race to the beleaguered camp, and when the charging Crows came up, they went smashing into the attacker's ranks. The pedestrian Assiniboine were obliged to retreat and seek cover among a cluster of trees in order to escape the flying hooves of Crow ponies.

When the Crows had first charged the Assiniboine Sore-Belly had been in the van, wielding a feathered lance high in the air and conspicuous by his double-tailed feathered war bonnet, the long trailers of which spewed out behind him as he rode. The Assiniboine, however, had retreated in good order and when reaching the timber, they quickly organized themselves in defensive positions and made ready to make a determined stand. This action caused the Crows to dismount and also fight on foot, and for many hours it was a hard fought contest.

Every now and then, one side or the other would execute a charge and engage their opponents in hand to hand combat before returning to their respective lines and in such a way the fight went on until late afternoon. It was then that the Crows with Sore-Belly again at their head, remounted their ponies and launched yet another charge upon the enemy. This time they threw the weight of their whole force at the Assiniboine position and succeeded in breaking through the latter's ranks. The enemy were forced to take to their heels in every direction in their efforts to escape. A running fight ensued; the Assiniboine on foot, the pursuing Crows both mounted and on foot, and in the course of which, many Assiniboine and several Crows were killed among others seriously wounded. Not until twilight descended did the Crows cease pursuing the fugitives. The Crows then returned to their camp, leaving the enemy to lick their wounds and count their dead.

A significant number of Crow women and children had been slain during the initial attack on the Crow camp before Sore-Belly and his warriors had come to their rescue. Thus, the earlier jubilation and excitement occasioned by the treasure trove of goods which came into their possession, was curtailed somewhat by losses incurred during the resulting battle. The Crows later admitted it was an event which would not have been severe, had they exercised their customary vigilance and had previously scouted the surrounding countryside for enemy sign. Instead, they had allowed themselves to become completely absorbed in the thought of easy riches gained by what they might salvage from the sunken goods. Today the Crows mention the event as having been,

*"A terrific battle, a number of well-known Crow warriors having fallen."* [5]

A few weeks later, Sore-Belly led his entire band back south across the Yellowstone and headed for that river's Clark's Fork tributary. This was in order to join again with Long-Hair's Mountain Crows so that the entire Nation could conduct its annual Medicine Lodge ceremonies together.

It was at this time [June 1832], that a portrait artist from the eastern United States named George Catlin, was visiting the American Fur Company Post Fort Union at the mouth of the Yellowstone. While at the fort, Catlin had the opportunity to paint from life several well-known Crow, Blackfoot, Assiniboine, Cree and Chippewa Indians as they came in their separate bands to trade at the fort. By the Indians Catlin subsequently depicted, he left us an authentic contemporary view of Sore-Belly's associates, - both hostile and friendly, - then in the prime of their influence and fame in the Upper Missouri Country.

Catlin was impressed by the Crows. He expounded what he saw as their virtues such as honesty, honour and high-mindedness in addition to their personal cleanliness. This was in contrast to what some other contemporary observers reported, who saw the same people as liars, thieves and vagabonds. Catlin, though, was somewhat corroborated in his view by his host Kenneth McKenzie, who told the artist that he considered the Crows to be,

*"... The finest Indians of his acquaintance."* [6]

Catlin also expressed his sympathy for the plight of the Crows when he wrote,

They [the Crows] are a much smaller tribe than the Blackfoot, with whom they are always at war, and from whose great number, they suffer prodigiously in battle, and probably will be in a few years entirely destroyed by them." [7]

The artist was, therefore, a little surprised while domiciled at Fort Union to witness mortal enemies such as Crows, Blackfoot, Assiniboine and Cree, talking and smoking amicably together within the fort walls. Although the Indians were then without weapons in compliance with McKenzie's firm dictate, that all Indians should disarm before entering the post gates.

It is a pity that Catlin did not personally meet the Crow chiefs Long-Hair and Sore-Belly, as he might then have left for posterity the likenesses on canvas of these two great men. He did, though, while at the fort, execute portrait images depicting several of their illustrious comrades-in-arms. These included Four-Wolves [a signer of the so-called Friendship Treaty of 1825], Red-Bear and his woman, Lives-in-the-Bear`s-Den, and Two-Crows the younger. Of this last-named, Catlin wrote,

> "He was one of the most extraordinary men in the Crow Nation…from his extraordinary sagacity as a counsellor and orator, even at an early stage of life." [8]

$$- 0 - 0 - 0 - 0 - 0 - 0 - 0 - 0 - 0 - 0 - 0 - 0 - 0 - 0 -$$

## CHAPTER 21.

## VENGEANCE ON THE ATSINA.

The next Crow fight of importance under Sore-Belly`s leadership, was against old-time antagonists and sometime friends, the *Api-Wishe* or Hairy-Nostrils; i. e. the Atsina. The event appears to have occurred as a consequence to the previously recounted conflict involving Chief Big-Bowl`s band on Crow Creek, previously referred to as, "The Big-Prisoner Affair."

The Atsina were known among other tribes as a somewhat fickle lot, who would often act on impulse rather than rational expediency. It has been noted in earlier chapters how, during previous decades, the Atsina with smiling eyes had several times held out the calumet of peace to the Crows, and the latter had accepted the offer in good faith. Always, however, it had been the Atsina who had broken the pact, and in the process of which, the Crows had invariably suffered the loss of several tribesmen treacherously killed by the Atsina. Only the previous year due to the trader McKenzie`s persuasion, the Atsina had again requested a pact with the Crows, to which the latter agreed. But as far as the Crows themselves were concerned, the Atsina a few months later had broken the pact yet again, by joining forces with Cheyennes and Arapaho during the aforesaid "Big-Prisoner Affair."

Since that time the Crows had waited patiently to wreak their vengeance on the Atsina for their perfidy, and in July this year [1832], their patience was rewarded. [1]

Now it had happened three years earlier as a result of the Atsina again severing their trading contacts with posts of the Hudson`s Bay Company, due to Atsina hostility against that company`s establishments and employees, and also - as Atsina oral tradition states - because a young brave of their tribe had fled south to the Arapaho with the wife of the Atsina head chief Old-Bald-Eagle, that in order to get back his wife and open trade with the Arapaho, the said chief had led half the Atsina tribe south, and actually joined with the Arapaho and Cheyennes on the South Platte and Arkansas River in what is now Colorado. This Atsina band of some two-hundred and thirty lodges had remained in the south until spring 1832, when an outbreak of smallpox among the Arapaho and Old-Bald-Eagle having retrieved his wife, induced the Atsina to return home in order to reunite with the rest of their tribe in the Milk River country of the north.

Upon entering southwestern Wyoming on their return journey, these same Atsina were wandering around in two separate groups in the Green River district and further north, generally making themselves a nuisance to white trappers and traders of the region; skirmishing with them at intervals and stealing their horses and scalps.

At the same time in mid-July, the annual rendezvous for the various groups of Mountain Men in the beaver country of the Upper Missouri, was being held at a place known as Pierre's Hole in what is now eastern Idaho. This being an extensive stretch of lush grassland at the foot of the Three Teton Mountains on their west side. Here were encamped over two-hundred white trappers and as many Flathead and Nez-Perce warriors with their Indian families, along with some three-thousand horses and mules, spread out for a considerable distance across the prairie.

On the morning of July 18th, a small group of mounted trappers led by Milton Sublette and a man named Alexander Sinclair, had only recently started out to hunt, when they espied a column of people and horses emerging slowly from one of the distant mountain passes as they snaked their way down into the valley below. Upon closer inspection, it was discovered that the emerging column consisted of a small group of mounted warriors in the van, along with a larger number of men, women and children; most of whom were on foot, following some distance behind. The Indians had also seen the white men and as was their custom, a number of mounted warriors let out a series of terrific war-whoops and careered their ponies towards the trappers, who soon recognized the charging Indians as Atsina. The trappers immediately presented a defensive stance ready for battle and upon this, the charging Atsina suddenly reined in their ponies and stopped some respectful distance from the white men. An Atsina chief then made the sign of peace and in response, two of Sublette's men rode out to meet him whilst also making signs of peace. The chief rode forward holding a pipe in both hands with out-stretched arms. When coming close one of the trappers held out his hand to shake that of the Atsina, but as soon as the chief did likewise, the trapper held him fast while his companion shot him dead. The two trappers then galloped back to their own line, one of them waving the dead chief's red blanket as he rode.

Realizing that a battle was imminent, the Atsina van guard rode away and joining the rest of their group, ensconced themselves in a swampy area formed by an abandoned beaver dam covered with willows and vines. In this area surrounded by willows, the Atsina herded their ponies then took up defensive positions. The women and children among them began digging trenches and building a low barricade of dead logs, over which they draped buffalo robes and blankets to hide themselves from the trapper marksmen, whom, the Indians suspected, would soon appear in strength.

Sure enough the trappers, along with a host of their Indian allies, did appear in strength, and the fight began in earnest.

One among the Atsina realized the predicament he and his people were in. He called out to those besieging them saying, that not far away were more than four-hundred Atsina warriors who would soon arrive on the scene to avenge their deaths.

Perhaps the chief's words were misinterpreted, for it was quickly circulated among the trappers and their Indian allies that there were four-hundred lodges of Atsina nearby – when there were little more than two-hundred and thirty lodges at most, - and that the trapper's rendezvous camp at Pierre's Hole now virtually undefended, would soon be under attack from the bulk of the Atsina force. At once, most of the trappers and their Indian allies left the battle ground and raced back to their camp to fend off the expected assault. By the time the camp at Pierre's Hole was reached and found to be safe, it was deemed too late in the day to return to the Atsina position and as darkness fell, only a handful of men were dispatched to watch the enemy, lest they attempted to abscond in the night.

The next morning, after those from the rendezvous camp returned to the battle ground, they were surprised to see that not a buffalo hide or piece of blanket could be found once belonging to the foe. The entire Atsina force bar one wounded woman, had somehow crept away in the dark, taking their belongings and surviving horses with them. On the periphery of and within the abandoned barricade itself, the trappers found thirteen Atsina corpses, while thirty dead horses were also discovered within the enclosure. Obviously, several more Atsina had been killed and others seriously wounded, but these had been carried off and years after the event, the trappers were told by the Atsina themselves that seventeen of their warriors had been killed outright that day, not to mention those who died later from wounds received in the fight.

The fleeing Atsina eventually reunited with the other group of their tribe's folk under Old-Bald-Eagle, after which their combined force started again on its journey north to their own country along Milk River, as originally had been intended before their confrontation with the trappers.

The Atsina had taken a good licking. In order to avoid further trouble whilst on the rest of their trek, their cavalcade was traveling a wide detour so not to cross the Three Forks of the Missouri region where other bands of trappers, Flathead and Nez-Perce enemies might be encountered. They were also under the impression that the Crows were then roaming much further east in the Big Horn River area, and supposing it was safe, the Atsina altered their route and turned northeast, heading towards the headwaters of Rosebud Creek, a branch of the Stillwater west of the Big Horn. Upon reaching Rosebud Creek the Atsina began travelling slowly down that stream intending to cross the Yellowstone, and thence continue northeast towards their own domain north of the Missouri.

It was five days after the Pierre's Hole fight, that a small band of Atsina stragglers who had not yet left the Green River area, met Captain Bonneville's party of trappers then encamped somewhere along that same stream.

Bonneville's men were ensconced in a strong defensive position, but as yet, knew nothing of the recent battle at Pierre's Hole. As it was, the meeting passed off peaceably enough, even though two Crows among the Captain's party had urged the white men to kill the Atsina visitors.

It then happened only two days after this encounter, whilst the now combined Atsina column was continuing its journey downstream along the course of Rosebud Creek, that a number of warriors broke off from the column's line of march. These Atsina separatists came upon four or five Crows out hunting from their main camp which, unbeknown to the Atsina, was actually located only twenty miles to the northwest on the upper waters of Clark's Fork. As was typical of the Atsina who, as previously noted, often acted on impulse, they attacked the small Crow party killing two in the process and rode away with their scalps. The Crow survivors immediately took word of the deed to their own people, along with intelligence that the main body of Atsina was moving down the Rosebud branch of the Stillwater not too far from where the Crows themselves were encamped. In fact, the whole Crow Nation was still together at this time in their Medicine Lodge camp, so that their entire fighting force comprised between six and seven-hundred warriors.

At once a large war-party was organised including both River and Mountain Crows, and under the leadership of Sore-Belly, the warriors started forth, not only in an endeavour to avenge the recent deaths of their two tribesmen, but also to wipe out the stain of humiliation which, the Crows felt, they had suffered during the Big-Prisoner affair the previous summer, and the supposed treachery of the Atsina on that occasion.

In the meantime, the Atsina had reached the middle course of Rosebud Creek and set their tepees on the west bank of the stream. It was about then that Sore-Belly dispatched a number of scouts to reconnoitre the enemy encampment and ascertain how many lodges it contained. With such information, the great chief could estimate the number of Atsina warriors his own force would have to contend with, and could plan his intended action accordingly.

As a rule, one could count at least two males of fighting age per lodge as regards most Plains Indian tepee villages, and when Sore-Belly's scouts returned they informed him that the Atsina camp comprised some two-hundred and thirty-three lodges. Thus Sore-Belly could easily calculate that the camp probably contained no more than four-hundred and sixty-six fighting men at most, and that his own number of warriors would prove more than a match for the enemy. With this knowledge Sore-Belly instructed his scouts to go out again. This time to keep watching the enemy and to send a report to him regarding the latter's every move.

Evidently the Atsina themselves were unaware that Crows in such formidable number were so near. Rather than prepare defences of any kind, the Atsina arose from slumber each morning and after packing their lodge covers and belongings on pony drags, resumed their slow journey down Rosebud Creek in their customary column formation.

As they travelled downstream along the west bank of the creek, now eight days after the fight at Pierre's Hole, the Atsina filed through a certain gap in the hills which led onto an open Plain.

Having been thus informed by his scouts, Sore-Belly declared that now they should strike. He led them to a place surrounded by low hills and timber a pistol shot from the Atsina cavalcade, and ordered his force to wait out of view from the enemy, until he himself gave the war-cry which would open the attack. If the Atsina had their own scouts out, then they were not alert enough to notice any sign of the hidden Crows. Although it is probable that the majority of Atsina were ignorant of the two scalps recently taken by other members of their tribe, and still believed the Crows to be further east at this time. It is also said, however, that having previously been at peace with the latter, the Atsina were under the delusion that the Big-Prisoner affair had merely been a slight upset with only one band of Crows, and that the Crow Nation as a whole, would still be tolerant enough to allow the Atsina to travel through their country unmolested. Perhaps it was for this reason that the Atsina force most of which was on foot, but still with a large number of pack ponies and pony-drags among them, travelled along in a seemingly carefree manner. One of the important Atsina chiefs led the way on horseback, whilst cavorting around him on foot were a number of young women and girls, laughing and joking in a playful mood.

The hidden Crows could observe all that was going on, although their own presence still remained concealed from the enemy.

At length, when deeming the column to have reached a point on the trail which was advantageous to his design, Sore-Belly with Little-White-Bear at his side, shrilled aloud the Apsaalooka war-cry and suddenly, a host of Crow warriors be-feathered and painted, charged from concealment up and over the surrounding hills and across the open ground towards the Atsina column. In all six-hundred and more screaming Crow braves mounted on fleet ponies, the twenty-four-hundred hooves of which pounded the prairie floor like a continuous roll of thunder.

An Atsina chief at the head of the column – perhaps Old-Bald-Eagle himself - was first among his people to be struck down by a tomahawk blow to the head, and as the Crows continued broiling over the hills and open ground, they went smashing into the column.

Many of the Atsina warriors had only lances, bows and arrows and tomahawks with which to defend themselves, having previously exhausted their powder and ball during the recent fight at Pierre's Hole, and they were completely overwhelmed. A good many of those on horseback simply turned their mounts around and fled towards a distant stand of timber. Although at the same time, a number of Atsina warriors led by a chief named Iron-Robe, did face the charging Crows and held them back for a while as the mass of Atsina pedestrian non-combatants also raced for the timber, many abandoning their pack ponies and pole-drags and even each other, in their panic-stricken efforts to escape.

The Atsina did not really have a chance. The Crows soon put the warriors facing them to flight and pursued them closely; knocking many to the ground with their horses and killing them with musket balls, arrows, lances and hatchets. A large number of the fleeing women and children were rounded up in bunches by Crow warriors and taken captive, along with a countless number of Atsina ponies.

242

The Mountain Man James Beckwourth, later professed he himself had been with the Crows in this fight. One among the enemy, Beckwourth said, was a powerfully built man who aimed a blow at Beckwourth with a battle-axe, but was lanced through by the Crow female fighter Woman-Chief who deflected the blow and which instead, struck the horse Beckwourth was riding, felling the animal to the ground. Beckwourth further said that he himself that day was wearing a feathered bonnet trimmed with white weasel tails, and during the battle, three of the feathers were cut away by a musket ball which actually grazed his head, inflicting a wound that scarred him for life. In addition, he declared that he managed to take captive a young Atsina woman who afterwards, he gave to a friend among his adopted Crow people.

Certainly the Crow female warrior Woman-Chief, albeit having been born an Atsina but taken captive by Crows when young and since raised into womanhood by her adopted people, was conspicuous in this fight. It is said that she alone killed several Atsina warriors and counted many *dakshey* that day. She later joined the Crow warriors in their victory dances, not merely as a female participant, but as an honoured and respected fighter whose deeds during this and previous engagements, had actually surpassed many among her male comrades-in-arms.

In the event, the initial attack by the Crows had caused an utter rout of the Atsina, although a good number did manage to reach the safety of the timber into which the victorious Crows were reluctant to enter, as a missile of death might issue from behind every tree. The Crows hovered around on their ponies at the edge of the Atsina position, shouting abuse and challenges to the enemy to come out into the open and fight. Meanwhile, as had been done only eight days earlier at Pierre's Hole, the Atsina women and children hastily dug rifle pits and constructed a barricade from brush and logs. Behind these defences they intended to protect themselves, lest the Crows should make another massed assault in an attempt to finish them off completely. Thus within a comparatively short while, the intense part of fighting came to an end. There then ensued a series of one to one combats, as lone champions from among the Crows and those among the entrenched Atsina who still had a horse to ride, battled it out in the no-man's land between their opposing forces.

One who was prominent among the Atsina that day was the aforementioned Iron-Robe [probably the same called Iron-That-Moves by Karl Bodmer who painted his portrait in 1833]. The Crows many years later still remembered this Atsina chief as being particularly active, and one who performed many brave deeds during the fight. Without this man in their ranks, say the Crows, many more Atsina would have been killed and, perhaps, their entire band annihilated. But such was Iron-Robe's fighting fury and leadership skill that he, along with those warriors who at first stood their ground holding back the Crows, allowed both time and space for hundreds of their fleeing non-combatants to reach the timber unscathed. It is further said that none of the Crows who afterwards met Iron-Robe in single combat, could stand against him.

Within the Crow ranks there was a chief known by the name of Wrapped-Hair or Ties-His-Hair, who had been yet another signer of the Atkinson – O`Fallon Friendship Treaty of 1825. He is said in Crow oral tradition to have taken the most number of captives that day during the initial charge upon the Atsina column. He was also duly recognized for performing brave deeds later on in the fight when taking up challenges from several Atsina champions, one of whom he overcame in single combat before being engaged against another contestant when he himself was wounded in the side by an Atsina lance, said to have been wielded by the Atsina chief, Iron-Robe himself. Fortunately, the Crow Wrapped-Hair eventually recovered from his wound, having managed to hang on to his pony and ride safely back to his own lines before his adversary could finish him off. Other note-worthy deeds, it is said, were performed by the Crow warriors Long-Horse, Bear`s-Head, Grizzly-Bear and Twines-His-Horses-Tail, and thus was the order of fighting for the rest of the daylight hours.

The Crows did not again assault the enemy in force and as twilight descended, the fighting ceased abruptly and most of the Crows returned to their village on Clark`s Fork. They intended to renew the fight come morning, and only a small number of Crow warriors remained at the scene of conflict in order to raise the alarm if the enemy attempted to move off in the night. However, when darkness did cover the land, the surviving Atsina, including all the men, women and children - as also they had done during the Pierre`s Hole fight eight days earlier – crept quietly away undetected by the Crows. At first they continued following the course of Rosebud Creek downstream and then crossed the Yellowstone, their tattered and depleted tribal remnant having lost nearly all their horses, camp equipment and provisions.

Nevertheless, and notwithstanding their defeat, the following morning while the bulk of the Atsina survivors were hurrying north, a body of Atsina warriors after rallying their broken force and mounted on the few horses they had left among them, did attempt a dawn counter-attack upon the Crow village. This was in order to retrieve at least some of their women and children carried off by the victors, along with a number of horses to facilitate better their ongoing trek. The attack, though, was easily repulsed and the Atsina driven off, although they did succeed in obtaining a small number of loose ponies for their trouble. They were, though, obliged to leave their lost women and children in the hands of the Crows.

It seems that the number of captives taken by Crows during the fight was so great, that they were considered too many to accommodate on a practical basis, being a large amount of extra mouths to feed and persons to care for. It was because of this that as an act of expediency several days after the battle, Sore-Belly told his people to set the captives free. Thus most, although not all the Atsina captives were subsequently provided with food and released. These set off at once on foot from the Crow village, traveling east, and upon reaching Rosebud Creek they followed the northern trail left by their fleeing tribe`s folk.

After only four or five days and nights of hard traveling, the released captives caught up with their own people then encamped along the Musselshell north of the Yellowstone, and when reuniting with their kinfolk, what was then left of the Atsina column now almost entirely on foot, continued its journey northeast. This time without being further molested as they headed towards Milk River and their home country, which they had left three long years before.

In total, the Crows say, the Atsina had lost sixty-seven killed in the attack on the collumn, in addition to some one-hundred and twenty women and children captured, and at least five-hundred ponies with a large amount of domestic baggage and other paraphernalia taken as spoils by the victors. It was for this reason that the Crows after the abortive dawn raid on their camp, had not pursued the enemy. The Crows were already over-laden with booty and captives, and grand scalp-dances were held for many weeks thereafter. Yet again, the great war-chief Sore-Belly's acclaim was sung and heralded among his people.

By Beckwourth's count, the Crows had suffered only twenty-nine of their own warriors wounded during the all-day fight, while they themselves had killed one-hundred and seventy Atsina, taking their scalps and one hundred and fifty women and children captive, not to mention a vast quantity of baggage, weapons and horses which also fell into Crow hands. An alternative account, however, penned by the Fort Union trader Edwin Denig, stated that twenty-two Crows had actually been killed outright that day, although others had been so badly wounded that they died later from their injuries. One-hundred and upwards of the enemy [who Denig termed Blackfoot] lay dead, while two hundred and thirty women and children had been taken captive along with some five-hundred ponies. Joe Medicine Crow merely remarked that the Crows did not scalp half their fallen Atsina enemies, as there were so many that they soon tired of the chore.

A more terse account later told to Edward S. Curtis by Atsina informants, in essence agrees with Denig's version, by recording that half the original number of Atsina women and children in the column had been carried off by the victors. It is also said that such was the respect the Crows had for the bravery shown by the Atsina chief Iron-Robe, they sent messages and gifts to him via the released captives, as tokens of their esteem.

Whatever the true number of casualties on either side, this event coupled with the earlier defeat at Pierre's Hole proved a terrible blow to Atsina morale. Never again did they recoup their one-time reputation across the Plains. A fact which certainly curtailed to a significant degree, their previous propensity for unrelenting war against most other Indian peoples, and especially as regards their erstwhile constant aggression towards white traders and trappers in the Upper Missouri region. Truly, it had been a combination of unforeseeable circumstances, or simply "*bad medicine*," which had caused the double catastrophe for the Atsina at that time.

Soon after this fight with the Atsina and whilst still encamped on Clark's Fork, there occurred another great fight between Crows led by Sore-Belly against a large force of Lakota led by the Oglala chief Old-Man-Afraid-of-His-Horses. Both forces were in formidable strength, and the Lakota had previously blackened their faces as a sign of their resolve to win a great victory on this occasion. The

245

fight lasted all day, consisting of charges and counter-charges, and several were killed and wounded on each side before the respective combatants retired from the field, both supposing they themselves had won the day. [2]

It was, though, while the Crows were celebrating this supposed victory, that a party of Hidatsa arrived from their earth-lodge towns on the Knife. They brought word of a recent disastrous attack by a combined force of Lakota and Cheyennes, and during which event, one of the Hidatsa towns had been destroyed by fire; many Hidatsa killed, and a number of women and children taken captive. This obviously refers to the same episode mentioned in the American-Horse Oglala winter-count for the year 1832, but which merely states,

"They [Lakota] killed many Gros Ventres [Hidatsa] in a village which they assaulted." [3]

The Hidatsa visitors told the Crows details of the affair, which the Crow informant Barney Old-Coyote conveyed to the present Author in the summer of 2010 from Crow oral tradition. [4]

It had happened as the sun came up one morning, a host of allied Lakota and Cheyennes suddenly appeared outside the Hidatsa town on the north bank of the Knife, and without hesitation, had attacked in force. The town in question was protected by a stout palisade and at first, all the allies could do was to gallop their ponies around outside the town hurling lances and shooting arrows over the wall, relying on chance if they found a mark or not. At the same time they shouted abuse at the Hidatsa defenders, taunting them to come out into the open and fight. The defenders had remained calm, casually taking pot-shots at the enemy with their trade muskets through loop holes in the stockade. But there had been one weapon against which the Hidatsa could not fight. After the attackers had grown tired of galloping around the village to little avail, the allies tied wads of grass to their arrow shafts; lit them and sent them thumping into the stockade posts and into the grass roofs and dry timbers of the earth-lodges themselves. The stockade quickly took light and soon, it seemed, the whole town was ablaze. As some among the occupants clambered onto the earth-lodge roofs attempting to extinguish the flames, the allies had pin-cushioned them with arrows, and as parts of the stockade weakened, the attackers butted their ponies backwards onto the stakes and pushed until the stockade collapsed. The blood-thirsty allies then poured into the town and began murdering all in their path. The Hidatsa defenders were falling one after another to the war-clubs and arrows of the enemy. Those remaining fled as best they could to their kindred town across Knife River on its south bank, although since the occupants of the kindred town had seen smoke billowing up from the village on the north bank, additional numbers of Hidatsa warriors had already started swimming their horses and paddling bull-boats across the river in an attempt to turn the tide of battle. Unfortunately, by the time Hidatsa reinforcements; most of whom were on foot, reached the beleaguered village, the damage had already been done, and the allies themselves in the process of leaving the scene.

The Hidatsa reinforcements had then advanced towards the foe, and as their numbers swelled to between three and four-hundred braves, the allies - comprising a slightly less than equal number, - bunched themselves together. They sat their ponies some distance from the dilapidated town, and braced themselves for the expected Hidatsa counter-attack. However, while the opposing forces were facing each other in battle array, neither side, it seemed, had actually been eager to resume the fight. The Hidatsa feared for the safety of the families they had left on the other side of the river, if the allies who had a superior number of horses, should ride through the Hidatsa ranks and assault the other town and its unprotected inhabitants before their own warriors could re-cross the river to protect them. The Lakota and Cheyennes on the other hand, had been content after their earlier sacking and plundering, and withal, they had taken many scalps, - over four-hundred, it is said, - along with a number of women and children captive. They had only faced the Hidatsa reinforcements as a matter of formality with no real intention of actually prolonging the conflict. At length, the allies had turned their ponies around and ridden away, while the Hidatsa looked on amid heart-rending wailing from the relatives of those slain and for those carried into bondage.

After hearing this sad report, the Crows were sympathetic to the plight of the Hidatsa. But the Crows themselves were then relaxing after their own recent battle with the Atsina and the Lakota fight which followed, and Sore-Belly was not inclined to organize another formidable war-party so soon, in order merely to chastise the culprits on behalf of his Hidatsa cousins. Instead, the Crows soon after, disbanded their Medicine Lodge village on Clark's Fork, and dividing into their respective bands, wandered off in different directions each towards its chosen hunting ground.

Having said this, a small party of Crows from the Kicked-in-the Belly band did, soon after, visit the Hidatsa villages whilst on their way to Kipp's new trading post Fort Clark next to the Mandan towns. In this particular party was James Beckwourth, along with a number of important warriors of the Apsaalooka, including the chief, Wrapped-Hair who had distinguished himself in the earlier fight with the Atsina.

According to Beckwourth, whilst en route to the Hidatsa towns, this same Crow band accidently encountered a party of eleven Cheyennes on the open prairie. The Crows being superior in number attacked at once, and wiped out the whole Cheyenne party, taking scalps, weapons and ponies as booty. When arriving at the Knife River villages, the Crows presented the Hidatsa the eleven scalps as token compensation for the destruction of the latter's village at Lakota and Cheyenne hands, and scalp dances were performed for many nights thereafter. [5]

A few days later after arriving at Fort Clark lower down the Missouri, and during an additional celebration of their current victory, this same band of Crows paraded in all their finery in front of the white traders and trappers much to the delight of all, and among whom was the previously mentioned George Catlin, who, whilst on his return trip down the Missouri from Fort Union, had since been domiciled at Fort Clark not long prior to the arrival of the Crows. Thus he met these same Crows from the Rocky Mountains and, subsequently, painted the

portraits of a number of important men among them. These included Two-Crows the elder, and two signers of the so-called "Friendship Treaty" of 1825 named He-Who-Jumps-Over-Everyone-Else and Wrapped-Hair, or - as Catlin called him and by which name he is entered on the treaty paper, - He-Who-Ties-His-Hair-Before,
6

$$-0-0-0-0-0-0-0-0-0-0-0-0-0-$$

## CHAPTER. 22.

## OF PIKUNI, DREAMS AND PACTS.

Having separated from other Crow bands after the conclusion of the Medicine Lodge ceremonies, Sore-Belly and his River Crows headed north; crossed the Yellowstone, and re-entered the region through which flowed what the Crows called *Buluhpashe,* i.e. Plum River, but now known as the Judith .[1] This was fine buffalo country during the late summer months frequented by several tribes, and often there were bloody contests between various war-bands roaming the region.

Now it had previously been agreed at the Medicine Lodge gathering, that Chief Long-Hair with fifty lodges of Mountain Crows of the Sore-Lip clan would again join Sore-Belly's people during the following moon [August], and conduct their late summer hunts together. So it was when Long-Hair's band finally arrived at the trysting site, a host of Apsaalooka were again congregated in one great village.

It happened that a Pikuni Blackfoot camp of eighty lodges was then in the Musselshell district on the north side of that river not too many miles from the Crows, and it was not long before each other tribes' presence was reported to their respective chiefs. In response, Sore-Belly, as the recognized paramount war-chief of the combined Crow bands, dispatched a number of scouts to reconnoitre the camp and determine the enemy's movements.

A number of scouts returned in due course, saying that the Pikuni camp was much smaller than that of the Crows and seemed to be preparing for a prolonged stay. Upon this intelligence, Sore-Belly devised a plan by which he intended to again trick the Pikuni and achieve a great and decisive victory over his people's mortal foes.

Having suspected that the Pikuni would have their own scouts out, Sore-Belly made it appear he was leading his people south; out of the country, but was actually manoeuvring them in such a way as to draw the enemy into a trap.

Next, Sore-Belly set up a number of empty lodges in a conspicuous and accessible place on the open prairie, along with a quantity of second-rate horses left to wander across the adjacent grasslands as an inducement for the Pikuni to attack. The Crow warriors themselves, some four-hundred in number and mounted on their fleetest war-ponies, Sore-Belly concealed in an extensive declivity not far from the unoccupied lodges. He told his warriors to wait patiently for the enemy to assault the deserted camp, and then they could make their presence known and take the enemy by surprise.

As anticipated, Pikuni scouts soon discovered the Crow decoy lodges and the scattered herd of ponies grazing nearby. So sure were the Pikuni of achieving an easy victory over what appeared to be an unsuspecting Crow camp much smaller than their own, that their chiefs immediately held a council of war to determine their plan of attack. During the ensuing discussions, it was agreed they would first send out a body of young braves who had not yet earned war-honours, to surround the Crow camp and keep watch through the night, lest the supposed occupants decided to move. The following morning, the chiefs said, the young men could begin an assault on the lodges, for by that time the rest of the Pikuni warriors would be racing to the scene to join in the fight, and their victory would be complete.

It does appear that so confident were the Pikuni of an easy victory, that the older warriors were desirous of a good night's sleep before the actual battle commenced. Thus the council had instructed the young braves alone to suffer a cold night's vigil around the Crow camp. But whatever the case, it is certain that the enemy had fallen completely for Sore-Belly's ruse.

Unfortunately for the Pikuni the night was very dark with only a quarter moon to give light. As a consequence, the first party of young men lost its bearings and when dawn broke, they were a long way from their intended objective. The rest of the Pikuni warriors meanwhile, had risen early from their slumber and at dawn as previously planned, were racing their war-ponies towards the Crow lodges, expecting to see their young braves already engaged with the foe.

Sore-Belly and his warriors waited patiently and in silence until the charging Pikuni were at the very door-flaps of the empty lodges. Then, in one great wave, the whole Crow force suddenly rode up and out from their concealed position and yelling the war-cry "Koo-Koo-Hey," raced their ponies headlong into the enemy's ranks.

Too late the Pikuni realized their blunder and at once turned to flee. But the Pikuni horses were jaded after their hectic race to the camp. The charging Crows easily caught them up and a bloody melee ensued as the Crows lanced their fleeing enemies from behind and knocked them on the head with war-clubs and iron-bladed hatchets. It was an utter rout. The Crows fought horseback hand to hand with the foe, even after the latter in their retreat had reached the tepees of their own village from whence they came.

There in the Pikuni village, a number of women and children were captured as they tried to escape on foot from their Crow pursuers. Many ponies were also rounded up by the victorious Crows along with muskets, smooth-bore fusees and other weapons, including a large quantity of ammunition all taken as booty, besides blankets and robes and much domestic paraphernalia.

One account states that the Crows lost only four killed during the fight, but of those injured several died later of their wounds. The Pikuni, on the other hand, according to an estimate given by the Mountain Man Warren E. Ferris, [2] lost seventy warriors killed, while Beckwourth, – prone to his customary exaggeration - said four-hundred. [3]

Whatever the true number of Pikuni killed and of captives taken, many of the captives remained among the Crows, eventually marrying within the tribe and raising new families of their own. [4]

The event indeed, was regarded by the Crows as yet another resounding victory. Several warriors received praises for the valiant deeds they had performed, but none had counted more *dakshey* that day than Sore-Belly himself. Praises were sung of his prowess for many weeks thereafter, while his buffalo hide lodge was decorated with crude portrayals depicting his and the deeds of other warriors in the fight. The many Blackfoot scalps - after being danced and sang over – were attached to the lodge poles of Sore-Belly`s tepee and sewn as fringes onto his war-shirt, leggings and robe. This last being an exceptional mark of distinction, afforded to few persons throughout the long and gory history of the Apsaalooka.

Soon after this affair Long-Hair`s fifty lodges returned south heading towards the Big Horn Mountains, while Sore-Belly and the River Crows also moved south, but only as far as the south bank of the Musselshell, and by early September, *"The Moon when cherries are ripe,"* they were once again meandering through the region between that river and the Yellowstone.

It was then that Sore-Belly experienced a powerful dream in which *Akbaa-tadia* the Great Spirit, he said, had informed him that if he took another war trail north, then he and his party would again take captives, albeit this time without any loss among themselves.

Having made his dream known to several companions, it was not long before word spread around camp that their great chief was determined to go again to war, and many warriors asked to accompany him on his venture. Soon after this, early one morning before the rest of the camp occupants stirred from their pallets, the great chief with a large party of followers including Twines-His-Horses-Tail and Bear`s-Head and the renowned Crow Amazon, Woman-Chief, started out on horseback riding north; looking for enemies as seen in Sore-Belly`s dream. [5]

After re-crossing the Musselshell the party arrived again in the Judith Basin, and here they made temporary camp among a small range of hills overlooking Judith River. The day was hot and balmy and as yet, no enemies had been sighted. Scouts were sent out to reconnoitre the surrounding country as was always the case when Sore-Belly carried the pipe. He did not suppose for one moment that he and his warriors were themselves immune from surprise attack by foreign War-bands.

Around midday the scouts returned and reported excitedly that in the distance ahead, perhaps two or three miles or so, they had seen rising smokes from a tepee village, although the lodges themselves had been obscured from the scout's view by intervening ridges and trees so they could not determine what tribe they belonged to. However, not far ahead of where the Crows were positioned, the scouts had also spied a group of women *awala-diille*, and who, evidently, belonged to the village in question. They seemed to be heading for an expanse of plum-bushes not far away and most likely, were intent on picking the wild fruit which was ripe at this time of year, for such was a delicacy among all tribes, and ideal for making pemmican to see the people through the winter months.

250

Here was an opportunity to take captives which Sore-Belly could not pass by. Surely, the chief thought, this was the promise received from *Akbaa-tadia* now being made manifest before his eyes.

Rather than raid the village itself for horses and scalps, which action might incur the loss of some of his own warriors in the process, the chief decided instead to take full advantage of what was now before him. Quickly he and his party prepared themselves for battle and rode towards the patch of plum-bushes with all haste. When arrived near their objective, Sore-Belly bade his warriors dismount and secrete themselves out of view, while they waited patiently for their female quarry to reach the bushes.

It was not long before the small group of people around sixty in number, all women but for three men, who, it was later learned, had included themselves for their own amusement, came ambling along laughing and chattering, oblivious to all but themselves. By the women's style of dress and language they proved to be Pikuni, and the hidden Crows first allowed them to get among the bushes and actually engage in their intended business. Then at a given signal, the Crow warriors raised themselves from concealment and after making their presence known with a lone cry of *"Koo-Koo-Hey,"* they immediately charged on foot into the bushes. They quickly surrounded their victims before the latter even had time to flee. The three men originally observed among the pickers were suddenly nowhere to be seen, and the Crows for all their searching could find neither hide nor hair of their presence. They therefore assumed they had made their escape when first the Crows had raised themselves from cover, and the Crows; wishing to extricate themselves from the area as soon as possible, did not bother to search for the missing men. Instead they concentrated on herding together the women they had captured and of whom, it is said, actually made little effort to escape. They seemed to be resigned to their fate and allowed themselves to be rounded up with ease.

Being always eager to take young attractive females as potential wives from their enemies, the Crows really had no need for the old grandmothers in the bunch, or even for those past their prime or considered as being of an ugly disposition. Thus the warriors only selected those who appealed to their desires and set free the rest, allowing them to return to their own people.

The Crows then hurriedly set off with the remaining captives mounted behind them on their ponies. They rode south as fast as their horses could gallop, lest Pikuni warriors from the nearby village should take up the pursuit in great force once the freed women told their people what had happened.

In Beckwourth`s account of the affair, it is stated that the Crow party [of which Beckwourth said he himself was a member] got away with fifty-nine women that day and upon reaching their home camp, the women were distributed among a number of selected unmarried Crow warriors to become their wives. [6]

Again according to Beckwourth, the Crow female warrior Woman-Chief herself took two captives at that time, while Beckwourth took four, who, he professed, he afterwards presented to his wife's family to be raised among the Crows. [7]

Lieutenant Bradley on the other hand, having likely heard the story from his Crow informant Little-Face many years later and, perhaps, also having heard the Pikuni version from the trader Alexander Culbertson with whom Bradley was in contact, was told that only twenty-six of the handsomest women captives were actually retained by the Crows from those captured in the plum-bushes. Some of these, Bradley added, managed to escape whilst being carried south of the Musselshell. Of those remaining among their captors, the majority were subsequently adopted into the Crow tribe, and at least three of these captives were still living among the Crows in 1875 when Bradley obtained his information. [8]

What we do know is that upon the Crow party's victorious return south of the Musselshell, there was as usual much rejoicing among the people. The powerful *medicine* of Sore-Belly had proved itself yet again. Esteem for the great chief was raised to even greater heights so that his very person was held in holy reverence and awe because - so his followers believed – he was undoubtedly favoured by *Akbaa-tadia*. And yes, there were more battles to come, albeit the Crows did not always achieve the victory anticipated.

On another occasion a week or so later in mid-September, after Sore-Belly`s people had returned south to the Big Horn region, a patch of plum bushes again played an important role. It was an event involving two separate Atsina war-parties which had started south on foot from the mouth of the Marias.

Both parties of Atsina were travelling towards the Big Horn Mountains to war against the Crows. One party comprised only nine warriors led by an Atsina chief named Sun-White-Cow, while the other – a much larger party – had the Atsina head war-chief Sitting-Woman as its Partisan. Sun-White-Cow and his comrades were first to reach the Crow country, and when nearing the Lodge Grass branch of the Big Horn River, they discerned in the distance a mixed band of Kicked-in-the-Belly and River Crows, traveling leisurely upstream with travois and hundreds of loose ponies in tow. Some among the Crows were singing victory songs, whilst others beat on hide-covered drums still celebrating coups gained in the Assiniboine fight one whole moon earlier. [9]

Near where the smaller party of Atsina was positioned when first discovering the Crow cavalcade, was a wide patch of plum-bushes adjacent to a copse of aspens. Expediently the Atsina fled into the bushes and hid themselves, scattered here and there in small groups of twos and threes and continued to observe their traveling enemies.

Unfortunately for the Atsina, a number of Crow women broke off from their line of travel in order to gather a quantity of plums. The foremost Atsina in concealment recognized one of these women as once belonging to their tribe, and who was now known by her Crow name of Woman-Chief. It was she, however, who first noticed the hidden warriors and immediately raised the alarm that enemies were among the bushes. An Atsina fired a shot at Woman-Chief but missed, and Woman-Chief; being unarmed, ran with her companions back to the column. In response, a great number of Crows quickly surrounded the bushes, and the Atsina began digging pits with their knives and musket butts to gain some protection from Crow missiles all at once being discharged at them. One Atsina

252

was killed outright; shot between the eyes, whereupon his comrades kept changing position to confuse their besiegers. Another Atsina was shot in the chest, although not a fatal wound, and several Crows were also hit, one of whom whilst charging on foot close to the bushes in an endeavour to count *dakshey*, was shot in the mouth by an entrenched Atsina named Running-Bear. The rest of the Crows, however, were more cautious, and would not assault the enemy head on owing to the latter's deadly marksmanship.

The contest dragged on; continuing through the afternoon and during which time, an Atsina known as Red-Eyebrow several times stood up alone outside his entrenchment. In full view of the enemy he shot off his musket and each time he did so, he either killed or wounded a Crow.

During a lull in the fighting a woman among the Crows known as Two-Strikes, who herself had been captured from the Pikuni by Sore-Belly's party little more than one week earlier, crept close to the bushes and hollered out in the Blackfoot tongue which the Atsina readily understood. The woman told them they should do their best to escape as the Crows were set on killing them all. It would soon be nightfall, she said, and already the Crows were gathering great piles of brushwood in order to light fires around the Atsina position so they might not escape in the dark. The Atsina thanked the woman for her advice, and one among them named Wolf-Chief then called out to the Crows saying, *"I am he who is known as Iron-Robe."* [10]

By so saying, Wolf-Chief was hoping to either discourage the Crows or appeal to their sense of honour by letting he and his comrades live. Well he knew that the Crows held the Atsina warrior Iron-Robe in high regard, having sent him presents as tokens of respect for his bravery after the battle with the Atsina column on Rosebud Creek where the Crow Wrapped-Hair had also boosted his fame. But no reply came from the Crows.

Now it happened that whilst the small party of Atsina was defending its desperate position against the over-whelming number of Crows, the second Atsina party led by Sitting-Woman, had at last reached a point not far from where the Crows had left their baggage and travois along with a sizable herd of ponies now virtually unattended. All the Crows including the old people and women and children had since followed behind their warriors, and were watching from clear but safe vantage points as the fight around the plum-bushes progressed. Sitting-Woman had previously been informed by his scouts what was going on some distance ahead, and of the dire situation facing Sun-White-Cow and his comrades. There was, it seems, some bad feeling between the two Atsina leaders, and this, coupled to the fact that Sitting-Woman's party was in no way strong enough to actually assist the besieged party in any practical manner, Sitting-Woman refused to risk his warriors in what could only result in a foolhardy rescue attempt which, most certainly, would result in the annihilation of his own party also. Instead, he and his warriors drove off a large number of ponies from the unprotected Crow baggage train, hoping this would distract the Crows from their present fight, and thereafter rode hurriedly north, leaving Sun-White-Cow's party to its fate.

As regards Sun-White-Cow and his comrades, when darkness fell the Crows did as the woman had told the Atsina, and lit fires to light up the area around the bushes. There remained only one among the Atsina who had not yet been wounded in the affair, and in the dark it was he who slipped away from the bushes, searching for a way through the Crow lines without being seen. This man did not return to his companions, and as no shouts of victory or gun shots had been heard, it was thought by the remaining Atsina that he must have succeeded in making his escape. Thus only a short time later, the rest of the Atsina also crept away going in the same direction as had their comrade, and coming to a stretch of creek not guarded by the Crows, they followed its course to the Big Horn Mountains and from there, albeit on foot and each bearing wounds of various number and degree, they headed north for home. Eventually after many weeks of suffering, they reached their home camp above the Musselshell without further miss-hap. Their leader Sun-White-Cow had actually been wounded nine times in this engagement alone, but both he and his surviving comrades lived to fight another day.

The next morning the Crows were in a quandary as to how their enemies had eluded them. But, they supposed, if indeed they had been pitted against the great Iron-Robe himself, then no wonder they had been out-manoeuvred on this occasion. There was then, some grudging respect accorded to the small Atsina party, notwithstanding that the Crows themselves had sustained a number of casualties during the conflict. Several of their warriors had been killed outright and there were a number who would surely die later from their wounds. Their deaths needed to be avenged, and there was also the desire to chase up the larger Atsina party under Sitting-Woman which had escaped with a significant number of Crow ponies.

This being so, Sore-Belly himself at once raised a formidable force of some 150 warriors, and started north in pursuit of the Atsina. What the details were concerning this retaliatory move, we are not told. Crow oral history merely states that Sore-Belly returned home victorious with a large drove of ponies, although it is not known if these were actually recaptured from the Atsina, or wrested from some other tribe during the expedition.

Either way, it was soon after this and Sore-Belly's return to the Yellowstone, that rumours of another intertribal peace initiative began rippling across the Plains.

As mentioned earlier, albeit that the Crows were again at war with the Assiniboine, the latter's old-time Beaver Hills Cree allies were still in friendly contact with Sore-Belly's River Crows, and yet again, at logger-heads with each of the Blackfoot-speaking tribes.

Before the end of September [1832], owing to continued Blackfoot harassment and a need to replenish a dwindling supply of horses, Chief La Quarter's Cree band again came south from the Fort Edmonton district on the North Branch of the Saskatchewan and camped alongside the River Crows on the Yellowstone. For several weeks the two bands socialized and traded in perfect harmony, and in October, a large combined River Crow and Cree war-party conducted a large-scale hostile foray north against the Pikuni. [11]

What the outcome was regarding this episode, likewise, is not recorded. It was, though, probably the last major hostile expedition undertaken by River

.255.

255255255255

25 5255255.5555

Crows against the Pikuni for little short of two years, owing to a long-standing truce soon after being arranged between their peoples.

This pact, primarily, was due to recent reverses suffered by the Pikuni at Crow hands, which had created a significant reduction regarding the number of women as opposed to men in Pikuni camps. It was because of a need to address this anomaly by rehabilitating those women and children captured by the Crows, and secondly, in order to comply with Sanford and McKenzie's repeated proposals that Pikuni new-comers to Fort Union should renew their previous short-lived pacts with all their old enemies, that a number of Pikuni and Crows whilst trading at the Fort, were persuaded again to smoke the calumet of peace between them. They then returned to their respective villages and informed their head chiefs what they had done. The Pikuni went further thereafter, by sending emissaries to the River Crows and to Sore-Belly specifically, holding out the proverbial olive branch, along with an invitation to attend a grand intertribal get-together on an open stretch of grassland abutting Warm Spring Creek, a branch of the Judith River in north Montana.

One among the Pikuni emissaries was the white man Hugh Munroe, who, for many years, had lived among the Small Robe Pikuni band. He had recently acted as a Free Trapper for the now abandoned Fort Piegan originally established for the Blackfoot trade near the mouth of the Marias, but had since been at Fort Union as an employee of the American Fur Company. Munroe's biographer James Willard Schultz, recorded more than one version regarding this Crow–Pikuni pact and of the two tribes coming together at that time. Each of these accounts regretably, are quazi-historical, if not to say romanticized versions which cannot be accepted entirely as historically or chronologically correct. It is for this reason that they are not included here in detail, although in essence they are likely authentic, and Schultz did in one version, give the correct date covering the beginning period for the aforesaid pact in his autobiographical work *"My Life as an Indian,"* wherein it is stated,

> "In 1832, the Blackfoot made a treaty of peace with the Crows at Fort Union, which lasted only two years." [12]

Corroborating the above statement is the Piegan Blackfoot winter-count of Teddy Yellow-Fly. This is usually sound in content, and herein a reference is made to such a pact in his entry for the winter of 1832 /'33,
> *"Crow Indians make peace."* [13]

We do know from present-day Crow oral tradition, as related by Joe Medicine Crow and others, that in 1832 Sore-Belly and a subordinate chief named Spotted-Buffalo of the River Crows did agree to meet with their erstwhile Blackfoot foes at Warm Spring Creek, and that a mutual pact was subsequently concluded. The resulting peace, however, only really applied to the River Crows and Pikuni, or, more specifically, to the Small Robe Pikuni band. It did not deter the Bloods and Siksika [even though Bloods were present at the meeting] from continuing their raids against the Crows, and such raiding parties often included non-Small Robe Pikuni warriors. Certainly, members belonging to other Pikuni bands not dissuaded by any recent pact, still persistently joined their Blood and Siksika relatives on hostile ventures into Crow country. Nevertheless, peace with the Small Robe band as a tribal body held fast for a while at least, and did allow Sore-Belly's people some respite. The Small Robes were a populous Blackfoot-speaking group of around two-hundred and fifty lodges who's general stomping ground was in the Musselshell and Three Forks districts. This was the most southern territory claimed by Blackfoot peoples and in close proximity to that of the River Crows

It was a similar situation with the Small Robe's close confederates the Atsina. In so much as they, too, had lost a good number of their people taken captive during recent conflicts with the River Crows. Thus the Atsina likewise, were desirous of entering into yet another truce with Sore-Belly's people, if only to get their own captive kinfolk returned. It is not documented or remembered in Crow oral history today if the Atsina were actually present during the afore-mentioned peace-making at Warm Spring Creek. Although several months after the event, Prince Maximilian Zu Wied whilst visiting among the Mandan and Hidatsa during the winter of 1833 /'34, heard that the Atsina, or Gros Ventres as he called them,

> "...had lately been compelled to make vigorous efforts to ransom about thirty of their men, who had fallen into the hands of their enemies –the Crows. In their engagements with this tribe, they lost so many men as to occasion among them an undue proportion between the sexes." [14]

That Maximilian mentions a ratio of more women than men among the Atsina at that time, does confirm the release of Atsina non-combatants after the Crow attack on the Atsina column the previous year and of so many young Atsina males then held by the Crows. On the other hand, according to the tribal historian Joe Medicine Crow, the Atsina male captives mentioned by Maximilian, likely refers to another event at which time, Joe was told, a number of young Atsina warriors had been taken captive during that same year when attempting to steal horses from Sore-Belly's camp. Before the Crow warriors could kill them, Sore-Belly had intervened and by his rhetoric and force of personality alone, had convinced his warriors that rather than continue at war with the Atsina, they should spare the lives of the thieves. He then had sent a message to the Atsina chiefs, saying they could ransom back their tribesmen and by so doing, cement a new peace between their tribes. [15]

Thus Joe Medicine Crow implies by his terminology, that the River Crows if not Long-Hair's Mountain band, did also make a temporary peace with the Atsina at that time, which remembering hostile Crow –Atsina encounters earlier in the year, was; most likely concluded during the same gathering some months later between the Crows and Small Robe Pikuni at Warm Spring Creek. What the statements from both Maximilian and Joe Medicine Crow do indicate, is a degree of compassion and practical thinking on Sore-Belly's part. This would be consistent with the character of the great war-chief of the River Crows, when determined to do what he believed, would be best for his people as a whole.

Overall this McKenzie inspired Crow and Pikuni truce further facilitated Crow access to the American Fur Company post Fort Union, along with McKenzie's design of enticing Crow trade away from the rival Rocky Mountain Company. To this end, before mid-summer of 1832, Mackenzie had already dispatched Samuel Tulloch [known to Crows as The-Crane owing to his supposed long neck] and a number of employees among whom was James Beckwourth, to erect a new post officially named Fort Cass [colloquially known simply as the "Crow Fort" or "Tulloch's Post"] on the right or east bank of the Yellowstone two or three miles below the mouth of the Big Horn. Before the post was completed, Beckwourth himself visited the various Crow camps and succeeded in obtaining that tribes' allegiance to the American Fur Company alone. Now at last, could both the Mountain and River Crows again have direct access to the white man's goods in their own domain, particularly of guns and ammunition, necessary to maintain an equal footing against their enemies.

However, the tribe's new loyalty to the American Fur Company was to create some serious dissention between the Crows and other white trappers and fur companies in the region. Indeed, come late summer, a detachment of twenty white trappers belonging to Captain Bonneville's expedition, but at the time separated from him, were in Crow country trapping beaver along a number of streams flowing into the Yellowstone from the south. Falling in with a band of Crows, the majority of the aforesaid trappers were persuaded to desert their employer Bonneville and join the Indians, carrying Bonneville's traps, horses and equipment with them. When the trapper's leader or partisan – who still professed his loyalty to the captain – tried to retake the deserters, the Crows threatened the partisan in a violent manner and made it clear that as far as the Crows were concerned, the errant trappers now belonged to the American Fur Company. Bonneville's partisan and those still adhering to his authority, then made their way to the newly erected Fort Cass where they sat out the winter rather than continue their journey to re-join the captain and the rest of the brigade on Salmon River west of the Rockies, as they would not dare traverse the hostile country in between with such a small force as remained. While at Fort Cass, even those trappers supposedly still loyal to Bonneville, were cajoled into trading the Captain's pelts to American Fur Company employees for whiskey, and after this, they, too, also cast their lot in with the rival concern, undoubtedly through the instigations of that company's agents James Beckwourth and Samuel Tulloch. [16]

After leaving the fort with a few 'Free Trappers' hired in place of the deserters, the same unnamed partisan had all his horses stolen by wandering Arickara near the head of Powder River. Two of the thieves were later captured by the trappers, and when the main group of Arickara refused to exchange the stolen horses for their tribesmen, the trappers raised a burning pyre and threw the two luckless thieves on it to roast slowly to death, in full view of their astonished tribesmen. [17]

Such barbarity as practiced by respective antagonists in the Far West at this time, merely perpetuated the ongoing resentment between Indians and whites, while increasing the savage propensity of both. Still, it seems, – more so than other tribes - the Crows could not help themselves in stealing horses and at times equipment from the more itinerant white men they met. It was a situation which even the white men themselves accepted as a necessary hazard to their day to day existence in Indian country, and more especially, when in the country of the Crows.

Thus it had not been surprising when earlier, in November 1832 near the headwaters of Colorado River adjacent to the Rocky Mountains, between seventy and eighty Crows visited a camp of white trappers some seventy strong belonging to a brigade led by Captains Gant and Blackwell, and among whom was Zenas Leonard who left an account of the event. [18]

The Indians professed to being a war-party out against the Shoshoni They showed much friendship towards the white men and after a few hours took their leave. But that same night under cover of darkness, a number of Crows returned and stole five of the trapper's finest horses. Upon discovering their loss come morning, the trappers at once took up the trail of the thieves. They followed it northeast across the mountains to the headwaters of the Missouri, and still following the trail, came at length to the mouth of Stinking [now Shoshoni] River west of present-day Cody, Wyoming. Turning north, they were travelling down the Big Horn when they came upon Long-Hair's Mountain Crows among whom were then fifteen lodges of River Crows, including Chief Sore-Belly and his family, briefly pausing on their way to visit Flatheads west of the mountains. [19]

Here, so Leonard reported, they met a Negro man who declared he had been with the Crows for 10 or 12 years and had four Crow wives. Who this man was, Leonard does not specifically say, although most likely, owing to later passages in Leonard's account [see appendix C.], it applies not to Edward Rose, but rather to James Beckwourth, and refers to when Beckwourth had merely first entered Crow country as a member of Ashley's trapper brigade in 1823.

The Negro told the trappers that Crows had stolen their horses because they thought the whites were intending to trade with their enemies, and if the trappers gave a few "trifling presents" in return, then the said horses could be retrieved. Such accordingly was done, and friendly relations between Crows and white men were revived on this occasion. Thus, notwithstanding the propensity of some incorrigibles among the Crows to persist in committing irritating mischiefs against the more vulnerable bands of white trappers, both Long-Hair and Sore-Belly were still adamant in their efforts to promote Crow friendship with all white men, and according to a contemporary account, Sore-Belly used logical argument to support his aim, saying,

*"If we keep friends with the white man, then we shall have nothing to fear from the Blackfoot and can rule the Mountains. [20]*

In fact, the Gant and Blackwell brigade remained among the same Crow lodges until January 1st 1833, at which point the white men finally departed from their hosts. Sore-Belly and his fifteen lodges then continued on towards the Flatheads, while Long-Hair's people began moving down river, first to hunt in the Buffalo Pasture and after a brief stay at that place, to move southwest to the forks of Stinking River, which area provided good forage for horses and was sometimes chosen by the Mountain Crows as a wintering ground owing to little snowfall in the region.

By this it is apparent that as regards both Long-Hair and Sore-Belly, their people's continued friendship with the white man was still of paramount concern. But there were also other thoughts which began haunting Sore-Belly's vision of the future, rather, that is, than the stealing of a few horses from those his people knew as Yellow-Eyes.

During Sore-Belly's younger days buffalo had been very numerous on the Northern Plains, It was then said among the Crows, *"bishee ammachuhka shipita,"* i.e., Buffalo darken the Prairies." However, by Sore-Belly's middle years, their numbers were no longer infinite. In 1830, Crows had shown the trapper Zenas Leonard a site filled with bones, the result of but one recent kill when some seven-hundred buffalo had been slaughtered in a single hunt by only one *small* band of Crows. This number, which was duly repeated twelve and sometimes fifteen times a year, and enjoined with what other tribes to the north, east and south also slaughtered to supply their own needs, and additionally, what the half-breed *Metis* from the North and *Ciboleroes* [Pueblo and Mexicans] from the South also slaughtered in twice-annual hunts which filled their many hundreds of two-wheeled carts to overflowing with meat and hides, made the number of buffalo killed on an annual basis by Plains people alone, astronomical. Once a year, small herds were slaughtered individually by various tribes merely for the animal's tongues as required in certain religious ceremonies such as the Sun-Dance, and at such times, between six and seven-hundred lodges would be camped together for two weeks and more, requiring the slaughter of some one-hundred and fifty buffalo per-day to sustain the population. Already, there was a thriving market for buffalo tongues in St. Louis and other white settlements east of the Mississippi, and in the procurement of which, often the rest of the carcass was left to rot on the prairie. Coupled to this, beginning around 1832, there was emerging a fast-growing commerce in Plains Indians selling bison robes to white traders in place of beaver pelts, the latter of which; due to over hunting and changing fashions in the white man's world, were producing reduced profits as a commercial commodity. This new trade in buffalo robes was very quickly creating an additional and even more rapid diminishing of the herds, and with the establishment of numerous trading posts along the North and South Platte and the Arkansas, the buffalo-hide trade soon after, was greatly accelerated.

Natural predators such as wolves etc.; took their toll of calves and breeding cows, a fact adding greatly to a further reduction among such animals and which together, with the aforementioned slaughter by Human hunters who likewise, generally preferred the tender meat of cows to that of bulls, was already proving an unsustainable situation for the continued proliferation of the herds.

Sore-Belly could see this plainly, and foresaw what was destined to befall his people. As indeed, would be the fate of all tribes reliant on buffalo for their existence. Too well, Sore-Belly knew, the Crows would eventually have to adapt to the white man`s way, if, that is, they were to survive intact as a people no longer able to survive as hunting nomads on the High Plains. And such a time, he suspected, would not be long in coming.

Be this as it may, and over-ridding the great chief`s apprehensions of what future years would bring, there were still numerous foes such as Cheyennes and Lakota among others to contend with.

Indeed, even while Long-Hair`s village was moving towards the Buffalo Pasture after playing host to the Gant and Blackwell party, their progress was suddenly halted when messengers brought word of the recent destruction and slaughter of a Crow village and its occupants. Such news caused Long-Hair to instead turn north back towards the Yellowstone, and join with the main camp of River Crows during the Nation`s time of grieving.

And so, for the present, notwithstanding recent pacts with the Pikuni and Atsina, the Crows still had to concern themselves with defending their lands and families against other enemies, and to undermine by counter-attacking those hostile tribes, which persisted in their endeavours to claim the fine Crow country for themselves.

- 0 - 0 – 0 – 0 – 0 – 0 – 0 – 0 – 0 – 0 – 0 – 0 – 0 – 0 - 0 – 0 –

**CROWS TAKING AN OATH TO THE SUN.**
Edward S. Curtis photo 1908. *[Author`s collection]*

**ROBERT CAMPBELL. 1867.**
*[Denver Public Library]*

**CROW WARRIOR, LONG-OTTER.**
*[Smithsonian Institution, Washington D.C.]*

**Crow Indian, Crazy-Head.**
*[Son of James P. Beckwourth by a Crow wife]*

**Crow Indian, Two-Crows, the Younger.**
*[George Catlin, 1832.]*

**JAMES P. BECKWOURTH.**
*[Courtesy of the Denver Public Library]*

**SORE-BELLY'S "*MEDICINE*" SHIELD WITH BIG-EARED FIGURE
EMBLAZONED ON IT.**
*[Photograph from an exhibit in the Museum of the American Indian, Heye foundation.
New York. U.S.A.]*

264

CROW CHIEF, RED-BEAR.    WOMAN-IN-A-BEAR`S-DEN [WIFE]
[Both painted by George Catlin from life at Fort Union in 1832]

VIEW OF FORT UNION FROM THE SOUTH.
From an aquatint by Karl Bodmer in 1834.   [Author`s collection]

Left to right; Bull`s-Back-Fat [Blood] and Spotted-Elk aka Bear-Chief [Piegan] [Karl Bodmer aquatint from life, 1834.]

Crow warrior Stump-Horn.
Also known as Elk-Horn,
Prominent in the Grapevine Creek fight.
[Painted from life by Alfred Jacob Miller
in 1837. [*The Gilcrease Museum*]

Crow Warrior, Two-Whistles.
*[Edward S. Curtis photograph.]*

# PART I11.

## DECLINE OF THE CROW ASCENDANCY

**MAP OF COUNTRY NORTH OF THE UPPER MISSOURI RIVER.**
*Map from the front piece of "The Vengeful Wife" by Hugh H. Dempsey. 1903.*
*[Author's collection]*

268

## CHAPTER 23.

## THE DESTRUCTION OF DANGLING FOOT`S PEOPLE.

By the latter part of 1832, Sore-Belly had reached the apex of his popularity and influence among his people, and his fame as a fearless fighter and strategist was acknowledged among all tribes of the Upper Missouri and Rocky Mountain regions. Long-Hair still held the titular position of "Chief of Chiefs" of the whole Crow Nation, along with the respect and reverence accorded such standing, but through a combination of tribal popularity and allegiance, it was Sore-Belly who now actually controlled the people`s more important military ventures, and dictated tribal attitude when dealing with both whites and Indians on a political level. It was Sore-Belly also, who alone finally put an end to the inter-clan disputes which, in previous years, had not only been detrimental to Crow – white relations, but had threatened to tear the Nation apart by the sometimes violent squabbles such inter-clan rivalry created. A long-term ongoing quarrel between the Whistling-Waters and Treacherous Lodge clans being a case in point.

This same year [1832], the head man of the Treacherous Lodges was a noted personage named Raven-Face. Earlier, in mid-summer the previous year when the whole Crow Nation had congregated to conduct its annual religious ceremonies, word was brought to him that his brother Arrow-Head, the same who with his small *Bilapilutche* - Dried-Out-Furs - band of dissidents had spent a prolonged period in the south, had just been killed by a Whistling-Waters chief named One-Heart, who himself, was the younger adopted brother of the paramount chief, Long-Hair. [1]

Raven-Face was a brave, albeit reckless warrior. Upon hearing of the death of his brother, he had at once mounted his favourite war-pony; took gun in hand and rode unhesitant to where the Whistling-Waters` lodges were pitched. When he was seen riding brazenly into the Whistling-Waters` camp, those responsible for Arrow-Head`s death huddled together and sensing what the lone rider was about, one of their number raised his gun and fired, wounding Raven-Face in the shoulder. Still, however, Raven-Face came on; his now useless arm hanging limp at his side.

The Whistling-Waters might easily have killed him and were in a mind to do so, had it not been for the timely intervention of a man named Dangling-Foot. This man, although a Whistling-Waters clan member himself, had been a close childhood associate of Raven-Face, and now he rode bravely over to his old friend in order to protect him from further harm.

At the same time other groups of people among both the Whistling-Waters and Treacherous Lodges, not themselves involved in the current feud and having remained neutral throughout, were also stirred into action. They placed themselves between Raven-Face and those opposing him and in such a way,

269

managed to keep the antagonists apart. The Whistling-Waters dissidents could not get near enough to finish Raven-Face off or to do him further mischief.

This action for the time being, had put an end to the affair and Raven-Face, still with Dangling-Foot by his side, returned safely to the camp of the Treacherous Lodges. Soon after this, the combined Crow camp had disbanded and the respective clans gone their separate ways.

The following summer [1832], when the whole Crow Nation had again congregated in one united camp then on Clark`s Fork of the Yellowstone, both Raven-Face and Dangling-Foot having since become even closer friends and constant companions, went out together to hunt. They had made a successful kill, and were busily engaged in butchering the animals and loading the meat on a pack-pony, when the same Whistling-Waters chief One-Heart suddenly appeared accompanied by his usual retinue of belligerent companions.

Intending to avenge the affair of the previous summer, these Whistling-Waters immediately attacked the two hunters; notwithstanding that Dangling-Foot was of their own clan. They were convinced he had both shamed and dishonoured them in full view of the people when he had taken the side of the Treacherous Lodge chief, and so were prepared to kill him also.

It was Dangling-Foot who first saw the Whistling-Waters riding towards him and his companion. Quickly he mounted his pony; notched an arrow to his bowstring and rode forward in a threatening manner. The Whistling-Waters Chief One-Heart immediately reined in his horse and called to Dangling-Foot saying,

"Why do you face us with the weapons of war; can you not see we are your own people?" [2]

But Dangling-Foot, who had never been cowed by the superior number of his adversaries, answered thus,

"Thou knowest this man called Raven-Face! Know it then, he is my brother-friend and long-time companion. What you wish to do him, you must first do to me, for I am obliged to honour and protect my brother here before you." [3]

Having said these words, Dangling-Foot did not wait a reply. He loosed off an arrow at his antagonist One-Heart which struck the latter squarely in the chest. Then, as Dangling-Foot rode around him, he sent another shaft into One-Heart`s back so that the blood pumped up through his opponent`s mouth before falling from his horse a dead man. Dangling-Foot dismounted; plucked out the arrow from his victim's back and in a show of contempt, wiped its bloody point on One-Heart`s head.

Upon seeing their leader fall, the rest of One-Heart`s Whistling-Water companions made a precipitous flight back the way they had come. Dangling-Foot, though, was not finished. He followed them up and although they shot at him many times with both muskets and arrows, they failed to bring him down. Still Dangling-Foot pursued them; caught them up and rode right through their ranks, unseating several warriors from their saddles and trampling them under hoof.

At length, Dangling-Foot returned to where his friend Raven-Face was standing. He told Raven-Face to scalp the prostrate One-Heart, for he himself, he said, had already done harm enough to his own clan people.

So it was that when Dangling-Foot and Raven-Face returned to where the Treacherous Lodges were encamped, they had their faces painted black as a sign of victory. They also held aloft willow wands, from the ends of which were attached pieces of One-Heart`s scalp.

Meanwhile, many Whistling-Waters clan members cried over the death of their chief. They spoke bad words against Dangling-Foot for what they saw as his dishonourable act. In truth, he had only done which in any other circumstance, would have been expected of him in order to protect his brother-friend.

Long-Hair, as titular head chief of the Nation, could not rightly physically involve himself in intra-tribal squabbles. He did, though, mourn and fast because of his adopted brother's death, and prophesied that before the year was out, Dangling-Foot would be killed by foreign enemies as punishment for his bloody deed.

The situation had now reached such a serious point, that through the instigation of Sore-Belly, supported by those neutral factions among both clans in question who had not actually taken sides in the feud, a special council was convened between the opposing clans, and a prolonged period of talking and compromise ensued. The result was that the Whistling-Waters and Treacherous Lodges were won over by Sore-Belly`s rhetoric and their differences finally resolved. They agreed thereafter, to live in peace with one another and to put their grievances behind them.

It had been supposed by the rest of the tribe, that this had put an end to the matter. But such was not to be as far as Dangling-Foot`s involvement was concerned.

There were those among his own clan folk who were not prepared to forgive his part in the feud for having taken sides against them. Constantly, it seemed, his own people were saying bad things about him and often pointed an accusing finger when he passed.

In the meantime, in early autumn 1832, the time now reached in our narrative, Raven-Face who was now titular head of the Dried-Out-Furs after the demise of Chief Arrow-Head, had left the Big Horn country for that lying between the South Platte River and the Arkansas. Soon after this, Dangling-Foot, who was himself a war-chief of some renown and a close friend and confident of Sore-Belly, decided that he would take those who still adhered to his authority - which together constituted thirty-eight lodges - and also move far away from the main tribal group, intending to follow Raven-Face and the Dried-Out-Furs south. He would stay away from the main Crow group for a satisfactory period, he said, and during which time, he hoped the people might forget the past and cease their gossiping about him.

Before Dangling-Foot left, Sore-Belly who was then visiting Long-Hair`s village on the Big Horn, counselled with him, and pointed out the error of removing his people from the protection of the united camp. He warned his friend saying,

> "It is a dangerous thing to do. Enemy war-bands are roaming the country and if your party be attacked, it will surely be destroyed." [4]

Dangling-Foot, however, heeded not Sore-Belly's words. He was still resolved to go south for the duration of the coming winter and spring, although first, he said, he would lead his small group into the Black Hills region in order to hunt, and as a compromise to Sore-Belly's concern, he further declared that he would return to the North country by the time the Nation gathered again to hold its summer festivals.

Now it had happened during the early part of summer, the whole Cheyenne Nation had come together in a grand encampment adjacent to the Tongue tributary of the Yellowstone. There that people's head chiefs and holy men had held council, to decide if they should abandon their old hunting grounds in the Powder and Cheyenne River country and move south between the South Fork of the Platte and the Arkansas, which latter country was now deemed more conducive to their needs. This proposed Cheyenne movement had been encouraged on one hand by the continued encroachment of Lakota into lands which, previously, had been regarded as belonging exclusively to the Cheyennes, and on the other, through the persuasions of the white trader William Bent, who had suggested to the Cheyenne and Suhtaio that they take up residence close to his new trading post on the Arkansas, from where, he said, he could supply their whole tribe with all the trade goods they required.

The result of the council induced the more northern Cheyennes, including the Watapio, Oivimana, Hevietanio and one or more Suhtaio bands to move south. By mid-summer the same year, they had already vacated the Cheyenne River and Black Hills districts entirely, in favour of the South Platte and Upper Arkansas region of the Southern Plains. In confirmation of this date of movement, William Bent later told his son George that his first meeting with the Suhtaio [as yet a separate tribe albeit closely confederated with the Cheyennes], was while he was building his new adobe fort on the Arkansas. This was the first time to his knowledge that the Suhtaio had come so far south to camp on a permanent basis.

Word of the Cheyenne migration had been carried to the Crows who believed it a permanent move, and it was this intelligence which had induced Chief Dangling-Foot to lead his small band of followers into the Black Hills along the Belle Fourch branch of the Cheyenne River. He thus believed that his people's mortal enemies the Cheyenne, were then too far south to pose a significant threat.

However, by the end of summer, 1832, the trader Bent had still been in the process of building his new adobe-bricked post, which stood on the American north side of the Arkansas between where the towns of Las Animas and La Junta now stand, twenty-five miles or so west of a thirty mile stretch of cottonwoods known to several tribes as "Big Timbers."

Before the construction of the fort was completed, smallpox had broken out among Bent's Mexican labourers, and he was obliged to temporarily abandon his task until the disease burned itself out. He sent runners to the Cheyenne and

Suhtaio telling them not to come near the Arkansas at that time to prevent their contracting the contagion. As a consequence, those Cheyenne bands which only recently had forsaken their lands in the north, and who knew from past experience that the best way to avoid infection was to put distance between themselves and its source, took heed of Bent's advice and fled precipitously back to their old haunts. It was for this reason, moreover, rather than being chased out of the Arkansas country by the Comanche as Edwin Denig supposed, that these particular Cheyenne and Suhtaio bands had expediently returned to their old home to escape the epidemic then raging across the entire Central and Southern Plains. Thus - unbeknown to the Crows at that time, - by early Autumn, 1832, several Cheyenne bands were again roaming and camping in the North Platte country, whilst the Suhtaio were back in the Black Hills, far north of the Arkansas River.

The Crows used to say that Cheyennes were always looking for someone to fight, and especially so, if they stumbled upon those they regarded as "easy prey." Any people appearing as such would most likely run afoul of that tribe's scalping knives. Such a fate was to befall this small band of Crows led by Dangling-Foot, who, like innocent children, came stumbling on, They were meandering through the Black Hills, completely unaware of the real danger of being assaulted by Cheyennes.

It was not long before Cheyenne scouts discovered the presence of Dangling-Foot's small band. At once they took news of the discovery to their main body, whereupon the Cheyenne war-chiefs began preparing for a fight.

The Cheyennes had the element of surprise on their side and were resolved that none of their Crow enemies should escape their wrath. For several days Cheyenne scouts 'dogged' Dangling-Foot's column as it moved disconcertedly across the region. The Cheyennes were waiting patiently for the Crows to reach what they considered would be a convenient spot to launch an attack, and so, still undetected, Cheyenne scouts continued to watch as the unsuspecting Crows set up their lodges at the end of each days march.

At length, after several more days of close observation, the Cheyenne scouts were satisfied with the location the Crows had chosen to pitch their camp.

The lack of diligence among Dangling-Foot's people, had caused them to site their village where it would be at the mercy of any enemy force which might stumble upon it either by accident or design. Indeed, at a later date, both Crows and Cheyennes agreed that the camp at that time had been situated in a very vulnerable position. This being on an open stretch of grassland where a small camp could easily be surrounded, and was some distance from any protective feature where the occupants could have taken cover in the advent of assault This was, in fact, close to where the present-day town of Rawlins, Wyoming is now situated near the headwaters of Cheyenne River.

The Cheyenne scouts, meanwhile, raced back to their base camp and reported this intelligence to their chiefs. It was then decided to move out that very night and the following morning, attack the Crow camp and destroy it. Hopefully, they thought, they would then drive off the entire pony herd in the process; along with killing as many Crow warriors as possible and taking the women and children captive.

So it was that the whole Cheyenne force comprising some two-hundred and more fighting men, set out from their war-camp that very night, and next day, just as dawn was breaking, the warriors got ready to charge on their objective.

Before they did so, a party of Crow hunters on horseback was observed leaving the camp and the Cheyennes decided to wait until the hunters had ridden a long way off. Then when they assaulted the camp, there would be fewer Crow warriors to contend with.

Such was the Indian philosophy, which always considered it to their credit if they had an overwhelming advantage over the enemy and lost as few of their own fighting men as possible. It was not the intention of the Cheyennes, of course, to offer what might be regarded as "fair play," by allowing the enemy the chance of a more equal contest.

After an appropriate hiatus in order to allow the Crow hunters to put some distance between themselves and the camp, a sudden shrill-pitched Cheyenne war-cry rang out over the shimmering grasslands. This was followed by a horde of painted and be-feathered warriors mounted on fleet war-ponies, all at once converging on the small cluster of tepees.

The Cheyennes rode toward the camp from two directions and moments later, had it completely surrounded. They then began bulldozing their way in and out among the lodges and into the camp interior itself with musket balls and arrows flying. At first the Crows were stunned by the lightening effect. But then a few Crow men-folk who had not gone out with the hunters and had their fastest horses picketed close to their lodges, quickly mounted up and fled the scene along with a sizeable number of women and children only moments before all escape routes were cut off. Their unfortunate kinfolk left in camp, could do naught but suffer the deadly fate now looming over them.

Of those Crow men-folk who did remain in camp, there was no time to don war clothes or *medicine* charms. Almost as quickly as they strung their bows or loaded their fusees, they were laid low. Some few Crows on horseback were toppled from their saddles and whilst the children screamed, several Crow women in fits of desperation, picked up their fallen husband's weapons and bravely carried on the fight for survival. All these women were also either shot or clubbed to death and left lying on the blood soaked ground, their bodies then scalped and pin-cushioned with arrows, as had been done to their slaughtered men-folk.

Miraculously, Chief Dangling-Foot was one of those who did break out of the beleaguered camp. Single-handed with his trade fusee and an ample supply of powder and ball, he had battled his way through the tightening ring of encircling enemies and managed to entrench himself in a small hollow not far from where most of the fighting was raging. From his position he succeeded in keeping the Cheyennes at bay for a long time. The Cheyennes later admitted to the Crows that this man had been very brave, and had killed and wounded several of their warriors before he himself was finally slain. It is additionally stated by the Crows that after the fighting ceased, the Cheyenne chief had looked down upon the lifeless, bloodstained corpse of Dangling-Foot and said to those around him,

"See this enemy lying stiff and lifeless who has given his body to the wolves. He was a brave fighter. Do not take his scalp. Treat him with respect as befits a fearless warrior." [5]

This, say the Crows, the Cheyennes did, and it is also said that the victors then washed the blood from the body of Dangling-Foot; dressed the corpse in their own fine clothes, and laid it to rest with the same ceremony as would be customary for one of their own.

As for the remaining Crow warriors who had no means of escape, they also had fought as bravely and as desperately as any when outnumbered at least three to one. But it was not long before all resistance had been subdued and Cheyenne moccasin feet stood among the slain. Every adult Crow male trapped within the camp had been killed, along with a number of females, while of those women and children who did survive, they were carried into captivity by the victors. In the aftermath, the Cheyennes ransacked the tepees and camp baggage, taking as booty everything of value and of novelty, and the rest, including the tepees, was put to the torch. The Cheyennes then rode away triumphant, driving scores of Crow ponies and women and children captives before them.

Almost as suddenly as the battle started - it was ended, and only Cheyenne victory songs fading into the distance broke the once again still and peaceful prairie air.

The Crow fighting men in Dangling-Foot`s village had originally numbered between seventy and eighty warriors, although at least half that number had been away hunting at the time the battle took place. When finally the absentees returned to their then smouldering, corpse-littered camp, they were filled with grief. Immediately they started south in search of Raven-Face and his Dried-Out-Furs band, whilst two of the survivors returned north to the main camp of Sore-Belly`s River Crows then located along the Yellowstone to inform him what had happened. Sore-Belly himself was not, though, in camp at that time, having gone to visit the Flatheads west of the Rocky Mountains.

In reality, according to Joe Medicine-Crow`s information concerning the affair, the total number of Crow men-folk actually killed during the fight, was no more than thirty or perhaps forty persons at most. On the other hand, of between one-hundred and one-hundred and fifty women and children constituting the non-combatants of Dangling Foot's thirty-eight lodges, the Cheyennes took a little over one-hundred prisoners. Of these, several later escaped back to their own people in the north, or were traded to or captured by other tribes with whom the Cheyennes were in contact. A sizable number of captives, however, were taken south by the Cheyennes when the latter returned to Bent`s post on the Arkansas later that year. Many of these likewise managed to escape from their captors, and after wandering around for some time in the southern country, eventually joined the Kiowa - then enemies of the Cheyenne – where at last they found succour and safety and among whom, the small remnant of the Dried-Out-Furs band of Raven-Face was by then, already ensconced.

According to most accounts narrated by the Crows in their oral traditions, it had been around this same date that the Dried-Out-Furs finally achieved their old Chief Arrow-Head`s aim of fighting all peoples they came in contact with, until they themselves were wiped out or no longer existed as a viable body. Details concerning the final defeat of the Dried-Out-Furs are not, though, remembered, although the Comanche have a story which also relates to this period of the early 1830s. It tells how they, the Comanche, once came across a small remnant of people somewhere in the eastern part of Colorado. These people were dressed in the Crow style and whose main body had only recently been massacred by some enemy tribe. Either then, this refers to the survivors of the Dried-Out-Furs band or to those belonging to Dangling-Foot`s village or to both. Certainly, the Kiowa who were very close allies and confederates to the Comanche, state that the survivors of Dangling-Foot`s Crow group soon after their defeat, joined the Kiowa. They eventually married Kiowa men and women with whom they raised families, and thereafter, became completely absorbed among that tribe.

The Kiowa, of course, had long been friends of the Crows and since some two or three generations past when residing in the Three Forks district of the Upper Missouri and at a more recent date, in the Black Hills of South Dakota, they had been the latter`s close allies and confederates. Thus it does appear most likely, that the Kiowa had willingly adopted these refugees from among Dangling-Foot`s people, and also, the remnants of the Dried-Out-Furs who, in time, likewise became completely assimilated among their foster tribe. They, too, married Kiowa men and women so that finally, they lost their Crow identity. Even today, not a few Kiowa claim a blood relationship with the Crows, particularly those who can trace their ancestry back to one or another of these same Crow survivors of both the Dried-Out-Furs band and of Dangling-Foot`s ill-fated followers.

A small number of Crow captives from Dangling-Foot`s band did remain among the Cheyennes, and two of these at a later date became important personages among that tribe. One, a boy was later known as Stands-All-Night [not the noted Cheyenne tribal historian of the same name who was Arickara by birth], whilst the other, a young woman called Pretty-Lance by the Crows, but known as Blackbird-Woman among the Cheyenne, also married into her adopted tribe and became the mother of the famous Southern Cheyenne war-chief Lame-White-Man. This man was later killed whilst doing brave things during the infamous "Custer Fight" on the Little Big Horn in 1876. [6]

Over all, the destruction of Dangling-Foot`s village was a severe blow to the whole Crow Nation. There was much grieving and oaths of vengeance were taken against those culpable. The most important issue as far as Crow warriors were now concerned, was to wreak vengeance again on the Cheyennes, and all the people`s energies seemed to be directed towards that purpose.

- 0 - 0 - 0 – 0 – 0 – 0 – 0 – 0 – 0 – 0 – 0 – 0 – 0 – 0 - 0 – 0 –

## CHAPTER 24.

## SORE-BELLY`S REVENGE and SMALLPOX AMONG THE LODGES.


It has been noted that when some of those who fled the attack on Dangling-Foot`s village eventually reached the River Crow camp on the Yellowstone, they found Sore-Belly was absent, being on his way to visit the Flatheads west of the Rocky Mountains. Runners were dispatched to inform him what had happened to Dangling-Foot`s people, and almost immediately, Sore-Belly changed direction and headed back towards the Yellowstone to be among his people during their communial time of grief. Likewise, as previously noted, news of the disaster had also been carried to Long-Hair`s Mountain Crows, and even though Long-Hair had harboured no personal liking for Dangling-Foot, the slain chief and his followers had, nonetheless, been Crows, and their loss was keenly felt as a significant blow to the Nation as a whole. In response, Long-Hair had abandoned his trek towards the Buffalo Pasture and Stinking River Forks, and had in the meantime, sent runners to all the scattered Crow camps with word that notwithstanding the winter season, they should gather as soon as possible at the place known as "Where the Mountain Lion Sits," and there the whole Nation could grieve its loss in the customary exaggerated manner so dear to the Crows at that time. This designated place of rendezvous was, and still is, regarded by the Crows as a sacred site. It stands on the south side of the Yellowstone and is known today as "Pompey`s Pillar." [1]

So it was during early January, 1833, in compliance to the wishes of Long-Hair, some nine-hundred and more clay-whitened, buffalo-hide tepees were erected in one great camp in several concentric circles, with others scattered among the cottonwoods growing along the south bank of the Yellowstone. Thousands of ponies milled around on the adjacent prairie looking like dark mottled patches, and every hour, it seemed, hunting parties were going out or coming in. For such a large village required a great quantity of fresh meat to sustain its population.

Although several weeks had passed since having received news of Dangling-Foot`s demise, no retaliatory action had been forthcoming. Indeed, the Crows had been so engrossed in lamenting their loss, they had not time even to contemplate what to do next. Now, though, with the full might of the Nation encamped together in one place, the people again felt strong and able to avenge themselves upon any foe in some spectacular manner, and not least, upon the "Stripped-Arrow-People," who since the dissolution of their pact with the Crows, were now again, considered among the latter`s foremost antagonists.

The coming together of all the Nation's fighting men was cause also, for clan relatives and close friends of Dangling-Foot`s slaughtered and otherwise missing people to launch themselves into yet another overt frenzy of grief. Bereaved womenfolk with blood streaming from self-inflicted wounds and screeching hideous laments, ran up to the important warriors, beseeching them to avenge their loss that the widows might cease their mourning. They wiped their blood on the warrior's heads and bodies and held up mutilated hands, now missing a recently lopped off finger joint so as to incite more pity.

The warriors could not help but be moved by such gory spectacles, which seemed to follow them everywhere around the camp.

This being so, it was not long before a number of warriors dressed themselves in their finest regalia and with a pack-pony loaded with gifts, carried a war-pipe around the camp before finally stopping at the door flap of the large red and black-painted lodge belonging to the head chief, Long-Hair. The warriors sang a wolf song outside his tepee to indicate they wished to conduct a raid deep into the enemy's own country and avenge the slaughter of Dangling-Foot's people. The Crows alone among other Plains Tribes, actually chose to mount grand hostile expeditions during the depths of winter, at which time enemy camps were often immobile and more likely to be taken by surprise.

Long-Hair summoned the leading men among the party to enter his tepee, wherein, after seating themselves in a half circle upon the buffalo robe covered ground, the war-pipe was charged and lit, then passed left to right from one mouth to the next. The last to be offered the stem was Long-Hair himself. But he refused to smoke. Instead he declared he would not accompany such a raid, as it would only bring more grief upon his Apsaalooka people if, it too, should end in disaster. The emissaries were taken aback at the chief's response. They rose to their feet in dejected silence and left the lodge and thereafter, walked around the village bewailing aloud that there was no great man among their people who would lead them to war.

It must be noted with regard to Long-Hair's decision, that an important part of his personal *medicine* power, was that he could not personally advocate the slaying of his own tribal people, and this applied to the Cheyennes as they had so many Crow captives since their victory in 1820 on Otter Creek, that Crow persons were sure to be killed if any Cheyenne village was attacked en masse by the Crows. This then was the logic behind Long-Hair's refusal to join the raid, although it should not have prevented him from sanctioning such an action by others.

In the meantime, while all this was going on, Sore-Belly had been sitting quietly in his own lodge listening to what was being said and bewailed through the camp. He now told one of his servants to go outside and remind those who carried the pipe, that their great war chief and protector had not yet been asked to lead their party, and to inform them further, that if he was not included and lacking his guidance, no success would attend them if they went without him against the foe. The servant did as directed, but acted as if what he said was on his own volition and in his own words, the gist of which was rendered thus,

> "Thou art fools. What do you expect to do? It is vain to go against the enemy without the guidance of Alapooish, and he is not among you. You have not even consulted him. Go now and persuade him to become your leader." [2]

Heeding these words, the warriors packed even more gifts on the pack-pony. They then carried the pipe to Sore-Belly`s lodge and stood outside the door flap while together, they again sang their wolf songs. The great chief bade them enter and they did so, their leader holding the war pipe in both hands with arms outstretched. After seating themselves around the central fire, they smoked the pipe in turn as it passed from mouth to mouth, and finally, the pipe was offered to Sore-Belly who sat silent and impassive at the rear of the lodge. Unlike Long-Hair, Sore-Belly grasped the pipe with both hands, placed his lips to the mouthpiece and inhaled and exhaled the four required puffs, thus signifying his acceptance of being the elected leader of the war-trip his visitors were proposing to take.

All the warriors shouted in unison, "Ah-ho, Ah-ho" as an expression of approval, and left the lodge in a body, joyous in both heart and mind.

Around mid-morning the next day, the old warrior Hanging-Raven rode around the lodges. He was crying aloud to the people words which Sore-Belly himself had again instructed him to say. This man Hanging-Raven had been a great fighter in his youth, and he it was who had accompanied the Crow hero Plays-With-His-Face when, twelve years before, the Cheyennes had been led into a trap at Horse Creek after the destruction of Long-Hair`s village. Hanging-Raven was regarded as a very brave man and was also known by the name "Good-Herald" for the obvious reason of now being the tribe's recognized camp crier. Such was the respect accorded this man, that whenever he appeared in his role as tribal spokesman, all the adults came out of their lodges to listen attentively to what he said, and which on this occasion ran as follows,

> "Crows, these words I speak are the words of your chief, Sore-Belly. Soon our Nation`s best warriors will go and meet the "Striped-feathered-Arrows" and many of your loved ones may not return from the fight. You women, cook your finest meal and feed yourselves and the young men. Be kind to one another; put your differences on the ground and speak no harsh words to one another. Let all those who wish, now talk to the women of their choice without constraint, and any man who wishes to talk to another man's woman - then let that too be done without shame on either side. Soon these brave men may leave their bodies lifeless on the prairie when they meet the foe in combat." [3]

After a significant pause Hanging-Raven addressed them further. He told the young men to clear the snow and level the ground at the north end of the village, then to gather up a great quantity of buffalo chips from the surrounding prairie. These, he said, they should place in a pile on the levelled ground to form a bank five or six feet high, and around the base of the bank, they should spread bunches of sweet-smelling sage. Whilst doing so, others among the women-folk should saddle and decorate the war-ponies and after which, all the people must gather around the pile of chips ready to welcome their great chief when he presented himself before them.

These instructions were duly carried out and only then, did Sore-Belly appear on the scene.

He was dressed in the entire skin of a young buffalo bull calf with horns and hoofs attached. The hind part of the robe including the tail was tucked over and under his wide, beaded waistband in the manner of a breech-clout, while the forelegs at their extremities, were tied about his wrists. His face, torso, arms and legs were painted black, while the edge of his lips where they curled slightly upwards; his lower eyelids and the apertures of his nostrils were daubed with bright vermilion. On his head, the side hair was cut short, whilst that over his forehead had been clipped square and raised with bear grease and yellow clay and withal, attached to his crown and hanging down his back, was a long horse-hair queue. Around his neck he wore a shiny otter skin and fastening his bull-calf robe at the front, were two eagle wings which served both as pin and clasp. In addition, a heavy rawhide strap was stretched across his chest, supporting his large *medicine* shield which rested on his back.

The people were amazed to see their chief's imposing and singular appearance. They stood in reverential awe; their eyes and concentration transfixed upon him.

Majestically and slowly, Sore-Belly walked a few paces towards the pile of buffalo chips, then sat down cross-legged and sang a sacred song. He then arose and walked a few paces more before sitting down again, and this procedure he repeated another two times making the sacred number four. After reaching the base of the pile he called to Hanging-Raven to stand behind him, and bade him repeat the words he, Sore-Belly, was about to say to the host of people milling around.

Once again Hanging-Raven addressed the people with Sore-Belly's words. He told them their great chief would sing another song four times and then attempt to climb the chip pile to the top. He further said that when the chief sang his song the fourth time, all the warriors should shout their war-cries and the women raise the tremolo, and this they must continue to do until Sore-Belly reached the summit of the pile. However, if he failed to reach the top, then it would be a bad omen and a sign they should not go to war at this time. Thus while still seated at the base of the pile, Sore-Belly began singing one of his personal *medicine* songs, and after repeating it a fourth time, he rose to his feet and started to climb the buffalo chip pile. After stumbling once or twice; which action sent numerous chips tumbling to the ground, he finally stood on top of the pile. The people, meanwhile, continued voicing their adulation and raising their war-cries, the sound of which became even louder when they saw him standing thus.

Sore-Belly next took the two eagle wings from where they fastened his robe, and holding one in each hand with arms out stretched on either side, began imitating the actions of a bird. The eagle was symbolic of the 'Thunder Spirit' which was Sore-Belly's own sacred *medicine* helper, and now he was invoking its power and benevolence for the benefit of the people.

He then placed the wings carefully on top of the chip pile next to where he stood; took the large shield from his back and held it up with both hands, so the people could clearly see the sacred big-eared emblem of `Spring boy` painted on its surface. Sore-Belly then said,

> "This shield I shall roll along the ground. I shall sing another song
> four times and you must again make a loud noise. The young men
> by patting a hand over their mouths; the old men by singing praise
> songs and the women raising the tremolo. When I roll this shield, if
> it lands face down then I shall not go to war, but if it lands face up
> looking at the sun, then I will lead you against the foe. Together, we
> Apsaalooka shall `eat up` our Striped-Arrow enemies and make the
> ground muddy with their blood." [4]

Having said this, with a downward thrust he cast the famous shield on its rim before him, so that it hit the ground and rolled forward on its edge across the open space below. At the same time the people again raised their voices in a great tumult, while all eyes were on the shield as it rolled; began to slow and wobble, then came to a halt; keeled over and fell flat, its painted side facing upwards.

In response Sore-Belly raised himself to his full height. He cried aloud above the noise of the people,

> "Aho, Crows, see this one`s shield looking at the sun. On the far
> side of the mountains are the enemy, their bodies lying
> dismembered, yet not one Crow have they killed." [5]

By this Sore-Belly meant the Crows would easily defeat the Cheyennes and take many scalps, and although there were some who were not convinced that none of their own warriors would fall during the impending conflict, they had now, they believed, been shown a strong sign of being victorious. Thus, even the sceptics among the people departed in good spirits, all eager to start upon, *"The Red Road to war."* [6]

The following morning, all the chiefs and warriors intending to take part against the Cheyennes began assembling on the open prairie, preparatory to mounting a grand parade past the village entrance.

It was not, however, until noon when Sore-Belly himself again appeared before the people. This time he was bedecked in fine apparel and mounted on a beautiful white-faced pony adorned with feathers, paint and flying strips of red and blue strouding attached to its main and tail. In one hand the chief carried an eagle-feathered lance, while on his left arm, he bore his sacred *medicine* shield. On his head was the double-tailed, eagle-feathered bonnet which touched the ground when he walked, and over his shoulders, his scalp-fringed robe emblazoned with crude depictions of his many coups. He took a position at the south entrance of the tepee circle and made ready to inspect the fighting men who were to ride past him on the open Plain, they, too, adorned in all their Native splendour, and at length, around mid-afternoon, the grand parade got under way.

First came the fifteen subordinate chiefs of the Nation, including Little-White-Bear, High-Bull, Yellow-Belly, Two-Face, Mad-Bull, Atsina-Horses, Three-Crows, Wooden-Bowl [Big-Bowl], Bear`s-Tooth, Grizzly-Bear, Sore-Tail [Rotten-Tail] Spotted-Water, The Rain [Big-Rain], Four-Wolves, and the female fighter Woman-Chief.

Each of these renowned personages was attired in a beaded, hair and ermine fringed war-shirt, while some wore feathered bonnets and others sported the raised scalp-lock over the forehead, made prominent by the addition of white or yellow clay and hair-pipe side pieces, and withal, two or three eagle feathers sticking upright from the crown with strands of red or yellow horse hair flying from the tips. Most carried a lance of some description, but trade muskets with their barrels cut down were also in evidence, and all were mounted on the finest buffalo-runner in their possession, the animals likewise decorated with feathers, hawk bells, strips of strouding and paint.

Behind these came the rank and file members of the soldier societies, which included the Foxes, Lump-woods, Muddy-Hands, Big-Dogs, Bulls and Half-Shaved-Heads. These comprised some twelve-hundred braves in total each mounted on a fine pony, the riders for the most part, wearing buckskin shirts and leggings decorated with beads, human hair and ermine tails. Others rode naked but for breech clout and moccasins, their bodies profusely daubed with paint of various colours in various designs. The two bravest warriors of each society rode at the head of their contingents, each carrying a lance shaped and decorated as was peculiar to their respective fraternities. These warrior societies constituted the flower of Apsaalooka manhood and in their finery, were regarded by friend and foe alike, as the most handsome body of fighting men on the Plains. They sang loud their society songs and raised war-chants in between blowing on eagle-bone whistles, as they rode majestically past the great Sore-Belly and to the adulation of all those looking on. As they passed, they raised their weapons above their heads while continuing to whoop and sing, and Crow hearts heaved with pride as the grand procession snaked its way past the camp entrance and out across the adjacent prairie.

Sore-Belly watched as the warriors rode by, observing minutely the quality of their mounts and weapons. To those whose mounts and weapons did not appear to the great chief as adequate, he told them drop out of the parade and that unless they replaced them with those of acceptable quality, then they would not be allowed to join the venture. Only the best equipped warriors, he said, would he lead personally to war.

It was because of Sore-Belly`s scrutiny, that when the grand war-party finally started forth, it comprised only some four-hundred picked warriors from a total Crow fighting force of twelve-hundred and more. But even four-hundred warriors deemed as being well-equipped and resolute would, Sore-Belly believed, be more than adequate to achieve the party's ultimate objective. Which was to bring destruction upon the slayers of Dangling-Foot`s people.

So it was the very next day as a winter sun sank slowly in the west, a formidable Crow force at last started out from the great village sited in the shadow of Pompey`s Pillar; looming large and evocable on the open Plain.

The chant of praise-songs for husbands, sons and sweethearts coupled with a reverberating tremolo, rang out high from the throats of the women-folk and other non-combatants, and this, mingled with the steady throb of war-drums and a high-pitched trill of eagle bone whistles, caused the whole Crow population to feel elated and confident of success.

Thus a long, multi-coloured column began snaking its way south, as these Crow warriors embarked upon the first leg of their merciless mission. A number of women and boys were included in the party, to help cook the warrior's meals and tend to the horses as was customary on such occasions. Although they would not be expected to get close enough to the enemy to be in danger.

The grand host travelled through that night and rested the following day. Scouts were then sent out to reconnoitre the surrounding countryside to the front and on the flanks, and in such a way utmost vigilance was employed. Sore-Belly who always rode at the head of the van, considered it imperative for the success of the venture that the Cheyennes did not have warning of their coming. If so, they would be sure to disperse and hide from such a large enemy force which could do them much damage. Truly, the Crows were determined that this time, the Striped-Arrow-People would pay dearly for their exultant scalp dances a few moons earlier.

Before sunset on its second day out, the column was off again. Now it headed specifically towards the Black Hills region, intending to visit the site where Dangling-Foot`s village had been destroyed.

After a cautious, slow, meandering march, the party at last came upon the battleground; still littered with the remains of their slaughtered kinfolk. The flesh had been picked and gnawed from the bones by beast and fowl, and withal, previously mutilated and abused by human hands so as to be unrecognizable even to a relative. Each skeleton lay pin-cushioned with arrows, the flights of which were of wild turkey and sage hen feathers which was a peculiarity of Cheyenne manufacture. Every skull had been smashed in; the limbs amputated, and all, of course, missing their scalps.

It was agreed among the Crows that the bones lying asunder, were all that was left of Dangling-Foot`s people [the Crows not knowing at this stage that survivors of the battle had taken refuge among the Kiowa]. They further discovered by lingering tell-tale signs that the Cheyenne band responsible belonged to the Suhtaio, and had not long fled the country, perhaps in fear of retribution.

However, upon the sight of the mutilated remains, the onlookers were again overcome with grief and great anguish. Outlandish oaths were retaken as old wounds, self-inflicted during the previous period of mourning, were savagely reopened, and it seemed that the guardian spirits of the Apsaalooka now cried with them over what they beheld. It is said that *Akbaa-tadia* then put the spirit of demons into their hearts, causing the Crows to again swear vengeance upon the perpetrators of the deed - or themselves to die in the attempt.

They gathered up the scattered bones and deposited them in large pits in the ground, which they then covered with earth and rocks as a safeguard against further despoilment from passing foes and animals, and when this was done the avenging host started forth again, this time in broad daylight with more vigour and resolve than before.

Having picked up an old trail leading south from the battlefield, the party continued in a southerly direction and followed the trail diligently. They hoped it would lead them to the specific Suhtaio band involved, and woe be to those people, as yet ignorant of their impending peril.

It was mid-January 1833, the tenth sleep after leaving the village on the Plain before Pompey`s Pillar, that the Crow war-party came at last into a snow-covered valley watered by the Arkansas. This was a long way indeed from their own Crow country in the north, and here they made camp. Again scouts were sent out, and these soon brought word that a Suhtaio village was in the vicinity near the place known as "Big Timbers." In those days, this was a notable landmark on the Southern Plains. It consisted of a stretch of cottonwoods bordering both sides of the Arkansas for a distance of nearly thirty miles, and about the same distance due east from where Bent's new trading post stood on the same river some twelve miles from the mouth of Purgatory Creek. [7]

Upon this intelligence, Sore-Belly sent out more scouts in order to ascertain the exact topography surrounding the village, and also, in order to observe any activity in the camp which might indicate whether or not the latter were aware of a Crow presence in the region. In due course the scouts returned with information that the Suhtaio appeared oblivious to the close presence of enemies. In response, Sore-Belly held a war-council with his leading chiefs and warriors to discuss their next move. And thus it was as the moon rose high in a star-sprinkled heaven, the great war-chief devised his plan of attack.

Meanwhile, within their temporary camp, the rank and file Crow warriors began preparing themselves and their war-ponies for imminent battle.

"`Chilia, kaashi-kaashi chilia` it is said, "Cold, much, much cold." [8] But notwithstanding, many striped to breech clout and moccasins so as to be free of restricting garments, and daubed either red, yellow, white or green pigment over their arms, legs and torsos. They streaked their faces with the same colours in hideous designs peculiar to their individual dreams and visions. Horse tails were cut short or tied up with brightly coloured ribbons in `bob` fashion, and eagle feathers tipped with red or yellow horse hair were entwined in manes and tails. At the same time, low eerie Crow war-chants and kill-songs began to drone monotonously through the still and fresh Arkansas night.

When at last the chiefs concluded their council, he who had been selected as camp herald, made it known that all the warriors should leave their excess baggage - and the few non-combatants who had accompanied the cavalcade so far - behind in the temporary war camp, while the warriors would start out at once for the enemy village so by traveling through the night, they might reach their objective come dawn.

The Suhtaio at this time were encamped between two heavily timbered creeks known as Horse Creek and Big Sandy Creek, both of which flowed north to south parallel to each other and into the north bank of the Arkansas. The village itself stood on a stretch of open grazing land between the two streams, and milling around at the southern end of the lodges was the Suhtaio pony herd. It was Sore-Belly's plan to send two separate parties of Crows along each creek from the south end of the village. These two parties would then drive the herd through the village to its north end and beyond, which action Sore-Belly anticipated, would bring forth the owners from their lodges and in pursuit of the thieves. The main body of Crows, meanwhile, would be positioned further north between the creeks, a large party led by Sore-Belly behind a ridge on one side of the open ground; a second party oposite behind a corresponding ridge and led by the great warrior Little-White-Bear, along with another then simply known as Blackfoot, but in later years, by the name of Sits-in-the-Middle-of-the-Land. Their forces would be obscured by timber bordering both creeks, and when the Crow decoys who first had stolen the enemy's herd raced along the open land between the creeks and flanking ridges, the Suhtaio in pursuit would be drawn into a trap executed by the two lines of hidden Crows.

Thus, early next morning, as the sun rose above the eastern horizon and lit up the strip of land where stood the Suhtaio village, nearly four-hundred Crow braves were already hidden some distance away, waiting with grim anticipation of their comrades bringing the Suhtaio to them. As they waited, some warriors calmly removed the fringed and beaded covers from their lance-points. Others strung bows and fitted an arrow to the string, while those with guns primed the powder pans of their fusees and waited patiently for the battle to commence.

There were warriors, no doubt, who knew too well that some among their own number would be going home this day to the Spirit World beyond after travelling the dark road of no return. But if this should be, then they were fully prepared to do so, and hoped to take as many of the enemy with them as possible.

And then it happened.

The two small parties of decoy Crows, comprising seven warriors in each group and having previously positioned themselves at the south end of the Suhtaio village, suddenly let out ear-splitting war-whoops and charged headlong into the Suhtaio pony herd. They shouted and sang at the tops of their voices and at the same time, waved and whirled blankets above their heads whilst others beat quirts on hide-covered shields, in all creating a terrifying din. All at once - neighing and kicking - the whole herd was aroused and began stampeding through the village towards its north end in a panic-stricken mass, churning up the snow and kicking up large clods of earth as they bolted.

Amid the confusion and commotion, the drowsy Suhtaio quickly summed up the situation as they believed it to be. Merely that the attack was nothing more than a daring dawn raid for horses by a small number of enemy opportunists.

Accordingly, eighty or more Suhtaio braves grabbed weapons and mounted ponies which having been tied securely to picket pins at the door-flaps of the lodges, had been prevented from joining the stampede. These Suhtaio immediately rode off in pursuit of the thieves followed by others on foot, all exultant in the thought of easily obtaining fourteen enemy scalps. Such was the Suhtaio naivety of the real seriousness of the raid that many of the men-folk remained within their tepees, content to let the younger warriors count the coups on this occasion, and thus outside the village the chase was on.

The Crows so not to be hampered, were soon obliged to abandon the stolen herd in order to elicit more speed, but still the Suhtaio continued in hot pursuit. However, as the chase went on, it seemed the Crow mounts were slackening speed due to the gruelling pace the pursuers set. But just when it looked as if the Suhtaio were gaining, sudden spurts of energy left the pursuers far behind. Once more the Suhtaio were gaining, and yet again the Crows pulled away from almost arm's reach, and try as they might, the enraged Suhtaio could not overtake their quarry. In such a manner the game was played and replayed, the Crows all the time drawing their enemies further from the village and in the direction of their painted and be-feathered Crow comrades.

As the chase progressed, the Suhtaio were led into a wide area of open ground flanked on either side by the tree-covered ridges, and all at once, those same ridges sprouted feathers as a host of Crows suddenly appeared atop each crest.

The fourteen Crow decoys then veered off in as many different directions, and the next instant, had vanished from sight of the pursuing Suhtaio. Too late the latter realized their blunder. They were caught in one of the oldest; but as to prove most effective traps of Indian strategy, and for a moment the two sides stared at each other - one with a look of triumph - the other with that of despair. A single Crow cry of *"Koo-Koo-Hey"* resounded from the throat of Little-White-Bear who sat his horse atop one of the ridges, and with it, the whole Crow force suddenly charged down the slopes on both sides of the Suhtaio.

The very ridge flanks seemed to move and the ground tremble and the Suhtaio for the present, could do no more but watch the cavalcade of colour, as four-hundred Crow ponies and riders thundered down the flanking slopes like raging human torrents. The Crows did not stop. They came on at breakneck speed careering into the midst of the Suhtaio who milled about on their ponies, looking desperately for a way out of the trap. Within minutes they found themselves completely surrounded.

The Suhtaio knew they were doomed, and could only prepare to sell their lives dearly in the advent of their complete annihilation. And so it was after only a short while, agonizing moans of dying braves resounded from among the Suhtaio ranks, as warrior after warrior was dropped from the saddle and lay twitching in death throes on the blood-soaked ground.

The Crows say today that their own warriors concentrated their movements in the manner of a circle, and continually rode around the Suhtaio, hurling arrows, lances and musket balls into the huddled bunch within. In such a way they wreaked a dreadful toll in both dead and wounded upon the enemy, and on their fifth or sixth circumference, the Crows finally reined in their mounts and turned to face those of the enemy still standing. They then threw themselves at them and in one swoop knocked the remaining Suhtaio to the ground and rode them under hoof. It was said by Crow veterans of the fight that when the Crows looked back over their shoulders, not one Suhtaio had been left alive. All had felt

286

the under-estimated might of Crow ferocity, and were well on their way to the Spirit Land of their ancestors.

The bordering creeks ran red with blood; many *dakshey* had been counted, and at least eighty bloody Suhtaio topknots dangled from Apsaalooka waist belts.

By this time, those Suhtaio who had preferred to remain in the village had heard the din of battle, and now came racing to the scene; some on horseback and many on foot. Their additional numbers, however, were still no match for the Crows and many met the same fate as their already prostrate comrades. The Suhtaio expediently soon gave up the fight, their depleted force turning around and racing back to the village in order to protect their women and children. But the exultant blood-crazed Crows harried them all the way, cutting down the stragglers as they went, and soon the Crows reached the village itself. Without hesitation they rode right in amongst the lodges, striking and killing every Suhtaio warrior they could lay hands on, and every woman and child who offered the slightest resistance to their wrath. Today, Crow oral tradition accredits the then aspiring Kicked-in-the-Belly Crow warrior later known as Spotted-Horse, as having been particularly conspicuous during this part of the fight, counting many *dakshey* and taking at least seven female Suhtaio captives in the event. [9]

Indeed, it is also said by the Crows that for the most part, the Suhtaio women and children could only watch helpless as their men-folk were slaughtered and their bodies mutilated before their eyes. Much of the Suhtaio incentive to continue the fight had been quickly lost and their defence turned into a rout.

A number of the village non-combatants managed to flee including a small group of men-folk, although a significant number of Suhtaio warriors did stay by the women and children, valiantly; but vainly, resisting the Crow's mad onslaught. At length, they were either shot down or in some other way killed where they stood. Some few others actually left the line of retreat and bravely returned to throw themselves into the thick of the blood-bath still raging, merely in the hope of preventing a direct pursuit of those fleeing the scene, knowing, of course, they would never again look upon the faces of those they were endeavouring to save, least ways, not in this world. No quarter was asked, or given. The Suhtaio had done the same when they had wiped out the village of Dangling-Foot.

It was not long before noon when the fighting finally ceased. Perhaps the fleeing Suhtaio did not stop to look behind them. If they did, they would have seen the glowing flames of their lodges which the Crows put to the torch, and heard the piercing screams and wailing of their womenfolk and children then captives among the victors as they lamented their fate. The Suhtaio had taken a whipping not to heal for many a year, as long as intertribal warfare blighted the Plains. Too well the Suhtaio had paid the price for their earlier victory, and the philosophy of the Indian – death for death and blood for blood - had been exacted in full.

The victorious Crows claimed as booty hundreds of Suhtaio ponies along with warrior equipment in weapons and shields, and had looted the domestic paraphernalia of the camp before setting the tepees ablaze. According to the trader, Edwin Denig, the Crows killed over one-hundred of the enemy in total, and took around two-hundred and fifty women and children into captivity, while the Crows themselves, he added, lost only five warriors killed and between ten and fifteen wounded.

Whatever the real number of enemy killed and of captives taken, the Crows then returned to their temporary base camp in a jubilant manner. They were filled with confidence regarding their own warrior prowess, due alone; they thought, to their indomitable Chief Sore-Belly and his omnipotent all-protective *medicine.*

Of the Suhtaio including men, women and children who survived the attack by escaping from the village, they waited until late in the afternoon when they were sure the enemy had left the region. Only then did they come out from hiding and return to the site where once stood their camp. An old man among them walked around the ruined scene calling to the remnants of the people, and continued calling until, it was thought, all the survivors were assembled together. The Cheyennes at a later date [1930s], told Stanley Vestal that the people then had no horses to ride and that all their food, bedding and tents had been destroyed. Some of the survivors were almost naked, not having had time to dress before fleeing the camp. The weather was very cold, it being in the depth of winter. But notwithstanding, they started out on foot, and enduring much hardship, they travelled in a northwest direction towards the South Platte, hoping to find others of their Nation who would take them in. [10]

Thus was the result of Sore-Belly's grand revenge expedition, which only served to add further to the great war-chief's fame in the Upper Missouri region.

## SMALLPOX AMONG THE LODGES.

It was no doubt, a number of warriors from the same grand war-party against the Suhtaio, who, during their return journey to the Yellowstone in late January 1833, broke away from the main group, and stole a number of horses belonging to Gantt and Blackwell's newly-erected trading post on the Arkansas, about one-hundred miles west of Big Timbers. [11]

The famous trapper and frontiersman Christopher [Kit] Carson had been in charge of the horses. With eleven companions, among whom were two Cheyennes visiting the post at that time, Carson set out on horseback after the thieves. There was much snow on the ground; the weather bitterly cold, and after a gruelling trek north some forty miles or so, the pursuers at last caught up with the thieves. These were about sixty in number ensconced in two separate war-lodges. Obviously the Crows had decided that the weather was too severe for the owners of the stolen horses to follow.

Disregarding the disparity in numbers, Carson was determined to attack. To this end he directed the two Cheyennes to run off the Indian's horses, while he and his companions left their own horses tied to trees some distance in their rear, and took up positions from where they could fire upon the Crows when they emerged from their war-lodges to see what was happening. The two Cheyennes successfully carried out their mission and when the Crows appeared as anticipated, the white men opened fire. Several Crows were wounded, but when they realized it was only a small party to contend with, they charged the trapper's position but were repulsed by a sustained fire directed at them. The Crows retreated, fleeing in several directions, and Carson's party retrieved all their stolen horses. The white men could be sure at least of two dead Crows, although of several others who had been wounded, some may have died later from their injuries.

Earlier, however, whilst residing at the Gantt and Blackwell post during the summer months of 1832, Carson among others; although later cured, had contracted smallpox. The disease was then prevalent also among William Bent's Mexican labourers lower down the Arkansas at the latter's new adobe fort still in the process of being built. It may then, have been from infected blankets on the horses stolen from Carson's men how some among Sore-Belly's victorious warriors afterwards contracted the disease, although it was then raging all over the Southern and Central Plains. Whatever the case, by the time Sore-Belly's war band returned to the Yellowstone, the contagion had already passed to the rest of the Crows. It quickly took a firm hold and spread rapidly among the people. At that time, it is said, most of the Crow Nation was encamped on Alkali Creek not far from where the town of Billings, Montana, now stands. Many children and teenagers among the Crows died, not having built up an immunity during the outbreaks of earlier years. Thus instead of celebrations, which in other circumstances would have followed Sore-Belly's triumphant return, there was only sorrow and grief before the contagion eventually burned itself out.

The indomitable Crow warriors Plays-with-his-Face and his brother Two-Face, met their demise at this time. Plays-With-His-Face had contracted the disease but survived along with his mother and his brother Two-Face. A new wife of Plays-With-His-Face named Blue-Bird-Woman, however, succumbed and with her died whatever other relatives Plays-With-His-Face and his brother had left. Because of their own now pitted and scarred disfigurements due to the contagion, and in their earnest beseeching to the Great Spirit to preserve the remainder of their people, both Plays-With-His-Face and Two-Face vowed to sacrifice their lives to show the sincerity of their pleadings. And so it was that they blindfolded their horses and then themselves, and without further hesitation, rode their horses off the great sandstone bluff towering above the Yellowstone River in the vicinity of Metra Park of present-day Billings. Both horses and riders went crashing to their deaths on the rocks below and ever since that time, the site in question has been known among the Crows as "Suicide Bluff," and alternatively as "The Place of Skulls." [12]

By the time the contagion finally ran its course, of the previous nine-hundred Crow lodges and more, only one third remained.

Conversely, the trader Edwin Denig reported from hearsay that of eight-hundred Crow lodges prior to this particular outbreak, in its aftermath only three-hundred and sixty remained, and further stated that no more than one in six or seven persons among the Crows actually survived. This, of course, is a preposterous count, although Crow numbers as previously mentioned, were certainly significantly reduced. Of the Kicked-in-the-Belly band, their earlier number of one-hundred and fifty lodges was reduced to seventy and hereafter, the Kicked-in-the-Bellies moved west into the Pryor Creek district in order to be nearer their Mountain Crow brethren, and to put distance between themselves and their enemies whilst they recuperated from their ordeal. In the main, though, it was the children and young adults who suffered worst, and Denig was probably also in error when he blamed white emigrants for transmitting the disease among the Crows – albeit unintentionally – when, most likely, it came from Crow contact with Sore-Belly's victorious party, members of which had been in contact with white trappers and Indians in the southern country. Only rarely if ever did white emigrants choose to travel during the winter months.

This being said, the Crows later blamed Robert Campbell and William Sublette for their decimation, by accusing them of leaving a mule with an infected pack in Crow country late in '32. But this also is unlikely, and both Campbell and Sublette vehemently denied any such inference.

- 0 - 0 – 0 – 0 – 0 – 0 – 0 – 0 – 0 – 0 – 0 – 0 – 0 -

## CHAPTER 25.

## THE PIKUNI PEACE IS BROKEN.

Notwithstanding the destruction of Dangling-Foot's village and smallpox among the lodges, the Crow people suffered yet another disaster in early spring, 1833, before the last of the snows melted. The consequence of this event proved a significant factor, which Sore-Belly foresaw as likely to threaten the eventual extermination of the entire Apsaalooka Nation. Such was brought about, however, by a most treacherous act perpetrated by some Crow tribal members themselves. [1]

Peace-making with the Pikuni at Warm Spring Creek in 1832, although still in effect one year later, was not proving satisfactory as far as the Crows were concerned. While it is true that Pikuni bands as a whole had kept their part of the bargain, their Blood and Siksika relatives had continued to harass Crows on every occasion. Sometimes they assaulted the latter's villages, but moreover, it was their constant stealing of Crow horses and taking a scalp or two when the opportunity arose. There had also been occasions when small groups and individual warriors from among the Pikuni had acted in concert with the war-bands of their relatives, a fact which had not gone entirely unnoticed by the Crows. Oft-times, they had recognized noted Pikuni warriors among their assailant's ranks.

Be this as it may, the cumbersome loss of population attending the Crows due to the continuing contagion, caused Sore-Belly to advise restraint among his warriors and for a period, at least, to desist from reciprocating in rash ventures against their enemies. Instead, he induced them to shore up their tottering pact with the Pikuni, before matters got out of hand and again erupted into all-out war between their peoples. To this end, he held council with all the nation's subordinate chiefs in order to decide how best this should be done.

After a period of much deliberation, it was decided that a delegation should go into Pikuni country, and inform that people that they and the Crows should again meet together at a certain place to be determined, and renew the fragile pact between them. A renowned Crow war-chief named Bird-Comes-Back, along with another whose name is not remembered, were selected to head the proposed emissaries numbering more than fifty warriors in total.

One party member was himself a Sarsi, who had been taken captive by the Crows several years earlier. He it was who would act as interpreter, as he could speak Blackfoot and had also learned the Crow language to a tolerable extent. And so it was in early April, *"The Moon when buffalo and horses fill out,"* that the Crow ambassadors after receiving blessings from the holy men of the village along with words of good fortune from Sore-Belly himself, finally set out from their camp at the head of Lodge Grass Creek near the Big Horn Mountains. The party went *Awala-diile,* although they had a number of fine pack ponies in tow loaded with gifts. These last comprised feathered ornaments, weapons, and various richly decorated items of clothing, all of which they intended to present to their Pikuni hosts as tokens of good will. Being on a mission of peace, the leaders each carried a long-stemmed red-stone pipe which all tribes respected, for such were regarded as sacred objects and even enemies if encountered, would be obliged to receive the bearers in friendship once such a pipe had been offered to them.

Thus with the two leaders at their head, each carrying a pipe in the crook of his left arm, while Bird-Comes-Back in addition, bore a red-painted shield on his back with pendent eagle feathers attached to its rim and held in place by a wolf-fur strap straddling his chest, the Crow ambassadors travelled north to the mouth of the Big Horn. Thereupon they crossed the connecting Yellowstone River, and continued north towards the Musselshell.

At this same time, the several Pikuni bands were only just starting to move into their customary summer locations. Usually they spent the winter months in the Three Forks district of the Upper Missouri, but this winter of 1832-.'33, they had spent most of that season travelling to and from the Hudson's Bay trading post Chesterfield House far northeast on the lower Saskatchewan above the International border. They had only recently started south, and so were some way from their summer camping grounds along the Marias, Teton and Sun rivers of northern Montana.

The Crow peace party was unaware of this. As a consequence, they continued at a moderate pace ever northwards. Upon reaching the Missouri across from the mouth of the Marias, they crossed to the north bank on rafts fashioned from brush and hides, then moved west to the Teton and followed that river's course upstream, hoping to locate their quarry.

They were surprised not to find the Pikuni where they thought they should be, and so spent some time searching the surrounding region looking for sign of the latter's whereabouts. They often took time out to hunt and being in no particular hurry, they were wandering around on foot, inspecting the country at their leisure. It began to snow, and it was at this point that the Crows divided their force into several small parties. These comprised from four, six, eight and more warriors in each group, which fanned out over the prairie in different directions looking for game and any sign of the Pikuni.

One of these small groups comprising six warriors and among whom were included two brothers, by chance came upon four horseback Pikuni traveling leisurely over the prairie with a spare horse in tow. One among these six Crows had with him his own long-stemmed pipe, although this was not regarded in the same high degree as were the red-stone ceremonial pipes carried by the Crow Pipe-holders who were then with another of the separate Crow groups. This man took his pipe from its hide covering, and holding it in his left hand before his chest, advanced boldly towards the strangers, who in turn, calmly sat their ponies waiting to see what would happen next.

As the lone Crow came close, he used sign-talk with his right hand to greet his erstwhile enemies and suggested they smoke the proffered pipe together. The rest of this small Crow group soon after came up, and the four Pikuni supposing these the only Crows in the vicinity, dismounted, and all sat down on the grass facing each other in a circle. The Crow with the pipe charged it with tobacco; lit it with the aid of a white man's tinder box and after drawing four puffs from the stem, he handed it to the Pikuni leader. This man proved to be a noted Pikuni chief named Big-Snake, [the first of that name], who with his three companions had, in fact, been recent members of a much larger Pikuni war-party that had gone to raid Flatheads west of the Rocky Mountains.

For some reason the Pikuni war-party had divided its force, and these four warriors now sitting down with the six Crows, had been in the process of returning to their home camp on their own. Big-Snake, although his people ostensibly, were already at peace with the Crows, was at first apprehensive regarding the sincerity of the latter, but not to show fear, he did accept the pipe and inhaled its smoke four times. After this the Pikuni felt more relaxed, for having smoked the pipe not even enemies, it was thought, would dare defile its sacred bond by soiling the ground with blood. One among the Pikuni then presented the Crow pipe-bearer the spare horse as a gift, whilst another presented a second Crow his gun, both as tokens of their newly made pact and goodwill towards each other. The two parties thereafter, talked among themselves with the aid of signs, and upon learning that the Crows were looking for a Pikuni camp in order to deliver their message for renewing the peace between their tribes, the four Pikuni offered to ride along with the Crows and show them the way.

So they travelled on in the ilk of new found friends, the Pikuni horseback; the Crows on foot, sign-talking and laughing together in what appeared to be perfect harmony. The two Crow brothers, though, had other ideas.

Now it had happened a month or two earlier, after a number of Blood Blackfoot had visited the River Crow village in order to trade and visit relatives taken captive by Crows in past battles, that the same Blood party after starting their return journey north, had killed two Crows and stolen a number of horses from the Crow village for good measure. The two killed had been close relatives of the Crow brothers now ambling along with Big-Snake and his companions, and the brothers had earlier taken a vow that they would avenge their kinsmen upon the next Blackfoot-speaking people they should meet, never mind if the latter's particular band affiliation made them innocent of the crime or not. These four Pikuni, unsuspecting as they were, thus appeared convenient persons upon whom Crow vengeance could be exacted.

The rest of the Crows in this small group must have been agreeable to the brothers' designs, for while passing through a narrow gorge in a rocky outcrop, all the Crows suddenly attacked their Pikuni companions with flaying war-clubs, and bludgeoned them to death. They each then counted *dakshey* on the bodies and took the scalps as trophies of their treacherous deed. One account adds that the Crows buried a beautiful quill-embroidered robe which the Pikuni Big-Snake had been wearing, with the intent of retrieving it on his return journey home. They also slaughtered the Pikuni horses, and hid the animal carcasses along with the human corpses under piles of leaves and sagebrush which they then covered with snow, in order to conceal them from any Blackfoot party that might happen to pass that way.

The Crows then returned to their main body, the bloody scalps stuffed in their bullet pouches, but told no one else what they had done.

Soon after this, the whole Crow party of emissaries having again come together, continued on its way, and the following morning they spied two more Pikuni - a father and son it transpired - mounted on running horses. These two Pikuni were merely out hunting buffalo on the open prairie between Brown Butte and Square Butte, not far from where Fort Shaw later stood in the Sun River valley about twenty miles north of the Missouri.

The whole Crow party had stopped in its tracks, but the Sarsi Blackfoot-speaking captive among them walked a few paces off to one side of his companions, and called aloud to the Pikuni while supplementing his words with signs,

"Come join us, let us smoke together. Our hearts are good. Let us be at peace with one another." [2]

At first the two Pikuni were hesitant to comply, but again the man called to them saying,

"Come join us; we are Crows; let us be friends and smoke together." [3]

There were more than fifty Crows and only two Pikuni. But thinking that the man in Crow attire must be one of their own kin by his command of the Blackfoot language, the latter decided to accept the offer of friendship, and rode over to meet them.

This Pikuni man was, in fact, a bold and well-known fighter named Spotted-Elk [later known as Bear-Chief], while his ten year old son riding alongside, was famed at a later date also by the name of Bear-Chief and even later by the name Three-Suns. His father Spotted-Elk was then around thirty-nine years old and a leading war-chief among the Grease-Melters Pikuni band.

Spotted-Elk and the Crow leader Bird-Comes-Back - who the Pikuni later referred to as Red-Shield [or Painted-Shield] because of such an item he was carrying - sat down together on a buffalo robe placed upon a dry patch of prairie hastily cleared of snow, and smoked a pipe together. After this formality they talked on various topics, employing the Sarsi captive among the Crows to interpret between them. Bird-Comes-Back then explained his peaceful intentions, whereupon the Pikuni Spotted-Elk agreed to lead the Crows to the nearest camp of his people on the Marias, and so saying, the two Pikuni remounted their ponies and riding ahead of the Crows who followed on foot, set out in that direction.

At length, the combined party reached the Pikuni camp situated on a beautiful stretch of open grassland close to the Marias River. It was a small village consisting of around forty lodges whose head man was a Pikuni chief named Eagle-Flag. Upon the Crows` arrival at the camp, Eagle-Flag went out to meet them and to welcome them in friendship. All the villagers milled around eager to get a glimpse of their erstwhile foes, who now came walking brazenly into their midst. But there was no sign of hostility and in accordance with Indian protocol when visitors came in peace, the Crows were feasted and regaled by their hosts. Two large lodges were made available for their convenience, one of which belonged to Eagle-Flag himself, the other to his son. The sacred red-stone pipe was then passed around and smoked, and all the chiefs and important men of the Pikuni camp, along with everyone else present, appeared to be at ease with the fifty and more Crows and joyous of the occasion.

The Crows were next ushered inside a large tepee known variously as the "Rattle" or "Rattling Lodge," the owner of which, sat at the back of the lodge and bade Bird-Comes-Back to sit left of him, and the other Crow chief to sit on his right. The lodge owner then took up his pipe. He lit it with a burning ember, drew four puffs from the stem then shook a rattle four times. The pipe thereafter was presented to Bird-Comes-Back and to the latter`s fellow pipe-holder with a request to smoke, and likewise in turn, to every Crow warrior in the tepee. The Crows complied with the request, but insisted that after each had puffed on the stem, the rattle should be shook four times as the owner of the lodge himself had done. Such was contrary to the rules attending this particular ceremony among the Pikuni, who viewed the Crows` actions with disdain, but the Crows were suspicious of the significance of the rite and requested exactly what the Pikuni pipe owner himself had done; so that what might befall the owner – good or bad – would be no different for the Crows. It was only when the ceremony drew to a close that a more congenial atmosphere again settled over the gathering.

If the two Crow chiefs broached their message at this point, suggesting the proposed peace gathering of their two tribes, then they did not as yet receive a reply. It was considered good manners among Indians not to hurry matters, but to leave all important issues to a more appropriate time, after, that is, the customary formalities of welcome and general exchange of news and gossip had been concluded.

As twilight descended, and after a period of dancing and singing within the camp in celebration of the Crow visitors, the latter in two groups, took their repose for the night in the lodges set aside for their use.

However, during the night whilst the Crows were deep in slumber, a Pikuni woman crept into one of the lodges, and set about rummaging among the belongings of the Crows in the hope of finding something of value to steal. This, of course, was not unusual practice among Plains Tribes, and if the thief managed to get away without being discovered, it would have been considered acceptable, and actually warrant a degree of envy from one's peers.

By chance, this woman happened to open the bullet pouch of one of the Crow brothers, and discovered a freshly-taken scalp hidden therein. Pulling it from the bag, to her horror she immediately recognized it as belonging to someone she had known. It consisted of the skin and hair from the right side of the head attached to a long, grey, braid, its end wrapped with otter fur while attached to the head piece itself, was a conspicuous dantalium shell pieced with seven holes representing the star constellation known among the Blackfoot as the "Seven Persons" [i.e., the Big Dipper]. [4] This, she knew, had been the personal *medicine* emblem of Chief Big-Snake, who along with three companions had not returned from the war-path. The woman had no doubt that this same party of Crows must have met the absentees whilst the latter had been returning home to the Pikuni camp, and had killed them all.

Quietly leaving the lodge, the woman at once carried the scalp to the war-chief Spotted-Elk and showed it to him, and who in turn, showed it to the camp's head chief Eagle-Flag.

Eagle-Flag was livid that he should have been so trusting of the Crows. He at once ordered a number of warriors to go out and back-track on the Crow trail before they had met with Spotted-Elk, in order to see if they could discover any sign of Big-Snake's resting place and to ascertain the manner of his death. This the warriors did, and as the tracks were now frozen hard in the snow, the trail was easy to pick up and follow. Thus it was not long before the searchers discovered the carcasses of both men and horses and, of course, the quill-embroidered robe of Big-Snake buried under brush topped with a thin layer of snow. Hurriedly, they took word of their findings back to the Pikuni camp, whereupon, seeing the quilled robe in front of him, Spotted-Elk was at first of a mind to wipe out the whole party of Crows there and then for their evil deed. Spotted-Elk, though, was a sensible man. He realized that it was really too dark to act at present, as some of the enemy would be sure to escape and furthermore, he considered the fact that the Pikuni and Crows had smoked the sacred calumet together. It would not be proper, therefore, to shed Crow blood within the camp, as that would violate the sanctity of the pipe and bring the odour of disrepute upon Pikuni hospitality. Instead he went silently around the village, visiting one lodge after another, telling the head warriors to gather in his large tepee in order to discuss the matter of the scalp, and what should be done about it.

When all the important Pikuni had gathered in the lodge of Spotted-Elk, the question was deliberated upon in earnest. Some of those present were of the opinion that Big-Snake may have brought his demise upon himself, whilst others said they should kill all the visitors anyway and have done with it. The ultimate decision, however, to which all finally agreed, was that they would wait until morning, then confront the Crows with the scalp and robe and hear their explanation before deciding whether to kill them or not.

In the meantime, a messenger was immediately dispatched to the Small Robe village then on the north bank of the Missouri, with a request that the latter's great chief, Big-Lake, should bring a large party to the aid of Eagle-Flag's much smaller camp. It is also said that Spotted-Elk ordered that the Pikuni womenfolk, if they had the opportunity to do so, should spike the firearms of the Crows as they lay sleeping, by inserting small twigs in the touch holes of the gun locks, so that when the triggers were pulled, the spark from the flash pan would not enter the barrel and the weapons would misfire.

Whatever the case, come morning the Crows awoke to find eighty and more Pikuni warriors; some mounted, others on foot, but all painted and armed, milling around outside their two lodges as if to give instant battle. Most of the Crows must have been a little unnerved to say the least, as all but few of their number had any idea why the attitude of their hosts should have changed so suddenly from that of the previous day.

It was not long before Spotted-Elk summoned the Crows to an even larger council lodge which had been fashioned from the skins of two tepees. There within, Spotted-Elk, being the band's leading war-chief, sat at the back of the lodge, his headmen and important warriors sitting on either side around the tepee wall.

The Crows could do naught but obey. When they entered the lodge, they were told to sit down in a body surrounded by the Pikuni chiefs and warriors. According to Father DeSmet's account, the Pikuni Chief Spotted-Elk then stood up and addressed the Crows as follows,

> "Strangers, only yesterday you arrived in our camp. We listened to your message. Your words and propositions seemed reasonable and advantageous. All our lodges have been open to you; you have shared in our feasts and hospitality. But, before discoursing further, I have a question to ask you. Crows! On this I must have an answer; and that answer will decide whether a lasting peace be possible between us, or whether a war of destruction must continue." [5]

Spotted-Elk then showed the Crows the Pikuni scalp and continued,
"Tell me Crows, whose hair is this? Who among you claims this trophy?" [6]

None of the Crows replied and most looked askance at one another; bewildered at the appearance of the scalp. The Pikuni war-chief then summoned the woman to his side, and bade her point out the man from whose bullet pouch she had taken the scalp. The woman complied with the request, and no sooner had she done so, when one of the Crow brothers suddenly leapt to his feet and took his stand beside Spotted-Elk. This Crow had a defiant air about him, and he addressed the Pikuni chiefs and warriors, saying in his defence,

> "You Pikuni, I fear you not! It is I who took the scalp! If I endeavoured to conceal it, I did so with the desire of doing more evil! You ask me whose hair this is. Look at the hair fringes on your shirt and on your leggings. In my turn, I ask, whose hair is that? Belong it not to my two brothers slain by thee or thine hardly two moons ago? Or belongs it not to the relations of some Crow here present? 'Tis vengeance brings me here! My brother holds in his shot-bag the companion of this scalp. We determined before leaving

the camp to cast into your faces these bloody tufts as a challenge of defiance." [7]

If the gist of these words as rendered by DeSmet were truly spoken by the accused, then we might take it that this man fully realized the consequences of having been found out. Thus he knew full well that the lives of he and his companions would be forfeit, and had attempted to put a brave face on the situation. Such was not an uncommon occurrence among Indians when they knew their own deaths were likely imminent.

The Crow`s reply had been brave talk, and the Pikuni always respected a brave man. In response the Pikuni war-chief congratulated the Crow on his admission of guilt. He then went on to explain that having previously smoked the pipe together, no blood should be spilt on the ground where now they stood. Instead, Spotted-Elk first told the Crows that a host of warriors from Big-Lake`s camp on the Missouri not far distant, was already on its way to assist his own braves, and seeing the look of despair on nearly every Crow face, he commanded that the whole body of Crows accompany him outside the lodge, after which he pointed to a certain hill some distance south of the camp and said,

"See Crows, the hill before you!. It is in the way that leads to your own country. As far as that hill, we Pikuni allow you to go unmolested. You may take your weapons with you, for as soon as you reach that hill, I and my warriors will pursue you until your scalps dangle on our waist-belts." [8]

The Crows were well conversant with this Blackfoot custom, which was regarded as a game among that people. But the Crows knew it would be a race for life or death to those being pursued. The Crows, though, in order to show their courage, casually accepted the offer, albeit a very slim chance for their survival.

The weather by then was turning decidedly colder, but at once, the Crows began striping down to breech-clouts and moccasins to enable themselves to run more freely. They discarded their robes and buckskin leggings which would have protected them from the bitter cold and from the rough underbrush and prickly pears strewing the prairie over which they would be obliged to travel, and when the Pikuni chief deemed they were ready, he cried aloud, *"Now run Crows, run! - save yourselves if you can."* [9]

At first the Crows merely walked across the open prairie towards the designated hill, obviously to conserve their stamina for when the chase proper began. The Pikuni meanwhile, numbering some three-hundred and more persons including all the Pikuni men, women and children, watched them go, and waited impatiently for the Crows to reach the hill, at which point the Pikuni warriors themselves would tear after them, and play their game of death.

After ten minutes or more, which to the Pikuni seemed much longer, a great howl arose from their three-hundred throats. This was the exact moment that the Crows reached the hill, and at least eighty Pikuni warriors - some on horseback, many on foot - set their steeds and limbs in motion and sped across the prairie in pursuit of their prey.

The Crows had started running as soon as they reached the hill, although they knew they had little real hope of escape. They were not likely to outrun the mounted Pikuni warriors, even if they succeeded against those on foot. But still they ran as fast as they were able. At the same time they were looking constantly around, hoping to find a suitable place from where they could make a stand and sell their lives dearly in the event.

Now in that part of the country between where Fort Shaw later stood and the Great Falls region of the Missouri, there are numerous shallow ravines or coulees running in various directions across the grasslands. And so it was that as the Crows ran on, they at last spied a small coulee cutting across the prairie floor on the north side of what the Pikuni knew as "Point of Rocks River," but today known as Sun River, a small tributary of the Marias. The Crows all at once headed towards it, deeming it an appropriate place from which to defend themselves.

At this stage the Pikuni pursuers were still far behind, and by the time they reached the hill from where the Crows had started to run, the latter had already concealed themselves behind the low walls of the coulee and were nowhere to be seen. The grass about the hill was starting sharply, and the Crow trail at this point had already disappeared. Subsequently, Spotted-Elk dispatched scouts to run across the prairie in several directions in order to pick up the trail further on, before it, too, was lost completely. Two of these scouts named White-Wolf and Cut-Ear did finally pick up the trail and saw that it led to the coulee wherein the Crows lay crouched, hiding themselves from view. Taking word of their find to their main body, the Pikuni horde immediately raced off in that direction, whooping and yelling as they went.

It was not long before the Pikuni came to the coulee, whereupon the Crows knowing themselves to be discovered, raised their heads above its lip and shouted to their foes,

"Come Pikuni, we have been waiting for you and are ready to fight!" [10]

The Pikuni were overeager to get to grips with their quarry. All at once some on horseback made a headlong charge at the Crow position. They intended to dislodge the defenders and drive them onto the open prairie, where the rest of the horseback Pikuni could run them down with ease.

Apparently, the Pikuni womenfolk could not have been very successful the night before if they had attempted to spike the Crow guns, for the Crows still had a good number of workable firearms and bows and arrows between them, and with these they opened a desultory fire of musket balls and arrows upon their attackers. Again according to DeSmet, this had the effect of dropping eighty Pikuni warriors, although the true number was more likely eight, if indeed, quite as many as that. But whatever the exact number of casualties, the Crow response did cause the charge to break. The Pikuni were forced to disperse in some disorder out of gunshot range a significant distance from the coulee.

Those of the Pikuni who had made the initial assault had all been mounted, and only after their ignominious retreat did the rest of their force on foot eventually reach the scene. The Pikuni then changed their tactics and began creeping forward under the cover of thick brush and prairie grass which mostly obscured them from view. Now and then, a Pikuni would stand up and show himself whilst taking aim with a trade musket at one or another Crow head appearing momentarily above the lip of the coulee. But too often did a Crow get off a shot before his adversary could do so, and in such a way, the Crows prevented any real damage being inflicted upon their own number. Some among the Pikuni would occasionally make a lone dash toward the position, in an endeavour to count coup by striking one of the defenders, or even the lip of the coulee itself with either gun barrel, lance, or a peeled willow stick sporting a single eagle feather attached to its striking end, although many warriors attempting to do so, were dropped by Crow musket balls before they actually reached their objective. However, one or two Pikuni did succeed in reaching the coulee to engage themselves in hand to hand struggles with one or more of the defenders, before being killed or making their escape back to the Pikuni lines.

The Crows, it seemed, had selected a strong position which was proving almost unassailable to the enemy. All the time, that is, the Crows had an adequate supply of powder and ball to recharge their guns and an ample supply of arrows for their bows. Thus for several hours the siege continued, and for all the efforts of the Pikuni they could not overrun the Crow position, or dislodge them from it.

A good number of Pikuni had either been killed or seriously wounded, whilst the Crows, as far as the besiegers could determine, had not yet lost a man.

It was then that Pikuni reinforcements from Big-Lake`s Small-Robe band arrived on the scene, and the fight took on a more serious aspect. Big-Lake himself took sole command of the situation. Calling his warriors around him, he suggested that all should shoot their guns and arrows at the same time towards the enemy. This action, he said, would keep the Crows crouching at the bottom of the coulee to avoid the barrage of missiles directed against them. Then, he continued, with himself at their head, they should charge the position on foot and by sheer weight of numbers, overwhelm the defenders and finish them off with knives and war-clubs.

The Pikuni warriors agreed, and a few moments later, a thick barrage of musket balls and arrows showered the defenders from all angles. Even before the barrage had ceased, the Pikuni, Chief Big-Lake himself let out his wild war-whoop and bounded forward, whereupon a host of Pikuni warriors followed in his footsteps. The chargers did not break their stride and before the luckless Crows really knew what was happening, scores of the enemy were jumping into the narrow defile and flaying about them with knives and war-clubs; slashing and stabbing; hacking and bludgeoning, until the Crows were slaughtered one and all.

It was said among the Pikuni that so successful was their ruse in keeping the Crow heads pinned down to avoid the initial barrage, that in this last bloody phase of the fight, not one Pikuni was killed or even wounded. The Pikuni account further states that those of the Crows not killed outright but severely wounded, very soon froze to death in the cold. Indeed, by then the cold had become so intense, that after scalping all the dead Crows, the victors lifted the stiff frozen bodies from where they lay and in their morbid humour, propped them up in standing positions along one side of the coulee. Spotted-Elk, the Pikuni war-chief, then gave his ten year old son a slender willow stick, and bade him touch each one of the frozen Crow corpses in the act of counting coup. Spotted-Elk for his part in the affair received much acclaim. He was accredited with having been instrumental in capturing the Crow party by having brought them to the Pikuni camp in the first place. Subsequently this man changed his name from Spotted-Elk to Bear-Chief, but for a while after the slaughter of the Crows recounted above, he had also been known simply as Crow-Chief.

The victorious warriors collected up the Crow's discarded guns and other paraphernalia as booty, including the latter's bullet pouches and bandoliers, and also carried away the red-painted shield of the Crow leader Bird-Comes-Back as a much sought after trophy. They then retired jubilantly to their camp, whereat they paraded around the lodges chanting their victory songs and waving the bloodied hanks of hair taken from fifty and more Crow heads, triumphantly in the air.

The Pikuni women then went out to inspect the scene of conflict; some with travois upon which to carry home the corpses of their own dead. A few days later, others seeking vengeance, also went out, but this time to mutilate the Crow bodies with their butcher knives, and this they did by dismembering the hands, feet and heads from their still propped-up lifeless foes. They even cut into small pieces what remained of the Crow torsos and scattered them far and wide over the prairie. This was done so that the body parts could not all be gathered up by the relatives, when and if a Crow party came later to visit the site and retrieve the remains of their kinfolk. A quantity of the dismembered limbs the Pikuni women did carry to their camp as grisly mementoes of the event, and these were attached to their husband's lance points or to long willow wands to be sung and danced over during the victory celebrations held for many a week thereafter.

That coming summer during their Sun-Dance ceremony, the Pikuni and Small-Robes offered up thanks to the Great Spirit for their victory, and since that time the annihilation of the Crow peace party has ever since been known among all Blackfoot tribes, as, "The Sun-Dance Massacre."

It was several moons later before Sore-Belly and the rest of the Crows learned the fate of Bird-Comes-Back and his delegates of peace. News of the disaster was eventually sent by runner from the American Fur Company trader David D. Mitchell at the newly built Fort Piegan at the mouth of the Teton, to its sister post Fort Cass on the Yellowstone near the mouth of the Big Horn. From there it was relayed to the Crows when a small party of the tribe appeared a few days later at Fort Cass on a trading expedition.

The news must have come as a great blow to Sore-Belly, as he, perhaps more than anyone else among the Apsaalooka, knew that peace with the Pikuni was now irretrievably lost. Again there would be total war between his people and the entire Blackfoot confederacy; a situation which could only invite disaster for the Crows. And true it was that a war of attrition did hereafter commence between the Crows and each of the Blackfoot-speaking tribes, which endured unabated [but for two short periods of peace] for another fifty-five blood-drenched years. At the same time, Lakota, Suhtaio and Arapaho attacks upon Crow hunting parties and villages began increasing at an alarming rate, and the resulting death toll among Crow warriors, eventually caused them to ponder upon their own imminent extinction as a separate tribal entity.

- 0 - 0 – 0 – 0 – 0 – 0 – 0 – 0 – 0 – 0 – 0 – 0 – 0 – 0 - 0 –

## CHAPTER 26

## SHOSHONIES, TRAPPERS AND A PRINCE.

Even before Sore-Belly had received word of the slaughter of Bird-Comes-Back and his party, the subsequent loss of population attending the Crows due to the aforesaid contagion, coupled with the deaths of the well-respected Plays-With-His-Face and Two-Face, had already caused Sore-Belly and his subordinates to reappraise their people's current situation. Thus Sore-Belly had further decided to make peace with all others of his people's old enemies; if possible, or, at least, listen to proposals from them. A case in point was an altercation between the Crows and Shoshoni which, in early summer this year of 1833, again put both tribes on a potential war footing against each other.

The Shoshoni were often both visitors and hosts to their linguistic cousins the Ute who lived further south, and although the Crows at this period were ostensibly at peace with the Shoshoni, they were always the inveterate enemies of the Ute. Only occasionally did Crows and Ute meet in tolerable circumstances and then, when accidently coming together in one or another Shoshoni camp. At such times, tribal protocol alone usually prevented a hostile confrontation, but in early June, 1833, a small party of Crows on a trading trip to a Shoshoni camp on Green River met a large number of Utes who happened to be visiting the same Shoshoni camp at that time. Even though the visit passed off without violence, tension between the Crows and Utes had been high. Having finished their trade the Crows deemed it advisable to leave their hosts sooner than anticipated owing to the aggressive atmosphere around them. But on their return journey home, they were followed by a superior Ute force and attacked. A running fight ensued during which the Crows lost six warriors killed before the rest of their party could reach the Big Horn Mountains and safety.

When word of the affair was made known to the Crow chiefs there was much anger among them and subsequently, a large war-party was organized and set out towards Green River and the Shoshoni camp to exact revenge.

According to the Beckwourth account, the Shoshoni were,

"…overthrown and dispersed with severe loss" and only a short time later, the Shoshoni sued for peace. [1]

In fact, it was a well-known Shoshoni chief named Iron-Wrist-Band who, wishing to avert another all-out war with the Crows, offered the proverbial olive branch on this occasion. This chief employed the services of Robert Campbell, who not long after the battle was residing in Iron-Wrist-Band's lodge, to act as a go-between, as Campbell was then on good terms with the Crows. Campbell mentioned this in a letter to his brother dated July 10th, 1833, in which he said,

> " ...It seems that a misunderstanding had arisen between the Snakes and the Crows, - not so serious as to lead to immediate open hostilities, - yet sufficient to render it doubtful whether they could meet as friends...Write a letter" said he [the Shoshoni chief] "to the Crows. Let it be in two parts. Tell them my people wish to know their intentions. We are anxious to go to war with the Black Feet Indians, we do not wish to fight with our former friends and allies the Crows, nor to divide our strength by keeping some war parties at home to protect our squaws. No – we wish to be friends with the Crows, we wish to join them against the Black Feet; - we wish to smoke, trade and intermarry with their people. If they agree to this, we shall be happy; - we will love them as neighbours – as friends – as allies." [2]

The second part ran as follows,

> "Should the Crow Indians reject these offers of peace, then the Snakes hurl defiance at them. Let them come. There are many heros among us who have never known fear. We shall meet them with as much ferocity as enemies as we could have cordially greeted them as friends. We are not afraid. We shall call on our friends the Shians, Aripahoes, Utaws and Navahoes before the snow comes, and will grind them to death." [3]

The Shoshoni chief then told Campbell to divide the two messages and if the offer of peace be accepted, then to destroy the other, but if not, then to give the Crows the Shoshoni chief's defiance and tell them to `come on. ` Iron-Wrist-Band then continued,

> "Eight years ago when we first saw the Long-Knife [General Ashley] there had been war between us and the Crows. We had killed many of them. They were as children in our hands." [4]

Campbell duly relayed the missives as requested, and the Crows after suffering great loss due to smallpox among them, and realizing they themselves needed all the allies they could get, acquiesced to the Shoshoni request for peace. So it was before the summer was out, a deputation of forty Shoshoni chiefs and warriors including a big medicine man among them, visited the Crow village and smoked the calumet together. Thus peace was once again restored between their peoples.

Meanwhile, regarding the current smallpox epidemic among the Crows, notwithstanding from whom or where it originated, by the beginning of August 1833, the disease had finally burned itself out.

Such is evident by the fact that two white traders in the guise of Louis Vasquis and Charles Larpenteur with a party of trappers, were then driving a small number of cattle before them en route to the recently erected Fort Cass at the mouth of the Big Horn. They would not, of course, have been doing so if smallpox was still raging in that district, and it did happen that when nearing their objective, Vasquez, who had gone on ahead to scout, returned saying he had sighted three Indians on the east side of the Big Horn. He suggested that the three Indians were probably Blackfoot, and that he and his companions should move closer to the river bank and erect some kind of barricade, lest they be attacked by the rest of the Blackfoot, who, Vasquez believed, were sure to be close by.

As the trappers neared the river bank, they were suddenly confronted by a horde of Indians massed on the river's far side. Vasquez at once ordered his companions to take up defensive positions with loaded muskets, but not to fire until he himself gave the command to do so. Soon a tall Indian on the opposite bank holding aloft a long stick with a white flag attached, began advancing across the river. At the same time, he was shouting aloud the name Apsaalooka and telling the white men in Crow not to fire their guns. One among the trappers, Paulette DesJardins, could understand a little of what the Indian said. He told his comrades that the Indians were Crows which meant that the whites would be safe, although he added that the Crows were also "great thieves." The Indians were thus allowed to come close and were even offered a feast of buffalo meat by the whites. The Crows ate heartily and then indicated in a defiant tone that they wished to trade. The trappers did not feel at liberty to refuse. Larpenteur later complained that he was obliged to part with all his new blankets, and, to boot, his own twenty-one dollar sky-blue capote blanket coat of which he was particularly fond. Nevertheless, albeit having been somewhat bullied by the Indians who had set their own prices in the trade, the meeting did pass off amicably, and the Crows departed in good spirits.

Here there is no evidence of Crows then still being ravaged by smallpox, and we further learn that soon after the above mentioned encounter, the same band of trappers whilst resuming their journey towards Fort Cass, had gone but three miles more when another group of Indians numbering ten warriors, came galloping towards them. Seeing that these Indians were also Crows, the trappers allowed the latter to come close, whereupon the white men were greeted by the head Crow war-chief Alapooish - the great Sore-Belly himself. The white men were cordially invited to camp with the Crows, and were actually billeted in the lodge of Sore-Belly who attended to their every comfort. This was for the trapper's own protection, Sore-Belly explained, as a band of Atsina [erroneously termed Blackfoot by Larpenteur] was nearby and on its way to visit his camp with a view to making peace with the Crows. If Vasquez and his men were to run afoul of the Atsina party, Sore-Belly added, then the latter would undoubtedly rub them out. Thus the trappers remained among Sore-Belly's people until the Atsina peace party duly arrived, whereupon the trappers departed, continuing their way towards

Fort Cass. Suffice to note that the sky-blue capote blanket coat purchased from Larpenteur by a particular Crow at that time, was to figure predominantly in a future Crow battle with the Atsina of which we will speak later.

As regards the Atsina, on August 17th, whilst en route to the Crows, the same Atsina peace party had stopped at Fort Cass, where Nathaniel Wyeth and his party of trappers happened to be residing at that time. Wyeth had then recorded in his dairy,

> "...Just as we arrived we saw 31 Indians with two American flags come to the other side of the river. They were Gros Ventres Du Baum [Atsina], the same we fought with last summer at the Trios Teton [Pierre`s Hole]. They came to make peace with the Crows. They were treated civilly at the fort and before night, followed the river up to the Crow village, where I expect their scalps will be taken, for the Crows informed us that not long since, a few Blackfoot came and made peace with them [Crows]. Shortly after three Crows went to the Blackfoot, two of which they killed and they were determined to make no more peace with them [5]

The above episode referred to by Wyeth pertaining to two of three Crows killed by the Blackfoot, appears to have been a reference to the earlier event during the month of March when the party of Bird-Comes-Back had been rubbed out by the Pikuni. Wyeth must then have miss-construed the actual number of Crow casualties on that occasion, and evidently the Crows, in accordance with their earlier decision, did take seriously the above mentioned Atsina peace delegation which, as previously noted, was subsequently cordially entertained in Sore-Belly`s village.

Perhaps, however, it was due somewhat to Crow anger of their tribe having contracted smallpox [which the Crows knew could only have come from white men no matter what the circumstances of how it reached the Indians], that in early September this same year, a group of Rocky Mountain Company employees were severely harassed and robbed by Crows. The event did have a negative effect upon subsequent attitudes towards the Crows by many of that tribe`s erstwhile white friends, and certainly, it increased fur company feuding for a number of years thereafter.

It has been mentioned earlier how the respective Fur Companies in the Upper Missouri country were in great rivalry with one another, each striving to obtain the most amount of furs and pelts possible; if not to monopolize the source for their individual companies. Dishonourable tactics were sometimes employed against competitors, and one particularly dastardly act was perpetrated by Crows later this year of 1833, having been encouraged to do so by American Fur Company employees to discomfit those belonging to the Rocky Mountain Company specifically. On this occasion our old friend James Beckwourth was foremost involved, or at least, highly instrumental in the affair, albeit in cahoots with fellow Company employee Samuel Tulloch along with another known simply by the name of J. P. Winter, who like Beckwourth, then actually often resided among the Crows. In Beckwourth's later reminiscences he went to great pains to exonerate himself from any culpability, although by other accounts he was guilty as charged. However, it is not the purpose of the present study to analyse the evidence or to attach blame, and we are only concerned here with the involvement of Crows during the event in question.

Moreover, it was Sore-Belly's River Crows who patronized the American Fur Company posts of Fort Union and Fort Cass, whilst Chief Long-Hair's Mountain Crows generally traded with the itinerant traders of rival companies.

It happened that a party of twenty-five to thirty trappers belonging to the Rocky Mountain Fur Company with one-hundred horses, equipment, and trade goods, and led by old 'Broken-Hand' Thomas Fitzpatrick, was encamped in the valley of Tongue River only some three miles distant from a large Crow village. On September 5th 1833, Fitzpatrick and a few companions paid a friendly visit to the village, having left their own camp in charge of a new-comer to the mountains, a Scotsman by the title of Captain William Drummond Stewart. At the Crow village Fitzpatrick was well received, but while he was away, a party of over one-hundred Crows led by a chief named High-Bull visited the trapper's camp, and their attitude was all but friendly. In the event, the Crows bullied and intimidated the small party of trappers who could do little in the way of resistance, lest they be massacred on the spot. They could only stand by as the Crows ransacked the camp. Actual bloodshed was averted, but when the Crows finally departed, they took with them all the white men's beaver traps, guns, powder, ball, blankets, trade goods and furs, along with almost all the horses and even the Captain's pocket watch from about his person. [6]

When Fitzpatrick returned and was informed what had happened, he immediately set out again for the Crow village and demanded from its chief that all which had been stolen be restored without delay. But notwithstanding his anger, only a few horses, mules and guns in addition to a little powder and ball were forthcoming, and Fitzpatrick was obliged to take his men out of the country as quickly as possible, still without most of what they had lost.

Of the animals Fitzpatrick succeeded in retrieving at the Indian village, during his party's trek out of the country, Crows again raided his camp and made off with a number of horses and mules from among the few the trapper's had left.

If this action on the part of the Crows was not blatant enough to show their current hostility, later that same month, albeit in another district, Captain Bonneville's brigade had their own brushes with belligerent parties of Crows.

Bonneville and three companions had separated from his main party and whilst traveling north from a point on Green River towards the Wind River valley, his party was constantly dogged by Crows. The white men only managed to avoid being molested by changing their route several times and by utmost diligence on their part. When finally reuniting with the rest of his party on the eastern slopes of the Wind River Mountains, the Captain was told that this other group during its own wanderings had also been followed by Crows who had fired upon them and stolen a horse. Three days later, after the then combined brigade of trappers continued moving through the valley, one among them named David Adams along with a few companions, left the party to trap beaver on the stream known as the Popo Agie..

Adams, being some distance from his comrades, suddenly found himself surrounded by Crows led by another subordinate Crow chief named High-Lance. The Crows robbed Adams of everything he had including his clothing and he was forced to stand naked before them, which the Indians thought was highly amusing.

The Crows did eventually give him an old and tattered buffalo robe to put over his shoulders and left him otherwise unharmed before going on their way. After reuniting with his comrades and returning to Bonneville's party, the humiliated Adams told what had happened and further reported that among the twenty-six horses and mules the Crows had with them, he had recognised a number of animals that had once belonged to Fitzpatrick's party before being robbed on Tongue River earlier that month. However, only a few days after this, three more Crows; evidently from the same band, brazenly entered Bonneville's camp and walked among the trappers with an air of arrogance and indifference. Now the trappers were doubly on their guard, and although treating his visitors in a customary warm and friendly manner, Bonneville made it abundantly clear that the white men would not tolerate any pilfering of their belongings, horses or equipment. The Crows appeared to take the hint, but notwithstanding, they stayed in the trapper's camp the rest of that day and coming night. Only at daybreak did the unwelcome visitors finally decide to leave.

The Captain and his brigade, having previously turned down an offer to accompany the three Crows to their camp, then continued their trek, heading south on their return journey to Green River.

Whilst en route, they crossed the trail of the same Crow band recently located nearby, and which appeared to be still following close behind. The trappers could tell by the size of the trail that there must be three-hundred or more warriors present, who could have made short shrift of the entire brigade if, that is, their earlier meeting had escalated into a fight. As luck would have it a heavy snowfall quickly obliterated the white men's tracks and, at last, they finally shook off their unwanted followers. Bonneville's brigade eventually reached a friendly Shoshoni camp, where they found Fitzpatrick with his own recently robbed party already ensconced.

Come October, however, Long-Hair's Mountain Crows were far distant from the trappers, having moved east to the Little Big Horn while Sore-Belly's band was on Grey Bull River, flowing east into the Big Horn. [7]

It was then that Sore-Belly and seventy lodges undertook a visit to the Hidatsa far down the Missouri, and whilst encamped adjacent to one of the latters towns, the chief was introduced to the German scientist and explorer, Prince Maximilian Zu Weid.

The Prince and his retinue were intending to spend the winter of '33 /'34 at Joseph Kipp's newly established trading post Fort Clark close to the Mandan villages. The Prince was a meticulous observer, although he did not mention Sore-Belly's great victory on the Arkansas. He did report that the Assiniboine and Cheyenne were at peace with the Crows, which statement, obviously, refers to the earlier pacts initiated by Kenneth McKenzie and Major Sanford in 1832, and of which the Assiniboine – Crow pact was then still in force. The continuance of the pact between Cheyennes and Crows applied only to one or another Cheyenne-proper band, and not to that Nation as a whole, and certainly, not to the latter's Suhtaio confederates who long-since, had broken their agreement with the Crows by the afore-noted attack on Dangling Foot's camp. At this date, the Suhtaio; under the alternative names of `Staihitans` and `Flyers,` were still acting as an independent element to the Cheyennes, and did not amalgamate fully with other Cheyenne-proper bands until 1834. This being in part, no doubt, due to the previously recounted destruction of an entire Suhtaio band by Sore-Belly's revenge expedition, and which event, by the time of Maximillian's observations during the winter of `33 /`34, had already led to a resumption of the Crow - Cheyenne war

Neither, however, did the Prince mention the Bird-Comes-Back fight, if indeed, he was aware of the event, although he did mention that the Atsina were still endeavouring to ransom thirty Atsina males who had fallen into the hands of the Crows,

Here the Prince was alluding to those captives taken as horse thieves, a short time after Sore-Belly's attack on the Atsina column following the latter's fight at Pierre's Hole more than a year earlier, and had been the reason why the Atsina party had visited Sore-Belly's camp in August 1833 after meeting Nathanial Wyeth at Fort Cass. What, though, is more important regarding the Prince's visit, is that whilst at Fort Clark he actually met with the great Sore-Belly himself, and it is from Maximilian's pen that we have our first and only contemporary eye-witness description of our subject. The Prince reported as follows,

> "....The Mandans, Manitaries [sic], and Crows, of which tribe there were now seventy tents about the fort, differ very little from each other in appearance and dress.....The haughty Crows rode on beautiful panther skins, with red cloth under them, and, as they never wear spurs, had a whip of elk's horn in their hand...with their diversely painted faces, feathers in their long hair, bow and arrows slung across their backs, and with a musket or spear in their hands, were a novel and highly interesting scene....The tents of the Crows are set up without any regular order. On the poles, instead of scalps, there were small pieces of coloured cloth, chiefly red, floating like streamers in the wind...Mr. Sanford had a conference with *Eripuass* [the Rotten Belly] [sic], the distinguished chief of the latter. We accompanied Mr. Sanford to this meeting. *Eripuass*, a fine tall man, with a pleasing countenance, had much influence over his people; being in mourning he came to the fort in his worst dress, his hair cut close, and daubed with clay. Charbonneau acted as interpreter in the Manitari language. Mr. Sanford recommended to the chief's continued good treatment of the white people who should come into his territory, hung a medal round his neck, and, in the name of the

government, made him a considerable present of cloth, powder, ball, tobacco, etc.;, which this haughty man received without any sign of gratitude; on the contrary, these people consider such presents as a tribute due to them, and a proof of weakness. The Crows, in particular, as the proudest of the Indians, are said to despise the Whites. They do not, however, kill them, but often plunder them. At nightfall we visited *Eripuass* in his tent. The whole camp of the Crows was now filled with horses, some with their foals, all of which had been driven in, to prevent their being stolen. This Nation, consisting of 400 tents, is said to possess between 9,000 and 10,000 horses, some of which are very fine....The interior of the tent itself had a striking effect...the chief sat opposite the entrance, and round him many fine tall men, placed according to rank, all with no other covering than a breech-cloth. Places were assigned to us on buffalo hides near the chief, who then lighted his Lakota pipe, which had a long flat tube, ornamented with bright yellow nails, made each of us take a few puffs, holding the pipe in his hand, and then passed it round to the left hand. After Charbonneau had continued the conversation for some time in the Manitari language, we suddenly rose and retired....About six years ago, the Crows are said to have had only 1,000 warriors, at present they are reckoned at 1,200. They are skilful horse men and, in their attacks on horseback, are said to throw themselves off on one side, as is done by many Asiatic tribes. They have many bardaches [sic], or hermaphrodites among them, and exceed all the other tribes in unnatural practices....of the female sex, it is said of the Crows, that they, with the women of the Arickara, are the most dissolute of all the tribes of the Missouri...."
8

The reason why Sore-Belly was in mourning at this time, was due to the recent death of a relative, if not, of course, regarding Bird-Comes-Back and his party. But alas, there would be more sad news to come, which would affect Sore-Belly to much greater extent than all those brave Apsaalooka who had gone before.

Indeed, if the Crows had not suffered enough throughout the year, on November 12th, a Leonid meteoric shower appeared in the night sky over the entire Northern and Central Plains. All Indians were awe struck at such a phenomenon as the very stars seemed to cascade from the sky. They saw it as a portent of misfortune destined to befall their respective tribes, and in some cases, as an indication of their personal doom. Some among the Crows thought it heralded the potential demise of a great man among them, and certainly, all Crows thought it a warning that yet another dire misfortune would again attend their people in one guise or another, before the leaves should fall again.

$$-0-0-0-0-0-0-0-0-0-0-0-0-$$

## CHAPTER 27.

## LITTLE-WHITE-BEAR`S LAST FIGHT.

As already noted, by August 1833 the smallpox contagion once raging across the Southern and Central Plains, had finally burned itself out. But still the New Year did not bode well for the Crows.

The moccasin grapevine had carried word of the Crow peace party`s defeat at Pikuni hands far across the Plains, and it was this same intelligence which helped inaugurate the disintegration of the Crow's recent, albeit fragile, pact with the Atsina.

It has previously been recounted how the Atsina themselves had again held out the olive branch to the Crows after their appearance at Fort Cass in August 1833. But it had soon become clear, this was a move by the Atsina only through expediency in an attempt to redeem the thirty male captives held by the Crows. At that date the Atsina were still confederated with each of the Blackfoot-speaking tribes, who once more, were engaged in all-out war with the Crows.

At the same time, not having suffered the recent ravages of smallpox among themselves, the Atsina remained numerically strong as compared to the Crows, and they had not forgotten several defeats suffered at Crow hands prior to their recent pact with that people.

Added to this, the Atsina had always harboured hostile feelings towards the white man, and generally, held the Crows in contempt for the latter`s apparent open and intimate association with white trappers and traders, some of whom resided permanently in Crow lodges. The Atsina did at intervals visit certain posts in order to obtain necessary supplies of powder, ball and metal implements. Although not infrequently they were at loggerheads with the traders and at such times, their contempt for the Crows became even more pronounced.

The aforesaid Crow-Atsina pact was thus proving a tenuous situation, likely to erupt into open warfare at any time, and in truth, it seemed; the Atsina were no longer concerned if their fragile truce with that people was thrown to the wind. For a while at least, there still existed a period of apparent calm. Yet beneath the surface was a veritable powder-keg awaiting the spark to ignite it in some spectacular manner, and plunge both peoples again into a state of bloody, total war.

Now it had happened that the grieving period for those slaughtered with Bird-Comes-Back and others taken by smallpox had lasted many moons, and it was not until spring, 1834, before Crow warriors began to think again of going to war. Their reason was sound enough. The spirits of dead relatives killed with Bird-Comes-back needed to be avenged. But there was also the necessity to restock the tribe's pony herds in order to compensate for animals lost during the many moons of sickness within the tribe, when the Crows had been least on their guard.

Whilst in their weakened state, the Crows had suffered devastating losses to their herds. Many animals had simply strayed away to become lost, although many more had been stolen by stealthy thieves. The Crows had not always then had the opportunity to follow up the thieves and sometimes, had even lacked the incentive to do so, while most of their concentration had been taken up caring for their sick and dying relatives.

Now, however, with the end of winter and reappearance of spring, the people's despondent spirits were re-invigorated, and their bellicose instincts again brought to the fore.

An old River Crow medicine man declared, that his sacred spirit helper had told him in a dream, to get together a war-party and go north again into the land of the Pikuni. There, he professed, they would find a small village of enemies situated at a certain place, and from where they could steal a large number of ponies without being discovered, or of suffering any casualties during the trip.

There were a number of Crows who trusted fully in the power of the old man's *medicine*, and agreed to go on the raid. Among these was the famous fighting chief, Little-White-Bear, who was himself a relative and close friend and confident of Sore-Belly. Also included was the female warrior Woman-Chief and even a white man known by the name of Hunter, a Kentuckian from the East. This man was an employee of the American Fur Company who spent much time residing among the Crows, and, it is said, he wished to go on the war-trip merely for the excitement of the venture.

Prior to the war-party`s departure, Little-White-Bear visited Sore-Belly in his tepee and offered him the war-pipe, thereby requesting that Sore-Belly himself lead the expedition. To Little-White-Bear`s surprise the great chief refused the pipe. Instead he told his friend with words to the effect,

> "It is not a good time for war. Our people have lost worthy warriors slain at the time buffalo and horses fill out. Others have passed away during sickness among us. We Crows are weak. We cannot stand another loss if your raid should meet disaster....First let us regain our strength; replenish our arms and ammunition from the white man trader, and look to our women until they are done with grieving." [2]

Sore-Belly then went on to express his additional feelings of apprehension, for he himself had dreamed that ill-luck would surely befall his friend Little-White-Bear along with many of his comrades if they went at this time to war. The chief then said he himself must not go, for his personal *medicine* father, the `Thunder` had warned him of his own demise if he did so.

Little-White-Bear respected Sore-Belly`s *medicine* and, no doubt, listened attentively to the chief's warnings. But he had already given his word that he would accompany the old shaman's party, and to drop out now whilst others were still eager and happy to go, might lose Little-White-Bear`s high standing among the people.

So it was that contrary to Sore-Belly`s advice and premonitions of impending doom, Little-White-Bear, albeit somewhat reluctantly, continued in his resolve and prepared for the trip.

It was soon after this that Little-White-Bear and his companions, some sixty in number, with shields and lances and short-barrel fusees and led by the old medicine man in a distinctive blue blanket coat [likely the same traded from Charles Lapenteur the previous year], started on foot from their camp on the Yellowstone, and headed for Pikuni country in the north.

As the days went by the party crossed the Musselshell, then turned northwest travelling up Box Elder Creek to its head. Thence they continued north to the Missouri, which they reached at a point across from the mouth of the Marias where the charred remains of old Fort Piegan were then still visible. Scouts were sent ahead beyond the Missouri and a short way up the Marias itself, then west to Teton River before returning south across the Missouri.

Throughout their wandering, the only sign of the enemy was a long-abandoned Pikuni camp on the Teton. This led the party to assume that their quarry had left the country, as indeed was sometimes the Pikuni habit this time of year, in order to trade at the Hudson's Bay post Chesterfield House far northeast on the Lower Saskatchewan.

Consequently, not suspecting Pikuni in the vicinity, the Crows relaxed their vigilance and neglected to send out more scouts to continue reconnoitring the country. They then actually divided their number into small groups, each of which went off in different directions to hunt. These hunters compounded matters further by shooting their guns off at any game they saw, which was sure to attract the attention of other people who might be passing through the region at that time.

True it was, of Pikuni there were none, but of Atsina there were many.

The Atsina told the Crows several years later that they had only just entered the country abutting the south side of the Missouri, when some of their own scouts reconnoitring the way ahead, noticed a small herd of buffalo in the distance moving rapidly over the prairie. Such a circumstance invariably indicated the presence of human hunters, whose actions were forcing the animals to move before them. They then heard the sound of gunfire carried on the wind, and rode off in the direction from whence came the shots. Soon they spied several groups of people all on foot, although they were not close enough to determine if they were members of a war-party, or to what tribe they belonged. Hurriedly the scouts took news of their discovery to their camp, which consisted of some four-hundred lodges comprising the entire Atsina tribe encamped between the forks of the Marias and the Teton. At once a strong party of around two-hundred braves led by the famous Atsina chief, Sitting-Woman, started out on foot toward the place their scouts had indicated in order to determine who the strange people might be. But they failed to find their quarry.

The Crows by then had congregated again into one group and still not sensing danger, had ensconced themselves among a few trees and rocks not far from the sandy bluffs of Shonkin Creek six miles southwest of the newly erected Fort McKenzie at the mouth of the Teton. The Crows roasted and ate a hearty meal of fresh buffalo meat, then prepared to bed down for the night, intending to start again on the war-trail come morning.

311

The Atsina war-party, meanwhile, had since moved over to Crow Creek at a point near where it enters the Missouri and set up a temporary war-camp, whereupon Sitting-Woman again dispatched a number of scouts to continue searching the whereabouts of the strangers.

Before the sun went down, the Atsina scouts had finally discovered the stranger's resting place. One look told them they were Crows by the latter`s distinctive raised hairstyles and vermilion daubed foreheads, and this intelligence the scouts took back to their camp.

From the scout`s report, the Atsina chief realized his own party must outnumber that of the Crows by more than three to one, and so could easily engage and overwhelm them. As to the peace supposedly then still in effect between his people and Crows, Sitting-Woman excused his intentions by declaring that this was Atsina country and these Crows were trespassers in it. However, before the Atsina moved out, one among them decided to call upon what his people referred to as a Ghost-Helper. This involved asking a particular ancestor spirit what the outcome would be when the warriors came face to face with the enemy. The Atsina believed that such a spirit could not only foretell forthcoming events, but could also assist their warriors in time of need. Thus a pipe was duly filled and lit and offered to one of the party whose ancestor the Ghost-Helper was. This man was first bound hand and foot and along with the pipe, placed within a small hide tepee-like structure erected for the purpose and which hid him from view. Such a shelter was similar to those used during the "Shaking Tent" rite among the Cree and other Northern Algonquian tribes, and was employed for the same purposes of foretelling things to come; discovering objects lost or stolen, and even the fate of missing persons. On this occasion the Ghost-Helper when called upon, told the man in the shelter that Crows were about to raid the main camp the Atsina had recently left, intending to steal a large number of horses.

The Crows, though, the spirit continued, were now heading towards the very place along Crow Creek where the Atsina war-party was positioned, and would arrive in early morning the following day. The spirit then went on to say that among the Crows, there was one who was wearing a blue blanket coat and that this particular man was very brave and dangerous. He should be killed early in the fight, the spirit said, after which the rest of the Crows could easily be wiped out, while none among the Atsina would be killed and only two of their number would suffer wounds; albeit of slight degree. The spirit then went on to warn the Atsina that if the man in the blue blanket coat should not be slain, then a number of Crows would escape and complete victory for the Atsina would slip from their grasp.

These words from the Ghost-Helper gave the Atsina added impetus. Their Chief Sitting-Woman thus decided to move out at once, in order to secrete his warriors closer to the enemy, and having done so, many stayed awake through the night to be sure of attacking the Crows at dawn.

As appeared the first rays of sunrise, the Crows had barely risen from slumber when, suddenly, the sound of ear-piercing war-whoops rang out, and a horde of Atsina warriors began shooting arrows and musket balls into the huddled group of Crows. The latter had been taken by surprise. Most of the Atsina were on foot, but one old man among them who was mounted, rode to the top of a nearby knoll where he could get a clear view of the fight. The Crows saw this man and believed they were soon to be assaulted by a host of mounted enemies. The cry went up, *"Iichilaa, Ahkaashi Iichilaa,"* `horses, many horses,` and such an idea caused the Crows to panic. Being themselves on foot, they looked around frantically for a place where they could gain cover and make a stand. Nearby was a line of bluffs bordering Shonkin Creek. All at once the Crows raced off in that direction and started scrambling up the slope of one of the bluffs before the Atsina could surround them.

Part of the bluff side was composed of soft dirt and sloping; the rest grassy and steep. The Crows scrambled up the soft dirt side and entered a shallow cave near the summit, the recess of which gave protection from the barrage of missiles already being directed at them.

In their initial effort to cut off the Crow stragglers from reaching the bluff, the pedestrian Atsina had all at once raced across the prairie, and one Crow, at least, did not make it to the cave. This Crow was a middle-aged man. Whilst running towards the bluff, an Atsina musket ball struck him above the knee shattering the thigh bone which caused him to fall to the ground. His Crow comrades were in such haste they dared not stop to assist him, and so the disabled Crow was obliged to sit where he had fallen, facing the oncoming foe alone. He was armed with a bow and arrows, and such was the skill with which he used them, he did for a while manage to keep the Atsina at bay, although he could not but realize his time had come. He could see the Atsina gradually creeping closer, and knew they would soon have him at their mercy.

In between loosing off arrows at any Atsina who exposed himself as a target, this lone Crow shouted to his opponents and taunted them thus,

> "Ho, Hairy-Nostrils; Come on and fight; I have been waiting for you. Many of your scalps and horses have I taken, and your Atsina women have warmed me in my pallet, `though not as good as our Crow women. Now I have grown tired of fighting. I am tired of killing your warriors, there has been no honour doing so. Your warriors cannot match the bravery of us Crows. Come now, it is time you killed me; I am tired of fighting and have grown too old for war." [3]

Having spoken these words, the lone Crow shot away the last of his arrows and only then, did all the Atsina rise from cover. They saw his helpless plight, but showing no compassion, rushed upon him, and finished him off with axes and war-clubs before pin-cushioning his body with arrows. They next blasted his head to atoms with several close-range musket shots, then cut his corpse into little pieces which they scattered over the ground about them.

Fortunately for the rest of the Crows, the killing of their disabled comrade had distracted the Atsina from their initial assault on the bluff, and the surviving Crows had taken full advantage of the interlude. With knives and bare hands they had hurriedly dug pits in the sandy floor of the cave, then heaped up loose stones and soil to form a flimsy breastwork at the cave opening, and behind this they hoped to defend themselves more effectively.

So it was that when the Atsina warriors resumed their assault, the Crows were well-prepared in a strong defensive position, and were able to repel them.

Of the few mounted Atsina, they attempted to ride their ponies up the grassy steep slope of the bluff, whilst others scrambled on foot up the soft dirt side. But before they could get near enough to strike the defenders, a sudden hail of missiles was discharged from the Crows, which sent all those scrambling up the slope tumbling back down, and scampering away in search of cover.

The Atsina Sitting-Woman now instructed his warriors to desist from launching another direct assault. Instead, he told them to keep firing at the mouth of the cave, and to momentarily expose themselves every so often, in order to lure the Crows into expending their ammunition. When this was achieved, he said, the defenders would be at their most vulnerable and the whole Atsina force could then scale the slope together and rub them out.

In their turn, the Crows thought the Atsina rather timid by their actions. Every now and then, three or four Crows would brazenly step out from the cave opening and show themselves in full view of the enemy. These would then fire a volley of musket balls and arrows at the foe, before darting back behind their defences where they were obscured again from the Atsina, and this procedure they repeated many times while their ammunition lasted.

In the meantime, small groups of Atsina were forever attempting to creep nearer the cave mouth, hoping to gain a position from where they could lean over the wall, and fire directly on those within.

There was one particularly brave Crow, who every time he thought one or more of the enemy was getting too close, he would suddenly jump over the low breastwork and stand brazingly with gun in hand, threatening to shoot first one and then another of the foe, and all the Atsina would race back down the slope in hectic flight.

Several times this brave Crow performed his deed, and each time he laughed heartily as he watched the Atsina in their hurried retreat, and which was so precipitous, that many tripped and stumbled as they ran. In their haste they bumped into one another, causing some to tumble head-over-heels all the way down to the base of the bluff.

It is said that another brave Crow; believing he and his comrades could not escape their dire situation, all at once ran from the cave entrance and actually jumped bodily from the bluff some fifteen feet and more, and landed amid a thick bunch of the enemy. With only a knife to defend himself, he then fought among the Atsina hand to hand - until eventually he was overwhelmed; cut down and killed.

And thus the siege continued.

At length, some among the Crows had exhausted their ammunition and by that time, a number of Atsina warriors had at last managed to scale the bluff and had positioned themselves on each side of the cave entrance. The lip of the cave, supplemented as it was with the low breastwork hastily erected, still obscured the Crows from view and none of the Atsina were brave enough, or perhaps, foolish enough, to poke their heads over the wall to inspect the state of things inside. Instead, they began shovelling up handfuls of sandy earth and small stones which they then tossed into the cave opening, and the fine consistency of sandy soil momentarily blinded those within. Many of the Crows were also hit by the stones raining in on them, as they could not see adequately to shield themselves from their path. This, the Crows thought, was a humiliating situation, and some among them were not inclined to endure it for long.

Little-White-Bear cried aloud to his comrades that here they were, cowering like dogs while being showered with dirt and stones. This was not a good way for a Crow to die. Rather, he said, they should attempt to break out and if only a few of their number managed to escape, then at least of those killed in the attempt, it could be said died like warriors. [4]

Most of his comrades agreed, and replied that if Little-White-Bear led the way, they along with others who wished, would follow in his wake.

The Crow partisan in his blue blanket coat then told his comrades that if they made a run for it, they would likely suffer great loss, but if they stayed where they were and made a stand, then perhaps many would survive. Most of the Crows disagreed, although between fifteen and twenty did refuse to risk a breakout. These believed themselves more secure in their present refuge and supposed that come nightfall, the enemy would grow tired and withdraw, leaving those in the cave to escape with their lives. Little-White-Bear and those willing to make a break were not of this opinion. On the contrary, their past war experiences had convinced them that to stay where they were meant certain death, and not being able to persuade more than two or three of the dissenters to join them, they individually prepared to meet their ancestors, which, either way they thought, would soon to be their fate in one guise or another.

Accordingly, when Little-White-Bear and forty or more Crow warriors were ready, and among whom were included Woman-Chief and, surprisingly, the old shaman in his blue-blanket coat, they all at once rose up in unison; leapt over the barricade and yelling war-cries, began racing down the bluff headlong towards the enemy milling around its base. It was the Atsina who were then taken by surprise and at first, they opened up their ranks for the charging Crows to run through for fear of shooting their own people in a cross fire. The old medicine man in the blanket coat was leading the Crows and being a strong runner, was soon racing ahead of his comrades. The Atsina then closed ranks and half their number began pursuing the Crows, shooting arrows and muskets as they ran. But their belated attempt to destroy their fleeing foes was of little avail. In desperation the Crows; with shields slung over their shoulders to protect their backs, were slashing and swiping with their knives, or swinging iron axes and stone-headed war-clubs both left and right, striking any Atsina in reach.

A Crow brave in the manner of a suicide warrior suddenly stopped running. He turned around and faced the oncoming Atsina warriors with musket levelled at his nearest adversary. There was an Atsina named Bear-Robe who came close to this man, and as the Crow discharged his piece, a second Atsina knocked the Crow`s gun to one side just as it was fired. The ball tore through Bear-Robe`s arm from elbow to wrist; knocking him down with the impact. But Bear-Robe quickly regained his feet. He ran right up to the Crow and actually snatched the now empty gun from his opponent`s hands and also a lance strapped to the Crow`s back, before eventually killing him with his war-club.

Yet another brave Crow then turned in his tracks and he, too, made a lone stand facing the horde of enemies in an effort to put distance between his comrades and pursuers. An Atsina named Crow-Moccasin struck him with a tomahawk, causing the Crow to stagger and drop his gun, although the Crow did manage to take hold of his opponent`s arm which held the axe, and after reaching for his own knife sheathed in front of his crotch, the Crow slashed the arm of his opponent; broke free, and turned to follow up his comrades. However, another Atsina took aim with a musket and fired, killing this second Crow outright as he fled.

The white man named Hunter was also with this group of Crows running across the open ground at the base of the bluff. In the event, he received a musket ball in the back which broke his spine. For a short while he continued to run as best he could just ahead of his pursuers. The Crow Little-White-Bear was close by. He grabbed hold of Hunter's hand to assist him in his flight. But the white man's wound was a death wound and after only a few steps more he stumbled and fell. Almost at the same time Little-White-Bear, too, was struck several times by musket balls, one of which caused a mortal wound, and he likewise fell to the ground. Later, when the Crow survivors eventually reached home, they told their friends that when last seen, Little-White-Bear was sitting on the ground next to his dying friend Hunter. Some among the Crows had called to him to get up and they would help him along, but Little-White-Bear replied he would not leave the side of his white friend. Having said this, he suddenly slumped over Hunter's body and died. Thus was the sad yet heroic end of a great and honourable warrior, the news of whose demise would fill Sore-Belly with grief.

Meanwhile, the rest of the Atsina continued shooting arrows and musket balls into the fleeing foe, and by running in separate groups, they did at length succeed in surrounding the Crows. However, such was the determination and ferociousness of the Crows in order to extricate themselves from the scene, that they put fear into many an Atsina heart, and once again the Atsina ranks actually opened up allowing a gap to appear, and of this the Crows took immediate advantage. They ran through it, although it was at this point that an Atsina musket ball tore off a little finger of the female warrior Woman-Chief. This, though, was her only wound, and she bravely fought her way right through the Atsina warriors and made her escape from what, only moments before, had seemed like certain death. The rest of her comrades also broke through and managed to reach a stand of timber bordering Shonkin Creek.

While all this was going on across the flat land stretching from the bluff base, those who had opted to remain in the cave were now at the mercy of the remaining Atsina. They had ran out of ammunition and once the Atsina who had continued the siege realized this was the case, they entered the cave, and in a very short while had slaughtered all those within. The Crows here, apparently, did not put up much of a fight without ammunition and adequate weapons with which to defend themselves, and not one Atsina was killed or even injured in the event.

The informant Joe-Medicine-Crow stated that of the original sixty-man Crow party, a good many actually escaped that day and lived to tell the tale, having expediently taken refuge among the trees and brush along Shonkin Creek where the Atsina were reluctant to follow. On the other hand, according to the white trader Edwin Denig`s account, only four Crows from a party of thirty escaped the slaughter and managed to get home safely, while Lieutenant Bradley`s informant Alexander Culbertson, declared that of forty party members, twenty-seven Crows and the white man named Hunter were killed. James Beckwourth, conversely, gave the number as twenty-four killed out of an original compliment of sixty Crows who had made up the war-party at the start, and Frederick P. Gone was told by Atsina informants during the 1940s that as many as forty Crows were killed and only a few escaped. Frederick Gone was also told by his Atsina informants that the fight was long known among them as *"The Massacre of the Chiefs,"* owing to the large number of important Crow warriors slaughtered at that time.[5]

Thus the Atsina themselves still had some memory of the affair as late as the middle years of the twentieth century, although by that time they could not recall the number of their own dead and injured. One suspects, however, that their casualties were slight and certainly, much fewer than those sustained by the Crows. But whatever the exact amount of dead and wounded on each side, it was a severe defeat for the Crows, and considered a great victory by the Atsina.

In the aftermath of the fight, even though a number of Crows had escaped their scalping knives, the Atsina were content with their victory. They had not thought it prudent to continue fighting the Crow survivors, who after their hectic flight over the open ground had taken refuge in a thick grove of timber adjacent to the creek. To drive them from the timber, the Atsina Sitting-Woman knew, would likely involve the loss of many of his warriors, as the Crows could then shoot at them with ease while remaining hidden behind the trees and camouflaged among the dense underbrush and thickets which enveloped their position.

Added to these considerations, it was then around mid-afternoon and the weather had turned bitterly cold. Sitting-Woman thus decided to call it a day and bade his warriors return to their main village. By so doing the Atsina allowed the surviving Crows to escape, and to make their way home on foot as best they could.

Regarding the surviving Crows, they must have thanked aloud their guardian spirits for their deliverance. They knew, though, it was a very long way to their home camp on the Yellowstone and if the weather deteriorated further, they were likely to freeze to death en route. The old Crow shaman still wearing his blue blanket coat was one of those included among the survivors, and it was he who, in order to alleviate their situation, suggested a daring enterprise. He told his comrades with words to the effect that the Atsina camp could not be far away. The Atsina themselves would be holding scalp and victory dances for many nights to come and would be sleeping late in the mornings. As a Consequence, they would not be on guard against thieves and certainly, would not expect a small band of Crows, the same who had survived the recent battle, to attempt a raid on their herds, and in the Atsina camp there were many horses; more than enough to carry he and his comrades home in comfort.

To raid the Atsina herds was a desperate measure to contemplate, as the Crows had little ammunition left with which to defend themselves if attacked again. But all agreed it was the most practical way to obtain mounts, of which their forlorn party was now in most dire need.

So it was, notwithstanding their recent drubbing, that just before dark the Crows began following up the trail of the victorious Atsina which led north across the Missouri. They travelled through the night and hid during the daylight hours, and it was several days before they reached the vicinity of the Atsina camp, since relocated on the west bank of the Teton about fifteen miles above that river's mouth. Once more the Crows went into hiding, and waited patiently for darkness to fall again.

True enough, as had been suspected, the Atsina were still fully occupied holding their victory celebrations. They sang and danced throughout the afternoon and continued late into the night, and not until long past midnight did the village become quiet, its occupants at last retiring to their lodges and falling asleep on their pallets. The Crows continued waiting until just before dawn. Then, in twos and threes, they crept cautiously among the grazing herd which milled around unattended, because, so the Crows were later told, the Atsina had not thought it necessary to station guards owing to the great size of the camp, which also caused them to think themselves safe from enemy raiders.

Each of the Crows, meanwhile, selected what he thought was a fine sturdy animal, a fast runner, and led it off quietly to a prearranged rendezvous a short distance from the village. When all had returned safely, they mounted up on the bare backs of the stolen ponies and together, rode downriver in the direction of the recently erected trading post Fort McKenzie, then sited on the north bank of the Missouri near the mouth of the Teton.

Now at this time, the above mentioned Major Alexander Culbertson was in charge of the fort, with a complement of twenty wilderness-hardened employees mostly of French-Canadian stock.

It had happened only a few days prior to the Crow survivors stealing the Atsina horses, that four Blood Blackfoot - three men and one woman each of whom was on foot - had stopped at the fort on their way south to steal horses from the Crows. The Major by his own account, had by earnest entreaty induced the Bloods to give up their intention, saying it would be a dangerous venture and that they would likely all be killed in its undertaking. The four Bloods had heeded his advice and abandoned their original design. Instead they had started on their return journey back to their own country in the north. Unfortunately, this was the very day the same Crow party mounted astride the recently stolen Atsina ponies, arrived in the vicinity of the fort.

Two or three miles distant at a place then called by the whites *"Cracon du Nez,"* the four Bloods were surprised by the Crows, who instantly fired upon them before they had a chance to flee. In so doing, they killed two of the Blood warriors outright and wounded the third, but this wounded Blood proved himself a brave and determined fighter. As the Crows came galloping towards him, he struck his nearest opponent with the stock end of his musket; toppling his adversary from his mount, then sprung himself upon the animal`s back; took up the discarded lance of the fallen Crow, and raced back the way he had come. He alone of his companions returned to the fort where Major Culbertson attended his wound. [6]

The next day or so, both he and the Major went out to inspect the scene of conflict, and to retrieve the bodies of the slain Bloods. These they carried back to the fort where they were duly interred in a Christian manner.

The Blood woman - so it was later learned - had become a captive of the Crows who took her with them on their return journey south. Eventually, she did escape back to her own people, but seems to have been the captive of the female warrior Woman Chief, who we know, was among the Crow survivors on this occasion. The Blood woman later told Culbertson that whilst being conveyed south to Crow country, she was compelled to,

*"...sleep with a lynx-eyed squaw* [obviously a member of the war-party] *whom the slightest movement awakened."* [7]

The survivors of the Crow war-party did then, achieve a degree of success to help compensate their misfortune at the hands of the Atsina. Now, at least, they had a number of horses; an enemy captive and two scalps to show for their ill-fated journey. But they were still a long way from their own Crow lodges in the south.

One of the older warriors among them, according to Beckwourth`s account, had lost a son killed during the flight along Shonkin Creek. Throughout the party's entire journey south he cried aloud continually lamenting his loss, until eventually he became hoarse and could cry no more.

It also began to snow. The temperature dropped below freezing and the party's progress became hard going. Virtually no game was sighted to sustain them on their miserable trek and some warriors suffered frostbite to their hands and feet. Truly, it was a sorry dishevelled, more dead than alive party which finally reached its home camp on the Yellowstone. [8]

Back in *Echeta Casha*, the survivors of the disastrous expedition were initially greeted with joyous rapture. But it was terrible news the returning ones brought to the widows and orphans of those warriors lost, and especially so, pertaining to the death of Little-White-Bear. This man had been highly respected by his people and beloved by all. His wife who had recently given birth to a son named Rawhide [killed during "The Battle When the Boat Exploded" in 1861], was particularly grieved as, too, was the indomitable Sore-Belly. Little-White-Bear had been the chief's close friend, upon whose support and loyalty Sore-Belly had always depended. In truth, it was a loss the chief never quite got over, and a factor soon to mark the demise of Sore-Belly himself. [1]

- 0 - 0 – 0 – 0 – 0 – 0 – 0 – 0 – 0 – 0 – 0 – 0 – 0 – 0 –

## CHAPTER. 28.

## BESIEGING THE WHITE MAN`S FORT.

Not alone in sadness were Little-White-Bear`s immediate kin and close friends. When news of the returning party's misfortune was heralded around the various Crow camps, the whole Nation was plunged into a prolonged period of mourning. Throughout that time the people lamented the demise of many other brave warriors, whose previous prowess in battle would be greatly missed. The population could not stand such heavy losses to its fighting strength if the people were to survive intact among the host of belligerent tribes around them.

Sore-Belly was fully aware of this fact and its dire implications. He knew well that renewal of war with the powerful Pikuni and now with the latter`s Atsina confederates - whilst also defending themselves against the ever encroaching Lakota and Cheyennes, - must only spell doom for his people. Perhaps the Crows would be expelled once and for all from their beloved *Echeta Casha*, if not eliminated as a tribal entity on the Northern Plains.

Contrary, however, to Sore-Belly`s apprehensions, tribal custom decreed that a revenge raid be conducted against the killers of Little-White-Bear and his comrades, and their remains gathered up and brought home to be properly honoured and re-united with their tribes-folk.

It was then, for this purpose in early summer 1834 that Sore-Belly led a formidable war-party north into Atsina country, to avenge those slain with Little-White-Bear and to repatriate their bones.

Along a stream known as Wolf Creek flowing into the Judith south of the Missouri, Sore-Belly`s party came face to face with a large body of Atsina, again led by the latter`s indefatigable war-chief Sitting-Woman. The Crows happened to be in larger number, although the Atsina had many guns traded from the Mandan and Pikuni allies which should have given them an advantage in the conflict. As it transpired, after a series of charges and counter-charges against each other`s ranks, the Crows, it seemed, were winning the day and the Atsina began holding back, hesitating to get to grips with the Crows. It was at this crucial point that a young Atsina warrior belatedly arrived on the scene. [2]

This lone Atsina, it is said, had not yet been to war and was so poor he did not even own a horse to ride. He had, just prior to the fight, been fasting on a hilltop and at which time, received a vision and strong *medicine* helper which promised to protect and make him feared among his enemies. Now at the same time as the Atsina warriors were engaging the Crows, this young man had only just returned to camp, and being informed of the battle then going on, he immediately dressed himself for war; mounted a fine pinto pony which actually belonged to Chief Sitting-Woman himself, and followed the Atsina war-party`s trail. Upon coming up with his warrior comrades this man did not hesitate, but with reckless abandon, charged headlong into the Crow ranks, striking left and right with his tomahawk and knocking several Crows from their horses. Such was his fury that he alone caused the Crows to draw back, while the rest of the Atsina warriors –encouraged by their lone comrade-in-arms – all at once rallied their once dispirited force and together, charged back into the fight. A number of Crows were severely wounded during this ferocious stage of the melee, and as an act of expediency, Sore-Belly ordered a tactical withdrawal from the field.

The Crows had inflicted a number of casualties upon the enemy, and so deemed the affair sufficient to uphold Crow honour by their having achieved albeit in a small way, a degree of vengeance for those killed along Shonkin Creek. The Atsina, though, rightly considered themselves the victors on this occasion, while Sore-Belly viewed the affair a stale-mate, and carrying their dead and wounded with them, the Crows turned their horses around and made their way back towards the Yellowstone and home.

Whilst travelling south, Sore-Belly and his party adhered to the other part of their mission for going north in the first place, and made a detour in order to visit the site where Little-White-Bear and his comrades had fallen. There they would retrieve the now bleached bones lying scattered along the line of the Crow's flight across the open ground bordering Shonkin Creek, and of those of the latter's dead comrades in the cave of their last refuge.

When Sore-Belly and his party finally gazed upon the remains of their slaughtered tribesmen, they shed copious tears and howled laments amid sacred oaths of vengeance. Sore-Belly himself was so moved that in his moment of grief, he made a solemn promise there and then that he would more fully avenge the death of Little-White-Bear, or leave his own body to the wolves if he failed in the attempt.

At length, having thus vented their grief and anger, the Crows gathered together the dismembered bones and skulls and carrying them wrapped in blanket bundles, continued their journey home.

The trader Culbertson at a later date, told Lieutenant James Bradley that when the Crows inspected the site, they had found only the unrecognizable bones and skulls of their kinsmen. But Joe Medicine Crow had been told that the skull of the white man Hunter was easily recognized by his decayed teeth, which seemed to be grinning up at them, and so the skeleton lying next to him must have been the bones of the Crow champion Little-White-Bear. [3]

Needless to say, when returned home the said remains were dully honoured, and interred in a sacred manner as customary for fellow tribesmen, and so the expedition overall was deemed a success.

It was after the aforesaid party's return to *Echeta Casha* and the Big Horn country, that Sore-Belly and his subordinate chiefs discussed between themselves their recent brush with the Atsina. All agreed that the lone Atsina warrior on the pinto pony had been the hero of the day, and as a token of respect for that young man, Sore-Belly in his sporting way, sent a message to the Atsina Chief Sitting-Woman via Fort Union traders, saying that they, the Atsina, should treat their young hero well as befitted such a brave warrior among them. [4]

At the same time, Sore-Belly and his chiefs also deliberated upon the fact that the enemy during the recent fight, had been superiorly armed with guns and ammunition obtained, the Crows knew, from the newly established Fort McKenzie operating specifically for the Blackfoot and Atsina trade. Many among the Crows knew that the superior numbers of Blackfoot and Atsina combined now coupled with the latter being well-supplied with firearms, must prove a situation which could not bode well for the Crows.

It was in order to counter this threat and gain some advantage over his people's enemies; no matter how little that might be, that Sore-Belly soon after his return from the Atsina country – and rather reluctantly it must be said – agreed to a bold enterprise broached by his subordinate chiefs, who suggested they cut off the supply of guns and ammunition to both the Pikuni and Atsina and thereby, deprive those enemies from having the means by which to match Crow warriors in the field.

Such misgivings on the part of the Crows were not without foundation. Until the early years of the eighteen-thirties, the latter had still regarded the region between the Yellowstone and Musselshell as Crow country, even though for several decades Pikuni, Bloods and Atsina had been trying to establish a foothold therein, and claim it for themselves.

As yet Sore-Belly had thwarted any attempts by the last-named tribes to do so, although since the peace-making of 1832, Sore-Belly had turned a blind eye to the Small-Robe Pikuni band which, generally speaking, remained somewhat aloof from other Blackfoot-speaking groups, and had been allowed by the River Crows to enter the aforesaid district, albeit on a temporary basis, in order to obtain a winter supply of meat and hides.

Now, though, since the permanent establishment in 1833 of the new American Fur Company post Fort McKenzie situated near the mouth of the Teton just west of the Marias, other Blackfoot bands from north of the Missouri were being lured south in great number to become permanent residents on the very edge of the Crow domain. This, of course, posed a very real and significant threat to the safety of Crow hunting parties and their villages, which were suddenly within easy travelling distance of Blackfoot and Atsina war-bands.

Fort McKenzie itself was a formidable structure intended to withstand Indian attack. After Fort Union it was considered the next most prominent landmark in the Upper Missouri country. Its predecessor Fort Piegan had been built at the mouth of the Marias in late autumn 1831, and by the same James Kipp who was then head trader at Fort Clark near the Mandan and Hidatsa villages lower down the Missouri. Fort Piegan, though, had been short lived. It was vacated early the following year and soon after, burned down by the Blackfoot; the very people it had intended to serve. Thus in midsummer 1832, another company employee David D. Mitchell, had been sent upriver from Fort Union to build a new post to replace Fort Piegan. Its location, although still on the north bank of the Missouri, was sited closer to the mouth of the Teton some six or seven miles west of the Marias. However, in early 1833 a more impressive structure was superimposed on the same site, and this new facility was named Fort McKenzie in honour of Kenneth McKenzie, the American Fur Company's head factor at that time.

322

Edwin Denig, for a long time senior clerk at Fort Union knew Fort McKenzie well. In 1856 he described it as follows,

> "The fort was built of logs enclosed with high and string pickets forming a square with the houses ranging along the sides and bastions on two corners, built so as to command the four sides of the picketing. These bastions were furnished with canon of small calibre, which with a good number of muskets, were always kept loaded in readiness for any attack from the savages. From thirty to fifty men were usually stationed here during the fall and winter; most of them however, were sent down the Missouri with the boats containing the robes and skins early in the spring, leaving some ten to fifteen persons to pass the few summer months in the fort. In the month of August or September, the annual supplies were received by a keel boat sent upriver from Fort Union, hauling the same with a *"cordelle,"* manned with thirty or forty boatmen. Thus the Fort received it's reinforcement of men and stores before the Blackfoot returned from the English posts in the north, whither they always went in the summer." [5]

Between the years 1834 and 1836, this famous fur-trading post was administered by the earlier mentioned Major Alexander Culbertson, a most able and conscientious employee, but who, apparently, favoured his Blackfoot-speaking customers sometimes to the detriment of the Crows.

Again according to Edwin Denig who during his time of residence in the Upper Missouri country was intimately associated with the Crows, and had known many of Sore-Belly`s old cronies personally, the Crows had long harboured a desire to rob each of the successive posts at the mouth of the Marias and on the Teton. Well they knew that white men at those establishments traded guns and ammunition to enemy war-parties when stopping at the post on their way south to raid Crow camps.

These same white men, Sore-Belly also knew, openly purchased both horses and captives taken on such forays against the Crows, when the aforesaid war-parties again stopped at the posts on their way home to their own lands in the north. Coupled to this, during the period when smallpox had been burning through Crow lodges, the men-folk had done little hunting over and above their immediate and personal needs. So at this time; mid-summer of 1834, they actually had very few surplus beaver pelts, furs and buffalo robes with which to trade in exchange for the white man's guns and ammunition, deemed necessary to enable the Crows to defend themselves against attack, let alone in pursuing their own warlike endeavours.

Of the large number of guns previously found among the Crows, many had since been buried with their owners who had succumbed during the previous year`s contagion, so that the spirit of the weapon itself would accompany the deceased warrior into the land of the hereafter. In addition, the Crows did not even have enough surplus ponies with which to trade at the posts, and for all these current ills both real and imagined, many Crows blamed the white man in the guise of trader and trapper who, the Crows believed, had cast an evil spell upon the Apsaalooka in order to disperse them from the land and claim the fine Crow country for themselves. Yet the Crows had to have the white man's goods in order to survive in the manner to which they had grown accustomed, and indeed, if these items could not be obtained one way - the more dissident Crow warriors proclaimed - then why not obtain them by another, even if it meant actually robbing the traders and posts of their merchandise.

It was this same group of dissidents who began clamouring to avenge themselves upon the traders for arming their foes. They badgered Chief Sore-Belly to take appropriate action against the "Yellow Eyes;" or at least, to neutralize the current situation which, they rightly supposed, threatened the destruction of their people.

In earlier years Sore-Belly had been adamantly averse to being a party to any such action which might upset the whites. But he had since changed his mind somewhat, and even though at first obdurate in his conviction of keeping peace with the white men, often advising restraint and that the warriors desist from any hostile acts upon them, as Head chief he would be obliged to go along with public opinion if the majority thought it the right thing to do.

Notwithstanding, however, the many voices of discontent against the posts, there were others among the Crows, predominantly followers of Chief Long-Hair, who were also against upsetting their people's harmonious relationship with the traders. Thus a grand tribal council was arranged to which all the Nation's head men were summoned to attend, in order to debate the issue together.

By tribal custom even the great Sore-Belly and Long-Hair could not, in theory, override the council's decision. Although in practice it would have been easy for Sore-Belly to have ignored it. Especially for a man like himself, who had the might of the military societies behind him to support almost everything he did or proposed. Yet to the full credit of the great war-chief, Sore-Belly never did abuse his powerful standing within the tribe, and in this instance, he remained consistent to that rule.

During the council some were those who, like Sore-Belly, declared it would be a very precarious undertaking to attack any of the white man's posts, for not only were the traders and their retainers always well-armed and expert marksmen with the musket, along with plentiful supplies of powder and ball, but in the aftermath, whether the Indians succeeded in their design or not, the traders might refuse to supply the Crows with goods in the future. Such would then cause the latter to be at the mercy of the many superiorly armed enemy tribes surrounding them.

This argument, of course, made good sense and after a period of further deliberation, it was agreed with the dissident faction which previously had clamoured for war, that only the Blackfoot post of Fort McKenzie should be targeted, and for the sole reason of preventing guns and ammunition being traded to the Blackfoot and Atsina enemies of the Crows. Sore-Belly did manage to gain the proviso that none of the white men at the post should be killed or physically harmed in any way, and that the Crow force should merely lay siege to the post until through hunger or despondency, the white men were forced to evacuate the site; abandon the supplies stored therein, and remove themselves and the post from the district once and for all. However, notwithstanding Sore-Belly`s pleas for restraint from those seeking a confrontation with the `Yellow Eyes,` and of who, he said, were *"without ears that they did not listen to his advice,"* [6] in his position as head war-chief, it was he who was expected to take charge of the undertaking proposed.

Now at the time Sore-Belly was making his plans, the annual trapper rendezvous between late June and mid-July 1834, was being held on Ham`s Creek, a tributary of the Black`s Fork branch of Green River in what is now southwestern Wyoming. In years past, Crows had sometimes attended these gatherings, but this year no Crows other than a few individuals were present. Too many white engages from the trading posts and trapping brigades were then in attendance along with great numbers of Shoshoni, Flathead and Nez-Perce, who at this period in time, were actually on a potential hostile footing against the Crows. Contrary then, to what some recent scholars have stated, Sore-Belly was not present at the trapper`s rendezvous this year. There was, though, a Nez-Perce chief in attendance, who having been wounded in the abdomen during the fight with the Atsina at Pierre`s Hole two years earlier, had since been known by the same name of Rotten-Belly or Sore-Belly, and it was this man who has been mistaken for the great Crow chief himself. It was, in fact, by knowing that the majority of white trappers in the Rocky Mountain region would be at the rendezvous, which had convinced the Crow chief to execute his planned attack against Fort McKenzie at this particular time. For as Sore-Belly rightly assumed, there would then be no formidable force of white men nearby, who might endeavour to bring relief and reinforcements to the occupants of the Crow`s intended objective.

So it was after the chiefs agreed to his strategy, Sore-Belly instructed a group of around thirty warriors to go on ahead. He bade them reconnoitre the country through which the main Crow force would have to travel in order to reach the fort, and determine if any enemy groups such as Blackfoot or Atsina in large number were encamped in the vicinity. The main host of Crows, he said, would follow in about ten days' time with all their lodges and belongings, along with a string of one-thousand pack ponies - one account states - upon the backs of which, the Crows intended to transport the vast quantity of trade goods and other plunder they expected to carry from the post, once it had been abandoned by its occupants.

It was, however, at the same time in the Crow camp on the Yellowstone where the discussions were taking place, that the Blood woman taken captive during the aforementioned fight with four Bloods after the debacle along Shonkin Creek, seized her moment to escape. She managed to get away without being detected and started north on foot towards Fort McKenzie. Somehow or other she knew the Crows were preparing to raid the post, and was determined to warn the white men of their intention.

It was five or more days later according to Major Culbertson, when he himself noticed someone moving around in the bushes across the river from the fort. He crossed over to see what or who it might be, and there discovered the dishevelled almost naked person of the Blood woman. She was dirty and emaciated from lack of food, and her feet badly cut and swollen because of having walked many days over thorns, prickly pear and sharp stones in order to reach the fort. It was indeed a miraculous escape and a commendable feat of endurance on the part of the woman. The Major took her into the fort; dressed her wounds and fed her, and cared for her until she fully recovered from her ordeal.

The woman then duly informed the Major of the Crow's hostile design, which, she said, was to attack the fort and destroy it. In response the Major began preparations for defence and immediately put all his post employees on a war footing.

The Crow scouting party, meanwhile, had set off from their camp and according to plan, they scouted most of the country to the immediate south, east and west of the fort. They did not see any sign of enemies or their abandoned camps and thus they reconnoitred the fort itself in order to note its defences and how many white men it contained. From a distance the fort appeared most vulnerable, and it was suggested among the scouts that it would be an easy task to run off the post's horses which would put the white men in a more disadvantageous position when the main Crow force arrived. This they agreed to do, and settling down for the night hidden amid a stand of timber under a bluff bordering the Teton River a short distance from the fort, they waited patiently for an appropriate opportunity to execute their plan.

Come morning the post employees as usual, drove their horses out through the main gate of the fort to allow them to graze on the adjacent prairie. The Crows had been watching the white men's every move, and decided that this was the chance they had been waiting for.

As soon as the white men left their horses and returned inside the stockade, a number of Crows suddenly rode in amongst the herd. The Crows were shouting at the tops of their voices whilst at the same time, they waved strips of red and blue strouding above their heads [breechclouts?] which frightened the animals into a stampede. In such a way they drove off around thirty head, these being all the horses belonging to the fort. So sudden and rapid was the raid, that the fort occupants did not even have time to level their muskets at the thieves, before the latter and the herd disappeared from view.

Whether the horses were stolen in compliance with Sore-Belly`s instructions to gain more bargaining power with the whites, is not determined. Yet in accordance with Indian character in general, it would seem more likely that the scouting party had merely taken the initiative on this occasion, not being able to resist such a tempting; and as it proved, so easily acquired prize.

Certainly, their action now convinced the Major and his employees of the veracity of the Blood woman's warning, that Crows were on the warpath against them. At once the Major began preparing everyone and everything in the fort, to be ready to withstand an impending attack.

The only commodity lacking within the fort itself was an adequate quantity of food. Meat was generally procured by post hunters as needed, and sometimes from the Indian customers themselves. But for the present no Indians other than those hostile toward the whites were on hand, and the only fresh game to be had was some distance from the fort on the open prairie. It was, though, now considered too dangerous to venture more than a few yards from the stockade walls, so that what food there was within the fort would have to be carefully rationed.

On the other hand, the daily water supply was usually obtained from the Teton River not one hundred yards from the fort. But even a trip that far was deemed not to be without serious risk. Consequently, a well some ten feet deep was dug inside the fort's interior and this provided the garrison with a constant and ample supply. Thus, as far as water was concerned, when the Crows did arrive on the scene, the white men would be well prepared to resist them.

It was during the latter part of July or early August, *"The moon when berries are picked,"* when the grand host of Crows comprising the whole River Crow band, finally made their appearance. According to the trader Edwin Denig, the Crows initially set up their tepees in the Pine Mountains about twenty miles east of the fort.

It was there, Denig said, that the Crows met a white trapper named John Coats who they knew well, and forced him to remain among them, as the Crows did not want the trapper telling those in the fort the Indian's true intentions.

For several days a body of Crows observed the fort from a position on the south bank of the Missouri, and it soon became clear that the building had since become a well-defended structure with its occupants ever on the alert. But notwithstanding, after a few days Sore-Belly decided to move the Crow village much closer to the fort, and had the tepees set up - some two-hundred and fifty in number - on the open prairie about one half-mile distant from the stockade.

It was soon after the relocation of the village, that Sore-Belly himself accompanied by a contingent of warriors, rode up to the fort. The chief hollered out to the proprietor, calling on him to open the gates and let him in.

The Major was a cautious man. He showed himself on the parapet of the gate wall and seemingly unnerved, shouted down to the chief saying, that a bunch of Crows had only recently ran off his entire herd which was tantamount to an act of war. Therefore, he continued, he would from here on only open the fort to those he regarded as friends.

Sore-Belly replied in a haughty tone. He proposed to talk the matter over with the Major and promised to make the thieves responsible give up the said horses, if only he, the Major, would rescind and let he and his warrior companions through the gate.

But the Major was adamant and again refused to allow them in. He further told Sore-Belly that he should return the horses anyway, which he could leave outside the gate in order to show his goodwill toward the whites. This, however, Sore-Belly refused to do without first being admitted inside. The chief then asked if he could speak to anyone in the stockade who knew the Crow language, which, of course, was a ploy to learn without the Major knowing, how many people were within, and what provisions they had to sustain them.

The Major, though, fully suspected Sore-Belly`s intention and did not respond to the request. Instead, this further act of defiance from the Crow chief only made the Major more belligerent. He actually ordered the chief and his warriors to depart, and added that if again they came to the fort fully armed, then he would not hesitate to empty the contents of his cannon amongst them.

At one stage during these verbal exchanges, the Blood woman once captive among the Crows, appeared atop the wall next to the Major. This was much to the astonishment of the Crows, who probably had assumed her dead from either hunger or exposure on the open Plains. What, though, was more important by her appearance, was that Sore-Belly now realized that the fort occupants must know the Crow's real intentions, and that even if his warriors were to assault the stockade, it would surely be a costly and, most likely, fruitless exercise.

The current situation was thus a stalemate.

After a while, Sore-Belly and his retinue returned to their lodges. But the Crows by their continued presence so near the fort, still prevented any of its occupants from venturing outside the stockade.

Obviously, the Major's threat to fire on the Crows if they returned with weapons in hand, had the desired effect. Hereafter, when groups of Crows came near the fort as they regularly did to take a closer look at the people they knew as "Yellow Eyes," they did so unarmed save their knives which were considered an indispensable part of everyday dress. Because of this, not a shot was fired by either Indian or white man and no blood had yet been spilt.

The next day the trapper John Coats, who until now, supposedly, had been forced to remain with the Crows, came to the fort alone and requested admittance. From his position outside the gate he told the Major the true purpose of the Crow's visiting the fort, and strongly advised him and his retinue not to let any of them in.

Perhaps this man Coats was genuine in his concern for the Major's safety and for all those within the fort walls. But even Denig; who was prone to give the lone trapper the benefit of the doubt, later admitted that the man Coates did appear to take more than a cursory interest in determining the amount of provisions among the defenders. Coats was, in fact, a free trapper with no allegiance to any particular trading outfit and, one suspects - as indeed some whites did at the time - that he had been and still was, actually in cahoots with the Crows, having been sent by Sore-Belly to gain information which the chief himself could not acquire. Either way, the Major would not let Coats through the gate, although the Major did give him several knives and a quantity of tobacco with which to present to Sore-Belly and his subordinate chiefs, as a token of the white man's continued propensity for friendship with the Crows. Coats then took his leave with his tail between his legs and rode off, presumably to make his report in the Crow village from whence he came.

As the days dragged by the supply of food within the fort became evermore scarce. When the meat and dried jerky was gone, the inmates resorted to killing and eating the post dogs, and after these poor creatures had been consumed, old parfleches and other scraps of leather including rawhide straps and the like, were boiled up into a glue-like soup and this alone sustained life among the defenders.

Soon, murmurings of discontent and of potential mutiny began to be voiced among the Major's men. Some even suggested they should give up the post to the Crows if the Indians would allow them safe passage down river to Fort Union. But Major Culbertson held fast. He was hoping the Crows would eventually tire of their sport and depart in peace, and by so doing, profitable trading relations might again be restored for the benefit of the Company and Indians alike. So it was that the Major would let none in the fort fire on the Crows, who in their small groups continued to come regularly to its walls, although mostly, it seemed, merely in order to converse with the whites upon various unimportant topics and to beg trinkets from them. But still the Crows would not leave. Several more days elapsed, by which time the very last piece of edible material in the fort had been accounted for.

At last, the Major decided that he and his men had endured all that was possible without resorting to violent retaliatory measures. He finally planned to take action which, he hoped, would relieve the situation one way or the other, even if it resulted in the death of himself and all with him.

As above mentioned, each day groups of unarmed Crows continued to congregate outside the stockade, and to some of those within, it seemed as if they were mocking the sufferings of the white men. It had been all the Major could do to keep his men from losing their nerve and firing on the besiegers. Now, however, it was the Major himself who was ready to retaliate with all the fire power at his disposal. Employing a number of Crows who happened to be at the stockade walls to act as intermediaries, he sent word to Sore-Belly saying that if he and his people did not soon vacate the region, then he would open war upon them and hurl his thunderbolts among their lodges and their people.

Sore-Belly, it is said, upon receiving the message, merely laughed at the threat and the Crows continued as they had been doing. Indeed, they were now under the impression that they themselves were on the verge of achieving their objective, which was to force the inmates to abandon the fort and supplies. But the Major was not one to make idle threats.

That same night the Major held a crisis meeting with those within the fort. He told them the situation in no uncertain terms. The crisis, he said, had now come to a head. He had been expecting his Blackfoot customers to return in force from their annual excursion to the Lower Saskatchewan, and their presence alone would likely scare the Crows into a precipitous retreat. Unfortunately, though, as they could plainly see, there was as yet no sign of their coming. Also late was the Fur Company's keelboat, usually sent up river from Fort Union and arrived by this time, carrying reinforcements in both men and provisions, and thus as a consequence of their present condition, their position was desperate in the extreme.

The Major went on to say that as he was the trader in charge, he alone was entrusted by the Company with the safety of the fort, along with all the merchandise stored therein. It was his responsibility, he said, to protect them both with his life if need be, or to relinquish his authority forthwith.

He then told his employees to charge the cannons and their muskets, for at the stroke of noon the following day, he intended to lead them out of the fort to take a stand against the Indians besieging them. He would offer the Indians battle, he said, or the chance to depart, and if still the Crows remained, then they - the white men - should be prepared to die fighting where they stood.

It was not an idea entirely welcomed by his men, but was nonetheless, deemed better than starving to death and no one among them so Denig`s account indicates, suggested any alternative action.

So it was the very next day that the Major and his employees got ready to sally out of the fort, and confront the Crows in mortal combat.

It was by divine providence, perhaps, that just before the appointed hour of midday arrived, a distant cloud of dust was observed to the north of the fort. This indicated either a herd of buffalo moving over the prairie, or a multitude of people and horses in the guise of a large Indian village, travelling in the direction of the fort.

The Crows, of course, had also discerned the same rising dust and already, scores of mounted warriors were hastily leaving camp in order to ascertain its origin.

It was not long before these Crows returned, and the intelligence they imparted to their people, must have been obvious even to the Major and his men, who themselves, could neither hear or understand properly what was said. But almost at once the young Crow boys began driving in the horses, while the women tore down tepee covers and started hastily packing belongings on pony drags. Within the hour, the whole site which once had been cluttered with tepees, was deserted, save a number of skeleton lodges scattered here and there, formed by sets of tepee poles left standing and abandoned in the people's haste to vacate the area completely. Even the great Sore-Belly could not restrain them, for the cause of alarm was that a strong force of combined Blackfoot and Atsina estimated as comprising some eight-hundred lodges, was within only a half-days travelling distance from the fort.

The white men, meanwhile, upon being made aware of this welcome news, raised their voices in a joyous and thankful uproar. At long last, they were delivered from the Crows and their expected fate.

The majority of Crows in turn, were already re-crossing the Missouri in as rapid a manner as possible, and soon began disappearing from view as they traversed the open grasslands stretching south.

Some warriors did loiter on top of low benchlands bordering the south bank of the river. As a final act of defiance, they fired a number of harmless musket shots at the white men who now stood along the parapet walls of the fort, watching and jeering as the main body of Crows faded into the distance.

The fort inmates had survived many days of fear and starvation, but had saved the fort and its stores and withal, the Fur Company's honour. The Crows on the other hand, and not least Sore-Belly, had been out-maneuverered and humiliated, a fact which would propell the chief in a future endeavour to erase the shame of failure, even if sacrificing his own life in order to do so.

James H. Bradley when writing of the affair some years later from information obtained from Major Culbertson himself, stated that the end of the siege had come about in a different way. According to his account, instead of

330

sallying forth with his men to actually confront the Crows man to man, the Major had one of the cannons in the fort loaded with solid shot and at noon on the day in question, had it aimed and fired into the Indian camp. The Crow men folk for the most part, were then off hunting and the shot landed dead centre of the camp causing great alarm among the Indian non-combatants. So surprised were the villagers, Bradley continued, that they immediately dismantled their lodges and departed the scene within the hour.

It is highly unlikely, however, that the white man's aim would have been so precise with their first shot, and the Crows anyway, would surely have then retaliated by storming the fort and taking revenge upon all those within. It must be remembered that Bradley stated elsewhere that it was always the Major's intention not to engage in hostilities with the Indians, which fact is corroborated by Denig. It seems, therefore, that if a cannon was at any time fired into the village, then it was in a moment of jubilant frustration after the besiegers had left, and incurred no actual injuries among the Crows, who were still regarded as potential customers if the current difficulties could be resolved.

There is also in the several accounts, a great deal of discrepancy regarding the exact length of time the fort and its occupants remained under siege. The James Bradley account says *"ten days,"* whilst Edwin Denig said, *"...nearly a month,"* and in a letter sent by the then trader in charge of Fort Union, one J. Archdale Hamilton to Kenneth McKenzie, dated September 17th. 1834, it is clearly stated that Culbertson and his people had been,

> *"...compelled by the Crows to live on cords parfleche for fifteen days."* [7]

On the other hand, the English naturist and artist John Audubon, wrote in his journal in the eighteen-forties from information copied from Culbertson`s own journal, that the siege had lasted only two days, i.e., between June 25th and 26th, and that Blood Blackfoot Indians had brought meat to the fort on June 30th.

Obviously this was either a slip of the pen on Audubon`s part, or a misunderstanding of the facts and, more likely, the text should have read something in the guise of "twenty days." Likewise, there appears to be some disagreement whether the siege took place in June, July or August. But here we have the diary entry of the Missionary Jason Lee for the month of June, 1834, which asserts that the Crows were then friendly towards the white men. Thus, the besieging of the fort one suspects, occurred after this remark, probably in late July, or, as the Denig account states, *"... early August ."* [8]

Be this as it may, and notwithstanding William M. Anderson`s understated comment in his diary penned August 24th, 1834, *"The Crows are becoming suspiciously audacious,"* [9] the whole affair as far as the American Fur Company was concerned, caused some disquiet among its hierarchy. Thereafter they instructed their employees to be on guard against further hostile acts perpetrated by Crows, although at the same time, it was also fully realized that the Indian intention had not been to harm the whites unnecessarily, but rather, merely to force them to abandon the practice of trading directly with that tribe's enemies so near Crow country. Because of this and for the time being, Fort McKenzie`s sister post Fort Cass near the mouth of the Big Horn continued to operate among the Crows, who were encouraged still to bring in their furs and buffalo robes without fear of recriminations for recent misdeeds. This is not to say that the affair at Fort McKenzie was soon to be forgotten. As late as May the following year of 1835, in a letter penned by a senior partner in the Company named Lamont, to Major Culbertson, who was then still in charge at Fort McKenzie, it is clearly stated,

> *"... should the Crow Indians come near you again this summer, do not spare them tooth or nail."* [10]

In other words, the Company's official line was to engage the Indians with all the fire power at Culbertson`s disposal, if again the Crows should show such hostility towards him. Although how practical this would have been if the occasion had again arose, must be open to debate.

Contingency plans, however, in the immediate aftermath of the event, were put into effect by the Company. One of which was to remove all employees from the fort at the time Crows were likely to appear in force, albeit such times being only during the absence of Blackfoot being encamped in the vicinity.

- 0 - 0 – 0 – 0 – 0 – 0 – 0 – 0 – 0 – 0 – 0 – 0 – 0 -

## CHAPTER. 29.

## THE SLAYING OF A CHIEF.

An important consequence regarding the aborted siege of Fort McKenzie, had been the humiliation suffered by the Crows, and which was likely to destroy the great Chief Sore-Belly`s own standing within the tribe. This Sore-Belly knew too well, for had he not also sworn to avenge the death of Little-White-Bear or die in the attempt? Yet whilst the Crows were travelling south, the recently arrived host of Blackfoot and Atsina against whom Sore-Belly could have carried out his vow, was encamped only one half-day journey north. But the rest of the Crows at that time had been in no mind to engage such a superior force, and especially so, whilst their own self-confidence and prowess had been somewhat undermined by a handful of white men behind a picket fence.

Such was typical of Indian character and, it must be said, the Blackfoot and Atsina upon being informed by the white men to whom they brought succour and relief, that the Crow force had only just departed and in which direction it was travelling, had themselves been reluctant to give chase. They suspected the Crows would be broiling for a fight, which would likely cost the Blackfoot and Atsina many casualties in dead and wounded before a victory might be had.

It was the conclusion therefore, among both Crows and Blackfoot, that their respective actions were expedient, and although it may have grieved Sore-

Belly that he personally had not got to grips with the foe, there was, it seemed, really no practical alternative whilst he had his people's women and children in tow. Thus the Crows continued their southward trek towards the Yellowstone and home. [1]

A more serious concern, however, was permeating through Sore-Belly's mind. Due to his personal involvement in besieging the fort, he suspected it had lost him any confidence and respect from those such as Kenneth McKenzie and Major Sanford, who, previously, the chief had always striven to court as friends to assist his people against their enemies. The fact that he had not over-ruled the populist decision of his rank and file subordinates to indulge in such a hostile act against the fort and its occupants, was, he thought, a serious failure on his part, and an indication of his inexcusable lack of judgement and persuasion at that time. Now Sore-Belly fully regretted his involvement, and deemed himself no longer capable of insuring his people's welfare, having supported what he had initially advised against and had really always known, would be a short-sighted action against the traders which could only be detrimental regarding his people's future. All white men, hereafter, would surely turn their faces from the Crows and refuse them guns and ammunition, thereby leaving them at the mercy of those tribes endeavouring to exterminate them and claim the Crow country for themselves. Already, Sore-Belly knew, some among his own people were uttering disparaging remarks regarding his seemingly diminished prowess and judgement, which caused him to feel that his time as their spiritual and unerring leader had likely run its course. He decided to give his people the opportunity to elect a new Head Chief, one who might better lead them and preserve the sacred land of *Echeta Casha*, - even if it meant that he [Sore-Belly], must forfiet his own life to do so. Thus, from hereon, he would merely wait an opportune time when he could put his commitment into effect.

The following morning after leaving the vicinity of the fort, the Crow column had not travelled far before a body of scouts having been sent out at dawn, came galloping back to the main party. They brought word they had discovered a small group of Atsina coming towards them from the south.

It was later learned that these Atsina were members of a war-party returning to their own country with horses, recently stolen during a raid on Long-Hair's Mountain Crow village on the Big Horn.

At once a large body of Crows including Sore-Belly, galloped off in the direction indicated by the scouts. The chief and a small group of warriors were far in the lead, and were first to come upon their quarry.

The Atsina party consisted of only twelve warriors. They were at that time sitting on the ground in a circle smoking pipes outside a rough barricade of logs, such as were often found scattered throughout the Upper Missouri country. Their horses were left unattended, resting and grazing nearby. The Atsina position was, in fact, a strong one in what was commonly known as a war-lodge.

War-lodges came in various shapes and sizes and in this instance, it consisted of a square formed by felled and rotten tree trunks, placed on top of one another some two to three feet high to that of a crouching man. The gaps between the logs had been filled with brush and overall, crude as it may have looked, it presented a formidable obstacle against pedestrian assault. At the same time it offered more than adequate cover for those seeking its protection. Many such structures were to be found in that part of the country where both trees and brush were abundant. Often they were repaired and utilized by successive war-parties when travelling war-trails to or from an enemy camp, regardless as to what tribe had previously used them, or to the tribal affiliation of their original builders.

Immediately, upon sighting the Atsina, the Crows charged towards them and the latter did not have time to mount their horses such was the momentum of attack. Instead, most of the Atsina retreated behind the protection of their barricade and prepared to defend themselves as best they could.

During the initial assault, the Crows succeeded in killing two enemy stragglers and took their scalps, while the rest of the foe secured themselves within their defences. In addition, the Crows captured all the Atsina horses and equipment, which the latter had abandoned in their haste to seek cover.

It was soon after this that the main body of Crows came up. But they realized the Atsina were in a strong position and well-armed with bows and arrows and also guns of English manufacture, far superior to those obtained from American traders south of the International border. The Crows themselves, as previously noted, had at this time very few guns of any description, not having had the required furs and buffalo robes with which to trade in order to replenish a supply of powder and ball needed to charge them. They knew it would not be to their advantage if they continued to oppose these enemies. For notwithstanding the latter's disparity in number, many Crows would likely be killed and wounded if they attempted to rub them out, or even to drive them from the barricades.

Sore-Belly, though, was determined to mount an attack and was only restrained from doing so by several of his warriors, who held fast to the bridle of his horse to prevent him riding off on his own into the midst of the enemy. They urged him by earnest entreaty to abandon such a reckless action, and at length, Sore-Belly was obliged to agree it would be expedient to leave the Atsina alone. His comrades suggested they should bide their time until circumstances were more conducive to obtaining an even greater victory, when they might avenge the death of Little-White-Bear in a more spectacular manner.

The Crow party thus gave up the fight and returned to camp - needless to say with a reluctant and despondent Sore-Belly among them. Most, however, were fully satisfied with the two Atsina scalps and captured ponies obtained without loss to themselves. But Sore-Belly had decided he personally was not long for the World, and was already preparing himself for another.

On their return, the Crow war-party found that the column of their non-combatants meanwhile, had set up camp for the rest of that day and did not intend moving again until next morning. So the returning warriors retired to their respective lodges in order to rest and eat, and shield themselves from the noon-day sun.

It was just after mid-day when Sore-Belly, who upon returning to the village had also retired to his lodge, suddenly reappeared in the centre of the camp.

Now he was mounted on his favourite war-pony and dressed in full war atire. This consisted of a long single-tailed eagle feathered bonnet; beaded and hair-fringed war-shirt and wrapped around his waist, his unique scalp-fringed red robe adorned with rude depictions of his many deeds. He also wore beaded and hair-fringed leggings, and beaded moccasins completed his attire. In his right hand he held a twelve-foot lance, whilst hanging from his left arm was his famous *medicine* shield with the image of the big-eared androgynous figure emblazoned on it. He was singing aloud a war-song, and all the people came out of their lodges and gathered around to see what he was doing.

When a large crowd had assembled, Sore-Belly calmly dismounted from his pony; stuck his lance upright in the ground and took the *medicine* shield from his arm. This he then held horizontally before him in both hands with arms outstretched, its painted side facing skywards.

Still holding the shield, Sore-Belly told those around him that he would cast it on its rim along the ground, and if the painted side should fall face down, then one great man among them would not return from the next fight with the enemy. But, he concluded, if the shield should land face up, then it would show that *Akbaa-tadia* still bestowed favour on the Crows, and that he, Sore-Belly, would continue to be their chief and protector.

He next walked over to where a pile of buffalo chips had earlier been raised in the centre of the camp. He climbed to the top of the pile and stood in full view of the people, who continued to stand motionless and in silence, watching attentively his every move. Then, as the great chief had done many times before, he tossed the shield on its rim along the open ground below him, which set the shield rolling, until it began to wobble before finally coming to a halt, whereupon it fell flat and landed on its painted side, so portending the death of a great man among the Apsaalooka.

Seeing the shield lying thus, Sore-Belly - with no discernible sign of emotion - remounted his pony and began riding slowly and majestically around the lodges. He spoke again to those looking on saying, two Atsina scalps were not enough to compensate for the death of Little-White-Bear. Neither did he feel he could protect his people further. He had warned them against causing trouble with the whites who must now hold the prowess of the Apsaalooka in contempt. The Crow people, he said, are fools, for their ears had not listened to the words of their chief who always had their best welfare at heart. They had ignored his advice and had raised their voices against his wishes, and thus by their actions against the white men, had now brought shame upon *Alapooish* and on themselves. He raised his eyes to the heavens and cried,

> "Oh, *Akbaa-tadia*. This one who stands humbled before you, offers
> a red blanket of his blood," [2]

He then continued berating those around him with words to the effect,

> "This great shame *Alapooish* shall wipe away; he no longer cares to
> live. He will give his body to the wolves and join his brothers in the
> `Other-side camp` of his ancestors. This one has been given a vision,

335

in which his stiff and lifeless body lay amid the corpses of his enemies. His *medicine* father the `Thunder` and the spirit of his brother-friend Little-White-Bear are calling to him, and hereafter, the Apsaalooka will regret not having heeded the advice of their chief." [3]

The women and old people still stood motionless and silent as they listened to his words. But they realized the mind of Sore-Belly was fully resolved in his suicidal undertaking. They were, however, not unduly surprised that such a dire event as the demise of their great chief would soon transpire. Only the previous night, it is said, the piecing shrill of a Screech Owl;- the harbinger of doom and death - had been heard repeatedly among the trees.

The warriors on the other hand, began whooping war-cries and singing *medicine* songs, for they knew a battle must be imminent. Soon the cry was for Atsina scalps, and all at once the warriors rushed to don their war-clothes. They then mounted ponies; took up weapons, and were ready and eager to follow their leader against the foe. And so it was before mid-afternoon, a host of mounted Crows including Sore-Belly, with the long feathered tail of his war-bonnet streaming in the wind, galloped from the camp and in the direction where, earlier that day, they had left the small band of Atsina behind their cottonwood breastworks.

During all this time the enemy had remained within their defences, as they had fully expected the Crows to return and resume their attack. The Atsina knew, of course, owing to the earlier capture of their horses, that if they abandoned their position and attempted to continue their homeward journey on foot, they would have much less chance of survival if caught in the open by mounted warriors, who would be able to run them down with ease and kill them one by one. They had decided therefore, to stay where they were, until they could be sure the Crows were not likely to return and were moving out of the region.

This the Crows had fully suspected and when they did arrive at the scene, they were not surprised to find the foe still behind their breastworks. But rather than immediately assaulting the position, the Crows reined in their mounts. Instead, they hovered tentatively around as if afraid to get to grips with the foe, whose guns and bows and arrows again bristled menacingly atop the barricade. It seemed, in truth, the Crows were undecided what to do next.

This was the chance Sore-Belly had been hoping for. If he could not regain lost prestige in any other way, then he would attempt to do so by performing some spectacular deed, by which even in death, his name would again be spoken with respect among his people and enemies alike, and his memory held in reverence ever more. He thus rode out alone in front of his warriors and in words narrated by Joe Medicine Crow, began addressing them as follows,

"The *Billebaachii* [White men] are on the great rivers [i.e. Platte and Missouri]. They are like ants. Already they have driven our red brothers west from where the sun rises, and many tribes no longer walk this earth. Soon we Raven Men also will be no more. Our enemies are strong and pushing us back beyond *Echeta Casha*. Truly, we, too, must go under; back to the red earth from whence we came. This one does not want to see this come to pass. He will go while his father the Sun and bright sky is above him.to where a Crow can continue as *Akbaa-tadia* intended, and again be with his brother Little-White-Bear, in the Spirit Land beyond." [4]

He then continued,

"Here you are my warriors facing the enemy, yet you stand off and tremble before him. Alapooish alone is not afraid. He shall be first to strike those who cringe behind their breastworks, 'though he will be killed in the attempt. If there are any among you who dare, let them follow Alapooish, and let it be known there are still brave men who call themselves Apsaalooka." [5]

Hardly had these words left his lips when, suddenly, Sore-Belly spurred his pony forward. He held his lance high, its iron blade pointing at the foe, and rode far in front of his warriors who, after some hesitation and thus some distance behind, also charged towards the barricades.

As the chief raced forward, all at once the Atsina guns began flashing and popping, and the musket balls, it is said, flew thick around him. But Still Sore-Belly came on, yelling the Apsaalooka war-cry *"Koo-Koo-Hey,"* and the Atsina shots went wild. With one great leap, Sore-Belly`s painted and be-feathered steed sailed right over the barricade and carried its rider in amongst the enemy. Almost immediately the Crow chief pinned one of his adversaries to the ground with his lance, while at the same time, a shower of arrows whistled towards him, for the Atsina had no time to reload their muskets.

Several Atsina arrows did find their mark, however, and punctured Sore-Belly and his pony in various places. One feathered missile, according to Winona`s account, was enough in itself to cause a death wound. This particular arrow was tipped with an obsidian point which struck just above the hip, and having been fired at an upward angle at very close range, its velocity drove the shaft deep into Sore-Belly`s torso so that its sharp point protruded from one shoulder. Several other arrows also struck the chief which were sufficient in themselves to cause serious wounds. Subsequently, Sore-Belly fell from his stumbling mount a dying man, even before his body touched the ground. [6]

By then, the rest of the Crow warriors charging forward in Sore-Belly`s wake had themselves reached the barricade, and the Atsina did not have time to set about the chief's body with their knives and axes. Both Crows and horses in overwhelming number leapt over the low breastworks, and went smashing into the huddled Atsina group within.

The Crows later said, that the few Atsina fought well that day and showed much bravery. But such was the fury of the Crows after seeing their great chief fall, that it took only moments before all were killed and their bloody scalps held aloft in the hands of the victors. The Crows then further vented their fury, it is also said, and cut the Atsina heads off.

The battle over, several warriors gathered around the prostrate form of their dying chief. Winona Plenty-Hoops stated that the pipe-holder Yellow-Belly who was a younger adopted brother of Sore-Belly, knelt beside the great chief and propped him up in his arms with the chief's head and shoulders resting on his lap. Two other pipe-holders, Tall [High] Bull and Grizzly-Bear also came close and together they listened, as Sore-Belly spoke. [6] With the last breaths of life, Sore-Belly uttered his final words in a scarcely audible tone. These came haltingly from his mouth, the gist of which according to Beckwourth, ran as follows,

> "Alapooish came here to die. Hear his dying words, for they are good words. Preserve the peace with the Yellow Eyes and do his bidding and you will always have guns and ammunition to defend yourselves...Leave the body of Alapooish where he has fallen, so your enemies will continue to fear his spirit. But when the flesh has gone, retrieve the bones, so that Alapooish may rest ever more in his beloved Crow country. [7]

The great chief then closed his eyes, and his soul wended its way to the 'Other-side camp' beyond.

To the end, Sore-Belly's *medicine* which protected him throughout his warrior life from iron-bladed weapons, iron-tipped missiles and leaden balls had remained strong. But it had been an obsidian-tipped arrow which finally laid him low.

With heavy hearts Grizzly-Bear and others placed the chief's lifeless form on a wolf skin. Next they lay his lance and battle-axe by his side, and wrapped the whole in a bundle composed of the dead chief's own scalp-fringed robe. In compliance with Sore-Belly's wish, they placed the bundle high in a tree straddling a natural fork in its branches and there the bundle would remain, defying his people's enemies when ere they crossed that trail. Eventually, the enveloping robe and cloth would disintegrate through the ravages of time and nature. The rotting flesh be picked by fowl of the air and the bones, after falling from their perch onto Mother Earth, would attract the beasts of the prairie to gnaw what was left. Such was the custom by which the great warrior was initially laid to rest, having been slain on the field of combat.

As the party made its weary way back to camp; it was a slow-moving morbid-looking column. Many warriors were crying aloud for the loss of their great mentor and protector, the greatest Crow war-chief of all. A few riders rode ahead to inform the villagers what had happened, and by the time the returning party came in, all the tepees had been dismantled and were lying dishevelled on the ground. This was a sign that a great catastrophe had occurred and hideous mournful wailings resounded from the people. As the warriors rode past, dozens - if not hundreds - of finger joints were already being lopped off, in expressions of the people's profound sorrow and respect.

It was not long before word of Sore-Belly's demise reached the head chief Long-Hair and the Mountain Crows. They in turn entered into a prolonged period of mourning and Long-Hair, it is said, actually cut off a large hank of his own hair which, by its luxuriant growth; cultivated and doted upon by its owner for many years, had been regarded as a potent protective *medicine* thought to guarantee the welfare of the Nation. Such was deemed appropriate to show how deeply the loss of Sore-Belly was felt, and to symbolize the high standing by which the great war-leader had been held among the people.

For many weeks both day and night the people mourned without respite, and it was some time before the clans finally moved off in their separate bodies towards their respective autumn hunting grounds.

## EPILOGUE

Notice concerning the death of Sore-Belly was variously recorded in contemporary Fur Company records in the guise of letters and journals written soon after the event. In the Fort Clark journal kept by Francis A. Chardon, we find under the date August, 8th 1834,

"...May [a company employee] arrived from the Gros Ventres [Hidatsa] with news of the death of Rotten-Belly [Sore-Belly], chief of the Crows, who was killed by the Blackfoot," [8]

Additionally, in a letter sent from Fort Union dated 17th September, 1834, it is confirmed that Rotten-Belly had been killed. Thus the date 1835 as given by Denig and Bradley is obviously in error, although both, no doubt, had obtained their information from Major Culbertson, who appears to have been the original source for miss-dating the event in the first place. Indeed, Culbertson often erred by one and sometimes two years in other instances of his recollections when; as an old man with a faulty memory, he was speaking to James Bradley many years later in the mid-1870s.

The exact site of the battle in which Sore-Belly died and the place where his body was left in the branches of a tree, must always remain in doubt. Beckwourth's account implied that the battle had taken place at a spot some two days travel north of the Yellowstone, whilst Edwin Denig - wisely one might suppose, - declined to give any specific location, merely stating that the event took place whilst the Crows were on their way home after the aborted siege of Fort McKenzie. On the other hand, Lieutenant Bradley's version, although brief, locates the scene as being near the particular eminence north west of Fort Benton [later built on the same site as Ft. McKenzie] called the *"Bosque D' Obard"* or "Goose Bill." However, this would then place the site in the very heart of Pikuni and Atsina country, and which appears unlikely when one considers that the Crows had been in the process of fleeing south, away from the formidable Blackfoot host then encamped within the vicinity of the fort.

Whatever the case, the renowned fighter Grizzly-Bear temporarily stepped into the position made vacant by the great chief's demise. But there were others such as Tall-Bull, Red-Bear and Bear's-Tooth who had no wish to accept Grizzly-Bear's overall authority. Thus a number of families from among the River and Mountain bands turned their backs upon the unity of the Nation, once achieved and kept in place by Sore-Belly himself. Instead, these dissident chiefs and their respective adherents chose to go their separate ways, to become individual camps and clans scattered throughout the country. By so doing they were, of course, putting themselves in a most vulnerable position, prone to enemy attack in formidable force upon one or another of their now isolated camps, such as had occurred fourteen years earlier when the "Eight-hundred were stolen."

Some months later on November 20th, 1834, warriors from a combined camp of Mountain and River Crows which had remained united and led by the newly installed war-chief Grizzly Bear, achieved a great victory over the Blackfoot. A sixty-nine strong Pikuni war-party was surrounded in a rocky place near No Wood Creek which flows into the east side of the Big Horn River, and during which event, Beckwourth was most prominent for his singular assault upon the enemy stronghold. The trapper Zenas Leonard who was present at the time, graphically described the event as follows,

"...Now was the moment for action. Each man appeared willing to sacrifice his life if it would bring down an enemy...Again and again did they return to the charge, but all was of no use...confusion began to spread through their ranks...the whole Crow nation was about to retreat from the field, when the negro, who has been heretofore mentioned, and who had been in company with us, advanced a few steps before the Crows and ascended a rockfrom which he addressed the Crow warriors...He told them that they had been making a great noise, as if they would kill the enemy by it, – that they had talked long and loud about going into the fort, and that the white men would say the Indian had a crooked tongue when talking about his war exploits. He told them their hearts were small, and that they were cowardly – that they acted more like squaws than men, and were not fit to defend their hunting ground. He told them that the white men were ashamed of them and would refuse to trade with such a nation of cowards – that the Blackfeet would go home and tell their people that three thousand Crows could not take a handful of them, - that they would be laughed at, scorned and treated with contempt by all nations wherever known...The old negro continued in this strain until they became greatly animated and told them that if the red man was afraid to go amongst his enemy, he would show them that a black man was not, and he leaped from the rock on which he had been standing, and looking neither to the right nor to the left, made for the fort as fast as he could run. The Indians guessing his purpose, and inspired by his words and fearless example, followed

340

close to his heels, and in the fort dealing destruction to the right and left nearly as soon as the old man…" [9]

The result was that the entire Pikuni force was rubbed out by the Crows, which was deemed a fitting episode to help compensate the loss of Sore-Belly.

However, notwithstanding this astounding victory and regarding the River Crows specifically, throughout the ensuing winter and coming spring, still no sizeable war-party from the River band actually ventured abroad. This was due to the continuing despondent attitude among the River Crows which the loss of Sore-Belly had brought upon them, and thus the winter passed with little combined hostile activity on their part.

Come mid-summer the following year [1835], the sub-chief Bear's-Tooth led a party of select warriors north to where Sore-Belly's corpse had been deposited, as it was time to gather up the dead chief's bones and bring them back into Crow country where they could be permanently laid to rest. By so doing, the dead chief's spirit, it was believed, would continue to protect the people as once, in mortal form, Sore-Belly had done so in life.

At the same time, Long-Hair, who was still the Nation's paramount chief, dispatched runners to each of the scattered camps of Mountain and River Crows, informing them that the people should again come together at a designated place along Rosebud River between the Big Horn and the Tongue. This trysting site was near the newly-erected Fort Van Buren close to the mouth of Tongue River built to replace the since abandoned Fort Cass, and there, while the Crows were holding their annual Medicine Lodge ceremonies, the bones of Sore-Belly would be ritually honoured and their final resting place agreed upon.

All the Apsaalooka people regardless of earlier dissensions, responded to the call. And so it was that Bear's-Tooth and his party after retrieving the bones of the great chief, carried them south to the grand tepee encampment on the Rosebud. There the bones were wrapped in a new bundle consisting of a richly decorated robe, and paraded on horseback in front of all the Crows with great ceremony. The hysteria of the occasion, though, caused the people's grief to be rekindled. Once again blood flowed profusely from hundreds of self-inflicted wounds. The very hills of the Wolf Teeth Mountains overlooking the camp, reverberated to cries of unbridled anguish mixed with doleful lamentations, and Beckwourth's account describes graphically the people's mourning at that time,

."…The cutting and hacking of human flesh exceeded all my previous experience; fingers were dismembered as readily as twigs and blood was poured out like water. Many of the warriors would cut two gashes nearly the entire length of their arm; then separating the skin from the flesh at one end, would grasp it in their other hand, and rip it asunder to the shoulder. Others would carve various devices upon their breasts and shoulders, and raise the skin in the same manner, to make the scars show to advantage after the wound was healed. Some of their mutilations were ghastly; but they would not appear to receive any pain from them." [10]

Anon, it was decided that the bones be deposited high on a butte, where Sore-Belly had often conducted his lonely vigils to fast and communicate with the Sacred Beings which had given him his protective powers. Accordingly; several days later, a great complement of chiefs and warriors started southeast toward the designated butte with the bones of their beloved leader re-wrapped in a red blanket bundle. The bundle itself was draped over the withers of a fine appaloosa pony, which trotted along with a solemn gait as if, it too, sensed the reverence of the occasion and the great honour bestowed upon it by bearing such a burden.

Coming to a halt at the base of a red rock eminence jutting up from the prairie floor, near where the small town of Dayton, Wyoming now stands, the bundle was laid to rest atop its crest, and with this ultimate act, the period of mourning within the Apsaalooka Nation at last came to an end, notwithstanding that Sore-Belly`s immediate relatives continued to express their grief for many moons thereafter.

Having returned to camp, Long-Hair held council with the Nation`s head men, and the position of Grizzly-Bear as new Head war-chief of the Crows was officially sanctioned as a permanent office. The initial dissent among other perspective candidates was quelled, and especially so, after Grizzly-Bear`s recent great victory over the sixty-nine Pikuni. However, Sore-Belly`s old Society of "Half-Shaved-Heads" was, hitherto, disbanded, as a token of respect for the dead chief; and the society`s redundant members joined the Lump-Wood Society in its stead. [11]

Before the grand gathering on the Rosebud dispersed, Long-Hair persuaded the people to again consolidate their scattered camps into larger bands. This to protect themselves more effectively by presenting a formidable military force which, in time of need, could combine to counter any large-scale attack from their many foes. By this arrangement the people again organized themselves into three divisions, and which together constituted the Apsaalooka Nation of River Crows, Mountain Crows and the Kicked-in-the-Belly band.

However, it was the demise of Sore-Belly which heralded the end of an era for the Raven Men of the Yellowstone.

In the immediate aftermath of Sore-Belly`s death, and due to the establishment of Sublette and Campbell`s trading post at the junction of the Laramie River and North Platte along with other posts which followed, Oglala, Miniconjou and Brule Lakota migrated west to that locality, lured by a rapid acceleration of the buffalo-robe trade. As a result, enemy peoples began populating what had been regarded as Crow Country in north-eastern Wyoming and south-eastern Montana, and for the next four decades, the Crows were continually resisting ever-increasing incursions from foreign invaders.

After suffering a catastrophic drop in population owing to recurring diseases throughout the 1840s and `50s, the Crows were obliged to relinquish their one-time predominance and that part of *Echeta Casha* east of the Big Horn River.

Even then, the writing was on the wall regarding the end of Crow freedom on the Plains.

But that is another volnme.

Here we have followed the life and passing of the great Sore-Belly, and with him, the ascendency of Crow military might in the Upper Missouri country. Many heroic persons and episodes continued to fill the pages of Crow history until intertribal warfare came to an end, and notwithstanding having lost a number of battles, they nevertheless won the war, and so remain an unconquered people who still hold an important part of *Echeta Casha* as their own. Such, however, has been made possible also by the Crow people's own individual determination and political diplomacy, rather than the bloodied axe of any one man's military leadership as Sore-Belly once exerted over the Nation.

This being said, it had been Sore-Belly alone who made the Crows the most resilient Indian group on the Northern Plains; respected by Indian and White man alike. Even today, the great chief's legacy can be observed in the pride and bearing of the Apsaalooka people, who through their many trials and tribulations, still stand tall and steadfast in the modern world around them.  *

## THE END

**\*A personal pipe and iron-bladed tomahawk belonging to Sore-Belly still survive, although more tangible to the great chief's memory is the continued existence of his famous *medicine* shield. This object was once regarded as an important tribal heirloom, and was employed many times even after Sore-Belly's death, in order to determine forthcoming events during hostile escapades in which Crows were involved. In 1923 it was successfully purchased by William Wildschut from Chief Bull-Tongue's widow, and fortunately for posterity, it survives today as an exhibit in The National Museum of the American Indian, New York.**

CROW WARRIOR, BULL-TONGUE.
*[Photo by Edward S. Curtis. 1907].*

CROW CHIEF, HIGH-LANCE.
*[Alfred Jacob Miller in 1837.]*

View of Shonkin Creek, looking west.     *[Author`s collection]*

344

APPENDIX A.

APPENDIX A.

## ANALYSIS OF THE ATTACK ON LONG-HAIR'S VILLAGE IN 1820.
### [DOCUMENTS AND RELATED MATERIAL]

Two accounts of the allied attack upon the Crow village of Long-Hair in 1820, were written by a Lieutenant James H. Bradley in 1876. He obtained his information from Crow warriors then employed as government scouts against the hostile Lakota and Cheyenne led by Sitting Bull and Crazy Horse. Bradley was in charge of the scouts, and being himself interested in the history of the old west and the tribes thereof, he made a point of collecting information from those around him whenever he had the opportunity to do so. In Bradley's longer version of the affair, the parts played by Red-Owl and Chief Long-Hair are given in detail, although in his second much shorter account, Bradley stated as follows,

> "...About the year 1822 [the Crows] were once more nearly one thousand lodges strong, when there occurred the most terrible calamity that ever befell the tribe, sweeping off in a single day about half their numbers and leaving the survivors impoverished. In the summer of this year a warlike fever seemed suddenly to have possessed the Crows, and party after party took the field, until eight large bands had gone forth, comprising the greater number of the warriors and the flower of the tribe. While in this condition of comparative defenselessness, the camp was suddenly assailed by a combined force of Sioux and Cheyenne numbering over one thousand men. Panic seized upon the Crows, and with little attempt at resistance they fled in wild confusion over the Plains toward the neighboring hills. The Sioux and Cheyenne were mostly mounted, and had only to ride after the fleeing throngs and slay them as they ran. Hundreds were overtaken and killed in the village and hundreds more in the subsequent pursuit, which continued for miles. The Plain was literally strewn for a considerable distance with the corpses of men, women, and children, and at last from the very fatigue of killing, and satiated with blood, the victors desisted from the pursuit. It had not been a battle but a butchery the most terrible that either in tradition or history has occurred upon the Great Plains of the Great West. At least five thousand of the Crows had fallen, but that was not all. All their lodges - a thousand in number - all the equipage of the camp, and hundreds of horses had passed into the hands of the victors, who also carried off as captives four hundred young women and children." March of the Montana Column. M H.S.C. p. 78. [Reprint] University of Oklahoma Press. 1991.

Here the number of Crow lodges supposedly destroyed, along with Crow persons killed in the attack are, of course, exaggerations. Although this might conceivably be an error in translation from Bradley's Crow informants, rather than a deliberate attempt to magnify an event which had been sufficiently severe in its own right not to warrant elaboration of the facts. Having said this, Bradley's account does compare favorably with that found in the memoirs of James P. Beckwourth, the mulatto Mountain Man adopted into the Crow tribe, and who dictated his life story to T.D. Bonner during the winter of 1854 / '55.

It has already been noted in the text that according to Beckwourth, he was first introduced to the Crows in 1829 by a fellow trapper named Greenwood [the memoirs erroneously give the date as 1827]. This man Greenwood, so the memoir says, told the Crows that Beckwourth, although born a Crow Indian, had been taken captive when,

> *"...so many winters ago, the Cheyenne defeated the Crows, killing many hundreds of their warriors, and carrying off a great many of their women and children."*

That the accounts of both Bradley and Beckwourth are indeed exaggerations of the 1820 episode in question, becomes apparent when we learn that prior to the disaster of that year, the Crow Nation comprised a number of autonomous bands, each of which was made up of several extended family groups constituting a clan. As a rule, other than times when annual religious festivals were held or during combined war ventures against an enemy, these separate clans spent most of the year camped apart from one another and followed their own whims of fortune, even to the extent that serious disagreements sometimes arose between one clan and another and internal fighting erupted within the Nation. It was as a result of the destruction of Long-Hair's particular Mountain Crow village, that the scattered Apsaalooka clans finally came permanently together for their mutual protection, in order to present a united force in the event of any future large-scale assault on their people. Of course, the whole Nation could not stay together for prolonged periods, owing to the amount of game needed to sustain such a large gathering in one area. For practical purposes the Nation divided itself into three main groups or divisions, which hereafter, became known as the Mountain Crow, River Crow and the Kicked-in-the-Belly band respectively. Of these, prior to yet another smallpox outbreak in 1833, the Mountain division was the largest, comprising between three-hundred and fifty and four-hundred lodges at any one time, whilst the River band never had more than three-hundred lodges at most, and the Kicked-in-the-Belly's considerably less.

Now before the second great smallpox epidemic which hit the Crows in 1801, the Crow Nation as a whole [according to information obtained by the French trader Francois Larocque during the summer of 1805], could count some two thousand lodges, but in the aftermath of the said contagion, their numbers had been reduced to half, i.e. around one thousand lodges in total. It was stated by some of those who had knowledge of the 1820 fight, that as a direct result of the allied attack this last number was again reduced, this time by a third, which would indicate a further loss of around three-hundred and thirty lodges. Assuming a population ratio among the Crows at that time of at least six or seven persons to a lodge, then their loss would suggest well over two-thousand persons, which is a preposterous figure and a gross exaggeration of the facts.

Of the several extant references concerning the fight, they all state that only one village of Crows was destroyed, and at a time before the tribe had consolidated its population for mutual defense. The particular village attacked was unlikely then, to have contained more than 250 lodges at most, and probably less. Allowing an average of two warriors per lodge, but of whom most would have been out looking for the allied camps and not in the Crow village at the time, then four or five non-combatants to each of the estimated 250 lodges in question, give a total of 1,250 persons at most. Thus after subtracting those killed or having escaped during the fight, somewhere around eight-hundred would be a more realistic number of captives. In corroboration of this, a recently discovered entry in the Hudson's Bay Company ledgers recording events between the years 1818 and 1821 and pertaining to the post at Lake Traverse, it is stated for November 9th 1820,

> *"The Chevall* [The Horse] *a Yankton* [Sioux] *chief arrived bringing some dried meat. He states that the Tetons went last Fall to war and returned a few days ago with 1100 horses and 800 prisoners of the Crow Indians."*

We must not forget also the assertion of Pretty-Shield, a Crow woman informant of Frank Bird Linderman who stated sometime during the early 1930s,

*"Once, a long time ago, the Lakota nearly wiped the Crows out, because all the men were gone to steal horses. Nearly all the women were killed, and all the old men that had been left in the village besides. But this was long before my time..."*

Most likely this statement was meant to refer to the 1820 fight, but Pretty-Shield who was not born until 1858, was not evidently acquainted with the exact details, as all other accounts are explicit in stating that most of the females were spared death and taken into captivity instead.

The Oglala Lakota artist and tribal historian Amos-Bad-Heart-Bull, included an event in his pictorial history of the Lakota, in which the Lakota had assaulted and destroyed a Crow village somewhere between the Lower Powder and Tongue River. The event was known among the Lakota as,

*"The battle when they fled around it."*

This refers to a particular butte near where the Crow village was apparently situated and assaulted. In their panic to escape, the Crows ran around the butte hotly pursued by the Lakota who destroyed the village and took many captives. According to He-Dog, who explained the Bad-Heart-Bull pictures to Helen Blish in 1929, this event, He-Dog said, had taken place *long before* his time. He-Dog was also an Oglala and a veteran of the intertribal war days who is said to have been ninety-five years of age when interviewed by Blish, and so must have been born around the date 1834. The details of the battle as related by He-Dog, conform favorably with the account given by Bradley concerning the attack upon the Crow village when the fugitives, along with Chief Long-Hair, had fled around the base of a nearby butte after the village had been invested by the allies. Now as there are no references to any other Crow village being destroyed by either Cheyennes or Lakota or both, when *"Many prisoners were taken"* between the years 1801 and 1830, He-Dog`s statement must be referring to the 1820 fight specifically. Bad-Heart-Bull`s caption on the other hand, also mentions that a Crow Indian wearing a peculiar styled four-horned war bonnet was killed, and further, that the particular Lakota force involved in the fight was the Hunkpapa band alone. However, the killing of the *"four-horned war bonnet man"* is an event well represented in several Lakota winter-counts, and is noted variously as having occurred sometime later during the mid-1850s. It would appear that the site referred to by both Bad-Heart-Bull and He-Dog as, *"When they fled around it,"* was actually the scene of two memorable episodes, i.e. that of 1820 concerning the destruction of Long-Hair`s Crow village; and that of a later battle of circa, 1855 / 56, when another bunch of Crows was chased around the same butte, but by the Hunkpapa Lakota, and during which event a Crow warrior wearing a four-horned war bonnet was slain.

It appears then, that Bad-Heart-Bull had fused together the earlier event of 1820 with that of the mid-1850s and referred to them as one specific fight, whereas He-Dog was commenting upon the 1820 fight alone. This is made evident by the fact that the creek flowing close by the butte in question was, according to He-Dog, known to the Lakota as, *"The creek where they cleaned up* [destroyed] *the village."* This stream is said to flow between the Tongue and Powder rivers, entering the Tongue near that river's confluence with the Yellowstone, and thus appears to be that known today as Otter Creek. It is likely therefore, to be the same site once pointed out by the Northern Cheyenne historian John Stands-in-Timber to Joe Medicine-Crow sometime in the mid-nineteen-fifties, as being the place where Chief Long-Hair`s Crow village was sacked.

Another Oglala Lakota named American-Horse, whose father or uncle had actually participated in the 1820 fight, stated that one-hundred Crow lodges were captured on that occasion. In the Lakota idiom this might refer to any number between eighty and one-hundred and fifty and more lodges, as Indians, generally speaking, did not differentiate precise numbers over and above what they could count on ten fingers. Instead they took the size of one group as being relative to another in comparison. White-Bull, however, a Southern Cheyenne informant of Michelson in 1910, when referring to the same event, asserted that 250 Crow lodges were taken, and in this White-Bull was probably correct, although he appears to have believed that a third of the whole Crow Nation was destroyed, rather than merely a third of the Mountain Crow division.

It seems more than probable that the figure of between two-hundred and two-hundred and fifty persons taken captive that day by the Southern Cheyennes alone [as given by George Bent and other informants], is also correct, and we learn from other sources that the Northern Cheyennes, including the Suhtaio, along with their Lakota allies, had themselves each taken as many captives again as had the Southern Cheyennes. Such would suggest a combined total of seven-hundred and fifty captives in all, and which compares favorably with the number of captives given in the Hudson's Bay Company account of around eight-hundred souls.

Tribal informants among the Cheyennes and Lakota and also among the Crow, agree that many of the said captives afterwards either escaped back to their own people, or were recaptured by the Crows, and before two summers had passed, only about one third of those originally taken remained among their captors. We do know that in 1839 a number of Crows were still living among Southern Cheyenne bands, either married into the tribe or actually preferring to stay with their captors. But of these some had been taken after the 1820 fight, and even then, their number was not large.

The Bradley material on the other hand, asserts that as late as 1876, the Cheyennes still had forty-four lodges belonging to their Nation, composed predominantly of Crow captives and their descendants [between 200 and 250 persons]. According to Bradley, these people by then, had intermarried within the Cheyenne tribe and at the time of his writing formed a separate camp or clan. Generally, they were to be found upon the headwaters of Powder River and usually kept aloof from most other Cheyenne bands, and even from the Crows. At that time [1876], there was a good deal of mixed blood among them, but the older members still spoke fluent Crow, even though their everyday language was Cheyenne. Bradley further stated that the Crows still thought of them as members of their own people, and declined to pursue hostilities against them, save their sometimes stealing their horses. The Cheyennes also desisted from harassing this band, but did not readily include them in the tribal politics which governed the rest of the Cheyenne Nation. The band apparently disintegrated shortly after 1879 or thereabouts, when the reservation system 'kicked in' so to speak. Some band members joined the Mountain and Kicked-in-the-Belly Crows in southern Montana; others joined the Northern Cheyennes, whilst a few families went south to be absorbed among the Southern Cheyennes in Oklahoma. There now remains little trace of their once separate identity. However, it appears likely that the small group of people once residing at Lame Deer on the Northern Cheyenne reservation and known as "Black Lodges," represented the remnant of the band in Montana, being so named owing to their close friendship and association with the "Black Lodge band of River Crows, whose own descendants yet reside around Crow Agency on the present-day Crow reservation.

It is interesting to note that in the year 1850, when Thadeus Culbertson then acting for the American Government undertook his survey of the "Western Tribes," he reported the existence of a Crow clan or band then known by the name *"Those whose camp is charged upon"* There seems to be no other reference to a Crow band or clan by that name either before Culbertson`s comment or after. Assuming that the name is a correct rendering, and that the band itself was extant at that date [circa, 1850], then perhaps the members of this group were, in fact, survivors from the same band of Mountain Crows under Chief Long-Hair, whose village had been assaulted and destroyed some thirty years earlier and its population so drastically reduced by the allied Cheyenne and Lakota. More specifically, the name may have referred to that group of Crows which had gone out with the adulterer Red-Owl the night before the village was attacked, and upon returning to the Crow camp the next day, had been "charged upon" by the allies and taken captive.

Whatever the case, it does seem that as Culbertson obtained the name from the Crows themselves, then the band or clan here referred to was probably the same as mentioned at a later date by Bradley, whose members, he said, were then of mixed Cheyenne and Crow parentage residing in a separate village somewhere near the headwaters of the Powder.

As to the actual date of the affair, Bradley says in one place 1822 and in another 1823. He had derived these dates from the age of his Crow informant Little-Face in 1876 who, Bradley supposed, was then in his early sixties, and from the fact that Little-Face had asserted that he had been seven or eight years old at the time of the attack. Beckwourth for his part, implied that the fight took place about twenty years prior to his induction into the Crow tribe, which would indicate a date of 1809 or thereabouts. This, though, is only Beckwourth`s assumption when he did not himself have a satisfactory date for the event, if indeed, he was not actually referring to the earlier destruction of another Crow village which, we know, occurred in 1801. There is no evidence that such a disaster befell the Crows around the date 1809 or near to it. But there is ample data for the calamities of 1801 and 1820 respectively, when in both cases, a Crow village was destroyed and its occupants either killed or carried off into captivity.

The eminent historian and anthropologist Doanne Robinson, did mention that in 1822 a combined Lakota and Cheyenne force then at war with the Crow, Mandan and Arickara, ambushed the Crows and won a great victory. Here, however, as both the Mandan and Arickara were earth-lodge dwellers along the Missouri, Robinson was likely confusing Crows with the Hidatsa who also were permanent Missouri River residents and close cousins to the Crows. In addition it has been said that the Lakota and Cheyenne once held a great council in order to decide how they were to wrest the Yellowstone country from the Crows. Likewise the date of this intertribal get together has also been erroneously given as 1824, when the actual date was 1820.

The latter-day Northern Cheyenne historian John-Stands-In-Timber, guessed that the time of the fight was around the year 1820, having come to this conclusion by working out the ages of his informants and of their parents and Grandparents, some of these last, having been Crow children taken captive on that occasion. Grinnell also used the same process of deduction and in his published version of the affair, also arrived at the date 1820 with which the George Bent material concurs. However, in Grinnell`s unpublished field notes and papers he gives the date as 1819 and thus, infers that the massacre of the thirty or more Cheyenne Crooked-Lance warriors, which had instigated the crusade against the Crows in the first place, had occurred the previous year, i.e. 1818. It would appear then, that Grinnell had later been persuaded to accept his informant George Bent's date of 1820, rather than rely upon his own calculations, believing Bent to be more informed than himself. Fortunately, though, we do have the corroboration of several Lakota calendar histories commonly known as Winter-counts, which fix the date of the destruction of Chief Long-Hair`s village more specifically as occurring in the year 1820.

These calendar histories were kept by certain individuals among various bands of Lakota, who recorded what they considered was the most important or most unusual happening of each year, and portrayed it thus in the form of a stylized pictograph, sometimes being more idiomatic as an aid to memory, rather than a realistic representation of the event. Each "winter" covered a part of a two year cycle, beginning with the spring of one year and ending with the close of winter of the next. It sometimes happens therefore, that a particular entry will conflict with our own conventional dating by one, and in some cases two years either way, although more often the entries do conform to our way of reckoning exactly. In the count accredited to Ben Kindle, an Oglala Lakota, the entry for the year 1820 / 21 is as follows,

"Two-Arrows made the Crow dance as a vow for brave men."

The meaning of this, conceivably, might be a reference to the origin of the "Crow-Lance-Owners" warrior society among the Oglala Lakota. This society was first organized at about this time, and its members carried as their insignia a fur-wrapped lance with a crook shaped end; the same, in fact, as carried by Lump wood warrior society members among the Crows. Perhaps it was in commemoration of the 1820 battle, when the Lakota and Cheyenne killed and captured a great number of Crows and, no doubt, took away as booty one or more ceremonial Lump wood lances which they most likely found in the ruined camp, that the idea for inaugurating a new warrior order among the Oglala came into being. This man Two-Arrows was the father of the great Oglala war-chief Red-Cloud [born 1822], and in all likelihood, had been an important participating member in the fight.

In another winter-count kept by American-Horse [previously mentioned] who also belonged to the Oglala band, and who produced one of the more precise of all the various Lakota calendars, the event in question is noted under the heading,

"Winter 1820/21, The Dakotas assaulted a Crow village of one-hundred lodges. They killed many and took many prisoners."

In the American-Horse pictogram, the central figure, even though singular in this instance, represents an unidentified number of enemies, while the red part of the head shows they had been scalped. Numerous dots surrounding the figure signify either flying musket balls, or more likely, horse tracks; indicating that the attackers had invested the camp. [It must be remembered that the allies at that time owned very few guns between them]. The whole is encircled by a ring of tepees, showing clearly it was a village that was taken.

Also important with regards to dating the affair, is an entry in the Winter-count of Iron-Crow, another Oglala Lakota, which records for the year 1819,

"They came home from killing Crow Indians."

As these `counts` were often a year or two out of date either way when compared to our conventional system, the event here recorded could just as well refer to the summer of 1820.

Two other counts, one kept by the Baptiste-Good, the other by High-Hawk, both members of the Brule Lakota, but who were closely associated with the Oglala, refer to the year 1821 as,

"The winter when in a war dance all wore Crow feathers."

Again these entries might refer to the year 1820, and especially so, as both these counts appear to be almost always one year ahead of the others. Thus the meteoric shower of November 1833 is properly recorded under its correct date in most other counts, but in that of Baptiste-Good and of High-Hawk, it is placed in the winter of 1834. The wearing of Crow feathers in the war dance may have been a symbolic act on the part of the dancers, to indicate that they had achieved a great victory over their Crow enemies or alternatively, it might refer to the wearing of captured ceremonial Crow war bonnets found within the lodges of the ruined Crow camp.

Yet another Lakota count records for the year 1819 / 20,

"They brought home curly horses."

350

This entry may be indicative of the great number of ponies captured during the aforesaid attack on the Crow village, by the fact that Crow horses were noted for their thicker, slightly curly coats because of there being stolen from more northern tribes, in whose country the winters were much more extreme.

We have also the winter count of the Miniconjou Lakota warrior Iron-Shell, who recorded an event which also occurred during the winter of 1820 as,

*"Crow Indian killed inside a tepee."*

It is said that the enemy Crow was killed within the Lakota camp. Perhaps this is an actual reference to the unfortunate Crow woman who was slain by vengeful Lakota in the latter's camp, after a Lakota warrior had died of wounds received during the fight at the Crow village. However, if Iron-Shell misunderstood the true meaning of the entry, the actual event having occurred many years before his birth, then it may refer more specifically, to Crow Indians having been killed within their own camp.

Likewise in the winter-count of the Oglala Lakota Red-Horse-Owner, it is recorded for the year 1818 that *"They* [Lakota] *went with the Skutani to fight."* Now the term Skutani cannot be translated from the Lakota or Dakota dialects, but it refers to the Cheyenne-speaking Suhtaio specifically, as is evident from other entries regarding the same name in the same winter count, and from a statement made by the wife of the later-day Miniconjou chief, John Grass in 1923, who inferred that the term Skutani was indeed, applicable to those known as Cheyenne [See http//www.welchdakotapapers.com]. In other entries in Red-Horse-Owner's winter count, it is also mentioned that the Lakota *"Went to the Skutani to fight,"* so that the entry for 1818 can only mean on that occasion, the Lakota actually accompanied the Skutani to war. In the same 'count' referring to the following year of 1819 it is noted, *"They went to buy back prisoners."* However, as there is no record of any Lakota being taken captive at or around the date 1819, the true meaning has most likely been misconstrued, and should actually read something like, *"They came to buy back prisoners"* and would then apply to the Crows trying to secure the release of their people captured by Lakota during the attack on Long-Hair's village in 1820. It is a fact that in this particular winter count, some of the year entries are out of date by one year at least, as is the case for the year 1822 in the same 'count,' which refers to the Major Leavenworth campaign against the Arickara, but which, of course, took place in 1823.

Further corroboration of the true date of the fight, although perhaps a little tentative, is that White-Haired-Killer, who was one of the female Crow captives taken during the fight and who remained with the Cheyenne the rest of her life, always declared that she was about ten years old when captured. She died around 1900 at an advanced age on the Washita River in Oklahoma. During her adult life she bore three children, one a daughter named Stands-In-The-Lodge [who was 64 years of age in 1891 and so was born in 1827], and two sons, the eldest of whom was named Iron-Crow, born 1829. A man named Wood, the second son was born in 1843. White-Haired-Killer was thus married when around seventeen years old, and so would place the time of her capture very near to the date 1820.

We know also that Long-Chin, the famous Suhtaio / Cheyenne Dog-Soldier war chief of a later date, was born in either the year 1802 or 1803. H always said that he had been a young warrior during the fight, about seventeen or eighteen years of age.

All being said, with the evidence of the above and including the Hudson's Bay Company ledger entry previously mentioned, it appears then that Bradley's estimate for the number of captives taken is at the least, a slight exaggeration, and that his dating of the affair is two years too late.

Perhaps we have a piece of additional corroboration for the date of 1820 which can be found in the journal of Edwin James. This he penned whilst a member of Major

Stephen Long's expedition from the town of Pittsburgh in the east, west to the Rocky Mountains between the years 1819 / 20.

The James' account informs us that whilst in the process of travelling downstream along the Arkansas River on the 28th August 1820, his party had a peaceful encounter with a band of Cheyenne who, James said, had seceded from their Nation, and for the previous three years had attached themselves to the great conglomerate of "Trading Indians" under the rule of an Arapaho chief named Bear's-Tooth. This conglomerate of peoples included Arapaho, Kiowa, Kiowa-Apache, Cheyenne and Oto.

What is pertinent regarding our present discussion, is that the Cheyenne band in question had a Crow captive [or captives] among them, and that at least one of these Cheyennes - seemingly a chief - was debarred from smoking in council with the James' party. James was told that this man could not partake of the pipe, for he had taken a vow never to smoke again. However, upon finding a small piece of paper discarded by a member of James's party, the Indian promptly rolled up a small quantity of tobacco in the form of a "seegar" [sic] and proceeded to smoke it with apparent relish.

Now among the Cheyenne, any tribesmen no matter what their rank or standing who had killed a fellow Cheyenne, was regarded as being 'unclean,' and as punishment for his crime, suffered banishment from the tribe for a period of four years. Also, from the time of the homicidal deed, the perpetrator was banned for life from smoking a ceremonial pipe, this being regarded as a sacred object and should not be contaminated by the touch or "bad breath" of the culprit.

Case histories show that such persons as were ostracized from the tribe, were usually joined in their enforced isolation by their families and members numbered among their close adherents. Thus they formed what might be regarded as a detached band of the tribe. Hereafter, although allowed back among the tribe after the four year term of banishment had expired, the murderer was not formally invited to share in any communal activity, which included organized tribal ventures against the enemy. Often he who was ostracized and his band would 'tag along,' so to speak, as a separate body and independently involve themselves in any tribal crusade, and more especially, when that nation's "Sacred Arrows" and "Buffalo Hat "were carried against the foe.

Just such an 'Outlaw' group were these Cheyenne met by the James' party in late August, 1820. They may have been the faction responsible for creating the civil strife during the victory celebrations in the allied Lakota and Cheyenne camps in the aftermath of the destruction of Long-Hair's Crow village. The Crow female captive or captives among this band of Outlaws when met by James, may well have been taken during the aforesaid attack on the Crow village that had occurred only some two months earlier.

Of the Crow prisoners that remained among the Cheyenne and Lakota, many became the mothers and Grandmothers of several later well-known chiefs and warriors of their adopted tribes. One of these captive women among the Cheyenne was simply referred to as Crow-Woman, but in her old age she was regarded as the best historian within the Cheyenne tribe. The Northern Cheyenne latter-day historian John-Stands-In-Timber, related an interesting anecdote concerning another of these Crow woman prisoners which runs as follows,

> *"One of the children taken that day was Old-Man-Medicine-Top's*
> *mother. She grew up and married among the Cheyenne, and years later*
> *some Crows came over to visit at the Agency where the Cheyenne were*
> *encamped. They were great people to ride along that way and see what the*
> *Cheyenne were doing. These four riders came by, and someone called to*
> *the old woman, "your relations are coming."*
> *"Tell me when they come close," she said, "so I can talk to them."*

*She was blind by then sitting under the wagons in the shade. They told her when they came near, and she hollered out to them in Crow. They stopped their horses and looked at her. Pretty soon they rode to the place and got off. And they were there a long time talking to that woman in the Crow language, and found out who she was and told her that she had Crow relatives still living. One was a man named Medicine-Top, and she had a Cheyenne son by the same name on the other side. And some other children that were captured at that time also found relatives many years later among the Crows."*

Hitherto there has been some doubt among Cheyenne informants themselves, with regard to whether their tribe's "Sacred Arrow" talismans were actually carried against the Crows on this occasion.

According to White-Bull, born 1834, a Northern Cheyenne of the Suhtaio band who was also the Grandson of Ice, the famous Contrary warrior who had played so prominent a role in the attack on the Crow village in question, the reason why the Cheyenne were so strong, he said,

*".....was because Mottsieve [Sweet-Medicine, the Cheyenne cultural hero who brought the Nation its "Sacred Arrows" in the first place], had a small piece of medicine which came from heaven. When the Cheyenne went to war against their enemies, whoever carried the bundle, opened the medicine and pointed it directly at the foe. He then blew the medicine through the bundle at the foe and then all the Cheyenne charged and exterminated them. The last attempt was made near the Black Hills when the Cheyenne fought the Crows. There were two-hundred and fifty Crow lodges which were wiped out, and this is the reason why so many Crow women were brought up by the Cheyenne."*

The first part of this statement refers of course to the "Sacred Arrows" being carried against the foe, while the second part refers specifically, to the expedition against the Crows in 1820. This statement corroborates the fact that the event was one of the few times in Cheyenne history when the *"Arrows"* were actually *"moved."* Further evidence is that an old Cheyenne informant of George Grinnell named Porcupine-Bull, who himself was a holy man of some repute and conversant with the taboos and history concerning the *"Sacred Arrows,"* when enumerating each time these tribal talismans had been carried to war, he included the expedition of 1820 on his list.

Yet another informant of Michelson whose name, coincidentally, was also White-Bull, but in this case a Southern Cheyenne born in 1846, when referring to the *"moves"* of the *"Sacred Arrows"* he said,

*"The Cheyenne went towards the Big Horns and kept going. They came near a big camp of Crows. They captured all the women; killed all the men and took all the Crow property, horses and everything."*

Again the above is referring to the allied expedition of 1820, but other than the Grinnell account [which for the most part was obtained third hand from George Bent], and that of Bradley's manuscript; coupled with the above mentioned references from Michelson and the various Lakota winter-counts, there are today remarkably few detailed accounts in tribal oral histories concerning the affair, which is surprising when one considers the scale and importance of the event.

353

Perhaps, though, there is another documented reference to this 1820 fight which again, is to be found in the memoirs of James P. Beckwourth. In this case he gives his rendition of a speech that the Southern Cheyenne Dog-Soldier Chief Porcupine-Bear supposedly made in 1841, when attempting to dissuade his people from trading away their buffalo robes for the white man's rot-gut whiskey, instead of for guns and ammunition with which to fight their enemies. Porcupine-Bear, according to Beckwourth's account, was particularly forceful on this occasion. He compared the then current high standing and prowess of the Crows among other tribes, to the perceived degeneracy into which the Cheyenne Nation had let itself slip, due to their habitual iniberism by partaking of the white man's debilitating "fire water." Referring to past glories, Porcupine-Bear had said,

*"...Once we could beat the Crows, and unaided destroyed their villages."*

Conceivably this was meant to apply to the similar event of 1801, albeit on a much reduced scale and more likely then, to the 1820 fight alone. The significance and scale of the more recent occurrence was, at the time of Porcupine-Bear's statement, still fresh in Cheyenne memories and hitherto, still regarded as the greatest of their tribe's military achievements. Indeed, George Bent in a letter he wrote in April, 1905 stated,

*".....The Cheyenne talk more about the fight on Tongue river [sic] than of any other...none are now living who were in that fight, but three or four years ago, White-haired-Killer died in the South, more than one-hundred years old. Her youngest daughter is still alive and about sixty-five years of age."*

Here, though, Bent uses the casual term, *"more than one-hundred years old,"* when White-Haired-Killer, according to present-day Cheyenne descendants, actually died in her early nineties, having been between ten and twelve years of age at the time the attack on Long-Hair's village took place.

The Northern Cheyenne tribal historian John-Stands-In-Timber, was adamant that the fight had taken place on one of the forks of Otter Creek, the aforementioned small tributary flowing into Tongue River on its east side near its confluence with the Yellowstone, and was no doubt, referring to this same attack upon Long-Hair's Crow village when elsewhere he stated,

*"Many years ago, the first trouble between the Cheyenne and the Crow was in this country over in [on] the east fork of Otter Creek. This is a tributary of the Tongue River east of the [Northern Cheyenne] reservation. Pumpkin Creek is east of this and the next creek is Box Elder. At this place [Otter Creek], the Crow and Cheyenne first fought. The Cheyenne captured the Crow village, the tepees and the homes [horses?] and they broke some cooking pots."*

Other Cheyenne informants said that Stands-In-Timber was mistaken on this point as regards the place and date of the actual event. However, it is known that some years after the fight of 1820, a war-party of Gros Ventres took to the crest of a similar butte in order to defend itself against a combined Miniconjou Lakota and Crow force, and was wiped out to a man. This particular fight occurred early in 1852 somewhere slightly west of Otter Creek and close to the South Fork of Rosebud Creek. It is this location, I believe, that has since been confused by later informants with the butte near Otter Creek. The fact that human bones and skulls were found in large quantity at the Otter Creek site, scattered around the base of the butte, whereas those of the dead Gros Ventres, whose doomed party had not exceeded sixty persons in the first place, were for the most part, left on top and on

354

the slopes of the butte near Rosebud Creek, make it more than likely that the Otter Creek site as pointed out to Joe Medicine Crow by John Stands-in-Timber during the mid-nineteen-fifties, is the true location of the destruction of Long-Hair`s village in 1820.

In corroboration of this, it is indicative to note that a Gros Ventre warrior named White-Shirt, who had actually been a surviving member of the ill-fated Gros Ventre war-party slaughtered on the hilltop near Rosebud Creek in 1852, eventually married a Crow woman and thereafter, remained among his wife's people along the Big Horn River. In 1893, he told a Northern Cheyenne named Vanishing-Head [an uncle of Henry Little-Coyote, keeper of *"Issiwun"* the Sacred Buffalo Hat of the Suhtaio], the story of that Lakota / Crow fight against the Gros Ventres, but not knowing the area too well, White-Shirt had assumed that the butte near Otter Creek, where; so Cheyennes had told him, a great intertribal battle once took place and a lot of human bones and skulls could still be found, must have been the same hill on which his Gros Ventre comrades had earlier been exterminated.

We do not hear the name Two-Twists again after the time of his victory over the Crows in 1820, but there is evidence to suggest that he may, in fact, have changed his name to that of High-Backed-Wolf, and thus would have been the same man as the illustrious head chief of that name. The evidence here is tentative, and perhaps more circumstantial than proven. However, both men were members of the Suhtaio Cheyenne-speaking band; both were chiefs of the Crooked-Lance Soldier Society, and both are said to have led the expedition against the Crows on the occasion in question. Both, it is said, were afterwards elected to serve as big tribal chiefs, obviously in the role of "Sweet-Medicine" chief itself, being the highest rank within the Cheyenne / Suhtaio Nation. Furthermore, a unique attribute associated with the character of High-Backed-Wolf was that he was renowned for charging alone into enemy camps, just as Two-Twists supposedly had done. It was he also who, in 1825, was recognized as the paramount chief of both the Suhtaio and Cheyenne, whose influence even extended over certain bands of Lakota.

If this was indeed the case, i.e. that the personages of Two-Twists and High-Backed-Wolf were, in reality, one and the same, [Two-Twists merely being his earlier name], then it was Two-Twists who carried the war-pipe to the various allied bands, and he alone who led the allied force into Crow country at that time.

It has also been said that Two-Twists was a Cheyenne Bowstring warrior, although an analysis of all the available evidence, coupled with a statement made by John Stands-in-Timber [who was himself of Suhtaio extraction], leaves little, if indeed any doubt, that Two-Twists was in truth a Suhtaio, and a member of the Crooked-Lance society more commonly known as Elks.

The confusion here may have arisen at a later date, owing to the fact that the carrying of a sword of some description, certainly after 1851, at which time swords were freely given out to the Cheyenne and other tribes by American Government officials during the so-called Fitzpatrick treaty of that year, became an essential part of Bowstring Society regalia. Perhaps the carrying of such a weapon by the said Two-Twists, had led some later-day informants to assume that Two-Twists was then a Bowstring warrior, rather than a member of the Crooked-Lance society.

As regards the Crow version of the affair, Grinnell obviously obtained some of his details from Crow informants, whilst Bradley's account, of course, came entirely from a member of that tribe. Nevertheless, a more informative Crow version has not apparently been forthcoming, and this for the reason attending all Plains Tribes, that they were reluctant to relate stories of past defeats, unless, that is, some exceptionally brave or unusual action had taken place on their part.

This being so, it does appear that even the great Crow Chief Plenty-Coups, prominent during the late nineteenth and early twentieth century, was actually referring to this same disaster of 1820, when he stated to his biographer Frank Linderman,

*"Once before my time, when many young men had left our village, the Lakota came and attacked it, nearly wiping us out. We have never been so strong since that terrible day."*

My good friend Joe Medicine Crow, present-day historian of the Crow tribe, put it succinctly when he told me that his old Crow informant of the buffalo days named Cold-Wind, had once said with regards to the same event,

*"The Crows do not like to talk of that fight; they do not like to talk of the dead."*

It is for this reason alone that a more detailed account of the event, notwithstanding its colossal effect upon both the population and minds of the Crows at that time, has not apparently survived into the present day among the Crows themselves.

In conclusion, the grand allied expedition against the Crows in 1820, was not just an endeavour to seek retribution for the deaths of a number of Cheyenne and Suhtaio warriors during past conflicts with that tribe. If indeed revenge alone had been the prime objective, then a confrontation with the enemy along traditional lines would have sufficed, and whereby, the invading force might have been content to show the enemy that their prowess was unabated, and to further indicate that they as a people, had not been cowered or intimidated by any recent reversal suffered at Crow hands. The death of one or two of the enemy would have been considered sufficient to compensate their own loss, and to appease the spirits of their dead tribesmen by the shedding of Crow blood - however little that might be. At the same time, a cursory show of force on the part of the allies, would also have been enough to uphold their position in the inter-tribal status-quo across the Plains.

On this occasion, therefore, revenge had really been the secondary objective, and nothing less than the complete dispersal of the foe would have satisfied the allied host. The ulterior motive then, as the presence of the Cheyenne and Suhtaio "Sacred Arrows" and the "Sacred Buffalo Hat" infers, was that of conquest, with a view to permanent occupation of the invaded territory by those two allied peoples.

This is further evidenced by the fact, that after this devastating attack of 1820, the Crows did for a while, relinquish their tribe's exclusive claim to the Tongue and Lower Powder River country. From that date on both the Cheyenne and Suhtaio along with one or two Lakota bands - albeit only during certain parts of the year - did occupy these rich hunting grounds at will.

If the allied expedition had only revenge as its motive, then even in the aftermath of their great victory they would still have regarded the invaded territory as rightfully belonging to the Crows. But it appears they did not. Neither did the thought enter their heads. Instead the Cheyenne and Suhtaio particularly, thereafter considered the invaded country as an extension of their own hunting grounds, and as a new location for their winter retreats.

On the other hand, if viewed as an attempt to destroy Crow military power in the High Plains, and as a Cheyenne and Lakota endeavour to keep the Tongue and Powder River area for their own exclusive use, then it must be admitted that the expedition was a failure, notwithstanding the immediate damage inflicted upon the enemy. What it did accomplish as a result of the destruction of the Crow village and the temporary abandonment of the region by that people, was to bring the Crows to the practical realization that they themselves, could not keep the Cheyenne and Lakota permanently out of the disputed area. The Crows instead, were obliged to tolerate a Lakota and Cheyenne presence in the eastern portion of their country, at least during a part of the year.

At the slightly later date of circa, 1822, upon the ascendency of the great chief Sore-Belly to the position of head war-chief of the entire Crow Nation, the latter did manage to reassert their claim to the relinquished districts and wrest them back from the allies, and which the Crows then held by force of arms for at least a decade more. But alas, even then it was always a disputed land - a war ground - until 1862 when yet another concerted Lakota and Cheyenne invasion into Crow country finally evicted the rightful inhabitants once and for all. The allies, thereafter, secured virtually the whole of the eastern half of the old Crow country for themselves now on a more permanent basis, their claim to those then conquered lands embracing the Lower Powder and Tongue River region, later being recognized by the United States Government at the Fort Laramie treaty of 1868.

## APPENDIX B.

### SLAUGHTER OF THE PIKUNI AND BLOOD COLUMN IN 1824.

Events pertaining to the destruction of the Pikuni and Blood column in 1824 and what happened in the aftermath of that fight, are remarkably similar to other engagements which, likewise, took place somewhere between the heads of the Judith Forks and the north bank of the Musselshell. During these other events, a large Crow force had also attacked a moving Blackfoot village and taken many scalps, horses and much camp equipment, along with a large number of women and children captives. In three of these events, the great Crow war-chief Alapooish or Sore-Belly is, ostensibly, accredited with leading the Crow force on those occasions.

There are extant, in fact, at least six separate accounts which relate to seemingly identical events, three of which were narrated by Hugh Munroe to the writer James Willard Schultz late in the nineteenth century. Hugh Munroe had lived as a fully-fledged member of the Pikuni Small Robe Blackfoot band for many years before his death at ninety-seven years old in 1896. He had, he said, actually been present fighting alongside his adopted Blackfoot people during each occasion of which he spoke, when Crows, he said, had attacked a moving Blackfoot village.

Earlier writers have been of the opinion that each of Munroe's various accounts really only refer to one particular occasion, even though their dating of the event has variously been given as either 1816, 1824, 1832 and 1845. The reality, however, is that at least two if not all three of Munroe's accounts, apply to completely separate episodes, but which, owing to a similarity of content, were confused in the retelling either by Munroe, or - and what is more likely - by his biographer James Willard Schultz. Indeed, Schultz admitted that at the time Munroe was relating his life story to him, the old man's memory was wanting and confused and he [Munroe], was often unable to specify the exact date and place of the event he was describing. Munroe was then a very old man, but according to Schultz, he could yet recall in detail his early years among the Blackfoot, as compared to his lack of ability to remember but very little concerning events thereafter.

Now the particular fight of 1824 previously recounted, would not have been an isolated episode in the history of any Plains Tribe. Rather, such would have been of comparatively common occurrence, as Indian villages were constantly being moved in pursuit of the buffalo herds from one hunting ground to another. Any wandering war-band would have been fully aware that a travelling column of people, encumbered with women and children, camp equipment and personal belongings piled on pole-drags, along with an immense herd of loose ponies, was always at a great disadvantage as regards defending itself, and the people themselves were likely to be easily scattered or captured and sometimes destroyed, if taken by surprise.

It is not unlikely - highly probable, in fact - that Hugh Munroe whilst an adopted member of the Piegan Small-Robe band for many years, did experience several attacks on the particular Blackfoot column he was travelling with at any one time, and on at least two occasions, the attacking force had been Crows. That three versions of such an episode as related by Munroe do actually refer to separate events, becomes apparent when one compares the finer details of each occurrence.

One of Munroe's accounts of an attack upon a Blackfoot column, according to Schultz in his book *"Rising-Wolf"* [1917], took place during Munroe's first year on the Northern Plains, which is said by Schultz and also by George B. Grinnell, to have been in the year 1816. Hugh Munroe, so it is stated, apparently at the ripe old age of seventeen years, had been appointed by the Chief Factor of the Hudson's Bay Company Post, Fort Edmonton, to live with the Blackfoot for one year in order to learn their language and their ways, which would then be of great benefit to the Company's future dealings with that people. So it was that whilst first travelling across the Montana prairies with his newly acquired Blackfoot hosts, Hugh Munroe was witness to one of the attacks of which he speaks.

It was in relation to this attack of supposedly, circa, 1816, when Munroe mentioned that a Small-Robe Pikuni chief named Lone-Walker, had a hand to hand fight with the enemy chief, whom he killed.

Munroe does not say that he himself did anything spectacular on that occasion, or received any personal injury during the fight, albeit, that this was his first experience of killing a man, which, of course, must have been as for anyone, a memorable and traumatic event in one's life. Munroe was also adamant that the enemy [whom he designates Crows] took no Pikuni captives at that time, although he did mention the killing of seven Crow scouts not long prior to the latter tribe's attack on the Pikuni column. In addition, he mentioned that soon after the fight, the Crows and Blackfoot made peace and immediately thereafter, went on a trading trip together to one of the white man's trading posts which, Munroe states, was operated by a Company Factor who Munroe simply calls `Hardesty.` This name can only refer to one Richard Hardisty, but who only became a Factor after the date 1824. The specific post mentioned by Munroe in this context, then stood north of St. Mary's Lakes [north Montana], which implies, therefore, that Munroe was alluding to either the Hudson's Bay Company sub-post named "Acton House," which stood on the North Branch of the Saskatchewan River near the mouth of the Clearwater, or to another post known as Rocky Mountain House which stood close by, and was known colloquially as " The Mountain Fort."

This is important, for we know that Acton House was only open seasonally and seems to have been abandoned between the years 1813 and 1819, while Rocky Mountain House was originally established by the rival "Northwest Fur Company" and did not come under British control until after the *"Nor`Westerners"* amalgamated with the Hudson's Bay Company in 1821.

James Schultz in *"My Life as an Indian"* [p.90], has Munroe asserting that he, Munroe, during his first year on the Plains, was sent out to the then *new* Hudson's Bay Company post known as the "Mountain Fort." Thus, as Mountain Fort was merely another name in the vernacular of the day for Rocky Mountain House, and that the post had been administered by the Northwest Company since as early as 1799, it must follow that Munroe could only have been referring to a time after the Northwest Company merged with that of the Hudson's Bay in 1821. At that date and for a number of years thereafter, the Mountain Fort would indeed, have been regarded as a *new* post by its employees, since coming under Hudson's Bay Company control.

Munroe also asserted that a famous Blood Blackfoot chief named Eagle-Ribs, was involved in peace-making with the Crows at the time of which he spoke. But Eagle-Ribs only became prominent during the early eighteen-twenties, and even then, was not recognized as a head chief in the proper sense of the term.

Certainly, pacts had been made from time to time between one and another band of Crows and one and another band of Blackfoot, such as that which due to the persuasions of Peter Skene Ogden of the Hudson's Bay Company, temporarily came into effect between the Crows and Small Robe Pikuni in 1825. The only official Government sponsored truce between Crows and Blackfoot, however, of which we have knowledge in the documented sources, prior that is, to the peace of 1855 known as *"The Stevens` Treaty,"* was that arranged in 1832 by a Major Sanford in conjunction with the fur trader Kenneth McKenzie and certain other associates of the American Fur Company. This pact between the tribes, as far as we know, was instigated and arranged from a central base at Fort Union, then the predominant trading post on the Upper Missouri near the mouth of the Yellowstone, but which was not fully operational before 1830 -`31.

Munroe himself [according to Schultz], did in another place *[My Life as an Indian. p.99]*, mention that Crows made a pact with one or another Blackfoot-speaking group in 1832. A truce, he said, which endured until sometime in 1834. This is corroborated by an entry in the North Blackfoot winter count of Teddy Yellow-Fly, which records for the period between the years 1831 and 1833,

*"A Crow Indian made peace."*

An alternative entry is inserted in a revised version of the same Yellow-Fly `count` for the year 1834, and it appears from a brief passage in James Beckwourth`s *"Life and Adventures,"* that this particular overture for intertribal peace with several tribes was actually inaugurated late in 1832, as Beckwourth states that when at the newly-erected Fort Cass [1832] at the mouth of the Big Horn, he received a letter from Kenneth McKenzie then at Fort Union, requesting him [Beckwourth],

> *"..To constrain the As-ne-boins into a treaty of peace with the Crows, in order that their incessant wars might be brought to a close, and the interests of the Company be less interfered with."*

Now in the Munroe account of a Crow attack upon a Blackfoot column as narrated in *"My Life as an Indian,"* Munroe is supposed to have asserted that during the melee, he himself was wounded in the leg, but made no mention of the hand to hand fight between the Crow and Blackfoot chiefs as recorded in *"Rising-Wolf."* He also stated in *"My Life as an Indian"* that the Crows took no captives on that occasion, neither did he mention that a truce was soon after effected between the Crows and Pikuni. The whole essence of the account in this second instance appears, moreover, to be referring to a similar Crow attack which, we know, took place in 1845 [although Munroe or Schultz erroneously inserted the date 1858] and it appears that three events of this nature as related by Munroe and printed in various publications, were fused into one by Schultz and merely repeated by more recent scholars on the subject.

The River Crows, if not the Mountain band, were at peace with the Piegan [Pikuni] in 1858, due to an American Government peace-making initiative known as the "Steven`s Treaty" three years earlier in 1855. Certainly, the Frontiersman William T. Hamilton mentioned in his memoirs pertaining to the year 1858, that the head Piegan Chief Little-Dog, was then encamped with the River Crows whilst on a friendly visit, and, perhaps, Munroe or Schultz confused this later period of peace-making with the earlier event of 1832, and had assumed, therefore, that the Crow attack on the Piegan column had occurred earlier in the same year of 1858.

It is not likely that if the several accounts as related by Munroe do refer to the same battle, then he would not have mentioned in each case, the fact that he himself had been wounded and likewise, no doubt, he would also have repeated the hand to hand duel between the Blackfoot and Crow chiefs, and this last especially so, as supposedly, it involved his great friend and mentor Chief Lone-Walker who Munroe, it seems, could not praise too highly in several of the stories he narrated to Schultz.

While it is true that Munroe, initially, was employed by the Hudson's Bay Company and was indeed, sent out alone to live among the Blackfoot at an early date, he was also in the service of other Fur Companies throughout his long and adventurous life on the Northern Plains. One of these employers was the American Fur Company, of which the trading post Fort Union was its most important establishment during the eighteen-thirties and forties. The existing 'Letter books' which record data for each of the American Fur Company posts, would show exactly when Hugh Munroe was in that company's employ, and might then clarify our dating for the aforementioned Sanford - McKenzie inspired Crow - Blackfoot peace sometime between 1832 and 1833 once and for all. Unfortunately, though, the Letter Books relating to those years are missing from the collection and their whereabouts at present unknown, if indeed they are still extant. What we do know is that late in the year 1832, Major Sanford - then acting as Indian Agent for the Upper Missouri Nations - did take a delegation of chiefs from several tribes to visit the Great White Father, the President, in Washington DC. Needless to say, before such an undertaking could have been accomplished, the warring tribes had first to be brought together to smoke the pipe of peace between them. Such pacts as then affected, however, were only likely to have been of short duration, given the belligerent attitudes and savage circumstances of the Indian environment at that period. Although as we have noted, there is extant a Blackfoot winter count entry for the period 1832-'33, recording that some Crows, at least, were at peace with the Blackfoot throughout that period and yet another entry for the year 1834, which attests to this pact with the Crows as then still being in vogue.

Certainly, in 1832 if not one year before, the Beaver Hills Cree had made an alliance with the Crows, predominantly for the benefits of mutual trade with each other, but which originally had been instigated through the persuasions of Major Sanford and Kenneth McKenzie, as earlier McKenzie had affected truces between the Assiniboine and Blackfoot and between the Crow and Atsina and the Crows and Assiniboine, and thus likely, between Crows and one or another Blackfoot-speaking tribe.

It is indicative to note that in yet another Blackfoot calendar history or 'winter count; ' once in the care of the North Piegan warrior Bull-Plume, it is recorded for the year 1816,

*"When the Piegan broke the River Peoples' line of March."*

The explanation for this entry further states that the Piegans came upon a camp of Pend d'Orielle on the move and attacked them.

If indeed, this was the same year when Munroe first joined the Small Robes as a lad of seventeen, as his biographers Grinnell and Schultz asserted, it might then be assumed that the interpretation by Bull-Plume for this year's entry was a mistake, and that the term "River People" applies to the River Crows, which in addition, would then mean that it had actually been the latter who attacked the Piegans, not the other way around. But as the Pend d'Orielle were known specifically as "River People" to all Blackfoot-speaking tribes, while the Crows were known by the collective name "Isahpo" meaning 'rock' or 'mountain,' it must be taken that the winter count is correct, and that it was not the Crows who were the culprits on that occasion, but the Pend d'Orielle in their stead, and thus the Bull-Plume entry would be compatible with the event given in the Munroe / Schultz account for the year 1816, although Munroe; due to a faulty memory in his latter days, had erroneously substituted Crows for Pend d'Orielle and reversed the order of attack.

Of late, however, considerable doubt has been voiced as to whether Munroe actually joined the Small Robes as an adopted tribal member in 1816, 1819 or 1823. The history of Munroe in the various accounts is confusing and often contradictory even as to his date of birth and death, although after careful scrutiny of other contemporary documented sources, a more likely scenario is that Munroe, did indeed join the Hudson's Bay Company in 1816, and at first, was sent to Fort Edmonton on the Saskatchewan in the capacity of clerk to begin a *mandatory* seven-year apprenticeship, as all young employees of the Company were obliged to do. As an apprentice, Munroe would not have been sent to live on his own and by his own devices with the Pikuni, as the Company during Munroe's indentured term, would have been legally responsible for his safety and well-being. However, Company records show that he was included as a member of the so-called Bow River expedition during the winter of 1822/'23, and the following Spring was sent among the Piegans during the latter part of his apprenticeship. He was at Acton House where he stayed until late 1823, then returned to Fort Edmonton carrying a letter from the Small Robe Piegan chief, who in turn, had received it from the Hudson's Bay man Finan McDonald, who himself, had met 400 Piegans earlier that year in the Three Forks district of the Upper Missouri. Obviously, Munroe was not then among the Piegans who met Finan McDonald and his party, for the meeting, although at first friendly, culminated in one of McDonald's men being shot by the Piegans and, soon after, a pitched battle was fought between the white men and Piegans during which McDonald's party lost 7 men killed and the Piegans 68. [Alexander Ross, *"Fur Hunters of the Fae West."* Vol. 2. Pp. 5 and 50. Oklahoma Press. 1956].

In addition, Munroe stated that he joined a big war-party comprised of Piegans, Bloods, Siksika and Gros Venters [Atsina] going south against the Shoshoni in 1825, because, he said, he wished to see the country, and which, of course, he would not have said if he had already seen the country alluded to during an earlier sojourn in 1823 as a member of the war-party which had the altercation with McDonald's men. It was while with the big war-party of 1825, that Munroe met William Sublette and Peter Skene Ogden at a point within sight of the Great Salt Lake, Utah, and at that time, the meeting between Indians and white men owing to Munroe's intervention, passed off peaceably.

Evidently then, whilst at Acton House, Munroe had become acquainted with the Small-Robe Pikuni band, and after returning to Fort Edmonton and after completing his term of apprenticeship, in the following spring of 1824 he was sent back into the Western Prairies to the newly acquired Rocky Mountain House, with instructions to live with the Piegan [Pikuni] in order to learn their language and ways, and thereby, facilitate better trade relations between the Pikuni and Hudson's Bay Company. Thus, it had been during the early days of Munroe residing among his Pikuni hosts, e.g., *"...his first year on the Plains,"* that he was involved in the great fight with Crows led by Sore-Belly, when the latter had attacked the moving Blackfoot column.

If therefore, the earlier date of 1816 for Munroe's first sojourn in the company of his Small Robe Pikuni hosts was correct, then his account of a Blackfoot column being attacked at that time, must refer to the same event involving the Pend d'Orielle as noted in the Bull-Plume winter count for that year. But if the later date of 1823 is correct for when Munroe first joined the Pikuni, then it refers to the attack by Chief Sore-Belly and his Crows which took place in 1824, and of which circumstances as recorded by both James H. Bradley and Edwin T. Denig, must be associated with those events recorded by Munroe via Schultz in the 1919 work *"Rising Wolf."* It would then, be the event of 1824 which Munroe or his biographer Schultz confused with not only the Pend d'Orielle attack of 1816, but also with a later-date occurrence of a Crow attack on a Gros Ventre [Atsina] column in 1832, and again, upon the Small Robe Pikuni column in 1845. It is also apparent from the Hudson's Bay records regarding appointments and service of its employees, that Richard Hardisty did not arrive in Canada until 1817, and did not have the chance or authority to be in command at Rocky Mountain House or even Acton House until 1825 at the earliest.

This being so, if Munroe had spent his 7 year indentured term as an apprentice clerk with the Company at Edmonton House on the Lower Saskatchewan, and which would have included a sojourn at Acton House, then the time of his roaming with the Pikuni in 1824 away from any of the Company's posts, would have constituted his *"...first year on the Plains."* It would appear then, that Schultz and Grinnell were wrong in assuming Munroe's first year at Edmonton House was his *'first year on the Plains,'* and, perhaps, were further miss-led by their having some knowledge of the 1816 Blackfoot attack on the Pend d'Orielle column that same year, but which they took as being compatible with the account given by Munroe of the Crow attack on the Pikuni column, albeit having actually occurred in 1824.

Concerning the 1824 Crow attack, Lieutenant James H. Bradley wrote in 1875 from Crow testimony, that sometime after the destruction of the Mountain Crow village under Chief Long-Hair by Lakota and Cheyenne [1820], a Crow force led by Chief Sore-Belly [*Alapooish*], achieved a great victory over the Blackfoot, at which time the Crows killed many and took a great number of captives. Bradley gave no specific date for the event. However, the Fort Union Trader Edwin Denig also gave an account of a similar victory of Sore-Belly over the same enemy people close to the Musselshell River, in which he stated, likewise, that the Crows killed many and took a large number of captives after attacking a moving Blackfoot column, and which runs as follows,

> *"Early in the day when the enemy's camp was on the move, scattered over a level Plain of some miles extent, he [Sore-Belly] gave the word to charge. Terrible was the storm that swept over the Blackfoot. The Crows were well-armed, mounted and prepared, the others embarrassed with their women, children and baggage. Their long and weak line of March was literally "rubbed out" by their savage foes. Whoever endeavoured to defend was killed, the women and children taken prisoners. Most of the men of the Blackfoot were in front of the travelling van. They soon rallied and returned the charge but were outnumbered. Although they fought bravely for some time they soon were obliged to leave their families and seek safety in flight. Others died defending their children...."*

Denig implied by his subsequent passages, that the event had taken place some years prior to 1832.

In yet another account of what appears to be relating to a similar event of Chief Sore-Belly gaining a victory over a Blackfoot column, James Beckwourth, although himself not specific as to time and place, does indicate by his peculiar chronological format that he was referring to mid or late summer of 1832. This last named account gives more detail than those of Bradley and of Denig, and is similar to Hugh Munroe's version of the event he narrated to Schultz and published in *"Rising Wolf"* regarding a Crow attack upon a Pikuni column and during which event, the Pikuni chief [Lone-Walker] had battled it out with the Crow chief in single combat. In Beckwourth's version, though, it is the Crow chief who was victorious, rather than the Pikuni as stated by Munroe. Beckwourth's account runs as follows,

*"On they [the Blackfoot] came - men, women and children - utterly unconscious of the terrible shock that awaited them....We [the Crows] were drawn up on a high table prairie, our whole force concealed from view at no greater distance than half pistol-shot.....The [Blackfoot] chief...was first to fall...and his attendants scattered like chaff before the wind. We were upon the warriors so unexpectedly that they had hardly time to draw their weapons before they were overthrown and put to flight They were encumbered with women and children and baggage..."*

Beckwourth adds that the Crows took Blackfoot women and children captives at that time - 150 by Beckwourth`s count, - and that a short time later, the Crows made a pact with the Assiniboine with whom for many years previously, the Crows had been at war.

This is important, as it corroborates the time period of the aforementioned Sanford - McKenzie inspired pacts between a number of tribes in contact with Fort Union, and among whom were included the Assiniboine, Plains Cree, Pikuni, Atsina and Crows, but excluding the Blood and Siksika Blackfoot tribes. The Pikuni in question were predominantly of the Small Robe band, and who at that time were briefly at war with their Blood and Siksika cousins.

In this instance, however, the event actually referred to by Beckwourth applies to the Crow fight with the Atsina in 1832 only a week and more after the latter`s defeat by white trappers and Indian allies during the famous "Battle of Pierre`s Hole," and so should not be confused with the earlier Crow attack upon the Blackfoot column as noted by Denig, Bradley and Munroe. In reality, Beckwourth and others among his contemporaries, invariably classified the Atsina as Blackfoot, owing to the close Atsina alliance with that people.

Whatever the case, it does appear that at least two separate events of Crows attacking a Pikuni column were recounted by Munroe, even though his chronology and details relating were somewhat confused, either by himself or his biographer Schultz.

Now concerning the Crow attack upon the Blackfoot column in 1845, we do have contemporary accounts in documented form from both Edwin Denig, head clerk at Fort Union at that date, and Father Pierre DeSmet, the famous Jesuit missionary to the Western tribes, and who received a report of the fight from a colleague who himself, was actually residing among the Blackfoot band involved only a short time both before and after the said attack. Each of these accounts compare favourably with one of the Hugh Munroe versions, specifically that recorded in *"My Life as an Indian,"* and wherein he states to have been wounded in the leg on that occasion. Munroe did not mention his killing a man during this event, neither that Chief Lone-Walker had his memorable hand to hand duel with the Crow chief. Furthermore, all the various accounts of the 1845 fight agree, that there were only eighty lodges of Blackfoot involved at that time. These belonged to the Small-Robe Pikuni band and a little over half that number of lodges were actually destroyed during the Crow attack led by the famous River Crow chief of that date named Twines-His-Horses-Tail, but who was not slain in the battle in a hand to hand fight, as he was still alive as late as 1867.

The Denig account does state that in an earlier attack by the Crow Chief Sore-Belly upon a Blackfoot column, the latter also comprised eighty lodges, although Denig, who obviously had knowledge of both affairs, that is, of 1824 and 1845, most probably misconstrued what he was told, or simply made a mistake as to the number of lodges involved. He would have been fully aware that both episodes applied to a Pikuni Blackfoot band, but at the same time, he may have confused the River Crow Chief Twines-His-Horse`s-Tail, who he knew well, but by this man's other name of Rotten-Tail [in the Crow language *"Cheesapoois,"*] with the great Crow Chief Sore-Belly, who Denig knew as Rotten-Belly [rendered in Crow as *"Alapooish"*]. Denig then, may have also confused the actual number of Blackfoot lodges involved in the two separate Crow attacks upon Pikuni columns, i.e., the occasion when Sore-Belly himself had led the expedition in 1824, and of the later-date event when Twines-His-Horse`s-Tail was chief in 1845.

In Munroe`s account of the battle, in which he said he was personally involved and during which the Small Robe Chief Lone-walker duelled with the Crow chief as narrated in *"Rising Wolf,"* he made it clear that most, if not the entire Pikuni division was then together and consequently, engaged in the fight at one stage or another. However, he also mentioned that no captives were then taken by the Crows and further stated, that the

Pikuni lost a total dead that day of *"...forty-one men, thirty-two women and girls and nine children,"* [eighty-two in total] whilst the Crows, he said,

> *"...lost sixty-one of their number and some of their wounded were sure to die."*

These figures are at variance to the one-hundred and thirteen Blackfoot killed during the similar attack as narrated by Munroe in *"My Life as an Indian,"* and to the number of Blackfoot slain as given by both Denig and DeSmet when referring specifically to the episode of 1845. These numbers are also at variance with Chief Sore-Belly's attack prior to 1832, when - again according to Denig, but who gave no date for the event,

> *"...One-hundred and upwards of the Blackfoot lay dead on the field. Two-hundred and thirty women and children were taken prisoners and more than five-hundred head of horses fell to the share of the Crows, besides all the lodges, camp equipment, provisions, etc."*

However, a correlation of the details given by Denig concerning this last-mentioned affair, ostensibly pertains to the fight of 1824, and is compatible with those details found in Hugh Munroe's *"Rising-Wolf,"* wherein it is stated that Munroe was personally involved as a young novice on the Plains under the protection of the Small Robe chiefs Rising-Head and Lone-Walker. This indicates that both accounts refer to the same singular event, and as the great River Crow Sore-Belly was then present according to the Bradley and Denig accounts, it must be referring to that particular episode which had taken place in 1824, and not in 1845, as we know that Sore-Belly himself had previously been killed by the Atsina in late 1834.

In addition, we see that in Munroe's account as published in *"Rising Wolf,"* it is stated that not long prior to the attack on the Small Robe column, a war-party of Blood Blackfoot wiped out seven Crow scouts who were members of a large River Crow force out on their way to the Shoshoni. Munroe further said that originally, there had been eight Crow scouts, but one must have escaped and taken word of the attack to the main Crow camp and of the position of the Small Robe village - albeit that the Small Robes themselves were innocent of being actually involved in the slaying of the scouts.

Here an added piece of corroboration can be found in the Piegan Blackfoot Winter Count of Bad-Head, wherein it is recorded for the year 1829,

> *"Seven Crow scouts killed."*

Perhaps this particular entry applies to the same event as mentioned by Munroe in *"Rising Wolf,"* and that the year indicated in the Bad-Head `count` should not be 1829, but closer to 1824. What we do know is that the Crows were at peace with the Shoshoni in 1824 and in 1845, as asserted in the contemporary writings of General John Charles Fremont and in certain Teton Lakota winter counts for those years. Whereas, the Crows were certainly at war with the Shoshoni in 1832, as both the Beckwourth and Ferris material make abundantly clear.

Munroe further stated that the peace gathering which then followed between the Crows and Blackfoot, after the attack on the Blackfoot column, was held north of the Musselshell on the flats abutting Warm Spring Creek, a tributary of Judith River which itself, runs from south to north into the Missouri. This area was always a favourite camping ground for the River Crows, and if Winona Plenty-Hoops is correct in designating the Plain adjacent to Pompey's Pillar as the trysting site for the Crow-Pikuni peace-making after the later- date destruction of the Small Robe column in 1845, then Munroe, surely, was referring to the earlier fight involving Chief Sore-Belly, and the subsequent Peter Skene Ogden inspired peace-making of 1825.

Hugh Munroe indeed, was a fully adopted member of the Small-Robe Pikuni band, which was the only Blackfoot-speaking group to actually claim the country immediately south of the Missouri as their hunting grounds, notwithstanding that the River Crows claimed that area also. During the season of their annual buffalo hunt in late autumn, the Small-Robes could usually be found in that region. This band before 1837, was comparatively large as compared to most other Pikuni bands and so could usually deter attack upon their village, solely because of the number of warriors they could put into the field at any one time. In 1832 the artist George Catlin was at Fort Union on the Upper Missouri, where he was told that the Small-Robes [who he wrongly stated were a separate Blackfoot-speaking division rather than merely one of the several Pikuni bands], comprised around 250 lodges. This number is consistent with Munroe's version of the attack as narrated in *"Rising Wolf"* and recorded by Schultz for the supposed date of 1816. More likely, though, it refers to the fight of 1824, at which time according to Denig's account, only eighty Blackfoot lodges were at first actually under attack, although Munroe himself admitted, that the attacking Crows were then only engaged with one part of the much larger Pikuni, Small-Robes and Blood force, and that the initial number of Blackfoot warriors holding off the Crows in the same *"Rising Wolf"* account, was, Munroe said, only some two-hundred strong before many more Blackfoot entered the fray, which fact he made clear by supplementary phrases in his narration, such as,

> *" Beyond, a great crowd of our men were riding at them [i.e. The Crows]."*
> *" Faced by ever increasing numbers of our [Blackfoot] warriors."*
> *" I looked back and the sight of hundreds of our men coming on was encouraging."*

Then follows the account of the duel between the Small Robe Pikuni Chief Lone-Walker and the Crow chief, who he does not name, the result of which after a hand to hand grappling match, was the death of the Crow chief. Munroe continued as follows,

> *"Their chief [the Crow] dead, and faced by ever-increasing numbers of our warriors, the Crows now turned and fled, but we did not chase them far; our men were so anxious about their families, to learn if they were safe, or dead, that they had no heart for the pursuit."*

So it would appear that on the above occasion of which Munroe speaks, a bunch of Pikuni was travelling as one small band some way in advance of the whole Pikuni division accompanied by the Small-Robes and a number of Bloods. Unfortunately, the foremost bunch was positioned at or near the head of the column when first they had been attacked and subsequently, suffered the most casualties as compared to their kindred Pikuni bands which included the Small Robes and accompanying Bloods. By this it must be construed that during this particular affair [1824], the arrival of Small-Robes, Pikuni and Blood reinforcements; having come forward from the middle and rear of the column, caused the attacking Crow force to retire from the field. The truth, however, seems to be that the Crows withdrew in an orderly manner rather than being driven in precipitous flight. As it is apparent that the Crows still retained their captives in large number along with all the booty they had taken. This, of course, would not have been the case if the Crows had been forced to retreat in disarray as the Munroe account suggests.

Munroe further stated that he was one of the foremost negotiators in arranging the subsequent truce between the Blackfoot and Crows. But this would surely not have been the case if he was only seventeen or eighteen years old at the time and not recognized as a warrior of any standing, as indeed, was Munroe's true situation in 1816. Later in life, when able to speak the Blackfoot language fluently and having achieved some distinction among his adopted people as a fellow warrior, he may well have been instrumental in negotiating a peace, being considered an important asset by both the Blackfoot and white traders as a go-between. But at the age of eighteen or thereabouts, he could hardly have had significant influence among the Indians, and especially so, in such important issues as serious peace-making between warring tribes.

What is interesting in the *"Rising Wolf"* account of peace-making between the Crows and Pikuni, is the appearance of a lone Blackfoot emissary entering the River Crow camp on a peaceful mission. This reminds one of an event recalled in Crow tribal tradition, which relates to a time when the head Crow chief, Grizzly-Bear, foretold the coming into camp of a lone enemy. Now Chief Grizzly-Bear, we know, was not in the position of head chief of the River Crow prior to 1834, having only attained the title after the death of Sore-Belly late that year. Coupled to this, Munroe by his own words, mentions his possession of what can only be conceived as a cap and ball pistol, which according to his account of his first year on the Plains and during an attack on the particular column he was travelling with, he used against the Crows to good effect. Such weapons were not readily available before circa, 1820.

Perhaps, then, Munroe's memory was not as faulty as his biographers James Schultz and George Grinnell asserted. But on the contrary, it was Schultz, moreover, who manipulated what he heard from the old man's lips in order to create more colourful stories for his readers. Thus he included details from several separate events, which he then wove together as he himself saw fit, without any real regard for historical correctness. *

In conclusion, it must be said that the Munroe account of a Crow attack on a moving Pikuni column as narrated specifically in the book *"Rising Wolf,"* applies not to 1816, 1832 or 1845, but to 1824. The account of a similar event recorded by Schultz in the book *"My Life as an Indian,"* would then, only apply to the event of the River Crow Chief Twines-His-Horses-Tail and his great victory over the Small Robe Pikuni in 1845.

Having said this, the Sore-Belly attack on a Blackfoot column in 1824 and that led by the later-day River Crow chiefs Twines-His-Horses-Tail and Bear's-Head in 1845, have also, it seems, been fused into one event in Crow oral tradition itself, again owing to the profound similarity of both episodes. But in reality, there can be little doubt that the two occurrences were completely separate affairs, isolated from one another in both time and detail, not to mention subsequent events occurring as a direct result of each fight.

- 0 - 0 - 0 - 0 - 0 - 0 - 0 - 0 - 0 - 0 - 0 - 0 - 0 - 0 - 0 - 0 - 0 - 0 –

*In *"The Metis Dictionary of Biography,"* dates pertaining to Hugh Monroe's birth, death and other dates are confused. In actual fact, Church records show that Hugh Munroe was born in the Three Rivers district of Quebec in August 1799, and was baptised two days later. Records also show that he died on the Blackfoot Reservation at Browning, Montana in 1896.

## APPENDIX C
## BECKWOURTH'S *"MEMOIRS"* AND LAKOTA WINTER-COUNTS AS SOURCES OF HISTORY.

Throughout the whole of Beckwourth's rambling narrative in his *"Life and Adventures,"* the number of warriors belonging to one tribal war-party or another when engaged in the numerous conflicts recounted therein, and especially with regard to the number of casualties sustained by one side or the other are, but for a few cases, greatly exaggerated, causing many of the said events to sound ridiculous if not to say, figments of Beckwourth's fertile imagination. For this reason above all, Beckwourth has often been branded a braggart and downright liar, yet there can be no doubt that he did, in fact, live among the Crows for several years and was certainly with them in more than one hostile engagement with that tribe's enemies. It is also true that he was prone to bouts of gross exaggeration when referring to the number of warriors involved in certain intertribal conflicts and particularly so, with regard to his own participating role and alleged high-standing among his adopted people. If, indeed, we took the number of enemies slain as recorded in Beckwourth's memoirs at face value, then we might assume that the Crows alone wiped out half the Plains Indian population of the Far West; having annihilated the Cheyenne Nation twice over. His knowledge, nonetheless, of Crow and Cheyenne military custom and of actual historical events concerning those tribes is essentially correct, and if one takes an objective view of his various accounts - ignoring the obvious embellishments of which not only he, but his biographer Bonner was probably also guilty - then much authentic information can be gleaned from his pages.

There are at least two examples in the published account of Beckwourth's adventures where he has, without question, deliberately manipulated the facts in order to give a false impression to his readers, although in both these cases, they concern altercations between himself and other white men and do not actually detract from his account of intertribal relations with which we are primarily concerned. It will become apparent that with the exception of the aforementioned episodes, in which the true details have been concocted to suit his own aims, Beckwourth's narrative is, in reality, a valuable and in essence a reliable sequence of events regarding Crow intertribal warfare according to his knowledge and personal experiences in the Far West during the period in question. That is, prior to the United States Government intervention beginning in the eighteen-fifties.

Beckwourth [b. 1798 – d. 1866] had been a member of Ashley's brigade of trappers and later, was employed by the American Fur Company. He was a true "Mountain Man" in every sense of the term. Therefore, in accord with his counterparts, he saw it as his prerogative to spin a good yarn - so to speak - and brag unashamedly of his own accomplishments be they true or false. He was also of mixed-race parentage, commonly known as Mulatto, and as a consequence, was somewhat looked down upon by his white contemporaries simply because of his Negro blood. During Beckwourth's time, black slavery, of course, was an accepted facet of American life and there were those who did not relish the idea of someone they considered a Negro, as being on a par with, if not actually better than themselves. Even after the abolition of slavery in that part of the world, both layman and scholar alike with but few exceptions, were still reluctant to accord Beckwourth just credit for his abilities and accomplishments, simply because of the colour of his skin. Certain derogatory comments pertaining to Beckwourth's race and character by a number of those who knew him personally and from others, who knew him only by reputation, are on record and merely confirm the widely held prejudices of the day.

The eminent historian Francis Parkman, who met Beckwourth in 1846, said of him in one place, *"...a mongrel of French, American and Negro blood,"* and in another passage described him as,

> *"...a ruffian of the worst stamp; bloody and treacherous, without honour or honesty; such at least is the character he bares upon the prairie."*

Robert Meldrum, also an American Fur Company employee, who himself lived among the Crows for thirty years beginning around the date 1827, told Lewis Henry Morgan in 1862 that he *"....had known Beckwith* [sic] *well"* and further commented,

> *"Beckwith* [sic] *was a humbug....The whole narrative was humbug ...He had Crow wives but was not a chief. He was adopted into a good family. His wife was not the daughter of a chief, a pretty woman but of low stock. His influence was little except while he was interpreter for the company. He never distinguished himself in fights."*

Meldrum went on to say,

> *"I was with him in three fights. He was not a coward but he [Beckwourth] was awkward,"*

And Morgan himself added,

> *"....James P. Beckwith said he killed the enemy, but Meldrum thinks he never did."*

Contrary to these views, however, was the opinion of Lieutenant George Templeton in his 1866 diary entry which states from personal contact, *"Beckwith* [sic] *with all his faults, was certainly a man of talent, very smart and a plesant man."* In addition there is a contemporary statement from the trapper Zenas Leonard [1839], in which he alludes to a Negro man with whom he and his party met in Chief Long-Hair's combined Mountain and Kicked-in-the-Belly Crow village during the winter of 1832 / '33. Leonard spoke of him in the highest terms and added, that the Negro in question, had first come to this country [the Upper Missouri] with Lewis and Clark,

> *"......with whom he also returned to the state of Missouri, and in a few years returned again with a Mr. Mackinney, a trader on the Missouri river, and has remained here ever since - which is about ten or twelve years.. He has acquired a correct knowledge of their [the Crows] manner of living, and speaks their language fluently. He has risen to be quite a considerable character, or chief of their village; at least he assumes all the dignities of a chief, for he has four wives with whom he lives alternatively."*

Although evidently mistaken in his reference to Lewis and Clark, Leonard's narrative when referring to a later event of 1835, actually gives an account of an exceptionally brave deed performed by the same or, perhaps, another Negro, which resulted in a force of combined River and Mountain Crows under chiefs Long-Hair and Grizzly-Bear, wiping out a war-party of sixty-nine Piegan Blackfoot. This episode was also mentioned by Parkman [Loc. cit.], who stated, rather reluctantly one might suppose,

*"....Yet in his* [Beckwourth's] *case, the standard rules of character fail, for though he would stab a man in his sleep, he will also perform most desperate acts of daring."*

Parkman then went on to describe Beckwourth's single-handed assault upon the Blackfoot [i.e. Piegan?] stronghold, of which event the aforesaid Zenas Leonard had personally witnessed.

The present Author has visited the site of this battle in the company of Joe Medicine Crow, the current Crow tribal historian, who informed him that Crow oral tradition also credits Beckwourth as being the perpetrator of the deed, rather, that is, one or another person of either Negro or Mulatto race who happened to be residing among the Crows during the first half of the nineteenth century.

Of course, Beckwourth himself was fully aware of the sometimes negative attitudes towards him and, no doubt, it was because of this that his ego found it necessary to boost his own importance, imaginary or otherwise, in order to show himself at least the equal of his white associates.

Among the Indians, however, he was in his element. Here there was no such thing as racial intolerance solely because of colour. Such an aspect of discrimination was not a concept in the Indian psyche. At a later period during the fierce and often bloody wars between the white invader and the red man, certain white men still continued to live among the hostiles, yet suffered no indignities simply for their having a white skin. A person was accepted or not on merit, good or bad, brave or otherwise and treated accordingly.

There can be no question as to whether Beckwourth was brave, and as such, that he was accepted among his adopted people as an equal. Although it is true to say that he did not in anyway, achieve the ultra-high status among the Crows of which he later professed. It is likely also, that Beckwourth abrogated to himself many deeds of the aforesaid Robert Meldrum, as the latter himself once asserted, whilst in addition, Beckwourth also attributed to himself, the high standing among the tribe of Edward Rose, who at an earlier date, had resided among the Crows and during which time, achieved a somewhat mythic-like warrior status.

The half-white half-Cheyenne, George Bent, in a letter to George E. Hyde dated 1905, referred to Beckwourth as *"The Yellow Negro"* [referring to colour rather than a slur on his character] and stated,

*"The Cheyenne knew him as the Yellow Crow Indian as he had been with the Crows a good many years."*

Bent elsewhere recalled that he himself had seen a good many Crow Indians in 1865 and that they knew nothing of Beckwourth. The old-timers, he said, thought that Beckwourth picked up the Crow language while working for the American Fur Company on the Yellowstone and in the opinion of Bent,

*"Jim Beckwourth wrote a poor book."*

As an agent for the American Fur Company, of which there is no reason to doubt and with whom the Crows specifically had dealings for many years, Beckwourth did exercise a certain authority as a go-between in his employer's relationship with that tribe and certainly, he had a great deal of influence among them. He married into the tribe and either of his two sons, one of whom he refers to in the *"Life and Adventures"* by the name of "Black-Panther," may well have been the same man of a later date known as "Crazy-Head," as some present-day tribal informants believe, and who later was noted among his tribe as an accomplished warrior. It is just as likely, however, that this man was the offspring of his Crow mother's liaison with the aforementioned Edward Rose.

369

It can be proven that Beckwourth did assist the Crows in more than one hostile encounter with that people's enemies and was recognized by them as a warrior who, during the course of his stay among the tribe, was known by various names such as "Antelope" and "The Bloody Arm." But again, it must be said, it is highly unlikely that he involved himself in anything like the number of engagements to which he later laid claim, even though he was obviously well-acquainted with the deeds and escapades of his Crow associates. In all fairness to Beckwourth, George Bent's contacts with the Crows in 1865 were, by his own account, hostile, and it does appear that Bent misconstrued the date of his friendly meeting with Crows, as indeed he often gave erroneous dates in his recollections. Actually he was referring to the period 1866-68, at which time Beckwourth was already dead, and Bent would have been in a position and situation to converse freely with Crow Indians, who visited certain army posts in the north where Bent was then in attendance. In truth, it would seem that George Bent had either little real knowledge of Beckwourth or, that for some personal reason, he had no liking for him.

It is not surprising that in later years the Crows did not apparently talk much of Beckwourth, perhaps because the particular Crow persons with whom George Bent was in contact, were probably of a different band to those of Beckwourth's acquaintance. Added to this, during the mid-eighteen - sixties, several white men were then living among the Crows and during the intervening years while Beckwourth was absent from their camps, at least one other Mulatto resided among them. The fact that Beckwourth after leaving the Crows, became so intimate with the Southern Cheyenne, may itself had been reason enough for the Crows to disclaim former knowledge of him or, at the least, were reluctant to acknowledge his one-time close association with them.

Later, though, the Crows must have relented, for they openly confessed their love for their old comrade-in-arms when in 1866, whilst on a return visit to a Crow camp, Beckwourth, then old and decrepit at sixty-eight years of age, suddenly died either in or near the Crow village; some say poisoned by the Crows in order to keep his spirit among them, but most likely from dyspepsia. Iron-Bull, a famous Mountain Crow chief and Beckwourth's host at that time, took it upon himself to dispose of the body, which he did by secreting it among the rocks, Indian fashion, thereby indicating a degree of respect for the old "Black warrior" of the past, at least from Iron-Bull himself.

It must be remembered that among the Crows as with most other tribes, it was not the custom to mention the deeds or even to speak the name of a departed warrior, until some significant time had elapsed after that person's demise. Therefore, if Bent's contact with the Crows was in the period 1866 to 1868 and not in 1865, it would then account for the refusal of the Crows to speak of Beckwourth so soon after his death.

As regards the numerous intertribal battles mentioned throughout the course of Beckwourth's memoirs, there are several independent sources to show that many did, in fact, take place, albeit, perhaps, without his personal participation and sometimes in varied detail when compared to Beckwourth's version of the same. It appears obvious that Beckwourth merely repeated the stories he had heard from warriors, who themselves, had actually taken part in the episodes described. He does, however, appear to have been aware of nearly every notable event relating to the particular Crow band among whom he resided, moreover, in relation to their military enterprises and more than twenty years later, could recall each event in its proper order of sequence along with the pertinent details.

Unfortunately, Beckwourth's narrative does not conform to the conventional sequence of chronology to which we are accustomed. But contrary to popular belief, although unconventional, his 'memoirs' do follow a specific chronological pattern which a close comparative study of related material makes abundantly clear. In order to understand this, we must first understand Beckwourth's personal concept of time and the methodology he used.

Unike most Mountain Men of his day, Beckwourth was articulate and literate, [having had at least two years formal schooling] and as documents and records attest, was overall, regarded as honest, trustworthy and generous. [See; Elinore Wilson, *"Jim Beckwourth."* Uni; of Okl; Press. 1983.] However, he does seem to have had very little knowledge of the science of "histography" as practiced in the more sophisticated world, and upon becoming a member of the Crow tribe, he readily adapted instead, to the Indian perception of time, along with the latter's concept of historical perspective.

To the Indian way of thinking, past events [and to a less degree certain historical episodes] were often "lumped" together, as it were, to form a whole. It was considered irrelevant whether one event should precede or succeed another in its proper order of occurrence, the content of the episode being the paramount concern. Thus when narrating events of the past within the confines of their own society, that is, before the outside influence of white historians and Anthropologists somewhat corrupted their philosophical outlook, one event was "tied" to another, as the Indians would say, if there was some comparison of content. The order in which historical storytelling was repeated was, in itself, a mnemonic device by which Indian history was kept alive in a semi-constant flow, each episode being connected to the last by some thread of similarity, the ethical or heroic lesson contained therein being of all importance.

This then appears to have been the idiom to which Beckwourth adhered during his time among the Crows. It was only natural, therefore, to narrate that particular phase of his life in a similar fashion. His biographer merely wrote down what he heard in the same order of sequence as the stories issued from Beckwourth's lips and thus, we have the seemingly erratic chronological format of the printed narrative.

It is apparent also that Beckwourth himself was not sure of the exact dates for all the events he described in relation to the white man's calendar; Yet he knew only too well their correct order of occurrence as one event followed on from the other. His recollections, though, were narrated in sections, each section comprising a number of related episodes told in their proper order of occurrence and covering anything from a one to three-year period in time. The confusion here is compounded by the fact that Beckwourth, - in accordance with the Indian idiom, - narrated these various "sections" in random order as he himself saw fit, without regard for their proper chronological sequence.

Of the few specific dates which do appear in the text, they were probably inserted by Beckwourth's biographer who himself, was not acquainted with the exact dates either. Neither, so it would appear, did he comprehend the manner in which his narrator was recounting his memoirs, i.e., in random sections. This is evidenced by the date of October 1832, given in the text as the time of the Leonid meteoric shower, which actually occurred in November of 1833. Beckwourth's biographer could easily have clarified and corrected this mistake, if indeed, he had been a little more conversant with the facts. Even the year 1826, included in the text as the date Beckwourth first took up residence among the Crows, is in error and should actually read, *"winter of 1828 / `29,"* which date is borne out by what are more discerning sources than Bonner alone concerning this particular point.

Other episodes related in the said memoirs can likewise be satisfactorily dated with the use of independent documentation and when taken together, do explain the peculiar chronology employed by Beckwourth himself.

This being so it soon becomes abundantly clear that rather than accuse Beckwourth of exploiting a fertile imagination, he did, in reality, possess a remarkable memory which would have surpassed many of the peers and betters of his day. His mind without doubt, was alert, keen and meticulous and able to retain the smallest detail pertaining to what some might describe as trivial and often repetitive experiences of his younger days.

It certainly cannot be denied, that Beckwourth's record of Crow Indian warfare during his time of residence among them, is a valuable and authentic account from someone who was actually on the spot at the time. Regrettably, his work has previously been much maligned. In the main because past scholars of the subject have either dismissed him out of hand due to his exaggerations, or simply not bothered to do their homework in order to verify the essence of his statements.

By employing solid historical data, it is possible to untangle the roundabout order of events as they are presented in the printed memoirs and thus, accept that many of the said events did in fact take place and at the time Beckwourth professed. An explanation of Beckwourth's chronological format is as follows.

Beginning with the winter of 1828 / `29, the time when Beckwourth first took up residence among the Crows, the text runs through to the autumn of `31. At this point in the narrative there is a hiatus before the text continues with the winter of 1832 / 33 and follows through to late summer of `34. Then the narrative returns to an event of September 1833, at which time Beckwourth had his altercation with Thomas Fitzpatrick and Rocky Mountain Fur Company employees; an episode which is well documented, although in order to add substance to his pleas of innocence, Beckwourth here includes in more detail, an event of the spring of 1830 which he had previously briefly referred to in the narrative in its proper chronological place and this is the account of Little-White-Bull's last stand.

The memoirs, seemingly, then jump back to where he had left off in recounting the events of September 1833, but actually the story follows on from the spring of 1830 with events of that year and the next which he had earlier omitted. As a result, after leaving out episodes from these years which had already been recounted, he picks up again with the events of the winter of '31 / '32, and continues by covering events which again the narrative had earlier neglected, until the autumn of 1832. From here, not surprisingly, the text leaps forward to the spring of 1835, [having previously related the happenings of 1833 and `34.] and thus follows through without further interruption to the spring or early summer of `37, at which time Beckwourth finally left the Crows for distant climes.

It has been noted above how Beckwourth's recollections are often prone to bouts of gross exaggeration, particularly when recording the number of Indian participants and casualties involved in any intertribal conflict. A typical example of this is to be found in his account of the Little-White-Bull affair. Here Beckwourth gives the number of Lakota and Cheyenne dead as thirty-four and in addition, includes the death of a white trapper among the allied host. This information, so Beckwourth said, he got later from Cheyenne participants themselves.

On the other hand, existing oral traditions of the fight obtained from both the Cheyenne and Lakota, mention only one Cheyenne as having been killed, while the Ferris version states that two of the allies were slain outright and several wounded. Only the Beckwourth material mentions the death of the white trapper.

From an analysis of these different accounts, we can only be sure of two allied deaths during the actual battle, notwithstanding those who may have been wounded and died later in their camps as a result. Of the former, one was a Cheyenne, the brother of Medicine-Water, the other perhaps being Beckwourth's alleged white trapper participant, who himself may not have been a member of the Smith and Jackson brigade, but rather a "Free" trapper, cohabiting with either the Lakota or Cheyenne on his own volition.

Even so, as Beckwourth did not over exaggerate this particular episode in his memoirs, - merely inserting the details of the affair in the wrong chronological place and that he did not claim any personal involvement in the fight - it may be that his original words were, *"three or four killed"* and that his biographer saw fit to alter this to *"thirty-four killed"* in order to add effect, [if not to be consistent with Beckwourth's usual propensity for exaggeration.]. Beckwourth was correct when referring to the number of

Crows slain on this occasion as twenty-three, which statement is corroborated by an entry in a particular Lakota winter-count pertaining to this same affair. It is not likely that Beckwourth would have had access to any of these Lakota calendar histories, either before or after his dictation to Bonner, so that the correlation on this point, must be more than coincidence.

Among the unpublished papers of George Bird Grinnell, there is also an account of a Cheyenne - Crow battle which, without doubt, refers to the Little-White-Bull affair. In Grinnell's version the name of the Crow partisan is not given, but there are added details such as the Crow leader's red blanket coat attire, along with some of the words spoken by the latter in defiance to his enemies. The death of Medicine-Water's brother wearing the coat of iron also comes from this source. Grinnell obtained his information from Cheyennes who were well-versed in the facts, although they did not apparently mention the presence of either the Lakota or white trappers. Neither did they give an exact date for the event.

Fortunately we have a more precise account penned by W. A. Ferris, who himself was a noted Mountain Man of the period. In all likelihood he had heard the story of Little-White-Bull's last fight first hand from trapper associates, who may have been resident in the allied camps at the time, even if they were not actual participants in the fight. This account is brief yet graphic and dates the event specifically as occurring during the month of March 1830. It is from this account also where comes the accusation that only three of the besieged Crows offered effective resistance, although as we have previously opined, it is more likely that most of the Crows had expended the last of their ammunition early in the fight, if indeed they had more than three guns among them in the first place. Furthermore, once their gunflints had become wet or damp, firearms such as the flintlocks they were carrying would have been rendered useless in their hands.

As late as the nineteen-thirties, the Crows themselves still had a quazi-historical account of the affair preserved in their oral traditions. Here Little-White-Bull's proper name of "Keeps-Looking-at-the-Albino-Buffalo" is given, along with a very brief description of the fight, but including the last actions of the Crow chief. The Anthropologist Robert H. Lowie published this account in 1931, but included a degree of mythological padding.

Be this as it may, the correlating factors between the accounts of Grinnell, Ferris, Beckwourth and Lowie regarding this particular episode, is that each describe the annihilation of a Crow war-party as occurring around the same date; the latter's defensive position in some kind of depression or hollow; the presence of snow and intense cold and in three of the versions, full credit is given to the bravery exhibited by the Crow chief concerned, coupled with similar quotes from the chief's harangue in defiance to his foes. All accounts are compatible in their essential details and therefore undoubtedly refer to the same event.

Further corroboration of Beckwourth's version can be had in several of the Lakota Winter-counts, which not only substantiate the exact date of the fight but also some of Beckwourth's details pertaining to it.

These "counts" were kept by certain tribesmen who recorded what they supposed, was the most important or unique happening of each year and portrayed it thus in the form of a stylized pictograph; often being more idiomatic as an aid to memory, than a realistic representation of the actual event. Each "winter" covered a part of two of our conventional years, beginning with the spring of one and ending with the close of winter of the next. It sometimes happens then, that an individual entry will conflict with our own dating by one year either way, although in many cases the entries do conform to our mode of reckoning exactly.

Perhaps the most widely publicized of all the various Lakota winter-counts, is that accredited to Lone-Dog. This man belonged to the Yanktonais Dakota, but his father and Grandfather had been Lakota of the Miniconjou band. Lone-Dog's Grandfather had first started the count, which was then continued by Lone-Dog's father and thus, the earlier part of this record relates to the Miniconjou specifically, that is, before Lone-Dog himself took up the count from where his father had left off.

Now the Lone-Dog entry for the year 1830 / `31 states,

*"A bloody battle with the Crows"* [along with the added notation] *"It is said that twenty-three were killed."*

The single icon depicted gives no indication of number, although as it shows a male figure with red body paint and red-colored feathered headdress, then perhaps it is highly indicative and descriptive of the event. The color red is invariably used in Indian symbolism as the conventional sign for "blood," even though in this particular instance, it may just as well denote the red capote-style coat worn by the Crow partisan at the time. The fact that a feathered bonnet is depicted, rather than a hooded coat, might serve to show that the figure portrayed was also the leader of the Crow party. In Lone-Dog's separate entry for the year 1834 / 35 a similar male figure is depicted, but here only the torso and tips of the feathers are painted red, with the accompanying explanation,

*"The chief Medicine-Hide was killed."*

Obviously the `count` keeper wished to convey a certain difference between the two events.

It is probable that Lone-Dog himself was not acquainted with the precise details of the 1830 fight and hence his notation, *"It is said that twenty three were killed."* It appears that Lone-Dog in this instance, had merely copied the earlier entries of the count from his Grandfather's and father's pictographs without knowing their exact symbolism and therefore, assumed that the profuse use of red paint in the 1830 entry indicated that the battle had been a particularly bloody affair. Why, though, this fight should have been considered more bloody than many other intertribal conflicts of a similar nature - of which there were many - or for that matter, why alone it should warrant such a singular appellation is not clear and especially so, when one recalls fights in which an even greater number of enemies had been slain and their bodies likewise mutilated in the customary savage manner. Unless of course the mutilations in this case were in excess of what was generally accepted as "customary" even among Indians themselves on such occasions.

More important, however, is Lone-Dog's comment that twenty-three Crows were killed, for this is precisely the number as given in the Beckwourth account. This correlation not only associates Lone-Dog's 1830 entry favorably with the Little-White-Bull fight, but shows that Beckwourth was obviously speaking the truth as far as he knew it, concerning most of the details regarding this particular event.

The winter count of Mato-Sappa [Black-Bear, Miniconjou Lakota] and that of White-Cow-Killer [Oglala Lakota], note the same event for the year 1830 / 31. Both these counts appear to be copies from that of Lone-Dog, although the Mato-Sappa count declares that the fight took place somewhere near Bear Butte in the northwest corner of what is now the state of South Dakota.

Another reference to the fight can be found in the calendar history of Cloud-Shield, also an Oglala, but of a different band to that of White-Cow-Killer.

Probably Cloud-Shield belonged to the same faction - albeit of a later generation - whose members had actually participated in the fight. This last is a more detailed entry while Cloud-Shield's calendar itself on the whole, is a more precise and probably more authentic record of Lakota history as compared to most other counts.

The winter heading on this count for the year 1830 / 31 is,

*"Many Crows were killed."*

Cloud-Shield himself gave the additional information,

*"The Crows were approaching a village, at a time when there was a great deal of snow on the ground. They, [the Crows] intended to surprise the camp, but some herders discovered them; The Dakotas went out, laid in wait, and killed many."*

The pictograph here is very graphic and to a large extent, self-explanatory. It depicts the head of a single Indian sporting the conventional Crow hairdo, encompassed by a circle which in itself, represents some kind of protective enclosure. The inward protruding lines emanating from the rim of the circle denote the flight of enemy projectiles, most likely bullets [musket balls] as opposed to arrows, whilst the few lines projecting outward indicate the inferior firepower from those within. A single character representing the head of an enemy usually suffices in such cases to denote an unspecified number of people, although in this instance, it may well depict Little-White-Bull himself who, so the allies declared, was the only one of the besieged Crows who on that occasion, was worthy of note.

A more obscure calendar originating among the Sans-Arc Lakota and now in the keeping of the Charger family at Pine Ridge [ a copy of which is in the present author's possession], is in the form of a typed manuscript transcribed in the Teton Lakota dialect without any pictographic representations. This suggests, however, that the count was set down from oral tradition alone.

The Sans-Arc were originally a part of that Teton Lakota group often rendered in early documents as "Saone," and whose stomping ground was on both sides of the Missouri river above its Great Bend. Until the early 1830s, the designation `Saone` then included those later independent Lakota Bands of Hunkpapa, Two Kettle, Sans-Arc, Blackfoot and Miniconjou, and thus the Sans Arc themselves were not, necessarily, personally involved in all the events recorded in this particular count. It is for this reason that many of the entries therein have no added details other than the "winter" caption itself. The entry in this count for the year 1830 only states therefore,

*"A bunch of Crows were killed."*

Nonetheless, this is significant, as the dating of the event surely associates it with the occurrence of the Little-White-Bull fight.

Perhaps there is yet another recollection of the Little-White-Bull affair which can be found in a winter-count belonging to the Yanktonais Sioux. This count of unidentified authorship, has an interesting pictograph entry for the year 1831. A caption written by hand in the Dakota dialect pertaining to this entry thus reads,

*"Wicasa num Kiciktepi."*

Which translates either as,

*"Man [men] two they came and killed," or "man [men] twenty they came and killed,"*

Such is the occasional ambiguity of the Lakota language when rendered in abbreviated form. The apparent discrepancy in the year number with that of the Little-White-Bull fight, can be satisfactorily explained by the fact previously mentioned, that sometimes a count entry does not conform exactly to our old- world system of reckoning, as each of these count "winters" cover a part of two of our calendar years. Subsequently, the above event can refer either to the year 1830, 1831 or even 1832. Having said this, what is most interesting in this particular entry is the pictograph itself.

Two opposing figures are shown, both wearing the enemy hairdo [in this case very long hair which often denotes the Crow tribe specifically], each of whom holds a knife-like object at the end of an out stretched arm. Perhaps this is meant to represent the two boy servants belonging to Little-White-Bull`s party, who according to the Beckwourth account, after being taken captive by the victorious allies, stabbed their guards before being slain themselves.

Two other Winter Counts, obtained from the Blackfoot band of Teton Lakota, which like the Sans-Arc once made up a part of the Saone group mentioned above, record for the winter of 1830,

*"One Cheyenne and twenty Crows were killed by Mandans at Bear Butte;"*

It seems unlikely that the interpreter of this last count really knew the proper meaning of the entry, for the Mandan of course, were the staunch friends and often allies to the Crows during the period in question, notwithstanding occasional petty disagreements which may from time to time have arisen between them. It might be assumed that the keeper of this count had heard some garbled version of the Little-White-Bull fight, and remembered that one of the parties involved had started forth from the vicinity of Kipp's trading post then on White Earth Creek very near the Hidatsa and Mandan towns. Thus the recorder was led to suppose that Mandans had been principally involved, whereas, in reality, two or three Mandan warriors may merely have accompanied the original Crow party when it first went searching for the stolen ponies. Of course, if a few Mandan warriors had actually been members of Little-White-Bull's group, then it would explain the varying number of Crows killed as given in the several accounts, including that of Beckwourth in his initial brief report of the affair, wherein he himself stated that only twenty Crows were killed, although this would then correspond, incidentally, with the W. A. Ferris version. It is true, however, that Beckwourth did mention another Crow party of twenty warriors that was also wiped out at around the same time as the party led by Little-White-Bull. Beckwourth, though, gave no details or any inclination as to where the wiping out of the twenty strong Crow party actually took place, and as yet, no other written reference to the event has been found. Perhaps then, the entries in the last mentioned Lakota winter counts, do apply to this same event as noted by Beckwourth, and not to the Little-White-Bull affair after all.

The site of Bear Butte, given in at least two of the aforementioned 'counts' as the location of the fight, rather than near the mouth of Powder River, probably likewise, derived from a misunderstanding of the facts, in so much as the affair would have been known to have taken place somewhere in the Cheyenne country as it was at that date and that Bear Butte, being regarded as the "Sacred Mountain" of that people, was considered the center of the Cheyenne domain. Perhaps then, this location is actually meant to be symbolic rather than historical fact. However, as late as the last quarter of the nineteenth century, certain Plains Tribes applied the name Bear Butte to several separate promontories, one of which was located in the south-eastern part of Montana near the lower course of the Powder and may therefore, have been misconstrued by later informants as pertaining to the more famous "Bear Butte" of southwestern South Dakota.

In yet another Lakota winter count composed by the Oglala named Left-Heron, it is recorded for the year 1830 / `31 that *"Many white buffalo were killed."* Now while it is true that if such an occasion had actually occurred, then it would well have warranted being entered in the 'count' as a most memorable event, it does, however, appear unlikely that `many white` buffalo would have been found in one herd at any one time. I therefore suggest that the entry here has been misconstrued somewhat, and was originally meant to refer to the Crow chief Little-White-Bull as having been killed at that time.

All being said, here we have abundant proof that a Crow war-party was annihilated by Lakota and Cheyenne during late winter or early spring of the year 1830, along with corroboration for Beckwourth's version of the event as being a factual account as far as his own sources of information would allow. We also have here corroboration for the correctness of our chronological reassessment of the Beckwourth material, and can then, with a great deal of justification, include other episodes from his `memoirs,` believing them to be of actual historical events relevant to any study of intertribal warfare, - particularly that between Crows and their Cheyenne, Lakota, Gros Ventre and Blackfoot enemies, -

albeit that the episodes have been related in a somewhat exaggerated form by Beckwourth himself.

$$- 0 - 0 - 0 - 0 - 0 - 0 - 0 - 0 - 0 - 0 - 0 - 0 - 0 - 0 - 0 - 0 - 0 -$$

## APPENDIX D.

## THE ARKANSAS RIVER FIGHT OF 1833.

Edwin T. Denig was employed as head clerk at Fort Union by the American Fur Company between the years 1840 and 1856. He naturally came into close contact with the Crows and other tribes of the Upper Missouri country and certainly, was one to take an avid interest in what was then going on around him and of what he was told. His information concerning this particular episode in Chief Sore-Belly's life, probably came in part from the Crows themselves, along with tales then current among itinerant trappers and traders told to him during his time at the said Fort. Perhaps his account of the Arkansas River fight is exaggerated to some extent, particularly regarding the number of Cheyennes both killed and taken captive on that occasion. Denig does not give a precise date for the event, saying only, *"The above circumstance brings up the life of the Crow chief* [i.e. Sore-Belly] *to the year 1833."*

Robert Lowie on the other hand, obtained a more detailed account of the affair from Crow informants during his research years among that tribe beginning in 1907. However, it is apparent after a careful scrutiny of his works, that Lowie as regards his version of the great victory of Sore-Belly over Cheyennes on the Arkansas River, combined two separate events into one. This, though, was not necessarily Lowie's fault, but moreover, the fault of Crow narrators themselves, in so much as by the time Lowie began collecting his information, the deeds and personage of the great Chief Sore-Belly had already become mythologized in Crow oral tradition. Thus the particular story of the great victory over Cheyennes on the Arkansas had, through the passage of time not to mention the storyteller's wish to create effect, become enjoined with that of an earlier, albeit another spectacular victory over the same tribal enemy. In Lowie's account it is further stated that during the episode in question, [1833], the Crow fighter Sits-in-the-Middle-of-the-Land, by employing some kind of *mystical* power, shot and killed the Cheyenne chief, Stripped-Elk [i.e. High-Backed-Wolf], and from such a great distance that the Cheyenne chief, in fact, could not then be seen. However, High-Backed-Wolf was actually slain by a fellow tribesman during a drunken brawl, albeit later in the same year 1833, and hence, because of the Cheyenne chief's demise close to the time of the Arkansas River fight, his death was thus attributed by the Crows to Sits-in-the-Middle-of-the-Land in the subsequent quazi-historical version of the fight which, many years later, came into being.

The same process which helps create an oral tradition is, of course, common throughout the world wherever non-literate cultures are found. It is often the result of incorporating mnemonic devices, and bringing past events and personages into a more recent time so as to keep the concept of the original story alive. In such a way, several separate occurrences pertaining to various persons or to several tribal heroes, become joined together to create a composite story, and which in due course, enters the realm of mythology. The Crows, it seems, were no different in this respect and, in reality, an analysis of Lowie's accounts show that the revenge attack of circa, 1821, led by Sore-Belly upon the Cheyenne in response to the destruction of Long-Hair's Crow village one year earlier, and during which occasion *no* Cheyenne prisoners were taken, is confused with Sore-Belly's later victorious escapade of 1833, when many Cheyenne prisoners *were* taken.

The Crows themselves only forty-three years later, it seems, did not appear to have been certain of the precise details concerning either of these two events. As the Crow informant Little-Face told Lieutenant James Bradley in 1876, garbled versions of the two battles of 1821 and 1833 respectively, but likewise fused the two events together as one. Little-Face – so Bradley assumed - was in his mid-sixties when he was talking to Bradley, although it would appear that Little-Face was then actually in his late fifties, as sixty would have been considered as being too old to go to war. Bradley was told by Little-Face as follows,

> *".. It happened when Arapooish was a young man, when the tribe [Crows] was still on the waters of the Arkansas River. The Crows were at war with four tribes viz., the Cheyenne, Arapahoe, Powder People and Wolves, but they were very powerful there and not afraid of them all. Once their scouts came in and reported a large village of their enemies higher up the river and it was resolved to leave behind the children and old men and women and proceed against the enemy with all the young men and women and warriors able to fight."*

This account then goes on to describe how Sore-Belly took up the war-pipe, and includes the story of the killing - against his orders - of a meadowlark, after which the account continues,

> *"... The expedition then moved on and in due time reached the village. Here they fought a fierce battle with their enemies and routed them with great loss, but the only one killed among the Crows was a young man, the brother of the girl who had struck and killed the bird with her riding whip."*

We can see from the Little-Face excerpt, if indeed it refers to either of the Sore-Belly victories in question rather than a completely different episode, that Little-Face gave the correct time period for the affair of 1821, which would have occurred before Little-Face was born, but confused this event with that of the fight on Arkansas River twelve years later when Little-Face would have been around fifteen years old. Thus, if we are to accept the Crow oral account as repeated by Lowie, Little-Face may indeed have been included as a young member of Sore-Belly's war-party against the Cheyennes in 1833.

The Cheyennes for their part, according to the works of George Bird Grinnell among others, did not mention the fight with Crows of 1833, although we know it was the habit among all Indians, not to mention in detail disastrous events in which their own people had been seriously defeated unless pressed to do so. Having said this, there remains the possibility that if the latter affair of 1833 *was* that mentioned by the Cheyennes, then Grinnell and his contemporaries may themselves have wrongly assumed that their informants were referring to the earlier event of 1821.

Could it be more than coincidence that the two episodes follow a similar pattern and indeed, that the two events are but varied accounts of the same fight? I think not. In the one it is Long-Hair's village which is first destroyed before the revenge attack by Sore-Belly in which the Crow warrior Plays-With-His-Face lured the enemy into a trap, and is said to have taken place either on, or very near the Horse Creek tributary of the North Fork of Platte River, in what is now the north-eastern part of Wyoming, and at which time, the Cheyenne village itself was *not* actually assaulted, neither were any Cheyennes taken captive.

In the other, it is the much smaller Crow village of Dangling-Foot which is at first destroyed, while the ensuing fight by Sore-Belly's revenge force took place much further south, either on or near the Arkansas in south-eastern Colorado between the tributary streams of Horse Creek and Big Sandy Creek, and during which event, so we are told, the Cheyenne village *was* assaulted and raised to the ground along with a sizeable number of captives taken. Perhaps then, the inclusion of the two Horse Creek locations in memories pertaining to each of the separate fights is what has confused the issue.

In 1851, when the so-called Fitzpatrick Treaty on the Laramie River took place, both Cheyennes and Crows who were in attendance at that time, discussed between them past conflicts with one another. Questions were posed by Cheyennes and Crows concerning both fights now under consideration, although again according to Grinnell`s information, the questions and answers given, referred only to the destruction of Long-Hair`s village of 1820 and the revenge attack by a Crow force soon after, during which a number of Cheyennes had been decoyed into a trap.

Fragments of the ensuing conversation which have come down to us through Grinnell`s writings, do suggest that such vivid recollections as were then recalled, although brief, indicate that the Crows were then meaning to refer to a much later episode than the destruction of Long-Hair`s village. The Cheyennes themselves may not have realized this and in the resulting confusion, the Crow mythological version which now combines the two fights, originally came into being.

Further discrepancies occur when we are made aware of the Northern Cheyenne Wooden-Leg`s opinion, as given to his biographer Thomas B. Marquis in the early 1930s, which states positively that as far as he [Wooden-Leg] was concerned, no Cheyenne women had ever been captured by the Crows. Obviously he was very wrong on this point, but then so too, was Edwin Denig when he gave the number of Cheyenne captives taken in the 1833 fight as two-hundred and fifty women and children. Such a large number of captives, surely, would not have gone unnoticed by the Cheyennes and certainly not forgotten. However, the more recent Northern Cheyenne historian, John Stands-In-Timber, said the same as Wooden-Leg, and when in 1930, an Indian pageant was being staged at the annual Sheridan, Wyoming Rodeo, both the visiting Crows and Northern Cheyennes were asked to stage an attack upon each other's villages representing some actual historical event between the two. The Cheyennes, it is said, then retold the fight of 1820, but the Crows could not seem to recall an occasion when their warriors had actually destroyed a Cheyenne village.

Notwithstanding these statements, some other Cheyennes, or rather, those among the Southern Cheyenne people at least, did apparently have some vague recollection of the 1833 fight which they imparted to Stanley Vestal in the early 1930s, and whose account of which runs as follows,

> *".... Somewhere near the Big Timbers a band of Cheyenne were in camp the fall of the year. They had just killed plenty of buffalo and were taking it easy while the women jerked the meat and dressed the robes. One morning while it was still dark a woman lying in her tepee suddenly awakened and felt the beat of galloping hooves against the ground on which she lay. The dogs began to bark loudly, she sat up, then scrambled to her feet just as a war-whoop shrilled at the far end of the camp. She ran out of the tent and looked around her. Enemies were charging the camp, which was suddenly alive....All around her was confusion. The old men were yelling advice. Young men dashed by to catch their horses or galloped past to meet their enemies. She could see the flash of guns and hear them crashing as the charge swept home...Women and children sped by her away from the battle, running in all directions to find a place of safety, mothers lugging their babies or dragging older children by the hand, matrons puffing for breath, hobbling old women making off as best they could with their sticks. Children cried, dogs yelped, horses reared and plunged, but above all she was conscious of the sound of shooting....Already the warriors were among*

*the tents, firing at everybody who came out of them. Some of the Cheyenne were killed before her eyes.... All this she saw in a moment. Then she was running as hard as she could go towards the bluffs, stumbling through the darkness. She could never remember how, but at last she arrived, panting and trembling, among the rocks. As it grew lighter she cowered back among them and found a shallow cave where she could hide....By that time her enemies had driven her people out of the camp and set the tents on fire. The Cheyenne had been surprised and overwhelmed by numbers. Shortly after sunup, her enemies took the captured ponies and rode away...."*

So we see from the above that the actual location of this fight, as given by Vestal's Southern Cheyenne informants as being near the place known as "Big Timbers," along with the fact that here the enemy are actually said to have destroyed the Cheyenne village, thus indicating that a number of Cheyenne captives were undoubtedly taken, would not only discredit both the Wooden-Leg and Stands-In-Timber assertions, but, I believe, proves beyond doubt the occurrence of a very similar, if not the identical event as befell the Cheyenne village assaulted by Sore-Belly and his Crows on the Arkansas in 1833.

The James Beckwourth material may well refer to the same fight of 1833, wherein he states that one of the two Head chiefs of the Crows, whom he later refers to as, *"the old chief,"* started out with a war-party of two-hundred selected warriors, intending to raid the Cheyennes in their own country. Beckwourth; abiding by his usual propensity for exaggeration, then states that the next night he himself also started out with two-hundred warriors against the same enemy. Accordingly, upon reaching a location between two streams [which Beckwourth calls the Laramie Forks], his party discovered a Cheyenne village; killed eleven Cheyenne hunters who for some unexplained reason had chosen to camp away from the said village for the night, and then returned home victorious with eleven Cheyenne scalps, nineteen horses and other plunder. The *"old chief"* so Beckwourth added, came home with his party three days later, bringing fourteen [Cheyenne?] Scalps *"...without having lost a single man."*

This account might possibly be alluding to the fact that although Chief Sore-Belly - as Denig says - had personally selected the host of Crow warriors for the proposed expedition, the force when it travelled [for part of the journey at least] actually did so in two separate bodies. One column of which would have been led by Sore-Belly, and the other by his second-in-command, Little-White-Bear. Certainly Beckwourth`s term of *"the old chief,"* is used throughout his memoirs to denote Sore-Belly specifically. Important, however, is that the name Little-White-Bear is not mentioned in the earlier account when Plays-With-His-Face decoyed the Cheyennes into the trap in 1821, neither is Little-White-Bear listed as one of the Crow Head men who put their marks on the so-called "Friendship Treaty" paper in 1825. This indicates that he was not then regarded as a chief of standing during that period, but which he certainly was in 1833. Also in the account leading up to the earlier fight of 1821, Young-White-Buffalo is mentioned as an important warrior and chief, and this is the same man also known as Looks-at-the-Albino-Buffalo, or more simply, Little-White-Bull. This man did put his mark on the treaty paper of 1825 and from documented evidence, we know he was killed in the early part of 1830, three years before Sore-Belly`s victory over Cheyennes on the Arkansas in 1833. The mention then of Little-White-Bull alone, shows that the fight during which Plays-With-His-Face acted as a decoy in 1821, should be regarded as completely separate to the fight more than a decade later, when Little-White-Bear led the decoys and a Cheyenne village was destroyed. Beckwourth, too, likely then confused the Horse Creek of the Arkansas with the Horse Creek tributary of the Laramie River further north

After a reappraisal of Beckwourth`s erratic chronological format, which is apparent throughout the whole of his narrative, the true dating of the episode he mentioned, appears to fit nicely with the early part of winter,1832-`33,whilst Beckwourth`s specific notation of, *"...without losing a single man,"* adds substance to the prospect of it being confused with the earlier event of 1821, as it is, perhaps, Beckwourth`s misconstrued reference to Sore-Belly`s *medicine,* but which in truth, having been broken by the killing of a meadowlark, the chief then prophesying rather, that *a single* Crow would be killed in the event. It is true that several other episodes related by Beckwourth, also bare a similarity with the Sore-Belly raid on the Arkansas in 1833. Although none of these offer enough corresponding details to make an association feasible.

Beckwourth had lived among the Crows as an adopted member of the tribe, as indeed, did several other white men during the same period, such as Robert Meldrum among others. Beckwourth, though, may not actually have been in residence with the tribe between the winter of 1832-`33 and the autumn of 1834, having by his own admission, been absent from the Upper Missouri country for fourteen months on other business. However, it would still be strange for Beckwourth not to have mentioned the episode of 1833, even if only briefly, and especially so, owing to the importance of the event among the Crows themselves, and the wide knowledge of it even among white trappers and traders of the Upper Missouri country. We should take it then, that Beckwourth was not present on that occasion, and probably was not fully informed of all the details thereof.

My own informants among the Crows such as Joe Medicine-Crow and Winona Plenty-Hoops, both told me on separate occasions, that in their youth they had heard from old-timers of the Buffalo days that Sore-Belly with a large force of warriors, had several times *"cleaned up on a Cheyenne village."* One particular occasion they both recalled, took place on Horse Creek soon after the destruction of Long-Hair`s Mountain Crow village, and another some twelve years later, which took place close to the Arkansas River far south in revenge for the slaughter of Dangling-Foot`s people. In the first instance, my informants said, no prisoners were taken; neither was the Cheyenne village destroyed, whereas in the second instance, the Cheyenne village was completely destroyed and a number of captives taken. Both Joe and Winona agreed that the account repeated by Robert Lowie in his *"Crow Texts"* does appear to combine the two events into one, but Joe especially was adamant, that they were separate episodes, distinguished in both time and detail.

When in 1952 the Crow historian Max Big-Man wrote about the Dried-Out-Furs band of dissident Crows having gone south, he also mentioned that he [Max Big-Man] had travelled far during his lifetime, and had visited a number of different tribes, among whom he inquired if they knew anything regarding the fate of the missing Crow band. He was told; presumably by Southern Cheyennes, that a big battle had once occurred involving Cheyennes and an enemy force, the result of which was that a camp of close to forty families was wiped out. This was said to have occurred one-hundred and nineteen years before Max Big-Man`s visit, thus dating the episode as of 1833, and which took place not far from the limits of the Southern Cheyenne reservation in western Oklahoma. Max Big-Man assumed that the event most likely, referred to the fate of the Dried-Out-Furs Crow band, although it could just as well refer to Chief Sore-Belly`s attack on a Cheyenne village somewhere in the lower Arkansas River country, and this especially so, as the Dried-Out-Furs band - so we are informed in the Crow tradition - did not comprise family groups, but was a war-band through and through, composed of fighting men with perhaps, only a small number of captive women among them. In corroboration, we find that Robert Lowie in another place, mentions from a Crow informant, that at one time *"...half the Crows went south and were massacred."* ["Societies of the Crow, Hidatsa and Mandan," P.163.], and which likely refers to either Dangling-Foots people of 38 lodges, or to the 80 lodges of the Dried-Out-Furs band of dissidents.

Yet another, although tentative reference to the fight of 1833, is to be found in one of the George Bent letters to George E. Hyde, dated, Jan. 21, 1915. Here it is stated,

*"...Some years after the Crow revenge raid upon the Cheyenne village on Horse Creek* [i.e., when Plays-With-His-Face had decoyed the Cheyenne into a trap; Present Author's parenthesis.], *another big fight took place between the Crows and Cheyenne, but did not really amount to much, and only a very few were killed on either side."*

Now the fact that Bent mentioned this last fight at all, and in the same breath as it were, as the two important episodes of 1820 and 1821, suggests that here he is referring to another event which had also been considered important by the Cheyennes, but owing to their own people having been severely beaten on that occasion, they had glossed over the actual details of the fight, as indeed, was customary among most tribes in relation to certain events in their history which they deemed derogatory to their own warrior prowess, let alone, not wishing to recall sad events of the past. Perhaps then, Bent was; albeit unwittingly, referring to the Sore-Belly attack of 1833 on the Arkansas River.

The truth of the matter seems to be, that the so-called Cheyenne village destroyed during the 1833 fight, had actually belonged to the Suhtaio, who at that time, although confederated and closely allied to Cheyennes, were not then regarded as fully integrated members of the Cheyenne Nation proper, and thus, they, the Suhtaio, still acted as an independent group. It has been noted that the trader William Bent who himself was well-acquainted with all other Cheyenne bands, declared that he did not meet the Suhtaio until sometime between 1832 and 1833, and mentioned further, that this was the first time the Suhtaio had come so far south to take up permanent residence in the region between the South Fork of the Platte and Arkansas River.

Having said this, it must have been warriors from one or another Suhtaio band who destroyed Dangling-Foot's Crow village, and therefore, as Sore-Belly's revenge expedition had been directed against those specifically responsible, it explains how the Crows had picked up the enemy trail in the beginning, and how they knew that the Suhtaio; who once had been their close neighbors and antagonists in the Powder River and Black Hills region, were those to blame. Indeed, the Suhtaio were also known to neighboring tribes as Kites or Flyers, and are noted in early 19th century documents as *Squihitans, Staitans, Staihitans,* and as *Skutani* in several Lakota winter-counts. There is indeed a reference to a band of so-called *Staitans* being virtually exterminated by an undesignated tribal war band, ostensibly, sometime during the early eighteen-thirties which is found in the 1895 writings of one Joseph H. Taylor which reads as follows,

*"The Staitans or Flyers, a band at the time numbering not more than one-hundred men....were exterminated, but just what tribe became executioners has never been clearly established...These Staitans were the most warlike and ferocious...They were the best mounted as well as the best horsemen of the Plains, and moved with the buffalo in their migrations, laying no claim to territory where buffalo were not found...Their hands were against every people not of their own, and every tribe on the Plains regarded the defiant Staitan as an uncompromising and inveterate foe...The Staitan Indian never yielded in battle. To meet an enemy was to fight him; to conquer him or to die. They never spared an enemy on account of age or sex. Their women rode in the ranks of every battle and fought as her mate fought and was as merciless and unsparing as he... Before their extermination, even certain societies or war-bands within several of the Indian tribes of the west [were] organized in partial imitation of the fighting codes of these Flyers of the open Plains. To have the unwavering courage of a Staitan was the loftiest ambition a warrior could aspire [to], and to be likened unto one, the highest*

*compliment his vanity could reach for."* Joseph H. Taylor, *"Sketches of Frontier and Indian Life."* Pp.24 and 25. Washburn. North Dakota. 1895.

It is most likely then, that the above except pertains to the great victory of Sore-Belly's Crow war band over Cheyennes on or near the Arkansas River in 1833, only that the enemy should be designated as Suhtaio, and who, indeed, were at one time also known as 'Staitans' and 'Flyers'.

The Cheyennes themselves, of course, even though having given these same Suhtaio a refuge after Sore-Belly's attack, would not have regarded the affair as being against their own people. Thus, other than having a vague memory of the event in later years, the Cheyenne-proper would not have recalled any specific details and most likely, the event had been completely forgotten by the majority of the tribe when Grinnell was undertaking his research, not being thought as being a part of the personal history of the Cheyenne tribe itself. The Crows had also regarded the Suhtaio as a somewhat separate tribe to the Cheyenne, albeit the latter's allies, and which explains why Crows when asked at the previously mentioned Sheridan Rodeo to recall an attack on a Cheyenne village, they did not regard the Sore-Belly attack on the Suhtaio in 1833 as then being pertinent.

$$- 0 - 0 - 0 - 0 - 0 - 0 - 0 - 0 - 0 - 0 - 0 - 0 - 0 -$$

## APPENDIX E.

### William Marshall Anderson's list of Crow chiefs and braves for 1834. *

| | |
|---|---|
| Old-Burns [Long-Hair] | The-Rain [Big-Rain] |
| Rotten-Belly [Sore-Belly] | Om-O-Tashi |
| Spotted-Water or War-Eagle | High-Bull [Tall-Bull] |
| Mad-Bull | White-Flower or Cherry- |
| Wolf [WHigh-Tail-Wolf] | Blossom [Woman-Chief] |
| Gros Ventre-Horse [Atsina-Horse] | Breast-Gives-No-Milk |
| Two-Face [Double-Face 2d] | Rotten-Tail [Twines-His-Tail] |
| Good-Fellow | Yellow-Bull |
| Three-Crows | Yellow-Belly |
| Pa-pa-ge | Mi-niki [?] |
| Wooden-Bowl [Big-Bowl] | Na-ki-o-shish |
| Bear's-Tooth | Burnt-Child |
| Lawyer | Tall-Lance [High-Lance] |

*"The Rocky Mountain Journals."* University of Nebraska Press, 1987. Pp. 232 and 235.

$$- 0 - 0 - 0 - 0 - 0 - 0 - 0 - 0 - 0 - 0 - 0 - 0 - 0 -$$

# NOTES AND SOURCES

## PART 1.

## DEFENDERS OF THE YELLOWSTONE COUNTRY

### CHAPTER 1. Rise of the Apsaalooka.

1.   Joe Medicine Crow to Author. Lodge Grass, Montana.
2.   "Ibid."
3.   "Ibid."
4.   Ladona Brave-Bull Allard, Hunkpapa Lakota to Author. Standing Rock. Summer, 2013.
5.   For an in-depth account of the origins and migrations of the various Crow bands, See; Keefe, Brian L. "Apsarokee," Chapters 1 to 6. The Choir Press. Gloucester. England. 2015. There are also definite comparisons in Siouan traditions, language and religious rites, with those of ancient Aramaic peoples, such as ancient Babylonian and Proto Assyrian and Persian groups. Cf; Akbaa-tadia and Allah-Akbaa, and the Mandan / Hidatsa "Okipa" with the Babylonian "Okeeda." Also the Great Flood tradition; Giants and Little People and the Mandan / Hidatsa "Ark" among other comparisons.
6.   Pius Real Bird, Crow informant to Author. Lodge Grass, Montana. June, 2010.
7.   Smith, G. Hubert, *"Explorations of the LaVerendryes in the Northern Plains 1738-1743,"* p. 64. University of Nebraska Press. 1980.
8.   "Ibid."
9.   Cocking, Mathew. *"Journal of Mathew Cocking,"* Pp.110-111. Royal Society of Canada. Ontario.
10.  "Ibid."
11.  Ferris, Warren A. *"Life in the Rocky Mountains."* Chapter LXV. Denver, Old West Publishing Company.1940.
12.  Rundle, Rev; Robert. *"The Rundle Journals."* Edited by Hugh A. Dempsey. P. 264. Historical Society of Alberta. Vol. 1. 1977.
13.  Pius Real Bird, Crow informant to Author. Lodge Grass, Montana. June, 2010.
14.  Various Dakota and Lakota Winter-Counts including Howard, James H. *"Dakota Winter-Counts."* Smithsonian Inst; Anth; Papers. No. 61. P.335ff; and Mallery, Garrick. *"The American Horse Winter Count."*
15.  "Ibid."
16.  Real-Bird, Pius. Crow informant to Author. Lodge Grass, Montana. June, 2010.

### CHAPTER 2. Sore-Belly`s Childhood Years.

1.   Crow informant Winona Plenty-Hoops to Author. Lodge Grass, September, 1994. Note book 1. [Author`s collection]
2.   "Ibid."
3.   "Ibid."
4.   Jackson, K. Gordon, *"The Adventures of Peter Fiddler of Bolsover, 1769 -1822."* P.75. Country Books. 1999.
5.   Mallery, Garrick. *"Picture writing of the North American Indians. Vol. 2. [The Lone Dog Winter Count.]"* Dover Publications. New York [No date].
6.   Joe Medicine Crow to Author. Lodge Grass, Montana. 1996. Note Book 2. [Author`s collection]
7.   Winona Plenty-Hoops to Author. Lodge Grass, Montana. Loc; cited.
8.   "Ibid."
9.   Tall-Bull, Bill, Northern Cheyenne informant to Author. Lame Deer, Montana. Sep; 1994. Note Book 1. [Author`s collection]
10.  Mallery, Garrick. *"The American Horse Winter Count."* Loc; cited.

11.     Winona Plenty-Hoops to Author. Lodge Grass, Montana. Loc; cited.

**CHAPTER 3. Hostile Interludes and the Yellow-eyes Cometh.**

1.      Winona Plenty-Hoops to Author. Lodge Grass, 2001.
2.      Lowie, R. H. *"Societies of the Crow, Hidatsa and Mandan Indians."* Anthropological Papers. American Museum of Natural History, Vol. X1 Part 111. P 195. 1913.
        An old warrior of intertribal war days named Hunts-to-Die, who was one of Robert H. Lowie's Crow informants in the early 20th century, stated that this particular Crazy-Dog-Wishing-to-Die event had occurred soon after a Crow band had been destroyed during his [Hunts-to-Die] grandfather's time. Hunts-to-Die was born in 1839, so his grandfather's time would have included the period 1801 – 1802, and at which date we know from Crow oral history and the American-Horse Lakota winter-count, a Crow camp of 30 lodges was wiped out by Lakota. In addition, the story pertaining to Crows being besieged atop a butte now known as Crow Rock in Harding County, South Dakota, and of the Lakota victors thereafter, contracting some deadly disease from the Crow corpses, was obtained by members of the South Dakota Historical Society from local tribal informants, but who dated the event as occurring in 1822. However, there is no evidence of any serious contagion among either the Crows or Lakota in or near the year 1822, whereas there is ample evidence for just such a scourge in 1801-'02, and which fits nicely with both the Hunts-to-Die statement and several Lakota winter-count entries, not to mention several white trader journals of the time.
3.      Crow informant Alex Birdinground to Author. Sep. 2001.
4.      This massacre of Crows on the butte, appears to be compatible with a current Lakota tradition which tells of a one-hundred and six strong Crow party surrounded by a formidable Lakota force that just happened to stumble across them. The Crows fled to the top of a nearby butte and a fierce battle commenced. At length, it is said, only one Crow was left alive, and this young man sang a last war-song before taking his own life rather than fall into the hands of his enemies. The Lakota thought this young Crow had been very brave and thereafter, they always referred to the butte in question as the "Young Man's Butte." Lakota informant Dakota-Wind. 2016.
5.      LeRaye, Charles. *"Travels through North America." Pp.191-192. South Dakota Historical Collections Vol.4.* Pp.150-180. Lakota Falls, S. Dakota. 1908. Although there is much debate whether LeRaye did personally undertake his supposed trip into the Upper Missouri country or not, it is clear from the information contained in the account, that he must have obtained his information regarding the Indians from another, who was well-acquainted with the region and had good knowledge of the tribes thereof.
6.      Pike, Zebulon M. *"Pike Expeditions, Vol. 2."* Pp. 756-58. New York. 1895.
7.      Abel, A. H. *""Tabeau's Narrative of Loisel's Expedition etc;"* P. 157. University of Oklahoma Press. 1968.
8.      Alex Birdinground to Author. Lodge Grass, Montana. 1994. Note book 1.
9.      Lewis and Clark. "Journals." See; August 31, 1804. University of Nebraska Press. 2004.
10.     Howard, James H. "The John K. Bear Winter-Count." Pp.21-73. Loc; cited,
11.     Lewis and Clark *"Journals."* See; August 31, 1804. University of Nebraska Press. 2004.
12.     McKenzie, Charles. In; *"Early Fur trade on the Northern Plains,"* Pp. 241-250. [Edited by W. Raymond Wood and Thomas D. Thiessen]. University of Oklahoma Press. 1985.
13.     "Ibid."
14.     "Ibid."
15.     Larocque, Francois. *"The Yellowstone Journal 1805,"* P.206. In; *"Early Fur trade on the Northern Plains,"* [Edited by W. Raymond Wood and Thomas D. Thiessen]. University of Oklahoma Press. 1985.
16.     "Ibid." Pp. 206.ff.
17.     "Ibid."
18.     "Ibid."
19.     "Ibid."
20.     "Ibid."

# *NOTES AND SOURCES*

### CHAPTER 4. The Great Fight at Pryor Gap

1. Joe Medicine Crow to Author. Lodge Grass, Montana. 1994. Note book 1.

   Lewis and Clark were in winter quarters close to the Mandan towns during 1804/`05, and in their journals for December 1804, it is mentioned that Cheyennes carrying a pipe visited both the Arickara and Mandan towns. However, Lewis and Clark continued on their expedition up the Missouri in early April of 1805, so were not aware of the allied crusade or its outcome. The trader Antoine Tabeau on the other hand, was actually domiciled among the Arickara from the summer of 1803 until May 1805. Thus he was witness in the summer of 1804, to the first-time arrival at the Arickara towns of Arapahos in company with the other tribes mentioned. But likewise, Tabeau had already left the country by the time the grand allied crusade against the Crows actually took place. Otherwise, we would likely have contemporary documented accounts of the event, penned both by Lewis and Clark and Tabeau. The trader Larocque who sojourned with the Crows for several months, left his hosts in early September of 1805 on the Yellowstone at the mouth of Pryor Creek. The Crows were still in the Pryor district in mid-September that year, but had not been assaulted by the allied crusade while Larocque was among them. Thus, it seems, that it was late September after Larocque had left, that the Crows were attacked, and this would be compatible with the allies having first conducted their Sun-Dance ceremonies in mid or late August, before starting out at a slow meandering pace to the Pryor country. It would seem also, by Larocque`s mention of the Atsina party visiting the Crows in early September, that it was the Atsina who actually warned the Crows of the allied crusade then marching towards them, and that it was this intelligence which instigated the Crows moving their camps to the more strategic location in the canyon recess at Pryor Gap.
2. Joe Medicine Crow to Author. Lodge Grass, Montana. 1994. Note book 1.
3. Howard, James H. *"Dakota Winter-Counts as Sources of History."* Pp.354-355. Smithsonian Institution, Bureau of Ethnology, 173. Washington D. C.1960.
4. "Ibid."
5. Beede, Dr. A. *"A Key to a winter-count."* [The High-Dog [Hunkpapa] Winter-count. Unit 3 Document Set 1; Winter Counts.
6. Howard, James H. *"Dakota Winter-Counts as Sources of History."* Pp.354-355.
7. McKenzie, Charles. In; *"Early Fur trade on the Northern Plains,"* Pp. 241-250. Loc; cited.
8. Henry, Alexander [The Younger]. "Journals." Pp. 4-5.
9. Howard, James H. *"Dakota Winter-Counts as Sources of History."* [Loc; cited.
10. "Ibid."
11. "Ibid."
12. "Ibid."

### CHAPTER 5. Hidatsa Scalps on Apsaalooka **Waist-Belts.**

1. James, Thomas, *"Three Years among the Indians and Mexicans."* Pp. 52-64. The Citadel Press. 1966. [Reprint].
2. "Ibid."
3. "Ibid."
4. Holmes, Rueben. *"The Five Scalps."* Pp. 12-18. Missouri Historical Society. *"Glimpses of the Past."* Vol. V. Jan-March Number 1-3. St. Louis. 1938.
5. Holmes, Rueben. *"The Five Scalps."* Pp. 12-18. Loc; cited, and Joe Medicine Crow to Author.

### CHAPTER 6. Sore-Belly Becomes a Pipe-Holder.

1. Winona Plenty-Hoops to Author. Lodge Grass, Montana.
2. "Ibid."
3. "Ibid."

4.        "Ibid."
5.        James, Thomas. *"Three Years among the Indians and Mexicans."* Loc; cited.
6.        "Ibid."
**7.**        Henry, Alexander [The Younger]. "Journals." Loc; cited.

### CHAPTER 7. Sore-Belly with Arrow-Head`s band and Edward Rose

1.        Winona Plenty-Hoops to Author. Lodge Grass, Montana.
2.        Irving, Washington. *"Astoria; Anecdotes and an Enterprise beyond the Rocky Mountains."* Pp.288-294. New York. [No date].
3.        "Ibid."
4.        Holmes, Rueben. *"The Five Scalps."* In *"Glimpses of the Past."* Pp. 53-54. Loc; Cited.
5.        "Ibid."

### CHAPTER 8. Big Victory over the Assiniboine.

1.        Joe Medicine Crow to Author. Lodge Grass, Montana.
2.        Bradley, James H. *"Manuscripts and papers."* Loc; Cited.

### CHAPTER 9. Thirty in the Hands.

1.        Joe Medicine Crow to Author. Lodge Grass, Montana.2001. Perhaps, also, Paints-His-Face-Rad was the same Crow chief referred to as, The-Man-That-Is-Red in Charles Augustas Murry`s *"The Prairie Bird,"* [Published; 1845], and who, according to the latter account, was killed during a fight with Dellawares near the Rocky Mountains around the date 1815.
2.        Glen BirdinGround [Crow informant] to Author. Crow Agency. August, 1994.
3.        "Ibid."
4.        "Ibid."
5.        "Ibid."
6.        "Ibid."
7.        Glen BirdinGround [Crow informant] to Author. Crow Agency. August, 1994.
8.        Clarence Spotted-Wolf, {Northern Cheyenne informant] to Author. Lame Deer. 2001.
9.        Joe Medicine Crow to Author. Lodge Grass, Montana. 2001. Additional information for this chapter supplied by Glen BirdinGround; the George Bird Grinnell papers and George Bent Letters to Hyde [See bibliography for locations].
        The Cheyennes always declared that if there had been only one village of Crows in the fight, then a good number of Cheyennes would have escaped. The presence of the whole Mountain Crow division had made their annihilation a certainty. When discussing the fight some years later at the Fort Laramie Treaty of 1851, Crow veterans who had taken part in the fight, described to the Cheyennes the man who had acted like a bird in front of the breastworks, but the Cheyennes could not determine who it had been. They did recognize One-Eyed-Antelope, when the Crows sang the song which the Cheyenne with the gun had sung each time he fired his weapon and killed a Crow. Why fire-power among the Crows had not annihilated the Cheyenne party much earlier than the two days and nights required, was probably due to the fact that old-time flint-lock guns employed by Indians at the time were of the smooth-bore type, obtained from Fur Company posts and manufactured specifically for the Indian trade. These firearms were generally of an inferior quality and being un-rifled, proved extremely inaccurate over fifty yards or so. Additionally, they often suffered the barrel being cut down to be handled more easily from horseback, while both lead shot and wadding was rarely rammed home sufficiently, thus further reducing the gun`s accuracy and velocity, and rendering such weapons ineffectual other than in close combat situations.
        Hitherto, there has been confusion as to whether the Cheyenne party was composed of Crooked-Lance or Bowstring Society warriors. Grinnell stated they were the former, whilst George Bent said Bowstrings, and John Stands-In-Timber stated they were Crazy-Dogs. This last-named

society belonged specifically to the Northern Cheyennes, and was the equivalent of the Bowstrings among the Southerners. However, the Crazy-Dogs did not come into being until after the separation of the Cheyennes into their Northern and Southern divisions about the date 1834. Neither were the Bowstrings in any great number in the North Country during the time of the aforesaid fight. It must be admitted, though, that the Crooked-Lances and Bowstrings were very closely connected, and that the original Crazy-Dogs had been made up in the first instance, from ex-Crooked-Lance and Bowstring soldiers combined. It is indicative also that two Cheyenne brothers slain in the fight had been Suhtaio band members, and that the punitive expedition undertaken thereafter by the Cheyenne Nation in order to avenge its loss, was, primarily, instigated and organized by the Suhtaio. It must then be assumed that the fight at Prairie Dog Creek had been a Suhtaio affair, and thus involved Crooked-Lance warriors which, certainly, was the predominant society among the Suhtaio and included at the date in question, i.e. 1819, for the most part only Suhtaio band members.

According to the Grinnell account, the Crows once called the site of the battle and its nearby stream, "Crow Standing Butte" and "Crow Standing Creek" respectively, in memory of the Cheyenne brave who had ran around outside the breastworks imitating a bird. The Cheyennes of old used similar appellations, but declared that the meaning was "Where they [Cheyennes] Stood off the Crows." On the other hand, a Crow informant of Joe Medicine Crow named Plain-Feather, stated that the Crow name should more properly be rendered "Where Owner-of-Raven was Killed," as for a long time the Crows had thought that the Cheyenne warrior prancing outside the breastworks had been soliciting the aid of his personal medicine helper, which, the Crows believed, took the form of a raven. Having said this, yet another Crow name for the site – as told to Tim McCleary by a Crow informant, is rendered "Where Raven-Owner was attacked," referring to the initial assault upon the Crooked-Lance Cheyennes, and is said by the same source to have occurred near the foothills just south of the present-day town of Story in the northern part of Wyoming.

The stream today is marked on modern day maps as Prairie Dog Creek, although in the 1860s when the military post Fort Phil Kearney stood nearby, it was known to troops stationed there as "Peno Creek." It is also said that the fight actually took place very close to where the Crow Cultural Hero No-Intestines [or a later protégé] first planted the Crow Nation's Sacred Tobacco Seeds. For this reason, the fight in question may have had a more significant impact on the Crows, who would have regarded the presence of enemies in that vicinity as a sacrilegious violation and trespass into an area revered by the Crows as a holy and inviolable place of worship and of religious mystery.

### CHAPTER 10. When Eight-Hundred Were Stolen.

1. Barney Old-Coyote to Author. Lodge Grass. August 2001.
   The details contained in this chapter are derived from; The James H. Bradley manuscripts, the George Bird Grinnell papers, and George Bent Letters to George E. Hyde. Additional data is derived from the present Author's personal interviews with Crow tribal members, Joe Medicine Crow, Winona Plenty-Hoops and Elias Goes-Ahead, along with interviews with Cheyenne tribal members, Clarence [Bisco] Spotted-Wolf, Wayne Medicine-Elk and James King, all previously cited.

2. An expression employed to denote contempt, compatible with the hissing sound of an animal when aroused to anger. See also; Edward S. Curtis, *"The North American Indian"* Vol. 2. P. 186. His-Fights Biographical sketch.

3. Bill Tall-Bull, Northern Cheyenne informant to Author. Ashland. Montana. 1994.

4. Winona Plenty-Hoops to Author. Lodge Grass, Montana. Joe also said that Long-Hair, as head chief of the entire Crow Nation, was also referred to as "Owner of the Camps."

5. Barney Old-Coyote to Author. Lodge Grass. August 2001.

6. Hudson's Bay Company records for the Lake Traverse post, Nov; 9th 1820. Loc; cited.

7. James King [Northern Cheyenne informant to Author. Lame Deer, Montana. 1994.
   A more detailed account of this attack on Long-Hair's village, appears in Brian L. Keefe's *"Red Was the Blood of Our Forefathers."* Pp. 1-42. Caxton Press, Idaho. 2010.

8. Cheyenne informant James King to Author. Lame Deer, Montana. 1994.

## CHAPTER 11. Regaining the Initiative and Vengeance on the Cheyennes.

1.    Details in this chapter are derived from interviews with Joe Medicine Crow, the James Bradley manuscripts and Wildschut`s *"Crow Medicine Bundles."* Museum of the American Indian. Heye Foundation. New York. 1975.
2.    Joe Medicine Crow to Author. Lodge Grass, Montana.
3.    Joe Medicine Crow to Author. Lodge Grass, Montana.
4.    Wildschut, William. *"Crow Indian Medicine Bundles."* Pp. 43-47. Loc; cited.
5.    "Ibid"
6.    "Ibid"
7.    "Ibid"
8.    Robert H. Lowie`s *"Crow Texts."* Pp.494-510. University of California Press. 1960. What follows unless otherwise noted, is derived from this source.
9.    "Ibid."
10.    "Ibid."
11.    Michelson, Truman, *"Field notes and Papers."* American Anthropological Archives. Washington D. C.
12.    Lowie, Robert H. *"Crow Texts."* Loc; cited.
    Joe said that Plays-With-His-Face was so named because he once tied ribbons to the horns of a live bull buffalo as an act of daring. Although not himself a member of the Crazy-Dog Society who were sworn to undertake reckless and suicidal deeds, Plays-With-His-Face was referred to as a "crazy person," and was also noted - on foot or on horseback- for often throwing himself into the very midst of the enemy without regard for his personal safety.
13.    Robert H. Lowie`s *"Crow Texts."* Pp.494-510. University of California Press. 1960.

## CHAPTER 12. Cleaning up on the Lakota and Arrow-Head`s band.

1.    Bradley, James H. *"Papers and Manuscripts."* Loc; Cited. This may well have been the same event mentioned by the Crow woman Pretty-Shield to her biographer Frank B. Linderman in 1931. She then told of a time when Crows, including Chief Silver-Tip [which was an alternative name for Chief Grizzly-Bear] brought back one-hundred captive women after a great Crow victory over the Lakota. [See; Linderman, Frank Bird, *"Pretty-Shield, Medicine Woman of the Crows"* Pp.173-79. University of Nebraska Press. 1972 edition.]
2.    Bradley, James H. *"Papers and Manuscripts."* Loc; Cited.
3.    Coues, Elliot. [Editor]. *"The Journal of Jacob Fowler."* Pp.57-92. Ross and Haines. 1965 [Reprint].
4.    Joe Medicine Crow to Author. Lodge Grass, Montana.
5.    Prince Maximilian Zu Weid. *"Travels in the Interior of North America."* London. 1844.
6.    DeSmet, Pierre. *"Western Missions and Missionaries."* P. 159. Irish University Press 1972.
7.    Denig, Edwin T. *"Of the Crow Nation."* Pp. 162-164. *"Five Indian Tribes of the Upper Missouri."* Edited by John C. Ewers. University of Oklahoma. 1961.
8.    Welch, Colonel A. B. *"Dakota papers, Indian Histories."* www.welchdakotapapers.com

## CHAPTER 13. Destroying the Blood and Pikuni Column.

1.    Schultz, James Willard. *"Rising Wolf. The White Blackfoot,"* Pp. 154-163. Houghton and Miffin Company. 1919.
2.    "Ibid."
3.    Joe Medicine Crow to Author. Lodge Grass, Montana. Note book 2. 1994.
4.    Denig, Edwin T. *"Of the Crow Nation."* P. 163. Loc; cited.
5.    Joe Medicine Crow to Author. Lodge Grass, Montana. Note book 2. 1994.

# NOTES AND SOURCES

6. Macgregor, J. G. *"John Rowand, Czar of the Prairies."* P. 65. Western Producer Prairie Books. 1978.

7. Dempsey, Hugh. *"Bad-Head's Winter-count."* P. 197. In; Adolph Hungry Wolf's *"The Blood People."* Harper and Row Publishers. 1977.

Further corroboration of this date can be found in the writings of James Willard Schultz who, when referring to events of 1867, he mentioned that a Small Robe Pikuni [who was born one or two years prior to 1820], when talking of his father or uncle named Chief Big-Lake, said as follows, "...One spring when I was a little boy of maybe six winters, the Crows did us much wrong. Big-Lake said, "We shall teach these dogs something, and they shall know our personality. " He called our brother tribes to join us, the Bloods, Siksika, our allies the Gros Ventre and even the Sarsi. Together we went south across Elk River [the Yellowstone] right into the heart of Crow country and remained there all summer. We camped all up and down Bighorn River and Tongue River, living upon Crow buffalos and other game and catching many Crow beavers. The Crows, they fled before us, some to the south; some to the mountains. All summer long our war-parties harassed them, taking many scalps and many of their fastest buffalo horses. Yes, truly, we taught them how powerful we are." See; *"The Trail of the Spanish Horse,"* Page 113. Houghton and Miffin Company. 1917.

## CHAPTER 14. Enter the American eagle and chastising the Hidatsa.

1. Pattie, James, *"The Personal Narrative of James O. Pattie of Kentucky."* Pp. 26-27. Cincinnati. 1831.
2. "Ibid."
3. "Ibid."
4. "Ibid."
5. "Ibid."
6. Holmes, Rueben. *"The Five Scalps."* Pp. 12-18. Missouri Historical Society. Vol. V. Loc; cited. Edward Rose along with fellow Mountain Man Hugh Glass and one other, while carrying messages to Fort Union and crossing the Yellowstone River on the ice near newly errected Fort Cass, were killed by hostile Arickara sometime during the winter of 1832 /'33. Hafen, LeRoy R, *"The Mountain Men and the Fur Trade."* Vol. IX. P. 345. Arthur C. Clark Company, Glendale, Cal; 1966.
7. Kappler, Charles, *"Indian Treaties Etc.;"* Government Printing Office. Washington D. C.
8. Beckwourth, James P. *"Life and Adventures."* Pp. 81-84. Ross and Haines [Reprint] 1965.
9. "Ibid."
10. Aeneas, Baptiste, *"William F. Wheeler Papers"* Box 1. Folder 13. Mt. His Soc.Archives.
11. Joe Medicine Crow to Author. Lodge Grass, Montana.
12. Jensen, Richard E. and Hutchins, James S. [Editors] *"Wheel Boats on the Missouri. The Atkinson and O'Fallon Expedition."* Pp. 142-160. Montana Historical Society. 2001.
13. Joe Medicine Crow to Author. Lodge Grass, Montana.
14. Winona Plenty-Hoops to Author. Lodge Grass, Montana.
15. Joe Medicine Crow to Author. Lodge Grass, Montana.
16. "Ibid."
17. "Ibid."

## PART 11

## DENIZENS OF THE UPPER MISSOURI.

### CHAPTER 15. Captured Ponies, Coups and Scalps.

1. Hudson's Bay Company Records. Winnipeg. Canada. [See Bibliography, this Volume].
2. Newell, Robert, *"Diary, 1829-'43."* MS. University of Oregon Archives. Eugene, Oregon.
3. Fort Edmonton Journal, Hudson's Bay Archives. Winnipeg. Canada.
4. Raczka, Paul M. *"Winter-Count."* P. 28. The Oldman River Culture Centre. 1979.

5.       Irving, Washington. *"The Adventures of Captain Bonneville."* New York 1860.

6.       Irving, Washington. *"Astoria."* Robert Campbell to Irving. Numerous editions.

**CHAPTER 16. James Beckwourth joins the Crows and Little-White-Bull's Last Stand.**

1       Beckwourth, James P. *"Life and Adventures."* Pp. 247-248. Loc; Cited. See also; Robert H. Lowie's *"Crow Texts."* Pp. 409 ff. University of California Press. 1960.

2.       "Ibid."

3.       Beckwourth, James P. *"Life and Adventures."* Pp. 247-248. Loc; Cited.

4.       Ferris, William A. *"Life in the Rocky Mountains."* Chapter LXV. Loc; Cited. Also; Northern Cheyenne informant James King [Mexican Cheyenne] to Author. Lame Deer. 1994.

5.       Barney Old-Coyote to Author. Lodge Grass. August 2001. See also; Beckwourth, James P. *"Life and Adventures."* Pp. 283-284. Loc; Cited. For a more detailed account of the Little White-Bull fight and episodes following, consult; Brian L. Keefe's *"Red Was the Blood of Our Forefathers."* Pp. 71-96. Caxton Press, Idaho. 2010.

6.       Barney Old-Coyote to Author. Lodge Grass. August 2001.

7.       "Ibid."

8.       Ferris, William A. *"Life in the Rocky Mountains."* Chapter LXV. Loc; Cited.

9.       Barney Old-Coyote to Author. Lodge Grass. August 2001.

10.     "Ibid."

11.     "Ibid."

12.     That white trappers were among the Sioux and Cheyenne allies at this time; i.e., during the winter of 1829-'30, is attested to in the trapper Robert 'Doc' Newell's *"Memoranda; Travels in the Territory of Missourie etc.;"* [The Champoeg Press, 1959], and in W. A. Ferris's *"Life in the Rocky Mountains."* Loc; Cited.

13.     Keefe, Brian L. "Red Was the Blood of Our Forefathers." Caxton Press. Idaho. 2010.

14.     Ferris, William A. *"Life in the Rocky Mountains."* Chapter LXV. Loc; Cited.

15.     "Ibid."

16.     Beckwourth, James P. *"Life and Adventures."* Pp. 247-248. Loc; Cited.

**CHAPTER 17. Defending the Pack-Horse Column.**

1.       Joe Medicine Crow to Author. Lodge Grass, Montana.

2.       Beckwourth, James P. *"Life and Adventures."* Loc; Cited.

3.       Joe Medicine Crow to Author

The particular Cheyenne band involved in this affair was again, most likely, the Watapio, under its rascally old Chief Bear-With-Feathers more commonly known as Old-Bark. At the date in question the Watapio usually spent the summer months between the two branches of the Platte, but during the autumn and winter seasons, were to be found further north anywhere between the western edge of the Black Hills, South Dakota, and the Lower reaches and tributaries of the Powder. They associated regularly with the Suhtaio of the Tongue River district, and were almost constantly in conflict with the Crows, including the River Crow, the Kicked-in-the-Belly and Mountain bands.

When in later years [after 1838], Beckwourth became a regular visitor among the Cheyennes in his role as a freelance itinerant trader, it was often to the Watapio Cheyenne band that he went. By which time, the Watapio had moved south and were then residing permanently in the country between the South Fork of the Platte and the Arkansas River. Beckwourth declared that he soon struck up a friendship with the Watapio chief Old-Bark and thereafter, often discussed details of past battles which had occurred between Old-Bark's Cheyenne band and the particular Crow division to which Beckwourth had once belonged. This fact surely, gives a degree of validity to Beckwourth's assertion that he obtained the Cheyenne version of certain fights, including the number of casualties they might have suffered on any particular occasion, from Cheyenne informants themselves. Although it would appear that access to such first-hand information did not preclude Beckwourth's natural propensity to exaggerate.

It is known that a man named Stands-In-The-Water was in later years, a high ranking chief among the Watapio Cheyenne. His name may well have been a variant version of Beckwourth's Leg-In-The-Water and thus, one and the same as the heroic Cheyenne warrior mentioned in the above account. Stands-In-The-Water, however, is said to have been born in or around the year 1814, which would make him only sixteen years of age or thereabouts at the time of the fight in question. While it was not uncommon for an Indian youth to have begun his training as a warrior at sixteen years old and even younger in some cases, such escapades were usually confined to stealing horses. Certainly it would have been unusual for a warrior of such immaturity to have performed such a reckless deed as Beckwourth attributes to the said Leg-in-the-Water, although to do so was not entirely unknown.

More feasible, perhaps, is that Stands-In-The-Water was the son, or more likely, the nephew of Beckwourth's Leg-In-The-Water and in accordance with Indian custom, had later been given the name of his illustrious relative. The Stands-In-The-Water who was born in 1814, later became head chief of the Southern Cheyenne Elk-Soldier society. Therefore, he may have been raised among the Suhtaio - among whom the Elk Society was predominant - before marrying into the Watapio band, as indeed his contemporary, Chief Black-Kettle, also originally a Suhtaio band member, was later to do. Stands-In-The-Water went to Washington in 1863, and was killed during the infamous slaughter at Sand Creek the following year.

### CHAPTER 18. The Battle at Grapevine Creek and the Big-Prisoner affair.

1. Winona Plenty-Hoops to Author. See also; James P. Beckwourth, "Life and Adventures." P.289. Either Beckwourth or, most probably, his editor T. D. Bonner confused the Stillwater River with the Sweetwater, but which would then place the event too far south. James H. Bradley on the other hand in "The March of the Montana Column," University of Oklahoma Press. 1961. P. 91-93, along with present-day map notations, leave no doubt that the Stillwater River and Bear Tooth Mountains are the correct locations for the episode in question.
2. Victor, Francis Fuller, "The River of the West." 1974.
3. Hudson's Bay Company Records. Winnipeg. Canada.
4. Hudson's Bay Company Records. Winnipeg. Canada.
5, Joe Medicine Crow to Author, from Crow informant He-Does-It.
6. Hudson's Bay Company Records. Winnipeg. Canada. See also; Elizabeth Losey, *"Let Them Be Remembered."* Pp.250-261. Vintage Press. 2000.

The Crows remember the story of the Grapevine Creek fight because of their champion Stump-Horn's deeds. There is no account today concerning the affair among the Blackfoot tribes themselves. This might seem strange, as so large a number of Pikuni had been killed during the fight in question. However, before the great smallpox epidemic of 1837-'38, during which at least one third if not half of the entire population of all the Blackfoot-speaking tribes was wiped out, the latter could boast some four-thousand warriors combined, and in which case, the loss of a sixty-strong party would not have had the same significant effect as at a later date, i.e., after the gross reduction of their manpower due to the aforesaid contagion. Having said this, sometime during the nineteen-fifties a number of Bloods, Pikuni and Siksika visited the Crows and actually inspected the site where, so some among the visitors had been told, the actual fight had taken place. The visitors said they knew of the fight and in total, fifty-nine Pikuni had lost their lives at that time and only one returned home. They further said that the doomed party had no business going to the hill to be "cleaned out." By this it was meant that the party should have merely conducted a raid on the Crow pony herds, and not entrenched themselves in their fortified position waiting for the Crows to attack. What is more likely, however, is that the Pikuni intention was to make several raids on the Crow herds, and that their entrenched position sufficed as a temporary war camp and point of rendezvous, and that being in open country devoid of trees and brush to any great extent, they had been obliged to construct a cluster of rock breastworks just in case they were forced to defend themselves. When the Pikuni party was discovered by the Crow hunters, the Pikuni knew it would not be long before the enemy came against them on horseback, and so would easily run them down if they attempted to flee across the vast expanse of open ground by which they were surrounded.

In James Beckwourth's *Life and Adventures*, there is mention of a big Crow – Blackfoot fight during the same period as that of the Grapevine Creek conflict, and which Beckwourth states occurred specifically in March of 1831. But either Beckwourth or his biographer T. D. Bonner chose to insert the details of a fight which actually took place at the later date of early 1835, when a band of Crows led by chiefs Long-Hair and Grizzly-Bear, wiped out a large Blackfoot party also besieged in a rocky position. Of this later-date event, there is a first-hand eye witness account by the trapper Zenas Leonard who was present on that occasion. Perhaps this is the reason why the Beckwourth material does not include details of the Grapevine Creek fight specifically, and also, when later referring to events of 1834 and '35, why he only mentioned in passing that Chief Long-Hair and his Mountain Crows had another big fight with the Blackfoot which, obviously, was meant to refer to the same later event witnessed by Zenas Leonard, but which Beckwourth had previously inserted in his "Life and Adventures" during March of 1831.

The finding of numerous .44 gauge red copper cartridge cases both in and around the Grapevine Creek battle site, have led some scholars to assume that the fight had taken place after the date such ammunition came into general use, i.e., around 1860. This, though, can easily be explained by the later presence of both Indian and White hunters in the area, as it was a popular hunting ground up until the bison were all but exterminated in the mid-1880s. See also; the Henry Stelfox [of Rocky Mountain House] papers. Glenbow Archives. Alberta.

7.     Winona Plenty Hoops to Author. Lodge Grass, Montana. 1998.
8.     Joe Medicine Crow to Author. See also; Grinnell, George Bird *"The Fighting Cheyennes;"* pp. 32-34. University of Oklahoma Press. 1956, and Hyde, George E *"Life of Bent."* Pp.28-29. University of Oklahoma Press. 1967.
9.     Joe Medicine Crow to Author. Lodge Grass, Montana. 1998.
10.    Grinnell, George Bird, *"The Fighting Cheyennes."* Loc; cited.
       Old-time Cheyenne informants told John Stands-In-Timber that Big-Prisoner; not long after the affair recounted, did return to visit the Crows and stayed among them sometime, and during which he was more than once on the Crow side in battles against the Cheyennes. However, he then returned to the Cheyennes and was engaged on the Cheyenne side in fights with the Crow. It was also said that he was a very brave man in battle, and often went back and forth, staying for periods among the Crow and then the Cheyennes as the fancy took him. See; Margot Liberty [Editor] "Cheyenne Voices. P. 195 and 315. " University of Oklahoma Press. 2013.
11.    Joe Medicine Crow to Author. Lodge Grass, Montana. 1998.


CHAPTER 19. Twenty Day Fight and Sore-Belly Saves His Son from the Enemy.

1.     Tall-Bull, Bill, Northern Cheyenne informant to Author. Lame Deer, Montana. Sep; 1994. Note Book 1. [Author's collection]
2.     Beckwourth, James P. *"Life and Adventures."*
3.     Tall-Bull, Bill, Northern Cheyenne informant to Author. Lame Deer, Loc; cited.
4      The wanderings of the Cheyennes at this time is construed from Edward S. Curtis in his *"The North American Indian,"* Vol. 4. *"Crow and Atsina,"* and Thomas B. Marquis in *"Wooden Leg, A Warrior who Fought Custer."* James P. Beckwourth is the source for Yellow-Belly's raid on the Cheyenne camp and details pertaining to it.
5.     Woman-Chief was an Atsina captured by Crows in 1815 when she was around ten years old. She thus grew up among the Crows and had a Crow husband and children. These alas, were all killed by enemies and thereafter, she took it upon herself to avenge their loss by becoming an active participant in war ventures against numerous foes. In this she was highly successful, and even took wives as would a male warrior, hunter and lodge owner. Eventually she was elected to the seventeen-strong chief's council of the Nation. Thus she is mentioned by William Marshall Anderson in his contemporary list of Crow chiefs for the period 1834 /'35 but by the name, Bar-chi-tuoki, i.e. White-

Flower or Cherry-Blossom. "The Rocky Mountain Journals." P.232. University of Nebraska Press. 1967. James P. Beckwourth in his memoirs referred to the then contemporary female Crow warrior as Pine-Leaf, although it is clear that he was alluding to the same woman better known to others and to history as Woman-Chief. The artist and adventurer Rudolph Kurtz met Woman-Chief at the Fort Union trading post in 1851 and said of her, who he termed the famous Absaroka Amazon, "…She looked neither savage nor warlike On the contrary, as I entered the room, she sat with her hands in her lap, folded as when one prays. She is about 45 years old; appears modest in manner and good natured rather than quick to quarrel." Whilst at Fort Union during the aforementioned visit, Woman-Chief gave the resident trader Edwin Denig a Blackfoot scalp that she herself had recently taken. This Denig later presented to his guest Kurtz as a memento of the meeting. Rudolph Kurtz "Journal" pp.213-214. Woman-Chief was a well-known figure throughout the Upper Missouri country during the 1830s and 1840s. She was finally killed by members of her own people, the Atsina, when on a peace mission to that tribe in 1854. For a brief biography of Woman-Chief see Edwin T. Denig`s, "Five Indian tribes of the Upper Missouri." [Edited by John C. Ewers] Pp.195-200. University of Oklahoma Press. 1961.

6.       Wooden-Leg`s descendent Wesley Whiteman, also a Northern Suhtaio tribal member, [died 1981], declared that as far as he knew, his Great Grandfather Wooden-Leg, originally came to the Cheyennes from the Crows, having been brought to them when still a young boy by his mother who had ran away from her own Crow people. Upon reaching the Cheyenne camp, the woman sought out the tepee housing "*Issiwun*," the Sacred Buffalo Hat of the Suhtaio, and took refuge inside it, knowing that she and her son would not be harmed once they had claimed the sanctuary of the holy tepee and the protection of the "Hat`s" keeper and his wife. The keeper and his wife protected them both as was their duty, and eventually allowed them to stay among the Cheyennes as adopted members of the tribe.

This account, however, appears to be a deliberate corruption in order to disguise the fact that Wooden-Leg and his mother had once been captives from an alien tribe, and not eligible, therefore, to be regarded as proper Cheyennes. Unlike other Plains Tribes, often among the Cheyennes, having a foreign ancestry especially as a captive taken in battle, undermined one's ability to reach the higher echelons in Cheyenne society, even though the tribe's people themselves as a whole, did not consider foreign blood in any way a disadvantage to earning respect and renown as a warrior. Chieftainship at its higher grade was usually unattainable, unless the recipients showed themselves to be of exceptional quality. Perhaps it did happen as Wesley Whiteman told it, but more probable is the assumption that the woman and child had at first been captured from the Crows and taken to the Cheyenne village as prisoners of war, and that only after this had the woman and her son taken refuge within the sacred "Hat" tepee. Either way, the Crow woman stayed among the Cheyennes until her death, having raised her son among the Suhtaio band as a Cheyenne-speaking member of the tribe. Not once, it is said, did Wooden-Leg or his mother show any signs of wanting to return to the Crows, although countless times they had the opportunity to do so. About the year 1840 or `41, Wooden-Leg married a Cheyenne girl named Living-Woman, and sired a daughter named Wise-Woman. As a warrior Wooden-Leg was known as a fearless fighter and was engaged in many a hostile escapade against the enemies of his adopted people. At one time he was captured by Blackfoot who kept him prisoner overnight intending to kill him the next day. Somehow he managed to escape and travelled alone and on foot many hundreds of miles before reaching his home camp and safety. After this episode, he began training seriously as a shaman and changed his name from Wooden-Leg to that of Black-Bear [even though his tribesmen continued to call him Wooden-Leg]. He became an important participant in Cheyenne ceremonies connected with the Sacred Arrows; the *Massaum* [Animal or Crazy Dance]; the Sun-Dance and as a priest during the performance of the Antelope-Pit rites among the Suhtaio, as well as those belonging to the Sacred Buffalo Hat or *Issiwun*.

Although having been brought up in the Powder River and Black Hills country of the north, he went south with Chief Roman-Nose`s band following the Sand Creek massacre of 1864, and participated in the so-called "Great raids" in the Central Plains. He was prominent during the subsequent wars between the Cheyennes and White men, and died in Oklahoma an old man around the turn of the nineteenth century. A nephew also called Wooden-Leg [born 1858], became a famous warrior among the Northern Cheyennes, and is widely known for his part in the Custer fight of 1876, but who should not be confused with the first-named Wooden-Leg here referred to.

# NOTES AND SOURCES

As for dating the time of the twenty-day Crow / Cheyenne fight here recounted, after a reappraisal of Beckwourth's chronological format, he appears to have placed the event as occurring either in late summer or early Autumn of 1831, whereas in the nephew Wooden-Leg's Cheyenne version, it is merely stated that the event took place many years before the nephew's birth, which we know was in 1858.

Nevertheless, by working back through the genealogy of at least one of the descendants of Crow captives taken at that time, Beckwourth's dating of 1831 can be reasonably substantiated. We know that the daughter of the Crow captive Wooden-leg married her first husband [a white officer stationed at Fort Laramie] in 1861, and assuming that she was then around twenty years of age; as would be customary among Cheyennes for a woman to wed, she was probably born about the date 1841. This would then make her father Wooden-Leg twenty years old at the time of her birth; certainly the right age for a Cheyenne man to take a wife. It was then, probably sometime in 1831 that the boy captive joined his adopted tribe after having been stolen from the Crows, and at which time, as asserted by his nephew, he was around ten years of age.

7.      Beckwourth, James P. *"Life and Adventures."* Pp. 228-231. Loc; Cited.
8.      "Ibid."
9.      "Ibid."
10.     Denig, Edwin T. *"Of the Crow Nation."* Pp. 177-182. Loc; Cited.

## CHAPTER 20. The Fight at Laramie Fork and Retrieving Sunken Trade Goods.

1.      Ewers, John C. *"Indian Life on the Upper Missouri."* Pp. 75-78. University of Oklahoma Press. 1968.
2.      "Ibid."
3.      Joe Medicine Crow to Author. Lodge Grass, Montana.
4.      Irving, Washington. *"The Adventures of Captain Bonneville."* P. 53. Loc; cited. The Irving account of Bonneville's travels gives the date as July 1st, although a close scrutiny of his work suggests the more realistic month of June.
5.      Joe Medicine Crow to Author. Lodge Grass, Montana.
6.      Catlin, George. *"The North American Indian."* London. 1841.
7.      "Ibid."
8.      "Ibid."

## CHAPTER 21. Vengeance on the Atsina.

1.      Joe Medicine Crow to Author. Lodge Grass, Montana.
2.      Humfreville, James Lee, *"Twenty Years Among Our Hostile Indians."* P.357. Hunter and Co; Publishers. 1899. Humfreville is not the most reliable of sources, as is apparent in his account of James P. Beckwourth and also, of the last fight and demise of Sore-Belly himself, found on pages 227-229 of the above cited work.
3.      Howard, James H. *"Dakota Winter-Counts as Sources of History."* Pp.354-355. Loc; cited.
4.      Crow informant Barney Old-Coyote as conveyed to the present Author in the Summer; 2001.
5.      Bonner, T. D. *"Life and Adventures of James P. Beckwourth."* Loc; cited Pp. 298-299.
6.      Catlin, George. *"The North American Indian."* London. 1841.

## CHAPTER 22. Pikunies, Dreams and Pacts.1.

1.      Joe Medicine Crow to Author. Lodge Grass, September, 2001. Note book 5. [Author's collection]. See also; William A. Ferris. *"Life in the Rocky Mountains."* Chapter LXV. Denver, Colorado. 1940

# *NOTES AND SOURCES*

2.        Ferris, William A. *"Life in the Rocky Mountains."* Chapter LXV. Loc; Cited.

3.        Beckwourth, James P. *"Life and Adventures."* Loc; Cited.

4.        Joe Medicine Crow to Author. Lodge Grass, Montana. Loc; Cited.

5         "Ibid."

6.        Beckwourth, James P. *"Life and Adventures."* Loc; Cited.

7.        "Ibid."

8.        Bradley, James H. *"Affairs at Fort Benton."*   Montana Historical Society. "The Bradley MS. Vol.

9.        This from an analysis of an Atsina oral account in *"War Stories of the White Clay People."* Pp. 24-43. Fort Belknap Educational Department.1982. The Sitting-Woman referred to in this account pertains to the first Atsina chief of that name, who was subsequently killed by Assiniboine led by their infamous Chief Tchatka, aka The Left-Hand or LaGauche, who's warriors destroyed Sitting-Woman's thirty-lodge camp sometime during the early part of the 1830s. Certainly the event was prior to 1838 when Tchatka himself died soon after the smallpox epidemic of 1837.

10.       "Ibid."

11.       Hudson's Bay Company Records. Winnipeg. Canada. [See Bibliography, this volume].

12.       Schultz, James Willard. *"My Life as an Indian"* P 100. Premier reprint edition. 1956.

13.       Yellow-Fly, Teddy. *"The Teddy Yellow-Fly Winter Count."* Glenbow Museum Archives. Alberta, Canada.

14.       Prince Maximilian Zu Weid. *"Travels in the Interior of North America."* London. 1844.

15.       Some other present-day Crow informants say, these Atsina young men were captured during the Atsina raid on the Crow camp after the Crows destroyed the Atsina column on Rosebud Creek.

16.       Irving, Washington. *"The Adventures of Captain Bonneville."* P. 53. Loc; cited.

17.       "Ibid."

18.       Leonard, Zenas. *"Narrative of Adventures."* Pp. 83-84. University of Nebraska Press 1978.

19.       Joe Medicine Crow to Author. Lodge Grass. Sep; 2001.

20.       Irving, Washington. *"The Adventures of Captain Bonneville."* P. 53. Loc; cited.

## PART 111.

### DECLINE OF THE CROW ASCENEDNCY.

### CHAPTER 23. The Destruction of Dangling-Foot's Village.

1.        The story of the feud between One-Heart, Raven-Face and Arrow-Head and of Dangling Foot's involvement, can be found in Robert H. Lowie's "The Crow Indians," and "Crow Texts," both published by the University of Oklahoma Press. In an alternative version of this story, it is stated that both Raven-Face and Arrow-Head were very handsome men, and that the men-folk among the Whistling-Waters were jealous of their women being attracted to them. It was for this reason alone, it is said, that the Whistling-Waters wanted to kill these two Treacherous clan tribesmen in the first place. Joe Medicine Crow to Author. Again according to Joe Medicine-Crow, both Raven-Face and Arrow-Head had been members of the Poor-War-Deeds clan, although as this last named clan was also very closely attached to both the Treacherous clan and Whistling-Waters, the confusion here is academic.

       Even today on the Crow reservation, clan rivalry is very apparent, although it does not nowadays result in physical conflict. It does, however, still effect the political situation within the tribe's self-governing tribal council, and often determines the allegiance of voters towards one candidate as opposed to another. The account of the attack on Dangling-Foot's village is from Lowie's *"Crow Texts"* with additional information from Winona Plenty-Hoops to the present Author. Details regarding the Northern Cheyenne and Suhtaio movement south can be found in Grinnell's *"The Fighting Cheyennes"* and George E. Hyde's *"Life of Bent."* Both published by the University of Oklahoma Press. Details concerning the Kiowa tribe as being a refuge for both Arrow-Head's and Dangling-Foot's survivors are from Joe Medicine Crow and Pius Real-Bird to the Author.

r

2.      Lowie, Robert H. *"Crow Texts"* Pp. 491-500. University of California Press. 1960. See also; Barney Old-Coyote, Crow informant to Author.

3.      "Ibid."

4.      "Ibid."

5.      Barney Old-Coyote, Crow informant to Author, Garryowen, Montana. 2010.

6.      Stands in Timber, John, *"Cheyenne Memories."* Loc; cited.

## CHAPTER 24. Sore-Belly`s Revenge and Smallpox Among the Lodges.

1.      Lowie, Robert H. *"Crow Texts"* Pp. 491-500. University of California Press. 1960.

2.      Barney Old-Coyote to Author, Lodge Grass. August. 2001.

3.      Lowie, Robert H. *"Crow Texts"* Pp. 491-500. University of California Press. 1960.

4.      Barney Old-Coyote to Author, Loc; cited. See also; Denig, Edwin T. *"Of the Crow Nation."* Pp. 177-182. In; *"Five Indian Tribes of the Upper Missouri."* Edited by John C. Ewers. University of Oklahoma. 1961.

5.      Lowie, Robert H. *"Crow Texts"* Pp. 491-500. University of California Press. 1960.

6.      Joe Medicine Crow to Author. Loc; cited.

     The location of the fight in question, must have been between the creeks known today as Big Sandy Creek and Adobe Creek close to "Big Timbers" some thirty miles east of where William Bent's new trading post once stood. The fight, in fact, occurred not far from the actual site of Sand Creek where, in 1864, a Southern Cheyenne village under Chief Black-Kettle was destroyed, and many of its occupants cruelly massacred by Col. Chivington`s regiment of ruffians.

.     Much of the material concerning this fight and activities in the Crow camp prior to setting out against the foe, is derived from both Edwin Denig`s manuscript entitled, "Of the Crow Nation," and from Robert Lowie`s several fine works dealing with that tribe, along with information from my own Crow Indian informants, Joseph Medicine-Crow, Barney Old-Coyote and Winona Plenty-Hoops.

7.      Hyde, George E. [Editor]. *"Life of Bent."* Loc; cited.

8.      Winona Plenty Hoops to Author. Lodge Grass, Montana. 1998.

9.      Winona Plenty Hoops to Author. Lodge Grass, Montana. 1998.

10      Vestal, Stanley, "The Santa Fe Trail." University of Nebraska Press. 1996.

11.      Carson, Kit. *"Kit Carson`s Autobiography."* Pp.24-28. University of Nebraska Press. 1966.

12.      There are several accounts of the suicide leap from the sandstone butte. I have selected that of Elias Goes-Ahead, who as a modern-day Crow historian, has himself decided on this account as being closer to the truth.

.     It is indicative to note with regard to the smallpox outbreak in the Upper Missouri region at this time, that a smallpox immunization program was actually already underway in order to protect the Indians. It had started the previous year of 1832, and was carried out by the Upper Missouri Super intendancy, in conjunction with the Fur trading Companies themselves. [The Plains Anthropologist, Memoir No. 23. 1987].

## CHAPTER 25. The Pikuni Peace is Broken.

1.      Joe Medicine Crow to Author. Lodge Grass, Montana. See also; Schultz, James Willard. *"Blackfoot and Buffalo."* Pp.252-263.University of Oklahoma Press.1962.

2.      "Ibid."

3.      DeSmet, Pierre. *"Western Missions and Missionaries."* Pp. 159-166. Loc; cited.

4.      Schultz, James Willard. *"Blackfoot and Buffalo."* Pp.252-263. Loc; cited.

5.      DeSmet, Pierre. *"Western Missions and Missionaries."* Pp. 159-166. See also; Barney Old- Coyote to Author.

6.      "Ibid."

7.      "Ibid."

8.      "Ibid."

9.      DeSmet, Pierre. *"Western Missions and Missionaries."* Pp. 159-166. Loc; cited.

## NOTES AND SOURCES

Information pertaining to this chapter is derived from 7 separate sources which include both White and Indian accounts. The result is a composite account that takes in all the details which appear consistent and relevant to the event. One other account that appeared in "The Sun Tribune" in 1891? is such a fanciful version, apparently cruelly doctored from a verbal account given to that newspaper's editor in good faith one supposes, by the Piegan Blackfoot informant Big-Plume, has little - if any - merit. It has, therefore, been omitted by the present Author as a source, and none of its details are included herein.

10.      Joe Medicine Crow to Author, Lodge Grass, Montana. Sep; 2000.

There is much dispute in the printed sources regarding the number of Crows comprising the peace party on this occasion. James Beckwourth who was on the ground so to speak not long after the actual time of the event, stated that 39 Crows were in the party, while Father Pierre DeSmet gives the Crows as numbering only 25 warriors in total. However, this last count would suggest rather a small party to risk traveling through such hostile territory in order to reach their goal. [DeSmet, Pierre. "Western Missions and Missionaries."]. Bradley's version on the other hand, likely obtained from the post trader Alexander Culbertson, mentions 40 Crow warriors as comprising the Crow peace party, whereas Blackfoot accounts taken from that people's oral history, give the Crow number as 53 in one place [Schultz, James Willard. *"Blackfoot and Buffalo."* Pp.252-263.1962.], and as 61 in another [Claude Schaeffer, m.100-152].Schultz, supposedly, obtained his information from the Piegan informant Three-Suns, who was the son of the original Spotted-Elk; aka Bear-Chief, who actually took part in the slaughter and in the aftermath of which, the then ten-year old Three-Suns himself had been a participant. In addition, the fact that the Pikuni chief Eagle-Flag felt it necessary to call up reinforcements from the much larger camp of Chief Big-Lake, indicates that the Crow party at the time, must have been in much larger force than the mere 25 warriors mentioned by DeSmet. I have, therefore, opted for the number of between 53 and 61 Crows as being most probably involved.

The James Beckwourth version states that on this occasion, the Crow leader's name was Constant-Bird [Beckwourth, James P. "Life and Adventures."]. This name has the same connotation as that of Bird-Comes-Back, given to the present Author by Joe Medicine Crow as being the Crow leader of the party in question. Certainly, there was a Bird-Comes-Back of that time, who is also mentioned in Crow oral tradition as having had in his youth, an altercation with the young Foolish-Boy, who later became the great Mountain Crow chief more commonly known as Long-Hair. [Winona Plenty-Hoops to Author. Lodge Grass, Montana. 1998]. Additional names given in the various accounts for the Crow chief or chiefs involved, are, respectively, Painted-Shield, [Schultz, James Willard. *"Blackfoot and Buffalo."* Pp.252-263.University of Oklahoma Press.1962]. Red-Shield [Claude Schaeffer, "papers." M.1100-135 -p.110. Glenbow Archives. Calgary. Alberta, Canada]. Painted-Wing and Spotted-Lip [Dempsey, Hugh A. *"The Vengeful Wife and other Blackfoot Stories."* Pp.29-35. University of Oklahoma Press, 2003, Split-Ears [Schultz, James Willard, "Schultz Papers" August 6th 1915. Montana State University. Montana], Scabby-Mouth and Red-Feather [Claude Schaeffer. *"Papers."* M.100-152 Glenbow Archives. Calgary. Alberta, Canada.]. Perhaps where two names are given, they represent the two Crow pipe-holders or even the two Crow brothers who had actually perpetrated the deed of slaying the Piegan Chief Big-Snake, and so were remembered in Piegan oral history, rather than the real Crow leaders of the party. However, as the name Red-Shield as given to Schaeffer by his Pikuni informant, was obviously dubbed upon the Crow leader because he carried about his person such an item, it might be taken that each of the other names given for the Crow leaders are wrong, apart that is, from that of Painted-Shield which would be but a variation on the name Red-Shield. Of course, the names Spotted-Lip and Scabby-Mouth probably refer to the same man, and may well have been other names for the Crow chief who earlier had made a pact with the Pikuni in accordance with McKenzie's wish at Fort Union in 1832, but who's proper Crow name was Spotted-Buffalo. See; Schultz, James Willard. *"Rising Wolf, The White Blackfoot."*

The Piegan Chief Big-Snake was the first of that name, also known as Big-Snake-Man or Big-Snake-Person. The second chief named Big-Snake was painted by Paul Kane in 1848, and drawn by Gustav Sohon in 1855. He was killed during a one to one combat on horseback with a Cree Indian in 1858.

DeSmet referred to the Pikuni war chief as Spotted-Deer, while Prince Maximilian uses the name Spotted-Elk and tells us that by the winter of 1833 /'34, the same Spotted-Elk had changed his name to Bear-Chief. Maximilian mentioned further, "He is the most respected chief among the Blackfoot at this time. His name was Spotted-Elk, who after a successful battle with the Flatheads, his name is now called Bear-Chief. " [Maximilian Zu Weid, *"Travels in the Interior of North America."* Vol. II. London. 1844]. Schultz`s Piegan informants stated that the same chief was, for a while after the Crow massacre, known as Crow-Chief, and only afterwards did he change his name to Bear-Chief. By the name of Bear-Chief he signed the treaty paper with the American Government known as the "Steven`s Treaty" of 1855, and was killed by either Crows or Cree during the winter of 1865 /'66. His son thereafter, took the name Bear-Chief for himself, but was later known as Three-Suns, and even later in life was nick-named Big-Nose. He, however, died peaceably in 1896, aged 73. [Schaeffer, Claude. *"Papers."* M.100-152-p. . Glenbow Archives. Calgary. Alberta, Canada].

Schultz also stated that not long prior to the Crow peace party`s arrival, there had been forty Pikuni lodges in Spotted-Elk and Eagle-Flag`s camp, but most of the people had since left the region, and only ten lodges remained. However, ten lodges would suggest only some twenty Pikuni warriors on hand, whose number would not then have posed any threat to the fifty or more Crows in their midst, and the Crows, when confronted aggressively by Spotted-Elk and his warriors, could not then have been prevented from wiping out the entire Pikuni camp before the reinforcements from Big-Lake`s village arrived.

In another account of the affair [Beckwourth in *"Life and Adventures,"* Loc; cited. Pp. 263-265.], it is stated that the Crow peace party had already left the Pikuni camp on its own volition, and was on its way home when the Pikuni followed up and slaughtered them all. However, how then could the woman have stolen the bullet pouch in the first place if the Crows had already left the camp? Even if she had, then why did she wait until after the latter`s departure before making her discovery known? Perhaps, though, if this version is what actually happened, then the Pikuni may at first have kept quiet about their find and instead, waited until the Crows had travelled some suitable distance from the camp so as not to violate the sanctity of the Sacred pipe, and only then had the Pikuni force set out to destroy them. Together, the various accounts do concur when relating to the more important elements regarding the event, although the details of the Crows having been given the chance to, "run for their lives," perhaps has merely been added by one and more informants, in order to symbolize more graphically, how and why the Pikuni had allowed the Crows to put distance between themselves and the camp. Either way, one must admit that the alternative version from Beckwourth which states that the Crows left the Pikuni camp on their own volition, would explain in a more logical way, how the Crows still managed to retain their weapons in the event.

## CHAPTER 26. Shoshonies, Trappers and a Prince.

1. Beckwourth, James P. *"Life and Adventures."* Loc; Cited.
2. Campbell, Robert. Letter to brother. *"The Robert Campbell Collection."* Missouri Historical Society. St. Louis.
3. "Ibid."
4. "Ibid."
5. Young, F. G. [Editor], *"The Correspondence and Journals of Captain Nathanial Wyeth."* In; *"Sources of the History of Oregon,"* Vol. 1, Eugene, 1899.
6. Irving, Washington. *"The Adventures of Captain Bonneville."* Loc; Cited.
7. Brooks, G. R. *"The Private Journal of Robert Campbell."* Missouri His; Soc; Bul; Vol.XX. October, 1953.
8. Prince Maximilian Zu Weid. *"Travels in the Interior of North America."* Pp. 346-351. In Rueben Gold Thwaites, *"Early Western Travels."* Vol. 24.

## CHAPTER 27. Little-White-Bear`s Last Fight.

1. Joe Medicine Crow to Author. Lodge Grass, Montana.

## NOTES AND SOURCES

2.  Joe Medicine Crow to Author. Lodge Grass, Montana. See also; Beckwourth, James P. *"Life and Adventures."* Pp. 313-316. Loc; Cited.
    Additional sources include, Regina Flannery, *"The Gros Ventres of Montana,"* A. L. Kroeber, *"Gros Ventre Myths and Tales"* the James H. Bradley Crow manuscripts, and Robert H. Lowie's works on the Crow.

3.  Beckwourth, James P. *"Life and Adventures."* Pp. 313-316. Loc; Cited.

4.  Joe Medicine Crow to Author. Lodge Grass. Montana.

5.  Montana State University library, Bozeman. Series 6. *"Indian Legends etc.;"* Box 19.

6.  Bradley, James H. *"Affairs at Fort Benton."* Pp. 218-219. Montana Historical Society. Montana. 1876.

7.  *Ibid.*

8.  Joe Medicine Crow to Author. Lodge Grass, Montana.

In another place, however, Bradley - although obviously referring to this same event – says, *"...ten Crows were killed along with Hunter."* Here Bradley unwittingly, may have been referring only to those killed during the actual breakout through the Atsina lines, or to those Crow warriors who had opted to remain in the cave.

James Beckwourth in his *"Life and Adventures,"* pp." 313-316. professed to having himself been a member of the above-mentioned war-party, It is, though, highly unlikely that he was present on this trip, but one must assume that he did have some first-hand knowledge of the affair, no doubt imparted to him by one of the participants - perhaps Woman-Chief herself with whom Beckwourth, apparently, had a close relationship during his time among the Crows. Edwin Denig also gave a brief account of this same episode, but which is at variance with some of Beckwourth's details. Specifically is Denig's assertion that the victorious party were Piegan Blackfoot led by the war-chief, Spotted-Elk. However, here it appears that Denig is confusing the earlier fight of the Crow peace party under Bird-Comes-Back, with that in which Little-White-Bear was slain. Beckwourth, though, was on the spot, so to speak, most probably being in the Crow camp when the survivors returned, whilst Denig merely quoted from hearsay some twenty or more years after the event. The main discrepancy as regards Beckwourth's version is, again alas, his confused chronological order of events, which appears to jump back and forth from one to another. This trait occurs all too often throughout the whole of Beckwourth's memoirs which relate to his time among the Crows. However, notwithstanding this peculiar trait, his pertinent details often remain sound and there is no reason to dismiss his recollections out of hand - as so many earlier scholars have chosen to do - simply because he has misdated an event, or which is sometimes the case, has deliberately inserted the event in the memoirs where he thought appropriate, in order to gain what either he or his biographer supposed, would add effect or at the least, present a more coherent account of his experiences.

Beckwourth actually places the affair in question as occurring after the death of Sore-Belly. Denig for his part, placed the death of Little-White-Bear before the siege of Fort McKenzie, and thus before the death of Sore-Belly, which latter event Denig states, was partly in response to the demise of Little-White-Bear in the first place. As Beckwourth, for obvious reasons, did not refer even cryptically to the besieging of Fort McKenzie, I have accepted Denig's chronology that pertains to the current sequence of events for the years 1833 and `34, as being the more accurate.

Lieutenant James H. Bradley also wrote briefly of the Little-White-Bear affair from, one supposes, a Crow informant named Little-Face and also, from Culbertson himself. Here Bradley implies the date as being 1835, although a study of his work suggests the real date to be early 1834. He mentions the event in two separate instances. In one account he states that the fight took place south of the Marias River near its junction with the Missouri, and in another, at the mouth of Shonkin Creek. Beckwourth stated that the fight took place on or near Little Box Elder Creek [a western tributary of the Musselshell], while Denig stated that the site was back of the fort which would indicate the Teton River. My own Crow informant Joseph Medicine-Crow, was, however, adamant that the site of this particular battle actually occurred near the mouth of Shonkin Creek.

Joe Medicine-Crow also said that a brother of the aforementioned Little-White-Bear, was with the party that retrieved the bones of the dead. This man, having found what he supposed was the skull of his deceased brother by it lying adjacent to the white man Hunter who was recognized by his

400

decayed teeth, carried it home and there extracted one of its teeth. He then incorporated the tooth into a certain *"war-medicine"* bundle as an integral part of its contents, and this particular bundle thereafter, proved itself very successful to all who carried it to war. At a later date, it passed into the hands of the Crow warrior Grey-Bull, who it is reported, bought it for the high price of ten ponies.

### CHAPTER 28. Besieging the White Man`s Fort.

1.       Joe Medicine Crow to Author. Lodge Grass. 1994. Note pad 1.
2.       Ibid.
3.       Ibid.
4.       Edward S. Curtis, *"The North American Indian,"* Vol. 4. *"Crow and Atsina,"*
5.       Denig, Edwin T. *"Of the Crow Nation."* Pp. 177-182. In; *"Five Indian Tribes of the Upper Missouri."* Edited by John C. Ewers. University of Oklahoma. 1961.
6.       Joe Medicine Crow to Author. Lodge Grass. 1994. Note pad 1.
7.       Archdale Hamilton letter to Alexander McKenzie. 1834.
8.       Denig, Edwin T. *"Of the Crow Nation."* Pp. 177-182. Loc; Cited.
9.       Anderson, William Marshall, *"Rocky Mountain Journals."* Bison Books. 1987.
10.      Lamont letter to Alexander Culbertson. May; 1835. Alexander Culbertson later married the daughter of the influential Blood chief, Sees-From-Afar, which was the reason, perhaps, why he subsequently and seemingly, showed preferential treatment towards that people. Denig`s account states further, that in an attempt to convince the Crows that the white men had an ample stock of food, they periodically threw small quantities of meat over the walls to the Indians loitering outside. Denig, Edwin T. *"Of the Crow Nation."* P. 179. Loc; Cited.

### CHAPTER 29 The Slaying of a Chief.

1.       Winona Plenty-Hoops to Author. Lodge Grass, Montana, August 1998. Most of the data pertaining to this chapter was verified by Crow informant Barney Old-Coyote to the Author.
2.       Winona Plenty-Hoops to Author, Lodge Gras. Montana. 1994.
3.       Joe Medicine Crow to Author, Lodge Gras. Montana. 1994.
      Beckwourth said that on this occasion, the enemy - whom he terms Blackfoot - numbered 14 warriors. Denig who also classifies the foe as Blackfoot, says 20. Bradley, however, rightly designated the enemy as Gros Ventre [i.e. Atsina], but gives their number as 12. As regards if they were Atsina or Blackfoot, the matter is academic. White men of that day did not, but rarely, distinguish between the two tribes, as both were staunch allies and confederate to each other during this period of their history.
4.       Joe Medicine Crow to Author, Lodge Gras. Montana. 1994.
5.       Joe Medicine Crow to Author, Lodge Gras. Montana. 1994.
6.       Winona Plenty-Hoops to Author, Lodge Gras. Montana. 1994.
7.       Joe Medicine Crow to Author, Loc; cited. Also; Winona Plenty-Hoops to Author. Loc; cited. And; Beckwourth, *"Life and Adventures,"* Pp. 259-268..
8.       Chardon, F. A. *"Chardon`s Journal at Fort Clark. "* P. 4. Univ. of Neb. Press 1997.
9.       Leonard, Zenas. *"Narrative of Adventures."* University of Nebraska Press 1978.
10.      Beckwourth, *"Life and Adventures,"* Pp. 259-268..
11.      Barney Old-Coyote to Author. Loc; cited.

$$- 0 - 0 - 0 - 0 - 0 - 0 - 0 - 0 - 0 - 0 - 0 - 0 -$$

# BIBLIOGRAPHY

## UNPUBLISHED MATERIAL.

The Public Archives of Canada; Hudson's Bay Company Records and Archives. Winnipeg, Canada.
[1] Bow River Expedition. Reel IM 20. 3 Nov. 1822.
[2] Edmonton Post Journal. Reel IM 50, 4. Sep. 1826.
[3] Ditto; Feb. 1827 and March. 1827.
[4] Ditto; Feb. 1828, March 12th. 1828 and Oct 8th. 1828.
[5] Ditto; Sep 2d and Oct 25th. 1832.
[5] Fort Pitt Post Journal. Reel IM 119. April 14th 1831 and Nov 4th 1831.
[6] Fort Pelly Post Journal. Reel IM 46. Nov 6th 1831.
[7] Lake Traverse Post records, 1818 to 1821. Nov; 9th 1820.


Claude Schaeffer. Papers. M.100-152-p. ff. Glenbow Archives. Calgary. Alberta, Canada.

Joseph Medicine Crow. Papers. Little Big Horn College Archives. Crow Agency, Montana.

James H. Bradley. Papers and Manuscript Vols 2, 3, 8, 9 and Book F. Montana State
      Historical Society. Missoula, Montana.
George Bird Grinnell. Papers and Note Books. Braun Research Library. The Southwest Museum,
      Los Angeles, California.
Colonel A. B. Welch. Papers. "Indian Histories" and "Notes on the Hidatsa." [retrieved]
www.welchdakotapapers.com
Brian L. Keefe collections.
      These include note books and audio tapes of interviews with tribal members from 1992
through to 2013. Information obtained from Crow Indians; Joe Medicine Crow, Winona Plenty-Hoops,
Lawrence Flat-Lip, Elias Goes-Ahead, Barney Old-Coyote, Pius Real-Bird, Glen Birdinground, Alex
Birdingground. Also interviews with Cheyennes; Wayne Medicine-Elk, James King [Mexican
Cheyenne], William Tall-Bull, and with the Lakota; Tom Bull-Head [Hunkpapa], Ladonna Brave-Bull
Allard [Hunkpapa], He-Owns-Her-White-Horses [Minniconjou] among others.


## PUBLISHED WORKS.

Abel, A. H. "[Editor] "Loisel's Expedition." [Tabeau's Narrative] University of South
      Dakota. 1932.
Ahler, Stanley A. [Editor], "People of the Willows," The Prehistory and Early History
      of the Hidatsa Indians." University of North Dakota Press. 1991.
Algier, Keith. "The Crow and the Eagle." The Caxton Press. Idaho. 1993.
Allen, Dr. William A. "Adventures with Indians and Game."A. W. Bowen. Chicago.
      1903.
Anderson, William Marshall. "The Rocky Mountain Journals." University of Nebraska
      Press. 1967.
Audubon, Maria [Editor]. "Audubon and His Journals." Dover Publications. 1960.
Bonner, T. D. "Life and Adventures of James P. Beckwourth." Ross and Haines [reprint]
      1963.
Bowers, Alfred. "Hidatsa Social and Ceremonial Organization." University of Nebraska
      Press. 1992.
      Mandan Social and Ceremonial Organization." University of Nebraska Press. 2004.
Bradley, James H. "March of the Montana Column." Montana Historical Society.
      Montana. 1876.
Brown, Mark H. Plainsmen of the Yellowstone." University of Nebraska Press. 1961.
Burpee, L. J. [Editor] "Journals and Letters of Pierre Gaultier de Verennes DaLaVerendrye and his
      Sons." Champlain Society Vol. 16. Toronto 1927 [Reprint].

Campbell, Robert. "Avadavit." See also; "Letters." Missouri Historical Society. St. Louis. Missouri.

Catlin, George. "Letters and Notes etc.; On the North American Indians." London. 1841.

Chittenden, Hiram Martin and Alfred Richardson [Editors]. "Life, Letters and Travels of Father Pierre DeSmet." 4 vols. New York, Arno Press. 1969.

Coues, Elliott. "The History of the Lewis and Clark Expedition." 3 Volumes.

Curtis, Edward S. "The North American Indian." Vol. 4. "Crow and Atsina."

Dale, Harrison Clifford [Editor] "The Ashley-Smith Explorations etc.;" The Arthur H. Clark Company. 1918.

Dempsey, Hugh A. "The Vengeful Wife and other Blackfoot Stories." University of Oklahoma Press. 2003.

Denig, Edwin. "Five Indian Tribes of the Upper Missouri." [Edited by John C. Ewers.] University of Oklahoma Press. 1961.

DeSmet, Pierre. "Western Missions and Missionaries." The Irish University Press. 1972.

Ewers, John C. "The Blackfoot, Raiders of the Northwestern Plains." University of Oklahoma Press. 1958.

Ferris, Warren. "Life in the Rocky Mountains." The Old West Publishing Company. 1960.

Fiddler, Peter. "Journal." Public Archives of Canada. Hudson`s Bay Company. Winnipeg. Canada.

Flannery, Regina. "The Gros Ventres of Montana." Part 1. Catholic university of America Anthropological Series. 15. [1953]

Elliott Coues [Editor]. "The Journal of Jacob Fowler." Ross and Haines, Inc. Minneapolis. 1965.

Grinnell, George Bird. "The Fighting Cheyennes." University of Oklahoma Press. 1966.

Harris, Burton. "John Colter, His Years in the Rockies." University of Nebraska Press. 1993.

Hayden, F. V. "Ethnology and Philology of the Hidatsa Indians." Transactions of the American Philosophical Society, Vol. XII. 1962.

Hayne, Coe. "Red Men on the Bighorn." The Judson Press. 1929.

Hodge, Frederick W. "Handbook of American Indians." [Two volumes.] Smithsonian Institution.

Holmes, Ruben. "The Five Scalps." Missouri Historical Society. "Glimpses of the Past." Vol. V. Jan-March, Number 1-3. St. Louis. 1938.

Howard, James H. "Dakota Winter Counts as Sources of History." Anth. Pap. Smith. Inst. Bull. 173. [1955].

Hoxie, Frederick E. "Parading Through History." Cambridge University Press. 1995.

Humfreville, James Lee, *"Twenty Years Among Our Hostile Indians."* P.357. New York. 1899.

Hungry wolf, Adolph. "The Blood People." [Contains the Bad-Head winter-count]. Harper and Row. 1977.

Hyde, George E. "Life of Bent." University of Oklahoma Press. 1968.

"Red Clouds` Folk." University of Nebraska Press. 1957.

"Indians of the Woodlands." University of Nebraska Press. 1962.

"Indians of the High Plains." University of Nebraska Press. 1959.

Irving, Washington. "The Adventures of Captain Bonneville." University of Oklahoma Press. 1961.

"Astoria." Anecdotes and an Enterprise beyond the Rocky Mountains. New York. [No date].

James, Thomas. Three Years among the Indians and Mexicans." [Reprint] University of Nebraska Press. 1984.

Jensen, Richard E. and Hutchins, James S. "Wheel Boats on the Missouri." [The journals and documents of the Atkinson – O`Fallon expedition of 1824-`26].

# BIBLIOGRAPHY

Keefe, Brian L.   "Red Was the Blood of Our Forefathers." Caxton Press, Idaho. 2010.
    "The Battle at Rainy Butte." English Westerner's Society. 2008.
    "Making Pacts with Old Enemies." English Westerner's Society. 2012.
    "A Double Defeat for the Atsina." English Westerner's Society. 2014.
    "Ma'heo's Children." The Choir Press. 2014.

Kelsey, Henry. "The Kelsey Papers." Editors; Arthur G. Doughty and Chester Martin. Ottawa; Public Archives of Canada. 1929.

Kroeber, Alfred, "The Arapaho." Bull. Amer. Mus. Nat. His., Vol. 18. Smithsonian Institution. 1902.

"Ethnology of the Gros Ventre." Anth. Pap. Ame. Mus. Nat. Hist., Vol. 1 part 4. Smithsonian Institution. 1908.

Kurtz, Rudolph F. "The Journal of Rudolph Friederich Kurtz." Smithsonian Institution, Bureau of American Ethnology. Bulletin 115.1937.

Lamb, W. K. [Editor] "Sixteen Years in the Indian Country." The Journal of Daniel W. Harmon. Toronto, Macmillan 1957.

Lahontan, Baron Louis Armand, "Lahontan's New Voyages." [Edited by Rueben G. Thwaites]. Chicago, 1905.

LaReye,   Charles. "Travels through North America."

Larocque, Francois, "The Yellowstone Journal. See; Wood, W. Raymond and Thomas D. Thiessen [Editors]. "Early Fur Trade on the Northern Plains." University of Oklahoma Press.1985. American Ethnology, Bulletin 198. Washington D.C. 1967.

Larpenteur, Charles. "Forty Years a Fur Trader on the Upper Missouri." [Reprint] Donnelley and Sons Company. Chicago. 1933.

Lehmer, Donald J. "Introduction to Middle Missouri Archaeology." National Park Service, Anthropology Papers 1. Washington D.C. 1971.

Leonard, Zenas, *Narrative of Adventures."* University of Nebraska Press. 1978.

Liberty, Margot. "Cheyenne Memories." Yale University Press. 1967.

Linderman, Frank B. "American." [The life story of the Crow Chief Plenty Coups]. John Day and Co. 1930.
    "Pretty-Shield, Medicine Woman of the Crows" John Day and Co. 1932.

Lowie, Robert H. "Crow Myths and Traditions." University of Nebraska Press. 1993. [Reprint].
    "The Crow Indians." Holt, Rinehart and Winston. New York. 1935.
    "Crow Texts." University of California Press. 1960.
    "Societies of the Crow, Hidatsa and Mandan."

Mallery, Garrick. "Picture-Writing of the North American Indian." [Dakota and Lakota Winter-counts].

McClintock, Walter. "The Old North Trail." University of Nebraska Press. 1992.

Mackenzie, Charles. See below; Wood and Thiessen, "Early Fur traders on the Northern Plains."

Marquis, Thomas B. "Wooden Leg, a Warrior Who Fought Custer."

Medicine Crow, Joseph. "From the Heart of the Crow Country." Orion Books. New York. 1932.

Meyer, Roy W. "The Village Indians of the Upper Missouri." Univ; Nebraska Press. 1977.

Michelson, Truman. Papers and Notes. American Anthropological Archives. Washington D.C.

Mooney, James. "Calendar History of the Kiowa Indians." Smithsonian Institution Press. 1979.

Morton, Arthur S. [Editor] "The Journal of Duncan M'Gillivary of the North West Company." 1929.

Nabokov, Peter. "Two-Leggings, "The Making of a Crow Warrior." [Edited by John C. Ewers]. Thomas Y. Crowell and Company. 1967.

Nye, Wilbur S. "Bad Medicine and Good; Tales of the Kiowas." University of Oklahoma Press. 1962.

# BIBLIOGRAPHY

Oglesby, Richard E. "Manuel Lisa and the Opening of the Missouri Fur Trade." University of Oklahoma Press. 1963.

Pattie, James O. "The Personal Narrative of James O. Pattie of Kentucky." Cincinnati. 1831.

Raczka, Paul M. "Winter-count; A History of the Blackfoot People." Brocket. Alberta. Oldman River Cultural Centre. 1979.

Robertson, R. G. "Competitive Struggle, America's Western Fur Trading Posts, 1764-1865." Tamarack Books, Boise, Idaho. 1999.

Roe, F. G. "The North American Buffalo." University of Toronto Press, 1970.

Rollins, Philip Ashton. "The Discovery of the Oregon Trail." University of Nebraska Press. 1985.

Ross, Alexander, " Fur Hunters of the Far West." University of Oklahoma Press. 1956.

Simms, S. C. "Traditions of the Crows" Field Columbia Museum, Anthropological Series, II, No. 6 [1903]

Schultz, Willard. "My Life as an Indian." Premier reprint edition. 1956.
    The White Blackfoot." Houghton and Miffin Co. 1927.
    "Blackfoot and Buffalo." University of Oklahoma Press.1962.

Taylor, Joseph H. "Sketches of Frontier and Indian Life." Washburn, North Dakota. 1895.

Thiessen, Thomas D. "People of the Willows." University of North Dakota. 1991.

Thompson, David. Travels."[Edited by William E. Moreau].Vols.1-3.McGill-Queens University Press.2009.

Trenholm, Virginia Cole. "The Arapaho, Our People." University of Oklahoma. 1970.

Trimble, Michael K. "People of the Willows." University of North Dakota. 1991.

Vestal, Stanley. "Jim Bridger, Mountain Man." University of Nebraska Press. 1970.
    "The Santa Fe Trail." University of Nebraska Press. 1996.

Victor, Francis Fuller, "The River of the West." Oakland Brooks-Sterling Company. 1974.

Warren, William. "A History of the Ojibway People." Minnesota His; Society Press. 1984.

Wildshcut, William. "Crow Medicine Bundles." Museum of the American Indian, Heye Foundation. New York. 1975.

Wilson, Elinor. *"Jim Beckwourth."* Universaity of Oklahoma Press. 1983.

Wilson, Gilbert L. "Agriculture of the Hidatsa Indians." University of Minnesota. Studies in Social Science. Vol. 9. 1917

Wood, W. Raymond. "An Interpretation of Mandan Culture History." Smithsonian Institution, Bureau of

Wood, W. Raymond and Thomas D. Thiessen [Editors]. "Early Fur Trade on the Northern Plains." University of Oklahoma Press.1985. American Ethnology, Bulletin 198. Washington D.C. 1967.

Young, F. G. [Editor]. "The Correspondence and Journals of Nathaniel J. Wyeth." New York; Arno Press. 1973.

Yellow-Fly, Teddy. "The Teddy Yellow-Fly Winter-Count." Glenbow Museum Archives. Alberta, Canada.

Zu Wied, Prince Maximilian. "Travels In the Interior of North America." London. 1841.

– 0 - 0 – 0 – 0 – 0 – 0 – 0 – 0 – 0 – 0 – 0 - 0 – 0 – 0 – 0 -